Second Edition

INTERNATIONAL MARKETING

Second Edition

INTERNATIONAL MARKETING

Dana-Nicoleta Lascu
University of Richmond

Cincinnati, Ohio
www.atomicdog.com

Book Team

Vice President/Publisher Steve Scoble
Managing Editor Kendra Leonard
Director of Interactive Media and Design Joe Devine
Production Coordinator Lori Bradshaw
Digital Designer Zack Hicks
Web Production Editor Angela Makowski
Director of Quality Assurance Tim Bair
Quality Assurance Editor Dan Horton
Marketing Manager Mikka Baker

When ordering this title, use ISBN 1-59260-167-7

To order only the online version (Online Edition) of this title,
use ISBN 1-59260-168-5

Dedication

This book is dedicated to the memory of Valeria and Isidor Lupse, who fostered an imaginative environment, and who taught me that anything was possible; to the memory of Daniel Suguru, my close friend and one of the first victims of AIDS; to Aloys Nyabutsitsi and his family, who lost their lives as proud members of the Watutsi tribe; and to Ofra Haza and Umm Kulthoum, the divas of music who inspired the world to unite through song.

Brief Contents

Contents

Part 3 International Marketing Strategy Decisions 129

Part 5   International Marketing Strategy: Implementation   373

Preface

International Marketing, Second Edition, is based on the enthusiastic feedback received on the first edition and on current developments in the international marketplace. The text has been thoroughly revised to reflect current international issues and concerns. The revised edition has new in-depth case studies integrated with each individual chapter and dynamic International Marketing Illustration boxes that address specific nuances of conducting business and marketing products internationally. The online study guide and end-of-chapter materials have also been fully revised to reflect the text changes.

The *International Marketing* textbook reflects the author's teaching philosophy: creating vivid, memorable examples that help students retain international marketing theory and facts. The author shares her own perspectives as a product of different cultures who has experienced and observed marketing on four continents, both as an expatriate and as a local, in a free-market system and under a repressive, anti-consumerist command economy. These experiences are further supplemented with material collected in the author's recent research and other fieldwork and with materials obtained from various international sources: newspapers and magazines (*The Financial Times, Le Monde, The Economist, The International Herald Tribune, Wall Street Journal Europe and Asia, Frankfurter Allgemeine, Süddeutsche Zeitung, Die Zeit, L'Express, Le Point, Jeune Afrique*, and local and international fashion magazines); government and nongovernmental organizations' publications (World Bank, United Nations Development Program, among others); as well as publications aimed at expatriates (*Delegates' World, Le Monde Diplomatique*).

The text adopts strategic, applications-oriented approaches to country- and region-specific environments. These are also illustrated, in the text and in the case studies, with interviews conducted with international and local marketing managers and with marketing theorists who uphold different international marketing philosophies.

Print Edition and Online Edition

International Marketing is available online as well as in print. The Online Edition chapters demonstrate how the interactive media components of the text enhance presentation and understanding. For example,

- Animated illustrations help to clarify concepts.
- Clickable glossary terms provide immediate definitions of key concepts.
- Highlighting capabilities allow you to emphasize main ideas. You can also add personal notes in the margin.
- The search function allows you to quickly locate discussions of specific topics throughout the text.

You may choose to use just the Online Edition, or both the online and print versions together. This gives you the flexibility to choose which combination of resources works best for you. To assist those who use the online and print versions together, the primary heads and subheads in each chapter are numbered the same. For example, the first primary head in Chapter 1 is labeled 1-1, the second primary head in this chapter is labeled 1-2, and so on. The subheads build from the designation of their corresponding primary head: 1-1a, 1-1b, etc. This numbering system is designed to make moving between the Online Edition and the print book as seamless as possible.

Finally, next to a number of figures in the print version of the text, you will see an icon similar to the one in the margin on the right. This icon indicates that this figure in the Online Edition is interactive in a way that applies, illustrates, or reinforces the concept.

Acknowledgments

The author expresses her deep gratitude for the immense support received in the process of developing this textbook. Many thanks go to the team at Atomic Dog Publishing for all their support and guidance in the process of accomplishing this project. Steve Scoble, Chuck Hutchinson, Lori Bradshaw, Kendra Leonard, Victoria Putman, and Ed Laube were instrumental in the materialization of the text; without their support through each stage of the project, this book could not have become a reality. The author also expresses thanks to Andrew Gross at Cleveland State University, to Al Rosenbloom at Dominican University, and to Bonita Kolb at Lycoming College for their valuable formal and informal feedback.

My gratitude to my parents, Lucia and Damian Lascu, and to Bram, Michael, and Daniel Opstelten for the formidable international experiences that this book is based on and for creating and facilitating the foundations for this text.

About the Author

Dana-Nicoleta Lascu

Dana-Nicoleta Lascu holds the 2005–2006 Fulbright Distinguished Chair in International Business at Johannes Kepler University of Linz, Austria and is associate professor of marketing and chair of the marketing department at the University of Richmond, in Richmond, Virginia. She has a Ph.D. in marketing from the University of South Carolina, a Master of International Management with concentrations in marketing and finance from the American Graduate School of International Management (Thunderbird), and a B.A. in English and French from the University of Arizona. She has taught international marketing at the University of Richmond for 15 years and has published her research in international marketing in journals such as *International Marketing Review, International Business Review, European Journal of Marketing, Journal of Euromarketing, Journal of International Consumer Marketing, Journal of Teaching in International Business,* and *Multinational Business Review.* She has organized a number of international conferences and published related proceedings (among them, the 1996 World Business Congress, in Bermuda; the Sixth Conference on Marketing and Development, 1997, in Romania; the Global Business and Technology Conference, 2003, in Hungary) and has participated as track chair, session chair, or conference co-chair in numerous other national and international conferences. She is on the editorial board of a number of marketing journals.

Dana Lascu worked previously as a simultaneous and consecutive translator for the Romanian government and for the United Nations, Kigali, Rwanda, where she volunteered as a translator of documents for the Round Table for International Aid. She also worked in international training in the United States, teaching managerial skills to civil servants from developing countries and developing related training proposals. She has consulted for international companies such as Stihl, Aquasource North America, Bailey's Irish Cream, Albright and Wilson, and Ford Motor Company, among others.

part 1

Introduction to International Marketing

 Scope, Concepts, and Drivers of International Marketing

Scope, Concepts, and Drivers of International Marketing

Chapter Objectives

By the end of this chapter, you should be able to

1 Define international marketing and identify the different levels of international involvement.

2 Describe the different company orientations and philosophies toward international marketing.

3 Identify environmental and firm-specific drivers that direct firms toward international markets.

4 Identify obstacles preventing firms from engaging in successful international ventures.

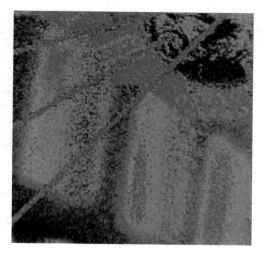

More than ever before, firms are looking for success beyond their national borders, partnering with foreign firms, or entering new markets on their own. In the past, internationalization was an option for large firms that had the necessary resources to enter and develop new markets. Today, small and medium-size businesses have access to international markets and can benefit from new venues—e.g., the Internet—and new markets—e.g., emerging markets worldwide—for selling their products.

Companies can look at international markets as a possible venue for distributing overproduction. Alternatively, they can look at international markets as a source of limitless opportunity. For example, Federal Express, when assessing its growth opportunities, states: "International, sky is the limit."[1]

Federal Express has traditionally pursued markets only in industrialized countries. In many developing countries (in Sub-Saharan Africa, for example), its competitor, DHL, was the first to enter the market, securing business from the national government, to the expatriate community, to local and international businesses operating there. When Federal Express decided these markets had potential, it had to spend large amounts of money to promote its services in these developing countries and to gain access there. Similarly, Pepsi set up strategic alliances with government agencies in Central and Eastern Europe in the late 1960s, at a time when Coca-Cola did not consider communist countries in Europe as attractive investment venues. As a first mover into this market, Pepsi was able to secure exclusive access and effectively blocked Coca-Cola's access for decades. In the 1990s, when these markets opened their doors to foreign investment, Coca-Cola had to spend huge amounts of money to overtake Pepsi's lead in these markets.

This chapter will introduce the different internationalization philosophies of international firms and address the drivers (environmental and firm-specific) of and obstacles to international expansion.

1-1 The Importance of International Marketing

The United States constitutes one of the most important world markets, providing and consuming a high percentage of worldwide products and services. Over time, it has become evident, however, that this percentage is getting smaller: less than 25 percent. For companies to achieve their full potential and to effectively compete with foreign companies in the same league, it is crucial that they expand into international markets to take advantage of global market opportunities, to keep pace with competition, and to maximize the potential of their product mix.

Throughout history, companies have achieved worldwide dominance in spite of the smaller size of their country of origin and their home country's limited market; it should be noted, however, that an international presence was essential for their success. Successful global companies from the Netherlands, a smaller country in Western Europe, have become giants of industry worldwide. Among them are Philips, a leading electronics manufacturer; Royal Ahold, a large retailer; Royal Dutch/Shell, a leading Dutch-British oil company; and Unilever, a leading Dutch and British consumer products company. Japanese firms dominate many industries; among them are Mitsui and Mitsubishi (electronics,

domestic marketing Marketing that is focused solely on domestic consumers and on the home-country environment.

export marketing Involvement in international marketing limited to the exporting function; although the firm actively seeks international clients, it considers the international market an extension of the domestic market and does not give it special consideration.

international marketing The processes involved in the creation, production, distribution, promotion, and pricing of products, services, ideas, and experiences for international markets; these processes require a substantial focus on international consumers in a particular country or countries.

multinational marketing Marketing in different countries without coordinating across operations.

banking, import-export, among others), Dentsu (advertising), Sony and Panasonic (electronics), Ito Yokado (retail)—and the list continues.

International companies such as General Motors, Mitsubishi, Microsoft, and Exxon earn profits greater than the gross domestic product of many developing countries; and their total market value is several times the size of their profits. Even successful small businesses can attribute their survival and/or success to international markets. Companies, to achieve their potential, must constantly monitor the international environment for opportunities. Since the 1990s, privatization in countries where government monopolies had dominated for decades has made it possible for multinationals to compete for local airline, railway, and telecommunications industries. In the future, postal services might constitute the new competitive territory of international companies. Already, in many markets, post offices are enterprising competitors to existing private sector firms, increasingly and effectively competing not only for mailing services, but also for banking services, as in the example offered in Figure 1-1.

1-2 Levels of International Marketing Involvement

All companies are affected by elements of the international marketing environment. In terms of international marketing involvement, however, companies have different degrees of commitment. A company engaging in **domestic marketing** has the least commitment to international marketing. This company focuses solely on domestic consumers and on the home-country environment. The home-country environment, however, is affected by developments in the international environment; furthermore, the local company is directly affected by local competition, which could come from global companies.

At the next level, **export marketing,** a firm could be involved in exporting indirectly—the company takes orders from international clients—or directly—the company actively seeks international clients. For both export marketers and domestic marketers, the international market constitutes an extension of the domestic market and is not given special consideration. Such firms have an ethnocentric philosophy to internationalization, as will be shown in section 1-3a, "Ethnocentric Orientation."

International marketing activities require a substantial focus on international consumers in a particular country or countries (when more countries are involved, international marketing is often referred to as **multinational marketing**). International marketing is thus defined as the processes involved in the creation, production, distribution, promotion, and pricing of products, services, ideas, and experiences for international markets. The international company is present in different countries with sales offices and subsidiaries, or is an active partner in strategic alliances with local companies. It is important to note that, in this case, international activities are not coordinated across the different countries, nor across different regions. An international company, according to this definition, has a polycentric or regiocentric philosophy to internationalization, as will be seen in sections 1-3b, "Polycentric Orientation," and 1-3c, "Regiocentric Orientation."

Global marketing involves marketing activities across different countries without focusing primarily on national or regional segmentation. Global marketing is possible due to the emergence of global consumer segments and due to efficient global allocation of company talent and resources. A company engaging in global marketing has a geocentric philosophy to internationalization.

It should be noted, however, that the terms defined in the preceding paragraphs are often used interchangeably by nonbusiness and business alike—even by international managers. *International, global,* and *multinational* are used to refer to any company crossing borders, without particular reference to the global strategy used. The descriptions of the levels of international marketing involvement should primarily guide one to understand when distinctions are made. A superior approach to distinguishing between companies' international orientation and philosophy is the EPRG Framework.

1-3 The EPRG Framework and International Marketing Concepts

Management's orientation toward the internationalization of the firm's operations affects each of the functional areas of the firm and, as such, has a direct impact on the marketing functions within the firm. Management's philosophy on international involvement affects decisions such as the firm's response to global threats and opportunities and related resource allocation. Companies' philosophies on international involvement can be described, based on the EPRG Framework, as ethnocentric, polycentric, regiocentric, and geocentric.[2]

1-3a Ethnocentric Orientation

Eli Lilly is an ethnocentric firm.[3] Top management at Eli Lilly places most of the emphasis on product research and development, in an effort to bring to the marketplace high-performance pharmaceutical products. Firms with an **ethnocentric orientation** are guided by a *domestic market extension concept:* In general, top management of firms with an ethnocentric orientation consider that domestic strategies, techniques, and personnel are superior to foreign ones and therefore provide the most effective framework for the company's overseas involvement; consequently, international operations and customers are considered secondary to domestic operations and customers.[4] Ethnocentric firms are likely to be highly centralized and consider that the purpose of their international operations is to identify markets that could absorb surplus domestic production; alternatively, international operations could represent a cash cow that generates revenue and necessitates only minimal attention and investment. Consequently, plans for international markets are developed primarily in-house, by an international division, and are similar to those for the domestic market.[5] Firms in the tobacco industry,[6] as well as firms at the forefront of technology, tend to have an ethnocentric marketing orientation.

It should be mentioned that, often, ethnocentric firms approach globalization by internationalizing at the level of the function, rather than the firm; for example, the marketing department may have a geocentric strategy even if top management has an ethnocentric orientation.[7]

1-3b Polycentric Orientation

Firms with a **polycentric orientation** are guided by a *multidomestic market concept.* Managers of polycentric firms are very much aware of the importance of individual international markets to the success of their business and are likely to establish individual businesses, typically wholly owned subsidiaries or marketing subsidiaries, in each of the countries where they operate. The assumption the company makes is that each market is unique and needs to be addressed individually. Consequently, the company is fully decentralized and engages in minimal coordination with the headquarters.

Each subsidiary has its own marketing plans and objectives and operates autonomously as an independent profit center on an individual country basis to achieve its goals; all marketing activities are performed in each country independently of the

global marketing International marketing activities that do not have a country or region focus and that are possibly due to the emergence of global consumer segments and efficient global allocation of company talent and resources.

ethnocentric orientation Company strategies consistent with the belief that domestic strategies, techniques, and personnel are superior to foreign ones and therefore provide the most effective framework for the company's overseas involvement; companies adopting this perspective view international operations and customers as secondary to domestic operations and customers.

polycentric orientation Company strategies predicated on the assumption that each country's market is unique and should be addressed individually, with a country-specific marketing mix.

company headquarters.[8] To address local consumer needs, marketing research is conducted independently in each overseas market, and products are fully adapted to meet these needs. Alternatively, separate product lines are developed to meet the needs of the individual markets.

In the process of developing individual strategies for each market, the company does not coordinate activities across the different countries and cannot benefit from economies of scale that such coordination would allow. Furthermore, numerous functions are duplicated, and, ultimately, final product costs are higher to the end consumer. For decades, Ford used a polycentric strategy in meeting the needs of budget-conscious consumers by developing a Ford Escort automobile for the United Kingdom that looked different from the one sold in the United States or Southeast Asia.[9] Currently, the automobile addressing the needs of the budget-conscious consumer, the Ford Focus, looks identical in each market: Ford has adopted a geocentric approach to product development.

1-3c Regiocentric Orientation

regiocentric orientation Company strategies that view world regions as distinct markets that share economic, political, and/or cultural traits that will respond to a regionwide marketing approach.

Firms with a regiocentric or a geocentric orientation are guided by a *global marketing concept*. Companies adopting a **regiocentric orientation** view world regions as distinct markets that share economic, political, and/or cultural traits such that they would be viable candidates for a regionwide marketing approach. A regiocentric orientation is now possible due to the success of regional economic and political integration that allows for implementing a uniform marketing strategy in the entire region. Member countries of the European Union, for example, are candidates for Pan-European marketing strategies, whereas signatory countries of the North American Free Trade Agreement (NAFTA) lend themselves to a successful marketing strategy aimed at the North American market. PepsiCo appears to have a regiocentric orientation: Its divisions are organized based on location, with regional offices coordinating all local marketing activities. For example, Pepsi's East European operations are coordinated by its Vienna (Austria) office, which devises the company's regional objectives and oversees the implementation of the company's marketing strategy in the region.

1-3d Geocentric Orientation

geocentric orientation Company strategies that are consistent with the belief that the entire world, without national and regional distinctions, constitutes a potential market with identifiable, homogeneous segments that need to be addressed differentially.

Firms in which top management adopts a **geocentric orientation** perceive the entire world—without national and regional distinctions—as a potential market with identifiable, homogeneous segments that need to be addressed with tailored marketing strategies, regardless of geographic location or nationality. Coordinated management policies are designed to reflect the full integration among worldwide operations.

The objective of a geocentric company is most often to achieve a position as a low-cost manufacturer and marketer of its product line; such a firm achieves a strategic competitive advantage by developing manufacturing processes that add more value per unit cost to the final product than its rivals.[10] McDonald's has been successful as a result of its geocentric philosophy. The company uses local products to ultimately offer a similar service to consumers from Mexico City to Mumbay. In Europe, McDonald's uses Polish potatoes, which do not lend themselves to a thin, McDonald's cut but are touted to be the best in the region. It also uses local beef from the European regions not affected or threatened by livestock disease. In India or Pakistan, for example, McDonald's serves lamb or vegetarian burgers. Throughout the world, it provides a uniform service that offers, in addition to the fast food it is known for, clean restrooms, air conditioning, and service with a smile—even in markets where a smile is a rare occurrence in a service encounter.

1-4 Drivers of International Expansion

Few companies operate in an isolated, country-specific environment, and even fewer can effectively avoid international involvement. Local firms manufacturing for local consumers are dependent on equipment, parts, and/or raw materials originating abroad. They sell to clients and final consumers who have had exposure to international trade practices and to international products. A complete isolation from international influence is possible only in a closed environment, in countries such as North Korea, where, for different reasons, consumers are shielded from international influence.

Increasingly, companies cannot afford to avoid involvement in international marketing. Avoiding international expansion could mean losing market share to competitors and missing numerous opportunities created by changes in the international environment. **Drivers in the business environment** and **firm-specific drivers,** addressed in sections 1-4a, "Drivers in the Business Environment," and 1-4b, "Firm-Specific Drivers," as well as Table 1-1, help international companies benefit from such opportunities.

1-4a Drivers in the Business Environment

Competition

Competitive pressure is frequently a driver of internationalization. McCann Erickson, a leading advertising agency, follows one of its longtime clients, Coca-Cola, in every country where the company is present around the globe; McCann Erickson has been handling the Coca-Cola account in 129 countries since 1942.[11] That often means McCann Erickson loses money in countries where its accounts are limited but where, nevertheless, it chooses to be present to serve the advertising needs of Coke. If McCann Erickson chose not to serve its client in a market, Coca-Cola might resort to the services of a competitor, and, based on the company experience with the competitor, Coca-Cola might replace McCann Erickson with the competing advertising firm.

Regional Economic and Political Integration

In addition to cultural similarities—language and religion, for example—economic and political integration play an important part in facilitating international trade. Regional agreements such as the North American Free Trade Agreement (NAFTA), the Southern Cone Common Market (MERCOSUR), and the politically and economically integrated European Union are examples of successful attempts at lowering or eliminating barriers between member countries and promoting trade within the perimeter of each common market.[12] The benefits of integration extend to companies from nonmember states as well. It permits subsidiaries incorporated in the respective markets to benefit from free trade within the region and allows firms outside the integrated regions to conduct business within the common market without the impediments typically posed by crossing national borders—customs paperwork, separate tariffs for each country, etc.

drivers in the business environment Elements in the business environment, such as competition, technology, and labor costs, causing the firm to become involved internationally.

firm-specific drivers Elements specific to the firm, such as product life cycle, causing the firm to become involved internationally.

Table 1-1   International Marketing Drivers

Business Environment Drivers	Firm-Specific Drivers
Competition	Product life-cycle considerations
Regional economic and political integration	High new product development costs
Technology	Standardization, economies of scale, and cheap labor
Improvements in the transportation and telecommunication infrastructure	Experience transfers
Economic growth	
Transition to a market economy	
Converging consumer needs	

A company from the United States exporting products to multiple countries in the European Union, for example, will cross borders once: The company will do the customs paperwork and pay the required customs duties only once, instead of applying for an import license and paying customs duties in every country where it exports products. A subsidiary of a company from the United States incorporated in any country of the European Union is a corporate citizen of the European Union. Consequently, the subsidiary does not have to pay duties when it crosses borders of European Union member states, nor foreign exchange costs, because all transactions are conducted in Euros. For example, although Ford is a U.S. company, Ford Germany is a citizen of Germany and the European Union. As such, Ford Germany can freely ship its Ford Focus, Ford Ka, Ford Mondeo, Ford Fusion, Ford Transit Euroline, and its other models to dealers in all the countries of the European Union without going through customs and engaging in related paperwork. Moreover, the company does not incur any foreign exchange cost because all the transactions take place in Euros.

Technology

Technology has created opportunities for firms involved in international business. In terms of media development, consumers worldwide are exposed to programming originating in other countries. Programming from the United States in particular dominates the international airways: *Law & Order* is followed by audiences worldwide, CNN is popular with businesspeople around the world, and NBC eagerly exports its mix of late-night comedy and news magazines to the rest of the world. Advertising also crosses borders, exposing consumers to brands from other countries. The Web and the Internet have revolutionized the way many companies conduct business, offering businesses instant and unlimited international exposure—something that brick-and-mortar stores and traditional manufacturers have taken years to achieve. Such exposure offers tremendous opportunities to small businesses that do not normally have the advertising budget to communicate with the international market. For example, a Havasu-owned business in Nevada, located two hours by car and another two on horseback from Las Vegas, can advertise weekend vacation opportunities to French businesspeople planning to attend Las Vegas conferences or to French couples looking for a unique honeymoon.

Improvements in the Transportation and Telecommunication Infrastructure

Closely linked to technology are the leaps in the area of transportation and, particularly, in the technology infrastructure. In the not-so-remote past, a Mercedes Benz service station in Bujumbura, Burundi (Sub-Saharan East Africa), attempting to contact the company factory in Stuttgart, Germany, to order a part, would tie up an English- or German-speaking employee for most of the day for this purpose. The employee would book the telephone call with the operator early in the morning and would typically be contacted by the afternoon. The call would be facilitated by an operator in Brussels, Belgium (all calls to Burundi went via cable from Belgium to its former colonies in East Africa), who would link the factory to the service station. The quality of the connection would often be problematic, necessitating a second request for a telephone connection. An alternative would have been placing the request via telex (faxing was not an option, nor was the use of email).

Today, a telephone connection to Burundi would be handled via satellite, at a significantly lower cost than previously, when it was handled via cable. The communication would be crisp and clear, especially if a cellular phone is used; analog telephones are still problematic. Teleconferencing is also becoming common in international business transactions. In addition, faxing and emailing constitute viable options for written communication between the service station and the German factory. In fact, much of the outsourcing of customer service to developing countries, such as India and China, is largely attributed to improvements in telecommunication. When consumers call CompuServe to obtain help with access or to pay bills, they are most likely to speak to a customer service representative in India; in fact, in this author's experience, it is almost impossible to speak to a representative in the United States.

Transportation has also greatly improved since the 1980s. The introduction of containers for international inter-modal (ship, truck, train) shipping greatly facilitates the transportation of physical goods. For passenger transport, efficient and rapid air travel has become more affordable, allowing for frequent interaction between expatriate or local employees and employees from the company headquarters. Alternatively, high-speed train travel on inter-city routes allows for rapid transportation in developed countries, such as Japan, and many countries in the European Union (see Figure 1-2).

Economic Growth

Economic growth constitutes a very important driver of internationalization. Economic development in general and increased buying power—attributed to the emergence of a strong middle class in large markets, such as those of Brazil and India, for example—have created great potential for international brands. Economic growth has also opened markets that were previously closed or that have limited international competition: A case in point is China, where consumers are no longer restricted with regard to their consumption and physical movement. China also welcomes foreign direct investment and supports large-scale privatization of state-owned enterprises. Emerging economies in general are more open to foreign trade and no longer severely limit international firms operating in these markets.

Transition to a Market Economy

The transition of the former Eastern Bloc countries and formerly closed economies, such as that of Vietnam, to a market economy has led to rapid economic development in these countries and has created important new markets for international brands. Another important outcome of the transition to a market economy has been the deregulation and privatization of former government monopolies; under the former Communist regimes, all industry was run by inefficient state enterprises. Opportunities exist for product manufacturers, such as Philip Morris, Whirlpool, Unilever, Procter & Gamble, Colgate-Palmolive, and other companies, to purchase or partner with local companies operating at a loss producing low-quality goods and to turn them around into successful enterprises. Similarly, service providers, from Accenture to Pizza Hut, are entering these markets, engaging in the highest level of commitment: foreign direct investment.

F i g u r e   1 - 2

An infrastructure that can support high-speed train travel is characteristic of large European cities.

Currently, international companies, joint ventures between multinationals and local companies, private local businesses, as well as some remnants of the former system—state-owned enterprises, for example—compete for local consumers in the transition economies of Central and Eastern Europe. At the same time, satellite television and the Internet expose these consumers to programming, to information, and to advertising for international brands, shaping consumer desires and brand preferences. Companies that have, over time, ignored these markets due to the obstacles they posed (limiting operations, limiting their access to hard currency, and restricting repatriation of profits) are now embracing the many opportunities open to international investors.

Converging Consumer Needs

Exposure to global brands in one's home country and, while traveling abroad, to media advertising these brands has created demand for many global products. Consumers worldwide are loyal to international brands such as Nike sneakers, Levi's jeans, Coca-Cola, Heineken beer, and Ralph Lauren shirts. Uniform consumer segments are emerging worldwide: Generation X consumers in the United States and in Southeast Asia are loyal to the same soft-drink brands, wear the same brands of clothing, listen to the same music, have the same idols, see the same television shows, and watch MTV for entertainment.

During their international travels, consumers purchase brands and services available in their home country, which they are familiar with. Most often, these offerings are successful international products and services. Alternatively, consumers traveling abroad bring with them product experiences and demand brands that may not be available in the home-country market. This would generate pull demand, whereby consumers request the product from the retailers, who subsequently convey the information up the distribution chain to wholesalers. The wholesalers would then order the product.

Firms facing similar consumers demanding in unison the same products have a relatively easy task in addressing the needs of these consumers, using a similar marketing strategy throughout the region. Entry in such uniform markets is facilitated by selling the same product regardless of market and by the use of the same advertising campaign to address Generation X in the United States, France, Malaysia, and El Salvador.

1-4b Firm-Specific Drivers

Product Life-Cycle Considerations

A main driver of international expansion is a firm's attempt to prolong the life cycle of its products. Products that are in late maturity, or even in the decline stage, can change their position on the global product life-cycle stage by going into markets where the product is in high demand. To illustrate this point, the cigarette industry is in either the late maturity stage or in the decline stage in many industrialized countries. By entering emerging markets where cigarettes are in the growth stage and consumers have increasing purchase power, such as China, India, and Central and Eastern Europe, the cigarette industry is in fact prolonging its products' life cycle.

High New Product Development Costs

The concept of high new product development costs is related to the product life cycle. Companies often spend long periods of time and significant amounts of money to develop new products. Nike, on the average, spends close to a year to develop, test, and manufacture new product designs that then last on the shelves in the United States for only six months. Despite the size and purchase power of the U.S. market, it is unlikely that Nike would fully recover its product development costs and make a profit as well if it limited its sales to this country. This is especially true for companies at the forefront of technology (manufacturers of high-tech equipment and electronics, pharmaceutical firms, and others), which need to tap large markets for long periods of time to recoup costs and to make a profit as well; as a result, for these companies, going international is not a choice—it is a precondition for survival.

Standardization, Economies of Scale, and Cheap Labor

During the maturity stage of the product life cycle, the core product is likely to achieve a standard in a particular industry: Competitors—typically an oligopoly—respond to consumer needs by offering products whose components are interchangeable and which converge toward the brand experiencing the greatest consumer demand. To offer historical illustrations, standards were established in the personal computer industry (the IBM standard) and the videocassette recorder industry (the VHS standard). Also during the maturity stage, firms increasingly compete on price: Typically, they attempt to lower the product manufacturing costs by achieving economies of scale in production. In addition, firms with mature brands also move manufacturing operations and facilities abroad, to developing countries, in an attempt to take advantage of significantly lower labor costs.

Experience Transfers

International firms benefit from lessons they learn in the different parts of the world. Colgate-Palmolive, for example, developed its successful Axion dish-washing paste for its Latin American market after noting that women washed dishes by hand, dunking their hands in a small tub with a few slivers of soap. The same product was then offered to consumers in Central and Eastern Europe after noting that they washed dishes using a similar method—and the product was a hit. Service providers such as Pizza Hut found that they were more successful with consumers in general, but especially with younger generations of consumers in Central and Eastern Europe, if they played pop music on the rather loud side in their restaurants. As a result, they started entering new markets by partnering with radio stations and discos.

Such experience transfers are not limited to product or service providers. The Tesco Extra hypermarket (superstore) in the city of Newcastle, United Kingdom, is based on a Tesco hypermarket first introduced by the same U.K. retailer in Hungary.[13]

1-5 Obstacles to Internationalization

Companies attempting to establish and maintain an international presence are likely to encounter **obstacles to internationalization** both from within the company and from outside. Such obstacles can be financial in nature: The company might not have the finances to expand beyond national frontiers. Others are psychological: Fear of an unknown international environment or of local business practices may keep the company from international engagement. These two types of barriers, however, could equally affect the company's local expansion efforts: Companies may not have the finances to expand beyond a small regional market, or they fear going into new markets where consumers may not be familiar with their products and hence may not respond to their marketing strategy.

Some obstacles are encountered only by firms in their process of internationalization—obstacles that they are unlikely to encounter in other expansion efforts. They are the self-reference criterion, government barriers, and international competition.

obstacles to internationalization
Impediments that the firm may encounter in the process of internationalizing.

1-5a Self-Reference Criterion

Of crucial importance to international operations is the ability of the firm, and especially of its marketing program, to adapt to the local business environment to serve the needs of local consumers and to address the requirements of local government, industry, and channels of distribution. An impediment to adaptation is the **self-reference criterion,** defined as individuals' conscious and unconscious reference to their own national culture, to home-country norms, values, as well as to their knowledge and experience, in the process of making decisions in the host country.

Self-reference can lead to a breakdown in communication between parties from different cultures. For example, an employee of a large multinational company from the United States has been trained by career counselors in the U.S. that looking one's counterpart in

self-reference criterion
Individuals' conscious and unconscious reference to their own national culture, to home-country norms and values, and to their knowledge and experience in the process of making decisions in the host country.

the eyes conveys directness and honesty. When this individual conducts business in Japan using direct eye contact, he is likely to be perceived as abrasive and challenging. Similarly, if an employee proceeds directly to transacting the business deal in Latin America or Southern Europe instead of first interacting in a social setting to establish rapport, he would be perceived as arrogant, interested only in the bottom line, rather than in a long-term working relationship.

A first step to minimizing the impact of the self-reference criterion is selecting the appropriate personnel for international assignments. Such employees are sensitive to others and have experience working in different environments. Second, it is important to train expatriates to focus on and be sensitive to the local culture, rather than limit their personal interactions to own-country nationals or to expatriates from countries with cultures that are similar to their own. In fact, it is advisable that firms institute an organizationwide general orientation that instills and demonstrates sensitivity to international environments and openly spurns value judgments and national stereotyping.

1-5b Government Barriers

National governments, especially governments in developing countries, keep a tight control over foreign investment. They scrutinize international market entrants, permitting or denying access to international firms based on criteria that are deemed important for national industry and/or security considerations. Among formal methods used by national governments to restrict or impede entrance of international firms in the local market are tariffs and barriers such as import quotas. Other restrictions may involve instituting policies of restricting import license awards, foreign exchange restrictions, and local content requirements, among others.

Member countries of the World Trade Organization, or members of regional economic and/or political integration agreements such as NAFTA and the European Union, find it very difficult to use tariffs as a means of restricting international expansion of companies in the countries' territories. Increasingly, they are using nontariff barriers, such as cumbersome procedures for import paperwork processing, delays in granting licenses, or preference given to local service providers and product manufacturing for all contracting work.

1-5c International Competition

Although competition can be a driver of internationalization, competitors can also erect barriers to new entrants in a market. In competitors' arsenals of barriers are, among others, the following: blocking channels of distribution, binding retailers into exclusive agreements, slashing prices temporarily to prevent product adoption, or engaging in an advertising blitz that could hurt a company's initial sales in a market and cause it to retrench. With heavy competition from new and lesser-known brands in Asia, Central and Eastern Europe, and North Africa and the Middle East, Marlboro created a strong defensive strategy for its cigarettes: It slashed prices by as much as a third and advertised heavily anywhere it was legal to do so, especially on billboards in the center of different capital cities and towns in the provinces.

As an example, sales of Marlboro in Southeastern Europe were hurt by various local competitors and, in particular, by a successful regional brand, Assos, from Greece. Assos was rapidly gaining a leading position in a number of markets in the region when Marlboro went on the offensive, limiting Assos's market share to a point where the company was forced to abandon many of its markets. Marlboro effectively put in question the international expansion of many new European and Asian brands, as well as new brands from the United States (it decimated, for instance, sales of new brands of U.S. cigarettes created specifically for the Russian market by small entrepreneurs).

Summary

- **Define international marketing and identify the different levels of international involvement.** Firms can elect to engage in different levels of international expansion. Domestic firms will focus on the domestic market and ignore international possibilities. At the next level, firms can export their products overseas, taking advantage of international opportunities to increase their sales and profits. Firms involved in international marketing are serving international consumers and are present in different countries (but do not coordinate between-countries activities under a regional office or subsidiary) with sales offices, subsidiaries, or in partnership with local or other international firms. Global marketing involves coordination of all marketing activities within a particular region or worldwide.

- **Describe the different company orientations and philosophies toward international marketing.** Depending on the type of industry or service they are in and depending on the extent to which companies have an international focus, companies adopt different orientations and philosophies toward internationalization. Ethnocentric companies consider domestic strategies, techniques, and personnel as superior to foreign ones; these strategies then provide the framework for the companies' overseas operations, which are secondary to domestic operations. Companies with a polycentric orientation focus on different international markets without coordinating between international activities. Companies with a regiocentric orientation coordinate their operations regionally, whereas companies with a geocentric orientation coordinate their marketing and management policies worldwide, fully integrating their operations and addressing uniform segments worldwide.

- **Identify environmental and firm-specific drivers that direct firms toward international markets.** A number of elements in the business environment direct firms to explore international opportunities. One such element is competitive pressure, the need to serve clients regardless of market attractiveness, preventing them from switching to the service of a competitor. Opportunities in the environment, such as worldwide economic growth and new emerging markets, regional economic and political integration and the removal of trade barriers, improvements in the transportation and telecommunication infrastructure, and advancement in technology worldwide also prompt international firms to pursue international markets. The advent of technology and media influence, economic prosperity, and consumer travel are creating uniform segments of consumers with similar preferences that international firms could serve effectively with standardized strategies. Firms facing decreasing sales attributed to a mature home market can extend the life cycle of their products by going international: Cigarette companies are in a late maturity stage in the United States but, most likely, in late growth stage worldwide. During the maturity stage, as products start competing on price, companies benefit from going international to take advantage of cheaper and yet competent labor and new markets.

- **Identify obstacles preventing firms from engaging in successful international ventures.** Obstacles to international marketing are the self-reference criterion—conscious and unconscious reference to one's national culture, to home-country norms, values, as well as to one's knowledge and experience, in the process of making decisions in the host country. Additional obstacles can be the local and national governments of the host country, which could impose entry barriers or prevent the companies from repatriating profits, and competitive barriers to entry.

Key Terms

drivers in the business environment
domestic marketing
ethnocentric orientation
export marketing
firm-specific drivers

geocentric orientation
global marketing
international marketing
multinational marketing
obstacles to internationalization

polycentric orientation
regiocentric orientation
self-reference criterion

Discussion Questions

1. Discuss the differences between firm internationalization philosophies.
2. Try to work backward from a company's web page and attempt to infer its internationalization philosophy. Look at the Procter & Gamble (www.pg.com) web pages describing the company's international involvement and its international product mix. What orientation do you believe this company has and why?
3. What are the drivers in the international business environment that lead a firm to engage in international operations? What are some of the firm-specific drivers leading to internationalization?
4. What is the "self-reference criterion"?
5. How can governments and competitors prevent a firm from entering a particular market?

You can find the correct answers to these questions by taking the quiz and then submitting your answers in the Online Edition. The program will automatically score your submission. Where you miss a question, the program will provide the correct answer, a rationale for the answer, and the section number in the chapter where the topic is discussed.

Chapter Quiz (True/False)

1. International marketing involves marketing activities that have a substantial focus on international consumers in a particular country or countries.
2. Firms involved in domestic marketing and export marketing are more likely to have an ethnocentric philosophy to internationalization.
3. Nontarriff barriers have been successful in restricting the international expansion of companies.
4. A regiocentric orientation calls for companies to focus on distinct markets and create country-specific marketing strategies.
5. Reducing the cost of labor is a basic business-environment driver.

Multiple Choice

1. International marketing obstacles include all the following EXCEPT
   a. the self-reliance criterion.
   b. competition.
   c. development costs for new products.
   d. government barriers.
2. Similarities of Generation Xers in the United States, France, and Malaysia create opportunities for international firms. Their similarity is in fact a business-environment driver, i.e.,
   a. economic growth.
   b. competition.
   c. converging consumer needs.
   d. regional economic and political integration.
3. Which internationalization philosophy best describes the Ford Focus strategy?
   a. geocentric orientation
   b. ethnocentric orientation
   c. polycentric orientation
   d. regiocentric orientation
4. CNN is known by businesspeople around the world mainly due to this driver.
   a. standardization
   b. competition
   c. technology
   d. economic growth

Endnotes

1. *FedEx Corporation Presents*, internal presentation.
2. Howard Perlmutter, "The Tortuous Evolution of the Multinational Corporation," *Columbia Journal of World Business*, January–February 1969.
3. Thomas W. Malnight, "Globalization of an Ethnocentric Firm: An Evolutionary Perspective," *Strategic Management Journal*, Vol. 16, No. 2, February 1995, pp. 119–142.
4. David J. Lemak and Wiboon Arunthanes, "Global Business Strategy: A Contingency Approach," *Multinational Business Review*, Vol. 5, No. 1, Spring 1997, pp. 26–37.
5. Ibid.
6. Ibid.
7. Malnight, "Globalization of an Ethnocentric Firm," pp. 119–142.
8. Lemak and Arunthanes, "Global Business Strategy," pp. 26–37.
9. Ibid.
10. Ibid.
11. Hillary Chura, "Coke Brands IPG as Global Ad Strategist," *Advertising Age*, Vol. 71, No. 50, December 4, 2000, p. 50.
12. Regional, economic, and political integration will be addressed at length in Chapter 4.
13. Alexandra Jardine, "Retailers Go on International Shopping Trip," *Marketing*, January 20, 2000, p. 15.

Case 1-1

Nanjing National Steel Company

Liu Hong, Director of International Accounts at the Nanjing National Steel Company, has just been summoned by the new company chairman. He is expected to provide viable solutions for the company that will enable it to compete effectively in an increasingly saturated international steel market. China's steel production is growing at breakneck pace. Its rapid growth is posing serious threats to the industry, and Nanjing National, one of the larger recently privatized steel companies, is part of the problem.

When Mao Tse Tung ordered an increase in the steel production as part of the Great Leap Forward, people left their fields, abandoned their work in agriculture, and fled to the large steel mills that produced millions of tons of useless substandard steel. Today, an enterprising China is taking another great leap, investing in industrial establishments, especially in the steel industry. The old, large steel mills have been privatized, becoming more efficient and producing high-quality steel, and investors are keen on banking on new and profitable steel mills.

According to industry reports, China has doubled its steel output since the year 2000, emerging as the world's largest producer, and it will double output again by 2007. At this pace, there will be an enormous glut of steel, which will lead to mass layoffs from Pittsburgh to Beijing. Under these circumstances, the Nanjing National Steel Company would have to cut its workforce—most of it recently hired—by two thirds. Such a move would displace many workers and their dependent families, and could very likely lead to political unrest in the Nanjing region, as elsewhere in China. In fact, China's State Council, its cabinet, is starting to discourage investment in new steel mills by making such investments less attractive for investors. However, such efforts at the national level are countered by local officials whose goals are to increase local job opportunities and taxes. Locally, there is a strong push for establishing new steel mills, with local governments offering incentives for such investment.

Liu Hong gazed at the steel mill's dock on the Yangtze River. So many of China's steel mills are located on the banks of this river, to facilitate the barge access of ore imports. The steel Nanjing National produces is used to meet domestic demand, but there are signs that China's economy is slowing down and demand is likely to decrease. The new investors in the newly privatized Nanjing National Steel Company need to be placated: a viable solution for the company in the future may be internationalization. And the chairman of the company needs to understand the importance of going international to be able to address the investors' questions.

Yet going international may be difficult in an environment that is fraught with unpredictability and protectionist measures. The world's largest steel consumer, the United States, is an important target market in Liu Hong's view. Yet dozens of U.S. steel producers are going bankrupt because they cannot compete with imports that benefit from state subsidies. As a result, in an effort to protect the U.S. steel industry, the U.S. government took a step that challenged the entire world trade establishment, charging tariffs on steel imports. Furthermore, the European Union is contemplating measures to block a flood of steel imports from Asian

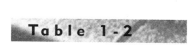

Table 1-2

The Major Steel-Producing and Steel-Consuming Countries

Major Steel Producers in 2002 and 2001 (million metric tons crude steel production)				
Country	2002		2001	
	Rank	Tonnage	Rank	Tonnage
China	1	181.6	1	150.9
Japan	2	107.7	2	102.9
United States	3	92.2	3	90.1
Russia	4	59.8	4	59.0
South Korea	5	45.4	6	43.9
FR Germany	6	45.0	5	44.8
Ukraine	7	33.4	7	33.1
Brazil	8	29.6	9	26.7
India	9	28.8	8	27.3
Italy	10	26.1	10	26.5
France	11	20.3	11	19.3
Chinese Taipei	12	18.2	12	17.3
Turkey	13	16.5	15	15.0
Spain	14	16.4	13	16.5
Canada	15	16.0	14	15.3

Major Steel Consumers in 2002 (world total: 845 million metric tons crude steel)	
EU (15)	16.8%
Other Europe	4.4%
Former USSR	3.7%
NAFTA	16.0%
China	25.8%
Japan	8.8%
Other Asia	15.9%
Africa	2.0%
Central and South America	3.5%
Middle East	2.0%
Australia and New Zealand	0.9%
Others	8.6%

Source: 2003 Edition, World Steel in Figures, International Iron and Steel Institute, 2003; www.worldsteel.org.

continued

countries—imports that normally would have had the United States as their destination.

Liu Hong realizes that he must present a balanced perspective on going international. The challenge is convincing the chairman and the investors that going international is essential for Nanjing National Steel Company. As a first step, he examines the data on steel production and consumption in Table 1-2.

Source: Adapted from "Another Leap by China, with Steel Leading Again," *The New York Times,* May 1, 2004, pp. B1, B3. Company and characters are fictional.

Analysis Suggestions

1. What arguments should Liu Hong offer the company chairman in favor of internationalization? What are the business environment internationalization drivers and the firm drivers that are likely to lead to the internationalization of the firm?

2. What product life-cycle stage is the steel industry in worldwide? Should Nanjing National Steel Company move its labor force overseas, to China's neighboring countries? Why? Why not?

part 2

The International Marketing Environment

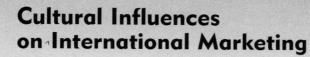

An Overview of the International Marketing Environment

Chapter Objectives

By the end of this chapter, you should be able to

1 Provide an overview of the world economic environment and examine different perspectives on economic development.

2 Address differences between countries of different levels of economic development and discuss the importance of emerging markets.

3 Examine the indicators of political risk and address international firm approaches to political risk management.

4 Describe how international law, home-country law, and host-country law affect international firm operations and address issues related to jurisdiction.

5 Discuss different legal systems, intellectual property laws, and national laws with extra-territorial impact that affect international firms.

6 Examine the natural and technological environments and the potential and limitations they present to international firms.

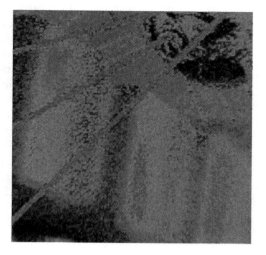

The transition economies that first opened their markets to multinational firms and privatized national industries experienced the greatest degree of growth and were most successful in developing national industrial sectors that competed effectively with the international firms. Yet, despite the clear, positive impact on economic development, successful multinationals face extensive criticism from developing countries in Africa and Asia. Their presence in these countries and their market dominance are often likened to a form of neo-colonialism—industrial colonialism.

Countries where multiple tribes have co-existed for decades without any conflict, where the president and his army have led effectively, spreading the wealth to the population and attracting in the country foreign direct investment, fall victim to a civil war. Multinational firms leave their assets open to plundering and promptly ship their expatriates to safety. This scenario is played over and over in the world: Multinational companies in Chad, Rwanda, Burundi, Sierra Leone, Haiti, Bosnia and Herzegovina, and Croatia have all experienced losses. Multinational companies are also victims of corporate terrorism, which is on the increase worldwide.

Some companies operate in environments where everything is forbidden unless expressly allowed. Other companies operate in environments where everything is perceived as allowed unless expressly forbidden. Companies operating in legally ambiguous environments face ethical and legal challenges from host-country national governments, para-national institutions, and the home-country government that they have to address effectively to be able to survive in international markets.

The natural environment of international marketing also poses challenges to businesses: Geology and the shortage of natural resources, coupled with a high population growth, can negatively affect market potential. Similarly, topography can affect access, and hydrology and climate can affect economic development. Phenomena such as a shortage of natural resources, the energy crisis, and the environmental quality crisis affect the business environment.

The technological environment of international marketing is rapidly opening international markets never before accessible to multinationals and is creating a viable future for small and medium enterprises that never before could have had such a broad exposure. The technological environment is also speeding the new-product development process and creating distribution potential never before attained in industry.

This chapter will focus on elements in the environment of international marketing. We will examine the economic, political, legal, natural, and technological environments on the international marketing operations of firms.

2-1 The Economic Environment of International Marketing

2-1a The World Economy

It is common today to hear that, when the United States sneezes, Europe and Japan catch a cold. This is an understatement. When the United States experiences a downturn in the economy, reverberations echo throughout the world: Central and South American countries need to be rescued by the International Monetary Fund; all the Asian economies flounder; banks in developing countries default on their debt. The United States is equally affected by the world economy. The Asian crisis of the late 1990s sent stock markets tumbling in the United States and in the rest of the world. In the Internet Age, countries are becoming more and more connected by trade, by capital markets, by the flow of technology and ideas across national borders, and by psychology: Rather than rising and falling separately, national economies increasingly respond to the same forces.[1] Interdependence has become the leading principle of globalization.

In sectoral examples, an excess of steel in the world markets, attributed to overproduction in Russia, led to restructuring of the industry elsewhere in the world, leaving only a few players in the world steel oligopoly. And underproduction of oil attributed to the control of the Organization for Petrol Exporting Countries (OPEC) has historically led to inflation worldwide. On the positive side, the boom in technology stocks in 1999 led to much—albeit short-lived—prosperity in many developed countries, as well as in countries that stress technical training and software design, in particular, such as India. Never in the history of mankind has there been such a degree of interdependence.

The international economy has indeed become one single unit. Major companies simply cannot afford a local, home-country focus: The market share game is played on a world scale. A one-world commercial future is close to becoming a reality: Whereas 60 countries (excluding Eastern Europe and countries with fewer than 1 million people) have a gross national product (GNP) of less than US$10 billion, 135 multinational firms have revenues in excess of that amount, in a world where multinationals are breaking down barriers that have withstood armies, missionaries, crusaders, and politicians.[2]

2-1b The Economic Development Disparity

In the current economic environment, firms from industrialized countries and their representative governments dominate the world economy, allocating resources worldwide based on market potential, rather than on local population needs, creating a growing gap between the *have* countries and *have-not* countries. Developing countries, on the other hand, control resources (raw materials, labor) that multinationals need, control access to local consumers, and frequently pose barriers to international business operations in an attempt to lessen the development gap. It is important, under this environment, to understand the existing dynamics between countries at different levels of economic and market development and the philosophies underlying those dynamics.

2-2 Perspectives on Economic Development

Two models of economic development have gained acceptance in the world: a Western model, best articulated by Rostow, and the **Marxist-Leninist development model,** which still constitutes a dominant development philosophy in some developing countries. It must be noted that the fall of communism in Europe and the structural changes in China and Vietnam have reduced considerably the areas dominated by the Marxist-Leninist philosophy on economic development.

2-2a The Rostow Modernization Model

According to the **Rostow modernization model,**[3] each stage is a function of productivity, economic exchange, technological improvements, and income. Economic growth requires advancing from one stage to another. The modernization stages are

- Traditional society
- Transitional society
- Take-off
- The drive to maturity
- High mass consumption

Marxist-Leninist development model A development model attributed to Karl Marx and Vladimir Lenin which maps the development of society from an agrarian, traditional society to a society characterized by shared ownership of the means and outcomes of production and an equitable resource allocation; advancement from one stage to another is based on class struggle and transfer of ownership from one class to another and, ultimately, to the state.

Rostow modernization model An economic development model attributed to Rostow, according to which each stage of economic advance is a function of productivity, economic exchange, technological improvements, and income.

Traditional Society

Countries in the **traditional society** stage are characterized by an economic structure that is dominated by agriculture. Minimal productivity occurs, and only a few exchange transactions take place. Economic change and technological improvements are not sufficient to sustain any growth in per capita output, which is low.

Transitional Society (Pre-Conditions for Take-Off)

The **transitional society** stage is characterized by increased productivity in agriculture, and modern manufacturing begins to emerge. In manufacturing, low productivity remains the norm.

Take-Off

During **take-off,** growth becomes the norm and improvements in production lead to the emergence of leading sectors. Income rises across the board, and a new class of entrepreneurs emerges.

The Drive to Maturity

In the **drive-to-maturity stage,** modern technology is fully adopted in all economic activity, and new leading sectors emerge. The economy demonstrates the technological and entrepreneurial skill to produce anything it chooses to. The economy looks beyond the country's border for development.

High Mass Consumption

In the age of **high mass consumption,** leading sectors shift toward durable goods. A surge occurs in per capita income and increased allocation to social welfare programs. The masses can afford goods beyond food, clothing, and shelter.

2-2b Alternative Models of Economic Development

The Rostow model of economic development is, in fact, a Western perspective of development. Alternative models exist in spite of the global triumph of the market system and the confirmation of a Rostow-type model in countries that have previously adopted alternative philosophies. One example is the Marxist-Leninist model, a competing alternative for developing nations seeking to avoid domination by advanced market capitalist economies. It endorses a collective orientation, one adopted by the more traditional developing countries, and competes with market-oriented capitalism, fueling anticolonial and anti-imperialist sentiments.[4] Socialist ideas of sharing wealth; leveling inequality; eliminating homelessness; and providing basic needs such as health care, food, education, and shelter to all citizens appeal to many in the poor, developing countries that were long suppressed and exploited by colonial and imperialist powers. At the heart of this philosophy are issues of equitable distribution of national income, improvement in the welfare of the masses, and economic justice.[5] For an illustration of the Marxist-Leninist model of economic development, read International Marketing Illustration 2-1.

In an attempt to counter these alternative philosophies, Western financial- and institutional-strengthening assistance to developing countries grew dramatically with the goal of solidifying the positions of their political and ruling elites and the regimes they operated and eliminating some of the hardships such as absolute poverty, hunger, and disasters the masses suffered; the result of this effort is mixed.[6]

2-3 Levels of Economic Development

There are many competing classifications of countries from an economic development perspective. Historically, the informal and frequently used classification in the West has referred to highly industrialized, developed countries as the First World, to socialist countries as the

traditional society A stage in economic development defined by Rostow as one in which the economy is dominated by agriculture and relatively few exchange transactions occur.

transitional society A stage in the economic development process described by Rostow as characterized by increased productivity in agriculture and by the emergence of modern manufacturing.

take-off A stage in economic development described by Rostow as one in which economic growth becomes the norm and improvements in production lead to the emergence of leading sectors.

drive-to-maturity stage A stage in economic development, described by Rostow, as characterized by the technological and entrepreneurial skill to produce anything society chooses to produce.

high mass consumption A stage in economic development, described by Rostow, as characterized by leading sectors shifting toward durable goods.

International Marketing Illustration   2-1

The Marxist-Leninist Model of Economic Development

primitive society The first stage of economic and political development, characterized, according to Marxist-Leninist theory, by the joint tribal ownership of primitive means of production centered on agricultural tasks.

slavery-based society A stage of economic and political development, which, according to Marxist-Leninist theory, emerges as a result of tribes' dominance over other tribes: Dominant tribes claim ownership of conquered tribes and their property.

feudalism A stage in economic and political development, which, according to Marxist-Leninist theory, is characterized by the dominance of feudal lords, who own the land and its dwellers.

bourgeoisie A dominant social class, which, according to Marxist-Leninist theory, establishes lucrative means of production and achieves high productivity at the expense of exploited workers.

The Marxist-Leninist model and its dialectic materialism theories approach economic development philosophy similarly to the Rostow model in the first stage. The subsequent stages are depicted as a class struggle ending in revolution, which is needed for advancement to the next stage. Advancement is a function of the control of means of production, production outcomes, resource allocation, and the development of a mindset devoid of materialist needs. The stages of this model are described next.

The Primitive Society

Countries in the **primitive society** stage are similar to those in traditional society. There is joint, tribal ownership of the means of production, which are minimal, primitive, and centered on agricultural tasks, for the use of all the members of the commune within the tribe. Much of the agriculture is slash-and-burn, with the tribes moving in the quest for new territory. All tribal members in this egalitarian society work for the common welfare of the tribe.

The Slavery-Based Society

The **slavery-based society** emerges as a result of tribes taking over other tribes and enslaving their population. Slaves are now property of the conquering tribe. Under Roman, Mesopotamian, and Egyptian rule, slaves toiled in agriculture and built infrastructures, such as access roads and irrigation systems. Tribal territory ownership is established as a first step toward establishing private property. Trading agricultural goods and tools between tribes becomes common.

Feudalism

Under the feudal society known as **feudalism,** feudal lords own armies, land, and the dwellers of the land. Land is primarily in the hands of the feudal family; production is still primarily agricultural. Guilds emerge as a production unit, manufacturing goods and training future manufacturers under apprenticeships. Trading is common and widespread, and exchange is now primarily based on gold as currency.

The Capitalist Society

The capitalist society is represented by two stages. The first stage is characterized by an emerging **bourgeoisie** (developed from the guild class) as a ruling class, alongside the aristocracy (the former feudal family). The bourgeoisie creates lucrative means of production, and it achieves high productivity at the expense of exploited workers. Production shifts gradually from the agrarian sector to the industrial sector.

The second stage of **capitalism** is multinational **imperialism.** Imperialist capitalism is characterized by a capital that loses its national identity by crossing borders; in fact, the export of capital international trade are a central mechanism of imperialism. The international firm is a double parasite exploiting its own working class, as well as workers in less-developed countries. Multinational firms represent the modality for national domination of developing countries, and for the domination and subjugation of workers and peasants worldwide. The creation of international monopolies (**monopolistic capitalism**) represents the most advanced stage of capitalist dominance.

The Socialist Society

The socialist society is also composed of two stages. The first, transitional stage, leads to the disappearance of private property—which is replaced by collective, state property. Countries in this stage typically are formally known as People's Republics.

Socialism in its more advanced stage takes the form of the multilaterally developed socialist society. Socialist Republics, as countries in this stage are referred to, are characterized by state ownership of all the means of production. The state also controls the modes of production, allocating resources to industry, agriculture, education, and health care based on societal needs. With the exception of some remnants of capitalism, such as private property limited to one's dwelling, and philosophies that need to be erased at the next stage— materialism, for example—the state has in place most mechanisms necessary for the transition to communism.

The Communist Society

No country has ever claimed to have reached the communist stage. Under **communism,** all means of production and private property are under state ownership and/or cooperative ownership. The state is in charge of allocation of resources to sectors as needed and to individuals (goods and services) according to their needs. Communism develops "the new man," who views work as a need and who will work according to his ability. There is no need for private property, and there is no materialism in society.

In the early stages of communism, Lenin argued that foreign capital is important in the development process as a source of advanced technology; his solution was a leasing system whereby foreign firms would participate in particular projects and regions in communist countries for a limited amount of time.[7] In practice, this concept was soon countered by the implications of the Cold War and by Stalin's theory of two parallel markets (capitalist and socialist), which stressed internal integration among socialist countries for mutual economic development; according to this theory, capitalist markets were inherently weak, and socialist countries needed to isolate themselves from the capitalist world.[8]

The Rostow and Marxist-Leninist models are comparable, up to a point. In Figure 2-1, the models work in parallel up to the level of the drive-to-maturity stage in the Rostow model and the capitalist stage in the Marxist-Leninist model.

capitalism A stage of economic and political development, which, according to Marxist-Leninist theory, is characterized, in its early stages, by an emerging bourgeoisie, the shift of production from the agrarian sector to the industrial sector, and, in its later stages, by imperialism, where capital loses its national identity by crossing borders and establishing monopolies.

imperialism A stage of economic and political development, in which, according to Marxist-Leninist theory, capital loses its national identity by crossing borders.

monopolistic capitalism A stage of economic and political development, in which, according to Marxist-Leninist theory, multinational companies establish monopolies and expand internationally with the goal of subjugating developing countries.

socialism A transition stage of economic and political development, characterized, according to Marxist-Leninist theory, by the disappearance of private property and its replacement with collective, state property.

communism A stage in economic and political development, which, according to Marxist-Leninist theory, is characterized by state and cooperative ownership of all means of production and property.

continued

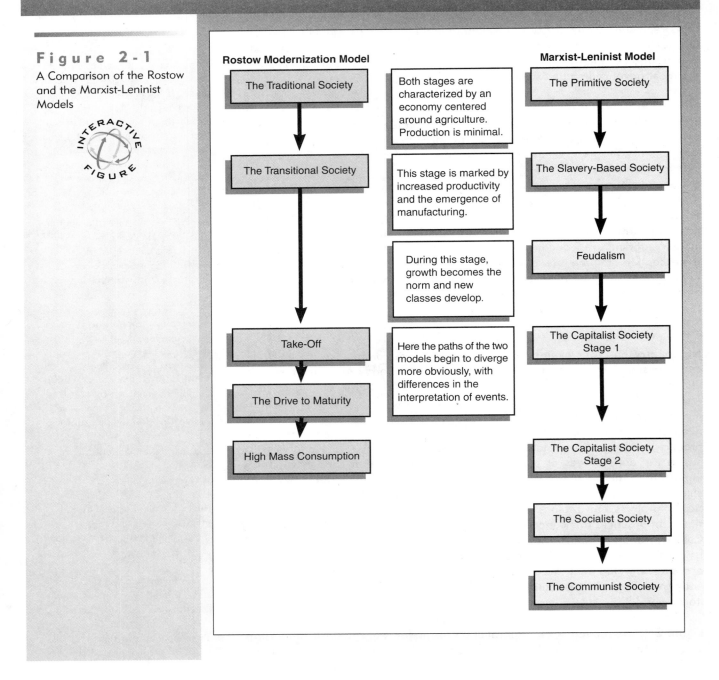

Figure 2-1

A Comparison of the Rostow and the Marxist-Leninist Models

Second World, and to developing countries as the Third World. Of this classification, only the term "the Third World" has been used widely, and it is still being used, even after the fall of communism. A United Nations (www.un.org) classification contrasts LLDCs (least-developed countries, and the lowest-income countries) and LDCs (less-developed countries, and lower-income countries) to developed countries. Yet other classifications bring in other dimensions, such as NICs (newly industrialized countries), in reference to Taiwan, Singapore, South Korea, and Hong Kong (known in the 1980s and 1990s as the *Asian Tigers*), and **emerging markets** (such as Brazil, Argentina, Chile, Peru, and the transitional economies of Central and Eastern Europe). For the purpose of this textbook, we will refer to three categories of countries, based on the classification used by the World Bank (www.worldbank.org):

- **Developed Countries**—These highly industrialized countries have well-developed industrial and service sectors. In this category fall newly industrialized countries, as well as countries that have had a developed status for many years. Although these countries present great potential because they have consumers with the highest per capita income, they also present challenges to international firms because their markets are in the maturity stage, consumers have established preferences, and competition is intense. The World Bank refers to the countries in this category as high-income countries, with a GNP per capita of US$9,266 or more.

- **Emerging Countries**—Countries considered emerging markets are both developing rapidly and have great potential. They are countries in Latin America, such as Argentina, Brazil, Uruguay, Paraguay, Chile, Peru, Bolivia, to name a few; countries in Asia, such as China, with its immense market, and India, with its substantial middle class; and the transition economies of Central and Eastern Europe, which are rapidly privatizing state-owned industries and adopting market reforms. Important in this category are **big emerging markets (BEMs),** which present the greatest potential for international trade and expansion. The World Bank refers to the countries in this category as middle-income countries, with a GNP per capita of US$766 to US$9,265.

- **Developing Countries**—Countries in this category are primarily agrarian, have low per capita income levels, and are located in different regions in Asia and in Sub-Saharan Africa. Developing countries are often neglected or underserved by large multinationals and consequently present great potential as niche markets. Even the countries with the lowest per capita income have a stratum of society that can afford global products. Furthermore, because they are primary recipients of international development aid, they present important opportunities for firms operating in the areas of infrastructure development and industrial sector development, and for related consultancies. The World Bank refers to the countries in this category as low-income countries, with a GNP per capita of less than US$755. It is important to note that these markets are grossly underserved by the international community and that consumer needs—even the most basic needs—in these markets are barely met by local administration. International Marketing Illustration 2-2 addresses challenges faced by poor consumers in developing countries.

The discrepancy between the countries in the three categories—developed, emerging, and developing—is evident: With regard to the GNP distribution worldwide, developed, highly industrialized countries account for close to 80 percent of the world's gross national product, whereas they account for less than 15 percent of the population (see Figure 2-2).

To illustrate, the United Nations Development Program monitors human development worldwide, publishing the *Human Development Report*. The report compares countries based on adult illiteracy, access to a viable water source, children underweight for their age, and the percentage of the population living on less than $1 per day. Table 2-1 compares countries in the low-human-development category on those dimensions.

2-3a The Importance of Emerging Markets

Countries with emerging markets present great potential to international firms. Their attractiveness lies primarily in their rate of economic growth—7 percent per year, in the

---

emerging markets Countries that are developing rapidly and have great economic potential; the World Bank characterizes them as middle-income countries, with a GNP per capita of US$766 to US$9,265.

developed countries Highly industrialized countries with well-developed service sectors, mature markets, and intense competition; they are characterized by the World Bank as high-income, with a GNP per capita of US$9,266 and above.

emerging countries Middle-income countries with a GNP per capita of US$766 to US$9,265, and with emerging markets that have great potential.

big emerging markets (BEMs) Large markets characterized by rapid economic development and high potential; big emerging markets set the pace for the economy in their geographic region.

developing countries Countries that are primarily agrarian, often neglected or under-served by large multinationals, and characterized by the World Bank as low-income countries, with a GNP per capita of less than US$755.

International Marketing Illustration   2-2

The Underserved Markets

In many developing countries, children must walk miles to reach their schools. In Adaboya, Ghana, for example, children must walk three miles to attend school even though a school building is located in the village; the local school is in disrepair and cannot be used in the rainy season. An average poor child in Mali has to walk five miles to elementary school. In Portero Sula, El Salvador, villagers cannot obtain health services at the local clinic because there are no doctors or nurses on staff. In the Mutasa district of Zimbabwe, women report that they were hit by staff during delivery of their babies.

Even in markets where services are available, the quality of services and their delivery are low. Absenteeism of doctors in Bangladesh is about 74 percent. Teachers in Ethiopia are absent a large percentage of the time. Children may attend school, but there may not be any teaching activity. Plus, 1 billion people lack access to adequate water sources, and 2.5 billion lack access to adequate sanitation.

The World Bank and the rest of the international aid community is taking forceful action to ensure that communities take concerted action to improve service delivery to these markets. For example, in El Salvador, community-managed schools, where parents are involved in their children's education and visit the school regularly, have a lower rate of absenteeism. In Bengalore, India, and in Cambodia, consumers have successfully penalized the poor delivery of services and forced local politicians and service providers to act.

For developing country consumers, priorities are highest for meeting basic needs. From a marketing perspective, however, these consumers are not a priority for most multinationals, but, rather, an afterthought, or a niche market at best. For now, local business will address the needs of these markets most effectively.

Source: World Development Report 2004: Making Services Work for Poor People; World Bank Group, http://econ.worldbank.org/wdr/wdr2004/.

past 20 years, compared to 2.3 percent for Western Europe and North America.[9] The following countries have been identified as emerging markets by *The Economist* in its regular reports on emerging markets:

- In Asia: China, India, Indonesia, Malaysia, the Philippines, Singapore, South Korea, Thailand
- In Africa and the Middle East: Israel, South Africa
- In Europe: The Czech Republic, Greece, Poland, Portugal, Russia, Turkey
- In Latin America: Argentina, Brazil, Chile, Mexico, Venezuela

Other countries are likely prospects for the emerging market category, based on their economic policies and performance in the past 20 years. Among them are Slovenia, Slovakia, Croatia, Romania, Bulgaria, the Ukraine, Latvia, Estonia, Lithuania, and Belarus in Central and Eastern Europe; and Colombia, Paraguay, Peru, and Uruguay in Latin America. These countries are rapidly privatizing their economies and adopting the economic reforms necessary to create a stable, growing economy.

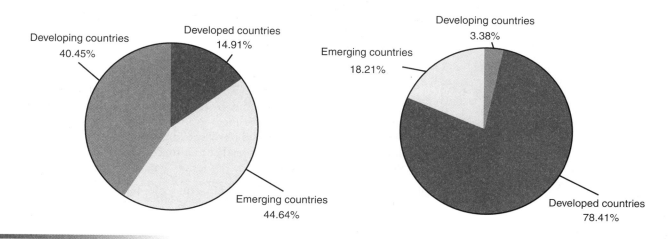

World Population Distribution

Developing countries
40.45%

Developed countries
14.91%

Emerging countries
44.64%

World GNP Distribution

Developing countries
3.38%

Emerging countries
18.21%

Developed countries
78.41%

Figure 2-2

An Illustration of Economic Disparity: Population and Gross National Product Statistics for Developed, Emerging, and Developing Countries

Source: Adapted from World Development Indicators, Washington, D.C.: World Bank, 2000.

Table 2-1
An Illustration of Human Development in Select Low-Human-Development Countries

Rank of Country (Total 175 Countries)	Birth Probability of Not Surviving to Age 40	Adult Illiteracy (%)	Population without Adequate Water Access (%)	Children Underweight for Age (%)	Population Living on Less Than $1 Per Day (%)
158 Rwanda	54.3	32.0	59	24	35.7
159 Benin	34.6	61.4	37	23	..
160 Tanzania	46.4	24.0	32	29	19.9
161 Côte d'Ivoire	51.7	50.3	19	21	12.3
162 Malawi	59.6	39.0	43	25	41.7
163 Zambia	70.1	21.0	36	25	63.7
168 Central African Republic	55.3	51.8	30	24	66.6
169 Ethiopia	43.3	59.7	76	47	81.9
170 Mozambique	56.0	54.8	43	26	37.9
171 Burundi	50.5	50.8	22	45	58.4
172 Mali	35.3	73.6	35	43	72.8
173 Burkina Faso	43.4	75.2	58	34	61.2
174 Niger	38.7	83.5	41	40	61.4
175 Sierra Leone	57.5	..	43	27	57.0

Source: Human Development Report, United Nations Development Programme, 2003, http://hdr.undp.org/reports/global/2003/.

Countries with emerging markets that are expected to have a successful economic future share a number of traits:[10]

- High political stability
- A sound currency
- A low level of inflation
- Privatization policies that reduce government deficit, create first-time share owners who vote for pro-business conservative policies, and diminish the power of trade unions
- Policies that facilitate repatriation of dividends and capital
- Policies that are in line with international accounting standards
- Open disclosure of directors' interests
- Policies that stress regular reporting of earnings and sales figures
- A sound and comprehensive system of corporate law
- A liquid and well-traded securities market reflecting fair prices
- A high savings rate
- Strong government support for internationalization
- A people characterized by integrity, a strong work ethic, and respect for the law

Of interest to multinationals are what the United States Department of Commerce refers to as big emerging markets. These markets share all the traits of emerging markets and present the most potential because they are large, have large populations, and, consequently, set the pace for the economy in the region. Among these countries are China and India (both with populations exceeding 1 billion), South Korea, Argentina, Brazil, Mexico, South Africa, Poland, and Turkey.

2-4 The Political Environment of International Marketing

- *Iran 1970, the period before the Islamic Revolution.* The Iranian government focused on projects aimed at increasing industrial development. Iranians were generally satisfied with the increased socioeconomic facilities. In 1976, dissatisfied groups engaged in scattered demonstrations against the Shah's regime. The demonstrations increased in frequency and resulted in the occupation of state-owned, American, and Israeli facilities, finally resulting in the Shah's leaving the country. In 1979, the government and the banking industries were paralyzed.
- *1979–1984.* After the 1979 revolution, the new government took hostile action against foreign multinationals, arresting expatriate staff and local staff related to the former regime, and confiscating multinational companies, especially those from the United States and Israel. Business in general deteriorated due to the political intervention and the Iran-Iraq war.
- *1985.* The Islamic regime consolidated and local businesses gained ground and stability.[11]
- *1997–Present.* The European Union is Iran's largest trading partner; companies from the United States are banned from doing business with Iran. The U.S. government continues to threaten sanctions against non-U.S. companies doing business in Iran, in spite of positive developments in Iran (reformist president Mohammed Khatami was elected in 1997 and subsequently re-elected to a four-year term in 2001).

The preceding time line demonstrates the volatile nature of alliances in the present world market. The United States enjoyed a close rapport with the deposed Shah Reza

Pahlavi, and U.S. businesses profited under his rule. The Islamic revolution targeted the Shah's allies in particular: U.S. firms had all their assets confiscated, and their international executives were forced to repatriate. Today, the business climate in Iran is promising, with reformist president Khatami still in power. Yet the United States continues to ban the involvement of U.S. firms in Iran and to threaten sanctions on foreign firms with U.S. interests if they engage in operations in the country. This section illustrates the political uncertainties involved in international marketing and the legal challenges that firms face in their international operations.

Companies contemplating any international involvement must have an in-depth knowledge of the political environment in the countries where they do business. This is especially important for companies involved in foreign direct investment—companies that undertake the greatest level of risk in a foreign market. Whenever there are discussions of **political risk,** they typically involve the host country—the country where a company engages in business in accordance with the respective country's political and legal restrictions. It should be noted, however, that the international company is also affected by political developments in its home country—the country where the parent company is headquartered. A U.S.-based company planning to enter Cuba in the late 1990s, when the Clinton administration appeared to relax anti-Cuba restrictions, had many more prospects than it had immediately thereafter, when the Bush administration attempted to enforce the embargo.

At the basis of international law lies the concept of sovereignty: Sovereignty is defined as a country's self-determination and independence from external interference in internal affairs, and complete authority over all nationals living in the country and beyond its borders (individuals and corporations). All countries in the world are sovereign, and yet all must curtail their sovereignty to co-exist in the world of nations and defend their national interests. By permitting international trade and by entering into international agreements, countries limit their sovereignty. When countries perceive that international firms, governments, or organizations have infringed upon their right to self-determination, they can invoke national sovereignty and take actions that erect barriers to trade or even jeopardize the presence of international companies within their borders.

Ideally, a firm crossing borders, large or small, will encounter an environment in both the host and home country that is politically stable and pro-trade. This is not the case for most firms all the time: The local government a company has established relationships with could collapse overnight, and its replacement could have ties with a competitor— or it could be against foreign business altogether, as was the case of Iran during the Islamic Revolution, described in the preceding paragraphs. International companies doing business in Cuba and Eastern Europe experienced a similar fate after the communist takeover.

Similarly, the stable environment where a business has operated for decades could suddenly be at the center of a civil war that nobody had foreseen: In the case of Rwanda and Burundi, many international businesses were forced to leave their inventory and buildings behind when the genocide began. With large labor reserves and low wages, Haiti seemed a promising market for U.S. firms until recently. However, after president Jean-Bertrand Aristide left the country in 2004, businesses allied with him personally and with his government quickly became the target of opposition party scrutiny.

In yet another example, a protectionist measure of one government could launch a series of retaliations both by the government and by the populace: When the United States instituted measures against European protectionism by increasing duties on nonessential European exports (cheese, perfume, soap, accessories), it had not expected the retaliations of Europeans against icons of U.S. business, such as McDonald's and Coca-Cola.

In 2004, the U.S. Department of State issued a warning about the heightened threat of terrorist attacks against U.S. citizens and interests abroad subsequent to the killing of the HAMAS leader Sheikh Ahmed Yassin in Gaza; in its Worldwide Caution Public Announcement, the State Department warned of demonstrations and violent actions

political risk The risk associated with actions of local, regional, and/or parastatal governing bodies affecting the international company, and with the overall economic and political stability within a particular country.

against U.S. citizens and interests overseas: An HAMAS spokesman specifically threatened revenge against U.S. business interests.[12]

2-4a Political Risk: An Overview

Evaluating Political Risk

A company has several resources at its disposal to evaluate country risk: The Department of State, the Department of Commerce, and other governmental and nongovernmental agencies provide data on country political risk that is current and continually updated to reflect new developments in each country around the world (see an example of country risk evaluation in Table 2-2). Some examples of useful publications providing periodic information on country risk are

- Business periodicals such as *The Economist* and *The Wall Street Journal*—particularly the European and Asian editions
- Commercial sources, such as *Country Reports*, the Economist Intelligence Unit, Ltd., Chase (particularly its guide for exporters), and RUNDT's World Business Intelligence. RUNDT's (S. J. Rundt & Associates, Inc.), for example, provides information on political developments, on currency, and on the regulatory environment; it provides insurance data and trade information, as well as a country risk rating on a scale from 1 to 10, and risk perception and collection experience for the previous four months.

Political Risk Signals

A number of country risk elements should be monitored on a regular basis to keep track of developments that might ultimately affect the international company. These elements are illustrated in Table 2-3.

Economic Performance

A poor economic performance and forecast are likely to lead to greater levels of unrest in the country. Of particular concern are high inflationary rates and high unemployment rates, both of which could lead to political instability.

General business performance is also important. Commercial payment terms and collection experience indicate the availability of hard currency reserves and access to hard currency. Default on loans is likely to be a threat to companies contemplating entrance into the market. Finally, an increase in regulatory restrictions on investment, capital, or trade flows should be closely monitored.[13]

Political Repression

Repression of certain ethnic groups is a signal of potential political instability. The repression of the Albanian minority in the former Yugoslavia resulted in war in the region, as did the repression of the Tutsi minority by the Hutu in East Africa. Other areas are also ripe for conflict: The repression of gypsies and Muslims in Central and Eastern Europe continues to create flare-ups. Anti-Semitism is rampant in France, and the French government is unable to subdue inflammatory rhetoric. It has recently enacted legislation that does not permit Muslim girls to wear traditional attire in school.

General repression by the elite—especially if the elite's position is not considered legitimate[14]—is always a signal of political instability. Personality cults in particular are problematic because they bring about widespread antipathy.

Internal Diversity and Incongruent Interests

Even if no political repression exists within a country, ethnic diversity and incongruent interests lead to a history of distrust and conflict (open or simmering) in the population. In Nigeria, the Ibo, Yoruba, and Hausa tribes have had a history of conflict, even though today, the country is relatively calm. Romania has a large minority of Hungarians who are

Table 2-2   Country Risk Score

Country	Ranking	Risk Score (Max=100)	Political Risk (Max=25)	Economic Performance (Max=25)
Luxembourg	1	99.44	24.59	25.00
Switzerland	2	97.36	25.00	22.39
United States	3	95.60	24.48	21.12
Norway	4	95.49	24.02	21.51
Denmark	5	94.31	24.25	20.41
Netherlands	6	93.48	24.82	18.69
Sweden	7	93.34	24.20	19.59
Austria	8	92.80	24.43	18.40
United Kingdom	9	92.57	24.59	18.02
Finland	10	92.13	23.45	18.72
Taiwan	27	77.42	19.32	12.13
Czech Republic	37	67.02	18.60	10.34
South Korea	38	66.97	17.50	12.43
Saudi Arabia	40	65.25	16.20	8.92
China	56	57.90	17.13	10.67
Iran	70	48.68	12.63	7.55
Vietnam	73	46.63	10.93	7.55
Russia	76	45.98	9.74	8.15
Cuba	181	3.44	3.39	7.22
Somalia	182	12.01	0.72	0.12
Iraq	183	6.39	1.93	3.62
North Korea	184	6.33	2.15	3.01
Afghanistan	185	3.07	0.00	2.23

Source: "Country Risk," *Euromoney,* March 2003, pp. 1–2.

Table 2-3   Country Risk Elements

Risk Element	Example
Economic performance signal	Turkey's stock market collapses in July 2001 and inflation is rampant.
Political repression signal	China arrests academics who have conducted research or presented papers in/on Taiwan.
Internal diversity and incongruent interests	Zimbabwe offers land to squatters on white-owned properties.
Political stability and the stability of government policies	Hong Kong reverts to China; commercial policies change only minimally.

actively advocating secession and annexation of the region where Hungarians represent the dominant population to Hungary. In more developed countries, substantial ethnic conflict still exists, not just between the established ethnicities—as in the case of Belgium, where the Flemish (Dutch) and Wallonians (French) often find themselves in opposition—but also between the new immigrants and long-established nationals—as in the case of Germany, where Turkish immigrants have been targets of hate crime.

Political Stability and the Stability of Government Policies

Although presidents and governments change every few years, with a few exceptions, national government policies do not necessarily change radically, nor does the level of political risk. On average, Italy has had a new government for every year since World War II, and yet its commercial policies have remained unchanged. Germany has had pro-business conservatives at its helm, followed by a government with a more socialist bent, with no substantial impact on international business. Former communists have succeeded democratic presidents in Central and Eastern Europe without any substantial change in the countries' pro-business attitudes. Hong Kong has become an integral part of China, and, to date, this has created more opportunities than threats for international business.

Yet political change can be a cause for concern for international firms. Companies that have operated in countries that have had decades of stability and prosperity under a one-party rule can be affected instantly by political turmoil. Although transition from a one-party rule can be peaceful, as in the case of Mexico, when Vicente Fox took over as president from Ernesto Zedillo and the PRI (the Institutional Revolutionary Party, the ruling party for more than 70 years), this is usually the exception. In the case of Central and Eastern Europe, such a change presented opportunities but also created regional instability, particularly in Serbia, Bosnia and Herzegovina, Croatia, and other regions. In addition to a change in the ruling party, companies should look for other signals that announce political instability: Tamil separatists in Sri Lanka, political riots in Indonesia, squatters in Zimbabwe, Rwandan refugees in Uganda—all spell trouble for the companies operating in the respective countries.

2-4b Nationalism

nationalism An expression of fierce nationalist sentiment in a country where a company is operating, which poses an implicit threat to the company and its operations.

The expression of fierce nationalist sentiment, or **nationalism,** in a country where the company is operating could constitute a cause for concern to the international company. The expression of nationalist feelings, such as pride in a country's history and accomplishments, is common in most countries.

Nationalist sentiment may signal attempts at separation from or isolation of a particular segment of society, which could lead to political instability in the country; this is the case of the Tamil separatist movement in Sri Lanka, which has led to economic chaos in the country. Particularly problematic for international business are expressions of antiforeigner sentiment and/or antiforeign business bias. Shared beliefs that engaging in international business represents selling one's country raise questions about the future environment in the respective country. In the United States, in the 1980s, the "buy American" slogans echoing especially in the automobile and textile industries presented great concern to European and Asian business and private investors. Of special concern to international marketing managers is *consumer ethnocentrism*—the belief that buying foreign goods will put local companies out of business and is, consequently, morally wrong.[15] Countries where such beliefs predominate are more likely to erect barriers to international trade.

2-4c Political Risks and Risk Management in International Marketing

Nationalism and claims to national sovereignty can lead to protectionist measures on the part of the host-country government, whereas political instability can lead to the failure of the economy. All can harm the operations of the company in the respective country, from hurting its sales and overall prospects in the market to completely losing company assets. In the sections "Risks Related to Government Trade Policies," "Risks Related to Government Economic Policy," "Risks Related to Labor and Action Groups," and "Risks Related to Terrorism," following examples of risks a company can experience in international markets are examples of risk management for each category of risk.

Risks Related to Government Trade Policies

The host-country government can erect trade barriers, imposing tariffs and nontariff barriers on international business, such as exchange-rate controls, voluntary export restraints and other types of quotas, and export/import license requirements. The company could also find itself falling victim to a trade war, in which the host country and home country reciprocally restrict the flow of goods. Or the company's home-country government can impose embargoes and sanctions on the host country, which could force the company to exit the market. All these issues are addressed at length in Chapter 3, "International Trade: Barriers and Facilitators."

Risks Related to Government Economic Policy

Local governments can use taxes as a means to control foreign investment: During downturns in the local economy, governments find that taxing foreign companies provides a source of valuable revenue. Under more extreme conditions, especially if accompanied by a radical change in the political leadership, change can lead to the (mainly involuntary) transfer of the firm's assets to local (national) ownership. Companies face the following types of risks:

- Confiscation
- Expropriation
- Creeping Expropriation
- Nationalization
- Domestication

Confiscation

Confiscation refers to the seizing of company assets and/or investors' assets without any compensation. In the 1940s and 1950s, most private companies operating in Central and Eastern Europe had their assets confiscated. More recently, all U.S. firms operating in Iran were confiscated when Shah Reza Pahlavi was dethroned. As a result of the confiscation of U.S. multinationals' assets in Iran after the Islamic Revolution, the United States imposed an embargo on trade with Iran.

confiscation The foreign government seizure of company assets and/or investors' assets without any compensation.

Expropriation

Expropriation involves some reimbursement for company assets, usually not at their market value. When Fidel Castro ascended to power in Cuba and a totalitarian regime was instituted, the assets of U.S. multinationals and U.S. citizens were seized. The Castro government offered payment that was deemed inappropriate, and, as a result, the United States imposed an embargo on trade with Cuba that is currently still in effect.

expropriation The foreign government seizure of company assets with partial reimbursement, usually not at market value.

Creeping Expropriation

Creeping expropriation refers to a condition characterized as "difficult bureaucracies, unreliable judicial systems, shifting regulations, and corrupt operating environments."[16] Although not explicitly, government actions discourage foreign investment, especially investment in nonessential sectors. This strategy typically uses additional barriers that are imposed on international trade.

creeping expropriation A situation characterized by bureaucratic red tape and corruption, an unreliable judicial system, and shifting regulations, where foreign government actions discourage foreign investment, especially investment in nonessential sectors.

Nationalization

Nationalization involves a takeover by the local government with the aim of creating a government-run industry. International law regards nationalization as legitimate as long

nationalization The takeover of company assets by a foreign government with the aim of creating a government-run industry.

as it is in the public interest and it offers fair compensation to the international company and to its investors. In 1997, the Korean government decided to nationalize the automobile company Kia Motors by converting the state-run Koreas Development Bank's debt into an equity stake in the company.[17] In the aftermath of the Asian crisis, governments began nationalizing ailing banks across the region: In Indonesia, the government controls nearly all the country's biggest banks and has taken over around 75 percent of all bank assets; whereas in Japan, as a result of nationalization, the government, instead of markets, now plays a larger role in determining the flow of capital.[18]

Domestication

domestication The process initiated by a foreign government leading to the gradual transfer of ownership and management to locals.

Domestication occurs when the local government requires a gradual transfer of ownership and management to locals. This transfer is usually completed over time, through consecutive government decrees aimed at reducing the presence of multinationals in nonessential local sectors (such as the consumer goods sector).

Companies can protect themselves against political instability by understanding the structure of the government, the political parties, and the ideologies of the ruling party, as well as the competing ideologies of the opposition. As a first step, companies must make every attempt to be exemplary corporate citizens in every country where they operate. A solid reputation for product quality and community involvement can create a general environment that is favorable toward a company's local operations.

A company also can minimize its risk by partnering with local companies, creating local expertise in product manufacturing and management, and/or using local suppliers. McDonald's, for example, frequently stresses the use of local ingredients in all its offerings. Similarly, companies that produce products deemed essential for local development, such as industrial products, high-technology products, or pharmaceutical products, are less vulnerable to changes in government policies than companies that manufacture goods that are considered nonessential, such as consumer goods.

Companies can obtain insurance coverage against nationalization from private insurance sources. For example, companies such as Global Risk Advisors insure against confiscation, expropriation, and nationalization, in addition to providing insurance against war risk; localized or subnational conflicts; kidnapping, ransom, and extortion; property terrorism; and currency inconvertibility; among others.[19] The U.S. government, through the **Overseas Private Investment Corporation,** or **OPIC** (http://www.opic.gov), also offers policies that insure companies against expropriation, nationalization, or confiscation by foreign governments. OPIC insures U.S. investments in emerging markets and developing countries against expropriation and political violence, such as revolution and war.

Overseas Private Investment Corporation (OPIC) U.S. government corporation that provides loans, guarantees and insurance to U.S. corporations investing in countries that present high political risk.

Risks Related to Labor and Action Groups

In many countries, labor unions are very powerful and can readily influence national policies. For example, layoffs by foreign companies can bring about negative feelings that are likely to affect these companies in the long term. Boycotts initiated by action groups can also negatively affect the companies. Esso (Exxon) was the victim of a "Boycott Esso" campaign aimed at the United States' environmental policies. These actions are not usually sanctioned by the national government, but they are, nevertheless, legal.

Companies have some control over the actions of labor and action groups. Although they cannot control market demand and derived demand for labor, companies can provide severance packages that are fair, as well as invest in the services of job placement businesses in an effort to seek placement for the employees who have been terminated. To avoid negative public sentiment, companies must be politically neutral and keep a distance from local politics. Too close an association with a regime could elicit a negative attitude toward the company and its products. Pepsi, unfairly, is perceived as the drink that greased the hands of the former communist elite in Central and Eastern Europe, whereas Coke is associated with the new, free society. It is important for a firm to be perceived as a good citizen of the country where it operates, as a company that has created opportunities for locals and that continues to serve their interests.

Risks Related to Terrorism

International terrorist attacks against multinational interests culminated with the September 11, 2001, attack on the World Trade Center in New York City. In the years preceding this attack, terrorist attacks steadily increased in frequency. Organizations or businesses with a United States connection alone were hit 206 times in 2000, up from 169 in 1999; internationally, private-sector facilities were attacked 384 times, up from 276 in 1999, while only 17 government facilities and 13 military facilities were similarly hit around the globe. Terrorism was most lethal in Asia in the year 2000, with 281 of the 405 international victims perishing there. Africa had the second highest total, with 73 dead.[20] In 2003, the number of people killed by terrorism was 625 (with 725 killed the preceding year); and 208 terror incidents took place, resulting in the injury of 3,646 people.[21]

The events of September 2001 have exponentially altered the trend of those statistics. In a choreographed operation, terrorists hijacked four planes that took off within minutes of each other, took control, and crashed into each of the World Trade Center twin towers and the Pentagon. Experts evaluated these attacks as the culmination of a 20-year trend toward assaults aimed to kill many people in technically complex operations.[22] A blow to the financial nerve center of capitalism,[23] the September 11 events disrupted financial operations worldwide, displaced hundreds of businesses in the area and beyond, and, for the first time ever, stopped all travel in U.S. airspace. An "attack on the world's … superpower, undertaken as a consequence of specific American alliances and actions,"[24] these actions are representative of **corporate terrorism** with the greatest of scopes.

corporate terrorism Terrorism that is targeted toward a particular company.

Companies have some control, however, in reducing their likelihood of becoming victims of terrorism by training employees in terrorism avoidance, such as briefing personnel on what to expect when entering high-risk areas and offering training for eluding roadblocks and avoiding hazardous encounters.[25] Companies can also purchase insurance against terrorist acts from private insurance companies. For example, Cigna International's International Specialty Products & Services offers insurance products that cover kidnapping, detention (kidnapping without asking for ransom), hijacking, evacuation, business interruption and extra expenses, product recall expenses, and expenses arising from child abduction (such as hiring private investigators or posting rewards for information).[26]

2-5 The International Legal Environment

International marketing is affected by three types of law:

- **International Laws**—A body of rules and regulations that countries agree to abide by. International law addresses agreements among countries with regard to trade, protection of property, and other issues in the political and economic sphere. International law agreements, although not enforceable, can be appropriately addressed by international law bodies.

international laws Rules and regulations that countries agree to abide by, addressing agreements among countries with regard to trade, protection of property, and other issues in the political and economic sphere.

- **Host-Country Laws**—Laws of the different countries where the company operates. The legal system in the host country could differ substantially from that of the company's home country.

host-country laws Local laws; laws of the different countries where a company operates.

- **Home-Country Laws**—Laws of the company's home country. Home-country laws follow the company all over the world.

home-country laws Laws of a company's home country that follow the international company all over the world.

U.S. companies must abide by all three types of law. For example, they must abide by international trade laws and agreements, such as World Trade Organization (WTO) trade regulations; they must abide by host-country laws governing every aspect of the company's operations; and they must abide by home-country laws, such as antitrust regulations and corrupt practices regulations.

2-5a Legal Systems

Three legal systems are predominant: common law, code law, and Islamic law.

Common Law

Common law is based on prior court rulings (legal precedent). It has its roots in English common law, on which U.S. law is based. This system of law is shared by many of the countries formerly colonized by Great Britain.

Code (Civil) Law

Code law—or civil law—refers to comprehensive written laws that specify what constitutes legal behavior. Code law has its roots in Roman law. This system of law is shared by most of the countries in the world, including most of Europe, Latin America, China, Taiwan, Japan, and South Korea.

Socialist countries still dealing with the legacy of communism are now converging on the adoption of civil law. Under the socialist system, countries of the former Soviet Union and the Eastern Bloc had a system of laws that allowed a large degree of flexibility in enforcement. All the nomenklatura (high-ranking communist party officials and their offspring) were largely exempt from enforcement, with some exceptions. For the commoner, however, activities deemed illegal—listening to Western radio stations, harboring a Western visitor—could place the individual in prison indefinitely. Such corruption appears to persist in this part of the world, where performance in the legal system is contingent on the firm's networks.

Islamic Law

Islamic law (sha'ria) is a system of law based on the interpretation of the Koran, Islam's holy book, and on interpretations of the practices and sayings of the prophet Muhammad. Islamic law establishes rules for business practices that can affect firms' operations. For example, it requires the sexes to be separate; in practice, this means that women cannot interact in any environment with men with whom they are not related. It bans the consumption of products such as pork and alcohol, it does not allow banks to offer or charge interest, and it requires Muslims to pray five times a day and to fast in the month of Ramadan.

All these factors have an impact on firms' local operations wherever Islamic law constitutes the basis of the legal system—in North Africa and the Middle East, and in Pakistan and Malaysia, among others. For example, business activities must be organized daily around prayer time. During Ramadan, business performance is generally low; in fact, many international businesses rely on the foreign, non-Muslim, workforce to carry out their firms' operations during this month.

2-5b Jurisdiction

With different legal systems worldwide, and with international laws, home-country laws, and host-country laws that govern all aspects of doing business internationally, it is important to establish **jurisdiction** in international legal disputes. No automatic supranational jurisdiction is assigned to an international court, unless the dispute takes place between companies and/or countries in the European Union; in this case, jurisdiction lies with the European Court of Justice (www.europa.eu.int). Legal disputes that arise between governments are usually handled by the International Court of Justice (www.icj-cij.org) in the Hague, within the United Nations system. International commercial law is usually handled in the home or host country of the company, or even in a third country, depending on the place where lies the jurisdiction for the matter under litigation. Because jurisdiction is often difficult to determine, it is advisable that each contract specifies the venue for handling the dispute and the procedure—a venue that is agreeable to all the parties involved.

The contract should also specify whether the dispute settlement process will involve procedures other than litigation, which is often too costly and leads to negative perceptions in the international business community of the companies involved. Such procedures may be as follows:

- **Mediation**—A nonbinding procedure that involves an independent third party. The disadvantage of mediation is that any decision of the mediator is nonbinding. The perspective of a neutral third party, however, could provide better insights into how the issue is perceived by the larger business community; moreover, not accepting the terms of mediation could signal to firms outside the conflict that the firm seen as being at fault might not be a reliable future partner.

> **mediation** Nonbinding procedure for conflict resolution involving an independent third party.

- **Arbitration**—A procedure that involves an independent third party; the outcome of arbitration is a binding decision. Agreeing to arbitration does not necessarily mean that the companies found to be at fault will adhere to the decisions; if they do not, however, their reputation in the international business community is likely to suffer. Arbitration is often preferred to litigation. It is a much faster procedure that is likely to cost the company much less than a lawsuit.

> **arbitration** Binding procedure for conflict resolution involving an independent third party; a faster and less costly procedure than a lawsuit.

2-5c Intellectual Property Rights Protection

Violation of **intellectual property rights** is the most significant threat to the competitiveness of companies involved in international business.[27] Intellectual property is the result of ideas and creativity transformed into products, services, and experiences that are protected for a specified period of time from unauthorized commercialization. Companies from developed countries manufacturing brand name products are the primary victims of intellectual property rights infringement and are leading the fight against violations. Losses attributed to the violation of intellectual property rights are estimated to be $60 billion a year, and its primary victims are the most innovative, fastest-growing industries such as software (with estimated annual losses at $11.4 billion), pharmaceuticals (with estimated losses at $1 billion), and entertainment (with estimated annual losses at $8 to $10 billion and expected to rise due to Internet piracy).[28]

> **intellectual property rights** Laws protecting the rights of the inventor or of the firm employing the inventor to use and sell an invention for a specified period of time.

Intellectual property protection takes on different forms:

- Protection of the rights of the inventor or of the firm employing the inventor to use and sell the invention for a specified period of time—this type of intellectual property is known as a **patent.** In many countries around the world, multinationals are racing to local patent offices to apply for patents to protect and enforce their technology. In Korea, for example, local memory chip and electronics firms are embroiled in patent disputes, fending off lawsuits initiated by multinational firms such as IBM and NEC, and the stakes are high: Losers will not only suffer financial setbacks in the form of paying royalties, but will also suffer the stigma of being labeled copycats.[29] This situation will ultimately be rectified by the World Trade Organization, which will institute uniform patent rules that all members are expected to follow.

> **patent** Protection of the rights of the inventor or of the firm employing the inventor to use and sell an invention for a specified period of time.

- Protection of the rights to an original work of art (literature, music, film, design, and other works), allowing the owner the right to reproduce, sell, perform, or film the work—this is known as **copyright.** National and international associations are actively fighting copyright infringement. In the United States, such an organization is the International Intellectual Property Alliance, or IIPA (www.iipa.com). The IIPA was formed in conjunction with the Association of American Publishers, the Business Software Alliance, the Interactive Digital Software Association, the Motion Picture Association of America, the National Music Publishers' Association, and the Recording Industry Association of America. In recent years, the IIPA filed petitions with the Office of the U.S. Trade Representative to investigate copyright infringement in the CD and CD-ROM markets in Brazil, Costa Rica, Guatemala, Russia, and Uruguay.[30]

> **copyright** The rights to an original work of art (literature, music, film, design, and other works), enabling the owner to reproduce, sell, perform, or film the work.

- Protection of a brand name, mark, symbol, motto, or slogan that identifies a particular manufacturer's brand and distinguishes it from the competitors' brands in the same product category—this is known as **trademark.** Trademark infringement occurs at many levels, from directly copying the product, as in the case of counterfeit Rolex watches and Gucci and Fendi purses selling for $30 in the streets of New York City, Hong Kong, and Paris and in many bazaars in developing countries. Brand name counterfeiting involves using the brand name, but not the product design, as in the case of Oleg Cassini and Christian Dior plain Egyptian cotton t-shirts selling in the streets of Cairo. Design copying, which is legal, involves using a popular design without the trademark, as in shirts with a crocodile or polo player that do not have the respective Lacoste and Ralph Lauren names, and Peugeot watches with designs that look just like the Rolex oyster.

- Protection of know-how, formulas, and special blends that are not registered, and thus not protected by law—these are shared with licensees, franchisers, or other partners and are known as **trade secrets.**

Factors Influencing Intellectual Property Rights Violations

The degree of intellectual property rights violation is influenced by a number of market factors,[31] such as

- Lack of appropriate legislation (e.g., for software)
- Lax enforcement, especially for local firms
- Unavailability of the authentic products, or when available, their high price provides justification for both the violators and the respective governments to allow the practice

Such violations are also influenced by cultural factors, such as

- Values that perceive imitation as a high form of flattery
- A culture characterized by interpersonal distrust and feelings of not getting a fair deal
- A culture characterized by an emphasis on acquisition of material wealth at the expense of caring for others; in such a culture, the focus of acquisition is status brands consumed and/or displayed publicly, rather than privately
- Beliefs that technology is in the common domain and that use of others' intellectual property is appropriate

Involvement in regional trade agreements and other trade organizations is also sought to diminish the likelihood that a country would tolerate violation of intellectual property rights. In fact, intellectual property rights used to be largely a domestic issue, with individual countries deciding on their own levels of legal protection and enforcement; today, countries that join the World Trade Organization, or WTO, (www.wto.org) must also sign on to the **Trade-Related Aspects of Intellectual Property Rights** (or **TRIPS**) agreement, an international agreement that sets out minimum standards for the legal protection of intellectual property.[32]

Multinationals seeking protection under TRIPS around the world still depend on each country's patent office to grant those rights and their judicial, customs, and police services to enforce them (in Europe, regionwide patents can be obtained). TRIPS offers rules describing the protection these systems must provide, including extending intellectual property rights to include computer programs, integrated circuits, plant varieties, and pharmaceuticals, which were unprotected in most developing countries until this agreement. According to TRIPS, patents can be granted for any new technological process or product, and the protection lasts 20 years from the date of application.[33]

In addition to TRIPS, and working in conjunction with the World Trade Organization, international conventions have been gaining strength. Among these conventions are the Berne Convention for copyrighted works, under the auspices of the World Intel-

---

trademark A brand name, mark, symbol, motto, or slogan that identifies a particular manufacturer's brand and distinguishes it from the competitors' brands in the same product category.

trade secrets Intellectual property such as know-how, formulas, special blends, and other elements that are not registered, and are thus not protected by law.

Trade-Related Aspects of Intellectual Property Rights (TRIPS) An international agreement, under the World Trade Organization, that sets out minimum standards for the legal protection of intellectual property. (See www.wto.org.)

lectual Property Organization;[34] the Paris Convention for the protection of industrial property; and the Madrid Arrangement, which established the Bureau for the International Registration of Trademarks.

Helping these organizations and conventions are, in particular, national governments of developed countries, which are protecting their multinationals. In the United States, the Patent and Trademark Office has an annual budget of $1 billion; a staff of more than 3,000 highly trained scientists, engineers, and legal experts; more than 600 judges to preside over patent disputes; and a vast customs service to clamp down on counterfeiting.[35] To protect intellectual property rights in the Internet Age, the United States government passed the Digital Millennium Copyright Act.

Developing countries frequently argue that intellectual property protection is yet another arm used in placing them at an economic disadvantage. From their point of view, patents and copyrights impose great cost on consumers in developing countries. In recent examples, AIDS activists and the government in South Africa argued that patents were killing the country's millions of HIV-infected patients who could not afford the drugs; Mexican peasants were enraged that a U.S. company received the exclusive right to market enola beans in the United States because they have been growing the beans for generations, and the protection restricts their ability to export the beans north of the border.[36] Activists argue that intellectual property protection allows Western multinationals to set up monopolies; to drive out local competing brands; to divert research and development away from the needs of developing countries; and to drive up prices while preventing poor people from getting life-saving drugs, interfering with age-old farming practices, and allowing foreign "pirates" to raid local resources, such as medicinal plants, without getting permission or paying compensation.[37]

2-5d Home-Country Legislation Affecting Multinational Firms Operating Overseas

Antitrust Laws

Antitrust laws of home and host countries are designed to prevent domestic anticompetitive activities, such as the creation of monopolies and cartels. The United States was among the first to impose its antitrust laws on firms in the United States and on U.S. firms operating abroad. Increasingly, governments of other countries are enacting and enforcing antitrust legislation that affects multinationals worldwide. In fact, antitrust enforcement in the United States often appears to be more lenient than in other developed countries. For example, the European Commission vetoed mergers between competitors after the United States gave these mergers a green light—as in the case of General Electric's failed takeover attempt of Honeywell and the MCI Worldcom and Sprint proposed merger.[38]

The United States allows certain types of collusion in the case of small and medium-size firms that might not have the resources to embark on a successful export program. The U.S. Congress passed the Export Trading Company Act in the 1980s to encourage firms to join forces in exporting by exempting them from antitrust laws.

Corruption Laws

Corruption laws of home and host countries are designed to prevent multinational corporations from using unethical means to obtain competitive advantage in a particular market. The World Bank surveyed 3,600 companies in 69 countries and found that 40 percent of firms paid bribes; this figure in industrial countries was 15 percent, and in the former Soviet Union, it increased to 60 percent.[39] Similarly, the European Bank for Reconstruction and Development (EBRD), which encourages investments in the former Eastern Bloc, has called Eastern Europe's bribe-seeking a deterrent to foreign investment.[40]

The U.S. **Foreign Corrupt Practices Act** (FCPA) makes it illegal for companies and their representatives to bribe government officials and other politicians or candidates to political office. The Act also prohibits payment to third parties when the company has

antitrust laws Laws designed to prevent anticompetitive activities, such as the creation of monopolies and cartels.

corruption laws Laws designed to prevent multinational corporations from using unethical means to obtain competitive advantage in a particular market.

Foreign Corrupt Practices Act Legislation that makes it illegal for companies and their representatives to bribe government officials and other politicians or candidates to political office, either directly or through third parties.

good reason to assume that part of that payment is being used for bribery purposes. U.S. multinational companies take such laws very seriously—some even address their commitment to reject bribery and other corruption in their mission statement (Caterpillar does so, for example)—even though forbidding these practices places U.S. firms at a disadvantage. In a number of high-profile cases, investigators found that illegal payments were made by firms operating in Canada, Colombia, Cook Islands, the Dominican Republic, Egypt, Germany, Iraq, Israel, Jamaica, Mexico, Niger, Nigeria, and Trinidad and Tobago; these payments ranged from $22,000 to $9.9 million and represented percentages of up to 20 percent of the business obtained. Seventeen companies have been charged under the FCPA, with fines ranging from $10,000 to $21.8 million.[41]

The United States is not alone in the fight against bribery. The Organization for Economic Co-operation and Development (OECD), which consists of 30 primarily developed member countries (Australia, Austria, Belgium, Canada, the Czech Republic, Denmark, Finland, France, Germany, Greece, Hungary, Iceland, Ireland, Italy, Japan, South Korea, Luxembourg, Mexico, the Netherlands, New Zealand, Norway, Poland, Portugal, the Slovak Republic, Spain, Sweden, Switzerland, Turkey, United Kingdom, and the United States) adopted a Convention on Combating Bribery of Foreign Public Officials in International Business Transactions in 1997. Other signatories include non-member countries Argentina, Brazil, Bulgaria, and Chile. The purpose of the Convention is to fight corruption in international business and to help level the competitive field for companies.[42]

2-6 The Natural Environment of International Marketing

The natural environment of international marketing addresses the relationship between natural resources worldwide and marketing. A country's geographic location determines how its key markets can be optimally accessed. Its climate determines its production and even its productivity capability. Geography facilitates or impedes relationships with other, international, markets. National boundaries determine access to the local market and the movement of goods, access to natural resources, and, overall, the potential for economic development.

2-6a Geology and the Shortage of Natural Resources

A country's access to natural resources determines whether the country can be a viable trade partner in the international market. Its geology determines the natural resources available in the country and its potential for prosperity. For example, oil in North Africa and the Middle East has brought prosperity to countries where the climate is a challenge and whose terrain contains a large desert expanse. Countries in Sub-Saharan Africa that have survived at subsistence level for centuries have found new prosperity from mining gold and diamonds. Botswana and the Central African Republic have attractive markets that are actively courted by multinationals.

Worldwide, a shortage of raw materials is slowly reverberating in most world markets, including the markets of industrialized countries. Prices of oil are steadily increasing, whereas access to oil sources is becoming more and more limited due to geologic and political factors. This shortage is translating to higher prices charged to consumers, which, in the long term, will lead to changes in consumption patterns. In the case of oil, it may mean that Northern Europeans will no longer count on their Southern European and North African vacations, which will, in turn, hurt tourism in Southern Europe and North Africa. Consumers in the United States may have to trade in their gas-guzzling monster trucks and sports utility vehicles for fuel-efficient smaller and/or hybrid vehicles.

2-6b Topography and Access to Markets

Topography is important because it determines access to the market and affects distribution decisions. For example, Holland has a flat terrain, allowing for efficient transporta-

tion. Holland has also altered its topography to increase access by creating an effective network of man-made canals that cross the country in every direction allowing for easy access to markets (see Figure 2-3). On the other hand, a mountainous terrain restricts access to markets. The Andes, for example, allow minimal access to local consumers, which can be accomplished only at great company expense. These restrictions are especially difficult to surmount in developing countries; developed countries have devised sophisticated access to some of the more remote areas, such as the canyons in Utah and the peaks of the Alps.

2-6c Hydrology and Economic Development

Hydrology determines access to local markets as well. Ocean access allows for the affordable shipping of goods to the local target market. Rivers and lakes offer access as well as potential for the development of agriculture and manufacturing. Hydroelectric power is essential for local development. In general, economic development is related to hydrology.

2-6d Climate

Climate is also an essential determinant of economic development. Arid lands, such as the desert lands of the Sahara and the Southwestern United States, are inhabitable only at a very high cost. Excessive rain and hurricane activity often lead to flooding and the destruction of the local infrastructure. On the other hand, a mild climate year round brings tourists to the Amalfi Coast of Italy, the islands of Hawaii, the beaches of the Caribbean, the shores of Tunisia, and the Sinai.

2-6e Population

One relevant aspect of the natural environment is the scarcity of natural resources, and especially raw materials, in light of today's high population growth. High population growth in spite of limited natural resources has led to famine and precipitated conflict in Ethiopia, Somalia, Rwanda, and Burundi in Sub-Saharan Africa. In these markets, the overall infrastructure is insufficient and cannot meet the basic needs of the population. The concentration of population in large cities of millions of inhabitants, such as Mexico City and Cairo, has taxed the infrastructure and impeded the optimal functioning of business. Most importantly, today, the world's population exceeds 6 billion and is growing rapidly, especially in developing countries. Table 2-4 illustrates the high annual population growth in low- and middle-income countries, compared to that of high-income countries. The population growth rate is highest for the developing countries of South Asia and Sub-Saharan Africa.

T a b l e 2 - 4	**Population Growth Trends**				
	Population (2002)	**Annual Growth (2002–2015)**	**Population Age Composition**		
			(0–14)	**(15–64)**	**(65+)**
Low-Middle Income	**5,232.4**	**1.2**	**31.2**	**63.1**	**5.7**
East Asia & Pacific	1,838.3	1.4	26.3	67.2	6.5
Europe/Central Asia	472.9	0.5	20.9	67.9	11.2
Latin America/Caribbean	524.9	1.3	30.9	63.6	5.5
Middle East/North Africa	305.8	2.6	35.3	60.7	4.0
South Asia	1,401.5	12.0	34.2	61.2	4.6
Sub-Saharan Africa	688.9	12.7	43.8	53.3	3.0
High Income Countries	**966.2**	**0.7**	**18.3**	**67.3**	**14.4**

Source: World Development Indicators, *World Development Report 2004*, World Bank Group, 2004, http://econ.worldbank.org/wdr/wdr2004/.

Population growth determines the types of markets that multinational companies, as well as small and medium enterprises, can target. In the high-income countries, marketers have a more mature market to contend with—markets with a substantial population aged 65 and older. Population growth also has implications with regard to access to goods and services, and to the environment.

2-6f Environmental Quality

Concerns about the effects of the overall population growth and industry on the natural environment have led to the active regulation of business, especially in industrialized countries. For example, the European Union actively regulates the use of hormones in raising beef and the use of pesticides in agriculture. It continues to raise taxes on gasoline to reduce consumption and encourage the use of public transportation. It charges localities huge sums for refuse and actively encourages recycling at the individual and community level.

Worldwide, there is a concerted effort to reduce air and water pollution, to control the amount and disposal of nuclear waste, to reduce deforestation and land erosion, and to limit fishing and hunting activity to preserve a viable natural habitat. The effort to preserve environmental quality limits infrastructure development in protected areas and charges businesses to take responsibility of consumption by encouraging bottle reuse and recycling, by limiting packaging to its more basic forms, and by producing products that can be consumed with minimal harm to the environment. Outside the United States, for example, Coca-Cola soft drinks and Heineken beer are sold in reusable glass bottles or in recyclable plastic bottles. Ford Motor Company competes in the international market by offering smaller automobiles with low gas consumption. And new, successful industries are emerging aimed at creating alternative energy sources and reducing the cost of electricity consumption. Windmills today populate not just the European landscape; they are increasingly present on the coast of California and on the East Coast of the United States.

2-7 The Technological Environment

The technological environment is changing rapidly. New product development is proceeding at breakneck pace, with thousands of patents and trademarks registered worldwide on a daily basis. The technology revolution since the 1980s has radically changed the face of international marketing. Hub and spoke networks, warehouse management systems, and electronic data interchange (EDI) systems, which allow intermediaries worldwide to share standardized inventory information, lower firms' inventory carrying costs, facilitating the flow of products, and make it easier to achieve the goal of making the distribution channel more flexible and responsive to customer needs.[43]

The Web allows for instant access to new international markets and creates potential for exchanges that have never been previously imagined. Multinational corporations, as well as small and medium enterprises, benefit from the long reach of the Web. Worldwide, more than 385 million people are using the Internet. The average amount of time each person spends on the Internet is 10 hours a month, visiting an average of 49 different sites, going online an average of 19 times per month. Table 2-5 provides statistics on the Internet penetration of the home market. The United States and the Netherlands have the highest penetration of active home users—39%—compared to the total population, Canada and Australia are next with 34%, followed by Great Britain at 30%.[44]

The Internet has profoundly changed the lives of individuals; but it has also changed the way international business is conducted. Consider these examples:[45]

- The Web hosts more than 4 million sites, with 235,000 new ones being added each month.
- The average email user receives 31 emails per day.
- Businesses will place orders totaling $3 trillion worldwide via the Internet.
- Twenty-five percent of all business-to-business purchases are placed through some type of Internet connection.
- Internet retail sales accounts for almost 2.5 percent of all retail sales.[46]

Numerous companies in the United States have been successful selling to international clients through the Internet. Nevertheless, there are some pitfalls. For example, the company may need to make use of freight forwarders, who handle transportation, insurance, and export documentation but also substantially increase the cost to the buyer. Companies must also determine the appropriate payment mechanisms. Countries differ not only with regard to the currency they use for transactions, but also in their methods of payments; for example, Europeans tend to use the Eurocard, which is a debit card, for

Table 2-5   **Internet Penetration of the Home Market: Sample Monthly Figures**

Country	Active Users (in millions)	Average Time Spent Online per Month	Average Number of Sessions per Month	Active as %
United States	110.9	13 hr 17 min	24	39
Japan	26.6	11 hr 44 min	21	21
Germany	22.0	10 hr 57 min	21	26
Great Britain	17.5	8 hr 52 min	17	30
Canada	10.5	10 hr 8 min	22	34
France	9.5	10 hr 37 min	21	15
Italy	9.2	9 hr 36 min	18	16
Brazil	7.5	11 hr 9 min	16	5
Australia	6.4	10 hr 3 min	17	34
Netherlands	6.4	9 hr 42 min	19	39

payments. Also, worldwide, there is a high rate of credit card theft, which increases the risks that sellers might face in the international market. Using the Internet to send Mother's Day flowers from the United States to one's mother-in-law in Holland is difficult, and using the telephone is not much easier because the local flower shops are reticent to serve when it comes to accepting credit cards from unknown buyers. Nevertheless, transactions never before thought possible are today commonplace due to the advances in the past two decades.

Summary

- **Provide an overview of the world economic environment and examine different perspectives on economic development.** Countries are becoming more and more interconnected by trade, and developments in one region have immediate repercussions in the rest of the world. There are divergent views on the economic development process: The Rostow model portrays economic development as a function of productivity, exchange, technology, and income. Alternative models portray development as a function of the control on the means of production, production outcomes, resource allocation, and the development of a mindset devoid of materialist needs and may fuel anticolonial, anticapitalist sentiment, while advocating a collective societal orientation.

- **Address differences between countries of different levels of economic development and discuss the importance of emerging markets.** Countries belong to different development categories. Developed countries are highly industrialized, have well-developed industrial and service sectors, and present great potential, with a GNP per capita of $9,266 or more; they also present a challenge because their markets are in the maturity stage, consumers have established preferences, and competition is intense. Countries with emerging markets are developing rapidly and have great potential, as they privatize state-owned industries and adopt market reforms; of these countries, big emerging markets present the greatest potential for international trade and expansion. These countries are middle-income countries, with a GNP per capita of US$766 to US$9,265. Developing countries are primarily agrarian, have a low GNP per capita (less than $755), and are located in different regions in Asia and in Sub-Saharan Africa; they tend to be neglected or underserved by large multinationals and thus present great potential as niche markets.

- **Examine the indicators of political risk and address international firm approaches to political risk management.** Several indicators signal political risk: economic performance, political repression, the existence of multiple groups with incongruent interests, rampant nationalism, and political instability. Some of the risks that companies can experience in foreign markets involve some level of dispossession, such as nationalization, expropriation, confiscation; risks related to action groups and labor; as well as corporate terrorism, is on the rise. Firms can reduce risk by being good corporate citizens, by partnering with local firms, and by purchasing risk insurance.

- **Describe how international law, home-country law, and host-country law affect international firm operations and address issues related to jurisdiction.** International companies are subject to multiple sets of laws: laws of the host country, laws of the home country—such as anticompetitiveness (antitrust) laws and corruption laws—and international laws, which could be laws of a regional governance body, such as the European Union, or laws of an international body, such as the World Trade Organization. Under this complex scenario, jurisdiction often becomes a problem; it is advisable that firms entering into agreements agree upon jurisdiction and on the procedure needed for conflict resolution.

- **Discuss different legal systems, intellectual property laws, and national laws with extra-territorial impact that affect international firms.** The three primary types of legal systems are common law, which is based on prior court rulings, with roots in English common law; code law, or civil law, which draws upon comprehensive written laws that specify what constitutes legal behavior, with roots in Roman law; and Islamic law, a system of law based on the interpretation of Islam's holy book and the practices and sayings of the prophet Muhammad. One issue facing multinationals today is the violation of intellectual property rights, which constitutes a great threat to firms' competitiveness. Protection of patents, copyrights, trademarks, and trade secrets is difficult to enforce due to lax attitudes attributed to cultural values and to economic and political motivations of national governments. This type of protection might have better prospects now that more countries have become members of the World Trade Organization and are signatories of the TRIPS agreement.

- **Examine the natural and technological environments and the potential and limitations they present to international firms.** Geography can offer opportunity for international business, or it can restrict access to the marketplace. Geography facilitates the relationship with other international markets, if those markets are located in the proximity of the home country or if the markets are located in the proximity of ports that allow easy access. Alternatively, geographical location that is remote from other international markets and that does not allow easy access impedes relationships. Geology determines the natural resources available in the country and its potential for prosperity, and climate and hydrology have a direct impact on a country's economic development. Population growth determines the types of markets that multinational companies, as well as small and medium enterprises, can target. In the high-income countries, marketers have a more mature market to contend with—markets with a substantial population aged 65 and older. Population growth also has implications with regard to the access to goods and services, and to the environment. The environment is continuously challenged by business interests; these challenges have led to extensive legislation aimed at limiting the negative impact of business on the environment. The technological environment is continuously evolving, rapidly opening international markets never before accessible to multinationals and is creating a viable future for small and medium enterprises that never before could have had such a broad exposure. The technological environment is also speeding the new product development process and creating distribution potential never before attained in industry.

Key Terms

antitrust laws
arbitration
big emerging markets (BEMs)
bourgeoisie
capitalism
code law
common law
communism
confiscation
copyright
corporate terrorism
corruption laws
creeping expropriation
developed countries
developing countries
domestication
drive-to-maturity stage

emerging countries
emerging markets
expropriation
feudalism
Foreign Corrupt Practices Act
high mass consumption
home-country laws
host-country laws
imperialism
intellectual property rights
international laws
Islamic law
jurisdiction
Marxist-Leninist development model
mediation
monopolistic capitalism
nationalism

nationalization
Overseas Private Investment Corporation (OPIC)
patent
political risk
primitive society
Rostow modernization model
slavery-based society
socialism
take-off
trade secrets
trademark
traditional society
Trade-Related Aspects of Intellectual Property Rights (TRIPS)
transitional society

Discussion Questions

1. Compare the Rostow and the Marxist-Leninist models of economic development. How do you explain the two models in light of developments over the past decade in Central and Eastern Europe? Why do developing countries continue to embrace the Marxist-Leninist model of economic development?

2. Describe indicators of political risk. Examine current events and identify some of the political risks that multinational companies face in the world today.

3. Discuss two home-country laws that affect U.S. businesses operating internationally.

4. What are some examples of violations of international property rights? Give some examples of counterfeiting.

Chapter Quiz (True/False)

1. Crises in one region of the world are likely to influence economic performance worldwide.

2. Developing countries fully control national resources (raw materials, labor), control access to local consumers, and frequently pose barriers to international business operations.

3. In the Rostow model, advancement is a function of the control of means of production, production outcomes, resources allocation, and the development of a mindset devoid of materialist needs.

4. The key political risk signals are ethnic diversity and incongruent interests.

5. Common law is defined as a body of written laws specifying what constitutes legal behavior.

6. The Foreign Corrupt Practices Act makes it legal for companies to bribe government officials and candidates to political office under certain circumstances.

7. A country's geology can determine whether the country can be a viable trade partner in the international market.

You can find the correct answers to these questions by taking the quiz and then submitting your answers in the Online Edition. The program will automatically score your submission. Where you miss a question, the program will provide the correct answer, a rationale for the answer, and the section number in the chapter where the topic is discussed.

Multiple Choice

1. The Rostow modernization model addresses all of the following EXCEPT
   a. high mass consumption.
   b. the drive to maturity.
   c. transitional society.
   d. the capitalist society.

2. A stage in which modern technology is fully adopted in all economic activity and new leading sectors emerge is known as the _____ stage.
   a. drive to maturity
   b. high mass consumption
   c. take-off
   d. transitional society

3. A stage in economic development characterized by leading sectors shifting toward durable goods is a
   a. transitional society.
   b. take-off.
   c. high mass consumption.
   d. drive to maturity.

4. _____ countries are characterized by consumers with established preferences and intense competition.
   a. Developed
   b. Nationalized
   c. Emerging
   d. Developing

5. _____ can impede the optimal functioning of business, tax the infrastructure, and lead to the scarcity of natural resources, especially raw materials.
   a. Economic development
   b. Population growth
   c. Technology
   d. All of the above

Endnotes

1. Michael J. Mandel, "In a One-World Economy, a Slump Sinks All Boats," *Business Week*, Industrial Technology Edition, No. 3738, June 25, 2001, pp. 38–39.
2. Russell W. Belk, "Hyperreality and Globalization: Culture in the Age of Ronald McDonald," *Journal of International Consumer Marketing*, Vol. 8, No. 3/4, 1996, pp. 23–37; and Leslie Sklair, "Competing Models of Globalization: Theoretical Frameworks and Research Agendas," working paper, London School of Economics and Political Science, University of London, London, United Kingdom.
3. See Walt W. Rostow, *The Stages of Economic Growth: A Non-Communist Manifesto*, London and New York: Cambridge University Press, 1960; ———, "The Concept of a National Market and Its Economic Growth Implications," in *Marketing and Economic Development*, ed. P. D. Bennett, Chicago: American Marketing Association, 1965, pp. 11–20; and ——— *The Stages of Economic Growth*, Second Edition, London: Cambridge University Press, 1971.
4. Barkley Rosser, Jr., and Marina V. Rosser, "Islamic and Neo-Confucian Perspectives on the New Traditional Economy," *Eastern Economic Journal*, Vol. 24, No. 2, Spring 1998, pp. 217–227.
5. Ali Farazmand, "Development and Comparative Public Administration: Past, Present, and Future," *Public Administration Quarterly*, Vol. 20, No. 3, Fall 1996, pp. 343–364.
6. Ibid.
7. Rosser and Rosser, "Islamic and Neo-Confucian Perspectives," pp. 217–227.
8. Roger Hayter and Sun Sheng Han, "Reflections on China's Open Policy Towards Foreign Direct Investment, *Regional Studies*, Vol. 32, No. 1, February 1998, pp. 1–16.
9. Robert Lloyd George, *The Handbook of Emerging Markets: A Country-By-Country Guide to the World's Fastest Growing Economies*, Chicago, IL: Probus Publications, 1994.
10. Adapted from Lloyd George, *The Handbook of Emerging Markets*, 1994.
11. Adapted from Amjad Hadjikhani, "Political Risk for Project-Selling Firms: Turbulence in Relationships between Business and Non-Business Actors," *Journal of Business & Industrial Marketing*, Vol. 13, No. 3, 1998, pp. 235–239.
12. U.S. Department of State, Office of the Spokesman, Worldwide Caution, March 23, 2004, http://travel.state.gov/wwc1.html.
13. Richard B. Loth, "How to Evaluate Country Risk," *Credit and Financial Management*, Vol. 88, No. 6, June 1986, p. 27.
14. Ilan Alon and Matthew A. Martin, "A Normative Model of Macro Political Risk Assessment," *Multinational Business Review*, Vol. 6, No. 2, Fall 1998, pp. 10–19.
15. Terence A. Shimp and Subhash Sharma, "Consumer Ethnocentrism: Construction and Validation of the CETSCALE," *Journal of Marketing Research*, Vol. 24, No. 3, August 1987, pp. 280–289.
16. Richard Karp, "Risk's Rewards," *Barron's*, Vol. 79, No. 16, April 1999, p. 16.
17. Sohn Young-Ju, "Saving Kia," *Business Korea*, Vol. 15, No. 1, January 1998, p. 15.
18. Henny Sender, "Reflation Is No Panacea," *Far Eastern Economic Review*, Vol. 161, No. 48, November 26, 1998, p. 93.
19. Karp, "Risk's Rewards," p. 16.
20. Michael Gips, "Businesses Bearing Brunt of Terrorism," *Security Management*, Vol. 45, No. 8, August 2001, p. 18.
21. David S. Cloud, "Bush Team Says Data Were Wrong on Terror Deaths," *The Wall Street Journal*, June 23, 2004, p. B2.
22. Joseph Kahn, "A Trend Toward Attacks That Emphasize Deaths," *The New York Times*, September 12, 2001, p. A18.
23. Steve Lohr, "Financial District Vows to Rise from the Ashes," *The New York Times*, September 14, 2001, p. A6.
24. Susan Sontag, "The Talk of the Town, Tuesday, and After," *The New Yorker*, September 24, 2001, p. 32.
25. "Counter-Terrorism Driver Training May Thwart Executive Kidnapping," *Best's Review*, Vol. 98, No. 2, June 1997, p. 95.
26. Ibid.
27. Ilkka A. Ronkainen and Jose-Luis Guerrero-Cusumano, "Correlates of Intellectual Property Violation," *Multinational Business Review*, Vol. 9, No. 1, Spring 2001, pp. 59–65.
28. Ibid.
29. "Copycats Beware," *Business Korea*, Vol. 18, No. 3, March 2001, pp. 44–45.
30. Heather R. Goldstein, David M. Lange, Andrew E. Roth, and James D. Lawrence, "International Intellectual Property Alliance Points USTR Toward Brazil, Costa Rica, Guatemala, Russia,

Uruguay," *Intellectual Property & Technology Law Journal*, Vol. 12, No. 11, November 2000, p. 27.

31. See Ronkainen and Guerrero-Cusumano, "Correlates of Intellectual Property Violation," pp. 59–65.

32. "Special: The Right to Good Ideas, Patents and the Poor," *The Economist*, Vol. 359, No. 8227, June 23, 2001, pp. 21–23.

33. Ibid.

34. Ronkainen and Guerrero-Cusumano, "Correlates of Intellectual Property Violation," pp. 59–65.

35. "Special: The Right to Good Ideas, Patents and the Poor," *The Economist*, June 23, 2001, pp. 21–23.

36. Ibid.

37. Ibid.

38. Edmund L. Andrews and Paul Meller, "EU Vetoes GE's Plan to Acquire Honeywell," *International Herald Tribune*, July 4, 2001, pp. 1, 5.

39. Aymo Brunetti, Gregory Kisunko, and Beatric Weder, "Institutional Obstacles to Doing Business: Region-by-Region Results from a Worldwide Survey of the Private Sector," *The World Bank Group Policy Research Working Papers*, 1997, http://wbln0018.worldbank.org/research/workpapers.nsf.

40. Jack G. Kaikati, George M. Sullivan, John M. Virgo, T. R. Carr, and Katherine S. Virgo, "The Price of International Business Morality: Twenty Years Under the Foreign Corrupt Practices Act," *Journal of Business Ethics*, Vol. 26, No. 3, August 2000, pp. 213–222.

41. Ibid.

42. Organization for Economic Co-operation and Development (OECD), www.oecd.org.

43. Sue Abdinnour-Helm, "Network Design in Supply Chain Management," *International Journal of Agile Management Systems*, Vol. 1, No. 2, 1999, pp. 99–106.

44. Nielsen Netratings, http://www.nielsen-netratings.com, March 8, 2003.

45. Al Nucifora, "Are You Preparing for the e-Business Revolution?" *Business First*, Vol. 16, No. 28, February 11, 2000, p. 17; Don Jeffrey, "Survey Details Consumers' Shopping Trends on the Internet," *Billboard*, Vol. 111, No. 22, May 29, 1999, pp. 47–48; Al Nucifora, "There Are Lots of Good Reasons for All the Internet Hype," *Pittsburgh Business Times*, Vol. 18, No. 42, May 7, 1999, p. 20.

46. Dana-Nicoleta Lascu and Kenneth Clow, *Marketing Frontiers: Concepts and Tools*, Cincinnati: Atomic Dog Publishing, 2004.

47. "Munich Re Posts $1.1B Loss," CNN.com Europe, http://europe.cnn.com/, November 29, 2001, p. 1 (web); February 21, 2002.

48. "What Exactly Does a Reinsurer Do?" *Jobs and Career*, Munich Re, http://www.munichre.com/index.html, February 25, 2002, p. 1 (web).

49. "Finance and Economics: Premium Rates; Reinsurance," *The Economist*, February 9, 2002, p. 79.

50. "Profit Through Pioneering Spirit," *History*, Munich Re, http://www.munichre.com/index.html, February 24, 2002, p. 1 (web).

51. "Corporate Responsibility," *120 Years of Innovation*, Munich Re, http://www.munichre.com/index.html, February 24, 2002, p. 1 (web).

52. Ibid.

53. "Reinsurer Munich Re Posts US $1.06B Loss, Keeps Damage Estimates from Attacks," *Canoe Money*, http://www.canoe.ca/MoneyEarnings/nov29_munichre-ap.html, November 29, 2001, pp. 1–2 (web); February 21, 2002.

54. "11th September 2001," *Munchener Ruckversicherungs-Gesellschaft*, 2001, p. 9.

55. "Reinsurers Double Terrorist Claims," *CNN money*, http://money.cnn.com/2001/09/20/europe/insurance/index.htm, September 20, 2001, p. 1 (web); February 21, 2002.

56. "Munich Re Posts $1.1B Loss," http://europe.cnn.com/.

57. Dan Ackman, "Insurers Make a Claim on Taxpayers," Forbes.com, http://www.forbes.com/, October 22, 2001, p. 1 (web); February 21, 2002.

58. Deborah Orr, "Risk Buster," Forbes.com, http://www.forbes.com/, January 21, 2002, pp. 1–2 (web); February 21, 2002.

59. Topics: Worker's Compensation Insurance IT Risks Investment Strategies," January 2004, http://www.munichre.com/publications/302-04044_en.pdf.

60. "After the Terrorist Attacks: US Rating Agencies Affirm Their Top Rating for Munich Re," *Munich American News*, http://www.marclife.com/news01/mr100501.htm, October 5, 2001, p. 1 (web); February 21, 2002.

61. "Reinsurer Munich Re Posts US $1.06B Loss, Keeps Damage Estimate from Attacks," p. 2 (web).

62. Meg Green, "Extreme Weather Patterns Pose Greater Insurance Risk," *Best's Review*, Vol. 104, No. 11, March 2004, p. 69.

63. Ulrike Dauer, "Munich Re Reports Net Profits as Write-Downs, Claims Decline," *The Wall Street Journal*, May 27, 2004, p. A6.

64. Green, "Extreme Weather Patterns," p. 69.

65. "Munich Re: Reinsurer May Trim Holdings; Will Tie Dividends to Profits," *The Wall Street Journal*, April 16, 2004, p. A7.

66. "11th September 2001: The Attack on the World Trade Center in New York from an Insurance Point of View," p. 2 (web).

Case 2-1

Munich Re

Background

On September 11, 2001, apocalyptic images from the World Trade Center and the Pentagon inundated broadcast and print media around the world. The events of 9/11 marked the beginning of new levels of vulnerability for businesses, for national and local governments, for airlines, and for individuals. The insurance and reinsurance industries experienced the largest aggregate losses ever as a result of the attacks. Half a world away, in Munich, Germany, the world's largest reinsurance company, Munich Re (in German, Münchener Rück), suffered a loss of $1.84 billion as a result of the terrorist attacks on U.S. soil.[47] In an effort to adapt to the new, post-September 11 business environment and its new challenges, the insurance and reinsurance firms were forced to change their entire marketing mix. One company that has undergone a complete overhaul of its marketing strategy is Munich Re.

The Reinsurance Industry

Insurance firms rely on reinsurance firms to minimize losses, allowing for costs attributed to insurance losses to be distributed among multiple companies; the reinsurance industry makes it possible for insurance companies to take risks that they would not otherwise,[48] creating new opportunities for increased revenue and market share. The amount of risk assumed by reinsurers varies with the market. When the market is optimistic, reinsurers are more likely to assume greater risks; more capital is available, so the companies are capable of underwriting additional risk.[49] In 2001, the faltering state of markets worldwide depleted the reinsurance companies' capital; reinsurance companies were further confronted by the implications of the September 11, 2001, terrorist attacks. As a result, the reinsurance industry is exploring the different ways in which it can alter the mix of products offered to insurance firms all over the world and their pricing strategies to most effectively operate in the present volatile environment.

Munich Re

Munich Re was founded in 1880 by Carl Thieme, who, with a vision far ahead of his time, created the reinsurance business: He convinced investors of the insurance companies' need for reinsurance as a means for redistributing risk (and loss) among insurance firms, thus allowing them to take advantage of opportunities that otherwise they could not afford to consider.[50] Munich Re is headquartered in downtown Munich, Germany, where it covers a couple of square blocks with impressive older and contemporary architecture. In front of its newest building, the tall figure of the Walking Man, by American artist Jonathan Borofsky, appears to leave the complex in a hurry (see Figure 2-4).

Inside the Munich Re complex, a Japanese garden offers an environment of meditation. Underground, all the buildings are connected with active corridors where color and light set a theatric stage; here, a second "downtown"—the downtown of Munich Re employees—exists in parallel to the bustling street, Leopoldstrasse. The environment projects a strong spirit of innovation, the very theme of Munich Re's corporate culture.[51] In addition to its quest for product innovation, Munich Re was the first German company to introduce English working hours in the nineteenth century, requiring shorter days from its employees and granting them greater

F i g u r e 2 - 4
The Munich Re Headquarters in Munich, Germany

leisure time; the company is also among a few in Germany that provide benefits such as access to a holiday home in the Alps and an on-site daycare—the Munich Re Giants Childcare Center.[52]

The Munich Re Product

With a dependable brand, international presence, and diversified product offering and 42 offices around the world, Munich Re has attracted customers and investors alike, and today it remains the largest reinsurance company in the world. The company offers several different types of insurance services, such as Alternative Risk-Financing and Risk-Transfer Solutions (ART), Agricultural Insurance, Managed Care Services, and Life Insurance. ART, including Finite Risk Reinsurance and Integrated Risk Management, supplements conventional reinsurance as a means of maximizing risk retention and discovering additional financial resources. This is an area that Munich Re has pioneered and that is especially in great demand today, after the September 11 events. Finite Risk Reinsurance allows the company to undertake more risk by using innovative financing techniques, rather than simply by transferring risk from the insured to the insurer.

Integrated Risk Management merges insurance risks with the risks involved in financial markets—for example, in currency fluctuation and in fluctuating interest rates. The objective of Integrated Risk Management is to achieve both the reinsurer's goals of the lowest possible risk and the client's goals of highest possible security and support.

Munich Re provides a number of other insurance services, covering all aspects of the economy. For example, Agricultural Insurance is a service that Munich Re has developed to protect commercial farmers in times of catastrophe and natural disaster. Its Managed Care Services, part of the Munich Re Health Division, are involved in evaluating each potential medical procedure that it insures to determine if, in fact, the procedure is essential. Finally, the company's Life Insurance services give the company access to final consumers—a different market than its traditional business-to-business market segments (its organizational consumers).

The September 11 Terrorist Attacks

Munich Re, much like other reinsurance companies, has had numerous challenges, many dealing with medical advances and genetics decoding, and others with natural disasters. For example, Munich Re had to absorb the costs involved in the recall of Lipobay, a cholesterol-reducing drug that was linked to death among users; a large typhoon in Taiwan; and a chemical plant explosion in France.[53] Yet these losses were dwarfed by the September 11, 2001, terrorist attacks, when terrorists crashed passenger airplanes demolishing the World Trade Center in New York and severely damaging the Pentagon in Washington, D.C. Total estimates for damages were between $10 and $12 billion; in addition to property costs and life insurance coverage, the insurance industry had to bear the costs for clean-up, replacement of items lost, and an array of other losses.[54] Original estimates were low, but by mid-September of that year the major players of the reinsurance industry had claims that totaled more than $3 billion for the disaster.[55] Munich Re's claims totaled $1.84 billion.[56]

Before September 11, 2001, terrorist attacks of this magnitude were inconceivable and were not considered in the calculations of premiums and the like. According to P. J. Crowley of the Insurance

Institute of America, "There has never been a premium dollar collected to cover terrorism."[57] Reinsurance firms had to reconsider their stance on what coverage they would offer in the event of future terrorist attacks. Many insurance and reinsurance companies included clauses in their policies that exclude the coverage of losses from any type of terrorism. Munich Re "was hit by the claims from September 11th more than other members of the reinsurance industry and thus it had to make careful decisions concerning what to do about providing protection against terrorist claims."[58] Today, Munich Re and most other insurers require exclusions in property insurance, for example; also joint ventures between state compensation and private insurance are becoming common.[59]

Reinsurance companies consider four primary criteria of general risk insurability:

- Assessibility; most of the reinsurance companies have been lax in the past about ensuring that insurance companies have a clear (transparent) assessment of potential risk.
- Randomness
- Mutuality
- Economic feasibility

Changing the Marketing Mix at Munich Re

Compared to competition, Munich Re has handled the aftermath of September 11 well. After the attacks, insurance and reinsurance companies were reevaluated by A.M. Best and Standard & Poor's to assess the appropriateness of rating that had been determined before September 11. Both raters agreed that their ratings of A++ and AAA/Stable, respectively, were still appropriate for Munich Re, based on the company's performance by the end of 2001.[60] Although the company had considerable losses, Munich Re reported an increase in premium income by 20 percent from the year 2000. Also, in the wake of claims payout from the terrorist attacks, Munich Re found itself with less competition in the reinsurance industry because a number of smaller reinsurers had losses attributed to the September 11 attacks that caused them to leave the industry altogether.[61] Subsequently, Munich Re experienced substantial losses: 557 million Euros in 2002. Economic losses from natural catastrophes rose sharply due to heat waves, forest fires, severe floods in Asia and Europe, as well as tornadoes in the Midwestern United States.[62] Its ratings dropped from AA, further to A-plus.

After deciding to underwrite more profitable businesses, however, Munich Re was able to rebound with a profit of 534 million Euros (US$646.4 million) in 2003.[63] This profit was gained in spite of severe natural hazard events, with the number of fatalities well above the average: More than 50,000 people were killed in natural catastrophes, such as more than 400 tornadoes in the Midwestern United States, California wildfires, hurricane Isabel, and snow and ice storms. In Europe, the company lost more than $13 billion due to the heat waves.[64] In the process, the company is working on improving its Standard & Poor's rating from A-plus to AA.[65]

No reinsurance company had ever considered terrorist actions of such magnitude when calculating Probable Maximum Loss (PML) for the properties insured. Insurance companies had to

continued

cover losses of more than 1,200 corporations housed in the World Trade Center complex, damage to the operating areas, loss of experienced employees, and destruction of business data and business income. More than 50 buildings were affected in addition to the World Trade Center, and 150,000 people were out of work permanently or temporarily.[66] These extreme circumstances led the reinsurance companies to change their marketing mix—especially the reinsurance product and its price.

According to Nicholas Roenneberg, senior executive manager, Corporate Underwriting/Global Clients division at Munich Re, if such a catastrophe were to happen, it did so at an opportune time for the company—when the company was renewing its policies for the year 2002 (most policies start at the beginning of the calendar year). At that point, the company placed all policy negotiations on hold so that it could reconfigure its marketing mix.

For the short term, Munich Re determined that terrorism was no longer insurable, given the high risks especially in high property concentrations. In these environments, it is impossible to estimate the frequency of such attacks and their total impact, thus presenting a situation in which an important criterion of general risk insurability, assessibility, cannot be met. In the long term, however, there may be some custom options for insurance for properties evaluated at more than 50 million Euros (more than $US50 million), on a case-by-case basis. Ultimately, all types of insurance options may be subject to negotiation. No terrorism exclusion, however, is imposed on life and personal accident insurance.

After the events of September 11, companies doing business with Munich Re were required to document all risks—many companies had not diligently met this requirement in the past. Transparency has become a most important criterion of insurability for Munich Re clients.

In terms of price, the company raised rates for aviation insurance by 80 percent; coincidentally, and to the advantage of Munich Re, aviation renewals were due on October 1, 2001, just after the September terrorist attacks. For property insurance, rates have gone up by 20 to 40 percent across the board.

With regard to promotion, the company has not changed its strategy substantially: It offers no advertising, no sponsorship. One of its main venues for communicating beyond its customer base is its website, which is comprehensive and well updated. Just after the September 11 attacks, the company undertook a tremendous public relations effort to inform shareholders about the impact of the attacks on the company's bottom line. The company increased the frequency of communication, particularly with large institutional investors; a preferred venue for such communication was telephone conferencing.

According to Christian Lahnstein, a specialist in genetic engineering law and liability law with Munich Re, there is an interest in the industry to learn from the experience of the September 11, 2001, events about the intervention of government in bailing out industries affected by disaster and about issues related to the equity of distribution of funds from the government and charitable sources. These findings may have an impact on the marketing mix of the company in the future.

Analysis Suggestions

1. Before analyzing the Munich Re case, address the political risk signals that brought about the September 11, 2001, terrorist actions. How can companies reduce their likelihood of becoming victims of terrorism?
2. As you conduct your case analysis, address the strategic changes to each element of the marketing mix at Munich Re as a result of the September 11 terrorist attacks.

International Trade: Barriers and Facilitators

Chapter Objectives

By the end of this chapter, you should be able to

1 Identify different trade barriers imposed on international trade and arguments used by governments to erect and maintain these barriers.

2 Provide an overview of key international organizations facilitating international trade directly or by promoting economic development.

3 Identify government efforts involved in promoting economic development and trade.

4 Describe other trade facilitators, such as foreign trade zones, offshore assembly plants, and special economic zones, and the Normal-Trade-Relations Status.

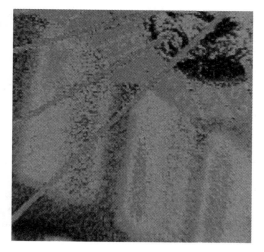

usinesses must face numerous barriers when entering international markets. Barriers to entry can be imposed by local and international competition, by the local channel structure, and by logistics and other firms offering marketing support. Factors in the economic, political, financial, and legal environment also can create barriers for businesses attempting to expand internationally—as discussed in Chapter 2, "An Overview of the International Marketing Environment." Even protectionist tendencies within a regionally integrated area could impose barriers to entry. For example, one of the first nicknames that the European Union acquired in the late 1980s was "Fortress Europe," for its potential to restrict access to this large, integrated market to companies from its member countries; that has not held true so far—but the possibility for it still remains. This chapter focuses on government-initiated protectionist strategies, such as tariff and nontariff barriers.

The reduction in trade barriers constitutes a main concern of multinationals and their representative governments. In addition to participating in numerous regional treaties, governments have joined forces to create forums for discussion of trade issues and mechanisms for the reduction of trade restrictions. One such organization, the World Trade Organization (WTO), has had a significant positive impact on trade, reining in protectionist strategies of important players in the world of trade, such as China, and opening formerly closed markets to international companies. Nevertheless, despite its accomplishments, this organization has met substantial opposition recently from groups that perceive globalization as the promotion of corporate interests to the detriment of the individual, of developing countries, and of the environment. This chapter focuses on facilitators to international trade and addresses the opposition to trade expansion by environmentalists and developing countries. Chapter 4, "Regional Economic and Political Integration," addresses regional economic and political integration as yet another mechanism used to eliminate trade barriers.

Protection of local markets from foreign companies constitutes an important mandate for national and local governments alike. Many political careers have been built and defended on market protection rhetoric. "We will not sell our country" has been a slogan of countries resisting foreign economic and political dominance in the past. Today, it is a slogan used against multinationals that are rapidly expanding, taking over emerging markets, and bringing with them a consumption culture perceived to go against local culture and traditions. These multinationals also are seen as eliminating small local producers and service providers, bankrupting formerly productive factories, and replacing abundant local labor with more efficient advanced technology, increasing local unemployment and disrupting political stability.

Some of the arguments for **protectionism** are indeed valid. The **infant industry argument** is aimed at protecting an emerging national industry from powerful international competitors, which could easily squeeze out a newcomer to the business merely with its brand name resonance and with pricing strategies that a new industry could not possibly sustain in the long term. The argument stressing the industrialization of developing countries also is valid for similar reasons. The national defense argument is regarded as justified in international trade forums and is widely accepted as a reasonable argument for protectionism.

protectionism All actions by national and local governments aimed at protecting local markets from foreign competitors.

infant industry argument A protectionist strategy aimed at protecting a national industry in its infancy from powerful international competitors.

There is also the argument for environmental protection and/or protection of natural resources and the need for maintaining standards to the benefit of all humankind; this line of arguments is also soundly reasoned. The problem with this defense of protectionism arises when the standards imposed are, in fact, simple protectionist arms that require foreign competition to go through excessive and unwarranted bureaucratic exercise, or when these requirements are imposed on international firms but not on local firms—or not to the same degree.

In general, it is believed that consumers pay the final price for the cost of protectionism strategies. Arguments for protectionism ignore the economic advantages of free trade and the importance of adopting open market mechanisms for optimal long-term market performance. In fact, history has amply demonstrated that a government's right and authority to pick and choose winners among industries and firms could be corrupted and distorted by local influential firms, power-seeking politicians, and favor-seeking lobby groups.[1] Politicians, particularly in the United States, favor trade barriers and vote for imposing them because such strategies appeal directly to the concerns of their constituencies regarding the possibility of losing their jobs. What these politicians do not consider is the subsequent retaliatory action of other governments that will negatively affect the domestic economy, the higher consumer prices attributed to the tax imposed to subsidize the domestic industry, and higher prices attributed to the reduction in competition in the local market.[2]

3-1 Arguments for Protectionism

Sections 3-1a through 3-1f describe arguments most often advanced to justify the imposition of tariff and nontariff trade barriers.

3-1a Protection of Markets with Excess Productive Capacity

Markets that have excess productive capacity have committed significant resources to their production facilities. In the case of Central and Eastern Europe, for example, the standard for production during the central planning years under communism was represented by enormous factories employing hundreds of thousands of workers, each charged with minuscule repetitive tasks under an elaborate division-of-labor program. The goal of such programs was both to ensure productivity and to assure a place of work to every individual, qualified or not. Such factories had, in addition to the workers, structures with directors and paradirectors, all served by several secretaries whose specializations varied from typing to answering telephones, to making coffee, to taking care of personal shopping for the director's family.

After the fall of communism, the new factory owners (often foreign) quickly realized that they needed only a fraction of the workers for optimal production and proceeded to fire the rest, leading to regional unrest. Currently, remaining factories are protected from foreign buyouts and are managed locally. Often they are state-owned enterprises. National governments protect them from foreign investors. They also protect these enterprises by limiting the entrance of competing products, such as superior steel and higher-performance tractors, by arguing that such restrictions are instituted for **protection of markets with excess productive capacity.**

protection of markets with excess productive capacity
A protectionist measure used to prevent foreign buyouts, invoking the protection of local labor.

3-1b Employment Protection and Protection of Markets with Excess Labor

Under the scenario presented in section 3-1a, "Protection of Markets with Excess Productive Capacity," the markets of Central and Eastern Europe—especially those in the countries of the former Soviet Union—are now experiencing high levels of excess labor and underemployment, all of which lead to flares of social unrest. As a result, local politicians actively lobby against granting import licenses for products competing with locally produced goods that are established in the market. Arguments invoking **employment protection** are used to ensure that competing multinationals do not import products manufactured elsewhere that might drive local manufacturers out of business and lead to local unemployment. The argument also is used against multinationals that might purchase local plants and fire most of the redundant workers to create acceptable levels of profitability. A related argument, invoking the **protection of markets with excess labor,** is also used to prevent more efficient multinationals from taking over local businesses and streamlining local operations.

> **employment protection** Protection of local employment by not granting import licenses for products competing with similar, locally produced, goods.

> **protection of markets with excess labor** The erection of barriers to imports of products competing with local offerings in an effort to protect local jobs.

3-1c Infant Industry Arguments and Arguments Related to the Industrialization of Developing Countries

The infant industry arguments and arguments related to the industrialization of developing countries are considered valid: Developing countries need to protect their markets from competitors from countries with an established industrial base. Foreign competitors would be able to offer higher quality products at lower costs and would undoubtedly undercut local manufacturers attempting to break into the market. Foreign competition would present the greatest challenge to local industries in their infancy.

3-1d Natural Resources Conservation and Protection of the Environment

The resource conservation argument is considered to be valid in international trade organization forums, especially in light of worldwide shortages of raw materials. Similarly, a balance sometimes has to be struck between free trade and legitimate arguments such as those centering on environmental protection, but governments still need to find a way of agreeing when curbs on trade can be an acceptable way to pursue a greater good.[3]

The problem with these two arguments arises when they are used arbitrarily, with a clear bias against international firms, either imposing the standards only on foreign firms or requiring them to meet higher standards than local firms.

3-1e Protection of Consumers

Protection of consumers is an often-echoed argument that ultimately favors local, over international, business. Standards that are rigidly applied against foreign businesses, quality controls that necessitate layers of costly bureaucracy, and arbitrary product origin requirements, among others, are invoked as a basis for this argument. Politicians in the European Union have argued that they were protecting consumers by imposing standards on imported beef: Listening to the unified voices of their constituencies and attempting to protect the local beef industry against the high-quality, cheap, corn-fed U.S. beef, the European Union banned its import, invoking the use of growth hormones in the United States. With the cattle in many countries of the European Union only slowly recovering from the mad-cow and/or hoof-and-mouth epidemics, this is an unequivocal demonstration that consumer-protection-gone-too-far is not necessarily in the interest of the consumer.

3-1f National Defense Interests

The national defense argument is also perceived as valid, and it is often invoked in international trade forums. Publications that attempt to destabilize the government, armament, and other similar products are often under an import ban. More recently, the national defense argument has been advocated by developing countries and/or by countries that attempt to control and restrict access of their population to Western influence. Such nations may perceive a threat in the unrestricted imports of information-based services through electronic channels; countries such as China, Singapore, and Saudi Arabia impose restrictions on and even ban ownership of satellite dishes, whereas other nations are attempting to control citizen access on the World Wide Web.[4]

3-2 Tools of Government Protectionism: Tariff and Nontariff Barriers

3-2a Tariffs

Tariffs are any type of tax imposed on goods entering a particular country. Tariffs are imposed to

- Discourage imports of particular goods, such as consumer goods, which often are not considered essential in developing countries.
- Protect local industry: for example, the United States imposed tariffs on steel imports to protect local steel manufacturers (however, the World Trade Organization ruled that the United States violated international trade rules).
- Penalize countries that are not politically aligned with the importing country, or countries that are imposing tariffs or nontariff restrictions on goods from the importing country.
- Generate revenues for the importing country.

In general, tariffs assessed by the United States are relatively low, less than 10 percent. Some developing countries set tariffs higher than 100 percent for products that compete with an infant industry. For example, countries attempting to develop their own automobile industry are likely to impose very high tariffs on all automobiles imported into the country.

3-2b Nontariff Barriers

Nontariff barriers include all measures, other than traditional tariffs, that are used to distort international trade flows; they raise prices of both imports and import-competing goods and favor domestic over foreign supply sources by causing importers to charge higher prices and to restrict import volumes.[5]

In the past 20 years, in an attempt to keep markets closed without going against the General Agreement on Tariffs and Trade (GATT) and the World Trade Organization (see Chapter 4, "Regional Economic and Political Integration"), governments have created new nontariff barriers, such as orderly market arrangements, voluntary import expansion, and voluntary export restraints, which limit market access for foreign businesses. These nontariff barriers have been erected by many countries, but most are imposed by the United States, members of the European Union, and other industrialized countries on exporting countries such as Japan, South Korea,[6] and developing countries.[7] But even local governments, such as the government of New York state, can erect such barriers, as International Marketing Illustration 3-1 describes.

Other, more traditional, nontariff barriers include quotas, currency controls, and standards—such as environmental, quality, performance, and health standards, all of which are expensive to provide and evaluate. Boycotts, embargoes, and sanctions are the most severe barriers to trade that are imposed usually to punish a company or a national government.

Nontariff barriers are constantly evolving: They are in a continuous process of refinement, aimed at avoiding scrutiny from the World Trade Organization or other trade organizations. Although the most frequently encountered nontariff barriers are described here, it is important to note that new variants of the barriers described are continuously emerging in the global trade arena.

Import Quotas and Orderly Market Arrangements

Quotas specify a maximum quantity (unit limit) or a value (usually specified in the national currency) of a product that may be imported during a specified period. Quotas are administered either on a global first-come, first-served basis or on a bilateral basis to restrict shipments from a specific supply source—such as the Multifiber Arrangement.[8]

International Marketing Illustration

3-1

Local Trade Barriers: An Example from New York State

Direct shipping laws provide an example of nontariff barriers to trade. Such laws enacted locally—by states, for example—restrict international trade. For example, New York state law denies all firms outside the state the ability to sell directly to New York consumers. These laws restrict consumer choice, and consumers have to pay higher prices because fewer competitors are available in the market. New York consumers could order wine from a company in Alsace, France, at a lower cost than buying the same wine from a New York retailer. The ability of New York consumers to purchase wine from abroad or from other states in the United States should increase competition and lead to lower prices and more wine choices for consumers. However, this is not possible: The New York law states that New York distributors must dispense every case of wine entering the state from foreign suppliers. In effect, New York distributors have a monopoly over the market. Retailers are also affected by this law because they, too, have to purchase their wine from U.S. distributors.

A comparison of wine prices reveals that states that allow direct shipping have a lower average price than states that do not allow it. The eight states surrounding New York have restricted wine trade in different forms. For example, New Hampshire, Connecticut, and Rhode Island allow direct shipping only with a permit, which has to be obtained from the state's Attorney General to allow shipping to consumers' homes.

Source: Robert Eyler, "Direct Shipping Laws, Wine, and Societal Welfare," *International Journal of Wine Marketing*, Vol. 15, No. 2, 2003, pp. 25–34.

The Multifiber Arrangement was initiated as a temporary measure in 1974 (but lasted 21 years!). Its articulated goals were to expand trade, to reduce barriers to trade, and to initiate a progressive liberalization of world trade in textile products, while ensuring the orderly and equitable development of this trade and avoiding disruptive effects in individual markets and on individual lines of production in both importing and exporting countries.[9] In reality, this was an **orderly market arrangement,** an intricate process of establishing quotas in the textile and apparel industries, initiated by the United States and Europe, whose textile operations were moving to Asia to take advantage of cheaper labor. The Multifiber Arrangement was nullified under the Uruguay Round of the General Agreement on Tariffs and Trade in 1995 but has since been replaced by similar nontariff barriers.

orderly market arrangements Protectionist measures involving intricate processes for establishing quotas in the textile and apparel industries.

Nonautomatic Import Licenses

Nonautomatic import licenses are issued on a discretionary basis and are used to restrict imports of a given product. Licensing requirements can restrict the volume of imports, as do quotas, or they can be used to impose on the exporter or importer specific conditions that will result in fewer imports.[10] It should be mentioned that the World Trade Organization presently requires member countries to ensure transparency of the import-license granting process; they are asked to do so by publicizing information concerning administration of restrictions, by listing information regarding the licenses granted over the most recent period, and, where practicable, by providing additional import statistics of the products concerned.[11]

nonautomatic import license A license issued on a discretionary basis to restrict imports of a given product and/or from a particular country.

Automatic Import Licenses

automatic import license A license granted freely to importing companies but may be used by government for the purpose of import surveillance, thus discouraging import surges, imposing administrative and financial burdens on importers, and delaying shipment.

Automatic import licenses are granted freely to importing companies. Automatic licenses are used by the importing country's government for the purpose of import surveillance: The licenses have the potential to discourage import surges, they place additional administrative and financial burdens on the importer, and they may also raise costs by delaying product shipments.[12]

Voluntary Import Expansion (VIE)

voluntary import expansion A government's response to protectionist threats from another country whereby it agrees to open markets to imports and/or to increase foreign access to a domestic market to avoid more severe protectionist action.

Under a **voluntary import expansion** (VIE), a country agrees to open its markets to imports. Voluntary import expansions increase foreign access to a domestic market, while increasing competition and reducing prices. Voluntary import expansions are not voluntary at all: A country agrees to import products as a result of pressure from another country. An example of voluntary import expansion is Japan's decision to avert U.S.-imposed trade sanctions by importing U.S. semiconductors.[13]

Voluntary Export Restraints (VER)

voluntary export restraints A government's self-imposed export quotas to a particular country that are established to avoid more severe protectionist action by the respective importing country.

Voluntary export restraints (VERs) are self-imposed quotas and constitute a barrier to trade often used in the 1980s to protect local industries. The United States, for example, used voluntary export restraints to protect local steel and automobile industries. Voluntary export restraints are agreed upon by both the importing and exporting countries. A country that is subject to voluntary export restraints limits the quantity of products it exports to another, primarily because it attempts, by doing so, to avoid more severe, future mandatory import restrictions. Voluntary export quotas are still used today even though they have been banned by the Uruguay Round of the General Agreement on Tariffs and Trade (and by the World Trade Organization) since 1999. The United States is imposing them informally, for example, for Japanese steel imports; this protection mechanism has been used since 1969 in the long history of trade protection of the U.S. steel industry.[14]

Price Controls: Increasing Prices of Imports

price controls Strategies requiring a product to sell for a particular price in the local market; price control strategies are typically used to increase the prices of imports to match the minimum prices of local competition.

Price controls have a direct effect on a product mix aimed at a particular market. Increasing the price of imports to match minimum prices of domestic offerings is one such strategy that is frequently used for both products and for retailers. For example, Japan uses such controls to ensure that locally produced rice is not at a disadvantage relative to rice imports from the United States, which are of equally high quality but are sold at much lower prices. In this instance, the prices of imports are held artificially high so that local consumers would not discriminate in favor of U.S. competitors. Similarly, Wal-Mart and other discounters and category specialists (see Chapter 12, "International Retailing") in the European Union are constantly scrutinized and often pressured by local authorities to raise prices; EU governments charge that these international retailers price products below cost to drive out smaller competitors.

Price Controls: Antidumping and Countervailing Duty Actions

antidumping Legislation designed to counter unfair price competition; lengthy antidumping investigations can also serve as an impediment to trade.

countervailing duty actions Investigations initiated to determine whether imports are sold below fair prices as a result of foreign subsidies and the subsequent establishment of measures to offset subsidies.

Antidumping and **countervailing duty actions** were designed to counter unfair competition, such as predatory pricing. Dumping refers to selling below fair value to undermine competitors' charging the market price and/or to get rid of excess inventory—with the same outcome, of undermining competition. When used as price controls, antidumping measures involve initiating investigations to determine whether imports are sold below fair value, imposing duties to offset dumping, as well as adopting other measures to counter the effects of dumping. Countervailing measures include investigations to determine whether imports are sold below fair prices as a result of foreign subsidies; such determination is usually followed by duties that are imposed to offset this practice and measures taken to offset effects of subsidies.[15]

To the detriment of international trade, such measures have become protectionist tools that are used to intimidate importers and restrict trade. The European Union has been under scrutiny in the past decade for excessive use of antidumping investigations. Such investigations probing into antidumping activity and countervailing duty investigations focus on a specific product from a particular supply source.[16]

Price Controls: Paratariff Measures

Paratariff measures are charges that increase the costs of imports in a manner similar to tariffs. Such measures include allowing an initial number of product units to enter the country duty-free and charging tariffs to subsequent shipments in excess of this quota; they also include advance import deposits, additional import charges, seasonal tariffs, and customs charges. The United States uses many of these paratariff measures to discourage shipment of certain agricultural products from developing countries.[17]

> **paratariff measures** Additional, nontariff fees that increase the costs of imports in a manner similar to tariffs.

Standards

Standards as barriers to trade are frequently used as barriers to imports, primarily imposed by highly industrialized countries. Most challenging are standards that are especially strict, such as those imposed by the European Union against hormone-fed U.S. beef and bio-engineered corn and soybeans on safety grounds. Standards that discriminate against foreign firms in particular, or that simply create more bureaucratic hurdles for importing firms, act as nontariff barriers to trade.

> **standards as barriers to trade** Trade barriers imposing performance, environmental, or other requirements that are primarily aimed at imports.

On the positive side, excessive standards could and often do help local and international industry alike, by deterring gray markets. For example, the United States has very strict environmental and manufacturing standards for automobiles. Importing an automobile that is not specifically designed according to U.S. specifications is very costly: One has to use expensive automobile conversion services and obtain the appropriate Department of Transportation authorization to use the vehicle.

Local Content Requirements and Foreign Ownership: Percentage Requirements

Governments of many emerging market economies mandate that a certain percentage of the products imported are locally produced: They mandate a **local content requirement.** This requirement can often be met by manipulating and/or assembling the product on the territory of the importing country—usually in a foreign trade zone. China, for example, has always presented a challenge to importing firms. Multinational firms often join with Chinese partners and agents to either package or manufacture enough of the product to have it qualify based on local content requirements; firms often do tricky calculations on local services and part values to meet such local content edicts.[18]

> **local content requirement** A protectionist measure requiring that a certain percentage of the products imported are locally produced.

In addition to the traditional local content requirements, there are other forms of favoring local contribution and labor. For example, governments often impose regulations to protect local carriers for passenger and freight transportation. An example would be restricting foreign airlines' landing rights or ability to pick up passengers at an intermediate stop ("third freedom" rights); this requirement favors national airlines operating on international routes.[19]

Foreign ownership restrictions also are widely used. Some ownership restrictions refer to the percentage ownership in a business—for example, requiring 51 percent or more of a joint venture to be owned by a national firm. Other restrictions are even more stringent and discriminatory in favor of nationals. The history of Indonesia's automobile industry is a case in point. Initially, the industry was in the hands of Indonesians from the military ranks or senior officials; as the "New Order" was instituted, the industry went into the hands of the ruling Suharto family and of the large Chinese conglomerates, creating a powerful lobbyist that was able to ban imports of motor vehicles until 1993, when the ban was replaced by tariffs in the range of 175 to 275 percent.[20]

Service industries in particular are subjected to regulations that invoke foreign ownership restrictions. Creative strategies that employ an ambiguous legal environment are used to block entry of international service providers or to place them at a disadvantage relative to local competitors.

Boycott

A **boycott** is usually initiated as the result of an action group calling for a ban on consumption of all goods associated with a particular company and/or country. Often, boycotts target a company that is representative, or even synonymous, with its country of origin. For example, when the uprising in the West Bank and Gaza erupted, Coke sales in neighboring Egypt and Jordan were hit by local boycott calls.[21] McDonald's restaurants were the target of French protesters, who were against tariffs imposed by the United States on European Union countries. Exxon-owned Esso was the target of a high-profile boycott campaign by groups angered at its support of the U.S. government's rejection of the Kyoto climate change pact.[22] In another example, British Muslims have called for boycotting all the firms doing business with a U.S.-based marketing and military intelligence firm, CACI, in protest for prisoner abuse in Iraq.[23]

Embargoes and Sanctions

Embargoes and **sanctions** are imposed by a country (or a number of countries) against another country. An embargo prohibits all business deals with the country that is the target of the embargo, often affecting businesses from third countries that do business with both the country (or countries) imposing the embargo and the country under embargo. The embargo could be limited to a particular product and/or to particular circumstances. For example, "smart sanctions" were imposed by the United States and the United Kingdom on Iraq's oil exports, modifying the oil embargo against Iraq to allow for use of oil revenues aimed at humanitarian purposes. (The embargo has since been lifted.) Liberia is presently experiencing an arms embargo imposed by the United Nations Security Council as a punishment for its support of Sierra Leone's Revolutionary United Front.

The United States has imposed, for decades, a full embargo against Cuba. The embargo covers any commercial and noncommercial relationship with Cuba, and it even prohibits visits to the country by U.S. citizens, with some exceptions. Furthermore, multinational companies from other countries doing business in the United States are prohibited, under the embargo, from engaging in any business deals with Cuba. Unfortunately for the United States, this strategy does not appear to reach its goal—punishing Fidel Castro, Cuba's president since the onset of the embargo, and his communist regime, by derailing its economy. On the contrary, Cuba is reaching out to the world by transforming itself into a hub for information technology, one where U.S. companies may be at a disadvantage relative to competition in the future.[24]

Finally, a form of nonretaliatory embargo exists: It is imposed when imports into a country that has established quotas for a particular product exceed those quotas.

Currency and Capital Flow Controls

Strategies involving **currency and capital flow controls** are used in economies under tight government control and/or experiencing hard-currency shortages. In the case of capital flow, countries use arguments of self-determination to ensure that regions in the country are uniformly developed or that there would not be a capital flight from the country. Such strategies affect international businesses in that they restrict market-dictated activity in the name of protectionism.

Governments use currency flow restrictions primarily to influence the stability of the national currency. Such restrictions, however, directly affect the flow of imports into the country, by giving priority to desirable goods and restricting the import of less desirable goods and services. Among the currency controls used by governments are the following:

- Blocked currency
- Differential exchange rates
- Foreign exchange permits

Blocked Currency

A country using a **blocked currency** strategy does not allow importers to exchange local currency for the seller's currency. This strategy can be used as a political weapon, to create obstacles for international businesses attempting to enter the country. More often, however, the strategy is used because the country is experiencing acute balance-of-payments difficulties. Firms fortunately have at their disposal countertrade strategies to address this type of barrier. Under a typical scenario, the exporter sells goods in exchange for local currency and uses the proceeds to purchase local goods for sale abroad; U.S. companies in the past often bought goods from Mexico and from Eastern Europe with local currency to address this barrier.[25]

Another method that firms can use to bypass blocked exchange rates entails using unofficial (and, from the perspective of the importing country, illegal) exchange offices. Such offices exist both abroad and in the importing country; however, they offer unfavorable exchange rates and expose the company to the risk of government action against it.

blocked currency A strategy that does not allow importers to exchange local currency for the seller's currency or a currency that the seller is willing to accept as payment (hard currency).

Differential Exchange Rates

Two types of **differential exchange rates** can be used. The first, which is government imposed, refers to a strategy the government uses to promote imports of desirable and necessary goods, such as armament and petrol, and to discourage imports of less desirable and necessary goods, such as consumer goods and services, entertainment, and the like. Offering a less favorable exchange rate for international products and services reflects a government strategy that ultimately increases the cost of this second category of products to the final consumer and discourages its purchase.

A second type of differential exchange rate is favorable to the international firm importing products into this market. In this situation, a difference exists between the black market exchange rate and the official government exchange rate, with the black market rate being higher than the government rate. The rate difference is a reflection of economic distortion: A high black market exchange rate can signal a likely depreciation of the local currency, or foreign exchange rationing by the government, or both. A large difference between the government and the free exchange rate can also be interpreted as a tax on exports and a subsidy on imports, stimulating the diversion of resources from the official to the black market sector.[26]

differential exchange rate The rate imposed by the local government to promote imports of desirable and necessary goods; it also can be the difference between the black market exchange rate and the official government rate.

Foreign Exchange Permits

Countries attempting to control foreign exchange often require the use of **foreign exchange permits.** Such permits are typically provided by the Central Bank. They also give priority to imports of goods that are in the national interest and delay access to foreign exchange for products that are not deemed essential. An exchange permit can also stipulate differential exchange rates. Most countries that experience a shortage of hard currency require foreign exchange permits. China and countries in Sub-Saharan Africa currently require such permits. In the past, Latin American and Eastern European countries relied heavily on the use of foreign exchange permits for imports.

foreign exchange permit A permit that is generally provided by a country's Central Bank in conjunction with the Department of Trade (Ministry of Foreign Trade) and that gives priority to imports of goods considered to be in the national interest.

3-3 International Trade and Trade Facilitators

Several important international and local institutions play an active role in promoting international trade and have a considerable impact on the development of international trade and marketing operations. International trade and development organizations and governmental organizations alike are working individually and jointly to increase the flow of goods, to open access to products and services, and to minimize costs to companies and final consumers by limiting or eliminating the layers of bureaucratic interference in the firms' international operations. Sections 3-3a through 3-3d address Ricardo's theory of comparative advantage and discuss some of the most prominent international trade and development organizations. They also address the role of national governments in promoting the international involvement of local business and in opening local markets to foreign investment—particularly foreign direct investment. It should be mentioned, however, that equally important strides have been made to date by trade agreements. The levels of economic and political integration such agreements have achieved permit free movement of labor and capital and open or nearly open access to markets by firms operating in the region; this topic will be addressed in the appropriately titled Chapter 4, "Regional Economic and Political Integration."

3-3a The International Trade Imperative

comparative advantage The premise that countries benefit from specialization in an industry where they have comparative advantage and from trading with one another.

Free trade is essential to economic development. One argument for free trade is based on economist David Ricardo's theory of **comparative advantage.** The premise for the comparative advantage argument is that countries benefit from specialization in an industry in which they have comparative advantage and from trading with one another. For example, India specializes in the software industry, achieving economies of scale in training its workforce in the necessary skills for optimal production, and in the production process itself. India thus acquires the income to import other goods that meet the needs of the population. At a worldwide scale, this improves overall productivity and output of goods and increases the economic wealth of nations.

Consider the example of two countries, East and West:[27] In a year, an Eastern worker makes two bicycles or produces four bushels of wheat. A Westerner can produce only one bushel or one bike. Each country has 100 workers split evenly between producing bikes or wheat; thus, East produces 200 bushels and 100 bikes, and West produces 50 bushels and 50 bikes. East thus has absolute advantage in producing both; West has no absolute advantage, but it does have comparative advantage in producing bikes. According to the comparative advantage theory, the two countries are better off in specializing in the industry in which they have comparative advantage. If East specializes in growing wheat, moving 10 workers from making bikes to wheat, it will produce 240 bushels and 80 bikes. If West moves 25 workers from wheat production to bike manufacturing, in which it has comparative advantage, it will produce 75 bikes and 25 bushels. Subsequently, consumers in both countries can enjoy more bikes and wheat if they trade at terms at which both gain—at one and a half bushels (sold by East) per bike (sold by West).

Other arguments for free trade suggest that opening up the home market increases competition, thus lowering prices for local consumers. Also, the presence of efficient multinationals will encourage efficiency in local manufacturing and services as well—yet another benefit to the final consumer. Free trade also means that firms no longer have to limit themselves to the local, national market. The companies themselves can afford to increase production, achieve economies of scale, and offer lower prices to world markets.[28] In other words, free trade also means economic growth. Table 3-1 offers figures on trade and foreign direct investment as a percentage of GDP in different regions of the world.

3-3b International Trade and Economic Development Organizations

This chapter provides an overview of the most important trade and economic development organizations worldwide in terms of their overall impact on companies and markets. It must be noted, however, that, in addition to these organizations, other entities provide similar, but typically more targeted, input into the international trade process. They do so directly, by facilitating trade, or indirectly, by developing national infrastructures essential to the flow of goods and communication. For example, the Belgian government and the Dutch government have specific structures that operate individually and jointly, with other international development organizations, to help former colonies in East Africa and Asia, respectively. The French Ministry of Cooperation has a similar mission.

This discussion centers primarily on the World Trade Organization and the organizations that have made significant inroads with regard to the liberalization of trade in the past two decades, facilitating the marketing of goods and services in markets previously

Table 3-1 **Trade in Goods and Gross Foreign Direct Investment**

	Trade in Goods (% of GDP)	Gross Foreign Direct Investment (% of GDP)
Low-Middle Income Countries	**51.8**	**3.3**
East Asia & Pacific	63.4	4.1
Europe/Central Asia	64.3	3.7
Latin America/Caribbean	41.2	4.0
Middle East/North Africa	50.5	0.9
South Asia	24.2	0.7
Sub-Saharan Africa	55.3	2.2
High Income Countries	**37.6**	**6.6**
Europe (EMU)	56.3	14.8
United Kingdom	39.9	23.8
United States	18.3	2.4

Note: Trade in goods as a percentage of gross domestic product (GDP) is the sum of merchandise exports and imports divided by the value of GDP in U.S. dollars. Gross foreign direct investment includes reinvested earnings, equity capital, and other short-term capital.

Source: World Development Indicators, *World Development Report 2004*, World Bank Group; http://econ.worldbank.org/wdr/wdr2004/.

deemed inaccessible and reducing barriers to trade worldwide. It also focuses on the two Bretton Woods organizations, which have provided support for development and trade in the free world since 1944—the World Bank and the International Monetary Fund.

The World Trade Organization (WTO) (www.wto.org) and the General Agreement on Tariffs and Trade (GATT)

The **General Agreement on Tariffs and Trade (GATT)** was signed by 123 nations agreeing to promote trade and eliminate trade barriers. Under the agreement, the signatory countries committed to open their markets to international business and to use the GATT forum to resolve trade disputes. In practice, however, trade disputes took too long to be resolved, and GATT had no enforcement power. GATT's Uruguay Round, which took place between 1986 and 1994, and was subsequently finalized at Marrakech in 1995, substantially changed international trade regulation, replacing the original GATT regulations with a newly empowered **World Trade Organization (WTO),** which currently has 147 member countries from a world total of 192. The WTO is forever changing the way countries regulate international business on their own territory and beyond. The organization's most important trait is that membership is predicated on full implementation and adherence to all GATT agreements.

World Trade Organization candidate countries often must radically change their trade practices and, implicitly, their internal economic structures, to gain membership. For example, China attempted for 15 years to gain membership in the World Trade Organization, before being accepted in December 2001. Its impediments to access were attributed primarily to its trade restrictions (attributed to concerns about the impact of open markets on its economy) and its demands to be allowed to subsidize agricultural output at the rate of developing countries; to gain access to the WTO, China had to lower tariffs on imports such as automobiles and new technologies and to make it easier for foreign companies to establish certain types of businesses in the country.[29]

General Agreement on Tariffs and Trade (GATT) The international trade agreement promoting trade and eliminating trade barriers, opening markets to international business, and creating a forum for resolving trade disputes; GATT issues are now addressed by the World Trade Organization. (See www.wto.org.)

World Trade Organization (WTO) The largest and most influential international trade organization whose primary goal is ensure the free flow of trade; WTO's agreements (negotiated and signed by member countries, ratified in their parliaments) represent trade rules and regulations and act as contracts guaranteeing countries trade rights and binding governments to trade policies. (See www.wto.org.)

The WTO is run by member governments, and its decisions are made either by governments' trade ministers (the organization's highest authority), who meet every two years, or by official representatives, who meet regularly in Geneva, Switzerland, the organization's headquarters. Routine issues are addressed by councils, committees, working parties, and negotiating groups.[30] Ministerial meetings have met with substantial opposition in the past few years. For example, the 1999 ministerial meeting faced 50,000 protesters in Seattle; this may explain why subsequent meetings were organized in locations such as Doha, Qatar, where the government bans activities of all organizations that are critical of any other Arab government or of institutions that the respective governments are members of.[31] It is significant that opposition groups see in globalization the promotion of corporate interests to the detriment of the individual, of developing countries, and of the environment.

The WTO's main functions are

- Providing assistance to developing and transition economies.
- Offering specialized help for export promotion, through the International Trade Center.
- Promoting regional trade agreements.
- Promoting cooperation in global economic policy-making.
- Reviewing members' trade policies.
- Engaging in routine notification when members introduce new trade measures or alter old ones.[32]

WTO agreements cover goods, services, and intellectual property and address issues such as[33]

import quota The maximum quantity (unit limit) or value of a product that may be imported during a specified period.

- Reducing tariff and nontariff trade barriers on specific categories of goods and services. In this regard, the WTO has made important strides in the area of manufactured goods, as well as in the area of information technology. It is still working on eliminating barriers in the area of agriculture, where GATT allowed, until recently, government subsidies and **import quotas.**
- Opening service markets to international business. The General Agreement on Trade in Services (GATS) has established rules for specific sectors, outlining principles that require countries to offer access to their markets. GATS initially covered banking, securities, and insurance.
- Regulating the protection and enforcement of intellectual property rights for trademarks, patents, and copyrights—under the Agreement on Trade-Related Aspects of Intellectual Property Rights (TRIPS).
- Dealing with antidumping activities.
- Addressing subsidies and trade restrictions designed to safeguard domestic industries such as technical regulations and standards, import licensing, rules of origin, and other measures that impede international trade.

Group of Seven (G7) A group of the seven most industrialized countries: Canada, France, Germany, Italy, Japan, the United Kingdom, and the United States; the group also includes Russia and it is often referred to as a G8. The group addresses issues such as biotechnology and food safety, economic development, arms control and nonproliferation, organized crime, drug trafficking, terrorism, environmental issues, digital opportunities, microeconomic issues, and trade. (See www.g7.utoronto.ca.)

- Settling disputes. Member states cannot ignore any of the dispute resolution decisions handled by the Dispute Settlement Body—as they previously did, under GATT. Examples of disputes handled by the DSB are Venezuela's complaint against the United States over discrimination in gasoline imports (requiring higher standards for imports than for locally produced gasoline).
- Reviewing regularly individual countries' trade policies to ensure compliance with the WTO and transparency.

Group of Seven (G7)

Members of the **Group of Seven (G7)** most industrialized countries are Canada, France, Germany, Italy, Japan, the United Kingdom, and the United States. The Group was formed during the 1970s economic crisis, as a forum for addressing economic and financial issues. The organization's yearly meetings involve heads of state, government ministers, and directors of central banks. The G7 currently addresses issues such as biotechnology and food safety, economic development, disarmament, arms control and nonproliferation, organized crime, drug trafficking, terrorism, environmental issues, digital opportunities issues, microeconomic issues, and trade.

Russia, an observer in the group, first participated in the organization's meetings in 1991. Russia's economy, however, is the size of that of Denmark,[34] and its inclusion in the G7 was often questioned. Ultimately, most of the economic deliberations are done in the G7 format, without including Russia, primarily through the regular meetings of the G7 finance ministers. Moreover, because Russia is not a member of the World Trade Organization (WTO), it does not participate in deliberations concerning this organization. For example, Russia did not participate in the G7 discussions within the framework of the WTO ministerial meeting in Doha, Qatar, which addressed, among others, market access of and technical assistance to developing countries. More recently, at the 2004 Washington, D.C., meeting, it was suggested that China should be invited to subsequent summits in recognition of the country's importance on the economic scene.

The G7 has met with substantial criticism on a number of sectoral problems that it was unable to adequately address. Among its missteps and shortcomings are the following: a failed $24 billion aid program in 1992 to turn Russia into a market economy; the Group's inability to foresee the Mexican crisis in 1994 and the Asian meltdown in 1997; its failure to devise ways to make Japan's economy grow or Europe's to produce jobs and faster growth, and to adequately respond to globalization and the challenge of emerging markets.[35] The G7 has also been criticized for its failure to challenge China on its human rights record. Among the G7 successes are the unity developed within the group on a variety of issues. The group has addressed successfully topics ranging from debt to nuclear power control—at the very least by providing a credible forum for discussion of these issues. Of particular note is the 1989 G7 Paris meeting that created the European Bank for Reconstruction and Development to help Eastern Europe in its process of transition to a market economy.[36]

The International Monetary Fund (IMF) (www.imf.org) and the World Bank (www.worldbank.org)

The **International Monetary Fund (IMF)** and the **World Bank** were created at the United Nations Monetary and Financial Conference, as a result of the Bretton Woods Agreement in 1944, to address the need for global economic development, stability, and rebuilding after World War II and the 1930s' Great Depression. Both the International Monetary Fund and the World Bank are specialized agencies of the United Nations; membership in the World Bank requires membership in the IMF.

The goal of the IMF was to establish an innovative monetary system and an institution charged with monitoring it. The IMF is based on the proposals put forth by Harry Dexter White in the United States and John Maynard Keynes in the United Kingdom. At its foundation lies a system that would encourage the unrestricted conversion of one currency to another by establishing a clear and unequivocal value for each currency.[37] Currently, the organization, whose mission has significantly expanded since its debut, is located in Washington, D.C. The IMF comprises more than 180 member countries who are free to join the organization—as such, they are obligated to adhere to its charter of rights and obligations—or to leave the organization (as Cuba, Indonesia, and Poland have done in the past).[38]

The IMF directly links members' voting power to the amount they contribute to the institution; as such, the United States has more than 265,000 votes (18 percent of the total).[39] The organization's international civil servants are international experts and nationals of the different member countries and operate under a Managing Director, who is typically a European. Rodrigo Rato, former finance minister of Spain, was appointed in May 2004 to serve as Managing Director and Chairman of the Executive Board for a five-year term. He follows Horst Köhler, who resigned to pursue Germany's presidency, in this position.

International Monetary Fund (IMF) Traditionally the lender of last resort; the IMF also has assumed the position of mediator between debtors and creditors, imposing stabilization programs; debt-reduction guidelines; ceilings for bank credit, budget deficit, borrowing, and international reserves; and development programs for borrowing countries. (See www.imf.org.)

World Bank The World Bank Group, headquartered in Washington, D.C., that is one of the largest sources of funds for development assistance aimed at the poorest countries worldwide. (See www.worldbank.org.)

Traditionally, the IMF has played the role of lender of last resort; more recently, how-ever, it has also assumed the position of mediator between debtors and creditors. Through its stabilization programs, the IMF imposes debt reduction guidelines; ceilings for bank credit, budget deficit, borrowing, and international reserves; and particular development programs that the borrowing countries have to follow. In the recent past, the IMF offered countries in Central and Eastern Europe loans for restructuring their economies. Other recent bailout activities focused on Brazil, Argentina, and Turkey. The bailout of Argentina with an $8 billion package had a unique twist: Disbursement of $3 billion of the funds hinged on a reschedule of Argentina's public debt. Brazil received a $15 billion line of credit (following a $41 billion rescue package that Brazil received in 1998), con-tingent on its strengthening fiscal and monetary policies, and implementing a structural reform agenda.[40] These actions were necessary because these two important emerging markets were unable to attract foreign direct investment from developed countries such as the United States, Japan, and Europe, which were themselves going through a period of slow growth or recession.[41]

The IMF also offers training and technical assistance for monetary and financial strategists from borrowing countries through its field offices and publishes statistical information based on accurate data that member countries provide as a requirement for membership.

The World Bank is the largest international bank that sponsors economic develop-ment projects. The World Bank, headquartered in Washington, D.C. (see Figure 3-1), employs international specialists in economics, finance, and sectoral development. In addition, it has field offices in developing countries, overseeing projects in the area of industry, health, poultry and dairy production, among others. Whereas, in the past, the World Bank's focus was in the area of industrial and infrastructure development, its cur-rent priorities lie primarily in the areas of health (it provided a $500 million umbrella loan for programs to combat HIV/AIDS in Sub-Saharan Africa) and information tech-nology (in 2000, the World Bank awarded $1.5 billion in contracts to IT companies).[42]

Both the IMF and the World Bank have met with their share of criticism. The IMF has been criticized for imposing unduly rapid or overly detailed structural adjustment pro-grams; consequently, countries are unlikely to feel a sense of ownership of programs that stretch their capacity for implementation and, as a result, may lack the political will needed to carry them out.[43] The World Bank has been criticized for lending primarily to countries with access to private international capital; according to the Bank's own analy-sis, the countries that could make best use of its resources receive a comparatively small share.[44]

Figure 3-1

The World Bank, headquartered in Washington, D.C., works closely with the International Monetary Fund, which is located nearby.

Nevertheless, the accomplishments of the World Bank and the IMF and their impact on economic development and trade cannot be ignored. They have been instrumental in fostering economic and political stability in developing countries. They have protected banks from developed countries by preventing firms in volatile regions from defaulting on their debt. They have helped create viable industrial, agricultural, and infrastructure projects. Also, they have contributed substantially to the training and development of local expertise in different sectors. Furthermore, the two agencies provide reliable statistics in areas related to finance, economic development, trade, population trends, and national policies, among others.

Other Development Banks

A number of development banks with a regional focus also are instrumental in advancing economic development and in providing support for business and trade. Among the development banks are the following:[45]

- The **African Development Bank** (www.afdb.org), headquartered in Abidjan, Ivory Coast, has as a primary goal poverty reduction. It provides support and expertise in areas such as agriculture, human resources, and health services, and it emphasizes small businesses as its target recipients.

- The **Asian Development Bank** (www.adb.org), headquartered in Manila, the Philippines, focuses on the private sector. The bank sponsors projects aimed at increasing access to technology and improving the functioning of government. Together with the World Bank and the IMF, the Asian Development Bank was instrumental in Asia's recovery from the 1990s' financial crisis.

- The **European Bank for Reconstruction and Development** (www.ebrd.com) headquartered in London, United Kingdom, has as main goals reforming and strengthening markets in the transition economies of Central and Eastern Europe. Among others, it has played an important role in the development of legal and institutional frameworks, in reducing barriers to foreign investment, and in strengthening the countries' financial markets and their private sector.

- The **Inter-American Development Bank** (www.iadb.org), headquartered in Washington, D.C. (see Figure 3-2), has as primary clients companies that do not ordinarily deal with the large development banks. Like the other banks, the IADB funds private sector projects, but it also has as priorities modernizing the government, strengthening institutions, and overcoming the "digital divide."

African Development Bank
A bank, headquartered in Abidjan, Ivory Coast, that has as a primary goal poverty reduction in Africa, providing support and expertise in agriculture, human resources, and health services, with an emphasis on small business. (See www.afdb.org.)

Asian Development Bank
A bank, headquartered in Manila, the Philippines, that focuses on the private sector in Asia, sponsoring projects aimed at increasing access to technology and improving the functioning of government in the region. (See www.adb.org.)

European Bank for Reconstruction and Development
A bank headquartered in London, United Kingdom, which has as main goals reforming and strengthening markets in the transition economies of Central and Eastern Europe. (See www.ebrd.com.)

Inter-American Development Bank A bank headquartered in Washington, D.C., aiding companies in the Americas that do not ordinarily deal with the large development banks; this bank is involved in funding private sector projects, modernizing governments, strengthening institutions, and eliminating technology barriers. (See www.iadb.org.)

Figure 3-2

The Inter-American Development Bank, headquartered in Washington, D.C., funds private sector and public sector institutions in the region.

United Nations Organizations

A number of United Nations (www.un.org) bodies promote the economic and financial welfare of developing countries; in particular, these organizations focus on developing the industrial, communication, and transportation infrastructure of developing countries. The impact of such development on fostering trade and foreign direct investment in these markets is substantial. Among the United Nations agencies involved in economic development are the United Nations Development Program (UNDP), headquartered in New York. The UNDP assists, coordinates, finances, and supervises various projects, ranging from institutional strengthening and support to building factories, to developing methane gas extraction facilities, to financing the building of bridges and highways or telecommunications networks. In its efforts, the UNDP, primarily a human development organization, is assisted by other specialized **United Nations organizations**—about 16 in number. Among them and directly involved in economic development and the development of international trade are

- The United Nations Industrial Development Organization (UNIDO), headquartered in Vienna, Austria. UNIDO offers or subcontracts expertise in industrial project design and implementation, often providing turn-key factories to countries in need.
- The United Nations Conference on Trade and Development (UNCTAD), headquartered in Geneva, Switzerland. UNCTAD assists developing countries in developing international trade relations and promotes the integration of trade, environment, and development.
- The Regional Economic Commission for Africa; for Asia and the Pacific; for Europe, North America, and the Commonwealth of Independent States (CIS); for Latin America and the Caribbean; and for Western Asia. This regional arm of the United Nations offers support for the economic and social development of its member States, fosters regional integration, and promotes international cooperation for regional development.
- The Food and Agriculture Organization (FAO), headquartered in Rome, Italy. The FAO offers expertise in agricultural projects.

The United Nations agencies also provide statistical data on developing countries, with a focus on different industry sectors, health, and agriculture.

3-3c Government Organizations

Promoting international trade constitutes one of the more important tasks of the national and local governments of most countries. Most of the international marketing literature explores the different strategies used by government to protect local industry, trade, and service providers from international competition; such publications often ignore efforts of local and national government bodies in increasing exports and in promoting foreign direct investment locally. This discussion details the involvement of the United States' federal, state, and local governments in promoting international trade. Most developed countries have similar institutions to those described herein and offer similar support to local businesses attempting to market their products internationally and to international businesses entering the local market.

Regardless of the level of country economic development, most international trade issues are addressed by the national Department of Commerce, known as the **Ministry of Trade** or, more specifically, the Ministry of Foreign Trade. Frequently, the Ministry of Trade works in tandem with the State Department, known as the **Ministry of Foreign Affairs,** promoting the respective country's foreign policy.

United States Agencies: Federal and State Government

Many United States federal, state, and local government agencies promote the interests of U.S. businesses abroad, encouraging their international involvement in the form of export promotion or by providing foreign direct investment support. They also actively

United Nations organizations The totality of United Nations bodies created to maintain international peace and security; to develop relations among nations; to achieve international cooperation in solving international economic, social, cultural, or humanitarian problems; and to encourage respect for human rights and fundamental freedoms using the venues offered by the different UN organizations. (See www.un.org.)

Ministry of Trade The international institutional equivalent of the Department of Commerce; it coordinates a country's international trade relations.

Ministry of Foreign Affairs The international institutional equivalent of the State Department; it coordinates a country's involvement in international relations.

encourage foreign direct investment in the United States. Among the U.S. agencies supporting activities of international business are the United States Agency for International Development and the United States Department of Commerce.

United States Agency for International Development (USAID)

The **United States Agency for International Development (USAID)** is an independent agency of the federal government. Similarly to the United Nations Development Program and other development organizations, USAID engages in economic development–related operations. Unlike the development organizations previously discussed, USAID is an arm of the **United States State Department,** supporting the economic development of and trade with developing countries aligned politically with the United States. USAID's origins are traced to the Marshall Plan of reconstruction in Europe after World War II, and it was created to advance U.S. foreign policy in developing countries by supporting economic growth and agricultural development, global health, conflict prevention, and developmental relief. In doing so, USAID gives priority to U.S. contracting firms; it has working relationships with more than 3,500 U.S. companies.[46]

Yet, in spite of USAID's success, and that of other aid organizations, not all the contributions to development are appropriately used. A case in point is the example from the Kyrgyz Republic, illustrated in International Marketing Illustration 3-2.

> **United States Agency for International Development (USAID)** An independent agency of the federal government that supports the economic development of and trade with developing countries aligned politically with the United States. (See www.usaid.gov.)

> **United States State Department** The foreign affairs arm of the United States government, in charge of promoting relations with other governments. (See www.state.gov.)

International Marketing Illustration 3-2

International Aid in Private Pockets

The newly independent Kyrgyz Republic is one of the five countries of central Asia that have emerged from the former Soviet Union and one of the few in the former Union that is making important strides toward adopting a market economy. Firms are eager to profit from consumers who are predisposed toward Western goods, unlike those of Uzbekistan, who are embracing fundamentalism and rejecting Western influence. The international aid community rapidly embraced the Kyrgyz Republic as well: Germany, Japan, the Netherlands, Switzerland, Turkey, the United States, the European Bank for Reconstruction and Development, the European Union, the International Monetary Fund, and the World Bank have invested substantially in this country.

As aid continues to pour into the country, however, it is evident that much of it is squandered. For example, USAID sent large quantities of vegetable oil to help meet the needs of Kyrgyz consumers. However, the oil, labeled "not for sale," is sold at prices few can afford on the open market. Similarly, German buses were sent to replace the older Soviet models, yet few can afford the steep bus fares.

This example is not an aberration, but rather the norm in many developing countries. Agricultural automobiles are often used for personal purposes by rural mayors, aid products for flood victims often appear on local store shelves in areas of a country not affected by the floods, and government officials hire their relatives to ensure a distribution of aid products that most effectively serves their families rather than the broader target community of the aid effort.

Nevertheless, with adequate monitoring, international aid efforts ultimately raise the standard of living and the ability of countries to become attractive trade partners.

Source: Adapted from Leo Paul Dana, "Change and Circumstance in Kyrgyz Markets," *Qualitative Market Research*, Vol. 3, No. 2, 2000, p. 62.

United States Department of Commerce

United States Department of Commerce The U.S. governmental agency that oversees and promotes trade, offering export assistance and counseling to U.S. businesses involved in international trade, providing country information and country specialists, and bringing buyers and sellers together.

The **United States Department of Commerce** (http://home.doc.gov) engages in many activities that promote trade (see Figure 3-3). It offers export assistance and counseling to businesses involved in international trade, it provides country information and the assistance of country specialists, and it helps bring buyers and sellers together through trade shows and other trade-related events. Its International Trade Administration district offices are located in the United States and in key international markets; their mission is to promote trade interests of U.S. business abroad. The Department of Commerce also regulates trade by issuing export licenses and by offering food, health, and safety inspections and certification.

An important arm of the Department of Commerce is the Export-Import Bank of the United States (the Ex-Im Bank). The Bank, created in 1934, works with city and state governments to offer export counseling and financial assistance to companies doing business in or planning to do business in international markets. Examples of the Ex-Im Bank's financial assistance are export credit insurance, guaranteed loans, pre-export financing to small and medium-size exporters, grants for feasibility studies and project planning for projects in developing countries, and technical assistance grants, among others. The Ex-Im Bank also makes loans to foreign purchasers who purchase U.S. goods and services.[47]

State and Local Government Agencies

Examples of government agencies actively supporting international trade are the state economic development offices. Most of the 50 U.S. states have a department whose goal is to promote local firms internationally; this is typically the Department of Economic Development. States further international trade interests of local companies by setting up representative offices abroad, in key markets, such as the European Union and Japan. They often also target big emerging markets, such as those of China, Brazil, and India—countries with a large and increasingly prosperous middle class—as well as wealthier developing countries, such as oil exporting countries (for instance, Saudi Arabia, the United Arab Emirates, and Venezuela).

Among the trade services that state governments provide—often free of charge—are export counseling, full or partial sponsoring of trade promotion (primarily trade shows), and dissemination of market information.

State and local governments also actively attempt to attract international business. For example, the state of South Carolina was able to draw substantial investments from noteworthy international firms such as BMW, Michelin, and Fuji. As a result of foreign

Figure 3-3

The United States Department of Commerce provides assistance and counseling to businesses engaging in international trade. A small business in the United States would benefit from the help of country specialists that this Washington, D.C. institution can provide.

direct investment in the state, South Carolina was able to add numerous new jobs. In fact, the foreign-owned firms alone added 20,600 new jobs in the 1990s—most with higher-than-average salaries.[48] More recently, Michelin has undertaken an additional $400 million capital expansion in South Carolina: In 2004, the company employs more than 7,200 employees in the state. Similarly, BMW employs more than 3,400 employees in South Carolina. And Fuji's Medical Products Division in Greenwood, South Carolina, has just initiated totally integrated manufacturing of the newest generation of dry medical imaging film for the North American market.

3-3d Other Institutions and Procedures Facilitating International Trade

Foreign Trade Zones (FTZs)

A **foreign trade zone** (FTZ) is a tax-free area in a particular country that is not considered part of the respective country in terms of import regulations and restrictions. Products can be shipped to a foreign trade zone, undergo additional manufacturing processes, and then be shipped further to the target market. Such products are not assessed any duties and cannot be subjected to tariffs or quotas unless they enter the territory of the host country of the foreign trade zone. A foreign trade zone is a site within a particular country that is considered to be an international area; merchandise in the FTZ, both foreign and domestic, is outside the jurisdiction of the host country's customs services.[49]

> **foreign trade zones** Tax-free areas in a country that are not considered part of the respective country in terms of import regulations and restrictions.

Initiated by governments, foreign trade zones stimulate domestic and international commerce. In the United States, the Foreign Trade Zone Act of 1934 allows for the creation of foreign trade zones for the purpose of stimulating U.S. domestic and international commerce by allowing firms to decrease tariff-related costs through their trade operations in the foreign trade zones.[50] FTZs are usually located in or near a port of entry and are usually operated as a public utility by a public entity such as the Port of Portland, the Indianapolis Airport Authority, or the Crowfield Corporate Center in Charleston, South Carolina.[51]

FTZs are regulated by the U.S. Foreign Trade Zones Board, which is part of the U.S. Department of Commerce, and by U.S. Customs, as part of the U.S. Temporary Entry System—designed to encourage the export of goods with foreign content and the re-export of foreign goods and to reduce the costs of using foreign goods.[52]

Foreign trade zones offer advantages to both the host country and to international firms operating in these zones. In the host country, the foreign trade zone benefits

- Domestic manufacturers, distributors, and suppliers by creating demand for their services, products, and raw materials. FTZ activities may involve manipulation, such as product inspecting, labeling, repairing, and sorting; small- and large-scale manufacturing, including manufacturing, assembling, and processing; warehousing; exhibiting; and distributing to domestic and foreign markets.[53] Such operations also create jobs in the FTZ country.

- The country's trade balance. Re-exports from the country where the foreign trade zone is located add to the total number of exports from that country, thereby increasing its trade balance.

The international firm operating in the foreign trade zone benefits from the following:

- Foreign goods that enter the foreign trade zone are exempt from the usual customs duties, tariffs, and other import controls, as long as the goods do not enter the country.

- For firms that ultimately export to the country where the FTZ is located, the FTZ provides flexibility by lowering and/or deferring tariffs for goods that are subject to tariffs. There are no time limitations for the foreign goods' presence in the foreign trade zone. Thus, goods that are assessed tariffs on the imported components are placed in storage in the FTZ and are imported into the country only when demand for the product is high or when import quota opportunities open up.

- Rather than bringing the equipment directly into the country and paying duties immediately, equipment could be brought into the FTZ, shown to customers, and the payment of duties delayed until the goods are sold; this is especially beneficial for high-value items.[54]

- A foreign trade zone is also a location that is used for breaking bulk. Components that are purchased from a foreign supplier to be used in a just-in-time manufacturing environment can be shipped into the FTZ in bulk to optimize quantity discounts and shipping costs. When these components are in the zone, they are repackaged into smaller quantities for shipment to the manufacturing plants; this helps the company postpone the payment of duties until the items are shipped to the plant rather than when they arrive in the country.[55]

- A foreign trade zone lowers prices for goods sold in the importing country: Unassembled goods are cheaper to transport, and duties are assessed at lower rates for unassembled, than for assembled, goods. Furthermore, duties can be avoided for goods that have been damaged in transportation.

- A foreign trade zone also helps when an importing country imposes local content regulations on products from abroad: Local content is provided through the manipulation processes taking place in the FTZ.

- FTZs are usually bonded and must be secured and enclosed, which make them safer than most ports of entry, thus decreasing insurance costs for companies using them. In the United States, for example, unauthorized removal of goods from an FTZ is a federal offense.[56]

- Products that are manipulated in a foreign trade zone may be labeled as manufactured in the FTZ host country. A favorable attitude toward the respective country and its products (that is, a favorable country-of-origin effect) greatly benefits the companies selling the product.

Foreign trade zones can range from no more than an assigned building close to a river port or a floor in a building adjacent to the local airport, to a gigantic operation with fully integrated multimodal access (see Figure 3-4). An example of the latter is the Jebel Ali Free Zone of Dubai—one of the largest foreign trade zones in the world. The Jebel Ali Free Zone houses operations of more than 1,200 companies from 72 countries, offering state-of-the-art transport and communications facilities in its 100-square-kilometer site. More than 100 U.S. companies have manufacturing, maintenance, or transshipment operations there, including AlliedSignal, DHL, Federal Express, General Motors, Johnson & Johnson, Microsoft, and Union Carbide—and all are allowed 100 percent foreign ownership of operations, 100 percent repatriation of capital and profits, a 15-year corporate tax holiday, and a full exemption from personal income taxes.[57] In return for access to 1.5 billion consumers in the region (from countries surrounding the Persian Gulf and Red Sea), companies incur four up-front costs: a license ($954), registration as a Free Zone Establishment ($2,725), lease of space (prebuilt space and land start at $32,686 a year), and telecom hookup ($381).[58]

Other Types of Customs-Privileged Facilities

Worldwide, there are variations on the foreign trade zone. They are similar to the foreign trade zone in that they have some type of customs-privileged facilities that may be restricted to a region, to a plant (when such a plant is used for product assembly purposes, it is known as an **offshore assembly plant**), or to a bonded warehouse. **Special economic zones** in China and **maquiladoras** in Mexico are examples of customs-privileged facilities that typically exist in countries with low-cost labor. Under most arrangements, products are brought into an in-bond area, manipulated (processed, repackaged, assembled), and then re-exported to the country where the products originated. Low import tariffs are only assessed at this point, and only on the value-added processing that took place in the special economic zone. Some limits are typically placed on products that are imported into the special economic zone country to encourage re-exporting.

offshore assembly plants Plants located in customs-privileged bonded areas in countries with low labor costs, where products are manipulated and re-exported.

special economic zones Customs-privileged manufacturing facilities in China where multinational companies can take advantage of low-cost labor.

maquiladora Customs-privileged contract manufacturing facilities in Mexico that take advantage of low-cost labor.

Figure 3-4
The port of Rotterdam, in the Netherlands, is the largest in the world. The port area is a foreign trade zone, an area of heavy maritime traffic.

Normal-Trade-Relations (NTR) Status

An important trade policy tool that is used by the United States is the Normal-Trade-Relations (NTR) Status (previously known as the Most-Favored-Nation Status). This status grants equal tax treatment on imported products from most countries, with the exception of rogue nations. In the past, granting of the MFN clause was linked to U.S. foreign policy. Receiving the MFN clause was predicated on countries' human rights records (as in the case of China in the 1990s), or as a reward for alignment with U.S. interests (as in the case of Romania before the fall of communism, when the country opposed Soviet interference in the internal affairs of Warsaw Pact member countries).

Summary

- **Identify different trade barriers imposed on international trade and arguments used by governments to erect and maintain these barriers.** Governments impose barriers to international trade to protect national industries and nationals (consumers, employees). Arguments for protectionism include protection of markets with excess productive capacity, employment protection, protection of infant industries, protection of national resources and the environment, protection of consumers, and national defense. Governments can impose tariffs on foreign business, or nontariff barriers, such as import quotas, required import licenses, voluntary imports, or voluntary export restraints. They also can impose price controls, such as simply increasing the prices of imports, filing antidumping and countervailing duty actions to delay imports, or imposing additional tariffs (paratariffs) to shipments that exceed quotas. Alternatively, they can impose currency and capital flow controls by blocking local currency exchange, charging differential exchange rates, and restricting the number of foreign exchange permits issued. Standards are also used to restrict imports, as are local content requirements. Finally, boycotts, embargoes, and sanctions restrict international trade by blocking all trade to the targeted areas.

- **Provide an overview of key international organizations facilitating international trade directly or by promoting economic development.** Among the organizations that are most active in and have the greatest impact on promoting international trade are the World Trade Organization, which provides trade assistance and development assistance to developing countries, promotes trade agreements, and reviews member countries' trade policies to ensure that they conform to the organization's trade requirements; the Group of Seven, which is a forum of the most developed countries in the world that addresses economic and financial issues, with trade as a main focus; the International Monetary Fund and the World Bank, two specialized United Nations agencies that address the need of global economic development, imposing restructuring standards on aid recipients; other development banks; and the different United Nations organizations that promote the economic and financial welfare of developing countries, as well as their participation in international trade.

- **Identify government efforts involved in promoting economic development and trade.** National and local governments are active in promoting international trade and development through a number of agencies and departments. Among them are the United States Agency for International Development, which supports the economic development of and trade with developing countries that are politically aligned with the United States; the Department of Commerce, which engages in activities from promoting export assistance, to organizing trade shows and events, to providing financial assistance to international business; and various state and local government agencies whose primary mission is to promote international trade involvement of local business.

- **Describe other trade facilitators, such as foreign trade zones, offshore assembly plants, and special economic zones, and the Normal-Trade-Relations Status.** Foreign trade zones are tax-free areas in a country that are not considered part of that country from the import regulations' perspective and where products undergo additional manufacturing and are further shipped to other destination countries. They create employment in the host country, and they lower or defer import duties for the manufacturing firm. Offshore assembly plants and special economic zones are customs-privileged facilities in countries with low-cost labor where products are manipulated and then re-exported. The Normal-Trade-Relations Status offers equal trade status to most countries doing business with United States firms, with the exception of rogue nations that have been refused this normal trade relationship.

Key Terms

African Development Bank
antidumping
Asian Development Bank
automatic import license
blocked currency
boycott
comparative advantage
countervailing duty actions
currency and capital flow controls
differential exchange rate
embargo
employment protection
European Bank for Reconstruction and
     Development
foreign exchange permit
foreign trade zones
General Agreement on Tariffs and Trade
     (GATT)

Group of Seven (G7)
import quota
infant industry argument
Inter-American Development Bank
International Monetary Fund (IMF)
local content requirement
maquiladora
Ministry of Foreign Affairs
Ministry of Trade
Most-Favored-Nation Status
nonautomatic import license
nontariff barriers
offshore assembly plants
orderly market arrangements
paratariff measures
protection of markets with excess labor

protection of markets with excess productive
     capacity
protectionism
sanctions
special economic zones
standards as barriers to trade
tariffs
United Nations organizations
United States Agency for International
     Development (USAID)
United States Department of Commerce
United States State Department
voluntary export restraints
voluntary import expansion
World Bank
World Trade Organization (WTO)

Discussion Questions

1. Discuss the different arguments used by countries invoking the protection of national industry and consumers.
2. Look up recent articles regarding China's trade restrictions. Which of these arguments does it appear to advocate?
3. What are the different financial controls imposed on international trade, i.e., price controls and currency controls?
4. Describe the mission and accomplishments of the World Trade Organization.

5. How do international organizations overlap in their efforts to promote trade and economic development?
6. What are the U.S. equivalents of the Ministry of Foreign Trade and the Ministry of Foreign Affairs? How do they promote trade?

Chapter Quiz (True/False)

1. The infant industry argument used against international firms is related to the protection of local employment in the respective country.
2. The local content requirement requires that a certain percentage of a particular product be produced in a second country.

3. The premise for the comparative advantage argument is that countries benefit from specialization.
4. The United States Agency for International Development (USAID) has as a primary mission the promotion of trade.

You can find the correct answers to these questions by taking the quiz and then submitting your answers in the Online Edition. The program will automatically score your submission. Where you miss a question, the program will provide the correct answer, a rationale for the answer, and the section number in the chapter where the topic is discussed.

Multiple Choice

1. Tariffs are meant to
   a. discourage imports of particular goods.
   b. generate revenue.
   c. penalize countries imposing tariffs on goods from the importing country.
   d. all of the above

2. Restrictions imposed by the United States on Japan to protect the U.S. automobile industry are known as
   a. voluntary import expansion.
   b. voluntary export restraints.
   c. nonautomatic import licenses.
   d. automatic import licenses.

3. Which organizations were created as a result of the Bretton Woods Agreement in 1944 to address the needs of global economic development, stability, and rebuilding?
   a. GATT and WTO
   b. IMF and World Bank
   c. G8 and G7
   d. UNDP and FAO

4. Which United Nations organization assists developing countries in creating international trade relations and promotes the integration of trade, environment, and development?
   a. UNCTAD
   b. UNIDO
   c. FAO
   d. CIS

5. Foreign trade zones benefit international firms in all the following ways EXCEPT
   a. FTZs lower prices for goods sold in the importing country.
   b. FTZs are enclosed and safer than most ports.
   c. just-in-time inventory can be shipped in bulk to FTZs.
   d. labeling, repairing, and sorting create jobs in the FTZ country.

Endnotes

1. Victor V. Cordell and Erin Breland, "Conflicting Competition Policies in a Globalized Business Environment: Prospects for Cooperation and Convergence," *Competitiveness Review*, Vol. 10, No. 1, 2000, pp. 104–122.
2. Ibid.
3. "Leaders: Storm Over Globalization," *The Economist*, Vol. 353, No. 8147, November 27, 1999, pp. 15–16.
4. Christopher H. Lovelock and George S. Yip, "Developing Global Strategies for Service Businesses," *California Management Review*, Vol. 38, No. 2, Winter 1996, pp. 64–86.
5. Don P. Clark, "Are Poorer Developing Countries the Targets of U.S. Protectionist Actions?" *Economic Development and Cultural Change*, Vol. 47, No. 1, October 1998, pp. 193–207.
6. Cordell and Breland, "Conflicting Competition Policies in a Globalized Business Environment," pp. 104–122.
7. Clark, "Are Poorer Developing Countries the Targets of U.S. Protectionist Actions?" pp. 193–207.
8. Ibid.
9. Richard Hughes, "The Uruguay Round: New Approach for the Textiles and Clothing Sector," *International Trade Forum*, No. 4, 1995, pp. 4–11.
10. Clark, "Are Poorer Developing Countries the Targets of U.S. Protectionist Actions?" pp. 193–207.
11. Richard Brechter, "The WTO at a Glance," *The China Business Review*, Vol. 24, No. 3, May/June 1997, pp. 16–17.
12. Clark, "Are Poorer Developing Countries the Targets of U.S. Protectionist Actions?" pp. 193–207.
13. Theresa M. Greaney, "Import Now! An Analysis of Market-Share Voluntary Import Expansions (VIEs)," *Journal of International Economics*, Vol. 40, No. 1/2, February 1996, pp. 149–170.
14. Jae W. Chung, "Effects of U.S. Trade Remedy Law Enforcement under Uncertainty: The Case of Steel," *Southern Economic Journal*, Vol. 65, No. 1, July 1998, pp. 151–159.
15. Clark, "Are Poorer Developing Countries the Targets of U.S. Protectionist Actions?" pp. 193–207.
16. Ibid.
17. Ibid.
18. Jack Robertson, "Foreign Exporters Learn to Deal with China's Local-Content Rules," *Ebn*, Issue 1258, April 16, 2001, p. 43.
19. Lovelock and Yip, "Developing Global Strategies for Service Businesses," pp. 64–86.
20. Yumiko Okamoto and Fredrik Sjoholm, "Productivity in the Indonesian Automotive Industry," *ASEAN Economic Bulletin*, Vol. 17, No. 1, April 2000, pp. 60–73.
21. Peter Lagerquist, Charmaine Seitz, and Harry Maurer, "Where Coke Is It—If the Trucks Get Through," *Business Week*, Industrial/Technology Edition, No. 3743, July 30, 2001, p. 4EU2.
22. James Curtis, "Body Shop Plans to Scale Down Its Political Activity," *Marketing*, July 26, 2001, p. 3.
23. "CACI UK Hit by Iraq Torture Scandal," *Precision Marketing*, June 25, 2004, p. 1.
24. Davis P. Goodman, "Getting Over the Slump," *World Trade*, Vol. 14, No. 7, July 2001, p. 8.
25. Kwabena Anyane-Ntow and Santhi Harvey, "A Countertrade Primer," *Management Accounting*, Vol. 76, No. 10, April 1995, pp. 47–50.
26. Martha de Melo, Cevdet Denizer, Alan Gelb, and Stoyan Tenev, "Circumstance and Choice: The Role of Initial Conditions and Policies in Transition Economies," *The World Bank Economic Review*, Vol. 15, No. 1, 2001, pp. 1–31.
27. Adapted from Patrick Lane, "World Trade Survey: Why Trade Is Good for You," *The Economist*, Vol. 349, October 3, 1998, pp. S4–S6.
28. Ibid.
29. Elizabeth Olson, "Beijing Clears Major WTO Obstacles," *International Herald Tribune*, July 4, 2001, p. 9.
30. www.wto.org
31. Michael Maiello, "Hoisted by Qatar?" *Forbes*, May 14, 2001, p. 60.
32. www.wto.org
33. For a comprehensive overview of the WTO, see the Web site at www.wto.org.
34. Barry D. Wood, "Economic Summits from Rambouillet to Cologne," *Europe*, No. 387, June 1999, pp. 18–22.
35. Ibid.
36. Ibid.
37. www.imf.org
38. Ibid.
39. Ibid.

40. Joseph Kahn, "I.M.F. Ready for Brazil and Argentina Rescues," *The New York Times*, August 4, 2001, p. A4.
41. Ibid.
42. Erin Butler, "New Directions for Investment in Developing Countries," *World Trade*, Vol. 16, No. 6, June 2001, pp. 24–28.
43. Flemming Larsen, "The IMF's Dialogue with Nongovernmental Organizations," *Finance & Development*, Vol. 38, No. 1, March 2001, pp. 54–56.
44. "Reforming the Sisters: If America's New Administration Would Like a Challenge, It Can Try Changing the IMF and World Bank," *The Economist*, Vol. 358, No. 8209, February 17, 2001, pp. 23–24.
45. See Butler, "New Directions for Investment," pp. 24–28, for a more detailed account of each of these development banks.
46. www.usaid.gov
47. See www.exim.gov for information about the Ex-Im Bank.
48. Ryan Lizza, "Silent Partner," *The New Republic*, Vol. 222, No. 2, January 10, 2000, pp. 22–25.
49. George F. Hanks and Lucinda Van Alst, " Foreign Trade Zones," *Management Accounting*, Vol. 80, No. 7, January 1999, pp. 20–23.
50. Lynette Knowles Mathur and Ike Mathur, "The Effectiveness of the Foreign-Trade Zone as an Export Promotion Program: Policy Issues and Alternatives," *Journal of Macromarketing*, Vol. 17, No. 2, Fall 1997, pp. 20–31.
51. Hanks and Van Alst, " Foreign Trade Zones," pp. 20–23.
52. Knowles Mathur and Mathur, "The Effectiveness of the Foreign-Trade Zone as an Export Promotion Program," pp. 20–31.
53. Ibid.
54. Hanks and Van Alst, "Foreign Trade Zones," pp. 20–23.
55. Ibid.
56. Ibid.
57. Josh Martin, "Dubai: A Model FTZ," *Management Review*, Vol. 87, No. 11, December 1998, p. 25.
58. Ibid.

Case 3-1

Michael's Ice Cream: Opportunities in Thailand

Michael Alexander opened two successful ice cream stores in Southeastern Virginia in 2004. He discovered a blending process that creates healthy and crunchy ice cream and made a substantial profit in his first year. His former college roommate, a Thai bureaucrat with business smarts and ambition, visited him recently and, since then, both have been pondering a business venture: franchising the ice cream store, Michael's Ice Cream, in Thailand.

Their research has revealed that Thai consumers have a strong preference for international branded stores and that they are drawn by the modern appeal and quality products associated with international franchises. In fact, various retail and fast-food franchises have done well in this market, operating more than 6,500 outlets in the country; among the successful franchises are Baskin Robbins, Blockbuster, KFC, McDonald's, Sir Speedy, and TCBY. Michael researched the Thai market and found that the Thai government is currently shifting its focus from large-scale heavy industry to small and medium enterprises (SMEs). The U.S. Thailand Business Council in Washington, D.C., and its sister organization, the Thailand U.S. Business Council, in Bangkok, have formed a partnership with the U.S. Department of Commerce and the International Franchise Association to increase the number of U.S. franchises in Thailand. The U.S. Commercial Service has identified franchising to be one of the top Thai sectors that should be targeted for U.S. trade expansion.

Michael's former roommate informed him that the Thai government is eager to provide support to small and medium enterprises: In an effort led by Prime Minister Thaksin Shinawatr, a successful businessman, the government provides loans, business counseling, and venture capital for small business development. Michael's roommate was going to investigate these opportunities upon his return to Thailand.

Michael decided to inquire whether the U.S. government offers any incentives to small businesses attempting to expand by building franchises overseas. He found that the Department of Commerce has numerous programs that could help franchisors. One of the programs that he is planning to participate in is the Virtual Matchmaker. This program is facilitated by the U.S. Embassy in the target market—Thailand, in this case—and it will invite qualified investors to attend a videoconference presentation for Michael's Ice Cream. The Department of Commerce will iden-

tify investors and invite them to attend. Then Michael has 15 to 20 minutes to present information about the franchise, followed by a question-and-answer session.

U.S. Department of Commerce trade missions provide an additional marketing opportunity to groups of investors. Foreign commercial staff schedule meetings for about a dozen U.S. franchisors to discuss their franchises with prequalified investors, so practically the only things Michael would have to do are buy his plane ticket and reserve a hotel room.

Another alternative is to participate in the Golden Key program, whereby the U.S. Embassy would call and invite prospective investors to meet at the embassy. This tailored program is likely to yield useful results for the franchisors. Additional opportunities are provided by foreign franchise expos (trade shows), whereby Michael could elect to be part of the U.S. Pavilion, representing several franchisors. The latter is a less expensive venue for exposure, but a very effective one.

Michael is ready to prepare for his different opportunities presented by the Department of Commerce. In reading about the process, he has found that he has to put together an accurate description of what he thinks is an ideal partner. He is also trying to figure out what level of investment should be required for this venture so that he can adequately brief the commercial staff about the franchise.

Sources: Franchising World, "Thailand Holds Potential and Opportunities for U.S. Franchisors," Vol. 35, No. 2, February/March 2003, p. 45; Mike Minihane, "How the Government Can Help You," *Franchising World,* Vol. 34, No. 6, September 2002, pp. 58–59.

Analysis Suggestions

1. Prepare a list of organizations that could effectively be approached to help Michael's Ice Cream set up franchises in Thailand. Look at the opportunities in the case, and beyond the case, at the different development organizations.
2. Prepare a description of the ideal partner for Michael's Ice Cream in Thailand.

4

Regional Economic and Political Integration

Chapter Objectives

By the end of this chapter, you should be able to

1 Provide an overview of the determinants of regional economic and political integration.

2 Examine the different levels of economic and political integration and identify, within each world region, economic and political agreements that have met with success.

3 Examine the functions of the different policy and governance bodies of the European Union.

Not too long ago, shipping goods in Europe was a complicated process: Waiting in lines at the border, filling out paperwork, going through customs, and paying duties were all part of the border-crossing process. Today, much of Europe has customs offices only at airports or ports, and there, no companies from the European Union are subjected to customs processing and duties. Removal of restrictions in the European Union is not limited to the movement of goods; it covers movement of all capital and labor.

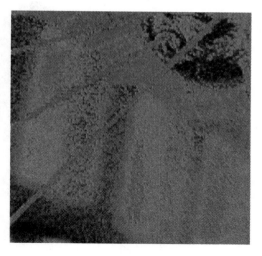

Countries in Europe that are not members of the European Union aspire to become part of the European Union and benefit from the many advantages of integration. Countries in the rest of the world are actively building similar regions aimed at removing trade and other barriers. Many countries hope to jointly create a world economic area where all countries can benefit from the free movement of goods.

Chapter 3, "International Trade: Barriers and Facilitators," examined the many initiatives undertaken within the framework of the World Trade Organization (WTO) to reduce trade barriers and promote unimpeded economic cooperation worldwide. A parallel effort aimed at economic, as well as political, integration is also attempted regionally, with various degrees of success. This chapter describes the determinants of regional economic and political integration, the different forms of integration, and, for each type of regional integration, it offers examples of successful agreements in all regions of the world.

4-1 Determinants of Economic and Political Integration

Numerous factors prompt countries to favor trade with other countries (neighboring countries in particular). Sharing a culture, a common language, a common history, or even common borders may lead countries to join forces in an effort to eliminate barriers to trade. The factors described in sections 4-1a through 4-1e compel countries to lower barriers and expand trade with each other for mutual benefit.

4-1a A Common Culture

Regardless of whether a common culture was fostered by a former colonial power, people in neighboring countries often share a language, as well as other cultural elements, such as traditions, norms, and religion. As will be addressed in Chapter 5, "Cultural Influences on International Marketing," many areas in the world are characterized by cultural similarity. For example, in North Africa and the Middle East, the preponderant language is Arabic, and the environment of business, as well as everyday life, is structured in accordance with Islamic law. Similarly, countries in Latin America share Spanish as the dominant language and Catholicism as religion; as such, individuals in the region share rituals, traditions, and personal values.

The commonality of language and other elements of culture facilitate interaction between neighboring countries and promote cooperation: In an economic relationship in which culture does not constitute a barrier to communication, individuals are more likely to understand their counterparts and their position. In addition, a common language

Figure 4-1
Consumers in Holland and Belgium would understand the product nutritional label on this Dutch brand.

facilitates commerce and marketing in particular. Figure 4-1 depicts a consumer in Holland reading the label of Appelsientje, a Dutch apple juice. This same brand can be marketed to Belgian consumers nearby, who speak the same language and would understand the Dutch labels.

4-1b A History of Common Economic and Political Dominance

A history of dominance by one nation in a region often leads to shared cultural elements among the different peoples in that region, as well as to similar economic and political structures. Russia's economic, political, and cultural dominance in the former Soviet Union has resulted, for example, in the use of the Russian language from the Baltics (Estonia, Lithuania, and Latvia) and the Ukraine, to the Asian republics of the former federation, such as Turkmenistan and Azerbaijan. The countries also shared economic and marketing structures, many of which continue to survive—for example, state-owned enterprises and large, nationwide distributors. In other examples, countries in East Africa formerly colonized by Belgium share a common second language (French), as well as extensive economic and political ties with the former colonist; and former colonies of the British Empire form the Commonwealth of Nations, a body that meets periodically to address issues of common concern and that recognizes the British Monarchy as its symbolic leader.

From a marketer's point of view, such similarities facilitate a standardized approach to the market. From the countries' perspective, regional economic integration is facilitated by the similarity of economic structures established by the former colonial power and the shared language and culture.

4-1c Regional Proximity

Regional proximity is an important facilitator of economic cooperation. Although countries do not need to have a common border to engage in cooperative agreements, access that is facilitated by direct and effective transportation and communication systems greatly increases the likelihood that the economic relationship will survive over time. In the case of the **European Union** (www.europa.eu.int), the member countries are quite dissimilar culturally; however, their regional proximity and the highly developed transportation infrastructure within the region, as well as economic similarity between the dif-

European Union An economic union consisting of most of the Western European countries; it is the only agreement that has achieved full economic integration and is now pursuing political integration. (See www.europa.eu.int.)

ferent countries, have all greatly contributed to the success of regional economic and political integration.

4-1d Economic Considerations

It has been amply demonstrated that countries characterized by a similar level of economic development are more likely to be successful in establishing and maintaining regional economic integration mechanisms than countries of different levels of economic development. In the latter case, it is typical that the larger, more developed economies are likely to further their interests at the expense of countries that lag behind on economic development. In effect, countries of similar development levels are more likely to create a successful common market that assures preferential treatment for goods manufactured in the region, while also securing a substantial local consumer market. As countries prosper further as a result of this proven mechanism, the regional market then opens to firms from outside its boundaries, benefiting international enterprise regardless of national origin.

As mentioned in section 4-1c, "Regional Proximity," the European Union is not characterized by a shared regional culture. The Union is successful primarily due to economic commonalities shared by member countries. Among others, they are

- A highly developed industrial base and overall productivity, translating into a high gross domestic product (GDP) per capita
- An extensive transportation and telecommunications infrastructure, which is indispensable in trading relationships
- Prosperous consumers who can afford to purchase the goods and services of local firms

It should be emphasized, however, that the member countries have developed at different levels, and, often, constituents of the wealthier countries (such as Germany and the Netherlands) have deplored having to adopt policies that would benefit the lesser developed countries in the Union. Furthermore, the member countries of the European Union and of other forms of regional economic integration often differ with regard to the economic and trade policies they advocate. For example, Germany and the Netherlands stress the importance of market mechanisms and interfere only minimally in the regulation of business, whereas France is more likely to intervene. France stresses social welfare at the expense of market development, and is often plagued by union activity that paralyzes different sectors of the economy (the post office and the national airline industry constitute just two examples). Similarly, in the case of the Southern Cone Common Market (MERCOSUR), the member countries disagree with the candidate members on the common external tariffs they should impose on international business entering the region.

It should be noted that, in the European Union, the economic disparity between the old members and the new members is leading to substantial controversy, as discussed in International Marketing Illustration 4-1.

4-1e Political Considerations

One of the more important obstacles to regional economic and political integration is the threat of losing national identity and sovereignty as part of the larger regional structure. Countries have many icons of national identity that generations have fought for centuries to maintain; such icons range from the form of government (republic, monarchy, and/or loose federation) to currency, language, and traditions. In the process of engaging in regional political and economic integration, member countries must choose, to a certain extent, to relinquish important aspects of their sovereignty and identity. For members of the European Union, such decisions have ranged, among others, from minor issues, such as the number of hours that civil servants have for a lunch break (in Spain, it is argued that it is the individual's right to have more than one hour), to completely

International Marketing Illustration

4-1

Creating a Level Playing Field in the New European Union

Meeting the new guidelines for the European Union is a challenge for the new members—eight formerly communist countries and Cyprus and Malta, the largest body of countries to do so in history. The EU member countries are facing new EU duties on imports from Asian markets and high expenses to meet EU safety, health, and other standards. For example, small farmers have to house pigs and cows in different buildings and build expensive septic tanks to conform to regulations. This standard greatly increases the farmers' expenses and potentially drives them out of business. The added hurdles and their often negative consequences as many small and medium enterprises are forced to fold are increasingly leading to calls for secession and renationalization from the new members.

Adding to the frustration of the joining nations are attitudes of the long-time members of the European Union, who are clearly not receiving the new members with open arms: Germany, for example, intends to keep citizens of the new member countries from working there for many years. And Denmark will not offer unemployment benefits to the Eastern workers who lose their jobs; to add insult to injury, these workers are forced to repatriate.

Moreover, Germany and Sweden repeatedly rebuke the new members for their low tax rates, which bring more jobs to the area—all the while the new members benefit from a generous aid package from the European Union. To illustrate, the corporate tax rates for the old EU members are much lower than those charged by the newcomers:

EU Member	Percentage (%) Tax Rate
Malta	35
EU-15 Median*	33
Czech Republic	28
Slovenia	25
Poland	19
Slovakia	19
Latvia	19
Hungary	16
Lithuania	15
Cyprus	10
Estonia	0

* Old EU member countries

Source: Adapted from Christopher Rhoads and Marc Champion, "Reshaping Europe: Affairs of State," *Wall Street Journal,* April 29, 2004, p. A1.

doing away with the French franc, the German deutsche mark, and the Italian lira in favor of the common currency—the Euro (see Figure 4-2).

A principal consideration in accepting to relinquish part of national identity constitutes the importance of the regional group as a whole to the advancement of national priorities. A successful regional economic and political integration is one that promises a more substantial and more rapid economic development for member countries than they would otherwise experience in isolation from the country group, and one that equitably addresses and protects regional, as well as national, economic and political interests. In the case of the European Union, considerations of national sovereignty and national pri-

orities take second place to joint interests in the creation of a viable, large market which provides a credible balance to large economic and political powers, such as those of the United States, Japan, China, and Russia, among others. The Southern Cone Common Market (MERCOSUR) accomplishes similar goals for its large and small South American member countries.

4-2 Levels of Regional Economic and/or Political Integration and Examples of Integration Successes

Typically, member countries go through different stages of regional economic and political integration. Although most member countries start at the industry-specific bilateral or multilateral agreement level, theoretically at least, more complex regional agreements could jump to a more advanced stage, such as a common market, while simultaneously setting up a framework for a free trade agreement and customs union. Most commonly, however, member countries could target a more advanced framework, as their name might indicate (e.g., Common Market), but go through the different steps nevertheless. Sections 4-2a through 4-2f present the different levels of economic and/or political integration agreements, from the more basic to the more advanced, along with current and some past examples within each category.

4-2a Bilateral Agreements and Multilateral Forums and Agreements

Numerous examples of bilateral and multilateral agreements exist. Some are industry specific, others involve some or all products exchanged between countries. In fact, most member countries of the more complex regional economic and political forms of integration engaged, as a first step, in some type of regional cooperation. Governments could enter into agreements that are limited to a particular industry; the agreements could involve the development of an industry sector, such as participating in the development of a hydroelectric plant in an area that would serve neighboring countries, or it could entail lowering or eliminating tariffs on certain goods that are traded between the member countries, such as coal and steel. The European Union had its earliest attempts at economic integration in the form of the **European Coal and Steel Community,** established in the late 1950s, and the subsequent structure, the **European Atomic Energy Community.**

What differentiates these agreements from the formal regional integration formats is that they are either limited to two countries (**bilateral agreements**), or, if they involve

European Coal and Steel Community An agreement that represents an early attempt at tariff reduction between members of the European Union.

European Atomic Energy Community A precursor to the European Union, it addressed issues related to the use and control of atomic energy.

bilateral agreement Regional trade cooperation between two countries aimed at reducing or eliminating trade barriers for all or for selected products.

multiple countries (**multilateral forums and agreements**), the agreements have a less formal structure and/or do not aim at regional integration. Examples of bilateral agreements are infinite, and they are often the foundation for the more formal regional integration attempts. Multilateral agreements that primarily provide a forum for regional cooperation endeavors are numerous. Some are industry specific, such as the **Organization for Petroleum Exporting Countries (OPEC).** Some are military in nature, such as the **North Atlantic Treaty Organization (NATO).** Others have an economic focus—for example, the **Organization for Economic Co-operation and Development (OECD).**

A noteworthy economic organization is the **Asia-Pacific Economic Cooperation,** or APEC (www.apecsec.org.sg). APEC was established to mitigate the economic block and trade protection trend prevailing in the 1970s and 1980s; it was established in 1989 at a ministerial meeting in Canberra, Australia, with the mission to create an open economic alliance in the Asia-Pacific region.[1] This trade group includes all the major economies of the region (the United States and Canada are member countries), accounting for 42 percent of global trade.[2] APEC provides a forum for economic cooperation and the gradual reduction of barriers to trade and investment between member countries. Although the group does not attempt to forge an institutional integration that would be required under a free trade association or a more advanced regional economic and political integration format, APEC has nevertheless been instrumental in fostering free trade. Most of its advances so far have been made in the area of computers and the Internet: APEC members agreed upon a moratorium on customs duties over the Internet, on safeguards against software piracy, and on eliminating tariffs on computers and semiconductors.[3] APEC also represents a forum for member countries to address issues critical to trade; for example, before its ascension to the WTO, China used the APEC forum to announce a number of important reductions in protectionism.[4]

An example of a political agreement—which we place in this category because of its failure to achieve a substantial level of regional integration—is the **Commonwealth of Independent States** (CIS). The 12 non-Baltic successors to the Union of the Soviet Socialist Republics (the Soviet Union) formed the Commonwealth of Independent States. This organization has never had a noteworthy economic content; and, even politically, the CIS became fractured in the second half of the 1990s with the GUUAM grouping (Georgia, Ukraine, Uzbekistan, Azerbaijan, and Moldova) operating explicitly as a counter to Russian hegemony.[5] The Union of Four (Russia, Belarus, Kazakhstan, and the Kyrgyz Republic) considered creating a customs union, with Russia's tariff as the putative common external tariff, but, apart from steps toward a bilateral agreement between Belarus and Russia aimed at creating an economic union, nothing has come to fruition.[6] Finally, the Central Asian states of the former Soviet Union have drawn up numerous plans for regional cooperation—they must cooperate on nontrade matters such as the desiccation of the Aral Sea—but the establishment of a Central Asian Economic Community has had little impact to date.[7]

4-2b Free Trade Agreements

A **free trade agreement** takes place between two or more countries and involves a reduction in, or even elimination of, customs duties and other trade barriers on all goods and services traded between the member countries. Countries are free to charge their own tariffs to all entities external to the free trade market. The following are present and past examples of free trade agreements:

- European Free Trade Association
- Association of Southeast Asian Nations
- ASEAN Free Trade Area
- North American Free Trade Agreement
- Free Trade Area of the Americas
- Southern African Development Community
- Arab Maghreb Union

The European Free Trade Association (EFTA) (www.efta.int)

The current member countries of the **European Free Trade Association (EFTA)** are Iceland, Liechtenstein, Norway, and Switzerland (see Figure 4-3); previously, Sweden, Austria, and Finland were also members but have since joined the European Union. EFTA has constituted for decades another example of successful regional economic integration in Europe—in addition to the European Union.

In 1993, EU and EFTA created the European Economic Area, representing the world's largest single market with 380 million consumers. Since then, however, the European Union has created new regulations with the Maastricht, Amsterdam, and Nice treaties, and has created new powers of authority in areas such as environmental and labor market policies.[8] Norway is the only EFTA country to participate in the Schengen agreement on the elimination of border controls, in the EU common foreign and security policy; none of the EFTA countries have joined the European Monetary Union.[9]

At present, politicians in the EFTA countries want to be at least unofficially part of the EU but believe that public opinion at home is against further EU integration. The EU, on the other hand, does not appear to be interested in new negotiations that would offer EFTA members a greater involvement in the EU. The focus of the EU is eastern expansion, and the members are faced with the following constraints:[10]

- Numerous complexities related to the different stages and phases of eastward enlargement
- Possibilities of looser associated memberships
- Special rights of nonmembers
- Periods of transition to membership and special arrangements

European Free Trade Association (EFTA) A free trade agreement between Iceland, Liechtenstein, Norway, and Switzerland; previously, Sweden, Austria, and Finland were also members, but they have since joined the European Union. (See www.efta.int.)

F i g u r e   4 - 3

Member Countries of the European Free Trade Association

In general, the perception of European Union members is that EFTA, especially Norway and Iceland, would like to have more impact on the decision-making process within the EU, in particular on legal decisions (where nonmembers have no influence at all), and share in the benefits of the single European market, but are not prepared to share in the costs and other obligations of membership.[11]

In spite of the national vote against joining the European Union, Switzerland is engaging in bilateral negotiations, securing agreements that would help it join: It has negotiated issues in the area of the collection of statistics, the environment, agricultural production and customs fraud, cross-border security, youth, and education, among others.[12]

The Association of Southeast Asian Nations (ASEAN) (www.aseansec.org) and the ASEAN Free Trade Area (AFTA)

The **Association of Southeast Asian Nations (ASEAN)** is the primary and most successful example of regional economic integration in Asia. Member countries are attempting to reduce tariffs and create an environment that promotes mutual involvement in industrial development in the region. The goal of ASEAN is ultimately to create a free trade area where tariff and nontariff barriers are eliminated and to provide a substantial market of more than 330 million consumers. Members of ASEAN are Brunei Darussalam, Cambodia, Indonesia, Laos, Malaysia, Myanmar, the Philippines, Singapore, Thailand, and Vietnam; they have signed the **ASEAN Free Trade Area (AFTA)** agreement (see Figure 4-4).

ASEAN countries are pursuing free trade agreements with countries such as Japan,[13] and even laying the groundwork for the formalization of currency swap agreements with Japan, South Korea, and China, whereby countries agree to give each other money to bolster foreign exchange reserves in the event of a currency crisis.[14] In addition, a China-ASEAN free trade area will be established in the near future.

Association of Southeast Asian Nations (ASEAN) A successful example of integration in Asia, creating an environment that promotes mutual involvement in industrial development in the region and a free trade area composed of Brunei, Cambodia, Indonesia, Laos, Malaysia, Myanmar, the Philippines, Singapore, Thailand, and Vietnam. (See www.aseansec.org.)

ASEAN Free Trade Area (AFTA) A free trade agreement signed by members of the Association of Southeast Asian Nations (ASEAN). (See www.aseansec.org.)

F i g u r e   4 - 4
Member Countries of the Association of Southeast Asian Nations

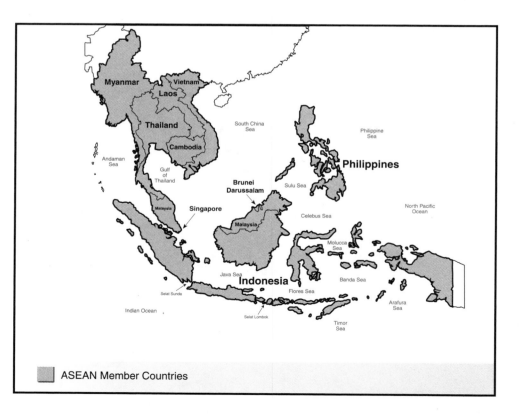

The North American Free Trade Agreement (NAFTA)
(www.nafta-sec-alena.org)

Signatory countries of the **North American Free Trade Agreement (NAFTA)** are the United States, Canada, and Mexico (see Figure 4-5). The goal of the 1994 treaty was to eliminate all tariff and nontariff barriers, such as import licenses and quotas, between the member countries and to offer free access to companies from member countries to a single market of almost 400 million consumers. As with other free trade agreements, member countries charge their own duties and other tariffs to companies from nonmember countries entering the respective markets. One of the more important decisions for NAFTA involves the rules of origin: To benefit from a duty-free status, goods must have a 60 percent North American content.

NAFTA initially generated great fears in the United States. It was described by a former presidential candidate and NAFTA opponent as the "giant sucking sound" that would move all jobs south of the U.S. border. Indeed, U.S. workers have experienced some level of job loss that can be directly attributed to NAFTA, in the lumber and textile industries, for instance. However, it also can be argued that NAFTA created jobs in the United States. For example, in terms of trade flow, NAFTA has fared very well: U.S. merchandise exports to Mexico grew fourfold, and the United States exports to Canada more than doubled; at the same time, Mexico currently purchases just under $100 billion in U.S. goods each year.[15] NAFTA has brought substantial foreign direct investment to Mexico ($85 billion),[16] creating stability in the country and lessening its dependence on the United States.

In spite of its free-market rhetoric, however, the United States has engaged in protectionist activity that hampers free trade among member countries; for example, in

North American Free Trade Agreement (NAFTA) An agreement between the United States, Canada, and Mexico, aiming to eliminate tariff and nontariff barriers between the countries. (See www.nafta-sec-alena.org.)

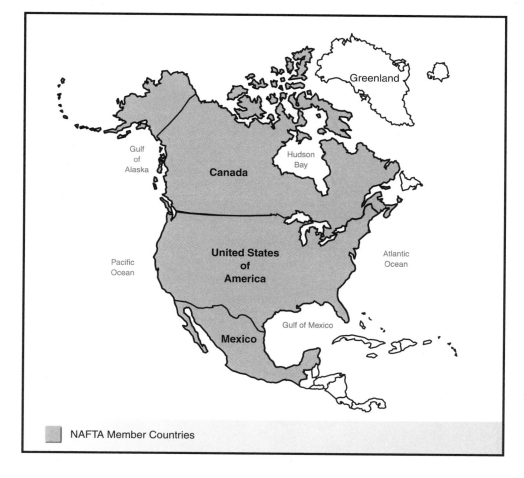

F i g u r e   4 - 5

Member Countries of the North American Free Trade Agreement

recent years, the U.S. Congress, pressured by domestic truck drivers, voted to keep Mexican truckers out of most of the United States.[17]

The Free Trade Area of the Americas (FTAA)

The **Free Trade Area of the Americas (FTAA)** is an ambitious plan to create a market of about 800 million people and an annual production worth $11 trillion in the Americas.[18] The organization has a goal to create a free trade association by 2007, but its progress has been greatly impeded by protectionist fears voiced in the United States, reminiscent of the unfounded dismal NAFTA predictions,[19] and Brazilian recalcitrance, as it attempts to maintain tariffs on manufactured goods, selectively liberalize services, and go slowly on intellectual property protection.[20] Member countries are the 34 democratic nations of North, Central, and South America.

The Southern African Development Community (SADC)

The **Southern African Development Community (SADC)** is a free trade organization that promotes economic cooperation among a coalition of 14 of Africa's more affluent and developed nations. The organization is designed to foster increased economic and governmental stability through the use of collective peacekeeping forces and should be credited for the recent relative stability of the region.[21]

Its member countries are Angola, Botswana, the Democratic Republic of Congo (DRC), Lesotho, Malawi, Mauritius, Mozambique, Namibia, Seychelles, South Africa, Swaziland, United Republic of Tanzania, Zambia, and Zimbabwe (see Figure 4-6).

The Arab Maghreb Union (AMU)

Better known as the Union du Maghreb Arab (UMA), the **Arab Maghreb Union (AMU)** has had less success than most of the examples of regional economic and political integra-

Free Trade Area of the Americas (FTAA) A plan to create a free trade association by 2005 that would comprise all member countries of the 34 democratic nations of North, Central, and South America. (See www.ftaa-alca.org.)

Southern African Development Community (SADC) A free trade organization that promotes economic cooperation among a coalition of 14 of Africa's more affluent and developed nations, designed to foster increased economic and governmental stability through the use of collective peace-keeping forces.

Arab Maghreb Union (AMU) An attempt, in the early 1980s, at creating a free trade area in the Southern Mediterranean area; it was not successful due to conflict.

F i g u r e   4 - 6
Member Countries of the Southern African Development Community

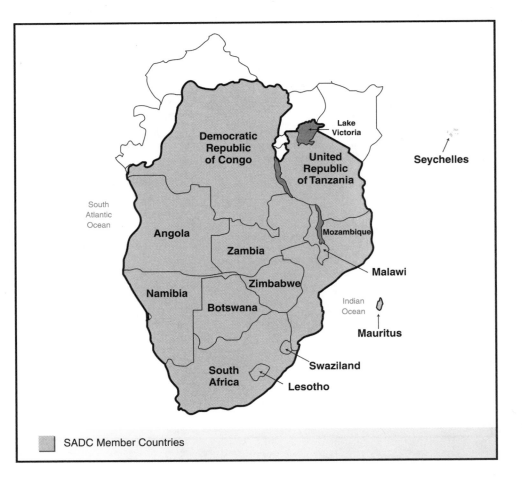

SADC Member Countries

tion associations mentioned here. Members in the AMU (Algeria, Libya, Mauritania, Morocco, and Tunisia) pledged to form a powerful economic bloc and a free trade area in the Southern Mediterranean region in the early 1980s. The organization has not operated since its inception in 1989, however, due to border disputes between Morocco and Algeria. It should be noted, however, that, within the group, bilateral talks have taken place between Morocco and Tunisia on issues of trade, investment, fishing, and tourism.[22]

4-2c Customs Unions

A **customs union** is a free trade association that may have either eliminated or greatly reduced all tariffs and other trade restrictions for member countries, and that has adopted common external tariffs on products imported from outside the free trade area. Although the Andean Common Market and the Southern Cone Common Market aspire to become a common market, at present they are only customs unions; they are, however, in the process of agreeing upon common external tariffs.

South African Customs Union (SACU)

Member countries of the **South African Customs Union (SACU)** are Botswana, Swaziland, Lesotho, and Namibia. The group's main trading partner is South Africa, and member countries have partially or entirely tied their currencies to the South African rand.

4-2d Common Markets

Member countries to a **common market** agreement eliminate all tariff and nontariff barriers to trade, adopt common external tariffs, and allow for the free movement of capital and labor within the common market. Although only the European Union has achieved (and surpassed) the common market stage, a number of other forms of economic integration are aiming to achieve this form of integration—among them, the Andean Common Market and the Southern Cone Common Market.

In Europe, member countries agreed, at the Treaty of Rome, to establish the European Economic Community (EEC), eliminating all internal tariffs and duties, establishing common external tariffs, and allowing for the free movement of capital and labor within its territory. At this point, member countries also set in place regulations and bodies that would ultimately form the basis for a monetary and political union—an event that was to take place in 1992, on the occasion of the **Maastricht Treaty,** commonly known as the eagerly anticipated "Europe 1992." Such regulations involved common trade policies, common agricultural and industrial policies, and common monetary and fiscal policies.

As an example of common monetary policies and precursors to a monetary union, member countries agreed to create a common float that would include the embryonic Euro, the then-theoretical currency of Europe. The float was known as the **European Exchange Rate Mechanism (ERM).** The ERM was also known as the "snake" because it changed its shape based on the fluctuation of the different currencies. According to the ERM, a currency could fluctuate only up to 2.5 percent of its value in either direction; when this value was consistently surpassed, the mechanism would adjust the currency upward or downward, respectively, creating a snake-like structure. A float that performed well was an important prerequisite to the success of a monetary union; this, as we will see in section 4-2e, "Monetary Unions," was not the case in 1992, the date established for the creation of the European monetary union.

Other examples of regional economic integration aiming to establish a common market are as follows:

- Latin American Integration Association
- Andean Community
- Southern Cone Common Market
- Central American Common Market
- Common Market for Eastern and Southern Africa

customs union A market composed of member countries imposing identical import duties and sharing import regulations.

South African Customs Union (SACU) A customs union that includes Botswana, Swaziland, Lesotho, and Namibia. The group's main trading partner is South Africa, and member countries have partially or entirely tied their currencies to the South African rand.

common market A market composed of member countries, characterized by the unrestricted movement of goods, labor, and capital.

Maastricht Treaty The treaty credited with establishing the European Union, eliminating all tariffs; establishing common external tariffs; allowing for the free movement of capital and labor within its territory; and setting regulations involving common trade policies, common agricultural and industrial policies, and common monetary and fiscal policies between member countries. (See www.europa.eu.int.)

European Exchange Rate Mechanism (ERM) A precursor of the Euro, a float that included the Euro, the then-theoretical currency of the European Union; the float allowed for variability in each currency.

The Latin American Integration Association (LAIA)

Latin American Integration Association (LAIA) Latin America's largest trade agreement striving to establish bilateral and multilateral agreements aimed at reducing tariff and nontariff barriers.

The **Latin American Integration Association (LAIA)** was created in 1980 to replace the **Latin American Free Trade Association (LAFTA).** LAFTA was an attempt by member countries to establish a free trade association. Its demise was attributed to the disparity in the level of development of member countries, and to the protectionist policies of countries with enormous foreign debt experiencing high inflation, currency devaluation, and economic crises. LAFTA is important in that it constituted a first step in an ambitious plan to create a common market that comprises all of Latin America, under the umbrella of the Latin American Integration Association.

Latin American Free Trade Association (LAFTA) An attempt by Latin American countries to establish a free trade association; its demise is attributed to the economic disparity between member countries and to protectionist policies.

The Latin American Integration Association member countries are Argentina, Bolivia, Brazil, Chile, Colombia, Ecuador, Mexico, Paraguay, Peru, Uruguay, and Venezuela (see Figure 4-7). Under LAIA, member countries are encouraged to establish bilateral and multilateral agreements aimed at reducing tariff and nontariff barriers. LAIA offers differential treatment to countries of different levels of development to avoid preferential treatment of the larger countries (blamed for the failure of LAFTA). Member countries are at present members of two successful common markets—the Andean Common Market (AnCom) and the Southern Cone Common Market (MERCOSUR).

Andean Common Market (AnCom) A trade group of the Andean countries that aspires to become a common market; it is currently in the process of agreeing upon common external tariffs. (See www.comunidadandina.org.)

The Andean Common Market (AnCom)

The **Andean Common Market (AnCom),** known previously as the Andean Pact, was established in the 1970s and renamed as the Andean Community in 1996. In addition to eliminating trade restrictions (tariff and nontariff) within the Andean region, AnCom also provides for uniform external tariffs and rules for foreign investment. Its member countries are Bolivia, Colombia, Ecuador, Peru, and Venezuela.

Figure 4-7

Member Countries of the Latin American Integration Association, Andean Common Market, and Southern Cone Common Market

▨ LAIA Member Countries	▥ MERCOSUR Member Countries	▤ Andean Common Market Member Countries

One of AnCom's accomplishments is that member countries have agreed on levels of external tariffs covering 95 percent of products, whereby raw materials and basic industrial feedstuffs pay a 5 percent duty, intermediate manufacturers pay a 10 or 15 percent duty, and finished goods are taxed at 20 percent.[23]

The Southern Cone Common Market (MERCOSUR)

The **Southern Cone Common Market (MERCOSUR)** is among the most successful common markets. Initially, it started as a bilateral agreement between Brazil and Argentina aimed at eliminating trade restrictions between the two countries. MERCOSUR now comprises two additional member countries—Paraguay and Uruguay. Two other members, Chile and Bolivia, have a pending status. Although Chile and Bolivia have both qualified for membership, the two countries continue to disagree with the other members on the common tariffs (Chile insists on a much lower external tariff than the agreement provides for) to be charged to companies from nonmember countries and consequently retain an associate status.

Initially, MERCOSUR was expected to look north, at NAFTA, for trade and cooperation accords; surprisingly, it has opted to first approach the European Union in an ambitious agreement that phases out all trade barriers.[24]

Southern Cone Common Market (MERCOSUR) A free trade agreement in South America that has met with considerable success; MERCOSUR is presently in the process of becoming a viable customs union. (See www.mercosur.org.uy.)

The Central American Common Market (CACM)

The economic agreement between Belize, Costa Rica, the Dominican Republic, El Salvador, Guatemala, Honduras, Nicaragua, and Panama, known as the **Central American Common Market (CACM),** includes plans for forming a regional economic union similar to the European Union, and to advance regional and international trade. The plan also encompasses political, cultural, and environmental measures.[25]

Central American Common Market (CACM) An economic agreement between Central American countries; this agreement includes plans for forming a regional economic union similar to the European Union, and to advance regional and international trade.

The Common Market for Eastern and Southern Africa (COMESA)

The **Common Market for Eastern and Southern Africa (COMESA)** plans full economic integration; it allows for the free movement of labor and capital, the free movement of people by 2014, and a currency union by 2025; it is, however, clear that the organization faces substantial political and economic obstacles given the political and economic instability in the region.[26] Specifically, the difficulties facing member countries include a poor compliance with tariff reductions and concerns over customs revenue losses; further complicating the matter is the fact that, despite diplomatic pressure, South Africa is not a member.[27] COMESA has 20 member countries: Angola, Burundi, Comoros, Democratic Republic of Congo, Djibouti, Egypt, Eritrea, Ethiopia, Kenya, Madagascar, Malawi, Mauritius, Namibia, Rwanda, Seychelles, Sudan, Swaziland, Uganda, Zambia, and Zimbabwe.

Common Market for Eastern and Southern Africa (COMESA) An agreement between 20 member countries aimed at achieving economic integration; COMESA is currently eliminating all tariff and nontariff barriers to trade and is in the process of adopting common external tariffs.

4-2e Monetary Unions

The establishment of a **monetary union** involves the creation of a unified central bank and the use of a single currency. The following are examples of successful monetary unions:

- European Monetary Union
- West African Economic and Monetary Union
- Economic Community of West African States

It should be noted, however, that successful monetary unions do not necessarily mean successful economic integration and the elimination of all trade restrictions.

monetary union A form of economic integration characterized by the establishment of a common central bank enacting monetary policy for the group.

The European Monetary Union (Euroland) (www.europa.eu.int)

The 1992 Maastricht Treaty had as a purpose to provide for the **European Monetary Union (EMU)** and to create the European Central Bank, a single currency, and fixed exchange rates. The creation of a monetary union was, however, hindered in 1992 by an

European Monetary Union (EMU) A union composed of the members of the European Union who adhere to the joint monetary policy enacted by the European Central Bank and who have adopted the Euro as the single currency. (See www.europa.eu.int.)

Figure 4-8

Member Countries of the European Union and the Euroland Countries

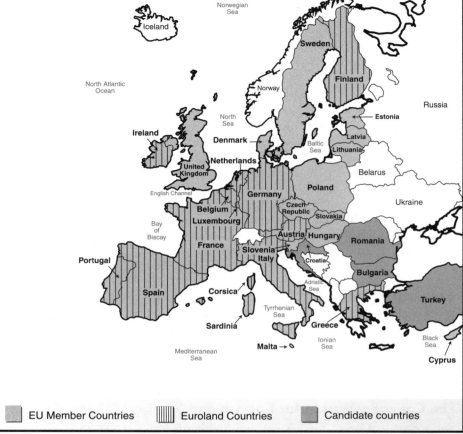

EU Member Countries   Euroland Countries   Candidate countries

Euroland The nickname of the European Monetary Union. (See www.europa.eu.int.)

West African Economic and Monetary Union (WAEMU) One of the first attempts at economic integration in Africa. Although it is successful as a monetary union that has adopted a single currency, trade is quite modest within the WAEMU. (See www.dakarcom.com/EconReports/econ_waemu.htm.)

Economic Community of West African States (ECOWAS) A free trade agreement that strives to achieve economic integration in West Africa; domination by Nigeria, civil unrest, and regional conflict have served as impediments in the group's success. (See www.ecowas.int.)

exceptionally strong German mark, boosted particularly by the financing of reconstruction for Eastern Germany (the former East Germany) and the high interest rates it offered to foreign investors. This, coupled with a recession taking place in Europe, led to a crisis that caused the British pound and the Spanish peseta to lose their value overnight and to float out of the European Exchange Rate Mechanism. To member countries, at the time, it appeared that the German Central Bank was likely to dominate the European body, and, for a while, the Euro lost popular support, especially in Britain.

Currently, countries that are full members of the European Monetary Union are Austria, Belgium, Finland, France, Germany, Greece, Ireland, Italy, Luxembourg, the Netherlands, Portugal, and Spain. These countries are often referred to as **Euroland** (see Figure 4-8).

The West African Economic and Monetary Union (WAEMU)

The **West African Economic and Monetary Union (WAEMU)** is one of the first attempts at economic integration in Africa. Although successful as a monetary union that has adopted a single currency—the CFA franc—trade is quite modest within the WAEMU.[28] WAEMU member countries are Benin, Burkina Faso, Ivory Coast, Guinea-Bissau, Mali, Niger, Senegal, and Togo.

The Economic Community of West African States (ECOWAS)

The purpose of the **Economic Community of West African States (ECOWAS)** is to achieve complete economic integration. At present, ECOWAS member countries are also attempting to address impediments to the integration process that are attributed to civil unrest, regional conflict, a lag in economic development compared to other market groups in the world, and the domination of the group by Nigeria.

ECOWAS's plans, however, are ambitious. Six of the 15 members—Gambia, Ghana, Guinea, Liberia, Nigeria, and Sierra Leone—have set up a monetary union and have committed to adopting a common currency and to merge with the WAEMU. In this regard, they have pledged to meet stringent convergence criteria, such as 5 percent inflation, a maximum budget deficit-to-GDP ratio of 4 percent, and central bank financing of the budget deficit limited to 10 percent of the previous year's tax revenue, among others.[29] ECOWAS member countries are Benin, Burkina Faso, Cape Verde, Ivory Coast, Gambia, Ghana, Guinea, Guinea-Bissau, Liberia, Mali, Niger, Nigeria, Senegal, Sierra Leone, and Togo.

4-2f Political Unions

A **political union** represents the highest level of integration; it assumes a viable economic integration and involves the establishment of viable common governing bodies, legislative bodies, and enforcement powers. Although there are many examples of political unions, the European Union (www.europa.eu.int) is the only example to date of successful voluntary political integration. In other examples, the countries of the former Soviet Bloc were members of the **Council of Mutual Economic Assistance (CMEA),** an economic body similar in nature to a free trade area, as well as members of the Warsaw Pact, a political/military body aimed at countering the North Atlantic Treaty Organization (NATO); under this format, member countries of CMEA also approached what would be considered a political union. CMEA did not survive beyond the fall of communism. Another example of political nonvoluntary integration is the Commonwealth of Independent States, discussed in section 4-2a, "Bilateral Agreements and Multilateral Forums and Agreements."

The European Union, composed of 25 member states, is well on its way to becoming a political union. In this regard, it has agreed on a common foreign policy, a common security policy that includes defense agreements, a common legal system, and a common enforcement system that works across borders for mutual purposes. As such, it has set in place a number of governmental bodies, as shown in Figure 4-9.

The **European Council,** in which heads of government meet, is the highest policy-making body of the European Union.

The **European Parliament,** located in Strasbourg, France (see Figure 4-10), is a body of 546 members elected every five years by direct universal suffrage. Seats are allocated among member states based on their population. The Parliament debates the policies and legislation in the European Union. In the past, it was mainly a consultative body that passed on most of the proposed legislation with a simple-majority voting. More recently, however, it has experienced extensive debate and lobbying from member countries on key international business issues. In one example, the Parliament killed a measure that would have made it easier to mount corporate takeovers; the vote is attributed to a string of hostile takeovers, such as Vodafone, the British mobile telephone company taking over its German rival, Mannesmann.[30]

The **Council of Nations** consists of representatives from parliaments of member states, and it acts as a constitutional council. It has the power to overrule the Court of Justice.

The **Council of Ministers,** the decision-making body (the legislature) of the European Union, is composed of one minister from each member country. The Council of Ministers passes laws based on proposals of the European Commission. Different ministers from each country, depending on the issue debated, meet at various locations to vote on directives advanced by the Commission. For example, EU energy ministers met in Stockholm to vote on EU electricity and natural gas directives to allow businesses and households to choose their electricity and natural gas suppliers.[31]

The **European Commission** is subordinated to the Council, as a civil service. The Commission consists of a president and commissioners who are appointed for a four-year term and are in charge of initiating and supervising the execution of laws and policies. This executive body of the European Union is located in Brussels, Belgium. It is important to note that the European Commission acts only on behalf and in the interest of the European Union, and not that of individual member states. It answers to the European Parliament.

Many of the European Commission rulings affect international business worldwide: A company that wants to do business in Europe must abide by the Commission's ruling.[32]

political union The highest level of regional integration; it assumes a viable economic integration and involves the establishment of viable common governing bodies, legislative bodies, and enforcement powers.

Council of Mutual Economic Assistance (CMEA) A trade agreement between the countries of the Soviet Bloc that disintegrated after the fall of communism. CMEA was an economic body similar in nature to a free trade area, and approached what would be considered a political union.

European Council The highest policy-making body of the European Union. (See www.europa.eu.int.)

European Parliament The Parliament of the European Union, composed of members elected every five years by direct universal suffrage; seats in the Parliament are allocated among member states based on their population. (See www.europa.eu.int.)

Council of Nations The constitutional council of the European Union consisting of representatives from parliaments of EU member states. (See www.europa.eu.int.)

Council of Ministers The decision-making body (the legislature) of the European Union, composed of one minister from each member country.

European Commission The body of the European Union in charge of initiating and supervising the execution of laws and policies. (See www.europa.eu.int.)

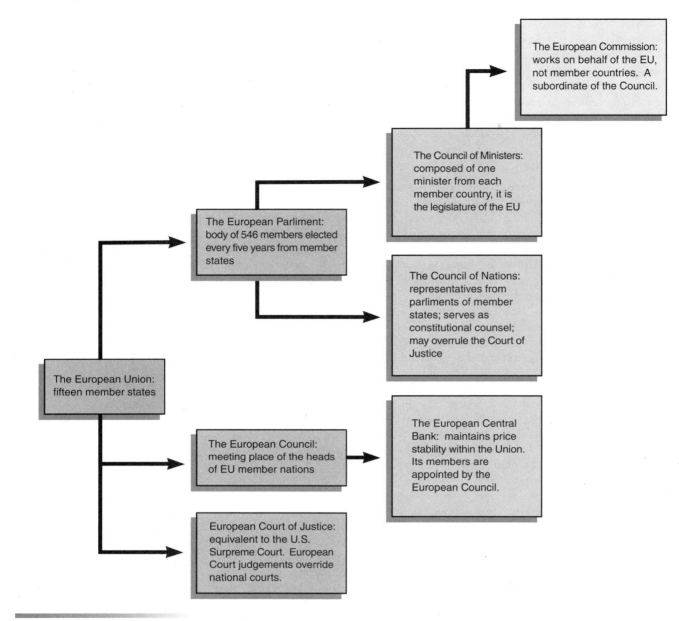

Figure 4-9
The Main Bodies of the European Union

For example, the European Commission blocked General Electric's $42 billion takeover of Honeywell International, due to the danger that GE could use Honeywell's strength in avionics equipment to expand its competitive strength in aircraft engines. The Commission rejected the merger of MCI Worldcom and Sprint on the grounds that the company would be able to dictate prices for Internet access in Europe, and it blocked a merger between two British travel agencies invoking the threat of collective dominance.[33] In another example, the European Commission raided nine mobile-service providers in Britain and Germany, including giants Deutsche Telekom AG, the Vodafone Group PLC, and France Telecom SA, looking for evidence of price fixing in setting roaming tariffs.[34]

The European Commission also recently enacted an important directive aimed at unfair commercial practices, described in International Marketing Illustration 4-2.

F i g u r e 4 - 1 0
The members of Parliament meet once a month in the European Parliament building in Strasbourg, France. This building ended the fight between Strasbourg and Brussels (Belgium) and the debate on the primary location of the European Parliament; it should be noted, however, that the work of the European Parliament is also conducted in Brussels and Luxembourg.

International Marketing Illustration 4-2

Unfair Commercial Practices: The European Union Perspective

In 2003, the European Commission published a Directive on Unfair Commercial Practices after years of consultation with consumer groups and businesses. The purpose of the directive is to address the tangle of national bans, limits, and other restrictions that impede small and medium enterprises from taking full advantage of the EU market and to provide consumers anywhere in the EU the same opportunities and protection as elsewhere in the market. The primary areas covered are misleading practices, aggressive practices, and facilitation of cross-border shopping.

Misleading practices are targeted in particular; for example, the directive would be used to outlaw the use of sports stars in food advertising directed at children. The directive bans bait advertising scams, whereby a product is advertised as a special offer without the retailer carrying it in stock in sufficient amounts. It also bans use of liquidation sales when in fact the retailer is not going out of business and use of pyramid schemes.

Aggressive practices are also banned; for example, harassment, coercion, and undue influence in sales are banned, as is excessive solicitation.

Consumers will also be able to confidently engage in cross-border shopping. Before this directive was enacted, consumers were worried that their rights would not be guaranteed to the same extent as in their home country and did not willingly purchase products over the Internet. This aspect of the directive also evens the playing field for companies in the EU. For example, companies that were unwilling to sell their products to consumers in untested areas because they were not familiar with national laws are now assured of the same protection anywhere in the European Union.

Sources: Adapted from http://europa.eu.int/comm/consumers/; and Lucy Alcock, Paul Chen, Hui Min Ch'ng, Sarah Hodson, et al., "New European Union Directive to Curb Unfair and Misleading Commercial Practices," *Journal of Brand Management*, Vol. 11, No. 2, 2003, p. 125.

European Central Bank The bank of the European Union charged with enacting monetary policy for the twelve countries that share a common currency, the Euro. (See www.europa.eu.int.)

European Court of Justice The Supreme Court–equivalent of the European Union. (See www.europa.eu.int.)

The **European Central Bank** is charged with enacting monetary policy for the countries that share a common currency, the Euro. Its goal is to maintain price stability within the European Monetary Union. The members of the European Central Bank board are appointed by the European Council by a simple majority vote. The equivalent of the Federal Reserve Bank for the United States, the European Central Bank tends to be more conservative and does not typically yield to individual countries' demands to reduce interest rates in an attempt to boost the economy during a downturn.

The **European Court of Justice** is the European Union's equivalent of the U.S. Supreme Court. The Court's decisions are final, binding to member countries, and cannot be appealed in national courts. Also, European Court judgments overrule those of national courts.

In addition to these bodies, the European Union has adopted other common policies; among them are commercial policies, foreign and defense policies, and policies concerning immigration and the granting of asylum.

Other Para-Statal Institutions in Europe

The European Union is not the only para-statal institution in Western Europe. Other para-statal institutions have no affiliation to the European Union, and yet they are significant players in the life of this region. One such example is the Council of Europe, which is composed of 40 European states that agree to accept the principle of the rule of law and guarantee of human rights and fundamental freedoms. The institution is involved in such areas as human rights; legal cooperation; cultural heritage; social, economic, and environmental planning; and local democracy. Two of its institutions are the Palais de l'Europe (see Figure 4-11a) and the European Court and Commission for Human Rights (see Figure 4-11b).

Figure 4-11

Institutions of the Council of Europe: (a) the Palais de l'Europe and (b) the European Court and Commission for Human Rights.

(a)

(b)

Summary

- **Provide an overview of the determinants of regional economic and political integration.** A number of factors prompt countries to favor trade with other countries. They are sharing a common culture, language, traditions, a history of common economic and political dominance, regional proximity, a similar level of economic development, and the desire to relinquish part of a nation's national identity in favor of advancing other national priorities.

- **Examine the different levels of economic and political integration and identify, within each world region, economic and political agreements that have met with success.** The first level of integration involves establishing bilateral and multilateral agreements; these agreements involve, to some extent, opening of markets and elimination of trade barriers. At the next level, a free trade agreement involves a reduction in, or even elimination of, customs duties and other trade barriers between member countries. Examples of free trade agreements are the European Free Trade Association, the Association of Southeast Asian Nations Free Trade Agreement, the North American Free Trade Agreement, the Southern African Development Community, and the Arab Maghreb Union. The Free Trade Area of the Americas is an ambitious plan to create a market of the democratic nations of North, Central, and South America. At the next level, a customs union is a free trade area that has eliminated or greatly reduced internal tariffs and that imposes common external tariffs. An example is the South African Customs Union. A common market is an agreement to eliminate all barriers to trade, to adopt external tariffs, and to allow for the free movement of capital and labor in the region. Examples of common markets are the Latin American Integration Association, the Andean Community, the Southern Cone Common Market (MERCOSUR), the Central American Common Market, and the Common Market for Eastern and Southern Africa. The establishment of a monetary union involves the creation of a common central bank and the use of a single currency. Examples of monetary unions are the European Monetary Union, the West African Economic and Monetary Union, and the Economic Community of West African States. The only viable political unions that have survived to date are the European Union and the Commonwealth of Independent States.

- **Examine the functions of the different policy and governance bodies of the European Union.** The different bodies of the European Union are the European Council, which is the highest policy-making body of the European Union, made up of heads of governments; the European Parliament, which debates policies and legislation of the European Union; the Council of Nations, which consists of representatives from parliaments of member states and acts as a constitutional council; the Council of Ministers, which is the decision-making body (the legislature) of the European Union that passes laws based on proposals of the European Commission; the European Commission, which is subordinated to the Council and initiates and supervises the execution of laws and policies; the European Central Bank, which is charged with enacting monetary policy for the countries that share a common currency; and the European Court of Justice, an equivalent to the U.S. Supreme Court.

Key Terms

Andean Common Market (AnCom)
Arab Maghreb Union (AMU)
ASEAN Free Trade Area (AFTA)
Asia-Pacific Economic Cooperation (APEC)
Association of Southeast Asian Nations (ASEAN)
bilateral agreement
Central American Common Market (CACM)
common market
Common Market for Eastern and Southern Africa (COMESA)
Commonwealth of Independent States (CIS)
Council of Ministers
Council of Mutual Economic Assistance (CMEA)
Council of Nations
customs union
Economic Community of West African States (ECOWAS)

Euroland
European Atomic Energy Community
European Central Bank
European Coal and Steel Community
European Commission
European Council
European Court of Justice
European Exchange Rate Mechanism (ERM)
European Free Trade Association (EFTA)
European Monetary Union (EMU)
European Parliament
European Union
free trade agreement
Free Trade Area of the Americas (FTAA)
Latin American Free Trade Association (LAFTA)
Latin American Integration Association (LAIA)

Maastricht Treaty
monetary union
multilateral forums and agreements
North American Free Trade Agreement (NAFTA)
North Atlantic Treaty Organization (NATO)
Organization for Economic Co-operation and Development (OECD)
Organization for Petroleum Exporting Countries (OPEC)
political union
South African Customs Union (SACU)
Southern African Development Community (SADC)
Southern Cone Common Market (MERCOSUR)
West African Economic and Monetary Union (WAEMU)

Discussion Questions

1. Identify the determinants of regional economic and political integration.
2. Describe the different stages of regional economic and political integration. What is the difference between a free trade association and a common market?
3. There are arguments that much of the groundwork for the Free Trade Area of the Americas already has been done by other free trade agreements in the region targeted for economic integration. Which free trade agreements are operating within this area?
4. Identify the different bodies of the European Union and describe their main function.

Chapter Quiz (True/False)

1. Determinants of successful economic and political integration include a common culture, a common history, and regional proximity.
2. Bilateral agreements and multilateral forums and agreements are different from formal regional political and economic integration.
3. The goal of NAFTA is to eliminate all tariff and nontariff barriers between the United States, Canada, and Mexico.

4. A common market is characterized by limited movement of goods, labor, and capital.
5. The European Parliament debates policies and legislation of the European Union.
6. The European Council is the highest policy-making body of the European Union.

Multiple Choice

1. All the following are examples of free trade agreements EXCEPT the
   a. Association of Southeast Asian Nations.
   b. North American Free Trade Agreement.
   c. Southern African Development Community.
   d. World Trade Organization.
2. Current members of the European Free Trade Association include all the following EXCEPT
   a. Norway.
   b. Liechtenstein.
   c. Sweden.
   d. Ireland.

3. Which agreement is credited with eliminating all internal tariffs and creating the European Economic Community?
   a. The Southern Cone Common Market
   b. The Treaty of Rome
   c. The Andean Economic Agreement
   d. The Maastricht Treaty

Endnotes

1. "The History of APEC," *Business Korea,* April 2000, Vol. 17, No. 4, April 2000, pp. 54–55.
2. Ibid.
3. Laura D'andrea Tyson, "The Message from Asia: Trade Locally, Think Globally," *Business Week,* December 4, 2000, Issue 3710, December 4, 2000, p. 28.
4. Ibid.
5. Richard Pomfret, "Reintegration of Formerly Centrally Planned Economies into the Global Trading System," *ASEAN Economic Bulletin,* April 2001, Vol. 18, No. 1, April 2001, pp. 35–47.
6. Ibid.
7. Ibid.
8. Robert von Lucius, "Nordic Neighbors Feel Snubbed," *Frankfurter Allgemeine Zeitung,* July 6, 2001, No. 154, July 6, 2001, p. 3.
9. Ibid.
10. For a discussion of the current conflict between the EU and EFTA, see Lucius, "Nordic Neighbors Feel Snubbed," p. 3.
11. Ibid.
12. Edward Taylor, "EU and Switzerland Resume Talks on Bilateral Accords," *Wall Street Journal Europe,* July 6–7, 2001, p. 2.
13. "Asia/Pacific Rim: Japan, ASEAN Set Up Free Trade Agreement Study Group," *World Trade,* July 2001, Vol. 14, No. 7, July 2001, p. 18.
14. Neil Saker, "The Foundations of Stability," *Far Eastern Economic Review,* May 24, 2001, Vol. 164, No. 20, May 24, 2001, p. 55.
15. Alan M. Field, "A New Vision for NAFTA," *Journal of Commerce,* June 28, 2004, p. 1.
16. Ibid.
17. "No Time for Protectionism," *Business Week,* July 23, 2001, Issue 3742, July 23, 2001, p. 98.
18. Ernesto Zedillo, Former President of Mexico, "Commentary," *Forbes,* July 23, 2001, p. 49.
19. Ibid.

20. Gary C. Hufbauer and Yee Wong, "Grading Growth," *Harvard International Review,* Vol. 26, (No. 2), 2004, pp. 72–76.
21. Ryan Fahey, "Congo Tensions: The SADC's Shortcomings," *Harvard International Review,* Vol. 21, No. 2, Spring 1999, pp. 14–16.
22. "International Economy: Africa," *Barclays Economic Review,* Third Quarter 1999, pp. 29–31.
23. Ibid.
24. Ibid.
25. Ibid.
26. *Country Monitor,* "Comesa's Free-Trade Area," *Country Monitor,* Vol. 8, No. 43, November 6, 2000, p. 4.
27. *Barclays Economic Review,* "International Economy," *Barclays Economic Review,* pp. 29–31.
28. Jacqueline Irving, "Point/Counterpoint: The Pros and Cons of Expanded Monetary Union in West Africa," *Finance & Development,* Vol. 38, No. 1, March, 2001, pp. 24–28.
29. Ibid.
30. Paul Meller, "EU Parliament Rejects Bill to Ease Takeovers," *International Herald Tribune,* July 5, 2001, pp. 1, 10.
31. "EU Energy Chief Expects Power Deal by the End of the Year," *Wall Street Journal Europe,* July 6–7, 2001, p. 3.
32. Brian M. Carney, "Mario Monti, Central Planner: Does the European Union's Competition Commissioner Really Believe in Competition?" *Wall Street Journal Europe,* July 6–7, 2001, p. 6.
33. Edmund L. Andrews and Paul Meller, "EU Vetoes GE's Plan to Acquire Honeywell," *International Herald Tribune,* July 4, 2001, pp. 1, 5.
34. Philip Shishkin, William Boston, and Almar LaTour, "Nine Mobile Firms Are Raided in Probe of Roaming Tariffs: EU Antitrust Officials Look for Evidence of Collusion in Germany, U.K.," *Wall Street Journal Europe,* July 12, 2001, pp. 1, 4.
35. http://europa.eu.int/comm/enlargement/bulgaria/
36. http://europa.eu.int/comm/enterprise/enterprise_policy/charter/

You can find the correct answers to these questions by taking the quiz and then submitting your answers in the Online Edition. The program will automatically score your submission. Where you miss a question, the program will provide the correct answer, a rationale for the answer, and the section number in the chapter where the topic is discussed.

Case 4-1

Damianov Press:
A Newly Privatized Printing Press Vies for the European Union Market

Damian Damianov is a retired director of a formerly communist metallurgic factory in Sofia, Bulgaria, with a lively enterprising spirit and a strong desire for success. He has identified a niche that may have great potential: He has bought an abandoned printing press with quality equipment in the outskirts of Sofia, the capital city, to produce art books for publishers in the European Union. The press, privatized in the early 1990s, after the fall of communism in Bulgaria, was recently abandoned by its previous owner because it was considered an environmental hazard by the state; the previous owner did not want to invest in new equipment that would meet environmental requirements of the European Union, which Bulgaria plans to join in 2007.

The fall of communism in Bulgaria created numerous opportunities for newly privatized larger companies, as well as small and medium enterprises. However, many businesses were greatly challenged by the 1996 crisis, and it took years for the economic recovery to bring back entrepreneurial enthusiasm. Since the 1996 crisis, Bulgaria has achieved macro-economic stability, it has a stable currency, and its real growth is accelerating significantly, becoming the most attractive of the 2007 candidates for membership in the European Union. Businesses from the EU and elsewhere are aggressively expanding in Bulgaria. And the government encourages the establishment of new small and medium enterprises, in line with the EU road map requirements. These requirements specify that Bulgaria should focus its efforts on resolving uncertainties in the legislative and taxation areas and reinforcing delivery mechanisms for promoting entrepreneurship; in this sense, Bulgaria is asked to implement the European Charter for Small Enterprises,[35] which would create a strong competitive position for Damianov's new enterprise.

Damianov is working with Bulgarian venture capitalists to establish a new enterprise, the Damianov Press. His goal is to produce quality art books at much lower prices than Western European publishers. At present, much of the art book production in the European Union takes place in Spain, where costs are somewhat lower than in the rest of the European Union. Damianov has returned from the Frankfurt Book Fair, where he met with a few of the German art book publishers: Prestel, Hatje Kanz, and Ravensburger. The Prestel representative appeared very interested in the possibility of producing lower-cost, high-quality art books. With the high costs of development, translation, and production, exhibition catalogues and art books in general are becoming quite expensive. If costs can be reduced on the production side, these books can have greater appeal to the art public in the German-speaking world and elsewhere. Damianov Press could produce those same high-quality, contemporary art books at a fraction of the cost.

Venture capitalists will gather at the proposed company's warehouse next week. Each has individually assured Damian Damianov that he is ready to work with the others to meet the financial needs of the company. They understand that their charge is to finance the refurbishing of old equipment and invest in new equipment. As soon as the equipment needs are met, Damianov Press must also conduct a study of environmental impact assessment, nature protection, and industrial pollution to ensure that the new company conforms to EU requirements. The study is mandated by the Bulgarian government for new manufacturing businesses. The new company also needs to conform to EU requirements in areas of antidiscrimination, equal opportunities, labor law, and occupational safety and health and ensure health and safety at work at the printing press.

Damian Damianov is in the process of preparing his speech to the venture capitalists. While going through his materials, he came across the European Charter for Small Enterprises, which was approved at the Feira European Council on June 19–20, 2000. The Charter calls upon Member States and the Commission to take action to support and encourage small enterprises in 10 key areas:

- Education and training for entrepreneurship
- Cheaper and faster start-up
- Better legislation and regulation
- Availability of skills
- Improved online access
- Ability to get more out of the Single Market
- Taxation and financial matters
- Stronger technological capacity of small enterprises
- Successful e-business models and top-class small business support
- Stronger, more effective representation of small enterprises' interests at Union and national level[36]

Damianov is attempting to devise ways of benefiting from Bulgaria's prospective entrance in the European Union and from the fact that Bulgaria is required to subscribe to the Charter.

Analysis Suggestions

1. Examine the European Charter for Small Enterprises. What are some benefits that Damianov Press could derive from Bulgaria adopting this Charter?
2. Prepare the speech that Damianov will deliver next week at the meeting with the venture capitalists.

5

Cultural Influences on International Marketing

Chapter Objectives

By the end of this chapter, you should be able to

1 Identify the elements of culture and examine how they affect marketing practices around the world.

2 Describe national and regional character based on dimensions such as time orientation, business practices, gift giving, socializing, gender roles, and materialism.

3 Discuss cultural variability in terms of the Hofstede dimensions with appropriate examples and address cultural change in a marketing context.

4 Address the self-reference criterion and ethnocentrism and describe how they impede mutual understanding and cooperation, with direct negative effects on marketing practices.

5 Describe the global consumer culture as it manifests itself around the world.

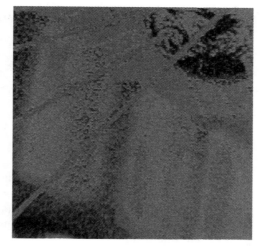

You are in the middle of negotiations with a potential Turkish client in Istanbul, over lunch, at the Conrad Hilton Hotel. You go to the self-service buffet and pile on your plate some tasty pork chops from a serving dish clearly marked "pork." You ask the waiter to bring a bottle of wine and offer some to your potential Turkish client; he declines. Your products are known for their quality in Turkey and elsewhere in the world, and your client seems receptive to your price quote. After lunch, the potential client invites you to his home for coffee; you decline and state that you need to stay at the hotel to get some work done and bid him good-bye. You come back to the United States and find that you cannot reach your Turkish client. His secretary always claims he is not in, and he does not return your calls. What went wrong? You subsequently learn that, in Turkey, the dominant religion is Islam, and Islam bans the consumption of pork and alcohol. Could your lunch have offended your client? Probably not too much because he still seemed receptive to your offer as you were eating the "dirty animal" in front of him. Could he have been offended by your not going to his house for Turkish coffee? Even though you refused, you did not tell him that you really hate the stuff and you were dreading spending even a few hours in 90-degree weather in a home that most likely was not air-conditioned. You were, after all, showing how dedicated you were to your job by staying at the hotel to work. Could the hotel staff have told him that you spent the evening next door, at another air-conditioned hotel, a former palace, having yet another bottle of wine?

This chapter will examine in depth the effect of different cultural influences on consumer behavior and on a company's international operations. It will examine national character and provide illustrations of behaviors in line with national character.

A full understanding of local culture in markets where one's firm is operating constitutes a minimal condition for successful global marketing operations. Although cultural understanding alone cannot guarantee a firm's success in a new international market, not fully understanding the local culture and engaging in marketing practices that may be discordant with the culture will guarantee failure.

- Many companies find that their new foreign firm is about to collapse because they have failed to learn that country's "customs, cultures, and laws."[1]

- One study conducted by Sami Abbasi and Kenneth W. Holman claims that two out of every three U.S. businessmen sent to Saudi Arabia are brought back home due to difficulties in adapting to the local culture. Such returns obviously become very expensive for the companies involved.[2] (See Chapter 15, "International Personal Selling and Personnel Management," for illustrations of expenses involved in sending expatriates overseas.)

- The wrong promotional strategies will quickly backfire for companies that do not fully research their target market. In the former Soviet Union, advertisements using the Marlboro Man did not produce much enthusiasm and did not initially enhance the adoption rate of the Marlboro brand of cigarettes; in spite of the popularity of Westerns, a cowboy was perceived as the U.S. equivalent of a peasant—an uncultured, poor individual with a low status in society. In general, advertisements that promise prosperity, higher status, and overall advancement tend to be more successful in this market.

When marketers are armed with knowledge about the local culture, they are in a better position to communicate effectively with the target consumer.

Culture is recognized as having a general influence on consumption; it is expressed in the consumption of numerous products and services, in homes, offices, stores and marketplace sites, with differences noted across various subcultures and nations.[3] Cultural factors also exert a profound influence on the firm's other stakeholders, such as government representatives, national and international consumer groups and interest groups, service providers, suppliers, channel members, and shareholders, among others. Culture is the key determinant of the manner in which individuals do business or respond to a company's marketing strategy.

5-1 Culture Defined

culture The continuously evolving totality of learned and shared meanings, rituals, norms, and traditions among the members of an organization or society.

Culture—a society's personality—is defined as a *continuously changing totality of learned and shared meanings, rituals, norms, and traditions among the members of an organization or society.*

Despite this definition, it should be noted that the notion of culture is relatively ambiguous and controversial among both practitioners and academics.[4] Some elements of culture, however, are thought to affect important aspects of marketing, and they are addressed in this chapter.

The pivotal constituents of culture are as follows:

ecology The manner in which society adapts to its habitat, i.e., the distribution of resources within an industrialized country versus a developing country; the desire for efficiency, space-saving devices, or green products.

- **Ecology**—The manner in which society adapts to its habitat, i.e., the distribution of resources within an industrialized country versus a developing country; the desire for efficiency, space-saving devices, or green products.
- **Social structure**—The organization of society.
- **Ideology**—The manner in which individuals relate to the environment and to others; this includes attitudes toward time, space, possessions, and referent others (peers).

social structure The organization of relationships in a society.

These areas are complexly interrelated.[5] In Section 5-2, "Elements of Culture," we describe the elements of culture that are most relevant to international marketing managers.

5-2 Elements of Culture

ideology The manner in which individuals relate to their environment and to others, including their attitudes toward time, space, possessions, and referent others.

5-2a Language

Language has a prominent role as an element of culture: The language one learns in the community where one is born and raised shapes and structures one's world view.[6] Some languages, such as the Bantu languages, are broad and do not differentiate, for instance, between the "here" and the "now."[7] Other languages are very precise, especially in domains such as agriculture; they may have several terms for an object or a body part, depending on the current function of the object or respective body part. For example, for the word "tail," Batwa languages have a term that refers to its use by cattle as protection against flies, another term as an illustration of joy, yet another as an indicator of attention, and so on. The key to communicating in a particular culture is understanding all the nuances and complexities of the language of the target market.

language The vehicle used for communication in a particular culture; includes spoken and written language and nonverbal communication.

A number of points are relevant in this regard. At a primary level, language has two aspects: the spoken/written language and the nonverbal language.

Spoken/Written Language

spoken/written language The language used in conversation/the language used in written communications.

Spoken/written language poses a number of concerns to marketers. First, in terms of translation, the diversity of languages creates difficulties for marketers operating internationally. Even if the same language is shared by different countries, marketers should be aware of differences in meaning: Procter & Gamble sells "nappies" in the United Kingdom, as opposed to "diapers"; the "boot" of the Ford automobile is actually its "trunk"; and housewives or househusbands who are "hoovering" in the United Kingdom may actually be "vacuuming" using an Electrolux vacuum cleaner.

Problems could arise in the process of translation: Firms have placed in jeopardy the viability of their brands by relying on primary translations and not ensuring that either the product name is appropriate in a given culture or that the communication actually conveys the intended message. Using procedures described in Chapter 6, "International Marketing Research: Practices and Challenges"—*back translation* (translation back into the original language) and *parallel translation* (translation by another translator for comparison purposes)—will diminish the likelihood that the company will commit blunders when communicating with the target market. Many companies have made translation blunders, and the marketing literature is replete with examples, from the chocolate and fruit product sold under the name *Zit* in English-speaking countries, to the *Fresca* soda pop sold in Mexico (where, in slang, this word means lesbian).[8]

Translation is expensive, especially in markets where multiple languages are spoken. For example, in India, there are more than 300 minor languages and 3,000 dialects. Only 15 distinct languages are widely spoken, however; Hindi, the official language, is spoken by 30 percent of the population, and English is widely used in administrative, commercial, and political life. To effectively communicate with this very promising multicultural market of approximately 1 billion, a firm's decisions on which language to use are crucial.

Marketing practitioners using the same marketing strategy in a unified market experience a similar dilemma: deciding which language to use or whether to use multiple languages. The European Union presents an interesting case: When companies target this market, product information is typically provided in two to three languages. A product that has French, Dutch, and German labeling is probably sold in France, Belgium (where both French and Dutch are spoken), the Netherlands, Germany, Austria, Luxembourg, Liechtenstein, and in the German and French regions in Switzerland.

Finally, it is important to communicate in the appropriate language with the target market in areas where multiple languages are used. Marketers selling their products in the United Arab Emirates will find that a significant proportion of consumers there do not speak the national language, Arabic; guest workers in these countries are predominantly Indian, Pakistani, and Southeast Asian. In targeting these markets, firms would benefit from using English, which is widely understood, and the main language used in business, rather than Arabic.

Nonverbal Communication

Nonverbal communication includes body language, gestures, facial expressions, eye contact, and even silence. Silent communications, especially gestures, have different meanings across cultures, and marketing managers must be aware of them to avoid embarrassing or costly mistakes. Examples of nonverbal communication are provided in International Marketing Illustration 5-1.

nonverbal communication All communication that is not written or spoken; includes body language, gestures, facial expressions, eye contact, and silence.

International Marketing Illustration 5-1

Nonverbal Communication

proxemics The amount of physical space individuals require to feel comfortable in the process of communication.

Proxemics refer to the relationship between physical space and the process of communication. One of the peculiarities of American culture that most foreigners find intriguing is the "bubble," the personal space around the individual, which, if one violates, one must apologize. In countries where standing in line means that the person behind another will periodically engage in a "poking exercise," pushing him or her lightly and hoping that he or she might

continued

advance somewhat, the bubble is unheard of. In these countries, even in polite society, apologizing for maneuvering too closely or cutting off another is not necessary.

In general, Greeks, Central and Eastern Europeans, Japanese, and South Americans feel more comfortable standing or sitting closer to strangers than do members of other nationalities.[9] Similarly, in the Middle East, even in the business world, men prefer standing close to people with whom they are conversing and take great offense if someone backs away from them.[10]

postures Individuals' physical postures during conversation.

orientations Individuals' positioning relative to their counterparts during conversation.

oculesics The use or avoidance of eye contact during communication.

Postures, orientations, and **oculesics** refer to individuals' positioning relative to their counterpart and the use or avoidance of eye contact during communication. Individuals' approaches to greeting, for example, differ in different parts of the world. In the United States, when shaking hands, one is supposed to look his or her counterpart in the eye; this should make an impression of being forthright, as well as having a take-charge attitude. The handshake should be firm and brief. This same handshake, however, would be perceived as arrogant and aggressive by an Asian counterpart. In Asia, a soft handshake, a humble posture, and avoidance of eye contact convey an attitude of respect. In Eastern Europe, a woman may expect to have her hand kissed (this also conveys respect for her as a representative of her gender), and men typically kiss each other on the cheeks. With an extensive Western presence in the countries mentioned, however, the expectation that foreigners should adhere to these patterns of behavior has diminished.

Certain sitting positions may even get one in trouble; for example, a person should not cross his or her legs or show the sole of his or her shoe to another person in the Middle East because the gesture implies that the person is "worthy of being stepped on,"[11] or, according to other interpretations, "likened to a shoe sole."

chronemics The timing of verbal exchanges.

Chronemics refer to the timing of verbal exchanges. Americans expect prompt responses and are uncomfortable with a slow response or silence. They attempt to fill in the silence and further probe into the issue at hand to ensure that their counterparts understand them. Other nationalities—the Japanese, for instance—prefer to use this "quiet time" as contemplation time, in which they evaluate the message. Often, translation comes in handy in this situation, especially if the negotiating parties understand each others' languages. Consecutive translation often provides the time necessary to digest and interpret messages, thus eliminating the need for the additional contemplation time. Often, the translator familiar with the Americans' discomfort with silence will intervene and explain that the time is being used for contemplating the deal.

haptics The use of touch while conversing.

Haptics refer to the use of touch while conversing. Again, this nonverbal communication is rarely used by Anglo-Americans, who prefer to keep others at the periphery of their "bubble." Latinate cultures tend to make extensive use of touch in order to convey their messages. A woman could expect to have not just her shoulders, arms, and hands touched, but also her hair and face, all with good intentions.

kinesics The movement of part of the body in order to communicate.

Kinesics refer to the movement of part of the body in order to communicate. Compared with many cultures, Americans gesture very little while communicating. The French and Italians, however, use hand gestures frequently to express themselves. It is important to understand the meanings of these gestures to function efficiently in these cultures. At the same time, it is wise not to assume that the gestures used in one's home country are identical with those used in other countries. It is possible, for example, that those gestures may have no meaning in other cultures, or, worse yet, they may have meanings other than those one would like to convey. For example, the sign of "OK" commonly used in the United States signifies "zero" in France, is a symbol for money in Japan, and is a vulgar gesture in parts of South America, as a company that had this sign printed quickly found out.[12]

One of the most difficult movements to interpret is head shakes. Western gestures such as shaking the head up and down to signify "yes" and from side to side to signify "no" have different equivalents in other cultures. In the Middle East, people raise their head in a haughty manner to say "no," while sometimes accompanying the gesture with a click of the tongue. "No" is conveyed with a wave of the hand in front of the face in parts of Asia, and with a shake of the finger from side to side in Ethiopia. On the other hand, the U.S. gesture to slit one's throat means "I love you" in Swaziland, folding one's arms conveys respect in Fiji and arrogance in Finland, and the list continues. . . .[13]

Paralinguistic refers to nonverbal aspects of speech that include emotional intonation, accents, and quality of voice. Again, a louder, more aggressive intonation denoting self-assurance and strength in some cultures, such as that of the United States, may be perceived as threatening or insulting by other cultures, where softness is equated with politeness and respect. In the cultures of West Africa, laughter indicates embarrassment, discomfort, or surprise, whereas in some other cultures, laughter is discouraged altogether.[14]

Although many people view North Americans as fairly loud and aggressive, the Spanish speak even louder, often shouting at each other to express enthusiasm.[15]

Appearances refer to one's physical attire and overall grooming. Each culture has its own expectations and norms with regard to what is appropriate in different circumstances. For example, Western business attire for men consists of a well-tailored dark suit, complemented by a conservative shirt and tie and elegant shoes; Western business attire for women may also consist of a well-tailored suit or a conservative dress and high heels. European dress codes allow for a more casual look or a more personal style than North American dress codes. In the Middle East, depending on the country, men's business attire may consist of a *gallabeya* (a long, typically white garment) and a head cover, whereas women in business may have their hair covered, while wearing an equally long, conservative dress, known as the *hijab*.[16]

In South Asia (India, Pakistan, Bangladesh, Nepal, and others), appropriate business attire for women may be the traditional *sari*, typically an exquisitely embroidered or designed material that is wrapped using a specific pattern. In Africa, women wear a similarly colorful outfit, but taking the form of a gown with country-specific prints—a *bou-bou* (pronounced "boo-boo"); men wear a short-sleeve shirt with a political party pin attached and a pair of slacks, with the exception of the most formal circumstances, when a coat and tie are worn.

Olfactions refer to the use of odors to convey messages. Typically, such messages have a religious meaning: Incense is frequently used to purify the air of evil presence in both temples and churches, as well as in private homes. Finally, odors are evaluated differently in different cultures. For example, U.S. culture finds body odors and garlic breath as offensive, whereas East Asian cultures avoid consumption of dairy products believed to cause intolerably bad breath.

paralinguistics The nonverbal aspects of speech that include intonation, accents, and the quality of voice.

appearances An individual's physical attire and overall grooming.

olfactions The use of odors to convey messages.

The Nonverbal Language and High- Versus Low-Context Cultures

low-context cultures Cultures in which what is said is precisely what is meant so that the verbal message carries the full meaning of the sentence.

The high-low context continuum defines the extent to which a spoken statement conveys a full message.[17] In **low-context cultures,** what is said is precisely what is meant. For example, in the United States, Canada, Germany, and Switzerland, a verbal message carries the full meaning of the sentence. In this environment, business is typically done at arm's length and change is readily accepted.

high-context cultures Cultures in which the context of a message—the message source, the source's standing in society or in a group, his or her expertise, tone of voice, and body language—are all meaningful parts of the message.

In **high-context cultures,** such as those of East Asia, the Middle East, and North Africa, the entire context of the message—the message source, his or her standing in society or in the negotiating group, level of expertise, tone of voice, and body language—is meaningful. Marketing managers must evaluate the nonverbal communication accompanying a message and interpret the full message accordingly. In low-context cultures, business is conducted via email or on paper, in contract form, whereas in high-context cultures, it is more important to establish solid personal relationships and trust in the process of conducting business. In general, relationships are highly valued in high-context cultures, and, on the social side of commerce, trust is crucial: A handshake in the Middle East is as important and reliable as a paper contract.

5-2b Religion

religion A society's relationship to the supernatural.

Religion defines a society's relationship to the supernatural and, as a result, determines dominant values and attitudes. Religious beliefs are important determinants of consumer behavior: Purchase motivation; consumption preferences and patterns; customs and business practices; attitudes toward authority, family, peers, and foreigners; as well as attitudes toward material possessions, cultural values, and norms, among others, can all be traced to religion.

Religion, then, can be linked to cultural behaviors that have an impact on economic development and marketing. For example,

- The Protestant religion stresses hard work and frugality and is linked to the development of capitalism and economic emancipation.

- Judaism, with its disdain for ignorance and sloth, stresses education and has led to industrial development.

- Islam dictates social etiquette and consumption and bans the use of interest rates, affecting, respectively, the relationship between men and women in society and in the workplace (as will be seen in the section "Religion and Gender Roles"); discouraging the consumption of pork products and alcohol; and requiring procedures to reconcile Islamic banking laws with Western banking practices—by, for example, charging periodic fees, rather than interest.

- The Hindu religion encourages a family orientation and dictates a nine-tier class structure and strict dietary constraints, affecting the workplace hierarchy and discouraging the consumption of animal products—beef, in particular.

- Buddhism stresses sufferance and avoidance of worldly desires, thus, in principle, rejecting most aspects of business.

Assuming that Buddhism has had a negative impact on marketing and economic development is erroneous, however, because a number of the more developed economies in Asia, for instance, are predominantly Buddhist. It is also erroneous to assume that Islamic law affects negatively all credit-granting activity or that, because of the restrictions imposed by gender isolation, marketing to women is impossible in Islamic societies—quite the contrary: These restrictions merely require the use of creative strategies and adaptation to local practices. For example, instead of selling on credit, businesses typically offer price discounts to individuals paying the full cash value, and no discount for those paying in installments. With regard to gender, women can use creative ways to interact (though not directly) with their male counterparts; more recently, the use of email has greatly facilitated a timely interaction between genders at work, even in the most conservative societies.

Finally, the restrictions on consumption do not mean that the respective products are prohibited in a particular country. For example, alcohol is available at diplomatic and other expatriate shops even in one of the most strict of Islamic countries, Saudi Arabia; it is also readily available at regular supermarkets in expatriate enclaves. Pork and pork products are readily available in Islamic countries and in Israel, targeted to the Christian population, and beef is available in India for consumption by Muslim consumers. Even in India, however, fast-food chains having to choose between offending Hindu consumers, by offering beef, or Muslim consumers, by offering pork, have elected to offer chicken, lamb burgers, or vegetarian burgers instead.

Discussions of religions and their relationship to overall consumer/market behavior and, specifically, consumption are offered in the sections "Religion and Business Days," "Religion and Gender Roles," "Religion and Gift Giving," and "Religion and Marketing Practices."

Religion and Business Days

In terms of working days, in countries where Christianity predominates, it is customary to work full days Monday through Friday and a half-day on Saturday. In Islamic countries, businesses are closed on Friday, the holy day of Islam. And, in Israel, the Shabbat (Saturday) is the day of worship when all businesses close.

In addition to noting business days, individuals doing business abroad must also note national holidays, when businesses are usually closed, and religious events/holidays. One religious observance that can substantially affect business operations is the month of Ramadan in the Islamic religion, when observers are not allowed to eat until sundown; this is typically not a productive time in the Near East and North Africa. In Israel, no business is conducted during the High Holidays (Rosh Hashanah and Yom Kippur).

During the regular work week, one should not be surprised if a Muslim with whom he is talking business abruptly ends the conversation by gathering his rug, kneeling on it, and then praying; Muslims are required to pray five times a day at specific times. In this situation, a businessman should just find a seat and wait quietly until the man is finished.[18]

Religion and Gender Roles

In the most traditional Islamic countries, women's business activities are channeled toward interaction in a women-only environment. As such, a salesman cannot engage in door-to-door selling in Saudi Arabia, for instance, in an effort to appeal to the woman of the house. In this country, women depend on men in the family for simple activities, such as driving them to and from a destination; the law does not permit women to drive cars. Personal services can be performed only by individuals of the same gender. For example, women can bank only at women's banks, can have their hair done only by other women, etc. The genders typically do not interact in the very traditional Islamic countries except within the family. Even in the less traditional Islamic countries, women often are seated separately from men (in a separate dining room or area).

Although business is male-dominated in Islamic countries, it should, nevertheless, be noted that women have historically held prominent government positions in countries such as Turkey and Pakistan, for example.

Religion and Gift Giving

A more in-depth discussion of gift giving is offered in section 5-2e, "National/Regional Character." This section will address religious holidays as important opportunities for sales. In countries where Christianity is predominant, holidays such as Christmas and Easter constitute important dates for product sales. In addition to these holidays, Saint Nicholas is celebrated on December 6, when gifts are offered to children, usually placed in their shoes, which are nicely lined up under a window. During the time predating these holidays, promotional activity (advertising and sales promotion) is intense. In Eastern Orthodox countries, such as Greece, Bulgaria, Serbia, Romania, Russia, and the other European countries of the Commonwealth of Independent States, among others, name days (days of the Saints after whom one was named) are celebrated, and gift giving is a must. Days for common names such as Sts. John and Mary are also national holidays.

Diwali is an important Hindu holiday, when the believers engage in a Puja (prayer) and typically wear new clothing. This day also is an important marketing event. The Jewish holiday of Chanukah is also an occasion for exchanging gifts.

Religion and Marketing Practices

Firms often must adapt their offering to the local culture to address consumers' religious concerns. Fast-food restaurants operating in Israel find that they can better serve their Jewish consumers by offering ample choices of vegetarian food, which does not compromise consumer kosher requirements. Keeping kosher requires, among others, the separation of milk products and meat products and implements used to serve or process them; vegetarian products are pareve—neutral, with regard to kosher requirements.

With regard to advertising, substantial censoring occurs in many countries. In Saudi Arabia, women should not be portrayed in advertisements; however, it is appropriate to show the covered arms and wrists of a woman demonstrating product use. For magazines of Western provenance, censorship is enforced; for example, when such magazines are brought into the country by individuals, or when delivered by mail, any area of a woman's uncovered body and her face in photographs are blackened with a marker. In other Islamic countries, such as Malaysia, women should not be portrayed sleeveless, whereas in the streets of Turkey, one can actually see Wonder Bra billboards.

5-2c Cultural Values

values Enduring beliefs about a specific mode of conduct or desirable end-state that guide the selection or evaluation of behavior.

Values are enduring beliefs about a specific mode of conduct or desirable end-state; they guide the selection or evaluation of behavior, and are ordered by importance in relation to one another to form a system of value priorities.[19]

Values guide individuals' actions, attitudes, and judgments, which are derived from and continuously modified through personal, social, and cultural learning, ultimately affecting their product preferences and their perception of products. Cultures are set apart by their *value systems*—the relative importance or ranking of values. Western cultures (North American and Western European) place more stress on success, achievement, and competitiveness, whereas Eastern cultures are more likely to be concerned with social welfare.[20] Examples of universally held values are provided by Rokeach[21] (see Figure 5-1).

Figure 5-1
Instrumental and Terminal Values (Rokeach)
Source: Adapted from Milton J. Rokeach, *The Nature of Human Values*, New York: The Free Press, 1973.

Instrumental Values (the means by which terminal values are achieved)	Terminal Values (goals reached by means of instrumental values)
Ambitious	A comfortable life
Broadminded	An exciting life
Capable	A sense of accomplishment
Cheerful	A world at peace
Clean	A world of beauty
Courageous	Equality
Forgiving	Family security
Helpful	Freedom
Imaginative	Inner harmony
Independent	Mature love
Intellectual	National security
Logical	Pleasure
Loving	Salvation
Obedient	Self-respect
Polite	Social recognition
Responsible	True friendship
Self-controlled	Wisdom

According to this classification, values can be related to goals (*terminal values*) or to the processes whereby one can attain those goals (*instrumental values*).

Members of a culture share a system of meaning, a set of beliefs about what is right or wrong. Values are learned from those with whom individuals are in contact: family, friends, teachers, clergy, politicians, and the media. The process by which individuals learn the beliefs and behaviors endorsed by one's own culture is known as **enculturation.** Learning a new culture, which most managers must do when doing business abroad, is known as **acculturation.** Acculturation encompasses intercultural interaction and adaptation, and it includes the **assimilation** of a new culture, maintenance of the new culture, and resistance to both the new and old cultures. *Consumer acculturation* refers to contact with a new culture and the resulting change for consumers in terms of their approach to consumption in the new environment, whereas *marketer acculturation* refers to contact with a new culture and the resulting change for the marketer.[22]

Acculturation does not necessarily mean abandoning all home country traditions; that is, it does not mean complete assimilation of the new culture. For example, recent Asian Indian immigrants to the United States are less likely to be assimilated in this culture because they maintain their original religious practices, language, food consumption, housing and friendship patterns, as well as contact with India.[23] Although Indian Americans are not easily assimilated, they are, nevertheless, acculturated in the U.S. culture: They consume fast food, shop at supermarkets, root for their favorite baseball team, and, overall, successfully integrate in the U.S. culture, without necessarily being assimilated. On the other hand, descendants of Japanese Americans tend to quickly acculturate to the U.S. culture, and, typically, by the third generation, they are likely to be fully assimilated.[24]

For the marketing practitioner, acculturation means adaptation to the new culture in a manner that would render him or her more readily capable of addressing the needs of the target market in that culture (see Figures 5-2 and 5-3).

enculturation The process by which individuals learn the beliefs and behaviors endorsed by their own culture.

acculturation The act of learning a new culture; encompasses intercultural interaction and adaptation.

assimilation The act of abandoning all home-country traditions while learning a new culture.

Figure 5-2

Exporting culture: Trends are quickly transferred from the United States. European stores carry a vast array of in-line skates and basketballs.

Figure 5-3

Exporting culture: Music from the Andean region in downtown Prague. From Paris to Prague, folkloric groups from Latin America share their musical traditions and market their CDs to European consumers in metro stations, parks, and on the main downtown thoroughfares.

5-2d Cultural Norms: Imperatives, Exclusives, and Adiaphoras

norms Rules that dictate what is right or wrong, acceptable or unacceptable in a society.

Norms are derived from values and are defined as rules that dictate what is right or wrong, acceptable or unacceptable. To be successful in the markets where the firm is currently operating or where it is planning a presence, marketers need to be capable of discerning between the following:

- What an outsider must or must not do (*cultural imperative*)
- What locals may do but an outsider cannot (*cultural exclusive*)
- What an outsider may or may not do (*cultural adiaphora*)[25]

Familiarity with the first two constitutes a minimum requirement for survival in a new country environment. Although most local employees are willing to accept that their foreign counterpart is not fully familiar with local practices, working for a firm that is planning a strong commitment to the respective market may render local representatives and clients less tolerant of ignorance of local customs.

Imperatives

imperatives The norms referring to what individuals must or must not do in a certain culture.

Imperatives refer to what one must or must not do in a certain culture. Respecting rank and position, especially in more formal societies, is crucial in developing a lasting relationship. In Germany, for example, individuals in a close business relationship would address each other formally, by their last names, for decades. A representative of a U.S. firm working in this environment would need to be aware of this expectation (although this individual may be afforded some lenience, as a foreigner, if he or she did in fact address his or her counterpart by first name).

Also, obtaining the appropriate approval before conducting a transaction constitutes an important consideration in doing business abroad. To conduct business in many developing countries, a company needs to become acquainted with local officials at all levels of government and to seek their expertise, as part of a close working relationship. If a company does not, any operation of the firm in the country could come under scrutiny and could be subjected to complications and higher costs. Obtaining the appropriate permissions before building on company-owned grounds, before conducting marketing research, or before approaching potential distributors is crucial in many countries. Among outcomes of noncompliance would be costly delays, the use of expensive alternative middlemen or subcontractors, or even interdiction of operations.

Other examples of imperatives are provided by the special situation women in management positions face when dealing with clients in North Africa and the Middle East. For example, women are not allowed, by law, to drive or walk in public unaccompanied by a male in Saudi Arabia. They are not allowed in the streets, nor in shops by themselves. A female marketing manager sent to this country would have to make arrangements to be chauffeured to client firms, to be permanently in the company of a male in public. She also would have to wear clothing to cover her wrists, ankles, hair, and face. Finally, in many firms, males are not permitted to interact with females. For example, female accountants communicate with male colleagues by sending a tray back and forth through a wall that divides the sexes.

Exclusives

exclusives The norms that refer to activities that are appropriate only for locals and from which individuals from a foreign country are excluded.

Exclusives refer to activities that are appropriate only for locals and from which an individual from a foreign country is excluded. For example, whereas a citizen of Kenya is likely to show allegiance to the government of Mwai Kibak by wearing a pin in his party's colors bearing his picture, a foreigner wearing such a pin would not only raise eyebrows, but he or she also may be perceived as attempting to interfere in the country's internal affairs.

Adiaphoras

Adiaphoras refer to customs that a foreign representative may engage in, but conformity in this respect is not required. Eating with chopsticks in East Asia, drinking banana beer in East Africa, and greeting a woman by kissing her hand in Hungary or Romania are all examples of adiaphoras.

5-2e National/Regional Character

Each country is thought to have a distinct set of behavior and personality characteristics, characteristics that may be shared by a number of countries in a certain geographical region.[26] This section discusses some of the **national and regional characters** that are likely to influence international marketing operations.

Time Orientation

An aspect of time relevant to marketers is related to the manner in which tasks are approached. **Monochronic time** (m-time) is attributed to individuals who usually do one thing at a time, and in sequence. These individuals tend to be prompt and to adhere strictly to agendas; countries where individuals typically operate on monochronic time are Germany, Switzerland, Austria, the Scandinavian countries and the countries of Benelux, the United States, and Canada. **Polychronic time** (p-time) is attributed to individuals who tend to perform multiple tasks at once; for these individuals, time is not linear but, rather, fluid. They are less likely to adhere to schedules, and they consider business as an opportunity for socializing. Countries where individuals operate on polychronic time are Italy, France, Spain, the countries of North Africa and the Middle East, and Latin America. This aspect of **time orientation** explains some of the examples provided in this section, describing attitudes toward time in different parts of the world.

North Americans like to plan their activities or to expedite matters by setting deadlines. Arabs facing deadlines, on the other hand, may feel threatened and would back into a corner.[27] A saying translated as "God-willing tomorrow" means, loosely, "If I feel like it and I have the time, I will take care of it tomorrow or any day thereafter." At times, businessmen in the Middle East arrive late for a meeting or do not arrive at all; they believe that Allah (God) controls time, so punctuality is unimportant. One should not be surprised if a Middle Eastern businessman is not ready for an appointment. It is imperative that one does not criticize this lateness or absenteeism because the individual would most likely become offended and resentful.[28] It should be noted, however, that this behavior cannot be generalized to all business conducted, especially in many of the larger cities or in international joint ventures operating in the region, where punctuality is mandatory and expected.

This behavior is not limited to the Middle Eastern context. In many countries in Sub-Saharan Africa, Southern and Eastern Europe, and Latin America, delays are common. Greeks feel that setting time limits is not only constraining, but also insulting. Latinate cultures, such as those of Latin America and Southern Europe, do not put much premium on punctuality. When one is invited to a dinner party, arriving at the specified time indicates poor manners, suggesting that the person may be very hungry. Arriving half an hour after the indicated time is considered being on time, while arriving one hour late is still no reason to apologize, especially if one is socially prominent. In these same countries, however, for business meetings, it is safer to arrive within 15 minutes of the agreed-upon time.

Business Hours, Business Days

The hours of doing business differ from country to country. The nine-to-five schedule prevalent in the United States is unusual in many countries. In countries where the climate is too hot to permit work at mid-day, businesses open early, at seven, and close for two to three hours at noon, to re-open again at two or three in the afternoon. This is also the case

---

adiaphoras The norms that refer to customs that a foreign national may engage in but is not necessarily expected to do so.

national and regional character A set of behavior and personality characteristics shared by individuals of a certain country or region.

monochronic time The interpretation of time as linear, such that individuals do one thing at a time, and in sequence.

polychronic time The interpretation of time as fluid, such that individuals can accomplish multiple tasks at once.

time orientation The manner in which individuals view time in relation to accomplishing tasks.

for businesses in Latin America and in many countries in Europe, where lunch time is spent at home having a large meal with the family, followed frequently by a nap.

In Spain, individuals and health experts have, for decades, argued for retaining the three-hour-long lunch period, despite changing standards attributed to regulations by the European Union. The long siesta time has been reduced to two hours (with the goal of further reducing it to one hour). At this time, stores are closed and no business is conducted. In recent years in Mexico, the federal government placed a new regulation into effect that brought a cultural revolution to this country: It required government workers to work from 9:00 A.M. to 6:00 P.M., with only one hour for lunch. In the past, as is still the case for most private businesses, employees had time for siesta, after which they had to return to work until later in the evening.[29]

In much of Europe, it is unusual to find someone at the office on Friday afternoons. In many European countries, there is a move toward shortening the work week. For example, the promise of 39 hours of pay for 35 hours of work was the campaign platform that catapulted Lionel Jospin's (former Prime Minister of France) coalition to power in 1997.[30]

As mentioned in section 5-2b, "Religion," working days differ, depending on the dominant religion in the different countries. Where Christianity is dominant, Sunday is a rest day; in Islamic countries, businesses are closed on Fridays; and, in Israel, businesses are closed on Saturdays. In Islamic countries, during the month of Ramadan, observers are not allowed to eat until sundown, and, during the regular work week, Muslims are required to pray five times a day.

Finally, vacation time—designated in Europe as the latter part of July, the entire month of August, and the last two weeks in December—tends to be slow and not very productive for most business activity, with some exceptions. Such exceptions are sales, which often are offered nationally in different countries for two weeks during the latter part of the summer. During this time, retail activity is brisk.

Gift Giving

Knowing what gifts are appropriate to give to one's hosts is very important. Some gifts are considered inappropriate in certain cultures, whereas others may be appropriate on certain occasions and inappropriate on others. In the United States, bringing a bottle of wine to one's host is perfectly appropriate; the same gesture would not be appropriate for a similar occasion in the Middle East, where Islamic religion prohibits alcohol. This rule holds true for any other gifts that may contain alcohol, such as chocolates. Also in the Middle East, bringing food or drink to the home of one's host could represent an insult, implying that the host's food is inadequate.[31]

Other inappropriate gifts are cutlery in Latin America, signifying cutting off a relationship,[32] or handkerchiefs in Latin America and in Southern and Eastern Europe, signifying a final, imposed separation, usually death; handkerchiefs and small hand towels are typically given as gifts at funerals of the Eastern Orthodox faith.

gift giving The norms regarding the gifts that are appropriate to give to others.

Although an even number of flowers (a dozen roses, etc.) constitutes the norm for **gift giving** in the United States, in Eastern Europe, odd numbers are expected, while even numbers of flowers and, especially, calla lilies, are offered only at funerals or religious commemorations. Giving one's host an even number of flowers or calla lilies could even trigger superstitious fears.

In developing countries, gifts of Western provenance such as good-quality pens or t-shirts with (preferably) English writing on them for children would probably meet with appreciation. So would some products that might be unimaginable as gifts in the United States, such as cigarettes, pantyhose, and hairspray. In fact, for more than two decades before the fall of communism, Kent cigarettes constituted the gift of choice in Romania, where they had the added value as commodity money.[33]

Even the manner in which gifts are given is very important. For example, in the Middle East, gifts should be presented publicly to avoid the appearance of bribery, whereas, in Asia, gifts of significance should be given privately, to avoid embarrassment.[34] Nevertheless, gifts such as pens with a company logo or insignia will be graciously accepted, regardless of timing.

Some rituals related to the giving and acceptance of gifts also should be noted. For instance, in many cultures, it is customary for the recipient to refuse the gift so vigorously that the gift giver may be tempted to withdraw it. Such a gesture, however, will meet with a noted disappointment; it is merely appropriate for the recipient to refuse the gift and then accept it reluctantly, but humbly and kindly. The ready, eager acceptance of a gift may be considered as a sign of bad manners or a confirmation of gift expectations.

In the Middle East, the mere admiration of any object in an individual's home will obligate the host to yield that object to the admirer. Although it may be appropriate to decline, such a gesture may be perceived, to a degree, as a rejection of the host's hospitality.

International Marketing Illustration 5-2 offers a synopsis regarding the ethics of gift giving.

International Marketing Illustration 5-2

Gift Giving or Bribe?

Bribing is a way of life in many countries. You cannot park your car without having to bribe the neighboring policeman. You cannot see a doctor without paying a bribe in addition to the doctor's fee. You cannot pass your medical boards, your entrance exam into college, or obtain an exit visa without bribing the appropriate authorities. Leaving the country as a tourist may mean bribing the baggage officer to put your luggage first in line to make sure you go through customs on time; bribing the customs officer to make sure that your luggage will not be turned upside down and inside out in the process of seeking for that elusive illegal gizmo, and bribing the health officer who will permit your exit from the country for a destination that may require immunizations. Does this sound outrageous? In this author's experience, it can take one case of Johnny Walker Red and a case of Kent cartons to pass the university entrance exam; the alternative is working in a factory as an unskilled worker. Does that sound attractive to the average high-school graduate? It could take a pack of Kent or Marlboro cigarettes to have access to quality red meat—meat you, of course, have to pay for. Or it could take two packs to see a marginally competent dentist—more, if he needs to work on your teeth.

Bribing is the price one pays for survival in Russia and the former Eastern Bloc, China, India, Egypt, Indonesia, and many other countries. In these countries, individuals and firms need to bribe to lead good lives, and firms need to bribe to make reasonable profits.

Companies attempt to institute a code of conduct worldwide. They have the same expectations for their operations in the United States and Singapore, where there is relatively strict adherence to norms that shun corruption, as for operations in countries where they would have to offer substantial gifts to government officials, such as expensive pens, watches, or even automobiles, depending on the importance of the contract. Caterpillar states in its code of conduct that, "in dealing with public officials, other corporations, and private citizens, we firmly adhere to ethical business practices. We will not seek to influence others, either directly or indirectly, by paying bribes or kickbacks, or by any other measure that is unethical or will tarnish our reputation for honesty and integrity. Even the appearance of such conduct must be avoided."[35]

The question remains: How can a company maintain such standards and work successfully within the constraints of the Foreign Corrupt Practices Act?

Socializing

If a marketing manager is planning on a working breakfast or a working lunch, or on discussing business over dinner, as is often done in the United States, it may be useful to first inquire about the extent to which such a practice is appropriate in the country where business is being conducted. Although many business partners may have been schooled in the United States and will, consequently, readily acquiesce to these types of working circumstances, other parties involved may feel uneasy if business is conducted during a meal.

In the countries of South America and in many countries in Europe, a meal is widely seen as an important occasion to personally get to know one's business counterpart; hence, the suggestion of a working lunch or dinner may indicate to the local representative a lack of interest in establishing a friendly basis for the future working relationship. For example, it is important not to plan a business meeting at first with a Mexican businessman because he usually prefers to become acquainted with his counterpart in a social atmosphere before doing business.[36]

Similarly, when first meeting a businessman in the Middle East, one should not begin right away with talk about the business at hand; instead, one should initiate "positive small talk." The first meeting in the Middle East is only to start developing a friendly relationship, not to secure business dealings.[37]

In countries such as China, knowing one's business partner socially is imperative because the relationship is seen as a long-term engagement, rather than a short-term, transaction-related one.

Gender Roles

When one engages in business internationally, it is important to understand the role that women are expected to hold in the respective society. In the countries of East Africa and in parts of West Africa (Nigeria, for example), the role of women in business, and particularly in running a business and in sales, is crucial and more important than the role of men. Men still hold an important decision-making role, however, when it comes to major sales or purchase decisions. In India and Pakistan, women share responsibility with men in business. It is noteworthy, however, that women play a more limited role politically, where only a few hold notable positions, despite the famous women leaders who have left important legacies in these countries.

A discussion of **gender roles** in Islamic societies, as well as their impact on marketing activity and consumer behavior, was provided in section 5-2b, "Religion."

gender roles The roles that women and men are expected to hold in a society.

status concern The value placed on symbols of status and on the attainment of high status in a society.

materialism Individuals' degree of concern with material possessions.

Status Concern and Materialism

Related to one's background is one's concern with status, or **status concern**—maintaining it or acquiring it—and with material possessions, or **materialism.** Individuals' concern with status is related to the values placed on symbols of status and on the attainment of high status. Often, the products consumed convey messages about the consumer in the same way that language does.[38] Status—like social class, to which it is related—is easier to transcend in industrially developed countries than in developing countries. In the United States, the Protestant ethic of hard work has led to centuries of individual prosperity and, at the individual level, status advancement; in the United States, it is not perceived as shameful for prominent politicians and businesspeople to refer back to their humble beginnings.

In other countries, including Great Britain, Spain, and many developing countries, one's social class is rigid, and, consequently, one's status remains stable. Expatriates from these countries who have transcended their social class in the United States, for example, typically hide their lower-class origins. Those from developing countries might state, for instance, that they came from the capital city when, in fact, they did not, because of the high likelihood of low-class provenance associated with a village origin.

Due to the influence of 800 years of Moorish control, Spain still has a rigid class structure described as feudal and autocratic.[39] However, countries that historically have had a polarized class structure (for example, Mexico) are developing a middle class or merchant class in response to expanding capitalism.[40]

Within the context of highly hierarchical Asian societies, individuals are always conscious of their place in a group, institution, or society as a whole and of the appropriate behavior, dress, and speech corresponding to status. They also are extremely aware of the need to maintain their own dignity, and face, and that of others. Careful attention is given to purchasing products whose price, brand, and packaging match one's social standing. In terms of personal appearance, the color, material, and style of clothing should match an individual's status, which is defined by age, gender, occupation, and so on. In Japan, for example, a married woman's kimono is much more subdued in color than a single woman's.

One region of the world where status has undergone great changes and individuals have lost "status security" is Central and Eastern Europe. A study on status changes in Romania[41] notes that status, guaranteed during the communist regime by the degree of affiliation with the communist party, has undergone significant changes with the advent of democracy. In the past, nomenklatura members (top communist leaders) enjoyed the highest status and living standard, despite the communists' goal to abolish differences between social classes. In Russia, this same privileged class, before the fall of communism, could rent 100 square meters of living space for a ridiculous price; had the free use of a country home (dacha) in a prime vacation spot; and conspicuously consumed caviar, sturgeon, salmon, and other goods not available at regular shops—something that the average person could not aspire to. They drove foreign cars with low license plate numbers (indicative of high governmental position) at high speeds and without concern for traffic laws, dressed extravagantly, and conspicuously flaunted their Western possessions.[42]

With the transition to a market economy, former party members and intellectuals found that, to survive, they had to accept jobs below their former status, as taxi drivers, sales clerks, and street vendors. At the same time, individuals who had previously held a low status, such as gypsies and blue-collar workers who started lucrative businesses, prospered and, as a consequence, engaged in consumption behavior previously reserved for the party nomenklatura.

Other Cultural and Behavioral Differences

Many other national and regional character differences also require companies to adapt their marketing practices. For example, as Figure 5-4 illustrates, people use different means of transportation to purchase products and get about in their daily lives. In the United States, most marketing strategies address a driving public, the shopper who can park at a strip mall and load the contents of an extra-large shopping cart into the family

Figure 5-4

Other cultural and behavioral differences: In Bangladesh, buses with upper-level decks are a common means of transportation, whereas, in Holland, bicycles are very common and they have their own paths that parallel most roads. In the United States, most marketing strategies address a driving public, but in other countries, marketers need to focus on the behavior of consumers using a different type of transportation.

van. In much of the rest of the world, things are quite different. For example, Western Europeans might take their bicycles to the supermarket and use automobiles only to drive to out-of-town destinations. In Central Asia and Sub-Saharan Africa, buses with crowded upper-level decks or trucks with protective bar grids are used for local and long-distance transportation. These consumers are likely to transport goods in crowded environments where they must also keep their balance. A typical fast-food drive-through is not likely to be the most efficient means for serving these consumers.

5-3 Cultural Variability

Cultural variability is the term used to identify differences between cultures using the Hofstede dimensions. All cultures can be classified based on a number of dimensions. Each dimension should be thought of as a continuum. Section 5-3a presents the Hofstede dimensions: power distance, uncertainty avoidance, masculinity, and individualism.[43]

5-3a The Hofstede Dimensions

Power Distance

Power distance refers to the manner in which interpersonal relationships are formed when differences in power are perceived. In some cultures, a vertical relationship is typical, whereas, in others, relationships are based on equality and informality. In the United States, for instance, individuals customarily address each other on a first-name basis, regardless of rank. Top managers often illustrate their solidarity with the lower ranks by engaging in work activities that they do, going to the plant floor or eating in the workers' cafeteria. In other countries (in Latin America, Eastern Europe, the Middle East, for example), it is a flagrant mistake to address a superior informally or for a superior to mingle with underlings. In these countries, most decisions are determined by the upper-level executives and only much later disseminated to individuals in the lower positions. This is one of the reasons why, in this environment, it is particularly important to address the senior management first, before addressing other individuals in the company.[44] When one does business in a country where relationships are of a vertical nature, it is important to find out who is one's counterpart in the partner firm or the individual in the government responsible for regulating the activities of one's firm before even approaching the business in question.

Uncertainty Avoidance

Uncertainty avoidance refers to the extent to which individuals feel threatened by uncertainty, risk, and ambiguous situations and thus adopt beliefs, behaviors, and institutions that help them to avoid the uncertainty. In countries where uncertainty avoidance is high, there is a feeling that what is different is dangerous: Consumers are resistant to change and focused on risk avoidance and reduction. In cultures low in uncertainty avoidance, there is a feeling that what is different, such as new products and services, is interesting and worth exploring.[45] In this regard, it is interesting to observe the changes taking place in the transition economies of China and Central and Eastern Europe. Traditionally, these cultures are high in uncertainty avoidance, primarily due to the communist system's assurances of work, a home, and a minimal standard of living. During the transition period, however, attitudes toward risk manifested themselves strongly, with some (especially the older generations) holding on to the status quo and rejecting privatization and all change, and with other, younger individuals taking unwarranted risks. Overall, most in this region continue to manifest symptoms of high uncertainty avoidance, electing (or supporting, in the case of China) conservative, welfare-oriented governments. Despite this trait, however, with regard to consumption, consumers here are eager to experience new products from different parts of the world and are open to new market offerings, such as food establishments and other services.

In another example, Belgian consumers, who are higher in uncertainty avoidance, prefer insurance that is higher in price but that does not have variable fees, whereas the Dutch, who are low on uncertainty avoidance, prefer lower-priced insurance with variable fees.[46]

cultural variability The classification of cultures on a number of dimensions, or continuums; Hofstede classified cultures on the dimensions of collectivism, masculinity, power distance, and uncertainty avoidance.

power distance The manner in which interpersonal relationships are formed when differences in power are perceived.

uncertainty avoidance The extent to which individuals are threatened by uncertainty, risk, and ambiguous situations and thus adopt beliefs, behaviors, and institutions that help them to avoid the uncertainty.

Masculinity

Masculinity is the degree to which a national culture is characterized by assertiveness, rather than nurturing. **Femininity** is the degree to which a national culture is characterized by nurturing, rather than by assertiveness. Masculine societies emphasize values such as wealth, material success, ambition, and achievement; whereas, in feminine societies, benevolence, equality, caring for the weak, and preserving the environment are emphasized.[47] In masculine societies, such as those in Australia, Canada, Great Britain, and the United States, successful marketing strategies focus on consumers' achievement motivation: Marketing communications should stress personal accomplishment and have ego appeal. In feminine societies, such as in Asian cultures, marketing strategies should steer away from a materialist, acquisitive focus and, instead, appeal to consumers' sense of good will.

> **masculinity** The degree to which a national culture is characterized by assertiveness, rather than nurturing.

> **femininity** The degree to which a national culture is characterized by nurturing, rather than assertive, values.

Individualism Versus Collectivism

Individualism refers to the degree to which people in a country prefer to act as individuals, in their self-interest, rather than as members of a group—which is a characteristic of collectivist societies. In individualist cultures, such as those of the United States, Great Britain, and Australia, the social fabric and group norms are much looser: People tend not to follow social norms but, rather, make decisions and initiate behaviors independently.[48] Such cultures stress the individuals' ability to achieve personal goals, make their way in life on their own, and, in the process, seek self-fulfillment and excitement. Collectivist cultures, such as those of Latin America, Asia, and the Middle East, stress subordination to the collectivity (group, business, family), and require acting in the interest of the group, rather than in one's self-interest. Cultures tend to evolve from collectivist to individualistic as countries become more industrialized,[49] and as individuals become less conformity oriented.

> **individualism** The degree to which people in a country prefer to act as individuals, in their self-interest.

Although Asia, with 50 percent of the world's population, is culturally more heterogeneous than, for example, Europe, the emphasis on social harmony is an overriding and unifying belief across all societies. Asian societies are fundamentally collectivist. This is considered necessary in order not to disturb social harmony. Such thinking grounded in Confucianism, Buddhism, and Islam contrasts sharply with Western individualism. The difference is profound and has major implications for consumer behavior. Whereas Asians tend to identify themselves in terms of their social frame or relationships, Westerners define themselves in terms of personal attributes or achievements. Despite the fact that individualism has come to be considered a natural component of "modern" society, Asian cultures are now challenging this assumption. Japan, a "modern," industrialized nation by any standard, is still strongly collectivist. South Korea, Singapore, and Taiwan combine features of modern societies with a firmly entrenched **collectivism** orientation.[50] See Table 5-1 for the cultural positioning of countries on the Hofstede dimensions.

> **collectivism** The degree to which individuals prefer to act in the interest of the group, rather than in their own self-interest.

Table 5-1	**Expected Country Dimension Scores (0=Low; 100=High)**		
Uncertainty Avoidance	**Power Distance**	**Masculinity**	**Individualism**
100			
Japan	China	United States	United States
			Australia
Eastern Europe	Eastern Europe	Argentina	United Kingdom
50			
United States	Germany, United States	China	China
1			

International Marketing Illustration   5-3

Learning about National and Regional Culture

Numerous resources can be used to learn about national and regional cultures. A valuable resource is the CultureGram produced by Brigham Young University. In addition to placing the country on the world map, it also provides country background information, such as information on the land, climate, and history, as well as information on the people—population, language, religion, general attitudes, and personal appearance. Information on customs and courtesies includes greetings, gestures, visiting, and eating, whereas lifestyle information addresses issues about the family, dating and marriage, diet, recreation, the arts, holidays, and commerce. Society-related discussions address the government, the economy, transportation, communication, and health. The CultureGram also has an events and trends section, a section that offers recipes and information on local famous people, the correct pronunciation of the country's name in the national language, and the national anthem.

To illustrate, for Bulgaria, the site offers a discussion of the preponderance of folk dance and traditions in the lives of Bulgarians. It also offers advice on interpreting gestures: For Bulgarians, "yes" is indicated by shaking the head from side to side, whereas "no" is expressed with one or two nods. The site also advises that leaving a party early is considered inappropriate and rude. In another example, we learn that Bahrain consists of 33 islands, of which only 3 are inhabited. Bahraini citizens are highly educated in the region, but they are the minority in a country where more than two thirds do not hold Bahraini citizenship. Access CultureGrams at www.culturegrams.com.

Additional sources for national culture information are the *Country Reports* of the Economist Intelligence Unit (www.eiu.com) and the Department of Commerce *Country Commercial Guides* (www.ita.doc.gov), among others.

International Marketing Illustration 5-3 discusses one resource that students can use to learn more about the culture within a country or world region: the CultureGram.

5-4 Cultural Change and Marketing

Being aware of the particulars of any culture may not be enough to succeed. Culture is undergoing continuous change all over the world as a result of external influences. For example, a manager obtains textbook training in business practices in a certain country. That textbook will probably not fully prepare the manager for all the changes in the cultural environment of the respective country that he or she can expect. Cultural training should involve immersion in the culture of the country, an understanding that goes beyond the world of business. Companies that are aware of the importance of such training go to great lengths to offer it. Consider, for instance, the case of Samsung, which spends $80,000 a year per person for employees to go abroad and literally goof off (go to malls, watch people, etc.), convinced that cultural immersion is likely to better help them understand what the customers of that country want.[51]

To appeal efficiently to a new market, marketers need to identify the symbolic elements and cultural meanings that are important to a market segment and use them effectively in creating the marketing mix. For example, the meaning of a fast-food joint in the United States is quite different from its meaning in other cultures. McDonald's and Pizza Hut are perceived in some cultures as trendy, fashionable places (see Figure 5-5).

Figure 5-5
The cultural meanings of McDonald's and Pizza Hut vary from country to country. In emerging and developing countries, they are not just fast-food joints; they are the hip place to take a girlfriend out on a date, the location where business is transacted, and where lifetime commitments are celebrated.

Marketers can use the following checklist[52] to integrate culture when designing a marketing strategy:

1. *Research* the present and possible symbolic elements and cultural meanings in consumers' lives.
2. *Identify* cultural meanings and physical properties of the product.
3. *Design* the product and packaging accordingly.
4. *Design* the marketing campaign using symbolic elements that carry cultural meanings.

5-5 The Self-Reference Criterion and Ethnocentrism

When interpreting cultural phenomena in other countries, marketers must avoid the unconscious reference to their own value systems, to their own way of doing things; that is, they should refrain from resorting to the **self-reference criterion,** as defined by Lee.[53] Instead, they should assess each culture as objectively as possible. Lee suggests a four-step correction mechanism to address individuals' tendency to resort to the self-reference criterion, which is herein adapted to a marketing context:

1. Define the marketing problem or goal in terms of one's home country's cultural traits, norms, and values.
2. Define the marketing problem or goal in terms of the host country's cultural traits, norms, and values.
3. Isolate the self-reference criterion influence and evaluate it to understand how it affects the marketing problem.
4. Redefine the marketing problem and, in the process, eliminate the self-reference criterion influence. Solve the marketing problem based solely on the unique conditions of the host country.

self-reference criterion
Individuals' conscious and unconscious reference to their own national culture, to home-country norms and values, and to their knowledge and experience in the process of making decisions in the host country.

Negative outcomes of using the self-reference criterion are inflamed nationalist feelings or antiforeigner feelings targeting a particular company—even if the foreign company relies extensively on local suppliers and locally manufactures most products. The French frequently perceive Americans as imposing their way of life and their culture on the rest of the world without any sensitivity to the local culture. For the French, symbolizing these views are, among others, McDonald's, Coca-Cola, and Disneyland Resort Paris; Disney has often been referred to as an attempt to "McDonaldize France." Americans are successfully selling their fast food in a country where food preparation and serving constitute an art form, they are successfully selling mindless Hollywood action movies in a country that prizes high culture and art films, and, more recently, Americans have been arm-wrestling Europe, where natural foods are prized, into permitting the imports of hormone-treated beef. As expected, Gallic resentment and retaliation are omnipresent: A few years ago, 150 farmers in southwestern France (in Auch) occupied a McDonald's restaurant and slapped posters that said "No to the American dictatorship" and "No hormones in foie gras country." Similarly, one restaurant, Creperie Domino, charged $8 per Coca-Cola bottle, instead of a little more than $1 (its regular price).[54]

Worldwide, there is a decline in the number of people who like and use, or desire to use, American brands: NOP World, a global research firm, found that McDonald's, Coca-Cola, Microsoft, and Nike were among the brands that suffered a decline in popularity and international consumer trust. A survey of 30,000 consumers in 30 countries outside North America found that the total number of consumers who use U.S. brands fell from 30 percent to 27 percent, whereas non-American brands remained stable. Blame can be attributed to U.S. actions in Iraq and the abuse of prisoners at Abu Ghraib, the refusal to sign the Kyoto agreement, and a general disaffection with U.S. culture and policies.[55]

ethnocentrism The belief that one's culture is superior to another and that strategies used in one's home country (presumably a developed country) will work just as well internationally.

Ethnocentrism is a belief related to the self-reference criterion, that a particular culture is superior to another and that strategies used in the home country (presumably a developed country) will work just as well abroad. Many examples illustrate the fallacy of this strategy in situations in which it is unwarranted. Attempting to sell clothes dryers in rapidly developing markets where the cost of electricity continues to remain high relative to a family's monthly income has resulted in failure, as have television advertisements aired in a conservative country, depicting a woman describing in detail the use of a feminine hygiene product.

A related concept is *consumer ethnocentrism*, the belief that purchasing foreign products is wrong because it hurts the domestic economy, causes loss of jobs, and is plainly unpatriotic.[56] Although ethnocentric attitudes are, to a degree, related to the standard of living and economic performance in a country at a particular point in time, it is important to note that consumer ethnocentrist tendencies frequently affect foreign firms. The North American Free Trade Agreement was, to a certain extent, diminished by ethnocentric feelings in the United States; similarly, in the 1990s, the potential of Japanese businesses in the United States did not entirely materialize due to strong ethnocentric feelings of U.S. consumers, many of whom felt that they had an obligation to buy American.

5-6 The Global Consumer Culture

Global consumer segments—consumers who associate similar meanings with certain places, people, and things—have developed worldwide and, with them, a global consumer culture. The global consumer culture is defined in terms of shared sets of consumption-related symbols, such as brands, and consumption activities that are meaningful to segment members. A global consumer culture is often attributed to the diffusion of entertainment from the United States to the rest of the world and to the dominance of English in both business and entertainment.[57] For example, MTV reaches viewers in more than 140 countries, and, among teens everywhere except for Africa, 8 out of their top 10 activities are media related. The direct outcome of this is a "global mall," whereby teens display the signs of this global culture by buying CDs, hamburgers, jeans, and running shoes—veritable emblems of the teen global culture.[58]

The global consumer culture has been identified as involving one or more of these trends:

- The proliferation of transnational firms and their brands worldwide and the related globalized capitalism
- Globalized consumerism and the desire for material possessions (the desire for fashionable or novel goods used to gain status and social acceptance)
- Global consumption homogenization, wherein consumers worldwide eat similar foods, desire similar brand names, and are exposed to the same entertainment

In addition to the described consumption behavior, certain gift-giving occasions have been adopted in many parts of the world where both traditions and religion are different from those in the industrialized Western world. Examples of such occasions are Christmas in Muslim countries where gifts are exchanged on New Year's Day, Valentine's Day in many countries of the world (including most of Western Europe) where it was not previously celebrated, and, increasingly, Halloween. Santa Claus (even in Buddhist, Muslim, and animist cultures), much like products such as Coca-Cola, represents the symbol of a consumer paradise widely imagined to exist in the United States.[59]

In response to an increasingly global consumer culture, marketers have devised marketing programs that appeal to individuals who would like to feel one with this culture. Among such messages are "United Colors of Benetton," "ADM, Supermarket to the World," and Philips' "Let's Make Things Better," which feature individuals and synopses from different countries. Such strategies are examples of **global consumer culture positioning** and identify a particular brand as a symbol of a given global culture.[60] Such positioning is typically accompanied by the extensive use of English in environments where English is not widely spoken: As the primary language of international business, the mass media, and the Internet, English currently represents modernism and internationalism to many consumers. It is also accompanied by aesthetic styles, which are increasingly identified to belong to the global consumer culture: among others, the use of widely known spokespeople in advertising.[61] Examples of such endorsers are Michael Jordan for Nike, Roger Moore for Lark Cigarettes, Harrison Ford for Kirin Beer, and Jodie Foster for different Japanese soft drinks.

According to Alden, et al., this strategy is different from **local consumer culture positioning,** which associates the brand with local cultural meanings, reflects the local culture, is portrayed as consumed by locals, and/or is depicted as locally produced for local people. For instance, Chevy trucks and Dr. Pepper have been positioned as part of the "American" way of life.

The strategy also differs from **foreign consumer culture positioning,** whereby the brand is positioned as symbolic of a foreign culture. For example, Hermes in the United States is positioned as a desirable French product. Yoplait yogurt also emphasizes its French origin with the slogan "C'est si bon"— "it's so good"—(whereas, in France, its slogan is "La petite fleur"—"the little flower"). And men in lederhosen sing into the Alphorn with the Matterhorn mountain as the backdrop for the Swiss Ricola cough drops, while Juan Valdez stresses the quality of pure Colombian coffee. In Japan, Coca-Cola advertising shows young Japanese driving on American desert roads, stopping for a drink at a remote truck stop, and instantly gaining locals' acceptance by consuming Coke. All these examples illustrate successful foreign consumer culture positioning strategies, focusing on desirable countries of origin for the different product categories.

global consumer culture positioning Marketing programs appealing to individuals who want to be part of a global consumer culture by purchasing a brand that is a symbol of that culture.

local consumer culture positioning Positioning that associates the brand with local cultural meanings, reflecting the local culture, and portrayed as consumed by locals and/or depicted as locally produced for local people.

foreign consumer culture positioning The positioning of a particular brand as symbolic of a desired foreign culture.

Summary

- **Identify the elements of culture and examine how they affect marketing practices around the world.** Culture, a society's personality, represents a totality of shared meanings, rituals, norms, and traditions shared by members of society. Its elements are language (verbal, written, and nonverbal), religion, values, and norms. They have a significant impact on consumer behavior and marketing practices in general, delineating gender roles, rules for gift giving, and appropriate behaviors in a business setting; they also create rules for individual interaction. International marketing managers must be familiar with local culture, practices, and expectations and behave in accordance with those rules.

- **Describe national and regional character based on dimensions such as time orientation, business practices, gift giving, socializing, gender roles, and materialism.** Traits such as time orientation, degree of status concern, and materialism at the societal level; rules for socializing; and gender roles are important to master for one to be able to perform optimally in a country's environment. Such knowledge should be used in determining the appropriate settings for transactions, the appropriate messages that should be used in advertising, and, in general, all interactions with local society.

- **Discuss cultural variability in terms of the Hofstede dimensions with appropriate examples and address cultural change in a marketing context.** Hofstede suggested four dimensions for classifying cultures that could benefit the marketing manager in deciding on the appropriate behavior. Those dimensions are power distance, which refers to interpersonal relationships when there are differences in power between the respective individu-

als; uncertainty avoidance, which refers to the extent to which individuals take risk in the respective culture; masculinity, which is the degree to which a culture is characterized by assertiveness; and individualism—the degree to which people prefer to act as individuals in their own self-interest—and collectivism—the degree to which people prefer to act as members of a group.

- **Address the self-reference criterion and ethnocentrism and describe how they impede mutual understanding and cooperation, with direct negative effects on marketing practices.** Two impediments to cross-cultural relationships are the self-reference criterion, which is the unconscious reference to one's own values and way of doing things, and ethnocentrism, the belief that one's culture is superior to others. Marketing managers must refrain from using self-reference or from adopting ethnocentric attitudes in the process of making decisions related to local operations.

- **Describe the global consumer culture as it manifests itself around the world.** The advent of a global consumer culture has created important opportunities for multinational firms: similar segments of consumers who share brand preferences; share a taste for similar consumer goods and services, such as fast food and entertainment; and respond similarly to a company's marketing strategies. Marketers are using three strategies to target consumers: global consumer culture positioning, which identifies brands as symbols of a particular global consumer culture; local consumer culture positioning, which targets the local consumer culture and portrays products as consumed by local consumers; and foreign consumer culture positioning, whereby the brand is positioned as symbolic of a foreign culture.

Key Terms

acculturation
adiaphoras
appearances
assimilation
chronemics
collectivism
cultural variability
culture
ecology
enculturation
ethnocentrism
exclusives
femininity
foreign consumer culture positioning
gift giving

global consumer culture positioning
haptics
high-context cultures
ideology
imperatives
individualism
kinesics
language
local consumer culture positioning
low-context cultures
masculinity
materialism
monochronic time
national and regional character
nonverbal communication
norms

oculesics
olfactions
orientations
paralinguistics
polychronic time
postures
power distance
proxemics
religion
self-reference criterion
social structure
spoken/written language
status concern
time orientation
uncertainty avoidance
values

Discussion Questions

1. How does religion affect international marketing and international business operations in a target market?

2. What are the different cultural norms and values, and how do they differ around the world?

3. Margaret Hogan is an international marketing manager planning to accept an assignment representing her company interests in Saudi Arabia. What are some of the cultural elements that will have an impact on her performance? How can she best prepare for this assignment?

4. Many messages aimed at consumers in Central and Eastern Europe have a status message. Why? If you were assigned to work in this environment, would you, as a manager, show solidarity with the workers and symbolically work alongside them in the factory? Explain.

5. How do managers use the global consumer culture to position their goods in the local market?

Chapter Quiz (True/False)

1. A sari is considered appropriate business attire for women in South Asia.
2. In high-context cultures, what is said is precisely what is meant.
3. Little attention to business is paid during the High Holiday month in the Islamic religion, when observers are not allowed to eat until sundown.
4. Acculturation is the learning of beliefs and behaviors endorsed by one's own culture.
5. Learning a new culture is known as assimilation.
6. In Japan, Coca-Cola advertising that includes a Japanese man driving through American desert roads is an example of foreign consumer culture positioning.

Multiple Choice

1. Which of the following is a terminal value?
a. ambition
b. cleanliness
c. freedom
d. joy
2. The process by which individuals learn the beliefs and behaviors endorsed by their own culture is
a. acculturation.
b. enculturation.
c. assimilation.
d. none of the above
3. The norms referring to what individuals must or must not do in certain cultures are
a. adiaphoras.
b. exclusives.
c. imperatives.
d. none of the above

Endnotes

1. Alan L. Gilman, "Stay Afloat in Foreign Expansions," *Chain Store Executive*, Vol. 70, No. 5, May 1994, p. 193.
2. Sami Abbasi and Kenneth W. Holman, "Business Success in the Middle East," *Management Decision*, Vol. 31, No. 1, 1993, pp. 55–59.
3. Lisa Penaloza and Mary C. Gilly, "Marketer Acculturation: The Changer and the Changed," *Journal of Marketing*, Vol. 63, No. 3, July 1999, pp. 84–104.
4. Raj Mehta and Russell W. Belk, "Artifacts, Identity and Transition: Favorite Possessions of Indians and Indian Immigrants to the United States," *Journal of Consumer Research*, Vol. 17, March 1991, pp. 398–411.
5. Michael R. Solomon, *Consumer Behavior*, Fourth Edition, Upper Saddle River, NJ: Prentice Hall, 1999.
6. Jean-Claude Usunier, *International Marketing—A Cultural Approach*, Upper Saddle River, NJ: Prentice Hall, 1993.
7. Ibid.
8. For this and many other examples of blunders of translation, see David A. Ricks, *Blunders in International Business*, Oxford, U.K.: Blackwell Publishers, 1993.
9. Ibid.
10. Abbasi and Holman, "Business Success in the Middle East," pp. 55–59.
11. Ibid.
12. Ricks, *Blunders in International Business*, 1993.
13. Ibid.
14. Ibid.
15. Roger Colles, "Spain—A Hot Prospect," *Resident Abroad*, November 1993, pp. 16–20.
16. In countries where this type of dress is expected of women, those same women will be encountered only in a business environment that excludes the presence of males.
17. E. T. Hall, *Beyond Culture*, Garden City, NY: Anchor Press, 1976.
18. Abbasi and Holman, "Business Success in the Middle East," pp. 55–59.
19. See Milton J. Rokeach, *The Nature of Human Values*, New York: The Free Press, 1973; and Jan-Benedict E. M. Steenkamp, Frenkel ter Hofstede, and Michel Wedel, "A Cross-Cultural Investigation into the Individual and National Cultural Antecedents of Consumer Innovativeness," *Journal of Consumer Research*, Vol. 63, April 1999, pp. 55–69.
20. Solomon, *Consumer Behavior*, 1999.
21. Rokeach, *The Nature of Human Values*, 1973.
22. Penaloza and Gilly, "Marketer Acculturation," pp. 84–104.
23. Mehta and Belk, "Artifacts, Identity and Transition," pp. 398–411.
24. See Darrell Montero, "The Japanese Americans: Changing Patterns of Assimilation over Three Generations," *American Sociological Review*, Vol. 46, December 1981, pp. 829–839; and Mehta and Belk, "Artifacts, Identity and Transition," pp. 398–411.
25. Ricks, *Blunders in International Business*, 1993.

You can find the correct answers to these questions by taking the quiz and then submitting your answers in the Online Edition. The program will automatically score your submission. Where you miss a question, the program will provide the correct answer, a rationale for the answer, and the section number in the chapter where the topic is discussed.

26. Terry Clark, "International Marketing and National Character: A Review and Proposal for Integrative Theory," *Journal of Marketing*, No. 54, October 1990, pp. 66–79.

27. Ricks, *Blunders in International Business*, 1993.

28. Abbasi and Holman, "Business Success in the Middle East," pp. 55–59.

29. Julia Preston, "A Downsized Lunch Unsettles a Mexican Rite," *The New York Times*, October 17, 1999, p. 7.

30. Suzanne Daley, "A French Paradox at Work," *The New York Times*, Business Section, November 11, 1999, pp. 1, 27.

31. Ricks, *Blunders in International Business*, 1993.

32. Ibid.

33. Guliz Ger, Russell W. Belk, and Dana-Nicoleta Lascu, "The Development of Consumer Desire in Marketizing and Developing Economies: The Case of Romania and Turkey," in L. McAllister (ed.), *Advances in Consumer Research*, Association for Consumer Research, Vol. 20, 1993, pp. 102–107.

34. Ricks, *Blunders in International Business*, 1993.

35. www.cat.com

36. Perry A. Trunick, "Culture and Custom Combine with Logistics," *Transportation and Distribution*, Vol. 35, No. 1, January 1994, p. 38.

37. Abbasi and Holman, "Business Success in the Middle East," pp. 55–59.

38. David K. Tse, Russell W. Belk, and Nan Zhou, "Becoming a Consumer Society: A Longitudinal and Cross-Cultural Content Analysis of Print Ads from Hong Kong, the People's Republic of China, and Taiwan," *Journal of Consumer Research*, March 1989, Vol. 15, March 1989, pp. 457–472.

39. Cyndee Miller, "Going Overseas Requires Marketers to Learn More than a New Language," *Marketing News*, Vol. 28, No. 7, March 28, 1994, pp. 8–10.

40. Trunick, "Culture and Custom Combine with Logistics," p. 38.

41. Dana-Nicoleta Lascu, Lalita A. Manrai, and Ajay K. Manrai, "Interpersonal Influences on Shopping Behavior: A Cross-Cultural Analysis of Polish and Romanian Consumers," in J. Bloemer, J. Lemmink, and H. Kasper (eds.), *European Marketing Academy Proceedings*, Vol. 3, 1994, pp. 1369–1371.

42. Ibid.

43. Geert Hofstede, *Culture's Consequences: International Differences in Work-Related Values*, London: Sage, 1984.

44. Abbasi and Holman, "Business Success in the Middle East," pp. 55–59.

45. Steenkamp, Hofstede, and Wedel, "A Cross-Cultural Investigation," pp. 55–69.

46. Ibid.

47. See Hofstede, *Culture's Consequences*, 1984; and Steenkamp, Hofstede, and Wedel, "A Cross-Cultural Investigation," pp. 55–69.

48. Steenkamp, Hofstede, and Wedel, "A Cross-Cultural Investigation," pp. 55–69.

49. Harry C. Triandis, "The Self and Social Behavior in Differing Cultural Contexts," *Psychological Review*, Vol. 96, July 1989, pp. 506–520; and John A. McCarty and Patricia M. Hattwick, "Cultural Value Orientations: A Comparison of Magazine Advertisements from the United States and Mexico," *Advances in Consumer Research*, Vol. 19, 1992, pp. 34–38.

50. Hellmut Schutte, "Asian Culture and the Global Consumer," *Financial Times*, November 1998, Mastering Marketing, Part Two: Understanding Consumers, pp. 2–3.

51. "Korea's Biggest Firm Teaches Junior Execs Strange Foreign Ways," *Wall Street Journal*, December 31, 1991, p. 1.

52. Adapted from Grant McCracken, "Culture and Consumer Behavior: An Anthropological Perspective," *Journal of the Market Research Society*, Vol. 32, No. 1, January 1990, pp. 3–11.

53. James A. Lee, "Cultural Analysis in Overseas Operations," *Harvard Business Review*, March–April 1966, pp. 106–114.

54. Craig R. Whitney, "Food Fight: French Impose Own Tariffs," *The International Herald Tribune*, July 31–August 1, 1999, p. 9.

55. "How the American Dream Became a Global Nightmare," *Marketing Week*, June 3, 2004, p. 32.

56. Terence A. Shimp and Subhash Sharma, "Consumer Ethnocentrism: Construction and Validation of the CETSCALE," *Journal of Marketing Research*, Vol. 24, No. 3, August 1987, pp. 280–289.

57. See Dana L. Alden, Jan-Benedict E. M. Steenkamp, and Rajeev Batra, "Brand Positioning through Advertising in Asia, North America and Europe: The Role of Global Consumer Culture," *Journal of Marketing*, Vol. 63, No. 1, January 1999, pp. 75–87; and Guliz Ger and Russell W. Belk, "I'd Like to Buy the World a Coke: Consumptionscapes of the 'Less Affluent World,'" *Journal of Consumer Policy*, Vol. 19, No. 3, September 1996, pp. 371–404.

58. Chip Walker, "Can TV Save the Planet?" *American Demographics*, Vol. 18, May 1996, pp. 42–49; and Alden, Steenkamp, and Batra, "Brand Positioning through Advertising," pp. 75–87; and Edna Gundersen, "MTV, at 20, Rocks on Its Own," *USA Today*, August 1, 2001, http://www.usatoday.com/life/television/2001-08-01-mtv-at-20.htm.

59. See Ger and Belk, "I'd Like to Buy the World a Coke," pp. 371–404.

60. Alden, Steenkamp, and Batra, "Brand Positioning through Advertising," pp. 75–87.

61. Ibid.

62. Harriet Marsh, "Variations on a Theme Park," *Marketing*, London, May 2, 1996, p. 14.

63. David Koenig, *Mouse Tales: A Behind-the-Ears Look at Disneyland*, Irvine: Bonaventure Press, 1994.

64. Ibid.

65. "Euro Disneyland SCA," International Directory of Company Histories, Vol. 20, December 1997, pp. 209–212.

66. Gail Ghetia, "As American as French Fries: Euro Disneyland, When It Opens, Will Feature Typically American Restaurants," *Restaurant Hospitality*, August 1990, p. 20.

67. "Euro Disneyland SCA," pp. 209–212.

68. "The Kingdom inside a Republic," *The Economist*, April 13, 1996, p. 66.

69. Juliana Koranteng, "Euro Disney Revenues Rise," *Amusement Business*, August 6, 2001, p. 38.

70. ———. "Future May Be Bright for Euro Disney," *Amusement Business*, May 21, 2001, p. 19.

71. "Euro Disneyland SCA," pp. 209–212.

72. Marsh, "Variations on a Theme Park."

73. Ibid.

74. Barbara J. Mays, "French Park Still Negotiating for Airline Partnership," *Travel Weekly*, April 20, 1992.

75. "The Kingdom inside a Republic," *The Economist*.

76. Barbara Rudolph, "Monsieur Mickey: Euro Disneyland Is on Schedule, but with a Distinct French Accent," *Time*, March 25, 1991, pp. 48–49.

77. Ibid.

78. Marsh, "Variations on a Theme Park."

79. "The Kingdom inside a Republic," *The Economist*.

80. Juliana Koranteng, "Taking It to the Tube: Parc Asterix to Unleash National TV Campaign," *Amusement Business*, February 11, 2002, p. 6.

81. Koranteng, "Euro Disney Revenues Rise."

82. "Business: Trouble in the Royaume Magique: Euro Disney," *The Economist*, Vol. 372, No. 8387, August 7, 2004, p. 57.

Case 5-1

Disneyland Resort Paris: The Challenges of Cultural Adaptation

Disneyland Resort Paris was known as Euro Disney in its first incarnation on the European continent. After its launch in April 1992, many name changes were made with the purpose of distancing the company from bad publicity.[62] After four different name revisions, the Disney Corporation has settled on Disneyland Resort Paris.

The idea of expanding the Disney magic to Europe proved to be a project that involved more attention to marketing than even this advertising giant could handle. Many Europeans did not want the American dreamland to distract their children, economy, and countries from their own home-grown successful entertainment. David Koenig, author of *Mouse Tales: A Behind-the-Ears Look at Disneyland,* commented, "To the Parisian intellectuals, Disneyland was a symbol of everything contemptible about America: artificial, unstimulating, crass, crude, for the masses. Yet here was a 5,000 acre Disneyland springing up half an hour from the Louvre."[63]

From the beginning, the Disney Corporation had the best of intentions for its European operation. After the successful opening of Disneyland Tokyo, the company was ready for its next international challenge. The company believed that locating the theme park in close proximity to Paris, France, would both ensure growth for Disney and offer an opportunity for it to incorporate different European cultures. It envisioned a Discoveryland that incorporated the histories of European countries through its fairytales: Italy for Pinocchio, England for Alice in Wonderland, and France for Sleeping Beauty's chateau.[64]

In its first incarnation as Euro Disney, the company failed in many aspects of its marketing strategy:

- Euro Disney failed to target the many different tastes and preferences of a new continent of more than 300 million people; addressing the needs for visitors from dissimilar countries, such as Norway, Denmark, and Germany, on one hand, and Spain, Italy, and France, on the other, was a challenge.
- Disney's high admission costs were 30 percent higher than a DisneyWorld ticket in the United States, and the company refused to offer discounts for winter admissions.
- Euro Disney ignored travel lifestyles of Europeans: Europeans are accustomed to taking a few long vacations, rather than several short trips, which would fit with the Disney model.[65] The company also neglected to consider national holidays and traditional breaks when Europeans are more likely to travel.
- Its restaurants did not appeal to visitors. Morris Nathanson Design in Rhode Island, which was responsible for designing the restaurants for Euro Disney, designed classic American-style restaurants. Most Europeans consider American-style

restaurants as exotic and unusual; unfortunately, the Europeans did not respond well to this format.[66]
- Euro Disney assumed that all Europeans wanted gourmet meals, which is not the case. Although French consumers tend to live a more lavish lifestyle and spend larger amounts for gourmet meals, many other consumers in Europe do not—especially when they have to also spend large amounts on air travel, resorts, and park entrance fees. Meal scheduling was also problematic: The French, for example, are accustomed to having all businesses close down at 12:30 for meal times, but the park's restaurants were not made to accommodate such larger influxes for meals, leading to long lines and frustrated visitors.[67] Finally, Euro Disney initially had an alcohol-free policy, which did not fit with local traditions, where wine is an important part of the culture.

Disney's failed marketing strategy for Euro Disney led to below-average attendance levels and product sales; the park was on the edge of bankruptcy in 1994, with a loss per year of more than a billion dollars.[68] Changing strategies—as well as its name, to Disneyland Resort Paris—led to increased revenues by 2001 of more than 4 percent, with operating revenues increasing by $32 million to $789 million.[69] Net losses also decreased from $35.4 million to $27.6 million.[70]

With a full-scale change in the company's marketing direction, Disneyland Resort Paris has been successful in attracting visitors from many countries. Access was a priority for Disney. The company worked on access to the park via the fast train—the TGV; it also worked deals with the EuroStar and Le Shuttle train companies.[71] Disney negotiated deals with trains and airlines to reduce prices—a move that ultimately benefited all; the price for transportation to Disney has dropped by 22 percent since the park's opening.[72] In 1992, the Walt Disney Company negotiated with Air France to make it the "official" Euro Disney carrier.[73] For visitors from the United Kingdom, British Airways is the preferred carrier of Disneyland Resort, and British Airways Holidays, its tour subsidiary, is the preferred travel partner.[74]

Disney also adapted targeting strategies to individual markets to address the interests and values of different segments of European consumers. It placed representatives around the world with the task of researching specific groups of consumers and creating the best package deals for potential visitors; new Disney offices were established in London, Frankfurt, Milan, Brussels, Amsterdam, and Madrid.[75] Research results led to the tailoring of package deals that were in line with vacation lifestyles of the different European segments. In addition to the package deals, Disney

continued

offered discounts for the winter months and half-price discounts for individuals going to the park after 5:00 P.M.

To better accommodate its guests, Disneyland Resort Paris revised its stringent no-alcohol policy, allowing wine and beer to be served at its restaurants. The resort hotels also lowered their room rates and offered less expensive menu choices in their restaurants.[76] The restaurants created more suitable food options, catering to different regional European tastes, but continued to offer large American-size portions.[77] Crepes and waffles are on the menu of almost every street stand in the park (see Figure 5-6).

Mickey Mouse and Donald Duck have French accents, and many rides were renamed to appeal to French visitors: in Adventureland, Le Ventre de la Terre (Galleries under the tree), l'Ile au Tresor (Treasure Island), La Cabane des Robinson (Robinsons' Cabin); in Fantasyland, Le Chateau de la Belle au Bois Dormant (Sleeping Beauty's Castle, rather than Cinderella's Castle at Disney World, United States; see Figure 5-7), Blanche-Neige et les Sept Nains (Snow White and the Seven Dwarfs), Le Carrousel de Lancelot (see Figure 5-8), Le Pays des Contes des Fees; and in Discoveryland, L'Arcade des Visionnaires, Le Visionarium (a time-travel adventure with Jules Verne), Les Mysteres du Nautilus (Nautilus's Mysteries).

The French-named attractions exist alongside attractions such as Main Street U.S.A., with its Main Street Station, vehicles and horse-drawn streetcars (see Figure 5-9); and Frontierland, with Thunder Mesa River Boat Landing, Legends of the Wild West, Rustler Roundup Shootin' Gallery, and other similar themes. The hotels also have more traditional American themes—New York, Newport Bay, and Sequoia Lodge.

Figure 5-6
This stand sells waffles for 2.45 Euros (waffles are primarily a dessert in Europe), Vittel water, Fanta, and Coca-Cola.

Figure 5-8
Le Carousel de Lancelot

Figure 5-7
Le Chateau de la Belle au Bois Dormant (Sleeping Beauty's Castle) in the background.

Figure 5-9
Main Street, U.S.A.: Disneyland Railroad Main Street Station

The park also has numerous attractions that appeal to European guests in general, such as Pinocchio's Fantastic Journey (see Figure 5-10), and Cinemas Gaumont, which feature live concerts with performers from around the world.

Along with creating an environment of greater appeal to European visitors, Disney changed the name of its resort to Disneyland Resort Paris. In its advertising strategy, the company decided to focus its efforts on brand building, initially targeting consumers with a new communication strategy implemented by Ogilvy & Mather Direct.[78] Disney changed its advertising, aiming its message at Europeans who did not grow up with Mickey Mouse; in the park's new commercials, parents and grandparents are shown delighting in the happiness of their children and grandchildren. The advertisements feature "children impatient to depart for and thrilled to arrive at the Magic Kingdom or a grandfather delighted by his grand-daughter's excitement at the prospect of seeing Mickey; or grown-ups sitting tensely before riding on the Space Mountain."[79]

The park is also working with Red Cell, a leading Paris-based advertising agency, for all its television campaigns for the park's new attractions.[80]

Disney capitalized on its European success by offering yet another grand theme park adjacent to Disneyland—the Walt Disney Studios. Disney promoted Walt Disney Studios in a manner that did not cannibalize attendance at Disneyland Resort Paris.[81] Among its attractions are a Rock'N'Roller Coaster Starring Aerosmith, capitalizing on the U.S. band's success in Europe; Animagique; and Cinemagique. The park is dedicated to the art of cinema, animation, and television, and it focuses on the efforts of many Europeans who made it all possible to bring fantasy to reality.

Yet not all is well in Mouseland. After the terrorist attacks of 2001, the number of foreign tourists visiting France fell significantly. The second park was supposed to boost visitor numbers from around 12 million to 16–18 million, a level that would bring profitability; yet years and 600 million Euros of construction costs later, there are still only about 12 million visitors for both parks combined. And new hotels not owned by Euro Disney are taking

Figure 5-10
Pinocchio's Fantastic Journey

away market share from the older Disney hotels. The difficulty can also be due to a mix of French political anti-Americanism and elite snobbery.[82]

Analysis Suggestions

1. How do the values and lifestyles of European consumers differ from those of consumers in the United States? Discuss the Disney failure to address European consumers' preferences based on the respective values and lifestyles.
2. A large proportion of the park's visitors come from Spain and Latin America. How can Disneyland Resort Paris appeal more effectively to this market? Design a new target marketing strategy aimed at the Spanish and Latin American market.

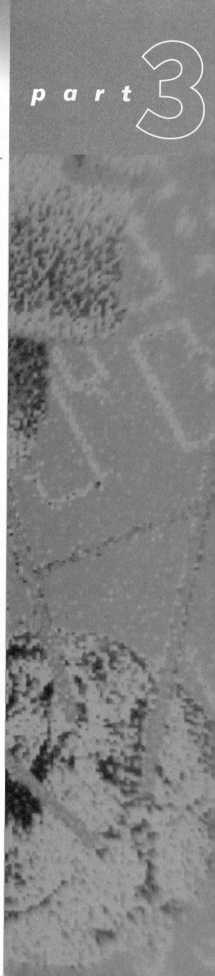

part 3

International Marketing Strategy Decisions

6

International Marketing Research: Practices and Challenges

Chapter Objectives

By the end of this chapter, you should be able to

1 Define international marketing research and provide a description of its immense scope; offer examples of each type of research conducted in international marketing.

2 Describe the steps involved in the international marketing research process while addressing, for each step, the international constraints involved.

3 Introduce the concept of decision support systems for international marketing and describe the sales forecasting process.

International marketing managers operating in unfamiliar environments need to have a thorough understanding of their target market if their marketing efforts are to be successful. Numerous marketing plans fail due to an incomplete understanding of the market. Companies selling consumer products are especially prone to experiencing difficulties in foreign markets. Many such examples exist: An American manufacturer of cornflakes tried to introduce its product in Japan but failed; the Japanese were simply not interested at that time in the concept of breakfast cereals.[1] Also in Japan, Procter & Gamble did not take

into consideration women's needs for a thinner diaper due to high frequency of changes and limited storage space, and their market share was quickly eroded by a local competitor that provided thinner diapers in line with market demands.[2]

Similarly, an ad for Procter & Gamble's Ariel detergent in Romania in the early 1990s portraying Dracula frightened at the sight of Ariel-cleaned white bedsheets assumed that Romanians were familiar with the Bram Stoker novel. TV viewers wondered at the count's reaction to a bedsheet, which had little to do with the story of Dracula as they knew it: Vlad the Impaler (Dracula) was a noble leader of the Romanian fight for independence from Ottoman dominance. Nowadays, the Bram Stoker version is widely known, and the P&G ad makes sense. One way to ensure that such blunders are averted is to engage in a thorough market analysis.

This chapter defines marketing research and examines its broad scope across all components of the marketing mix (product, place, price, and promotion). The chapter addresses the international marketing research process and the complexities of the process in an international setting.

6-1 The Need for International Marketing Research

Marketing managers need to constantly monitor the different forces affecting their international operations. Marketing information, which should constitute a basis for all executive action, must be taken into consideration to improve the chances of success in a complex global environment. Such information, though amply available in highly developed, industrialized nations, needs to be carefully evaluated and viewed in light of the purpose for which it was collected. In developing countries, relevant data may not be available at all, and, if available, it is often questionable in terms of both quality and integrity. For example, production and sales data reported may be tainted by pressures of governments on factories to exceed unrealistic plans or production quotas.

International marketing research is especially complex. International managers are likely to encounter not only the obstacles they have learned to master when conducting research in their own countries, but also obstacles laden with the specifics of the international market where they are conducting the research, specifics that may differ substantially from those of their national market. Consider, for instance, a male marketing researcher working for a haircare firm interested in launching its lines in the beauty salons of the Middle East. In the United States, it is perfectly appropriate for this individual to assess interest in the company's product line by collecting data in beauty salons. In most countries in the Middle East, however, women's beauty parlors cater exclusively to women (men's barber shops cater exclusively to men), and the presence of males in this environment would constitute a breach of Islamic law, which forbids males from seeing a woman's hair if they are not closely related.

Another aspect of the difficulty of engaging in research internationally is readily observable in Eastern Europe, where consumers remain suspicious of attempts by foreigners and locals to investigate local markets and related consumer behavior. Consumers are simply not accustomed to responding to opinion polls and regard such attempts as an intrusion or as suspect. And, since the transition to capitalism, prospective respondents are also likely to promptly demand payment for any time and effort demanded by the investigation.

These and many other environmental factors encountered in international marketing research complicate the task of marketing researchers, who should have not only an expertise in the most advanced techniques of scientific inquiry, but also a profound understanding of the markets under investigation.

6-2 Defining International Marketing Research

international marketing research
The systematic design, collection, recording, analysis, interpretation, and reporting of information pertinent to a particular marketing decision facing a company operating internationally.

We define **international marketing research** as follows:

> *International marketing research is the systematic design, collection, recording, analysis, interpretation, and reporting of information pertinent to a particular marketing decision facing a company operating internationally.*

This definition of international marketing research contains a caveat also present in the general definition of marketing research: an acquired understanding of the market environment. In an international setting, the environment is particularly complex, and it displays obvious and important subtle differences in culture, religion, customs and business practices, and general market characteristics from the environment of the company's home country.

6-3 The Scope of International Marketing Research

International marketing research has a broader scope than domestic research: Managers will need additional information to compensate for lack of familiarity with the foreign environment. Sections 6-3a through 6-3f describe some general research categories (see Figure 6-1).[3]

6-3a Research of Industry, Market Characteristics, and Market Trends

Studies of industry, market characteristics, and market trends—often in the form of acquisition, diversification, and market-share analyses—are conducted regularly by marketing research suppliers and shared with subscribers. This topic will be further addressed in the "Secondary Data" section. Export research is yet another type of research in this category; it is prompted by the shortening of the product life cycle and the intensity of international competition, as well as by the rapid technological change that increases the need to segment markets more frequently.[4] The research techniques range from formal methods, such as focus groups and concept testing,[5] to more informal approaches.

6-3b Buyer Behavior Research

buyer behavior research
Research examining brand preferences and brand attitudes.

Examining brand preferences and brand attitudes falls into the category of **buyer behavior research.** In recent years, this type of research was conducted by DuPont, which, for

Types of International Marketing Research

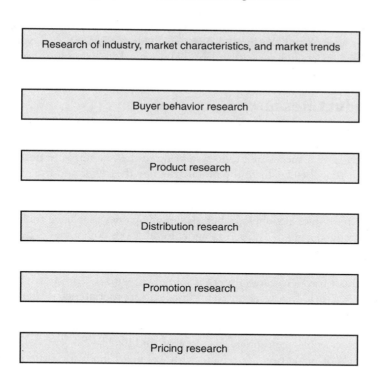

Research of industry, market characteristics, and market trends

Buyer behavior research

Product research

Distribution research

Promotion research

Pricing research

Figure 6-1
The Scope of International
Marketing Research

six months performed qualitative and quantitative research in 20 countries with more than 85,000 respondents. In the process, the company found that 64 percent of the consumers interviewed perceived clothing made with DuPont Lycra to be of better quality, whereas 45 percent indicated that they wanted stretch in their wardrobe, and a total of 30 percent actually asked for Lycra apparel.[6] As a result, DuPont launched its first global advertising campaign to promote Lycra apparel to men and women ages 21–49 with a household income of more than $35,000, and to teenage girls ages 12–17 throughout the Americas, Europe, and Asia.[7]

In most Asian countries, uncertainty is strongly avoided, resulting in high brand consciousness, brand loyalty, greater insistence on quality, and consumers' active reliance on reference groups and opinion leaders. People tend to shop in groups, and they are slower to accept new products. Whereas consumers worldwide are concerned about monetary, functional, physical, psychological, and social risks, Asians tend to be more sensitive to social risk than Westerners.[8]

Brand awareness research and **purchase behavior studies** are frequently conducted by companies to assess their position in the market. For example, the International Research Institute on Social Change, a consultancy based in Switzerland and active in 17 markets, launched a study of luxury goods in the United States. A total of 3,000 respondents were interviewed in person at home and were asked, among others, about their familiarity, at least by name, with a set of 34 luxury brands. They were asked the following aided awareness question: "Here is a list of luxury brands. Please indicate which ones you know least by name." The researchers found that, in the United States, brands such as Daum, Christofle, and Bulgari were relative unknowns. Consequently, consumers were less likely to indicate an intention to purchase these brands: The study concluded that the consumers' desire for the brands was limited because awareness was low.[9] The respective marketers could address this problem by launching an awareness campaign for their brands.

Other useful studies that belong to this category are **consumer segmentation studies,** which are conducted to identify profiles of heavy product consumers, as well as occasions for consumption. Using the previous example of the problems faced by Procter &

brand awareness research
Research investigating how consumers' knowledge and recognition of a brand name affect their purchasing behavior.

purchase behavior studies
Research aimed at evaluating consumers' reaction to and interaction with a company's products.

consumer segmentation studies
Research conducted to identify market segment profiles.

Gamble Japan when marketing Pampers to Japanese mothers, it is evident that the company might have benefited from a study of diaper use rate. Linking the heavy use of diapers (Japanese mothers change their children more frequently than mothers in other regions of the world) and the limited space available for storage in a typical Japanese home, the company could have easily identified the need for less bulky disposable diapers in this market.

6-3c Product Research

concept development and testing studies Concept tests usually performed in developed countries evaluating the product/service offering and the related marketing mix in light of the different international target markets.

Concept development and testing studies are usually performed in developed countries by the firms' research and development departments. When going international, firms usually already have a successful product to bring to the marketplace; nevertheless, it is still important that they evaluate the product/service they offer and the related marketing mix in light of the different target markets, regional and local.

brand name generation and testing The testing of brand names and logos, necessary when companies market their products internationally.

Brand name generation and testing is used not only in the consumer goods industry, where its importance is obvious, but also in companies that have traditionally marketed their products regionally, such as agricultural goods companies. These companies need to test brand names when they market their products internationally. For example, when American Cyanamid Company created a new global herbicide-tolerant crop production system, it used a research firm that started out with 600 possible names and then narrowed the list to 30 that were tested for linguistic appropriateness. After the company decided on the Clearfield brand, it then tested this brand and one other choice in seven different countries for six different crops. Testing showed the Clearfield name and logo to be meaningful, credible, appropriate, memorable, and likable.[10]

The annals of marketing are replete with examples illustrating the importance of testing a brand name in different countries. International Marketing Illustration 6-1 addresses challenges that marketing managers have faced in the process of deciding on brand names.

product testing Studies that estimate product preference and performance in a given market.

Product testing identifies the extent to which the product conforms to local tastes. For example, PepsiCo Foods International decided to undertake extensive product testing in China before introducing its Cheetos snack food brand. The outcome of the test was not favorable: Respondents indicated that they did not like the cheesy taste of the snack. As a result, PepsiCo's local joint-venture Guangzhou Frito-Lay decided to get rid of the cheese and replace it with cream and steak flavors. Sales increased dramatically.[11]

Other types of studies that would be appropriate are competitive product studies, which are helpful in determining the overall product strategy for the product, the price that the market will bear for the respective product category, the promotion that is appropriate in light of the competition, etc.

product packaging design studies Studies that evaluate consumers' reaction to a package, the extent to which the package adequately communicates information to the consumer, and the distribution implications of the package.

As for **product packaging design studies,** firms need to take into consideration consumers' reaction to the package, the extent to which the package adequately communicates information to the consumer, and the distribution implications of the packaging decisions. For instance, in many emerging markets, packaging distinguishes between local products and international products. In Poland and Romania, many local dairy products are available in recyclable glass jars, have no brand name (just the product name, such as yogurt, kefir, etc.), and may contain only the dairy's address information. International products, on the other hand, come in colorful, sophisticated, disposable packaging. To the local consumers, however, simple packaging represents freshness and a lack of additives; after researching this phenomenon, a Romanian-German joint venture offered to the market dairy products in simple, recyclable glass packaging, rather than in sophisticated, disposable packaging.

The choice of package color is another important dimension that necessitates researching. One color could have different meanings in different countries: Green signifies abundance in North Africa and the Middle East, disease in the Amazon region, and healthful contents in North America.

In another example, Primus, a Belgian beer manufactured under license in Rwanda, is sold in one-liter bottles, rather than in the 33cl bottles that most other Western beers

International Marketing Illustration

6-1

Naming the Brand

Marketers often rush to international markets with proven products. However, a product successful in the home country does not guarantee product success abroad. The reason for a product not performing optimally could be its brand name. Rolls-Royce planned on marketing its Silver Mist in German-speaking countries only to find out before the launch that "mist" means "dung" in German. Sunbeam Corporation, however, entered the German market without testing the name of its product, Mist-Stick, before introduction. In other examples, a Finnish brewery introduced two new beverages in the United States, Siff beer and Koff beer, both unsuccessful.

Adapting the brand name so that it will appeal to the local market can bring substantial benefits to the company. For example, U.S. brands enjoy substantial success in China in part due to their well-translated meaning; for example, in Chinese, *Coca-Cola* means "tastes good and makes you happy," *Keebler* means "rare treasure," *Ford* means "happy and unique or special," and *Marlboro* means "a road with 10,000 treasures." Choosing an appropriate brand name is more than simply a translation exercise; the translation should consider the local culture, norms, tradition, and history to ensure an optimal appeal.

In the case of global products, it is important to research their meanings in different languages. Kodak, Exxon, Xerox, and Ajax are examples of product names selected only after extensive testing. Frequently, companies may have to come up with different names for products to ensure their acceptance in each region or country. As a result of brand-name–testing research, Maxwell House introduced its product under the name Maxwell Kaffee in Germany, Legal in France, and Monky in Spain.

Sources: Lily C. Dong, "Brand Name Translation Model: A Case Analysis of U.S. Brands in China," *Journal of Brand Management*, Vol. 9, No. 2, 2001, pp. 99–115; Charlotte Clarke, "Language Classes," *Marketing Week*, Vol. 20, No. 17, July 24, 1997, pp. 35–39; and David Ricks, *Big Business Blunders*, Homewood, IL: Dow Jones, 1983.

use in this market. In researching the Rwandan market, Primus found that the Rwandan consumer typically drinks beer at night, sharing with family and friends. Research also showed that beer is usually purchased and transported on foot for distances of one or two kilometers. Consequently, the bottles are typically sold in crates of 12 fitted such that they could be easily transported on one's head, allowing the individual to also carry other goods.

Test marketing is another important research procedure belonging to the product research category. Procter & Gamble test marketed Swiffer, a disposable mop, in Cedar Rapids, Iowa, and Sens, France, among other disparate markets. The company hoped to craft an international new-product success with the goal of evaluating whether a consistent brand image could be achieved in a number of major markets.[12] This research was the first step that now defines the company's strategy: to introduce the product worldwide in 18 months, rather than in the traditional four to five years.[13] In other examples, Kraft Brand Foods International tested a branded coffee shop variety aimed at vendors and coffee shop operators; the company tested the brand in universities in the United Kingdom, Germany, and Sweden[14] and subsequently engaged in a successful launch.

test marketing Testing new-product performance in a limited area of a national or regional target market to estimate product performance in the respective country or region.

6-3d Distribution Research

The distribution function is particularly important in international marketing, where special attention should be given to import/export regulations and practices, and where companies are well advised to engage in comprehensive analyses. For example, **import/export analyses** aid companies in identifying the logistics companies most capable of handling the paperwork and getting products through customs in a timely and cost-effective manner. The U.S. government and state governments in the United States are often instrumental in helping with this type of research.

Researching individual exporter and importer expertise and local influence is crucial to the success of the firm in a particular market. In one example, a small U.S. firm attempted to export older, high-quality Louis XV armchairs from Romania to the United States. In the process, the firm obtained the appropriate documentation from the State Patrimonium Commission, attesting to the fact that these armchairs were not antiques, nor important local historical artifacts; however, at customs, the firm through its local export company (a vestige of the former communist firm ROMTRANS) encountered obstacles that prevented it from exporting the armchairs. Only after contacting a different and much smaller firm, owned by a close relative of a top government official in the former communist regime, was the U.S. firm given clearance to export the armchairs. This same influential firm arranged for the chairs to be shipped via the Romanian airlines Tarom directly to New York at a fraction of the cost of the initial shipment that would have taken one month by truck to Hamburg and by ship to New York. Had the U.S. firm researched the local import/export service providers, it would have found that influence is crucial for the success of transactions. Of course, it should be noted that this type of influence often crosses the boundary of ethics and legality and could, potentially, cause problems for the company.

Trade with Turkmenistan can serve as an example of the importance of researching specific requirements imposed on importers by the local government. The government of Turkmenistan tightly monitors all foreign trade through the State Commodity and Raw Materials Exchange. All import and export contracts must be registered with the exchange at a 0.3 percent commission. According to foreign companies, connections with someone holding a seat on the exchange facilitate registration. It is worth noting that the Turkmenistan president, Saparmurat Niyazov, plays an integral role in the economy. He and a close circle of advisors centrally direct market activity, making all key decisions. To conclude, opportunity for a foreign company wishing to export to Turkmenistan is largely defined by the government's "priority projects."[15]

Consider another example. Kazakhstan is a small but growing market for U.S. consumer goods. Distributing products in this large and sparsely populated country is a challenge. Geography and the inexperience of local wholesale distributors require exporters of consumer products to pay close attention to developing and maintaining a distributor network in this region—a task that is not easy to implement. Most of the population is located in two areas: the Southeast, around Almaty, and the North and Northeast, the republic's industrial and mining centers. Some existing infrastructure already supports distribution. An extensive railway network carries products within Kazakhstan, to other newly independent states (NIS), and to Europe. On the other hand, poor roads and bad telecommunications, when combined with geography, make it virtually impossible to rely on just one regionally based distributor. Smaller foreign companies may wish to start with a small, regionally located distributor and gradually build a countrywide network from there. Larger firms may consider a larger up-front investment to establish their own infrastructure in Kazakhstan.[16]

Another important type of study is that of **channel performance and coverage studies,** which may reveal either that channels need to be further developed at significant expense to the company, or that, in certain markets, particular channels dominate much of the activity in a particular area. Kraft, according to former Philip Morris U.S.A. (Kraft's former parent company) CEO William Campbell, had, for the longest time, delayed entering the Hong Kong market due to the high costs imposed by the dominant

---

import/export analysis Research that aids companies in identifying the necessary logistics that serve their needs in a timely and cost-effective manner.

channel performance and coverage studies Studies investigating whether existing channels are appropriate for communication, if channels exist at all, or whether they are appropriate for international marketing communications.

distribution companies. After many years and little progress in this market, however, Kraft decided, after all, to partner with the top distribution firm that had been instrumental to Kraft's success in Hong Kong.

Finally, **plant/warehouse location studies** are important, as are evaluations of the transport infrastructure (roads, shipping, and warehousing infrastructure). In countries with an underdeveloped infrastructure and/or a mountainous terrain, warehousing is available only in the main cities or just in the capital city. Consequently, distribution to a more remote location is complicated, and firms may elect to avoid it altogether. Research in this regard is important. For example, in the case of Ecuador, transportation between the capital city, Quito, and its second largest city, Cuenca, is facilitated by the well-developed highway system between the two cities, both of which are at a high altitude. Moving products from one location to another should not present problems because the transportation infrastructure is adequate and warehousing facilities exist in both cities. If, however, a firm is to transport goods to Guayaquill from the capital city, it is likely to encounter difficulties because the transportation infrastructure between these two locations is complicated by the terrain. Guayaquill is easily accessible by sea—the route taken by most imported goods and services aimed at the islands' tourist market. Goods from Quito are more likely to be transported by air than by truck.

plant/warehouse location studies Studies that evaluate the appropriateness of plant or warehouse location to ensure that it is in accordance with the limitations of the national environment and with the needs of a company.

6-3e Promotion Research

Promotion research is crucial for companies doing business internationally. By doing such research, the firm evaluates the extent to which it effectively communicates with the market, it ensures that certain promotional strategies are appropriate for that particular market, and, finally, it evaluates the extent to which the local media are appropriate for developing the intended message.

First, in terms of **studies of premiums, coupons, and deals,** it is important to identify the practices in each country where the specific promotion will run. When an agency has developed an idea to run in a number of countries, it first needs to check on the legality of premiums and coupons across those markets. For example, the sales promotion consultancy Black Cat has extensive experience in adapting pan-European strategies to different legislations in different countries. The agency ran a promotion for 3M diskettes, data cartridges, mini cartridges, optical disks, and transparency film, offering millions of prizes. In most European countries, this took the form of an "instant-win" promotion, with the game mechanism in the box; in some countries, such as Germany, however, the promotion had to be adapted to include a "write-in-a-slogan" competition.[17] Similarly, giving away money-off vouchers is legal in the United Kingdom, Ireland, and Spain but illegal in Germany, Norway, and Switzerland, whereas self-liquidating premiums are legal in the United Kingdom, Germany, France, and many other countries but illegal in Luxembourg, Norway, and Switzerland. They may be allowed in the Netherlands, depending on exactly what form these premiums take.[18]

studies of premiums, coupons, and deals Studies that help identify the practices in each target country where a promotion is planned by investigating the practice and legality of premiums, coupons, and special deals.

In addition to the legality of promotional practices, it is important to determine whether consumers are likely to respond to promotions as expected. According to sales promotions experts, the most difficult aspect about promoting in Eastern Europe is that consumers are just not accustomed to entering competitions and sending off coupons.[19] Alternatively, everyone may participate and overwhelm the postal system, as was the case when Pepsi offered a contest in which participants had to mail in bottle caps.

Advertising effectiveness research is frequently conducted to examine the effectiveness and appropriateness of advertisements aimed at individual markets. Frequently, ads that are initially developed for home-country markets and tested there are later used abroad; such ads are frequently dubbed and do not fit with the culture of the local environments where they are broadcast. One example is the Dracula Ariel advertisement previously discussed, but many other such examples exist. For example, Gitanes, a French cigarette maker, advertised its cigarettes on television in developing countries where the average monthly salary is less than $100 per month; the ad sold the good life

advertising effectiveness research Studies conducted to examine the effectiveness and appropriateness of advertisements aimed at individual markets.

by portraying a man driving a Porsche, with a beautiful, tall blonde on his arm (in a country where most women are petite and hardly ever natural blondes).

Media research also is important. First, in terms of media availability, developing countries pose the most problems. For example, in many countries in Central Africa, television is available only for a select few, via satellite. The majority of individuals have access to radio (local, or Deutsche Welle, the German broadcasting company) aimed at the individual countries in the region. The local radio station usually advertises only local service providers and only occasionally, whereas Deutsche Welle does not advertise at all. No advertising exists in locally available newspapers, nor in local magazines (Western publications, bought primarily by the expatriate community, have advertisements aimed only at Western reader markets). Most local advertising is limited to billboards on the main roads to the national airport in the capital city, and most are aimed at the business segment. Occasionally, one may see an ad advertising cigarettes, cola, or rum. In this type of environment, it would be difficult for a company to communicate with prospective customers using advertising; research would most likely indicate that the most effective communication would take place at the point of purchase.

In countries where various media venues are available, it is important to determine which channels, in the case of television, are likely to broadcast advertisements; frequently, the top television channel is government owned and does not carry advertisements (it receives revenues from private subscriptions). In many countries, advertising is broadcast only in between programs, rather than at 10-minute intervals, and consumers often use the advertising time to take a break from television.

Finally, studies pertaining to personal selling activities, such as **salesforce compensation, quota, and territory studies,** are crucial in helping to determine the appropriate strategies for different markets. This material will be examined in greater detail in Chapter 15, "International Personal Selling and Personnel Management."

6-3f Pricing Research

Internationally, pricing research is much more problematic than when it is performed locally, in a developed country. In addition to studies projecting demand, such as **international market potential studies, sales potential studies, sales forecasts, cost analyses, profit analyses studies, price elasticity studies,** and **competitive pricing analyses,** which are typical of most pricing research studies conducted by U.S. firms in the United States, the firm also must look at issues regarding countertrade and currency issues, inflation rates, and a national tradition of bargaining for every transaction, all of which have implications for pricing decisions. These points will be further addressed in section 6-4e, "Designing the Data Collection Instrument," as well as in Chapter 16, "International Pricing Strategy."

At the retail level, pricing decisions could make or break a product. In countries where salespeople typically keep the change, it is important to price the product a few pennies/centimes below the amount that can be paid using larger currency denominations. For example, for a product costing $10.00, pricing it at $9.50 will give the salesperson a $.50 "tip" because customers would not demand change—an important consideration, especially in markets where salespeople have a considerable latitude as to which product they make available to the consumer.

Marketers of consumer goods in Kazakhstan should research sales compensation practices. Potential distributors must be trained thoroughly in selling a given product. Many stores, although privatized, still have not grasped the concept of product marketing and often do not keep track of their inventories. As a result, it can be very difficult to build loyalty among retailers, who will often sell "whatever is available" at any given moment rather than try to establish a solid relationship with suppliers.[20]

Research in cost analysis would reveal that high product certification cost could significantly contribute to the price of a product and ultimately adversely affect its marketability. This is the case in Russia, where the lack of transparency connected with certifying products confronts both foreign and domestic companies. Although such com-

---

media research Studies that evaluate media availability and appropriateness of the medium for a company's message.

salesforce compensation, quota, and territory studies Different studies pertaining to personal selling activities; they are crucial in helping to determine the appropriate strategies for certain international markets.

international market potential studies Studies conducted to evaluate the potential that a particular country offers for a company.

sales potential studies Studies forecasting optimal sales performance.

sales forecast Projected sales for a particular territory.

cost analyses Methods used for projecting the cost of research.

profit analyses studies Studies that estimate product profit in specific international markets.

price elasticity studies Studies examining the extent to which a particular market is price sensitive.

competitive pricing analyses Pricing studies that determine the price the market will bear for the respective product category.

panies are awaiting political solutions to these problems, marketers should be aware and plan ahead for certification. Often, the process may be cumbersome. Generally, there is some choice among the certification centers inside and outside Russia that are accredited to certify a given type of product or equipment. In some cases, however, the product itself may fall into several categories, and two certificates may be required.[21]

6-4 The International Marketing Research Process

Effective international research involves the steps shown in sections 6-4a through 6-4g. Researchers attempting to obtain accurate and reliable information regarding a problem experienced in the firm's international operations are likely to encounter a number of difficulties, such as translation and cross-cultural comparison complications, which do not, as a rule, affect firms engaging only in domestic research. These difficulties will be addressed for each step in the subsections titled "International Constraints."

6-4a Defining the Research Problem and Research Objectives

The first step in the international marketing research process requires the international marketing manager and marketing researcher defining the research problem and jointly agreeing on the research objectives. The complexity of the environment of international operations does not afford marketing researchers the opportunity to have a very clear idea of the specifics that the research study should examine. Instead, they may need to engage in **exploratory research** of the problem to define the relevant dimensions of the problem investigated. Exploratory investigations may help to further define the problem, suggest hypotheses, or even actually identify additional problems that need to be investigated. **Descriptive research,** on the other hand, portrays a situation—for instance, how frequently shoppers in Cairo shop for food items; whether they prefer to shop for meat products in state stores, which are cheaper but offer inferior-quality products, or in private stores, which are more expensive but offer a higher quality and assortment of meat products. Finally, **causal research** examines cause and effect relationships, such as the extent to which Sony's offer of financial incentives to electronics salespeople in Ahmedabad, India, is likely to increase sales of the Sony brand.

> **exploratory research** Research conducted early in the research process that helps further define a problem or identify additional problems that need to be investigated.

> **descriptive research** All research methods observing or describing phenomena.

> **causal research** Research that examines cause-and-effect relationships.

Managers must note that a fine line should be maintained between identifying the problem too broadly—"What are French consumers' entertainment needs?"—or too narrowly—"Will enough French consumers pay an additional 4 Euros to gain access to a specific American movie channel to make an investment in such a business worthwhile?" Better questions are: "What should be the price of this service in order to draw sufficient subscribers?" "What is the interest of French audiences in the movies carried by this channel?" "To what extent would the recently rekindled anti-American feelings affect subscriptions?"

At this point, the researcher, in conjunction with the marketing manager, will set specific research objectives identifying

1. What is the interest of French audiences in the types of movies offered by the American movie channel?
2. How many subscribers will the company have if the subscription costs 4 Euros? 3 Euros? 2 Euros?
3. Will the channel gain customers in spite of the anti-American cultural-dominance feelings in France?

6-4b Developing the Research Plan

The research plan is a blueprint for the study, indicating all the decisions to be made with regard to information sources, research methods, data collection instruments, sampling procedures, data collection methods, data analysis, and, based on these decisions, the projected costs of the research.

6-4c Deciding on Information Sources

After the international manager and researcher define the problem and set the objectives, the researcher must determine the extent to which available information may shed further light on the problem at hand. The researcher will start by identifying information that may shed additional light on the problem and that has been collected either by the company itself (internal) or by some other firm or agency (external)—**secondary data.** The secondary data may, if needed, help the researcher more clearly define the problem and set better objectives. It will also help the researcher pinpoint the type of information that needs to be gathered for the goals articulated in section 6-4a, "Defining the Research Problem and Research Objectives"; the data collected to address the problem at hand is known as **primary data.**

secondary data Data collected to address a problem other than the problem at hand.

primary data Data collected for the purpose of addressing the problem at hand.

conceptual equivalence The extent to which meanings remain the same in different cultural environments.

International Constraints
(for Both Secondary and Primary Data)

Conceptual Equivalence. Concepts have different meanings in different cultural environments. For example, the meaning of "household" in the United States is different from the meaning of "household" in many developing countries. In the United States, a household typically consists of a nuclear family, although this meaning is changing to include increasing numbers of single parents with children or of households with roommates. In developing countries, the household may include the extended family with distant relatives, as well as servants who have chosen to live with the respective families for the rest of their lives.

The urban versus rural distinction also varies from country to country. In the United States, rural areas typically benefit from excellent access to infrastructure; whereas, in many developing countries, rural areas have no electricity, they have poor roads, and the poverty level is very high. In other countries, little distinction exists between urban and rural areas. In a number of communist countries, governments decided to do away with villages so that they could build high-rise apartment buildings to replace quaint village homes. At the same time, some urban areas were (and remain) in a high state of disrepair, such that the newly built villages look much more developed than these urban areas.

Another issue that deserves mention is that many marketing applications in the United States are designed for the typical American who drives a car, shops once a week at a supermarket, and, when the need arises, drives to the mall to purchase department-store goods. In most other countries of the world, however, the population is largely "pedestrian"; consumers shop daily for food (they are unlikely to have refrigerators, or, if they do, the refrigerators are small, fitting under the countertop) and may have to make special and costly plans to take a long trip—using public transportation, rather than a personal car—to a larger city to shop for department-store items. How, then, should researchers study these markets differently than they study the U.S. market? Clearly, practices such as mall-intercept interviewing are not applicable. Imagine, for instance, conducting a research study at the Khan El Khalili bazaar in Cairo or at the "Russian markets" in the Ukraine or Poland where Russians sell household goods. In both scenarios, even a study based solely on observation is logistically complicated, given the crowded, aggressive environment where consumers can barely keep their balance and get around, let alone respond to interviews.

Retailers and service providers differ greatly from one country to another. A drug store in much of the rest of the world outside the United States is known as a simple pharmacy. A pastry shop in the United States is usually a small Mom & Pop retailer selling warm pastries from behind the counter; elsewhere, it could offer an elegant environment much like that of a luxury restaurant that serves only desserts. Similarly, a mall in the United States typically is one huge structure anchored by large department stores; in other countries, a mall could be a centrally located shopping avenue that may or may not be covered (see Figure 6-2) or a pedestrian shopping zone (see Figure 6-3).

Functional Equivalence. Products themselves may be used for different purposes in different country environments. Whereas, in many countries, jewelry is used to advertise status and/or style and to reflect concern with appearance, in countries such as India and Pakistan, jewelry is used as a way to accumulate wealth.[22] Thus, a status scale containing a display of visible wealth such as jewelry will yield results that are not comparable across different environments.

functional equivalence The difference in the purposes for which products may be used in different country environments.

Figure 6-2

A mall is a popular retail establishment in the United States. In Europe, malls often take the form of covered alleys between centuries-old buildings.

F i g u r e   6 - 3
Pedestrian shopping zones are popular in much of Western Europe.

Also, if similar activities have different functions in different societies, they cannot be compared across the respective cultures. Refrigerators are used in some countries primarily to store frozen food, whereas in others, they are used for chilling water and soft drinks. Warranties also have different meanings in different countries. In China, for example, firms are expected to support their products indefinitely, whereas in the United States, firms are much less generous. Finally, in many developing countries in Sub-Saharan Africa and in Eastern Europe, products cannot be returned, even if under warranty.

Problems are particularly frequent in the case of consumer products, where many companies have encountered difficulties in gaining market acceptance. For instance, an American company assuming that similar languages indicate similar tastes found out the hard way that British men saw no functional value in the use of aftershave, considering the use of scents as effeminate. Similarly, Chase and Sanborn, a British company, met with resistance when trying to market instant coffee in France. In France, coffee plays more of a ceremonial role than in Britain; the preparation of "real" coffee represents a touchstone in the life of a French housewife.[23]

Problems also are encountered when companies assume that, if individuals have a certain purchasing power, the market is ripe for time-saving devices that appeal to Western housewives. Standard of living is not necessarily an indicator of such needs, however, particularly in countries where a wide gap exists between the haves and the have-nots. In many middle-class and upper-class families worldwide, household work is done by hired workers, and there is little likelihood that much thought would be given to facilitating their work. Servants themselves perceive time-saving devices as a threat to their job security.

In fact, the immense popularity of Western luxury goods among high-income earners and teenagers in Asia is not necessarily proof that they have joined the rest of the world's Western consumers. They may try some goods, but for different reasons. Brand name goods such as Louis Vuitton bags may be bought more for "face" reasons and the importance of the regard of others than from an individual preference for the product. Remy Martin cognac and Lafitte red wine may not be consumed because consumers really prefer it over local liquor or beer but because of peer pressure. Strong market position can therefore be built on foundations different from those in the West and require different marketing activities—in other words, an approach especially geared toward globalization but more efficient in terms of creating value for the consumers, and, as a result, earning higher returns.[24]

International Marketing Illustration 6-2 offers insights into retailing and consumer behavior in China.

International Marketing Illustration 6-2

A Comparison between Shoppers in China and the United States

A.C. Nielsen's annual reports on Chinese shoppers' habits suggest that foreign retailers have focused on the wrong things, assuming that consumers want a one-stop-shopping experience when, in fact, they do not. Mass retailers such as Carrefour SA and Wal-Mart Stores, Inc. have built hundreds of look-alike sprawling stores offering food, appliances, and housewares but met with declining sales per store and little consumer loyalty. What went wrong? These retailers built these stores around the Western one-stop, infrequent shopping concept. But Chinese consumers prefer to go daily to wet markets—open-air markets selling fresh produce, meat, and dry goods. In fact, wet markets account for more than 80 percent of food expenditures.

Yet, when Chinese consumers do go to supermarkets, they spend more than one hour there, expect the experience to be relaxing and entertaining, and spend relatively little money, compared to consumers in Europe and the United States. Indeed, U.S. consumers expect some entertainment—hence the success of creative supermarket retailers such as Stew Leonard's and the fun product sampling experiences provided by many retailers. However, in the process of enjoying their shopping experience, U.S. consumers spend substantially more compared to their Chinese counterparts.

In other differences, U.S. supermarket consumers shop in bulk at supermarkets once a week, loading the family automobile with large packages of food, freezing meat and vegetables for later consumption, or purchasing these products frozen; in contrast, Chinese consumers place little value on convenience. Overall, Chinese households spend 72 percent on fresh food, 9 percent on frozen food, 9 percent on convenience food and canned food, and the rest (10 percent) on basic necessity food items such as packaged rice, edible oil, sauces, and chicken stock. And, among the fresh food products most often purchased by consumers in China are the following: for fruit, oranges, apples, and bananas; for vegetables, choi sum (Chinese cabbage), lettuce, and beancurd; for meat, lean pork, pork soup bone, and pork spare ribs; and for fish, mandarin fish, golden thread, and big head fish.

Sources: "World Watch," *Wall Street Journal*, March 21, 2003, p. A12; www.acnielsen.com.hk.

Secondary Data

Researchers first must determine whether information is available, and if so, how much. Doing so may aid in gaining insights into the problem at hand. Secondary data are defined as *data collected for a problem other than the problem at hand.*

Secondary data are typically examined first, and they offer the advantage of low cost and ready availability in many of the more-developed countries.

The data that may be most relevant to the researcher's study, however, may not exist, or if it does, it may be dated or unreliable. For example, one company chose to cut costs and use research previously performed by a competitor on a specific Asian market. The study found that such investment had substantial support. After the firm built its plant, however, it noted that conditions had substantially changed since the study had been done. The company's use of an outdated feasibility study caused it to overestimate market potential.[25]

Secondary data can be categorized as *internal,* collected by the company to address a different problem, or collected by the company to address the same problem but in a different country, or *external,* collected by an entity not affiliated with the company.

Internal Secondary Data

internal secondary data Data collected by a company to address a problem not related to the current research question.

Assuming that Reynolds Aluminum Foil is available in Saudi Arabia but not in Sudan, and assuming that the firm has no prior experience in Sudan, **internal secondary data** are useful only if the company has collected similar information from relevant respondents in a country with a similar environment (Saudi Arabia). For example, after considerable research, Reynolds' advertising in Saudi Arabia portrays the hands (with the wrists covered) of a woman preparing a sandwich for storage; an authoritative male voice describes the use of the foil and endorses its use. Because, from a religious perspective, the two countries are similar (although Sudan is less conservative), transferring this advertisement to Sudan will probably work. In this case, an analogy approach is appropriate.

If the environments of the countries are different, however, internal secondary data collected in one country are not useful in the second country. For example, Philip Morris advertises its Lark and Parliament brands in Japan using glamorous American images—scenes of the New York skyline at night, the Golden Gate Bridge, or movie-like clips of 007 in a subway chase or escaping whiskey-drinking bad guys. These advertisements were created as a result of extensive research in Japan, which revealed that Japanese consumers are admirers of many things American. In advertising to the Chinese, Philip Morris found that it cannot communicate using such advertisements: The Chinese are reticent to fully buy into U.S. values; moreover, China bans mass-media tobacco advertising. Thus, the only type of broadcast communication Philip Morris offers this market is an elaborate advertisement, glorifying Chinese culture, on the occasion of the Chinese New Year. Transferring research findings in the Japanese market to China is clearly not appropriate.

External Secondary Data

external secondary data Data collected for purposes other than the problem at hand.

Marketing researchers in developed countries have ample access to different sources of **external secondary data.** They include government sources (provided by different government ministries/departments or bureaus—such as the Census Bureau), international agencies (such as the World Bank, the various United Nations agencies), professional associations, various publications, and Internet sources.

Secondary Data Sources

Researchers must check established sources of information on countries, regions, markets, competitors, and consumers. As a first step, researchers can conduct online searches using search products such as Dialog (Thomson), Lexis-Nexis (Elsevier) and others, as well as Google, Yahoo, and other similar search engines or portals. Additional useful country

Publications	Professional Organizations
Advertising Age	Academy of International Business
Adweek	Academy of Marketing (U.K.)
American Demographics	Academy of Marketing Science
Brand Marketing	Advertising Research Foundation
Brandweek	American Academy of Advertising
Catalog Age	American Marketing Association
Chain Store Age	American Psychological Association
Discount Store News	Asia Pacific Marketing Federation
Marketing	Association Française du Marketing
Marketing and Research Today	Association for Consumer Research
Marketing Management	Australia-New Zealand Marketing Academy
Marketing News	Center for Service Marketing
Marketing Research	Chartered Institute of Marketing
Mediaweek	Direct Marketing Association
Sales & Marketing Management	European Direct Marketing Association
Target Marketing	European Marketing Academy
	Hong Kong Institute of Marketing
	Institute for the Study of Business Markets
	Institut fuer Qualitative Markt und Wirkungsanalysen, Germany
	Interactive Marketing Institute
	Japan Marketing Association
	Market Research Society, U.K.
	Marketing Research Association
	Marketing Science Institute
	Medical Marketing Association
	Sales & Marketing Executives Association
	Society for Marketing Advances

Table 6-1

Sources for Secondary Data: Publications and Professional Associations

resources are the CultureGrams produced by Brigham Young University, previously mentioned in International Marketing Illustration 5-3 in Chapter 5, "Cultural Influences on International Marketing." They provide succinct country background information, information on the people, language, customs, lifestyles, government, economy, and other important facts useful for a summary country analysis (see www.culturegrams.com).

As a second step, researchers can access various publications and national and international marketing associations; examples are offered in Table 6-1.

Research suppliers such as A.C. Nielsen and others offer subscribers extensive information on different markets. Overall, secondary data collected by different research suppliers is quite useful. In the past, U.S. research suppliers dominated the market; nowadays, there are more and more international players. The leading firms in all areas of market research are ranked in Table 6-2.

Researchers searching secondary data internationally are likely to encounter a number of constraints, which are addressed in the next section.

Table 6-2

**The Top 10 Market
Research Organizations**

Rank	Company	Home Country	Global Research Revenues (US$ millions)
1.	VCU N.V.	Netherlands	2,814.0
2.	IMS Health Inc.	U.S.	1,219.4
3.	The Kantar Group	U.K.	1,033.2
4.	Taylor Nelson Sofres Plc.	U.K.	908.3
5.	Information Resources Inc.	U.S.	554.8
6.	GfK Group	Germany	528.9
7.	Ipsos Group S.A.	France	509.0
8.	NFO WorldGroup Inc.	U.S.	466.1
9.	Westat Inc.	U.S.	341.9
10.	NOP World	U.K.	320.0

Source: "Top 25 Global Research Organizations," *Marketing News*, Vol. 37, No. 17, August 18, 2003, p. H4.

International Constraints

In many international markets, information sources may be limited and inaccurate. Although information accuracy is usually closely linked to the level of country development, the data collected may have shortcomings attributed to factors other than development, such as translation, correspondence, etc. The following are some of the shortcomings of secondary data in international markets:

- *Availability*—In many markets, very little data are available. The detailed data readily available in developed countries may not exist in numerous regions in developing countries, where, for example, population censuses are frequently collected based on estimates made by village elders. If, for instance, demographic information—reliable and readily available in developed countries—is deemed important to the project but is not available for the local market to be researched, the researcher may have to collect this type of data. Also, data on income and sales from tax returns can be inaccurate in countries where this information is not declared.[26] Finally, state-run research organizations are often reluctant to disclose the details of the data collection method and process used; no information may be available on response rates, questionnaire development, and the nature of the sample.[27]

- **Reliability** and **Validity**—Governments in developing countries often exaggerate poverty figures to solicit international aid. On the other hand, in many dictatorial environments where the government desires to project prosperity, figures attesting to the success of the economic policies may be inflated. Such was the case for many of the communist governments of Africa, Asia, and Eastern Europe, where figures demonstrating that workers were surpassing the five-

reliability The extent to which data is likely to be free from random error and yield consistent results.

validity The extent to which data collected is free from bias.

year plans abounded, while, in fact, these same economies were experiencing severe shortages (typically attributed by government officials to consumer hoarding).

Errors also may be unintentional, attributed to lack of education or mere carelessness. Regardless, unless the researcher is convinced of the credentials of the research firm performing the study, it is best that the secondary data be regarded with skepticism.

Overall, the accuracy of government-published secondary data is questionable. Published statistics contain high margins of error, beyond the tolerance range of reliability.[28] In addition, published data may be fragmented or aggregated in inconsistent formats by different research organizations; researchers may pull the data for estimation, but, in most instances, they are likely to view the data with skepticism.[29]

Some reliable sources of data are those provided by the World Bank, the United Nations Development Program, and the Organization of Economic Co-operation and Development (OECD). Finally, even countries whose research reporting has been questionable for decades are revamping their data collection and reporting systems. For example, the Chinese government started to improve its marketing research infrastructure in the 1980s, introducing criteria for high-quality statistical service: accuracy, timeliness, relevance, diversity, and richness.[30] Overall, the State Statistics Bureau has expanded its role from data collection and compilation to a role similar to that of a business consultant.[31]

Regardless of the source, secondary data must be carefully scrutinized and interpreted. Researchers may construct a checklist to determine the extent to which the data are usable. This list may contain items such as

- Who collected the data and for what purpose? Was this actual research, or was it used to support a decision already taken (i.e., is it pseudo-research)?

- When was the data collected? What were the environmental country-conditions then?

- What stakes did the firm managers have in the study?

- What stakes did the researchers have in the study?

- Who else may have a stake in the findings of the study (government entities, businesses)?

- What methods were used?

- How consistently were the methods applied?

- Do the findings appear to be consistent with the findings of previous studies or with studies conducted in similar countries?

Primary Data

Primary research is used internationally far less than it should be. Cost-benefit analyses suggest that spending on research in remote markets of questionable value is unwise; consequently, the temptation is to use secondary data to serve all research functions.[32]

Often, even the largest firms use a wide variety of quick, ad hoc research techniques and look at databases and online information to get their projects off the ground.

Yet many U.S. firms are interested in conducting research in the international markets where they operate. In an interview of 313 executives at major U.S. corporations who were responsible for conducting research and hiring outside research firms, 61 percent indicated that they would devote a larger percentage of their research budgets to international research over the following three years.[33]

Most international marketing research projects involve the collection of primary data, *information collected for a specific purpose, to address the problem at hand.* It requires substantial expertise in both instrument design and administration and, as a consequence, it is expensive and time consuming.

International Constraints

Lack of Marketing Infrastructure. The costs of collecting primary data in foreign markets are likely to be much higher given the lack of a marketing infrastructure. Many markets do not have research firms or field-interviewing services; consequently, the sponsoring firm would have to invest in developing sampling frames and training interviewers.[34]

6-4d Determining Research Approaches

research approach The method used to collect data.

When collecting primary data, researchers may use qualitative and quantitative **research approaches.** Qualitative research methods typically have some of the following characteristics:

- Fewer respondents belonging to a nonrandom sample
- Open-ended answer format
- Nonsystematic observation
- Researcher involvement as participant

Qualitative Research

qualitative research Research that uses nonsystematic processes, such as nonrandom sampling and open-ended data, as well as involves the researcher as participant.

Qualitative research has been particularly useful either as a first step in studying international marketing phenomena—when conducting exploratory research—or as one of the methods of exploring the problem at hand in a multiple-method approach. Focus group research and observation fit in this category. In certain countries, such as France and Italy, there is a preference for qualitative data as a complement to quantitative data, whereas in others, such as Germany, the United States, and Scandinavian countries, quantitative data are deemed as most valuable.

Focus Group Interviews and Depth Interviews

focus group interview A qualitative research approach investigating a research question using a moderator to guide discussion within a group of subjects recruited to meet certain characteristics.

Focus group interviews typically involve from 6 to 12 participants recruited to meet some previously decided characteristics—for instance, ethnic background, certain age group, social class, tribal allegiance, and use of certain products—and a moderator who guides the discussion based on a certain discussion agenda. Frequently, representatives from the sponsor observe the group's deliberations through a one-way mirror or on close-circuit television. A video camera or tape recorder may also be used to record the group's deliberations on a certain topic of interest to the sponsor. The participants are typically given a small financial reward for participating in the study, or products such as free beer and food, product samples, etc.

depth interview A qualitative research method involving extensive interviews aimed at discovering consumer motivations, feelings, and attitudes toward an issue of concern to the sponsor using unstructured interrogation.

Depth interviews are one-on-one attempts to discover consumer motivations, feelings, and attitudes toward an issue of concern to the sponsor using a very loose and unstructured question guide. They are typically used if the issue under study is a complex behavioral or decision-making consideration or an emotionally laden issue.

International Constraints

Focus groups, consumer panels, and depth interviews are frequently problematic to apply in international settings. In Eastern cultures, responses are likely to be affected by "acquiescence bias" or "good-subject role," whereby consumers agree in order to please the interviewer. When conducting international research using focus groups, researchers should be aware of the significance of culture in the dialogue because many societies do not condone open exchange and disagreement between individuals.[35] Also, topics such as domestic habits or sexual behavior are considered too private and embarrassing to discuss with strangers. In these environments, researchers would benefit more from using observational approaches.[36]

Observation

One type of **observational research** that is particularly useful in international research is naturalistic inquiry. Naturalistic inquiry requires the use of natural rather than contrived settings because behaviors take substantial meaning from their context.[37] The researcher is the data collection instrument and part of the behavior—verbal and nonverbal. The analysis performed by the researcher is inductive, rather than deductive; that is, unlike in conventional research methods, the researcher does not rely on previous theory in the process of developing hypotheses, but, rather, theories are developed from data. Ethnography—the study of cultures—is largely based on naturalistic inquiry. Both academic researchers and practitioners have used observation to better understand international consumers and consumer motivations. It is frequently used by researchers who attempt to increase the validity of their studies by acquiring an intimate knowledge of a culture's daily life through personal observation.[38] See Figure 6-4.

Other observational methods—such as the study of garbage (garbology); physiological measurement methods, which measure a respondent's nonvoluntary responses to stimuli; eye tracking, which is used in packaging research and in advertising; and response latency, which measures the time interval between the question and the response to that question—are used only to a limited extent in international research, usually in developed

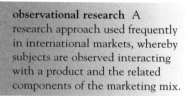

observational research A research approach used frequently in international markets, whereby subjects are observed interacting with a product and the related components of the marketing mix.

Figure 6-4

Observing a mother and grandmother shopping with their grandson would provide information on who the primary decision maker is in this shopping decision.

countries. They are very costly because they require sending expensive experts to the research site abroad and obtaining data only on limited, usually nonrepresentative samples.

Information technology provides new sources for observation-based information, such as point-of-sale (POS) store scanner data, which can offer outlets high-quality, instant, as well as longitudinal, information on the movement of goods. Such resources are amply available in the United States, Canada, and the countries of the European Union. Increasingly, they are available in Asia and in the emerging markets of Latin America. This information is used for tracking, as well as for managerial decision making. This topic will be addressed in section 6-5a, "Sales Forecasting." Other sources for observation-based information include people meters, used to identify television audience watching behavior; in the United States, A.C. Nielsen also links this type of data with self-reported purchase behavior of consumers.

International Constraints

Observation can have a number of shortcomings. Individuals in different cultures may react differently if they note that their behavior is being observed. Also, the observer may need to be familiar with all the different languages spoken at the study site; this is especially the case in Europe, where store research is relatively novel.[39]

Quantitative Research

quantitative research
A structured type of research that involves either descriptive research approaches, such as survey research, or causal research approaches, such as experiments.

Quantitative research methods are more structured, involving either descriptive research approaches, such as survey research, or causal research approaches, such as experiments.

Content Analysis

content analysis Method that assesses the content of advertisements in a medium with verbal and/or visual content.

Content analysis, an example of descriptive research, is a quantitative analysis that entails counting the number of times preselected words, themes, symbols, or pictures appear in a given medium such as printed material or any medium with verbal and/or visual content. Content analysis is particularly useful in international marketing research, helping international marketing practitioners understand the complex multicultural environments in which they compete. At the same time, content analysis makes them aware of the subtle qualitative differences—such as taste, tradition, and symbolism—that are especially useful in market segmentation.[40]

One area where content analysis is used extensively is advertising research, in an attempt to discover themes that are more popular in certain countries, for particular product categories. One study examined differences in the portrayal of women in magazines of different countries.[41] Using U.S. and international male and female judges, the study found that, in general, North American and Western European magazines portrayed women displaying more positive emotions, compared to Latin American, East European, and African magazines. In addition, the women from Latin America appeared to be older, sexier, and more aggressive than their Western counterparts. Table 6-3 is a partial content analysis questionnaire used to gather this data.

Survey Research

survey research Descriptive research that involves the administration of personal, telephone, or mail questionnaires.

Survey research, another example of descriptive research, typically involves the administration of personal, telephone, mail, or Internet questionnaires. The use of the questionnaires assumes that respondents are both capable and willing to respond to the questions. A cheap survey method involves the use of mail questionnaires; however, this method is fraught with obstacles in many developing countries. And, in most developing countries, there is a high level of illiteracy, which renders impossible the use of mail surveys. Nevertheless, this method is most popular in international marketing research, especially because it can be effectively used in cross-national comparisons.

Women are frequently used in advertising. Advertisers portray them differently, depending on the mood/feeling they would like to convey. Please look at each ad and indicate to what extent you believe that THE WOMAN IN THE AD appears to have the following characteristics by circling the corresponding number, as follows:

Table 6-3

Partial Content Analysis Questionnaire

1 = if the ad/woman DOES NOT AT ALL HAVE the respective characteristic

2 = if the ad/woman DOES NOT HAVE the respective characteristic

3 = if the ad/woman SEEMS TO HAVE the respective characteristic

4 = if the ad/woman HAS the respective characteristic

5 = if the ad/woman DEFINITELY HAS the respective characteristic

The woman in the ad appears to be...

Soft	5	4	3	2	1
Cool	5	4	3	2	1
Seductive	5	4	3	2	1
Scornful	5	4	3	2	1
Kitten-like	5	4	3	2	1
Optimistic	5	4	3	2	1
Maternal	5	4	3	2	1
Loving	5	4	3	2	1
Practical	5	4	3	2	1
Proud	5	4	3	2	1
Comic	5	4	3	2	1
Calm	5	4	3	2	1
Superior	5	4	3	2	1
Elegant	5	4	3	2	1
. . .					
Caucasian	5	4	3	2	1
AfroAmerican	5	4	3	2	1
Hispanic	5	4	3	2	1
East Asian	5	4	3	2	1
Asian Indian	5	4	3	2	1

The woman is looking at . . .

People	5	4	3	2	1
An object	5	4	3	2	1
Nothing	5	4	3	2	1
The reader	5	4	3	2	1
Herself	5	4	3	2	1

The woman's age is approximately _____ years.

International Constraints

Respondent Factors. In certain countries, researchers may not have access to certain household members. For example, a male researcher collecting data in Djeddah, Saudi Arabia, will not have access to female respondents; in fact, he may even get into trouble if he attempts to approach a woman in any environment. Companies are advised to hire local female interviewers for any study that may involve women and male interviewers for studies that involve male respondents. Procter & Gamble, for example, a Western company with a substantial presence in the Saudi market, conducted a study examining the consumer behavior of Saudi women. The marketing department invited the husbands and brothers of Saudi women to participate in a focus group study. In spite of its obvious limitations, the study produced useful results that helped Proctor & Gamble develop appropriate strategies for this market.[42]

In Eastern Europe, on the other hand, there is considerable suspicion of any attempts to gain personal information. In fact, the word used for "research" is a variant of the Slavic *ankieta,* meaning inquiry (of the same type as that conducted by the former, feared secret police). Intercepting consumers in the marketplace typically meets with minimal response and with possible attempts to discredit the interviewer. A better method is "the apartment intercept," whereby the interviewer randomly chooses apartment buildings—typical mass structures found in most communist and formerly communist countries—located in representative neighborhoods and then attempts to interview every nth individual. The individuals approached may either live in the building, visit someone who lives there, or do business (shopping, renting videocassettes, etc.) in one of the apartments. An advantage of this method is the private environment protected from weather elements that may impede interaction.[43] Yet even this method does not yield a very high response rate because respondents may still suspect the interviewer's intentions. Moreover, Eastern European respondents believe that, in capitalism, people do not give something for nothing, and they almost always ask to be paid for their time.

In conclusion, it is crucial that researchers have a good understanding of the culture and local practices to be able to obtain adequate response rates.

Infrastructure Factors. In many countries, the use of telephones limits the data collection to a handful of individuals who have access to a telephone. This problem may disappear as the country develops; however, even more developed countries such as Poland, Spain, and India do not benefit from a very efficient telephone network. And, in many countries where mail is unreliable and slow, companies cannot rely on this type of data collection approach, leaving the personal interview, focus group, or observation as the only feasible research approaches. Even in India, which has one of the best home delivery mail systems in the entire developing world, mailing surveys to consumers' homes or offices has never been a part of the business culture of Indian society; similarly, in Saudi Arabia, which has one of the most efficient mail systems in the world using the most modern technologies, studies cannot be conducted through this venue because the system restricts the use of mail surveys.[44]

Another illustration of obstacles to the mail survey approach is offered by Nigeria: Attempts to collect data using mail surveys is restricted by literacy rates, which eliminate most potential respondents. Further, the mail delivery system is limited to the use of postal boxes, with home delivery being almost nonexistent; Nigerian roads/streets are not named and homes are not numbered.[45]

Finally, the sampling frames (mailing lists, telephone books, or other relevant databases) may not be available.

Experimental Research

Experimental research has the highest validity and reliability of all types of research. This research looks at cause-and-effect relationships, eliminating or controlling other extraneous factors that may be responsible for the results, and eliminating competing explanations for the observed findings. It requires the use of matched groups of subjects who are subjected to different treatments, to ascertain whether the observed response differences are statistically significant.

Given the many constraints that this type of research imposes on the researcher, experimental research findings are difficult to transfer to other countries where the control factors behave differently. Given the fact that results are not easily generalizable to similar environments, and that this type of research can be very costly, experimental research is rarely used in international research.

6-4e Designing the Data Collection Instrument

International marketing phenomena are particularly difficult to measure and require an intimate knowledge of the culture. Themes that are functionally and conceptually equivalent across nations, such as the universal concept of "affection," manifest themselves differently in different environments; for instance, kissing, a common manifestation in the West, is inappropriate in Eastern cultures and taboo in others.[46] Given these differences, phenomena specific to each culture are best measured by **emic instruments,** which are constructed for each nationality to measure the particular factor. The instrument employed must then conform to the specific characteristics of each culture.

International managers are frequently faced with problems related to the need for survey instruments that can be used across different cultures, especially for comparative evaluation of market characteristics such as response to an advertising campaign and other types of multi-country research. For this type of study, **etic instruments,** which are culture free and extremely difficult to develop, can be used to measure the same phenomenon in different cultures. For example, when one refers to the distance to the nearest supermarket in the United States, one uses the driving distance, whereas, in the rest of the world, the distance to the supermarket is measured in pedestrian terms. In fact, the word "supermarket" itself has different meanings in different countries. The type of store referred to as a "supermarket" in the United States is typically a large store belonging to a national or regional chain. A typical supermarket in Romania, such as a *Unic*, is probably made up of different stores that carry an assortment of products and does not even come close to that of its U.S. equivalent, whereas a *Migros* in Switzerland, *Hertie* in Germany, and *Albert Heijn* in the Netherlands carry a larger variety of products, but not as wide an assortment of competing brands as their U.S. equivalents. Consequently, what would be the appropriate way to measure consumer shopping experience at these supermarkets? Surely, a forced-choice standardized questionnaire would not be appropriate for cross-national comparisons, unless it is properly modified to reflect these differences. And, should there be such modification, it is likely that the value of the direct comparison itself would be compromised.

When deciding on the **data collection instrument,** the researcher needs to come up with an appropriate format and to offer very precise instructions. Frequently, respondents may not answer entire sections of the questionnaire, unless advised that full completion is essential for the integrity of the study. A typical *semantic differential* scale, anchored by words with opposite meanings (good . . . bad, important . . . not important) could be confusing to respondents as well. Clear instructions, preferably with examples, would help respondents in filling out the questionnaire appropriately. A variant of the semantic-differential scale follows (note the detailed explanation of the numbers to be circled). The typical Likert scale anchored by "strongly disagree" and "strongly agree" is unfamiliar to respondents in many cultures. Explaining the procedure in detail, as well as the meaning of circling a particular response, is essential. See the questionnaire in Table 6-4 for a variant of the Likert scale.

experimental research Research that examines cause-and-effect relationships; it has the highest validity and reliability of all types of research.

emic instrument A data collection instrument constructed for each nationality to measure a particular factor; it is the best measure for culture-specific phenomena.

etic instrument A culture-free data collection instrument that can be used to measure the same phenomenon in different cultures.

data collection instrument The instrument used to collect data, such as a printed questionnaire, a paper-and-pencil measure, or an electronic measurement device.

Table 6-4   **Sample Partial Consumer Research Questionnaire (Version Translated into Romanian, Bulgarian, and Hungarian)**

Please indicate the extent to which you agree or disagree with the statements below by circling 5 if you strongly agree, 4 if you agree, 3 if you neither agree nor disagree, 2 if you disagree, or 1 if you strongly disagree with a statement. Please answer *every* question; the questionnaire cannot be used unless you do so.

	Strongly Agree				Strongly Disagree
1. I don't care to find out about what types of brand names of appliances and gadgets my friends have.	5	4	3	2	1
2. I often read advertisements just out of curiosity.	5	4	3	2	1
3. I rarely read advertisements that just seem to contain a lot of information.	5	4	3	2	1
4. When I hear about a new store or restaurant, I take advantage of the first opportunity to find out more about it.	5	4	3	2	1
5. Companies are usually out to make money even if it means violating ethics and taking advantage of consumers.	5	4	3	2	1
6. Most durable products could be made to last much longer but are made to wear out quickly to necessitate repurchase.	5	4	3	2	1
7. If people really knew what businesses do to deceive and take advantage of consumers, they would be up-in-arms.	5	4	3	2	1
8. Most Western products I buy are overpriced.	5	4	3	2	1
9. Most *LOCAL* products I buy are overpriced.	5	4	3	2	1
10. Businesses could charge lower prices and still be profitable.	5	4	3	2	1

open-ended questions Questions with free-format responses that the respondent can address as he or she sees appropriate.

An easier approach (from the point of view of the respondent, and certainly not from the perspective of the individual coding and analyzing the data) is to use **open-ended questions** that elicit the appropriate answer from the respondent. This format allows the interviewer to probe in depth into the issue at hand and the respondent to fully address the points.

International Constraints

Instrument Translation. Instruments developed in one country require translation into the language of the country where they will be administered. Many concepts, however, are likely to lose some of their meaning when translated into another language. Idioms are particularly problematic, and their literal translation has led to numerous marketing blunders.

In cross-cultural research, all steps should be performed by individuals fluent in both the original language of the questionnaire and in the language of the country where it will be administered. First, a questionnaire is translated from the language in which it was originally written into the language in which it will be administered. There are two possible alternatives to further ensure that the instrument has been translated as intended. One is **back translation,** whereby the translated questionnaire is again translated into its initial language by a different individual. Another possibility is **parallel translation,** whereby the questionnaire is translated from its original language by two different individuals and the two versions are compared. The successive translation (by different translators) of the instrument between the original language and the language of administration with the purpose of obtaining an instrument that is closest in meaning to the original questionnaire is known as **decentering.**

The consumer research questionnaire in Table 6-4 contains a number of scales developed in marketing in the United States, among which are attitudes toward business ethics, attitudes toward pricing practices, comparison shopping, dogmatism, fashion concern, dress conformity, and information searches. The translated scales performed well and were considered highly reliable when used in the different country environments.

Instrument Reliability. Even if the same scale is used in different cultures and has been subjected to decentering techniques, it is likely to have different reliabilities (i.e., the extent to which the scale is likely to be free from random error and yield consistent results) when administered in different countries because respondents in one country might be more likely, for example, to give answers that would please the interviewer. This provides yet another argument against simple comparison of research results in international marketing.[47]

Other Instrument Issues. In certain environments, such as the United States, respondents are unwilling to answer questions about income, whereas in others, such as France, respondents more readily volunteer such information. In other cultures, age is a taboo subject. It is important to take these differences into consideration when designing questionnaires. Creating categories of income, rather than asking the precise figure, tends to have a better success for data collected in the United States. Regardless, it is best if all demographic data are placed at the end of the questionnaire, to ensure response.

> **back translation** The translation of translated text back into its original language, by a different individual, to ensure that the instrument has been translated as intended.

> **parallel translation** The process of translating the original instrument by different translators and comparing the translations.

> **decentering** The successive translation (by different translators) of an instrument between the original language and the language of administration with the purpose of obtaining an instrument that is closest in meaning to the original.

6-4f Deciding on the Sampling Plan

The sampling plan calls for the manager and researcher to jointly decide on the following issues:

- **Sampling unit**—Determining who will be included in the survey
- **Sample size**—Determining how many individuals will be surveyed (the larger the sample, the higher the study reliability)
- **Sampling procedure**—Determining how the sampling units will be selected (the most representative sample is a random probability sample)

Determining the sampling plan is likely to be affected by some of the same problems discussed previously. First, the sampling unit itself may have a different definition, depending on the country where the data are collected. In developed countries, for example, research examining family consumption patterns will typically survey a nuclear family, whereas in many developing countries, an extended family, including relatives living with the nuclear family, will be scrutinized. Similarly, as already mentioned, the concept of household varies across different countries.

The sampling procedure also presents a problem, as previously discussed, especially the **sampling frame** (the list from which sample units are selected). Mailing lists are

> **sampling unit** The entity included in the study; it may be individuals or representatives belonging to particular groups.

> **sample size** The number of study participants necessary to obtain a high study reliability.

> **sampling procedure** A decision involving the selection of sampling units.

> **sampling frame** The list from which sample units are selected.

inadequate, and telephones are available to only a small percentage of the population in many countries of the world.

6-4g Collecting, Analyzing, and Interpreting the Information

In the final stage of the marketing research process, the researcher or research team is ready to collect the primary data. This expensive undertaking can be eventful. Researchers are frequently faced with respondents who have never had any experience participating in surveys. *Nonresponse* (inability or, more frequently, refusal to participate in the study) can be a particularly serious problem, as previously seen. Even lateral processes that do not involve data collection per se, such as *briefing the field force* (training the interviewers) and *evaluating the fieldwork quality*, can be particularly difficult if the marketing researcher is not a national because communication may be encumbered by language and cultural differences. Ideally, local researchers should be in charge of implementing the data collection process because they are aware of the particulars of the environment that may have an impact on the data collection.

Finally, it is important that marketing managers not base all their decisions on the data collected because even proper planning of the data collection effort does not exclude the possibility of shortcomings in the study. For example, after one market research firm indicated that there was a substantial market for a specific product, a Swiss pharmaceutical firm built an $8 million manufacturing firm in Southeast Asia. The researchers, however, overlooked an important aspect of that market: the black market controlled by government officials. The added competition of the black market led to lower earnings for the company.[48]

6-5 Decision Support Systems for Global Marketing

A **decision support system** is defined as "a coordinated collection of data, systems, tools, and techniques, complemented by supporting software and hardware designed for the gathering and interpretation of business and environmental data."[49] In a global environment, the environmental data takes into account home-country and host-country developments, as well as other developments in other global markets that may affect operations.

Ideally, a global marketing decision support system should be[50]

- *Computerized*—Having a computerized support system is now possible in the case of many global markets, including those of developing countries, due to the increase in the capability of personal computers to perform more and more complex tasks.

- *Interactive*—Managers can use online instructions to generate reports on the spot, without assistance from a programmer, who now may need to be present in the country of operations only periodically, for system updating and training. This, of course, reduces the number of expatriates necessary at the operations site and the overall costs to the company.

- *Flexible*—Managers can access and integrate data from a variety of sources and manipulate the data in a variety of ways (producing averages and totals, sorting the data, etc.). The system should allow managers to access information about firm operations in similar markets where the firm may be present and competitors' operations in the respective market where such information is available.

- *Discovery-oriented*—Such systems should produce diagnostics that reveal trends and identify problems.

In a global environment, there are different, country-specific information systems. Integrating the different approaches may lead to operational difficulties; managers must continuously take into consideration such differences as they interface with the system.

---

decision support system A coordinated collection of data, systems, tools, and techniques, complemented by supporting software and hardware designed for the gathering and interpretation of business and environmental data.

A number of areas lend themselves well to marketing decision support systems (MDSS). In section 6-5a, "Sales Forecasting," we discuss different possible applications for such systems.

6-5a Sales Forecasting

Different approaches to sales forecasting are discussed in this section. The more complex these techniques are, the more their efficiency can be improved in an MDSS environment. Nevertheless, input obtained from using the simpler methods (salesforce composite estimates, jury of executive opinion, and the Delphi method) can be used to cross-validate the estimates given by the more sophisticated forecasting techniques (time series and econometric models).

Salesforce Composite Estimates

Forecasts from **salesforce composite estimates** are based on the personal observations and "hunches" of the local salesforce. These people are in the closest contact with the international consumer, and they are likely to find out about consumer desires and overall changing market trends. The salesforce is likely to be constituted of locals who have a good understanding of the market. They, in turn, report to the manager, who may or may not be an expatriate sent abroad by the home office. Ideally, the individual occupying this position is schooled under both home- and host-country systems; if not, it is recommended that this individual should undergo at least some training in host- or home-country approaches, respectively, to doing business. This training is important because this individual is typically responsible for interpreting the predictions of the salesforce.

salesforce composite estimates Research studies wherein sales forecasts are based on the personal observations and forecasts of the local salesforce.

Jury of Expert Opinion

Forecasts from the **jury of expert opinion** are based on the opinions of different experts about future demand. The experts' opinions are then combined, and an aggregate demand estimation is offered. Because experts could come from both home and host country, as well as other countries where other companies, or the company in question, may face similar problems, obtaining a consensus perspective or aggregate forecast may be more difficult to achieve. At the same time, the awareness of the different possible outcomes or individual perspectives may prove invaluable in gaining insight on demand, particularly for a market new to the company.

jury of expert opinion An approach to sales forecasting based on the opinion of different experts.

The Delphi Method

The **Delphi method** entails asking a number of experts to estimate market performance, aggregating the results, and sharing this information with the said experts. This process is repeated several times, until a consensus is reached. Clearly, such an approach would be most cumbersome when dealing with a global company. First, in addition to impositions on executives' time, the company also must incur expenses related to the logistics of bringing together experts from different countries. Second, should the company attempt to use the Delphi method by mailing forecasting surveys, there is always the risk that international mail may impose, in addition to the high likelihood of noncompliance by executives, who may perceive such an exercise as an imposition on their time.

Delphi method A method of forecasting sales by asking a number of experts to estimate market performance, aggregating the results, and sharing this information with the said experts; the process is repeated several times, until a consensus is reached.

Time Series and Econometric Models

Time series models use data of past performance to predict future market demand. Typically, these models give more weight to more recent developments. These methods assume that the future will be similar to the past. Econometric models, on the other hand, take into account different deterministic factors that affect market demand—factors that may or may not depend on past performance trends.[51]

An example of an application of econometric models to global marketing is provided by the application of an autoregressive moving average (ARMAX) to predict consumer demand for beer in the Netherlands.[52] The variables used as predictors of the demand for beer were temperature, price, consumer expenditures, and company advertising expenditures. The study concluded that advertising expenditures are not good predictors for beer demand; the authors suspected that the reason is a saturated market where all competitors advertise extensively and where additional advertising efforts may go unnoticed.

Time series and econometric models are dependent on the availability of historical data, data that are mainly available in developed countries but not in developing countries. For these markets, then, it is appropriate to estimate demand *by analogy*, noting responses of markets with similar relevant characteristics, markets with similar levels of economic development, markets with similar cultural characteristics, etc.

> **time series and econometric models** Models that use the data of past performance to predict future market demand.

Analogy Methods

The **analogy method** is an estimation method that relies on developments and findings in markets with similar levels of economic development, markets where the product is in the same development stage, or markets with similar cultural characteristics, or it may be based on sales of a related product in the key market of study. For example,

> **analogy method** A method for estimation that relies on developments and findings in similar markets or where the product is in the same life-cycle stage.

- To estimate anticipated adoption rate of cell phones in Latvia, it may be appropriate to identify the proportion of new adopters in a more advanced country in the Baltics—Estonia, which is more developed—where cell phone service is widely available, but which shares a similar history and similar geopolitics with Latvia. This is an example of *country performance analogy*.

- To estimate the adoption rate of Internet service in Sri Lanka, it may be appropriate to evaluate the adoption rate of computers in this country. This is an example of *product performance analogy*.

Typically, in the country performance analogy, adjustments are made based on development level, cultural differences, trade barriers, competition, etc. In the product performance analogy, adjustments are made for consumer traits such as purchase power, consumer innovation rate, and competitive environment, among others.

Point-of-Sale–Based Projections

Point-of-sale–based projections are made with the help of store scanners, which are increasingly used by research suppliers, particularly in the United States (A.C. Nielsen and Information Resources, among others), to assess market share and other relevant market dimensions. Weekly or biweekly store audits reveal the movement of goods within the store and from warehouses. Internationally, although scanning technology is widely available, it is mainly used for inventory purposes, rather than for research purposes. For example, British retailer Marks & Spencer uses bar code and wireless local area network (LAN) technology to improve operations in its stores. The company installed a Symbol Technologies Spectrum24 wireless LAN, mobile computers, and bar code laser scanners to increase accuracy and efficiency and to improve customer service at its more than 300 European-based stores; the scanners send data over the LAN, allowing Marks & Spencer to reconfigure point-of-sale stations or add and subtract stations based on need.[53] Overall, scan rates are lower in Europe when compared to the United States, but higher than rates elsewhere around the world (with the exception of Canada); Europe, Great Britain, and France have 100 percent scanning for most food products.[54] Surprisingly, in the United Kingdom, unlike the United States, consumer data collection is dominated by face-to-face interviewing, which still accounts for more than 50 percent of U.K. research, whereas retail data collection is still dominated by the conventional retail audit. The use of scanners at POS and the difference in the level of development in the major store groups make it impossible to construct a nationally representative sample of scanner stores.[55]

> **point-of-sale–based projections** Market share and other relevant market dimensions assessed by the use of store scanners in weekly and biweekly store audits.

Summary

- **Define international marketing research and provide a description of its immense scope; offer examples of each type of research conducted in international marketing.** International marketing research involves gathering information for international marketing decisions. It is wide in scope, covering industry research, market traits and trends, buyer behavior, and the marketing mix. Examples of product research are product testing, product package studies, and competitive product analysis. Distribution research covers areas such as import/export analysis, international channel performance and coverage, as well as plant/warehouse location studies. Promotion research has the widest scope, with studies of premiums, coupons, and deals; advertising effectiveness; media research (which is especially important in highly industrialized countries); and salesforce analyses. Pricing research involves studies projecting demand, as well as international market potential studies, sales potential studies, cost analyses, and profit analyses, among others.

- **Describe the steps involved in the international marketing research process while addressing, for each step, the international constraints involved.** The first step of the international research process involves defining the research problem and setting the research objectives; this is usually done in conjunction with a local team and international experts and consultants.

The development of the research plan involves deciding on the information sources—primary and secondary (evaluating the validity and reliability of secondary data)—and determining the appropriate research approach. The research approach may involve collecting qualitative data, using focus groups or observation methods, or quantitative data, using descriptive (surveys, content analyses) or causal research methods (experimental research). They, in turn, determine the contact methods. The next step requires the researcher to design the data collection instrument and translate it into the local language(s). Next, the sampling plan must be determined: selecting the sampling procedure, sample size, frame, and unit. Finally, the researcher must collect, analyze, and interpret the information.

- **Introduce the concept of decision support systems for international marketing and describe the sales forecasting process.** Decision support systems represent a coordinated approach to collecting and interpreting business and environmental data. International sales forecasting techniques can be improved in this environment. Methods used in international sales forecasting are international salesforce composite estimates, jury of expert opinion, the Delphi method, time series and econometric models, the analogy method, and point-of-sale–based projections, all of which can be used in an international setting with various degrees of success.

Key Terms

advertising effectiveness research
analogy method
back translation
brand awareness research
brand name generation and testing
buyer behavior research
causal research
channel performance and coverage studies
competitive pricing analyses
concept development and testing studies
conceptual equivalence
consumer segmentation studies
content analysis
cost analyses
data collection instrument
decentering
decision support system
Delphi method
depth interview
descriptive research
emic instrument

etic instrument
experimental research
exploratory research
external secondary data
focus group interview
functional equivalence
import/export analyses
internal secondary data
international market potential studies
international marketing research
jury of expert opinion
media research
observational research
open-ended questions
parallel translation
plant/warehouse location studies
point-of-sale–based projections
price elasticity studies
primary data
product packaging design studies
product testing

profit analyses studies
purchase behavior studies
qualitative research
quantitative research
reliability
research approach
sales forecast
sales potential studies
salesforce compensation, quota, and territory studies
salesforce composite estimates
sample size
sampling frame
sampling procedure
sampling unit
secondary data
studies of premiums, coupons, and deals
survey research
test marketing
time series and econometric models
validity

Discussion Questions

1. Describe the broad scope of marketing research with a focus on promotion-related research.
2. You have been hired to evaluate the purchase behavior of adolescents in Latvia. What types of research studies could you conduct?
3. What are some of the limitations of secondary data available to international marketing researchers?
4. Describe the challenges that researchers experience when designing and administering questionnaires in countries that are culturally dissimilar from their own.

5. Discuss the quantitative data collection methods that researchers can use in an international study and the problems they pose to the validity and reliability of the findings.

6. Describe the international sales forecasting methods that marketing managers can use to better monitor and more efficiently react to information in the local environment.

Chapter Quiz (True/False)

1. Brand awareness research and purchase behavior studies are frequently conducted by companies to identify the profiles of heavy consumers of the product.

2. Advertising effectiveness research uses studies that evaluate media availability and the appropriateness of the medium.

3. Research that examines cause-and-effect relationships is also known as causal research.

Multiple Choice

1. Which product research method mainly deals with testing new-product performance in a limited area of a national or regional target?
   a. test marketing
   b. product testing
   c. competitive product studies
   d. brand name generation and testing

2. Which product research method attempts to identify the extent to which the product conforms to local tastes?
   a. test marketing
   b. product testing
   c. competitive product studies
   d. brand name generation and testing

3. Kraft's research on identifying the top distribution firm in Hong Kong is a good example of which distribution research method?
   a. plant/warehouse location studies
   b. channel performance and coverage
   c. import/export analyses
   d. none of the above

4. Which of the following is a stage of the research plan?
   a. deciding on the research methods
   b. deciding on the information sources
   c. deciding on the sampling procedure
   d. all of the above

5. Data collected by a company on previous occasions to address a problem not directly related to the current research question is also known as
   a. first-tier data.
   b. primary data.
   c. internal secondary data.
   d. external secondary data.

6. Qualitative research methods include
   a. survey research.
   b. focus group research.
   c. experiments.
   d. all of the above

7. A sampling plan relies on specific decisions for a
   a. sampling unit.
   b. sample size.
   c. sampling procedure.
   d. all of the above

Endnotes

1. David Ricks, *Big Business Blunders*, Homewood, IL: Dow Jones, 1983.
2. Alecia Swasy, *Soap Opera: The Inside Story of Procter & Gamble*, New York: Times Books, 1993.
3. This section is organized based on a framework provided in a table in Thomas C. Kinnear and Ann R. Root, eds., *1988 Survey of Marketing Research: Organization, Functions, Budgeting, and Compensation*, Chicago: American Marketing Association, 1989, p. 43.
4. See Rolf F. H. Seringhaur, "Comparative Marketing Behaviour of Canadian and Austrian High Tech Firms," *Management International Review*, Vol. 33, No. 3, Third Quarter 1993, p. 247; and James D. Hlavacek and B. C. Ames, "Segmenting Industrial and High-Tech

Markets," *Journal of Business Strategy*, Vol. 7, October 1986, pp. 39–51.
5. William L. Shanklin and John K. Ryans, Jr., "Organizing for High-Tech Marketing," *Harvard Business Review*, Vol. 62, 1984, pp. 164–171; and Seringhaur, "Comparative Marketing Behaviour," p. 247.
6. Kim Thuy Balin, "DuPont Lycra Goes Global," *Sporting Goods Business*, Vol. 32, No. 5, March 8, 1999, p.16.
7. Ibid.
8. Hellmut Schutte, "Asian Culture and the Global Consumer," *Financial Times*, November 1998, pp. 2–3.

You can find the correct answers to these questions by taking the quiz and then submitting your answers in the Online Edition. The program will automatically score your submission. Where you miss a question, the program will provide the correct answer, a rationale for the answer, and the section number in the chapter where the topic is discussed.

9. Bernard Dubois and Claire Paternault, "Observations—Understanding the World of International Luxury Brands: The 'Dream' Formula," *Journal of Advertising Research*, Vol. 35, No. 4, July/August 1995, pp. 69–74.

10. Erika Rasmusson, "Growing a Global Brand," *Sales and Marketing Management*, Vol. 151, No. 8, August 1999, p. 17.

11. Helen Johnstone, "'Little Emperors' Call the Shots," *Asian Business*, Vol. 32, No. 9, September 1996, pp. 67–68

12. James I. Steinberg and Alan L. Klein, "Global Branding: Look Before You Leap," *Brandweek*, Vol. 39, No. 43, November 16, 1998, pp. 30–32.

13. "P&G Goes Local," *Country Monitor*, Vol. 47, (No. 3), October 27, 1999, p. 9.

14. Julia Day, "Kraft Foods Moots Kenco High Street Coffee Outlets," *Marketing Week*, Vol. 23, No. 38, November 16, 2000, p. 9.

15. Irina Begjanova and Lisa Palluconi, "Trade with Turkmenistan," *BISNIS Bulletin*, September 1996, p. 5.

16. Kevin Lyons, "Distribution in Kazakstan," *BISNIS Bulletin*, November 1996, pp. 1, 5. This article was adapted from the *Country Commercial Guide* for Kazakstan, produced by the U.S. Commercial Service in Almaty.

17. Martin Croft, "War of Independence," *Marketing Week*, Vol. 17, No. 49, March 3, 1995, pp. 47–48.

18. Ibid.

19. Ibid.

20. Lyons, "Distribution in Kazakstan," p. 5.

21. Judith Robinson, "Product Certification in Russia," *BISNIS Bulletin*, August 1996, p. 6.

22. This example is taken from Yusuf A. Choudhry, "Pitfalls in International Marketing Research: Are You Speaking French Like a Spanish Cow?" *Akron Business and Economic Review*, Vol. 17, No. 4, Winter 1986, pp. 18–28.

23. Ricks, *Big Business Blunders*, 1983.

24. Schutte, "Asian Culture and the Global Consumer," pp. 2–3.

25. Ibid.

26. William R. Dillon, Thomas J. Madden, and Neil H. Firtle, *Marketing Research in a Marketing Environment, Second Edition*, Burr Ridge, IL: Irwin, 1993.

27. T. K. Sherriff Luk, "The Use of Secondary Information Published by the PRC Government," *Journal of the Market Research Society*, Vol. 41, No. 3, July 1999, pp. 355–365.

28. Naresh Malhotra and J. Agarwal, "Methodological Issues in Crosscultural Marketing Research: A State of the Art Review," *International Marketing Review*, Vol. 13, No. 5, 1996, pp. 7–43.

29. Luk, "The Use of Secondary Information," pp. 355–365.

30. Ibid.

31. Ibid.

32. Michael R. Czinkota and Ilkka A. Ronkainen, "Market Research for Your Export Operations: Part II—Conducting Primary Market Research," *International Trade Forum*, Vol. 1, 1995, pp. 16–26.

33. Allison Lucas, "Market Researchers Study Abroad," *Sales and Marketing Management*, Vol. 148, No. 2, February 1996, p. 13.

34. Ibid.

35. Czinkota and Ronkainen, "Market Research for Your Export Operations," pp. 16–26.

36. Choudhry, "Pitfalls in International Marketing Research," pp. 18–28.

37. See Yvonna S. Lincoln and Egon G. Guba, *Naturalistic Inquiry*, London: Sage Publications, 1985; Laura A. Hudson and Julie L. Ozanne, "Alternative Ways of Seeking Knowledge in Consumer Research," *Journal of Consumer Research*, March 14, 1988, pp. 508–521.

38. Jerome Kirk and Marc L. Miller, *Reliability and Validity in Qualitative Research*, London: Sage Publications, 1986.

39. Czinkota and Ronkainen, "Market Research for Your Export Operations," pp. 16–26.

40. David R. Wheeler, "Content Analysis: An Analytical Technique for International Marketing Research," *International Marketing Review*, Vol. 5, No. 4, Winter 1988, pp. 34–40.

41. Dana-Nicoleta Lascu, "Women in Advertising: A Cross-Cultural Study of Emotion," in *Proceedings of the Annual Meeting of the Academy of International Business, South-East 1997*, pp. 19–32. Presented at the Academy of International Business Conference, South-East (Atlanta, Georgia), November 1997.

42. Zafar U. Ahmed, Dana-Nicoleta Lascu, and D. Neil Ashworth, "International Management and Marketing Research in Developing Countries," in *Proceedings of the Sixth Annual Meeting of the American Society of Business and Behavioral Sciences*, Vol. 10, February 1999, pp. 9–14.

43. Dana-Nicoleta Lascu, Lalita Manrai, and Ajay K. Manrai, "Marketing in Romania: The Challenges of the Transition from a Centrally-Planned Economy to a Consumer-Oriented Economy," *European Journal of Marketing*, Vol. 27, No. 11–12, 1993, pp. 102–120.

44. Ahmed, Lascu, and Ashworth, "International Management and Marketing Research in Developing Countries," pp. 9–14.

45. Ibid.

46. The material in this section is adapted from Choudhry, "Pitfalls in International Marketing Research," pp. 18–28.

47. Ravi Parameswaran and Attila Yaprak "A Cross-National Comparison of Consumer Research Measures," *Journal of International Business Studies*, Spring 1987, pp. 35–49.

48. Ricks, *Big Business Blunders*, 1983.

49. William R. Dillon, Thomas J. Madden, and Neil Firtle, *Marketing Research in a Marketing Environment*, Burr Ridge, IL: Irwin, 1993.

50. Ibid.

51. Ibid.

52. Philip Hans Franses, "Primary Demand for Beer in the Netherlands: An Application of ARMAX Model Specification," *Journal of Marketing Research*, May 28, 1991, pp. 240–245.

53. "British Retailer Goes Wireless," *Automatic I.D. News*, October 1998, Vol. 14, No. 11, October 1998, p. 14.

54. Gerry Eskin, "POS Scanner Data: The State of the Art, in Europe and the World," *Marketing and Research Today*, Vol. 22, No. 2, May 1994, pp. 107–108.

55. Tim Bowles, "Data Collection in the United Kingdom," *Journal of the Market Research Society*, Vol. 31, No. 4, October 1989, pp. 467–477.

56. Interview with Mr. Ziad Tantawi, Director of Business Development, July 2002.

Case 6-1

Hilton Sorrento Palace

Two hours south of Rome to Naples, by the Eurostar, the Italian high-speed train, and an additional hour west along the Bay of Naples via the Circumvesuviana regional railway is the town of Sorrento. The Hilton Sorrento Palace reigns high on the hills of Sorrento, overlooking Mount Vesuvius, the now-dormant volcano (since 1944) that buried the towns of Pompeii and Herculaneum in the year 79 AD (see Figure 6-5).

Sorrento is a small resort town, known well throughout Europe, an ideal vacation destination for its picturesque location and mild weather. A favorite of British travelers, the town of Sorrento has 10,000 beds according to Mr. Ziad Tantawi, director of business development at the Hilton Sorrento Palace. The Hilton Sorrento Palace is the largest of all hotels in the small resort town, with 383 rooms. Owned by the Sorrento Palace Gruppo since its year of construction (1981), the hotel became part of the Hilton chain in May 2001, and is now under Hilton management. One of the few hotels open in the winter, the Sorrento Palace boasts an average occupancy rate of 60 percent, with an average occupancy of 30 percent from November to March and more than 85 percent from May to October.[56]

The Hilton Sorrento Palace faces competition from three categories of competitors. Bed and breakfast, family-run lodging is very popular. The bed and breakfasts are competitively priced at or below the room rates of leading hotels in the area. Most bed and breakfast accommodations are open year round.

Sorrento is also a popular destination for cruise lines during the summer months. For cruise ship passengers, Sorrento offers easy access to the ruins of Pompeii, Mount Vesuvius, and the Isle of Capri. Overall, prices for cruise ships are higher than that of hotels, but they include meals and entertainment, as well as airfare to Italy.

Other local hotels compete directly with the Sorrento Hilton. The historic Europa Palace Grand Hotel, for example, offers close views of the Bay of Naples and the cliffs of Sorrento.

The Hotel Offerings

The four-star Hilton Sorrento Palace is situated on a hill overlooking the town and the Bay of Naples, a short walk from downtown's busy tourist markets. Surrounded by residences and lemon and orange groves, the hotel is modern and elegant. Its restaurant, L'Argumento, is situated amidst blooming cannas and orange and lemon trees (see Figure 6-6). Le Ginestre has frescoes and elegant columns, and an indoor pool with a lush painted background. Its other four restaurants abound in blooming bougainvillea and oleander and have a splendid view of the Bay of Naples and Mount Vesuvius.

The indoor lounge, shown in Figure 6-7, has excellent performers scheduled every evening and boasts a view of the city and the Bay.

The executive lounge, shown in Figure 6-8, is situated on the top floor of the hotel and has a splendid view of the Gulf and town. It also boasts a swimming pool at the highest altitude in the region (see Figures 6-9 and 6-10). The lounge serves complimentary food and drinks to executive guests and to gold- and diamond-level Hilton Honors members.

Figure 6-5
The Hilton Sorrento Palace reigns high on the hill above the Bay of Naples.

Figure 6-6
L'Argumento Restaurant, among Orange and Lemon Trees

The hotel has a total of six outdoor swimming pools of different depths, flowing into each other (see Figures 6-11 and 6-12), a tennis court, and a relatively well-equipped fitness center. Among the services offered at the hotel pool are the Hilton Kids Club: Every day, from 10 to 12 and from 2 to 4 in the afternoon, the Hilton kids can enjoy entertainment by the pool (uno spazio giochi per bambini).

Marketing Strategies

The hotel's targeting strategies focus primarily on meetings: Its meeting space is one of the largest in Europe. The Centro Congressi (congress center) has a full range of rooms for conferences and conventions of any type or size, from the 1,700-seat auditorium to smaller rooms, a 2,300 square meter exhibition space, a banquet facility that can accommodate 1,000 people, and parking facility that can accommodate 300 automobiles. In addition, the Centro also offers conference interpreting systems (six conference interpreting booths) and audio-visual presentation equipment, including a megascreen, making it an ideal venue for international events. About 65 percent of all hotel guests are conference participants. Hilton's sales offices in Italy (Milan) and overseas (in

continued

Figure 6-7
The Lounge—Offering a Stylish Open Indoor Space

Figure 6-9
The Executive Lounge Swimming Pool Perched High Above the City, with a Bay View

Figure 6-8
The Executive Lounge—an Elegant Indoor Lounge with a Bang & Olufsen Stereo System

Figure 6-10
The View from the Sorrento Palace

Figure 6-11
A Partial View of the Swimming Pool

Figure 6-12
Perspective from the Swimming Pool Area

Germany, the United Kindgom, France, Sweden, and the United Arab Emirates) are responsible for conference sales.

Tour operators constitute a second target group, accounting for 25 percent of the hotel's business. Their demand is highest in the months of July and August, when demand exceeds supply—Sorrento's location on the Bay and up a steep hill does not allow for space that could accommodate additional hotels. Only 10 percent of the hotel's business comes from individual bookings, the Internet, and telephone reservations.

The Hilton Sorrento Palace's main target market is Italy. In addition, the hotel also actively targets groups from the United Kingdom, Germany, Belgium, France, and Japan—in that order, according to Mr. Tantawi. Visitors from the United States previously constituted an important presence at the hotel, particularly in the summer, in organized tours; however, after the terrorist attacks of September 11, 2001, demand fell sharply.

The hotel's management would like to direct the hotel's marketing strategies to the United States. In particular, it would like to increase conference attendance at the hotel, as well as the number of tour groups and individual tourists in the off-season (November to March). At present, the hotel draws guests primarily from Italy and the United Kingdom. However, because European economies tend to follow a similar cycle, it is preferable for the hotel to diversify to other markets. Recently, the hotel made extensive marketing attempts aimed at Japanese tour groups, with great success. Now the hotel's management would like to find a way to bring in more tourists from the United States.

Analysis Suggestion

How should the Hilton Sorrento Palace market more effectively to the U.S. market? Design a concept development and testing study that evaluates which combination packages would appeal most to the following U.S. consumer segments: (a) university students, (b) families, and (c) conference organizers.

Note: Conduct a complete research design and provide sample questionnaires that will be used in the research conducted with each segment.

7

International Strategic Planning

Chapter Objectives

By the end of this chapter, you should be able to

1 Develop a general understanding of international marketing strategy at the different levels of the international organization and provide some insights into the international marketing planning process of selected companies.

2 Identify the rationale for adopting a target marketing strategy in international markets.

3 Identify the requirements necessary for effective international market segmentation.

4 Introduce the concept of country attractiveness analysis and offer a blueprint for conducting the analysis.

5 Identify the bases for consumer segmentation and offer company application examples.

6 Describe the three targeting strategies used by companies worldwide.

7 Describe the six positioning strategies that international companies can use to position their brands in the minds of target consumers.

Ford, responding to rapid changes in the global economy, implemented a major reorganization, ending competing regional fiefdoms by consolidating engineering, design, and development within new global divisions. Motorola, faced with aggressive Asian competitors and falling profits, adopted a similar plan, replacing decentralized and competing businesses with three distinct global groups focusing on retail customers such as cell phone users, telecommunications companies, and government and industrial clients. Procter & Gamble initiated the broadest overhaul in its industry, transforming four business units based

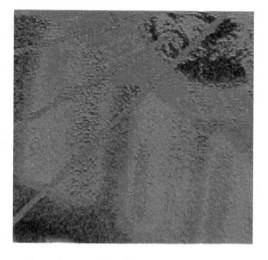

on geographic regions into seven global entities based on product lines such as Baby Care and Food & Beverage.[1] Firms need to consider the fit between their external environment and company characteristics and goals that optimally serve their target consumers.

This chapter offers an overview of international marketing strategy and provides insight into the international marketing planning process. The chapter covers tools for macro- and micro-segmentation and strategies for targeting international consumers; it also identifies the different product positioning strategies that companies use in world markets.

7-1 Developing an International Marketing Strategy

An international marketing strategy involves developing and maintaining a strategic fit between the international company's objectives, competencies, and resources and the challenges presented by its international market or markets. The international strategic plan forges a link between the company's resources and its international goals and objectives in a complex, continuously changing international environment. Given the changing nature of the environment, the international company's strategic plan cannot afford a typical long-term focus (a 5- or 10-year plan); rather, the planning process must be systematic and continuous, and it must reevaluate objectives in light of new opportunities and potential threats.

Another dimension of international marketing strategy is linked to the company's commitment to its international markets. Some companies use international marketing only to test the waters or to unload overproduction. This approach to international marketing, although it might open long-term opportunities to the company, does not indicate a substantial commitment to internationalization and is not a premise for success in the long term. A long-term international commitment that entails substantial investment in terms of resources and personnel is likely to bring the company the greatest rewards in the long run. Such a strategy will make the company a stronger competitor in the world market, as well as at home. Appendix A, "The International Marketing Plan," offers guidance for the development of an international marketing plan.

International strategic planning takes place at different levels (see Figure 7-1):

- At the *corporate level*, the strategic plan allocates resources and establishes objectives for the whole enterprise, worldwide. The corporate plan has a long-term focus and involves the highest levels of management. For example, PepsiCo Beverages

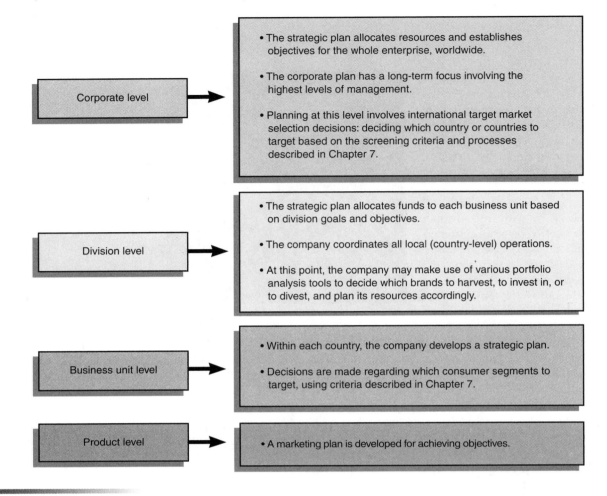

Figure 7-1

Planning Activities in the International Firm

headquarters (including its international headquarters) are located in Purchase, New York, USA. The company's corporate plan is developed there. Planning at this level involves international target market selection decisions: deciding which country or countries to target based on the screening criteria and processes described in this chapter.

- At the *division level*, the strategic plan allocates funds to each business unit based on division goals and objectives. In the PepsiCo example, its division for Eastern Europe is located in Vienna, Austria. From there, the company coordinates all local (country-level) operations. At this point, PepsiCo may use various portfolio analysis tools to decide which brands to harvest, to invest in, or to divest, and plan its resources accordingly.

- At the *business unit level*, within each country, decisions are made regarding which consumer segments to target, using criteria described in this chapter. At this level, PepsiCo develops a strategic plan.

- At the *product level* (line, brand), a marketing plan is developed for achieving objectives. PepsiCo's marketing plan for Poland, for example, might include increasing the consumption of Pepsi and Pepsi Light and launching Pepsi Max beyond the cities of Warsaw, Krakow, Wroclaw, and Poznan.

7-1a Developing an International Marketing Plan

At this stage of the planning process, the international company develops marketing strategies for the target market, deciding on the product mix for the local target market, as well as on the other components of the marketing mix (distribution, promotion, and pricing); plans the international marketing programs; and manages (organizes, implements, and controls) the marketing effort.

The decision on which elements of the marketing mix to use in a particular target market is closely linked to the product's life cycle and to the market entry strategy selected: A product in the early stages of its life cycle, such as the Palm Pilot, will most likely be sold to consumers in highly industrialized countries for a high price, accompanied by heavy promotion. A product will most likely be manufactured in a developed country and exported to the rest of the world. Alternatively, a product in the later stages of its life cycle, such as a videocassette recorder, will be sold to consumers worldwide, regardless of country development level. The company selling the product will heavily compete on price and, thus, most likely manufacture the product in a developing country, where labor is inexpensive, to sell all over the world. Most likely, the company will have at least one subsidiary located in the country of product manufacture.

Insights into the marketing strategies that companies use to target international markets reveal that marketing mix decisions are complex and based on extensive research. Kraft Foods (www.kraftfoods.com), a company based in the United States, has made interesting product mix decisions: It sells coffee products and confectionery products that cover the spectrum of target consumers—and the brands often cannibalize! In addition, Kraft Foods has different mix strategies for each market. And it sells to the U.S. consumer only a fraction of its international offerings, some of which are positioned as premium European imports. Kraft also has numerous brands that are restricted to a few markets. Among them are Daim, aimed at Scandinavian consumers, and Bis, aimed at Argentina and Brazil.

Among the many brands of coffee Kraft Foods offers are

- *Jacobs coffee*—This product sells mainly in Central and Eastern Europe. Jacobs coffee is popularly known as a quality German brand. Because consumers in Central and Eastern Europe have traditionally had frequent interaction with German consumers and have acquired a taste and preference for German brands, marketing the Jacobs brand in this region was appropriate. Had Kraft brought the product to the United States, it would have had to challenge quality perceptions of bulk coffee associated with developing countries in Latin America (Colombia and Guatemala, in particular) and Africa (Kenya, especially) and value perceptions held by store brands and other low-priced national brands such as Folgers and Kraft's own Maxwell House.

- *Gevalia coffee*—This brand is aimed at the Scandinavian market and imported into the United States as a gourmet product sold exclusively by mail order.

Among the numerous confectionery products Kraft offers are the following:

- *Milka*—Kraft Foods is now importing its European Milka brand of chocolate into the United States, selling it primarily through chain stores such as Target. Mass-market consumers in the United States are increasingly replacing favorite local candy bars with products that are perceived as more sophisticated and that are available at competitive prices. Competitors such as Ferrero Rocher and Dove have had great success with the premium chocolates they sell in the U.S. market, and they are increasingly placing their products in the impulse-purchase section, by the cash register. Kraft's Milka uses a similar strategy, selling its basic milk chocolate with the picture of a Swiss cow in the Alps on the packaging at Target stores. Milka also is available in a wider selection at shops that specialize in foreign gourmet foods.

- *Suchard*—Kraft Foods is restricting the distribution of its premium chocolate Suchard to Western Europe. Suchard has been for decades the traditional competitor to Lindt in the premium chocolate market in Europe. The Suchard name has long been associated with French-speaking Switzerland, and most European consumers do not know that it is owned by an American company.

- *Toblerone*—Kraft is distributing its Toblerone chocolate brand extensively all over the world.

Like Kraft, companies entering more and more countries in search of new markets are likely to face increasing difficulty in continuously monitoring and controlling their international operations. These firms must monitor not only the constantly changing marketing environment, but also changes in competitive intensity, in competitor product/service quality strategies, in supply chains, and in consumer expectations. In the process, they must carefully target their international market segments and appropriately position their products relative to those of the international and local competition.

7-2 The Rationale for Target Marketing

target marketing The process of focusing on those segments that the company can serve most effectively and designing products, services, and marketing programs with these segments in mind.

With the exception of very narrow markets, one single company, however large its resources and capacity, could not possibly serve all customers. Consumers worldwide are too numerous, and their needs and wants are too diverse. Companies must focus on those segments that they can serve most effectively and design products and services with these segments in mind; that is, they must engage in international **target marketing.**

International target marketing is used by companies to

- Identify countries and segments of international consumers that are similar with regard to key traits, who would respond well to a product and related marketing mix (international market segmentation).

- Select the countries and segments that the company can serve most efficiently and develop products tailored to each (international market targeting).

- Offer the products to the market, communicating, through the marketing mix, product traits and benefits that differentiate it in the consumer's mind (market positioning).

7-3 International Market Segmentation

segmentation The process of identifying consumers and/or international markets that are similar with regard to key traits, such as product-related needs and wants, and that would respond well to a product and related marketing mix.

International market segmentation involves identifying countries and consumers that are similar with regard to key traits, such as product-related needs and wants, and that would respond well to a product and related marketing mix. International **segmentation,** thus, must be performed at the country level (macro-segmentation) and at the consumer level (micro-segmentation).

At the country level, segmentation analysis identifies countries that are similar in aspects relevant to the company. If a company produces luxury goods, for example, economic variables can help determine whether a sufficient number of consumers can afford to purchase the company products. At the consumer level, segmentation analysis identifies consumers who are looking for the same benefits in the product. Although all consumers seek an efficient mode of transportation when they purchase an automobile, they also fulfill other desires. Consumers in rural Scotland may seek a small, versatile vehicle that can maneuver through tight single-lane roads, whereas executives in Muscat and Oman (one of the United Arab Emirates) may want a luxury automobile that exudes high status and elegance to navigate on the country's impeccable roads.

7-3a Requirements for International Segmentation

Regardless of whether the segmentation analysis is performed at the country level or at the individual consumer level, several requirements must be met for market segmentation to be effective. The requirements, which apply equally to country and consumer segmentation, are shown in Figure 7-2.

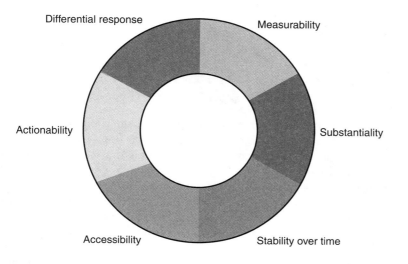

F i g u r e   7 - 2
Requirements for Effective
International Segmentation

Measurability

Individual market segments should be easy to identify and measure, thus ensuring **measurability.** International market segments pose numerous challenges in this regard. First, in many developing countries, reliable population statistics, including market size and economic development data, are difficult to come by. Even if the International Monetary Fund and other development organizations' data are reliable and valid, international companies still run into difficulties when evaluating culture-related dimensions, such as product preferences, especially food products, and benefits sought. Collecting data on such variables also presents many challenges.

For example, working backward, from product performance to segmentation, the Wonder Bra has sold very well in Islamic countries. What benefit could women seek when purchasing the Wonder Bra in an environment where many women are fully covered in thick clothing in public? Clearly, the product is not used to enhance one's attractiveness to the opposite sex. Research would find that women dress primarily to impress other women in many Islamic countries, in a friendly competitive way. To be able to reach such conclusions, the research study would have to explore motivations beyond basic product benefits. Furthermore, the subjects must be willing to share such information.

measurability The ability to estimate the size of a market segment.

Substantiality

The segment should be large enough to warrant investment. Assuming that the segment can be measured, this step—determining **substantiality**—is relatively easy. Even if research determines that the local market segment is not large enough, it can be grouped together with an identical segment in another country and targeted jointly. Another dimension that must be evaluated is the segment's growth potential. Such data must be evaluated with surrogate statistics, such as economic development measures (i.e., as an increase in GDP per capita or income per capita), employment data, the level of foreign direct investment in the country, exports from the country, and trends in consumer spending. An important consideration here is also the intensity of competition directed at the same segment. All of these examples constitute important variables that must be evaluated to determine the market's viability in the future. A substantial market is the World Beat consumer; see International Marketing Illustration 7-1.

substantiality The extent to which the market is large enough to warrant investment.

Stability over Time

In the past, stability of a segment over time was a primary consideration mainly for developed countries. Today, however, **stability over time** is an important consideration in a

stability over time The extent to which preferences are stable, rather than changing, in a market segment.

International Marketing Illustration

7-1

The World Beat Consumer: A Substantial World Market

World Beat is a popular genre of music that has been around since the early-1990s. It is a mix of techno and Latin beats, hip-hop, and African or Arab beats, with a synthesized ethnic melodic touch. This music is marketed effectively to the World Beat consumer segment worldwide. Jessica, a 22-year-old Swede of African ancestry and a World Beat star in her home country, first launched her CD internationally in the Asia-Pacific region before introducing it elsewhere—with rapid success: Her album went gold instantly in South Korea and began winning other markets around the world.[2]

World Beat (groups accessible at www.cdnow.com) ranges from more traditional Europop groups such as Enigma, with its haunting, sinful, seductive French whispers and interjections of Greek Orthodox church choir; to Alabina, a group whose Arabic-Latin music is heard even in U.S. supermarkets; Disidenten, a German group playing Arabic songs; and Gypsy Kings, a French group playing French music with a Latin beat. The late Israeli singer Ofra Haza attempted to bridge Israeli and Arab culture with her album "Shaday"; her song "Im Nin Alu," based on a seventeenth century poem by Rabbi Shalom Shabazi, propelled her to international superstar status.

The market for World Beat is the World Beat consumer. This genre of music appeals across cultures and across age groups; in Europe, Asia, and Africa, listeners range from teenagers to forty-somethings. The opportunities that this segment presents to entertainment companies are immense.

---

world environment where products are in different life-cycle stages and where preferences are continuously changing with the advent of the Internet and online ordering across borders from countries of all development levels. In a rapidly changing environment, it is important to constantly reevaluate this segment.

Accessibility

target market Consumers and/or international markets that are similar in aspects relevant to the company.

accessibility The ability to communicate with the international target market.

The ability to communicate with the **target market,** determining the market's **accessibility,** is essential as well. Internationally, the differences in language in individual countries may pose obstacles, greatly increasing the cost of advertising and other promotions. Marketing in large emerging markets, such as India and China, could present challenges for different reasons: Communicating with Indian consumers necessitates expensive translation into the local languages, whereas communicating with Chinese consumers may be difficult because the large rural population has only limited access to technology. The ability to serve the market is also essential. Companies should be able to freely access the market; the market must be open to international companies and reachable (its topography should permit access to the target market).

Actionability

actionability The extent to which the target market segment is responsive to the marketing strategies used.

Actionability refers to the idea that the market should respond to the marketing strategies used, assuming that the company is targeting the market with the appropriate marketing mix. Consider, for example, the Colgate-Palmolive strategy for Latin America and the Balkans. In both markets, the company noted that its dishwashing liquid was not selling well. Research revealed, for this large market segment, a different approach to washing dishes—using soap slivers in a tub. As soon as the company developed a tub with dishwashing paste and promoted the product to the market, sales took off. The segment responded as intended to the strategy: The segment was actionable.

Differential Response

The segments should be easy to distinguish from each other and should respond differently from other market segments to marketing strategies; they should have a noticeable **differential response.** If consumers all over the world are similar and/or have identical preferences—and this is hardly the case—there is no need for international target marketing.

> **differential response** The extent to which international market segments respond differently to marketing strategies.

7-3b Macro-Segmentation: Country Attractiveness Analysis

Companies have different criteria that they consider essential for committing to a particular market. PepsiCo International did not consider profit as the main criterion when it approached the former Soviet Union to establish a countertrade agreement; rather, market size and the ultimate potential of the market were the company's primary concerns. As a first step in the segmentation process, companies engage in macro-segmentation, grouping countries based on such criteria as economic performance, evaluating the potential of a particular market; on their political, legal, and financial environment; on their marketing support infrastructure; on the company brand's standing or potential standing relative to existing competition; and on the degree of market fit with company resources, policies, and goals, among others. These criteria, in turn, are used in the screening process to select and target the countries that present the highest potential to the company.

Firms could use the following criteria to group countries and, based on these criteria, select those countries that offer the most opportunity for the company and those countries that should be targeted:

- Market potential
- The political, legal, and financial environment of the country
- The marketing support infrastructure in the country
- Brand/company franchise relative to competing products/companies
- Degree of market fit with company policies, goals, and resources

Market Potential

Countries can be grouped based on market potential. The potential of a market can be evaluated based on the rate of economic development, as expressed through validated, reliable market indicators, such as

- Gross domestic product (GDP) per capita
- Industrial and agricultural sectors statistics
- Market size and potential
- Consumer buying power
- International investment figures, such as foreign direct investment data and other trade statistics

Such indicators identify countries and markets where the company should invest important resources and engage in long-term commitment. Attractive big emerging markets, such as Brazil or China, have initially presented many challenges to international companies. Brazil in the 1970s and 1980s was plagued by runaway inflation and instability, whereas China was an unpredictable market closed to international scrutiny and influence.

With time, both countries have opened their markets to international investment, which has led to rapid economic development and prosperity. In the case of Brazil, statistics demonstrate an enormous growth. With a population of more than 180 million, of which almost half are younger than 20 years old, and with a GDP growing from US$800 billion in 1997 to more than US$1.3 trillion in the year 2003, Brazil is performing very well. As a result, it has become a viable trade partner of the United States and the European Union, despite a few setbacks; Brazil was recently twice rescued by the International Monetary Fund.

Similar potential is now presented by the countries of the former Soviet Union. These countries, despite being plagued by inflation and instability, all have a literate, educated workforce and excess of highly qualified labor on one hand and a consuming public that is eager to experience new products on the other. Among attractive markets of the former Soviet Union are the Baltic Republics (Estonia, Latvia, and Lithuania), Russia, and Belarus, all of which are being actively targeted by multinationals. Of possible interest in the future are the Asian Republics of the former Soviet Union, such as Armenia, Azerbaijan, Georgia, Kazakhstan, the Kyrgyz Republic, Turkmenistan, and Uzbekistan. A number of these countries have made important inroads on the path to economic development and prosperity: Kazakhstan and the Kyrgyz Republic are rapidly developing their banking systems and have both adopted pro-market structural reforms. Uzbekistan is not far behind, nor is oil-rich Turkmenistan.[3] Many companies that have initially only exported to these countries are now committing greater resources but have still to embark on aggressive foreign direct investment.

The Political, Legal, and Financial Environment of the Country

Countries also can be grouped based on their political, legal, and financial environment. Some of the following criteria should be considered when evaluating a potential country for entry:

- Ethnic conflict in the region
- History of war engagement
- Antiforeigner rhetoric
- Recent nationalization activity
- Legal ambiguity—especially in business
- Trade barriers erected by government to protect local business
- Exchange rate controls

Companies are not likely to succeed in markets where there is high political risk. Sri Lanka, an attractive small country located southeast of the Indian subcontinent, is no longer even a viable export market. Tamil separatists have actively targeted Sri Lanka's airport and, consequently, have practically demolished an economy that was already on the decline.

Even oil-rich countries could present a risk for companies considering entering these markets. Sudan, for example, discovered substantial oil reserves; however, its initially modest exports (primarily to Singapore) have only further fueled an ethnic civil war that has been raging for more than two decades. Today, oil exports from Sudan are about 500,000 barrels a day,[4] bringing in large amounts of hard currency. However, in spite of a strong GDP growth, Sudan represents a risk for long-term investment due to continuing clashes between rebel factions and government armed militia.

Ambiguities in the legal system create an environment that renders companies vulnerable to competitive theft, lack of trademark protection, bribery pressures, and employee theft. In such an environment, where everything is perceived as allowed unless expressly forbidden, even exporting could pose difficulties. For example, it could force firms to incur bribery costs that cannot be justified to the headquarters, nor to the home-country government, for mere access to the market. Finally, exchange rate controls could restrict the types of products that can be exported to the target market and/or impede the repatriation of profits.

One related issue is whether the country is a member of the World Trade Organization or of a regional block, such as the European Union or the Southern Cone Common Market (MERCOSUR). Countries that adhere to regulations of the WTO and that have the supra-national controls of regional integration are more likely to have a stable environment that promotes trade and investment.

The Marketing Support Infrastructure in the Country

The marketing support infrastructure of the target country is an important determinant of country attractiveness. Important to international firms are the availability and reliability of distribution and logistics providers to ensure that the product is delivered in a timely fashion at locations convenient to consumers.

Countries also can be grouped based on the availability of competent partners for firms contemplating international partnerships. A firm entering a new market should have access to capable local firms. In many developing countries, only few such firms may be available, and all other competitors will attempt to approach them. For instance, for large multinationals attempting to enter the Turkish market, Sabanci Holdings is in great demand and already boasts joint-venture and distribution partners in companies as varied as Carrefour supermarkets, Danone dairy products, Dresdner Bank, DuPont, IBM, Mitsubishi, Philip Morris, and Toyota, to name a few.

The information technology available to members of the local distribution chain is an important consideration in that it maximizes supply chain efficiencies and minimizes warehousing and logistics costs to the company. The level of local telecommunications development is also essential in ensuring adequate data flow and access to suppliers, clients, and company headquarters. Countries also should be evaluated on the availability of adequate local advertising support, such as local advertising talent and open access to media for advertising and other communication purposes. Finally, the availability of other service providers, such as marketing research firms, financial firms, and management consulting firms, is also essential for company performance in the market.

Brand/Company Franchise Relative to Competing Products/Companies

Markets where a brand or company name is already established with local consumers—either by reputation, through advertising, or experience (for consumers who have bought the product abroad or have heard of the company)—offer greater potential to the company.

This situation is especially true if the company has only few viable direct competitors. Markets can thus be segmented based on the reputation of the product and/or company in the market, and on the competitive density in the market for the company's products. Here, a related dimension is also useful: that of *lead country* (a country where products are first adopted) versus *lag country* (a country where products are last adopted). The lead/lag concept also is closely linked to the level of economic development and is particularly relevant to firms at the forefront of technology. These firms usually first introduce their products in lead countries.

Degree of Market Fit with Company Policies, Goals, and Resources

For companies that have the resources and the goal to saturate the world market, such as McDonald's and Coca-Cola, no market is too small. Other companies that have the resources but whose products cater only to the luxury market will most likely ignore countries with a limited number of elite consumers and focus on industrialized countries, or countries with substantial revenues from national resources, such as oil and diamonds. Yet other companies have limited resources and can afford to target consumers in only one or a few countries. For these companies, it is essential to select those markets that are perceived as the most appropriate for their goals and that provide the lowest level of risk.

7-3c Micro-Segmentation: Focusing on the Target Consumer

The purpose of micro-segmentation is to identify clusters of consumers that respond in a similar fashion to a company's marketing strategies. Identifying individual market segments will enable the company to produce products that meet the precise needs of target consumers with a marketing mix that is appropriately tailored for those segments. The international company typically conducts extensive marketing research to identify such segments.

Bases for Segmentation

In the process of analyzing consumer demand and identifying clusters of consumers that respond similarly to marketing strategies, firms must identify those bases for segmentation that are most relevant for its products or service offerings. The features that identify the bases for segmentation that companies may use in the process of analyzing their international markets are described next.

Demographic and Psychographic Segmentation

Demographics are statistics that describe the population, such as age, gender, race, income, education, occupation, social class, life-cycle stage, and household size. Demographics are easy to measure and to compare across countries; for this reason, they are widely used by international companies.

Consumers worldwide exhibit many differences with regard to **demographic segmentation** variables. The following few examples demonstrate how these differences have important implications for marketing:

demographic segmentation The process of identifying market segments based on age, gender, race, income, education, occupation, social class, life-cycle stage, and household size.

- *Age*—Countries that have a rapidly aging population (the Scandinavian countries, for example) present different challenges and opportunities to international firms than countries with half of their population under the age of 20 (such as Brazil and most countries in Sub-Saharan Africa). See International Marketing Illustration 7-2.

- *Urbanization and social class*—Industrialized countries, such as the United States, Japan, and the countries of Western Europe, are primarily urban and have a large middle class with substantial buying power. China's rural consumers are poor and have limited buying power; its urban consumers fall into four segments: "working poor" and "salaried class"—together accounting for 80 percent of the urban population; "the little rich," 15 percent of the urban population; and "yuppies," representing nearly 5 percent of the urban households.[5] Although multinationals such as Coca-Cola and Kodak actively target middle class consumers in the industrialized countries with their global brands, in China, they target their global brands primarily to yuppies; for the remaining 95 percent of the population, they have developed or acquired local brands in addition to their premium global brands.[6]

- *Education*—Most developed countries, countries that were formerly communist, and countries that are under a communist rule (China, for example) have a high literacy rate and heavily emphasize education. In contrast, countries in Sub-Saharan Africa have a lower literacy rate; here, education is a privilege. Companies that target these consumers have to adapt the marketing mix, describing product use pictorially in their communications. Countries where education is stressed present opportunities for educational institutions intending to expand globally, to firms selling training technology and software, etc.

Demographics are closely linked to psychographics, which include lifestyles, values, attitudes, interests, and opinions. It is difficult to describe psychographics without demographics. Cultural variables such as religion, norms, and language influence consumer product preferences as well. As such, these variables can be used as bases for segmentation. For example, Hofstede's dimensions—described in Chapter 5, "Cultural Influences on International Marketing"—can be used to segment countries based on individualism/collectivism, masculinity/femininity, uncertainty/avoidance, and power/distance. A study conducted with consumers in Europe[7] found that consumers in the Scandinavian countries have a small power/distance (are more egalitarian), have a low uncertainty/avoidance (take more risks), rate high on individualism, and have a low level of masculinity (low ambition and competitiveness). These consumers share certain traits that marketers can stress: They seek variety and prefer environmentally friendly products.

Many management consulting firms have come up with systems for segmenting consumers, clustering them on different behavioral and psychological dimensions, or **psychographic segmentation.** In the United States, a popular classification system is *Acorn,* which classifies individuals based on ZIP code. Another classification of lifestyles is provided by SRI Consulting Business Intelligence, which offers the *VALS 2* (http://www.sric-bi.com/) psychographic consumer segmentation system. Upon completing a questionnaire containing lifestyle and demographic questions, individual respondents are categorized based on resources and on the extent to which they are action oriented. VALS also has a survey that is especially designed for the Japanese market.

Other approaches to psychographic segmentation have been used in Europe: The Anticipating Change in Europe program examined different types of European consumer segments. One large study conducted within this framework used a representative quota sample of 7,600 Europeans from the continent's five major luxury markets, attempting to identify the relationship between culture, trend following, income, and the acquisition of luxury goods.[8]

> **psychographic segmentation** The use of values, attitudes, interests, and other cultural variables to segment consumers.

International Marketing Illustration 7-2

The Global Youth Consumer Segment

Figure 7-3
Niek and Alexander are representative of the global youth segment. They listen to heavy metal and rap, play various instruments, and are fashion conscious.

Worldwide, the global youth consumer segment presents an important opportunity for U.S. corporations to leverage their investment. The global youth segment has a $100 billion purchasing power. Most importantly, worldwide, this segment is growing: In China, 25 percent of its population is under the age of 14; in India, 31.1 percent; in Malaysia, 34.5 percent; in the Philippines, 36.9 percent; in Vietnam, 32.1 percent; in Pakistan, 40.5 percent; in Brazil, 28.6 percent; in Argentina, 26.6 percent; and in Iran, 32.97 percent. The global youth consumer segment hungers for U.S. products and entertainment, fed via access to satellite television and the Internet.[9]

Teens are the products of two cultures: local and global. For global culture, they represent a homogeneous target that can be targeted with music, fashion, film, and videogames; Game Freak's *Pokemon, Rockstar Games,* and *Grand Theft Auto* have, in fact, a global cult following.[10]

Global youth purchase Levi's and Diesel jeans, Nike shoes, and Ralph Lauren clothing. They see newly released movies, listen to popular musicians, go to discos, and are very interested in music in general (see Figure 7-3). Marketers find this segment particularly attractive: Coca-Cola has successfully targeted global teenagers with messages that use local and international celebrity endorsers; Nike is continually producing new designs for them.

An interesting hybrid European segment is a combination of the global youth segment and the global elite, a youth-driven Euroculture in which national heritage has become less important for a multi-lingual, educated, and well-traveled cosmopolitan segment with commonalities based on continental values and lifestyles. For such consumers, European MTV can be used effectively to sell CDs and related products.[11] This Pan-European segment covers a broad spectrum of male and female consumers from ages 12 to 45.

global youth segment A psycho-demographic global group of teenagers considered to be astute consumers with precise desires for brand name clothing products and entertainment.

global elite A psycho-demographic group worldwide characterized by high income and desire for status brands and exclusive distribution.

Global market segments present important opportunities for standardized marketing. Among the global psycho-demographic (a combination of psychographic and demographic segments) segments that have emerged are the following:

- **Global youth segment**—Psychographically, teenagers are described as astute consumers with precise desires for brand name clothing products and entertainment. They are described in International Marketing Illustration 7-2.
- **Global elite**—The global elite have the highest income of all consumers. From a psychographic perspective, they travel the globe, often have homes in more than one country, and spend money on luxury brands, such as Rolex, Prada, and Mercedes

International Marketing Illustration   7-3

The High-Sensation-Seeking Market Segment

High-sensation seekers, regardless of background, thrive on high stimulation and hedonic consumption. Their behavior translates into a windfall for manufacturers of high-risk products and entertainment—and even for the armies of psychologists, psychiatrists, and geneticists who specialize in sensation seekers. Medical research has found that the traditional attribution of high-sensation seeking to high testosterone levels is, in fact, a myth and that people hooked on thrills have a low cortisol level, which is remedied promptly by high excitement. Marvin Zuckerman, a professor of clinical psychology who has studied high-sensation seekers for four decades and developed well-known psychometric measures for sensation seeking, has identified certain common characteristics of the sensation-seeking market. High-sensation seekers drive fast, are drawn to excitement and to exciting people, and, "in every aspect of their lives, they are looking for the latest thing."[12]

But psychologists have yet to explain why the high-sensation-seeking market is increasing exponentially and across demographics. Worldwide, there has been a rapid increase in the past three decades in the participation in high-risk activities such as parachuting, hang gliding, ultralight and glider flying, bungee jumping, scuba diving, ballooning, and white-water rafting.[13] And amusement parks from Los Angeles to Tokyo to Paris are perpetually bracing for visitors who are themselves bracing for adrenaline floods.

Francis Tetard, a professional living in the Montpellier region in Southern France, epitomizes the high-sensation seeker. He has traversed continents in search of excitement, flying into blazing volcanoes and speeding through banana plantations in Central Africa. He spends his free time as staff of the local Aero Club, flying gliders, planes, and helicopters. His current personal excitement arsenal includes a helicopter (see Figure 7-4), a glider (Figure 7-5),

Figure 7-4
A Helicopter, Used for Sensation-Seeking Pursuits

(E-Class and beyond). The marketing mix typically used to target this group focuses on status: exclusive distribution, high price, and status-oriented advertising messages.

Another global psychodemographic segment is the high-sensation seeker, described in International Marketing Illustration 7-3.

Benefit Segmentation

Benefit segmentation also is a very useful tool for identifying uniform consumer segments. Marketers who understand the motivation behind consumer purchases will be able to send the appropriate message to the relevant market segments. Internationally, important

benefit segmentation The process of identifying international market segments based on important differences between the benefits sought by the target market from purchasing a particular product.

and his almost-family-member historic airplane, Bebe Jodel (see Figure 7-6). When Francis is not airborne, surveying the sea, canyons, mountains, beaches, and lakes in the region, his secondary passion is tinkering with the respective high-sensation facilitators.

Figure 7-5
A Glider Used for Weekend Pleasure Activities in the Languedoc-Roussillon Area of Southern France

Figure 7-6
Francis Tetard, a High-Sensation Seeker, in His Airplane, Bebe Jodel

differences exist between the benefits sought from purchasing a particular product. Consumers in the United States purchase soft drinks such as Coke and Pepsi to quench their thirst on a regular basis. In Eastern Europe, these brands are purchased primarily as special-occasion drinks.

In other examples, the majority of consumers in developing countries are not as much interested in brand names as they are in product performance and value. Marketing strategies catering to these preferences have succeeded in China: Philips Electronics introduced a very popular combination video/CD player, which Chinese consumers perceived as good value for the money.[14] And, although consumers in the United States seek speedy service, quality food, and convenience in fast-food chains, consumers in emerging markets are particularly attracted to the clean environment, pleasant ambience, polite staff, and air conditioning.[15]

Usage and User Status Segmentation

Usage rate indicates the extent to which individuals are

- Nonusers
- Occasional users
- Medium users
- Heavy users

usage segmentation The process of segmenting markets based on the extent to which consumers are nonusers, occasional users, medium users, and heavy users of a product.

Consumers worldwide can be segmented based on these **usage segmentation** dimensions. Segments of consumers identified as heavy users of a product category would constitute prime target markets for new brands in the category. For example, French women are heavy users of perfume, have a refined understanding of scent, and use different brands (often of the same company) at different times of day and for different occasions. Similarly, German, Dutch, and Belgian consumers are heavy users of beer. In each country, hundreds of breweries carry specialty beers, and each country is also an exporter of global beer brands.

User status refers to the status as

- Users of competitors' products (nonuser)
- Ex-users
- Potential users
- First-time users
- Regular users

user status segmentation The process of determining the status as users of competitors' products, ex-users, potential users, first-time users, and regular users.

In terms of **user status segmentation,** the ideal consumer is the regular heavy user! Companies introducing a product for the first time to a market of nonusers face enormous and costly challenges, in that they have to educate consumers about the product and convince them to buy, but these companies also can reap huge rewards, especially if they are first in the market. The paper towel offering in Europe was rather limited before the introduction of the Procter & Gamble Bounty brand; consumers typically used cloth towels in the kitchen because the brands available locally did not have sufficient absorption capacity for cleaning jobs. Bounty introduced its quality, heavy-duty paper towels in the late 1990s, accompanied by heavy promotion—particularly direct mail samples. The brand quickly took off, and now most households have an accessory previously nonexistent in European households: a paper towel holder.

Geographic Segmentation

geographic segmentation Market segmentation based on geographic location, such as country or region.

Geographic segmentation can be performed at the macro-segmentation level—country analysis, membership in international trade forums, regional blocks, etc.—as well as within the country. Consumers differ within countries with regard to demographics and psychographics, such as ethnicity, religion, and language spoken. Even in small countries such as Switzerland, the marketing mix needs to be adapted for German Swiss, French Swiss, and

Italian Swiss consumers; they constitute segments that differ not only linguistically, but also with regard to other aspects of culture, and consequently are likely to respond differently to marketing strategies. Belgium also is a case in point: A Flemish culture thrives in the north; in the French-speaking south, people view themselves as Wallonians rather than Europeans or Belgians; and a small German community exists in the southeast.[16]

7-4 Targeting International Consumers

7-4a Target Market Decisions: Country Screening and Selection

Companies engage in processes that involve extensive evaluation of countries' attractiveness for the purpose of market entry. In this evaluative process, a company must ensure that it does not overlook countries with potential and that it does not target markets in countries that do not provide sufficient potential and/or that present a high risk. To ensure that markets that present the most promise to the company—based on the company's goals and resources—are selected, countries are submitted to a screening process. Most often, screening of potential markets follows a variant of these three stages:

- Assigning an importance score to country screening criteria
- Evaluating country performance on each of the screening criteria
- Calculating the country attractiveness score

Assigning an Importance Score to Country Screening Criteria

An international company would typically aggregate a selection of criteria—discussed in section 7-3b, "Macro-Segmentation: Country Attractiveness Analysis"—that the company deemed important. Among these criteria are market potential, determined using economic indicators; the degree of political and financial stability; the extent to which the legal system is transparent and predictable; the state of the marketing infrastructure in the country; the degree to which consumers have a preference for company brands; the extent of competitive intensity in the market; and the market fit with company goals, policies, and resources. The criteria deemed important are selected from brand managers in different international markets, salespeople, industry country specialists working for management consulting firms, and international suppliers and distributors, among others. Each criterion is then assigned an importance weight that denotes the extent to which the company considers a particular trait important in its decision to enter the market.

Evaluating Country Performance on Each of the Screening Criteria

In the second stage of country screening and selection, potential target countries are rated on each of the criteria enumerated. The rating process may involve the same evaluators as in the first stage.

Calculating the Country Attractiveness Score

In the third stage of country screening and selection, the importance score is multiplied by the performance score for each of the screening variables. The total score for each country is then calculated by adding the resulting scores; this is the country attractiveness score that can be used to compare between potential target countries.

7-4b Target Market Decisions: The Target Market Strategy

Companies that have ample resources can, and often do, address the needs of all segments of consumers. Procter & Gamble, Henkel, and Kraft attempt to target all consumers with the products they sell, filling the supermarket and discount store shelf space with what seemingly are competing brands and saturating the media with their communication, meeting all related needs of the global consumer at a nice profit. Other companies with sufficient resources choose to focus on one well-established brand, improving it continuously, offering alternatives under the same umbrella brand name. Boeing uses such a strategy and, to date, it has only one true direct competitor—Airbus Industries. Not all international companies have the resources of the companies mentioned here. Frequently, small and medium-size businesses are quite successful internationally, as they are in the home-country market, by best addressing the needs of one segment, or a niche. One common trait of all these international companies is that they research very closely their consumers, and target and position their products accordingly.

Companies can use the three main strategies in Table 7-1 to target their international markets.

Differentiated Targeting Strategy

differentiated targeting A targeting strategy identifying market segments with different preferences for a particular product category and targeting each segment with different brands and different marketing strategies.

Companies that use a **differentiated targeting** strategy identify, or even create, market segments that want different benefits from a product and target them with different brands, using different marketing strategies. Some companies have the necessary resources to offer at least one product to every conceivable market segment. Procter & Gamble, for example, offers a variety of laundry detergents in North America: Bold, Cheer, Dreft, Era, Febreze Clean Wash, Gain, Ivory Snow, and Tide. To European consumers, the company offers Ace, Alfa, Ariel, Bold 2 in 1, Bonux Biomat, Dash, Daz, Dreft, Fairy, Moher, Tide, Tix, and Vizir.[17] Each of these laundry detergents appeals to a different market: consumers who want a detergent that has an excellent cleaning ability, consumers who need whitening, consumers who need fabric softening agents in the washing process, consumers who need a product for sensitive fabrics or for babies' sensitive skin, and consumers who may be allergic, to name a few.

Concentrated Targeting Strategy

concentrated targeting The process of selecting only one market segment and targeting it with one single brand.

Not all companies can afford to offer something for everyone, and not all companies want to meet the needs of all consumers. In fact, many companies select only one market, and segment and target it with one single brand, using a **concentrated targeting** strategy. Mont Blanc, a company manufacturing pens and fountain pens, offers a relatively limited product selection that it markets using the same theme worldwide—"the art of writing." This product is targeted at the professional class.

Companies that cannot afford to compete in a mature market with an oligopoly may choose to pursue a small segment—a niche. This option may be the only one available for the company's limited resources. Retailers often use a niching strategy—even international retailers, such as The Body Shop, catering to consumers who are environmen-

Table 7-1   International Targeting Strategies

Strategy	Purpose
Differentiated targeting strategy	Differentiated targeting strategies identify, or even create, market segments that want different benefits from a product and target them with different brands, using different marketing strategies.
Concentrated targeting strategy	Companies select only one market segment and target it with a single brand. Companies that cannot afford to compete in a mature market with an oligopoly may choose to pursue a small segment—a niche.
Undifferentiated targeting strategies	The product is aimed at all markets using a single strategy, regardless of the number of markets and/or countries targeted.

tally concerned and who want to purchase natural products that have not been tested on animals. An Amsterdam retailer called de Witte Tanden-Winkel (the White Tooth Shop) shows how a small firm can compete successfully using niche marketing: It sells toothbrushes, floss, and dental products—and nothing more.[18]

Undifferentiated Targeting Strategies and Standardization

The existence of similar consumer needs worldwide presents opportunities for international firms. They can reap the benefits of standardization by achieving economies of scale in the manufacturing process, in distribution, and in promotion. Pure standardization can be described as an **undifferentiated targeting** strategy, in which the product is aimed at the market using a single strategy regardless of the number of countries targeted and regardless of the locations where it is marketed.

Yet even products that are created as pure global brands, such as Coke, are not marketed using a standardized, undifferentiated strategy. Coke is sold primarily in recyclable glass and plastic bottles requiring a high deposit in Africa and Europe, whereas, in the United States, it is sold in disposable cans and plastic bottles. Its taste differs depending on the market. Diet Coke is sold as Coca-Cola Light elsewhere in the world. Heineken, the Dutch beer that bills itself as the world's most international brewery, uses a global positioning strategy of premium pricing and high quality, whereas, in Holland, the beer is positioned as a popular-priced product and usually costs no more than mineral water in most bars and restaurants.[19] The Nissan Sentra name was created by a U.S. research firm as a global brand to avoid language translation blunders; yet Sentra in Holland is called the Nissan Sunny and other Nissan brands include Bluebird, Cherry, and Micra.[20]

Certain products, such as food and culture-bound products, and most services do not lend themselves to a standardized strategy; they need to be customized to meet the specific needs and preferences of consumers. In general, it is advisable that firms standardize the marketing effort over similar worldwide segments and differentiate it across dissimilar worldwide segments.[21]

undifferentiated targeting A targeting strategy aiming the product at the market using a single strategy, regardless of the number of segments.

7-5 Positioning the Brand

Positioning entails placing the brand in the consumer's mind in relation to other competing products, based on product traits and benefits that are relevant to the consumer. Such a process entails identifying the international and local competitors, determining how the competitors are perceived and evaluated by local consumers, determining the competitors' positions in the consumers' mind, analyzing the customers, selecting the position, and monitoring it.[22]

Brands are positioned using a theme—a unique selling proposition. This theme could be unique to each market, for companies that customize their offering to local markets, or uniform, throughout the world.

A third approach also is common: a uniform positioning strategy that still allows local offices freedom for adaptation, if necessary. Coca-Cola, for example, formulates its worldwide positioning at its Atlanta headquarters but enables its affiliates in different markets to alter the strategy as needed.

The six international positioning strategies are illustrated in sections 7-5a through 7-5f.[23]

7-5a Attribute/Benefit Positioning

Procter & Gamble focuses on product attributes and benefits to position its products. An **attribute/benefit positioning** strategy uses product or service attributes and benefits to position it in the consumers' mind relative to competitors' products and services. The following are examples of product positioning by the company:[24]

attribute/benefit positioning Positioning that communicates product attributes and benefits, differentiating each brand from the other company brands and from those of competitors.

- Bold is positioned as a powder laundry detergent with fabric softening and pill/fuzz removal.

- Cheer, in powder or liquid, with or without bleach, is positioned as protecting against fading, color transfer, and fabric wear.
- Dreft is positioned as a detergent that removes tough baby stains and protects garment colors.
- Gain, as a liquid and powder detergent, is positioned as having exceptional cleaning and whitening.
- P&G's premium product worldwide, Tide, in powder or liquid, with or without bleach, is positioned as a laundry detergent with exceptional cleaning, whitening, and stain removal.

Such precise positioning, which is reflected in the company's communication with its respective segments, clearly differentiates each brand from the other company brands and from those of competitors such as Unilever and Colgate-Palmolive.

7-5b Price/Quality Positioning

price/quality positioning A strategy whereby products and services are positioned as offering the best value for the money.

Products and services can be positioned as offering the best value for the money. The **price/quality positioning** strategy is especially useful for companies marketing in developing countries. Manufacturers such as Toyota, Daewoo, and Philips and retailers such as Wal-Mart and Sears emphasize the value aspect of their offerings.

Alternatively, products and services can be positioned at the other end of the price/quality continuum, as the best product that money can buy. In addition to stressing high price and high quality, such positioning also entails an exclusive distribution or access, an expert salesforce and service, and advertising in publications aimed at the global elite. Mercedes-Benz claims that, in a perfect world, everyone would drive a Mercedes. Kempinski Hotels and Resorts, an upscale German chain, "reflects the finest traditions of European hospitality, luxurious accommodation, superb cuisine and unrivalled facilities—complemented by impeccable service."[25]

7-5c Use or Applications Positioning

use positioning The process of marketing a very precise product application that differentiates it in the consumers' minds from other products that have a more general use.

applications positioning The marketing of a very precise product application that is differentiated in the consumers' minds from other products that have a more general use.

Uses or applications are often used to position products in the **use positioning** or **applications positioning** strategies, respectively. Procter & Gamble's Era is positioned as a high-technology detergent that pre-treats and washes fabrics to suspend dirt. This very precise application differentiates it in the consumers' minds from other laundry detergents that have a more general use.

Sometimes the uses or applications differ from one market to another: A bicycle manufacturer would most likely position its offerings in Asia and Europe as efficient transportation machines, whereas, in the United States, it would position them as high-performance recreation instruments.

7-5d Product User Positioning

product user positioning A positioning strategy that focuses on the product user, rather than on the product.

The **product user positioning** strategy focuses on the product user, rather than on the product. The marketing mix for the Mont Blanc pen is targeted at the business executive anywhere in the world. The pen is usually pictured along with a quality business letterhead, with a passport, and/or with an attaché case. In this case, the product is understood to be among the highest quality pens around, so it receives only associative emphasis.

7-5e Product Class Positioning

product class positioning A strategy used to differentiate a company as a leader in a product category, as defined by the respective company.

Disney sells magic, not just entertainment. Harley sells excitement, not just motorcycles. And Parliament sells a glamorous, romantic America all over the world, not just cigarettes. Products using a **product class positioning** strategy differentiate themselves as leaders in a product category, as they define it.

7-5f Competitor Positioning

When a firm compares its brand with those of competitors, it uses a **competitor positioning** strategy. Some comparisons are direct, if the local legal environment allows it. Others are somewhat subtle. When Airbus asks readers of *The Financial Times* whether they would be more comfortable with two or four engines when they are up in the air, it makes implicit reference to Boeing.

All positioning, ultimately, is relative to competition, only not always explicitly so. Even symbols hint at competition: Merrill Lynch is bullish on the market (it is embodied by the bull); all other competitors are probably wimps. Quick, a local competitor of McDonald's in France, advertises cheaper prices: Its restaurants are quick and they are cheaper than McDonald's—and they are right across the street. *The New York Times*' positioning as "all the news that's fit to print" ultimately states that, if it is not published there, it is not newsworthy. (This, of course, may be problematic because the paper is sold all over the world—even where the New York Metro section has minimal relevance to local readers.)

> **competitor positioning** The process of comparing the firm's brand with those of competitors, directly or indirectly.

Summary

- **Develop a general understanding of international marketing strategy at the different levels of the international organization and provide some insights into the international marketing planning process of selected companies.** Planning takes place at different levels. At the corporate level, the strategic plan allocates resources and establishes objectives for the whole enterprise, worldwide. At the division level, the strategic plan allocates funds to each business unit based on division goals and objectives, whereas, at the business unit level, within each country, decisions are made on selecting target consumer segments. At the product level (line, brand), a marketing plan is developed for achieving objectives. An important decision is which product mix to use in the different countries where the company is present.

- **Identify the rationale for adopting a target marketing strategy in international markets.** International target marketing is used to identify countries and segments of international consumers that are similar with regard to key traits, who would respond to a particular marketing mix (i.e., segmenting the market); to select the countries and segments that the company can serve most efficiently and develop products tailored to each (i.e., targeting the market); and to offer the products to the market, communicating, through the marketing mix (i.e., positioning), product traits and benefits that differentiate it in the consumers' minds.

- **Identify the requirements necessary for effective international market segmentation.** For segmentation to be effective, segments must be easy to measure, stable over time, accessible, actionable, and respond differentially from other segments to a company's marketing strategy.

- **Introduce the concept of country attractiveness analysis and offer a blueprint for conducting the analysis.** Country attractiveness can be assessed by measuring market potential using indicators such as GDP per capita, industrial and agricultural sectors statistics, market size, and consumer buying power. It also can be assessed by evaluating international investment figures, such as foreign direct investment data and other trade statistics; the political, legal, and financial environment in the country; the existing marketing support infrastructure; the existing brand and/or company franchise for the product and/or company, and for competitors' products and/or companies; and the degree of market fit with company policies, objectives, and resources.

- **Identify the bases for consumer segmentation and offer company application examples.** Consumers are segmented on demographics, psychographics, geography, usage and user status, and benefits sought from purchasing the product or service. International firms segment based on the criteria that are most appropriate for their product or service. The job of the international marketing manager is facilitated by the emergence of homogeneous demographic segments worldwide, such as global teenagers and the global elite.

- **Describe the three targeting strategies used by companies worldwide.** These strategies are differentiated marketing, whereby companies address the needs of different segments by offering them different brands and using different marketing mix strategies; concentrated marketing, whereby companies address a single consumer segment that is large and stable enough to warrant the investment; and undifferentiated marketing, whereby a company can reap the benefits of standardization by using the same strategy to market to all consumers worldwide.

- **Describe the six positioning strategies that international companies can use to position their brands in the minds of target consumers.** International companies can position products by focusing on product attributes or benefits; by positioning the brand as a high-price/high-quality product or as the best value for the money; by positioning the brand based on use or applications; by positioning the brand based on product users; or by positioning it as the best product in its class.

Key Terms

accessibility	differentiated targeting	segmentation
actionability	geographic segmentation	stability over time
applications positioning	global elite	substantiality
attribute/benefit positioning	global youth segment	target market
benefit segmentation	measurability	target marketing
competitor positioning	price/quality positioning	undifferentiated targeting
concentrated targeting	product class positioning	usage segmentation
demographic segmentation	product user positioning	use positioning
differential response	psychographic segmentation	user status segmentation

Discussion Questions

1. International planning involves planning activities at different levels of an organization. Describe the planning processes that take place at each level of an international company.
2. International marketing managers use a number of criteria to ensure that segments are useful. Describe the effective types of segmentation and offer examples for each.
3. Macro-segmentation refers to country-level segmentation, and micro-segmentation refers to consumer-level segmentation. What bases and strategies do marketing managers use for segmenting their international markets using macro- and micro-segmentation?
4. Describe the principal targeting strategies. Go to the Mercedes USA (www.mercedes.com) home page. What targeting strategy does the company use? Explain.
5. Go to the VALS 2 web page and read the description of each population segment; also, go to the PRIZM web page. What segments would you ascribe to Mercedes users based on VALS 2?
6. What are the six positioning strategies? What strategies does Mercedes USA use for its U.S. market? Does Mercedes use different strategies for its international market? (Go to the other English-language Mercedes sites to answer this question.)

Chapter Quiz (True/False)

1. International positioning involves identifying countries and consumers that are similar with regard to key traits and would respond well to a product and related marketing mix.
2. Measurability refers to the requirement that the segment should be large enough to warrant investment.
3. Actionability refers to the ability to communicate with the international target market.
4. Macro-segmentation involves grouping countries together based on their political, legal, and financial environments.
5. Identifying markets based on age and gender is an example of demographic segmentation.

Multiple Choice

1. Target marketing involves
   a. market segmentation.
   b. market targeting.
   c. market positioning.
   d. all of the above
2. Which segmentation requirement refers to the ability to communicate with the international target market?
   a. actionability
   b. substantiality
   c. accessibility
   d. measurability
3. Proctor & Gamble offers a variety of laundry detergent brands to European consumers, which appeal to different market segments. This is a good example of
   a. undifferentiated targeting.
   b. concentrated targeting.
   c. differentiated targeting.
   d. none of the above
4. Which type of positioning focuses on offering the best value for the money?
   a. applications
   b. price/quality
   c. product class
   d. attribute/benefit

You can find the correct answers to these questions by taking the quiz and then submitting your answers in the Online Edition. The program will automatically score your submission. Where you miss a question, the program will provide the correct answer, a rationale for the answer, and the section number in the chapter where the topic is discussed.

Endnotes

1. Jeffrey E. Garten, "Cutting Fat Won't Be Enough to Survive This Crisis," *Business Week*, No. 3603, November 9, 1998, p. 26.
2. entertainment.iafrica.com, "Jessica: Europop with Substance," September 5, 2001.
3. "Kyrgyzstan Leads the Banking Pack," *The Banker*, Vol. 151, No. 901, March 2001, pp. 53–54.
4. "Sudan Politics: Oil Is Driving the US Move on Sudan," *EIU ViewsWire*, July 15, 2004.
5. Geng Cui and Qiming Liu, "Executive Insights: Emerging Market Segments in a Transitional Economy: A Study of Urban Consumers in China," *Journal of International Marketing*, Vol. 9, No. 1, Spring 2001, pp. 84–106.
6. Ibid.
7. Sudhir H. Kale, "Grouping Euroconsumers: A Culture-Based Clustering Approach," *Journal of International Marketing*, Vol. 3, No. 3, 1995, pp. 35–38.
8. Bernard Dubois and Patrick Duquesne, "The Market for Luxury Goods: Income Versus Culture," *European Journal of Marketing*, Vol. 27, No. 1, 1993, pp. 35–44.
9. Arundhati Parmar, "Global Youth United," *Marketing News*, Vol. 36, No. 22, October 28, 2002, pp. 1–2.
10. Ibid.
11. Art Weinstein, "A Primer for Global Marketers," *Marketing News*, Vol. 28, No. 13, June 20, 1994, p. 4.
12. Sharon Begley, "Researchers Delve into the Darker Side of Scary-Ride Junkies," *The Wall Street Journal*, May 31, 2002, p. B1.
13. Richard L. Celsi, Randall Rose, and Thomas W. Leigh, "An Exploration of High-Risk Leisure Consumption through Skydiving," *Journal of Consumer Research*, Vol. 20, No. (1), 1993, pp. 1–23.
14. Cui and Liu, "Executive Insights," pp. 84–106.
15. Ibid.
16. Weinstein, "A Primer for Global Marketers," p. 4.
17. See www.pg.com.
18. Weinstein, "A Primer for Global Marketers," p. 4.
19. Ibid.
20. Ibid.
21. See Imad B. Baalbaki and Naresh K. Malhotra, "Marketing Management Bases for International Market Segmentation: An Alternate Look at the Standardization/Customization Debate," *International Marketing Review*, Vol. 10, No. 1, 1993, pp. 19–44; and, by the same authors, "Standardization Versus Customization in International Marketing: An Investigation Using Bridging Conjoint Analysis," *Journal of the Academy of Marketing Science*, 1995, Vol. 23, No. 3, 1995, pp. 182–194.
22. Adapted from David A. Aaker and Gary J. Shansby, "Positioning Your Product," *Business Horizons*, Vol. 25, No. 3, May/June 1982, pp. 56–62.
23. See Aaker and Shansby, "Positioning Your Product," pp. 56–62.
24. See www.pg.com.
25. See www.kempinski.com.
26. Developed with Matt Crumley, Lisa Myers, Pascal Ontijd, Taylor Roberts, Kerrie Robinson, and Sean Wygovsky.
27. Chris Reiter and Stephen Power, "Western Europe Car Sales Rise; Germany Shows Weak Demand; Asian Makers Gain Share," *Wall Street Journal*, July 14, 2004, p. B 3.
28. "The Worst Managers: Jurgen Schrempp; DaimlerChrysler," *Business Week*, January 12, 2004, p. 72.
29. Deborah Bonello, "Car Makers Find Value in the Web," *Marketing*, July 7, 2004, p. 14.
30. www.bmwgroup.com
31. Ibid.
32. Chris Reiter, "BMW Sees Profit Jump 18%; New Models Outpace Mercedes," *Wall Street Journal*, August 5, 2004, p. A3.
33. www.bmw.com, Products, February 25, 2002.
34. Ibid.
35. Ibid.
36. Chris Reiter, "BMW Sees Profit Jump" p. A3.
37. Gregory White, "High Style in a Tiny Package —Top European Makers Bet Little Cars Can Coexist with SUVs on U.S. Roads," *The Wall Street Journal*, October 17, 2001, p. B1.
38. Mark Ritson, "Safe Bets Can Be Huge Brand Extension Gamble," *Marketing*, July 28, 2004, p. 1.

Case 7-1

Bavarian Motor Works: Positioning Alternative Offerings and Retaining the Image of Its Prestige Brand[26]

Bavarian Motor Works (BMW) is a leading global manufacturer of luxury automobiles. High-priced, high-performance automobiles, BMWs have long been status products for consumers worldwide. Called the "Beemer" by consumers in the United States and the "BMW" (pronounced *Beh Em Veh*) by most consumers in continental Europe, this brand of automobile is a legend of style and class. One of the company's greatest challenges is retaining its leadership position in the luxury automobile market—a challenge that has been recently compounded by the decision to diversify into the lower-priced automobile market. In one of its most daring moves, BMW successfully launched the MINI—a very non–BMW-like automobile, the outcome of BMW's relationship with the British Rover group.

The Automobile Industry

Depressed consumer spending worldwide coupled with weak economic growth in the first part of this decade has created pressure for the automobile industry. Automobile manufacturers work in a global marketplace that is demanding and fickle. U.S. manufacturers are facing challenges from Asian automobile manufacturers, such as Japan's Toyota and Korea's Hyundai, not only at home, but also abroad. Likewise, European automobile manufacturers find themselves increasingly under siege from U.S. and Asian competitors, slashing prices to survive. Volkswagen, Europe's largest automobile manufacturer, has found its profits plunging by 80 percent, its market share in Europe is rapidly being eroded by Asian manufacturers, its profits in the United States are falling by double-digit numbers as it attempts to sell its aging Jetta and Passat models, and in China, where it is the market leader, it has been forced to cut prices. Other European automakers are also struggling: Daimler-Chrysler's sales fell in 2004, and Peugeot Citroen's market share is falling as well, challenged by Asian competitors Toyota and Hyundai and U.S. competitor General Motors.[27]

The mergers and acquisitions of the late 1990s have not necessarily resulted in the expected high profits for automakers. In 1998, when DaimlerChrysler's CEO Jurgen E. Schrempp sealed the merger of Daimler Benz and Chrysler Corp., he told shareholders to "expect the extraordinary" from the $157 billion new company: The company was expected to have a $2 billion profit in 2003, and had instead a $360 million loss for the year, due to a tough market in the United States and to challenges from Asian manufacturers.[28] DaimlerChrysler also invested in the Mitsubishi Motors Corp., which, in 2004, had an operating loss of more than $400 million.

In other developments, the Internet is revolutionizing automobile shopping, especially in the industrialized nations. Forrester Research found that one third of Internet users have researched cars online, and research by AOL, an Internet service provider, suggests that almost 80 percent of car purchases are researched on the web first. Car manufacturers found that the medium allows them to generate leads via websites and gather data on potential buyers; as a result, BMW and Peugeot have recently announced a substantial increase in spending on the medium, above the average of 8 percent of the automobile marketing budget.[29]

The Company

Karl Rapp created Bayerische Motoren Werke (Bavarian Motor Works) in 1913 as an aircraft engine design shop just outside Munich, the capital of the state of Bavaria, Germany. BMW made its first motorcycle in 1923, resuming its production of motorcycles in 1948, after the war. As an automobile manufacturer, the company was struggling at first. An attempt to buy out the company in 1959 was thwarted by a small car with an Italian design and a BMW motorcycle engine named the "lion-hearted weasel," the BMW 700.[30]

Today, with brands like BMW and Rolls-Royce Motor Cars, the BMW Group has been focusing primarily on premium segments in the international automobile market.[31] The company is also diversifying into lower-price markets: It recently launched the BMW 1 Series, touted as an expansion of the model range in the premium segment of the lower middle class, and the MINI, aimed at the same segment.

The BMW headquarters constitute a Munich landmark, reigning in its imposing three-cylinder building just outside the Middle Ring (the Middle Beltway) as the city's tallest structure (see Figure 7-7).

BMW AG continues to demonstrate its lead over Mercedes: Sales have been propelled by its new models, such as the X3 sport-utility vehicle and the 6-series luxury coupe; the company's net profits almost doubled to $1 billion in 2004 and continue to grow rapidly, in spite of falling motorcycle sales profits and falling sales in North America, the world's largest market.[32]

BMW has traditionally catered to the luxury market segment with its high-performance, high-style automobiles. The company has traditionally offered the 3 series as its more affordable luxury line, the 5 Series targeted at the mid-luxury market, and the 7 Series targeted at the high-end luxury market. BMW also offers sports cars and sports utility vehicles (SUVs). The BMW Z3 sports and the 1 series compact; it also brought out a convertible version of the MINI in 2004 and the new Rolls-Royce Phantom.[36]

Targeting to Lower-Price Segments: The MINI, the 1 Series, and Certified Pre-Owned BMWs

BMW is aggressively penetrating the small and compact car market. As a first step in this direction, the MINI brand extension was the first little luxury model to be introduced in the United States by European manufacturers. It is BMW's reinvention of the 1960's British classic, a four-seater that is less than 12 feet long and only 4 feet 7 inches tall—barebones transportation with heated mirrors, a computer navigation system, an air-conditioned glovebox, rain-sensing windshield wipers, and an eight-speaker premium stereo. This is one cute car that appears to smile, while sporting a top that looks like a cap and a speedometer that looks like a salad plate.[37]In the United States, the MINI is very popular in urban centers, where it zips through traffic and fits in tight parking spaces. The MINI does not have the BMW name or emblem and is not distributed by BMW dealerships.

The BMW's 1 Series was an important line extension for the company: It was an attempt to attract younger consumers to the brand and to get a larger piece of Europe's compact car market.[38] The automobile competes in Europe with the Mercedes A Class and the Audi A3. For now, the 3 Series is the smallest BMW brand available on the U.S. market and BMW has not yet signaled that it will sell a smaller series in the United States; however, that may change, given MINI's success with U.S. consumers.

Beginning in 2002, BMW began focusing its advertising efforts on its Certified Pre-Owned vehicles. The Certified Pre-Owned BMW is given a warranty and a series of checks in order to be classified as Certified. With this push toward selling used cars, BMW might again be risking a dilution of brand image with luxury-conscious consumers.

In the long run, it may be that making the BMW name a more affordable prospect to more segments of the population would reduce the prestige and luxury appeal of a BMW. The jury is still out, however, because the other luxury automobile manufacturers are also broadening the appeal of their established brands.

Figure 7-7
BMW Headquarters in Munich

car is available in a coupe or roadster with a 4- or 6-cylinder engine.[33] The BMW Z8 offers the highest quality and performance of any of BMW's products.[34] In addition, BMW produces the M Series, high-performance machines made especially for those individuals searching for very high performance, safety, and design.[35] In its traditional product mix are also motorcycles, apparel, and accessories.

The company first introduced the MINI, a small compact automobile, which has fared well. More recently, the company introduced the BMW 6 series coupe, the X3 sport-utility vehicle,

Analysis Suggestions

1. As you analyze this case, focus on segmentation, targeting, and positioning strategies used by BMW in marketing the 1 series, the MINI and the Certified Pre-Owned BMW.
2. How is the BMW positioned in the consumer's mind? Describe the typical BMW driver, using psychographic and demographic variables for the description. What leisure activities does this driver engage in? What are the driver's hobbies? What magazines does the driver subscribe to?
3. What strategy suggestions would you offer to BMW to ensure that the MINI, the 1 series, and the Certified Pre-Owned BMW do not dilute the BMW brand?

Expansion Strategies and Entry Mode Selection

Chapter Objectives

By the end of this chapter, you should be able to

1 Offer an understanding of company expansion strategies, entry mode selection, and the risks involved at each level.

2 Describe different types of strategic alliances involving international companies.

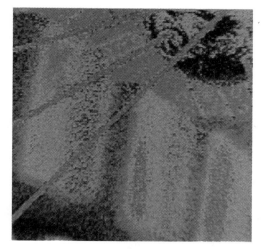

D ial your airline or your Internet service provider, and you will likely have someone in Bangalore, India, make your reservations or help you pay your subscription. You may be dealing with Delta Airlines, CompuServe, or many other services, but you will no longer hear a Southern accent at the other end—nor someone addressing you as "honey"; instead, you may hear a precise Indian accent with softened *v*'s that sound like *w*'s. And, if you make a joke, your customer representative may quickly steer you on to business, without letting on that he does not quite understand you. Ask your service rep where he or she is located, and the response may be India or China. And when you look around you in your community, you will find individuals recently laid off by service companies, such as credit card businesses, software companies, and customer service providers. The chances are high that their jobs were outsourced.

In other international trends, companies use strategic alliances to broaden their market access and appeal and to take advantage of economies of scale. National airlines become instant world-class carriers by establishing strategic alliances. For example, Delta Airlines started partnerships with Air France, AeroMexico, Air Jamaica, China Southern, Czech Airlines, Korean Air, Singapore Airlines, and South African Airlines, to name a few. These partnerships involve, in addition to mutual partner booking in areas not serviced by the airline, other types of advantages that ultimately benefit consumers, such as a frequent-flyer miles exchange. In addition to helping airlines cut costs and increase their customer base, the alliances may even help individual carriers weather temporary financial challenges. Other airlines actually share routes, with a flight bearing numbers of two airlines. Such sharing enables firms to have multiple flight options to a destination; it also lowers airport access fees. Examples of airlines sharing routes are United Airlines with German company Lufthansa, KLM Dutch Royal Airlines with Northwest (Northwest-KLM), and KLM with Alitalia.

This chapter will cover the international firm in the process of international expansion, exploring issues such as outsourcing and entry mode selection and evaluating the control and risks associated with each entry mode option.

8-1 Going International: Evaluating Opportunities

Managers of small and medium enterprises and multinational firm managers alike must evaluate the costs of delivering their products and services to their target markets. They need to take into consideration a number of important factors in their decisions related to the manufacturing and distribution of their goods. In Chapter 1, "Scope, Concepts, and Drivers of International Marketing," we examined the different drivers of international expansion in the environment, such as competition, regional economic and political integration, economic growth, technology and converging consumer needs, and the firm-related international expansion drivers, such as product life-cycle considerations, new product development costs, experience transfers, and labor costs. Many firms cross borders in search of lower factor costs, such as low-cost labor, capital, and land. As Table 8-1 illustrates, hourly compensation costs for production workers in manufacturing in the United

	Country	Compensation ($U.S.)
Table 8-1	United States	21.37
	Austria	20.83
Hourly Compensation	Australia	15.44
Costs in U.S. Dollars for	Brazil	2.58
Production Workers in	Denmark	25.16
Manufacturing	France	17.27
	Germany	24.31
	Israel	10.85
	Italy	15.07
	Japan	19.02
	Korea	9.04
	Mexico	2.61
	Netherlands	21.74
	Singapore	7.26
	United Kingdom	18.03

Source: http://stats.bls.gov

States are quite high, averaging around $21.00. However, in Singapore and Korea, average hourly costs are $7.26 and $9.04, respectively; considering the high productivity of these countries' highly educated workforce, Singapore and Korea may be attractive labor markets for skilled manufacturing work. Moving manufacturing to Brazil or Mexico would further lower labor costs to less than $3.00 per hour.

It should be noted, however, that wages are only part of the cost of production. Other costs are equally important—capital equipment, components, and land, for example. Firms must look at the full spectrum of costs and opportunities when deciding which markets to enter. An international manufacturing presence could ultimately mean greater access to the respective international markets facilitated by local governments that favor firms engaging in foreign direct investment. Companies need to examine the fit between the costs of international involvement (and the opportunity costs that they would incur if they ignore the international market), company resources, and market potential. They should also evaluate exactly how much risk they are willing to take in the process of going international and how much control they desire to maintain over the marketing mix.

8-2 Control Versus Risk in International Expansion

In broad terms, companies need to decide whether to use middlemen in the process of taking their products internationally or to market directly to the international market. Using middlemen requires a company to relinquish control: The distributors or agents sell the product. Middlemen allow the company to become involved in international business, while minimizing the typical risks involved in international marketing. On the other hand, direct international involvement exposes the company to substantial risk, but it also affords the company significant control of the marketing mix. Figure 8-1 illustrates the control and risk trade-off facing international firms in the process of selecting the international entry mode.

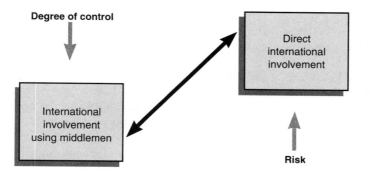

F i g u r e 8 - 1
Control and Risk for Entry Mode Alternatives

International expansion using middlemen may represent a first step in going international. Firms often test their international markets using distributors and, in a quest for higher profits and greater market share, eventually opt for direct international involvement. Section 8-3 addresses the different international entry mode selection and expansion strategies for international markets.

8-3 Deciding on the International Entry Mode

The **entry mode** classifications offered in sections 8-3a to 8-3i follow a general model of low to high control and risk, respectively. That is, company control over operations and overall risk increase from the export mode to the wholly owned subsidiary entry mode. In general, companies tend to use the export mode in their first attempt to expand internationally and in environments that present substantial risk, and they tend to approach markets that offer promise and lower risk by engaging in some form of foreign direct investment. There are, however, many exceptions: Companies that have been present for decades in attractive international markets, such as Airbus Industries and Caterpillar, continue to export to those markets, rather than manufacture abroad. Similarly, many new small businesses find that they can manufacture products cheaply abroad and distribute them in those markets without making a penny in their home country; this is increasingly becoming a possibility for companies selling using the Internet.

entry mode The approach to international expansion a company chooses based on desired control and on the risk it can afford.

8-3a Indirect Exporting

Indirect exporting means that the company sells its products to intermediaries in the company's home country who, in turn, sell the product overseas. A company engaging in indirect exporting can use middlemen such as export management companies, trading companies, or agents/brokers (described in Chapter 11, "Managing International Distribution Operations and Logistics") to distribute its products overseas. Alternatively, the company can use **cooperative exporting,** also referred to as **"piggybacking"** or **"mother henning."** With cooperative exporting, companies use the distribution system of exporters with established systems of selling abroad who agree to handle the export function of a noncompeting (but not necessarily unrelated) company on a contractual basis. Such companies are paid on commission or are charged a discount price for the product; they are larger companies with extensive experience in and knowledge of the target international market.

Using indirect exporting does not require market expertise, nor a long-term commitment to the international market. The company essentially sells its product to a distributor with little investment and without having to learn about the international market. The company's risk also is minimal; at most, it can lose a product shipment. Among disadvantages are lack of control over the marketing of its products, which could ultimately

indirect exporting An export entry mode whereby a company sells its products in the company's home country to intermediaries who, in turn, sell the product overseas.

cooperative exporting/ piggybacking/mother henning Using the distribution system of exporters with established systems of selling abroad who agree to handle the export function of a noncompeting (but not necessarily unrelated) company on a contractual basis.

lead to lost sales and a loss of good will that might ultimately affect the perception of the company and its brands in other markets where it has a greater commitment.

Some companies use indirect exporting as a first step toward a greater degree of involvement. After a sufficient consumer franchise is secured and the market is tested with the initial shipment, a company might commit resources for additional investment in the market. It should be mentioned, however, that indirect exporting in the long term does not necessarily mean that the company is not committed to the market; it simply means either that the company does not have the resources for greater involvement or that other markets are performing better and need more company resources. One of Europe's leading car makers, Germany's Volkswagen, operates through independent importers and distributors in Belgium, the Netherlands, Switzerland, and Austria, whereas in France, Germany, Italy, and Spain, which together account for the largest percentage of European sales, it controls its wholesale operations directly.[1]

8-3b Direct Exporting

direct exporting An export entry mode whereby a firm handles its own exports, usually with the help of an in-house exporting department.

Companies engaging in **direct exporting** have their own in-house exporting expertise, usually in the form of an exporting department. Such companies have more control over the marketing mix in the target market: They can make sure that wholesalers and retailers observe the company's marketing policies, charging the suggested sale price, offering the appropriate promotions, and handling customer requests promptly and satisfactorily. More control, however, is expensive. Companies carry the cost of their export department staff and the costs involved in selecting and monitoring the different middlemen involved in the distribution process—freight forwarders, shipping lines, insurers, merchant middlemen, and retailers—as well as other marketing service providers, such as consultants, marketing researchers, and advertising companies.

One venue that opens new opportunities for direct exporting is the Internet. With a well-developed website, companies now can reach directly to customers overseas and process sales online. And many companies do: Catalog retailers and dot-com companies, such as Lands' End and Amazon, respectively, long ago made their first international incursions by exporting their products to consumers abroad and have successfully expanded their international operations.

The challenges for companies using the Internet to export their products involve securing the appropriate credit in environments where credit cards and personal checks are uncommon and, finally, having sufficient sales to warrant staff expenditures needed to process and handle the international sales.

The primary export destinations for U.S. products are listed in Table 8-2. Note that our neighbors to the North and South—Canada and Mexico, respectively—are the primary purchasers of U.S. exports.

8-3c Licensing

licensing An international entry mode that involves a licensor, who shares the brand name, technology, and know-how with a licensee in return for royalties.

licensor The owner of a product license who agrees to share know-how, technology, and brand name with the licensee in return for royalties.

licensee The purchaser of the license who pays royalties to the licensor for the rights to use the licensor's technology, know-how, and brand name.

A popular international entry mode, **licensing** presents more risks to the company but also offers more control than exporting. Licensing also offers substantial flexibility to the company, allowing for rapid international expansion and high brand awareness worldwide. Licensing often does not require knowledge of the local market, and it may not even require any capital investment, allowing for a low-cost market penetration.

Licensing involves a **licensor** and a **licensee.** The licensor offers know-how, shares technology, and often shares a brand name with the licensee. The licensee, in turn, pays royalties. The licensor may license the product without the name, or it may license the product allowing the use of the brand name.

Licensing without the Name

A licensor is very selective when choosing a licensee, ensuring that products manufactured under license are of the highest quality. When quality cannot be guaranteed, either

Country	Purchases (Millions $U.S.)
Canada	169,770
Mexico	97,457
Japan	52,064
United Kingdom	33,895
Germany	28,848
China	28,419
South Korea	24,099
The Netherlands	20,703
Taiwan	17,488
France	17,068

Table 8-2

Top Purchasers of U.S. Exports in 2003

Source: http://www.ita.doc.gov/td/industry/otea/

because the licensee does not allow the licensor sufficient control and scrutiny, or because the licensee cannot guarantee quality, it is preferable for the products produced under license not to carry the licensor's brand name.

In the early 1970s, Italy's Fiat granted a license to AvtoVAZ, Russia's largest automobile manufacturer, to manufacture Lada, Russia's most popular automobile, and an important export to neighboring and other developing countries. Under a similar arrangement, France's Renault granted a license to build Dacia brand automobiles in Romania in the 1960s. Today, the automobile, which continues to sell under the Dacia name, is as popular as ever, and, in 1999, Renault acquired a 51 percent stake in the company.

Licensing with the Name

Licensors can decide to adapt the names of their products when they have a greater confidence in the capability of the licensee's workforce. One example is Poland's Polski Fiat. Fiat was confident of the reliability of Polish manufacturing and did not require the use of a different name for the product. Today, the company no longer licenses the Fiat name to Polish manufacturers; it has set up a subsidiary with multiple operations, Fiat SpA, which manufactures many of the Fiats sold in Eastern Europe under the Fiat brand name (primarily lower-priced models, such as Fiat Punto and Seicento).

Licensing is a lower-risk entry mode that allows a company to sell a product all over the world and offers the brand a global distribution. Beverly Hills Polo Club, for example, conducts business in approximately 85 countries around the globe, producing apparel licensed under its own name, all licensed apparel for Harvard University, as well as Hype, Karl Kani, and Blanc Bleu—a line that sells in upscale European retailers.[2] In fact, companies may choose to engage in trademark licensing, whereby brand names appear on merchandise without any design input from the parent company. For example, Eskimo Pie ice cream is sold around the world, but the product is not manufactured according to its U.S. recipe.

Licensing permits the company access to markets that may be closed or that may have high entry barriers. In the examples in the "Licensing without the Name" section, Lada, Dacia, and Polski Fiat were sold in the countries of manufacture at low prices, with few taxes, while automobile imports were charged tariffs at rates ranging from 50 to 100 percent.

Companies that engage in licensing agreements also limit their exposure to economic, financial, and political instability. In the event of a national disaster or a government takeover, the licensor licensing without the name incurs only the loss of royalties. The licensor that permits the use of the name may suffer a loss of reputation in the short term if the products are manufactured without licensor supervision and/or if they do not uphold the licensor's standard. In the latter case, the licensor has some control, at least in international markets. For example, it can bring to the attention of international trade bodies the sale of products that are illegally using its brand name, assuming the company has international trademark protection; in most markets, it also can sue the former licensee.

A downside of licensing is that it can produce a viable competitor in the licensee, who is well equipped to competently compete with the licensor. Training locals in company operations, particularly technology, can lead to the development of skills for future competitors.

8-3d Franchising

franchising The main international entry mode for the service industry, whereby the franchisor gives the franchisee the right to use its brand name and all related trademarks in return for royalties.

franchisor The owner of the franchise who gives the franchisee the right to use its brand name and all related trademarks and its business know-how, such as secret recipes and customer interfacing techniques, in return for royalties.

franchisee The recipient party to a franchise who pays royalties in return for the right to use the franchisor's brand name and related trademarks.

Franchising is a principal entry mode for the service industry, and it is the service industry's equivalent to licensing. The **franchisor** gives the **franchisee** the right to use its brand name and all related trademarks and its business know-how, such as secret recipes and customer interfacing techniques; the franchisor also may provide the franchisee with advertising and sales promotion support—all in return for royalties.

The popularity of U.S.-based franchises worldwide is undisputed: McDonald's Golden Arches decorate crowded Hong Kong streets, the picturesque Scottish countryside, elegant buildings in the downtown of centuries-old European cities (see Figure 8-2), and strip malls in Holland (where one franchise commissioned a giant Michael Jackson sculpture); they also border the suks (bazaars) in the Middle East. Among other fast-food franchises present all over the world are Pizza Hut, KFC, and Burger King. Many of these franchises are adapted to the local market, serving spicy vegetarian dishes (and no beef) in India and Sri Lanka and beer and wine in Europe. Although some of the products might differ (as do the sizes of portions—gigantic in the United States, minuscule in the rest of the world), the franchises look quite similar. They also offer the same courteous service, air conditioning, and toilets, and they run similar promotions.

Surprisingly, some franchises are successful even if the premise of the service's primary offering (hamburgers) runs counter to the local culture (religious ban on eating beef). When a company sets up franchises, however, it is especially important to evaluate the market's acceptance of the offering. For example, Starbucks decided in 2002 to compete with Austria's coffee houses. Although Austria is a good market for coffee consumption, with an annual consumption of 56.8 gallons per person, Starbucks encountered some challenges: It was unwilling to relax its global no-smoking policy, which is daring in a country with a high proportion of smokers. Also, the company's concept runs counter to an environment that perceives American coffee and the pace of life associated with American cafés as being different from the Austrian café business perfected over the course of 200 years[3]—the Kaffeehaus tradition. Nevertheless, the company has done well, positioned as a place to relax. Its signs inside read "Aroma protection through smoke-free spaces," and the company thanks customers for their understanding.[4]

The franchise, in its close association with the franchise country of origin (for consumers, the franchise may be representative of its country of origin), may be high on the target list for individuals who do not agree with the politics of the franchise home country, as exemplified in International Marketing Illustration 8-1.

The advantages and disadvantages of a franchise system are similar to those of licensing. The franchisor experiences less risk and a higher level of control over operations and offerings to the target market. Franchising also is a method that allows for very rapid market penetration, which is important especially when new markets open their doors to foreign firms. On the downside, franchising can create future competitors who know the ins and outs of the franchise's operations. In fact, one hears many stories of former employees from fast-food restaurants who offer a precise replica of the original franchise, while

offering better prices. Ideas of franchises can also be copied (see Figure 8-3). As soon as Esso (Exxon) stations in Europe started offering a Tiger Mart (a convenience store affiliated with the Esso franchise), local competitors immediately set up their own version that was even better adapted to local demands—selling, for example, potted flowers at discounted prices in affiliation with local growers.

It should be mentioned that licensing and franchising can be used instead of exporting, but also in addition to this approach to ensure rapid international expansion.

8-3e Joint Ventures

Joint ventures involve a foreign company joining with a local company, sharing capital, equity, and labor, among others, to set up a new corporate entity. Joint ventures are a preferred international entry mode for emerging markets. In developing countries, joint ventures typically take place between an international firm and a state-owned enterprise; in this case, the company's partner is the local government. As such, the company is assured instant local access and preferential treatment.

Many developing countries welcome this type of investment as a way to encourage the development of local expertise, of the local market, and of the country's balance of

joint venture A corporate entity created with the participation of two companies that share equity, capital, and labor, among others.

International Marketing Illustration   8-1

Successful U.S. Franchises in a Hostile World

Franchises have often been the scapegoats for action groups protesting U.S. politics, trade, and health policies, and globalization in general. In their use of English, with the corollary loss of stature of other languages, franchises are perceived as an imperialist enemy, driving out local traditional operations and imposing U.S. culture and traditions on developed and developing countries alike. KFC operations in India were closed by the government on grounds of compromised hygiene. A McDonald's franchise was vandalized in France and access to McDonald's was blocked in France and Belgium; a McDonald's was bombed in Xian, China, and another in Istanbul was a target of a pipe bomb. Other franchises were bombed in Beirut, Moscow, Ryadh, and in an eastern Indonesian town.

Still, U.S. franchises continue to do well abroad, even in hotbeds of anti-U.S. sentiment. Franchises stress the local origin of the products they sell, the local labor they employ, and their stature as local citizens. They even make fun of their U.S. origins to appeal to the local consumers; for example, in France, McDonald's ads feature cowboys who boast that the McDonald's franchises refuse to import American beef to guarantee maximum hygienic conditions.

U.S. franchises also support nationalist and local ethnic causes of broad appeal. For instance, in Serbia, McDonald's hands out free burgers at rallies and has added a Serbian nationalist cap to the golden arches, using the slogan "McDonald's is yours." And in Saudi Arabia, for every Big Mac purchased during a Ramadan promotion, McDonald's offers a 30 cent contribution to the Red Crescent Society and to a hospital in Gaza treating Palestinians.

The survival of U.S. franchises in a world that, for now, is somewhat hostile toward the United States is also due to the franchises' efforts to adapt to the local markets. They sell wine and beer in Europe, pastries in France, miso soup in Japan, and various other local dishes, pastries, and other consumer favorites. And, in spite of often-ignited anti-U.S. feelings, consumers worldwide maintain a certain preference for all things American, especially for an American education, medicine, airplanes, and the Internet—and for American franchises.

Source: Adapted from Philip F. Zeidman, "The Global Brand: Asset or Liability?" *Franchising World*, Vol. 35, No. 4, 2003, p. 52.

trade—assuming the resultant production will be exported abroad. In most developing countries, the international firm will typically provide expertise, know-how, most of the capital, the brand name reputation, and a trademark that is internationally protected, among others. The local partner will provide the labor, the physical infrastructure (such as the factory and access to the factory), local market expertise and relationships, as well as connections to government decision-making bodies.

It is typical for the local government of the developing country to limit the joint-venture ownership of international firms to less than 50 percent. It is also typical for the local government to encourage the reinvestment of profits into the firm, rather than the repatriation of profits by the international firm. As such, the government, in effect, leads the international firm to engage in transfer pricing, a method whereby the parent company of the international joint-venture partner charges the joint venture for equipment and expertise, for instance, above cost.

(a)

F i g u r e   8 - 3
Franchises often find that their concept is easily copied. McDonald's restaurants (a) in France often find a Quick copycat (b) setting up around the corner.

(b)

Joint ventures could constitute a successful approach to a greater involvement in the market, which is likely to result in higher control, better performance, and higher profits for the company. Successful joint ventures abound. In one example, British Petroleum PLC established a joint venture in Russia, under the name Petrol Complex, with ST, a powerful local partner with close ties to the Moscow city government. The company owns 30 BP gas stations, each of which sells an average of 3.5 million gallons of gasoline a year, four times the average of a gas station in Europe.[5] BP offers Russian drivers good service (a rare commodity in this market), as well as minimarkets with espresso bars and a wide selection of wines; this is in stark contrast to the Russian gasoline stations where customers pay for gasoline by stuffing cash through a tinted window and where they communicate with the salesperson through a microphone.[6]

The joint-venture entry mode is not limited to developing countries. Numerous joint ventures are operating throughout Europe, and they are increasingly coming under the scrutiny of the European Commission, which assesses their impact on competition. Typically, the Commission appoints a task force to investigate the impact of the joint venture on competition and then issues a statement of objections within six to eight weeks, giving the companies involved a chance to respond and request a hearing before the Commission makes its final decision with regard to the joint venture; whenever no such statement is issued, the deal is assumed to be on its way for approval.[7] One joint venture that the European Commission has examined involves the diamond giant De Beers Centenary AG (the world's largest diamond-mining company) and the French luxury goods company LVMH Moët Hennessy Louis Vuitton SA (which owns, among others, Christian Dior, Moët & Chandon, Louis Vuitton, and Donna Karan); the company would produce De Beers-branded jewelry and open a network of exclusive shops all over the world.[8]

Overall, 70 percent of all joint ventures break up within 3.5 years, and international joint ventures have an even slimmer chance for success.[9] Companies can, to a certain extent, control their chances for success by carefully selecting the joint-venture partner; a poor choice can be very costly to the company. Other factors that will increase the success of the international joint venture are the firm's previous experience with international investment and the proximity between the culture of the international firm and that of the host country; a greater distance erodes the applicability of the parent's competencies.[10]

Reasons for the failure of joint ventures are numerous. The failure of a partner can lead to the failure of the joint venture—for example, the joint venture between a mid-size company, Bird Corp. of Dedham, Massachusetts, and conglomerate Sulzer Escher Wyss Inc., a subsidiary of Sulzer Brothers Ltd. of Switzerland. Although the joint venture performed well, Bird Corp. experienced serious problems, with unsteady revenues and slim profits, leading to the failure of the joint venture.[11] Even a natural disaster or the weather could lead to failure: Zapata, a $93 million Houston, Texas, company involved in natural gas exploration, took a 49 percent share in a joint venture with Mexican investors with the goal of fishing on Mexico's Pacific coast for anchovies, processing them, and selling them as cattle and poultry feed. The weather system El Nino caused the anchovies to vanish, leading to the failure of the joint venture.[12]

Like licensing and franchising, joint-venture partners can turn into viable competitors that know the firm's operations and competitive strategies. In this case, the local partner will undoubtedly become a formidable competitor locally, where the firm will be protected by the government. Internationally, however, the international firm has some capability to combat the new competitors through controls and agreements with the supply chain and distributors that will prevent access to equipment or to markets, for example.

8-3f Consortia

consortia A company created with the participation of three or more companies; allowed in underserved markets or in domains where the government and/or the marketplace can control its monopolistic activity.

Consortia involve three or more companies. An example of a successful consortium that involves some companies with a substantial percentage of government ownership is Airbus Industries. Airbus is an international consortium involving France (Aerospatiale with a 37.9 percent ownership), the United Kingdom (British Aerospace, with a 20 percent ownership), Germany (DaimlerChrysler DASA subsidiary, with a 37.9 percent ownership), and Spain (Construcciones Aeronauticas, with a 4.2 percent ownership).

Most national governments and trade organizations are concerned with the monopoly effect that a consortium would create. In the case of Airbus, it was successfully argued that a single European country would not have the resources necessary to provide a challenge to Boeing, the U.S. manufacturer. In general, companies are allowed to set up consortia in the area of research and development, where they can share the cost of developing products that are at the forefront of technology.

Interestingly, consortia can have international subsidiaries. For example, Airbus has subsidiaries in the United States, Japan, and China. In the United States, the newest Airbus facility—and largest as well—is in Wichita, Kansas; it is the first design and engineering venture of the company in North America, and it has about 140 engineers working on the largest Airbus aircraft, the A380, the twenty-first century flagship airplane.[13] Most of the other non-European subsidiaries deal primarily with customer service training and support services.

8-3g Wholly Owned Subsidiaries

Companies can avoid some of the disadvantages posed by partnering with other firms by setting up wholly owned subsidiaries in the target markets. The assumptions behind a **wholly owned subsidiary** are that

- The company can afford the costs involved in setting up a wholly owned subsidiary.
- The company is willing to commit to the market in the long term.
- The local government allows foreign companies to set up wholly owned subsidiaries on its territory.

The company can develop its own subsidiary, referred to as **greenfielding,** which represents a costly proposition, or it can purchase an existing company through acquisitions or mergers. Many opportunities for acquisitions have recently emerged in developing and developed markets alike: Governments have been de-socializing services and industries, rapidly privatizing industries that were formerly government owned or operated. Opportunities have emerged in the area of telecommunications, health care, energy, and even the national mail service.

The most important advantage that a wholly owned subsidiary can provide is relative control of all company operations in the target market. In particular, a subsidiary offers the company control over how to handle revenue and profits. Wholly owned subsidiaries also carry the greatest level of risk. A nationalization attempt on the part of the local government could leave the company with just a tax write-off.

Additional difficulties could arise when a company decides to acquire or merge with another. In the case of DaimlerChrysler, Daimler quickly found out that the former Chrysler was not performing up to par and quickly proceeded to restructure, weeding out former Chrysler employees. In general, the company acquiring another or building its wholly owned subsidiary will not be able to share risks with a local partner, nor will it benefit from a partner's connections; it must build its own.

Even selling the subsidiary can eventually haunt the company years later. Harrods Buenos Aires was originally set up as a subsidiary of Harrods London but became an independent company in 1913 and changed hands several times. Today, Harrods Buenos Aires operates in Argentina and has no relationship whatsoever with Harrods London—which cannot address this issue successfully in the local courts in Argentina.

8-3h Branch Offices

The primary difference between subsidiaries and branch offices is that subsidiaries are separate entities, whereas branch offices are entities that are part of the international company. Companies that set up branch offices abroad often must engage in substantial investments. For example, Stihl, a German manufacturer of chainsaws, has a branch office in Bucharest, Romania, that handles all company operations in the country. In

wholly owned subsidiary The entry mode that affords the highest level of control and presents the highest level of risk to a company; it involves establishing a new company that is a citizen of the country where the subsidiary is established.

greenfielding Developing a brand new subsidiary.

addition to overseeing product sales, Stihl also ensures that servicing contracts are appropriately honored and that the representatives have adequate training. In low-income countries in Sub-Saharan Africa, where Mercedes is a standard of luxury, but where few locals and a handful of expatriates can afford to purchase the brand, Mercedes must still incur substantial investment costs. At the very minimum, it must invest in a sales office that has substantial staffing requirements and in a showroom that displays a few models. The company also is likely to engage in the distribution of parts to service stations and in the training of mechanics in handling Mercedes parts.

Branch offices of service providers typically engage in a full spectrum of activity in the domain of their specialization: The Chase branch offices in different European capitals handle the banking needs and credit to corporate and individual clients, in effect serving these markets the same way they serve the home markets.

Branch offices, like subsidiaries, also offer companies a high level of control over operations and profits in international markets. In terms of risk, however, the company invests much less in the market that can be lost in a government takeover attempt, compared to a subsidiary.

Companies also can have a presence in international markets in other formats that could be informal or more formalized. For example, the company could have a sales office (low risk, especially if the company does not carry any inventory in the country; some control). Alternatively, the company could be part of a strategic alliance, which will vary in the level of control it provides the international company, as well as in the level of risk to the company, depending on the type of alliance and resource commitments. Strategic alliances are described in section 8-3i.

8-3i Strategic Alliances

strategic alliance Any type of relationship between one or more companies attempting to reach joint corporate and market-related goals; term used to refer to most nonequity alliances.

All joint ventures and licensing and franchising agreements are occasionally loosely referred to as **strategic alliances** between companies attempting to reach joint corporate and market-related goals. This textbook, however, adheres to the mainstream thought that strategic alliances are formats that tend to be more short term in nature and that do not entail the same level of commitment as the previous categories. Such alliances crop up frequently and have various forms and degrees of "alliance." They vary from a contract manufacturing agreement that requires the contracting firm to provide raw material and training to the contracting factory in return for production that could last for two years, to an exchange of loyalty points (hotel, frequent flyer) between companies. The following are some examples of alliances:

- Manufacturing alliances
- Marketing alliances
- Distribution alliances
- Outsourcing

Manufacturing Alliances

manufacturing alliance A nonequity relationship between two firms, in which one firm handles the other's manufacturing or some aspect of the manufacturing process.

contract manufacturing A relationship between two companies wherein one company contracts with another to manufacture products according to the contracting company's specifications and for a specified period of time.

The category of **manufacturing alliances** covers many types of alliances, from **contract manufacturing** to technological, engineering, and research and development alliances. A typical example of a manufacturing alliance is that between the U.S. company Motorola, Inc., and Singapore's Flextronics International, Ltd., whereby the Singapore-based electronics manufacturer would make billions of dollars' worth of Motorola products. At present, Flextronics has manufacturing contracts for infrastructure and cell phones, among others.[14] In another example, Porsche has engaged in different types of technical alliances with Harley-Davidson, the U.S. motorcycle icon, primarily helping it develop low-noise, low-emissions motorcycles; most recently, Porsche helped Harley-Davidson develop its water-cooled Revolution engine.[15]

International Marketing Illustration 8-2 discusses two successful locations for contract manufacturing: Mexico and China.

International Marketing Illustration 8-2

Mexico and China: Factories to the World

Two of the most prominent examples of contract manufacturing locations are Mexico and China. Described previously in Chapter 3, section 3-3d, "Other Institutions and Procedures Facilitating International Trade," Mexican maquiladoras are examples of customs-privileged manufacturing facilities set up by U.S. businesses to take advantage of low-cost labor in Mexico. Maquiladoras, also known as "twin plants," were built in the 1960s along the Mexican border with the United States at a time when U.S. companies were trying to keep up with competition from Japan. U.S. companies were permitted by Mexican law to export components duty-free to the Mexican plants, where they were assembled using low-wage Mexican labor for re-exporting back to the United States.[16]

With the 2001 turndown in the U.S. economy, maquiladoras suffered, losing more than 300,000 jobs in three years. And they were further plagued by China's emergence as a strong competitor in areas where Mexico had thrived.[17] However, the tide has turned for the maquiladoras: The Mexican government has reevaluated its taxation, and U.S. firms have been deterred from moving to China after the financial crisis and the SARS health crisis. U.S. jobs continue to move to Mexico; for example, electrical parts manufacturer Kemet Corp. of Atlanta is relocating 500 jobs to Mexico, and Eastman Kodak announced that Mexico would receive jobs lost in Rochester, New York.[18]

The Chinese example is somewhat different. China is rapidly taking over as the world's top manufacturer: The world is looking at China as a primary source of low-cost labor. Its strategy has been to upgrade its technology through massive foreign direct investment and price competition based on comparative advantage in labor cost.[19] U.S. companies are increasingly resorting to outsourcing in China; for example, Sweetheart Cup Co., a manufacturer of plastic plates, cups, and utensils for McDonald's and Wendy's International, contracted with a Massachusetts consultancy, E5 Systems, to develop a system to track production processes at 14 of its North American factories. E5 is developing the system in China.[20]

Labor cost in China is so low that even Mexican maquiladoras are moving there. Yet, in addition to low-cost labor, China also benefits from admission to the World Trade Organization and a shift in political and economic philosophies designed to open the door to contract manufacturing and other businesses.[21] In addition, China is rapidly developing its telecommunication and transportation and logistics infrastructure, facilitating multinational business access to the local and international market alike.

Marketing Alliances

Some **marketing alliances** focus on all aspects of marketing. For example, Opel, the German subsidiary of U.S. auto manufacturer General Motors, signed a two-year contract to market its automobiles to 6.5 million America Online (AOL) subscribers in Germany by informing users about Opel and directing them to the Opel website.[22] The two companies are also considering a marketing alliance involving mobile Internet: Opel will equip its automobiles with mobile Internet connections, and AOL will supply

marketing alliance A nonequity relationship between two firms, in which one firm handles the other's marketing or some aspect of the marketing process.

content for the mobile service. Other marketing alliances focus on sales; for example, U.S.-based Northwest Airlines is in charge of all sales in the United States for the KLM Royal Dutch Airlines.

Distribution Alliances

distribution alliance A nonequity relationship between two firms, in which one firm handles the other's distribution or some aspect of the distribution process.

Distribution alliances are common as well. Mitsui and Mitsubishi have set up distribution alliances with Coca-Cola in Japan, bottling and distributing all Coke products in this market. Numerous distribution alliances exist under various formats and in countries of all levels of development. Emerging markets are well served by such alliances. In an example, Carrier Aircon distributes Toshiba's high-end air conditioners in India. The Toshiba air conditioners are positioned as a super premium product catering to a wealthy niche market. Carrier set up a separate exclusive distribution network for them.[23]

Outsourcing: A Rapidly Growing International Expansion Mode

outsourcing The strategic use of outside resources to perform activities that are usually handled by internal staff and resources.

Outsourcing is defined as the strategic use of outside resources to perform activities that are usually handled by internal staff and resources.[24] Outsourcing offers opportunities for strategic alliances for the service industry—and even for manufacturing businesses using outside resources to perform activities normally handled by internal staff. Outsourcing has been around for a long time, but until the late 1990s, much of the activity was in the realm of technology. Today, it is present in many domains and prominent in providing activities usually handled by internal staff, such as customer service and billing. The growth of the global outsourcing market has been phenomenal, and all indications suggest that this trend will continue, with the outsourcing market pegged at US$100 billion and growing.[25]

Asia has emerged as the outsourcing hub and back-office of the Western world, and India, China, the Philippines, and Singapore are competing for the business. India has initially received the lion's share of outsourcing opportunities, starting with information technology: A software developer in India costs US$6 per hour, compared to one in the United States, who costs US$60 per hour.[26] Subsequently, many other businesses turned to India for outsourcing, taking advantage of the low-cost, educated, and English-speaking labor force. As seen in the introductory section, Delta Airlines and CompuServe outsource many customer service functions to India.

China had initially focused on providing back-office support for financial services, telecom, software, and retailers in neighboring Asian countries because its operators can easily talk to people in Taiwan, Japan, and Korea in their native languages—China has plenty of Japanese and Korean speakers. However, China is rapidly making inroads as an outsourcing base for English-speaking nations, a business dominated by India.[27]

It should be noted, however, that many outsourcing alliances have failed in recent years. Companies should be aware that the success of outsourcing strategic alliances depends on a number of factors:[28]

- Outsourcing must be done carefully, and with clear objectives and expectations of outsourcing activities.
- Outsourcing partners must be selected based on their expertise in the outsourcing activity and based on their cultural fit with the firm.
- The outsourcing firm must provide its partner in the strategic alliance with adequate training and skills that will help the partner adapt to other cultures.
- The outsourcing plan should provide clear expectations, requirements, and expected benefits during all phases of the outsourcing activity.

Outsourcing is currently challenged in the United States, where government representatives urged on by their constituencies, are attempting to ban outsourcing, especially business process outsourcing. And this challenge may prompt other countries such as the United Kingdom and other European countries to contemplate banning outsourcing in the future. Yet, for every dollar going offshore, the U.S. economy gets back more than US$1.12 in income, while the countries doing the work gain 33 cents.[29]

Summary

- **Offer an understanding of company expansion strategies, entry mode selection, and the risks involved at each level.** A company can use different entry modes to enter a new market. They range from the lowest-risk mode and the mode that provides the least control to the highest-risk/highest-control mode. Exporting is at the lowest level of control and risk. Indirect exporting requires minimal internationalization and involves selling the product to distributors, such as export management companies, trading companies, or export agents in the company's home country, who then distribute the product internationally. Direct exporting requires in-house exporting expertise, usually in the form of an exporting department. Such companies have more control over the market-

ing mix in the target market than indirect exporters. Licensing and franchising are popular entry modes that allow flexibility and allow for rapid international expansion and high brand awareness. Joint ventures, consortia, and wholly owned subsidiaries are examples of foreign direct investment; wholly owned subsidiaries offer the greatest commitment to a particular market but also present the highest risk to investors.

- **Describe different types of strategic alliances involving international companies.** A company can use various forms of strategic alliances (manufacturing, marketing, distribution, and outsourcing alliances) to enter a new market. Such alliances are industry-specific, and they have various degrees of stability over time.

Key Terms

consortia
contract manufacturing
cooperative exporting
direct exporting
distribution alliance
entry mode
franchisee
franchising

franchisor
greenfielding
indirect exporting
joint venture
licensee
licensing
licensor
manufacturing alliance

marketing alliance
mother henning
outsourcing
piggybacking
strategic alliance
wholly owned subsidiary

Discussion Questions

1. What is the difference between international franchising and international licensing? Explain.
2. Briefly describe each type of international entry mode, from exporting to wholly owned subsidiary, and address the risks and controls characterizing each entry mode.
3. There are many types of international alliances. Go to the home page of U.S. Air (http://usairways.com/dividendmiles/index.htm) and identify the company's alliances.

Chapter Quiz (True/False)

1. Companies need to examine the fit between the costs of international involvement, company resources, and market potential.
2. Licensing is an international entry mode that presents less risk to the company but offers more control than exporting.
3. One of the benefits of franchising is that it keeps out new competitors.
4. Competing companies are allowed to work in consortia in industry sectors where the government can control their monopolistic activity.
5. Outsourcing involves the strategic use of outside resources to perform activities that are usually handled by internal staff and resources.

Multiple Choice

1. Which of the following is correct about using international middlemen?
   a. They increase company control over marketing strategy.
   b. They subject the company to less risk than direct international involvement.
   c. They maximize control for the company in the target market.
   d. All of the above
2. Direct international involvement has as a result which of the following?
   a. The company is exposed to less risk than if it used middlemen.
   b. The company has greater control over marketing strategies.
   c. The company faces greater risk in the market.
   d. b and c only

You can find the correct answers to these questions by taking the quiz and then submitting your answers in the Online Edition. The program will automatically score your submission. Where you miss a question, the program will provide the correct answer, a rationale for the answer, and the section number in the chapter where the topic is discussed.

Chapter 8

3. Companies may choose direct exporting because it allows them to
   a. monitor retailers.
   b. control suggested sale prices.
   c. observe the handling of customer complaints.
   d. all of the above

4. Franchising constitutes a primary entry mode for the _____ industry.
   a. automobiles
   b. technology
   c. service
   d. machine-tools

5. Which of the following is a reason for the failure of joint ventures?
   a. natural disasters
   b. poor performance by a partner
   c. partners becoming competitors
   d. all of the above

6. Porsche helping Harley-Davidson to produce its water-cooled Revolution engine is an example of which type of strategic alliance?
   a. distribution
   b. marketing
   c. manufacturing
   d. none of the above

Endnotes

1. Frank Bradley and Michael Gannon, "Does the Firm's Technology and Marketing Profile Affect Foreign Market Entry?" *Journal of International Marketing*, Vol. 8, No. 4, 2000, pp. 12–36.
2. Sherrie E. Zhan, "Choosing a Market Entry Strategy," *World Trade*, Vol. 12, No. 5, May 1999, pp. 40–46.
3. "Starbucks Targeting Austria's Coffeehouses," *International Herald Tribune*, Frankfurt Edition, July 5, 2001, p. 12.
4. "Starbucks Company Invades Austria," *Austria Information*, Vol. 55, November/December 2002, http://www.austria.org/nov02.
5. Sabrina Tavernise, "In Russia, BP Profits at the Pump," *International Herald Tribune*, Frankfurt Edition, July 5, 2001, p. 12.
6. Ibid.
7. Brandon Mitchener and Deborah Ball, "EU Clears De Beers-LVMH Venture," *Wall Street Journal Europe*, July 6–7, 2001, p. 3.
8. Ibid.
9. Dave Savona, "When Companies Divorce," *International Business*, Vol. 5, No. 11, November 1992, pp. 48–50.
10. Harry G. Barkema, Oded Shenkar, Freek Vermeulen, and John H. J. Bell, "Working Abroad, Working with Others: How Firms Learn to Operate International Joint Ventures," *Academy of Management Journal*, Vol. 40, No. 2, April 1997, pp. 426–442.
11. Savona, "When Companies Divorce," pp. 48–50.
12. Ibid.
13. www.airbus.com
14. "Motorola Scales Back Flextronics Outsourcing Deal," *International Herald Tribune*, Frankfurt Edition, July 4, 2001, p. 11.
15. Tim Burt, "Porsche Fires Revolution at Harley," *Financial Times*, July 14–15, 2001, p. 8.
16. Joel Millman, "Mexico's Maquiladoras May Be Putting Together a Comeback," *Wall Street Journal*, July 25, 2003, p. A12.
17. Ibid.
18. Ibid.
19. "China: Cheap Labor and Foreign Investment Aren't Enough," *Business Week*, November 18, 2002, p. 8.
20. Bruce Einhorn and Manjeet Kirpalani, "Move Over India, China Is Rising Fast as a Services Outsourcing Hub," *Business Week*, August 11, 2003, p. 42.
21. Perry A. Trunick, "Logistics Links Are Critical in China," *Transportation & Distribution*, Vol. 44, No. 8, 2003, p. 50.
22. Holger Schmidt, "Opel to Market Its Cars through AOL," *Frankfurter Allgemeine Zeitung*, No. 152/27, July 4, 2001, p. 5.
23. "Friendly Rivals," *Country Monitor*, Vol. 11, No. 16, 2003, p. 5
24. Dean Elmuti, "The Perceived Impact of Outsourcing on Organizational Performance," *Mid-American Journal of Business*, Vol. 18, No. 20, 2003, pp. 33–36.
25. Denis Chamberland, "Is It Core Strategic? Outsourcing as a Strategic Management Tool," *Ivey Business Journal Online*, July/August 2003, p. 1.
26. Pankaj Mishra, "US Proposes Ban on Outsourcing," *Asia ComputerWeekly*, February 16, 2004, p. 1.
27. Bruce Einhorn and Manjeet Kirpalani, "Move over India, China Is Rising Fast as a Services Outsourcing Hub," *Business Week*, August 11, 2003, p. 42.
28. Dean Elmuti, "The Perceived Impact of Outsourcing on Organizational Performance," *Mid-American Journal of Business*, Vol. 18, No. 20, 2003, pp. 33–-36.
29. Pankaj Mishra, "US Proposes Ban on Outsourcing," *Asia ComputerWeekly*, February 16, 2004, p. 1.
30. Developed with Maria Vornovitsky and Ramil Zeliatdinov.
31. www.vaz.ru
32. Ibid.
33. Ibid.
34. Carol Matlack, "Anatomy of a Russian Wreck," *Business Week*, No. 3594, September 7, 1998, p. 86b.
35. Ibid.
36. www.vaz.ru
37. Matlack, "Anatomy of a Russian Wreck," p. 86b.
38. Ibid.
39. Ben Aris, "A Tale of Two Car Companies," *Euromoney*, Vol. 393, January 2002, pp. 24–25.
40. "GM's Russian Partner," *Manufacturing Engineering*, Vol. 126, No. 2, February 2001, pp. 20–22.
41. Matlack, "Anatomy of a Russian Wreck," p. 86b.
42. www.vaz.ru
43. www.avtoreview.ru
44. Ibid.
45. Aris, "A Tale of Two Car Companies," pp. 24–25.
46. Jerry Flint and Paul Klebnikov, "Would You Want to Drive a Lada?" *Forbes*, Vol. 158, No. 5, August 26, 1996, p. 66.
47. Ibid.
48. Matlack, "Anatomy of a Russian Wreck," p. 86b.
49. Ibid.
50. Aris, "A Tale of Two Car Companies," pp. 24–25.
51. Flint and Klebnikov, "Would You Want to Drive a Lada?" p. 66.
52. Ibid.
53. "GM Seals AvtoVAZ Deal," *Country Monitor*, Vol. 9, No. 27, July 16, 2001, p. 8.
54. "GM's Russian Partner," *Manufacturing Engineering*, Vol. 126, No. 2, February 2001, pp. 20–22.
55. "GM Seals AvtoVAZ Deal," *Country Monitor*, p. 8.
56. "Auto Investment," *Country Monitor*, Vol. 9, No. 6, February 19, 2001, p. 2.

Case 8-1

AvtoVAZ: International Joint Ventures and Local Competitive Advantage[30]

AvtoVAZ, or Automobile Factory of the Volga Region, also known as VAZ, was created in 1966 by the Soviet government. The government had as a goal to create a venue for the mass production of affordable automobiles for the Soviet consumer. The company was built by transplanting a defunct Fiat assembly plant from Italy to Togliatti, a small industrial town on the Volga River shores.

AvtoVAZ in the Soviet Era

AvtoVAZ's first car, the Zhiguli (better known in the West as Lada), was built based on Fiat 124, an automobile produced in Italy 20 years earlier. This first Lada was produced on April 19, 1970, and quickly became Russia's most popular passenger automobile.[31] Its first model was VAZ 2101, which was endearingly called "kopeika" (the penny). It was considered to be of very high quality, and many of these models can still be seen on the road today. Russians were so infatuated with this automobile that there is a movie titled *Kopeika*, dedicated to this automobile, illustrating the life of the car and its owners.

Over the years, the factory began to gain popularity as it strove to "supply Russian citizens with cars especially made for the tough Russian climate and harsh road conditions."[32] During the Soviet era, AvtoVAZ quickly grew and expanded its production of the Lada. It later introduced Niva, a new model, in 1977, and Samara, in the 1980s. These efforts allowed the company to move ahead of other Soviet automobile manufacturers AZLK, producer of Moskvich, a higher-end automobile; and AvtoGAZ, producer of the Volga, an automobile used primarily for government officials and functions.

Post-Soviet AvtoVAZ

After 1989, the end of Communism brought drastic changes to the political and economic environment. In addition to the breakup of the Soviet Union, the drive toward a new market economy placed substantial pressure on the old state-owned enterprises. AvtoVAZ needed to implement important changes to continue to compete in the new transition economy and to operate successfully in an unstable economic environment. The company privatized immediately after the fall of Communism—it was the first automobile company in Post-Soviet Russia to adapt to a market environment[33]—and promptly lost its former government protection. It also became a target of corruption and mismanagement. At first, the Yeltsin government turned a blind eye to conflicts of interest and theft by corporate managers to win support for policies such as privatization. Today, Russia and AvtoVAZ are paying the price: Companies are held hostage by networks that rob the government of tax revenues, soak up cash needed for industrial modernization, and fuel organized crime.[34]

In 1989, Boris A. Berezovsky, a management-systems consultant to AvtoVAZ, organized a nationwide car-dealership chain that would later bring him vast wealth; he persuaded AvtoVAZ Chief Executive Vladimir Kadannikov to supply him with automobiles without up-front payment. As hyperinflation raged in the early 1990s, Berezovsky earned billions of rubles, partly by delaying payments for AvtoVAZ cars.[35] When the company privatized, in 1993,[36] Kadannikov and Berezovsky set up a company, called the All-Russian Automobile Alliance, which gradually amassed a 34 percent stake in AvtoVAZ. Other AvtoVAZ managers and employees own 35 percent of the company, and Automotive Finance Corp., an affiliate headed by Kadannikov, holds an estimated 19 percent.[37]

Subsequently, trading companies mushroomed around AvtoVAZ, taking advantage of its need for parts and its poor distribution network. The companies swapped components for cars—straight from the factory—at prices as much as 30 percent below market value. Many traders took cars without prepaying, often waiting months before settling. By late 1996, some 300 trading companies were operating with AvtoVAZ. While they raked in millions of dollars in profits, they also owed AvtoVAZ $1.2 billion, about 35 percent of annual sales, for cars delivered to dealers.[38] Furthermore, organized crime became involved in AvtoVAZ, requiring payments equivalent to $100 per automobile to ensure safe delivery. The late 1990s, however, announced a new period for AvtoVAZ, one in which the company was forced to address these irregularities. These changes, along with a slowdown in rampant inflation, helped the company turn around and enabled it to explore new growth options through joint ventures.

AvtoVAZ Today

Currently, AvtoVAZ has a substantial part of the Russian automobile market. A high percentage of automobiles on Russian roads (70.31 percent, or 960,000 automobiles) are produced by AvtoVAZ, whereas only 13.02 percent are produced by its largest Russian competitor, AvtoGAZ. In provincial Russia, there are primarily just two makes of automobiles: the Zhiguli, by AvtoVAZ, which has about 60 percent of the market share; and the Volga, by AvtoGAZ.[39] AvtoVAZ exports more than 98,000 automobiles yearly.[40]

Even though AvtoVAZ operates less efficiently than its foreign competitors (it builds an automobile in 320 hours, whereas an automobile at a European plant takes an average of 28 hours to build),[41] it is a perfect fit with the budget and aptitudes of the Russian consumer. AvtoVAZ touts itself as "optimal for the Russian market relationship between price and quality."[42]

Indeed, Russian automobile buyers spend an average price of $5,000 to $6,000 for a new Lada and have an interesting relationship

continued

to the automobile. For example, VAZ owners never use official dealer automobile services; instead, they prefer to use private garages, with self-taught mechanics. Russian automobile buyers are practical: They do not expect the automobile to function perfectly right off the assembly line; the automobile's performance problems are addressed by the private garages at a reasonable fee. Russians expect their brand new Ladas to have some sort of defect; it is recommended to take the car for tuning as soon as it is bought. The tuning consists of a complete change of transmission, some modification of the battery, and a complete change of brakes and tires.[43]

Russian buyers are not too concerned about design—their main consideration is price. Russians also make practical choices when it comes to automobile options: They prefer metallic color, which lasts longer; metal protection for the bottom against winter damage; and rubber mats so that they do not vacuum the automobile often. Russian drivers value Ladas for their simplicity, which allows them to fix the automobile themselves; for their durability in withstanding tough climate and road conditions; and for their small size, which makes driving and parking in cities easier.[44]

AvtoVAZ also introduced a new model, the Kalina, a cheaper car than the Lada, in fall of 2004; it sells for about $4,000.[45]

VAZ Competitors

In spite of the popularity of its Lada model, AvtoVAZ is rapidly losing market share to foreign competitors. Used automobiles from Europe, especially from Germany, compete directly with the VAZ automobiles, and especially with its latest models—2110, 2111, and 2112. German automobiles continue to function without needing any repairs after four years of operation. In fact, without duties on imports of up to 100 percent, Russian automakers would be out of business. Even with the duties, more than 400,000 automobiles are imported yearly.[46] But important drawbacks for imported foreign cars are parts, which are expensive, and service; moreover, neither exists outside Moscow and St. Petersburg.[47]

Competitors such as Daewoo Corporation (Korea) and Skoda (Czech Republic) are also assembling cars in Russia,[48] creating additional competition for AvtoVAZ.

Among Russian competitors, the worst of the local carmakers, AZLK (making the Moskvich) and truckmaker ZIL, are practically shut down. The viable Russian competitors, truckmaker Kamaz and GAZ, have seen production pick up in the past few years. The GAZ (Gorky Auto Works) factory complex was built in Gorky—known today as Nizhny Novgorod—in the 1930s, with help from Henry Ford. GAZ has a huge plant, with a capacity for 400,000-plus vehicles, including 300,000 medium-size trucks targeted to the military, agriculture, and industrial markets. GAZ has also created a light truck, the Gazelle, targeted toward Russia's new small businesses. The GAZ passenger car is the Volga, targeted initially for government use, which maintains its 1970s looks.[49] As the company is changing its focus from production to profits, the price of the Volga has been raised, which ultimately has hurt sales (its price is now close to that of many foreign automobiles); consequently, spare capacity was switched to making the more profitable light trucks and minibuses.[50]

Soviet planners decided to build the largest truck factory in the world: They built the Kamaz plant along the Kama River in Tatarstan, near the Urals. Kamaz covers 50 square kilometers with foundries, an engine plant, and an assembly line theoretically capable of producing 150,000 big trucks a year. (For comparison, the U.S. heavy truck market is about 150,000 in a normal year.) The fall of Communism led to a plummeting production, and the company was ripe for restructuring; costs were cut so that Kamaz would produce just 25,000 to 35,000 units a year, and the firm Deloitte & Touche was hired to keep the books and suggest improvements. The firm Kohlberg Kravis Roberts agreed to raise $3.5 billion over six years in exchange for 49 percent of Kamaz; the money was used to develop a new 25-ton truck for the oil and timber industries—a tractor trailer capable of competing with the best from abroad, with a diesel engine from U.S.-owned Cummins, a transmission from Germany's ZF, and a cab from the Netherlands' DAF—and a light truck to challenge the Gazelle. Kamaz is also moving into passenger cars, with a microcar, the 30hp Oka, which sells for $3,500. Kamaz loses $1,000 or so per automobile, but its goal is to be profitable at 50,000 units.[51]

The last of the still-healthy Russian carmakers is UAZ. It makes off-road utility vehicles and small buses, for a total of 93,000 yearly. The company, with designs that date back to the 1970s, has limited working capital.[52]

The AvtoVAZ–GM Joint Venture: Creating a Competitive Advantage

General Motors and the European Bank for Reconstruction and Development, whose mission is to finance economic development projects in Eastern Europe, created a new opportunity for AvtoVAZ: a $340 million joint venture to manufacture off-road vehicles in Togliatti. GM owns a 41.5 percent stake in the joint venture and invested $100 million; EBRD has a 17 percent stake, with $40 million, lending an additional $100 million; and AvtoVAZ contributed manufacturing facilities and intellectual property valued at $100 million, for a 41.5 percent stake. The new company produces the new GM-branded Niva, aiming for a maximum yearly output of 75,000 vehicles, of which more than half are built for export.[53] The new Niva is sold in Western Europe and to markets in Africa, Asia, Latin America, and the Middle East, where the old Niva was popular.[54] In Germany, the Niva is equipped with engines from Adam Opel.[55]

The joint venture attempts to maintain the price of the new cars below $10,000 (still beyond the reach of most Russian automobile buyers), but this requires dependence on domestic components; and lack of these components in sufficient volumes and at required quality levels have previously set back plans by Ford (U.S.) and Fiat (Italy) to produce for the Russian market.[56]

The Niva sport-utility vehicle looks very attractive and has an impressive design. However, Russian consumers, in addition to balking at its price, still perceive it as being of lower quality: The automobile is assembled on the VAZ platform by VAZ workers. Also, the automobile body is produced at VAZ facilities—not at new GM facilities—so the Niva buyers do not expect the automobile finishing to be superior and last longer than that of the Niva ancestor, VAZ 21213.

Analysis Suggestions

1. Discuss the positioning strategies of the different competitors in the Russian market. Are the competitors competing for the same segments? Explain.
2. Address the potential contribution of the GM–AvtoVAZ joint venture to creating competitive advantage for the AvtoVAZ.

part 4

Managing the International Marketing Mix

9

Products and Services: Branding Decisions in International Markets

C h a p t e r   O b j e c t i v e s

By the end of this chapter, you should be able to

1 Describe drivers for international standardization and offer an overview of the international standardization–local adaptation continuum and respective company strategies.

2 Examine country-of-origin effects on brand evaluations in relation to product stereotypes and consumer ethnocentrism.

3 Examine challenges faced by service providers in international markets.

4 Address issues related to brand name protection and the reasons behind widespread international counterfeiting.

5 Address the marketing of industrial products and services and related product and service standards.

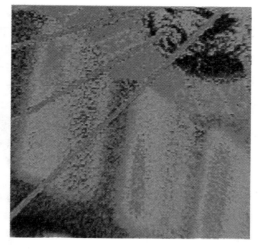

The world has been gradually moving toward one large, global marketplace. As Chapter 4, "Regional Economic and Political Integration," illustrated, a fragmented Europe is merging into one large, unified market, as is South America; the Asian market also is gradually removing barriers and allowing more access to Western multinationals. A number of mature products—consumer electronics, for instance—have succeeded in addressing the needs of consumers worldwide in essentially the same format, with only minimal market modifications.[1] Sony (Japan), for example, markets the Trinitron television set using similar marketing strategies worldwide; Braun and Krups (Germany) sells kitchen appliances using the same marketing mix across continents with only minor mandatory adaptations (voltage, cycles, television systems).

Similarly, franchises such as KFC, Pizza Hut, McDonald's, and Burger King are only minimally altering their offerings to meet local demands, offering wine and beer in some European countries and miso soup in Japan. Mineral water distributors—such as Gerolsteiner (Germany), Evian and Volvic (France)—and food manufacturers—such as the Kraft International company and Jacobs Suchard (Toblerone and Suchard chocolate, Jacobs coffee, among others)—are modifying only their labels to conform to local requirements when selling their products across different continents.

Yet, for certain product categories that appeal to local preferences, international firms have had to adapt their offerings to effectively compete with local manufacturers and service providers and to more directly cater to the individual needs of local markets. Advertising agencies and numerous financial and legal service providers, for example, typically partner with local firms to create successful campaigns and strategies aimed at individual markets.

This chapter examines the driving forces behind the decision to standardize, or to partially or fully adapt the offerings to individual international markets. It also addresses barriers faced by brands from private-label offerings and by service providers from local government. The chapter addresses brand name protection issues and reasons behind the proliferation of counterfeiting activity worldwide.

9-1 Standardization Versus Adaptation

The topic of standardization versus **adaptation,** to a certain extent, parallels the concepts introduced in Chapter 1, "Scope, Concepts, and Drivers of International Marketing," addressing geocentric, regiocentric, and polycentric orientations—with global standardization reflecting a geocentric company orientation, regional standardization reflecting a regiocentric orientation, and local adaptation reflecting a polycentric orientation, respectively (see Figure 9-1). It must be noted, however, that multinational companies may adopt a combination strategy, depending on the particulars of individual markets. For instance, PepsiCo is a global company with, most likely, a geocentric orientation; however, it has only recently moved from a localized strategy to a regional strategy in terms of its distribution and purchasing.

adaptation The strategy of altering a product to better meet the needs of a local market.

```
┌─────────────────────────────────┐
│      Global standardization      │
└─────────────────────────────────┘
                 │
                 ▼
┌─────────────────────────────────┐
│      Regional standardization    │
└─────────────────────────────────┘
                 │
                 ▼
┌─────────────────────────────────┐
│        Global localization       │
└─────────────────────────────────┘
                 │
                 ▼
┌─────────────────────────────────┐
│        Mandatory adaptation      │
└─────────────────────────────────┘
                 │
                 ▼
┌─────────────────────────────────┐
│   Local, non-mandatory adaptation│
└─────────────────────────────────┘
```

9-1a Global Standardization

global standardization The standardization of products across markets and, ultimately, to the standardization of the marketing mix worldwide; more commonly called glocalization.

Global standardization, frequently used interchangeably with the term "globalization," refers first to standardization of products across markets and, ultimately, to the standardization of the marketing mix worldwide. This latter definition will be used in this textbook.

Among the numerous arguments in favor of global standardization of the marketing mix are the following:[2]

- Global consumers
- International travel
- Consumer preference for higher quality and lower price

Global Consumers

global consumers The homogeneous consumer group worldwide sharing similar interests and product/brand preferences.

Consumers' interests and product/service-related needs are becoming more and more homogeneous worldwide. As a consequence, products and, indeed, brand preferences are gaining a common definition across continents, leading to the emergence of **global consumers.** In-line skating constitutes a favorite pre-teen pastime in New York, Warsaw, and Delhi. Blonde, svelte Barbie dolls and Barbie-doll look-alikes are on the wish lists of little girls in developed countries and developing countries. Little German viewers of the British *Teletubbies* television show watch Dipsy say "Winke-Winke" (bye-bye) and demand Teletubbies merchandise, as do toddlers in the United States. Professional loggers in the U.S. Northwest and those in the Scandinavian Peninsula perceive the German Stihl chainsaw as a high-quality product.

International Travel

As more and more consumers engage in international travel, they are confronted with advertisements for the same products that they have initially encountered in their home countries. Building brand awareness globally is simply easier, especially given the overlapping media in many countries and, consequently, the higher likelihood of exposure to the brand name.[3] Global brands also are more prestigious, signaling that the company has the resources necessary to back the respective brands.[4]

Consumer Preference for Higher Quality and Lower Price

Consumers worldwide are willing to sacrifice product-related features, function, and design to obtain higher quality at a lower price—achieved as companies acquire economies of scale in research and development, production, distribution, and promotion. To address uniform needs of consumers, Ford attempted a global product approach to vehicle design and production, building "world cars."[5] Its first such experiment was the launch of the Ford Contour/Mercury Mystique in the United States and the Mondeo in Europe in 1993.[6] This attempt was followed by the marketing of the Ford Focus, which is successful on both sides of the Atlantic.

The strategy used to address these needs is global branding. A global brand has the same name, logo, image, and positioning everywhere in the world. Main streets in most world capitals and malls worldwide advertise and sell brands such as Ralph Lauren, Escada, and Donna Karan, while logos of Pepsi-Cola, Coca-Cola, and Camel and Kent cigarettes adorn umbrellas in many central squares. These are global brands, enjoying worldwide reputation and recognition, demanded by consumers in Beijing, Antananarivo, and Paris alike. These brands have a high awareness among consumers worldwide and are perceived to be of high quality.

Standardization is particularly important for product research and development. Economies of scale can be achieved if there is a concentration in research and development, and coordination also gives a firm flexibility in responding to competitors' R&D efforts.[7] Such coordination is expensive; moreover, governments may restrain the flow of information and people, which are required to coordinate research and development activities.[8]

With regard to the other components of the marketing mix, advertising savings can be achieved by having a uniform advertising strategy in each country. PepsiCo, for example, saved an estimated $10 million as a result of using the same film for television advertising in different international markets.[9] Similarly, the standardization of supply chains has resulted in cost reductions in transportation and distribution, with significant cost reductions and overall shorter transportation times; and, finally, research and development, purchasing, packaging, and customer service, among others, also have benefited from standardization.[10] These issues will be examined in Chapter 11, "Managing International Distribution Operations and Logistics," and Chapter 13, "The International Promotional Mix and Advertising Strategies."

9-1b Regional Standardization

A variation of global standardization, a **regional standardization** strategy refers to the use of a uniform marketing strategy within a particular region. This strategy is becoming more appealing to companies as regional market integration is gaining strength worldwide, with the European Union, MERCOSUR, and NAFTA in particular gaining ground as veritable unified markets. Pan-European brands are becoming common, even for U.S. multinationals, such as Procter & Gamble (whose Ariel detergent was its first Pan-European product; today, the brand is available in most markets, with the exception of North America).

regional standardization The use of a uniform marketing strategy within a particular region.

In addition to regional branding strategies, companies also benefit from economies of scale by concentrating certain marketing activities regionally. PepsiCo, for example, centralized purchasing across all of its European businesses, thus achieving volume savings from sugar, cooking oil, flour, and packaging materials, for a total of $100 million per year.[11] In terms of distribution, Nike has traditionally utilized local warehousing to supply retailers; the company has replaced more than 20 national warehouses in Europe with one single distribution center located in Belgium, thus using a strategy similar to that used in the United States, where it has successfully centralized its American operations in Memphis.[12]

Mercedes-Benz (www.mercedes.com) is a brand that appears to have some degree of regional focus, targeting consumers in the United States differently than most other consumers. For example, its A-Class (a lower-priced series) is available everywhere except in

Figure 9-2

The A-Class Mercedes is about as large as a Ford Focus; it even looks like one.

the United States, where the company appears to have a different strategy altogether (see Figure 9-2). In the case of its compacts, the C-Class, for much of the rest of the world, Mercedes offers the Classic, the Elégance, and the Avantgarde models in the C-180, C-200, C-240, C-320, and C-220 CDI versions, whereas for the U.S. markets, the C-Class is limited to C-240s and C-280s. The different approach to the U.S. market is in large part attributable to the fact that Mercedes had to fight gray marketing channels until it instituted a strategy that made using alternate marketing channels a complicated proposition and took control of distribution under the Mercedes-USA umbrella organization.

A product often must be adapted to the demands of the local market because consumers might have certain specific preferences. Alternatively, adaptation might be dictated by the political and legal environment, by the technological environment, or by other particulars of the market (trade relationships, climate, etc.). The degree of economic development in a market also is a factor that determines the degree of product adaptation needed: The lower the level of economic and market development, the more the product needs to be changed to serve the needs and demands of the market.[13]

Host governments affect the globalization of products by imposing local content requirements, standards (technical, emission, etc.), and ownership restrictions and requirements on technology transfer; in the case of services, consumer participation in production may be affected by government barriers to global strategy.[14] Banking in the Middle East is gender-based: Women's banks are separate from banks used by men, and cross-access is restricted. Government restrictions affect not only international banking: China, Singapore, and Saudi Arabia ban the private ownership of satellite dishes, and China is restricting citizen access to the Web.[15]

9-1c Global Localization

In general, few products and services can succeed through a purely global strategy; a degree of adaptation to local conditions is frequently imperative for company success. According to marketing experts, the idea of marketing a standardized product with a uniform marketing plan around the world remains purely theoretical. Although a product concept may be universal, it must still be adapted to differences in local culture, legislation, and even production capabilities.[16] The term **global localization,** or **glocalization,** is frequently used to describe the practice of global branding and localized marketing adaptation.

global localization The practice of global branding and localized marketing adaptation to differences in local culture, legislation, and even production capabilities.

glocalization The standardization of products across markets and, ultimately, to the standardization of the marketing mix worldwide; also called global standardization.

Product managers must decide on which aspects of a product they want to standardize across markets and which aspects of the product to localize. In this decision, they resort to two approaches: One involves offering parts (modules) that can be assembled worldwide in different configurations, depending on the needs of the market—**modular adaptation;** the other, standardizing the core product/service, but allowing for easy modification from market to market—**core product strategy.** In an instance of the latter, the core product is identical from one country to another, but certain aspects of the offering differ from market to market. To illustrate this concept, marketers with brands heralded as global icons often act using a local strategy: McDonald's Golden Arches are omnipresent throughout the world. Its offerings, however, are adapted to the local culture; at its restaurants in New Delhi, where Indian consumers consider cows sacred and don't eat beef, McDonald's offers the Maharaja Mac (two all-mutton patties, special sauce, lettuce, cheese, pickles, onions on a sesame-seed bun).[17] Similarly, Volvo, unlike Mercedes (as mentioned in section 9-1b, "Regional Standardization"), has a similar core product in every market; however, it offers air conditioning as a standard feature for the U.S. market.

Similarly, other fast-food restaurant services have adapted their offerings from market to market (see Figure 9-3). The Tricon companies (Pizza Hut and KFC, in particular), Burger King, and McDonald's offer beer and wine in Europe, and most multinational fast-food companies offer miso soup in Japan. Along with this type of adaptation are other examples: McDonald's in the Netherlands offers its large Coca-Cola Light (Diet Coke)[18] in containers slightly smaller than the medium drink containers it serves in the United States. Pizza Hut in Germany sells cans of Pepsi from take-home windows—outside a café-restaurant on Leopoldstrasse, a street lined with cafés, in Munich, for instance. KFC found that, for its Japanese consumers, it needed to change its product's shape and size because they prefer morsel-sized food; similarly, Pampers disposable diapers were successful in Japan only after the size was adapted to accommodate smaller Japanese babies.[19]

9-1d Mandatory Adaptation

To render products usable, manufacturers of appliances adapt their products to local requirements. Such **mandatory adaptations** involve voltage—220 volts for Europe, whereas, in the United States, the standard is 110. Other such adaptations involve cycles

modular adaptation The localization across markets of the product by offering parts (modules) that can be assembled worldwide in different configurations, depending on the needs of the market.

core product strategy The strategy of using the same standard core product/service worldwide, but varying certain aspects of the offering (product ingredients, advertising) from market to market.

mandatory adaptation The adaptation of products to local requirements so that the products can legally and physically function in the specific country environment.

F i g u r e   9 - 3
This McDonald's in France advertises its "Croque McDo, à croquer dans ton Happy Meal"— a melted cheese sandwich, to munch on in your Happy Meal. The name of the Croque McDo is a play on Croque Monsieur, the traditional French cheese sandwich.

(50 versus 60), electricity and telephone jacks, and television/VCR systems (NTSC in the United States, PAL and SECAM I and SECAM II in the rest of the world).

In other examples, automobiles must be adapted to the left-hand driving requirements in the United Kingdom, Ireland, and Australia. The United States requires a conversion to local specifications (emissions and other standards) for any imported automobiles that were not manufactured according to U.S. standards; subsequent to conversion, the U.S. Department of Transportation must approve the conversion for the vehicle to be registered locally, which makes this, overall, a costly undertaking.

Other types of mandatory adaptation abound. For example, a number of Middle Eastern countries continue to restrict the import of products that have components manufactured in Israel. Food products, in particular, must be scrutinized: Alcohol content is prohibited from distribution without special and limited authorization in many countries in North Africa and the Middle East, and food products containing pork have very limited appeal and face inspections and other restrictions in this same region. Magazines are either marked with a black marker where a woman's body or face is evident or not allowed through at all in Saudi Arabia. And the list continues.

9-1e Local, Nonmandatory Adaptation

nonmandatory adaptation The strategy of adapting a product to better meet the needs of the local market, without being required to do so.

Many global companies adapt their offerings to better meet the needs of the local market, thus performing a local, **nonmandatory adaptation.** Examples of multinational companies offering products aimed at local markets abound. In most instances, the products result from a buyout. Unilever and Procter & Gamble bought numerous brands in Central and Eastern Europe; for instance, Unilever bought Romania's Dero, a detergent that is now part of the company's product mix in that country.

Multinational companies also have developed new brands for individual local markets: Häagen-Dazs Japan offers its customers Royal Milk Tea ice cream, a full-bodied, creamy green ice tea; Weight Watchers offers consumers in France Mousse Legeres in two different four-pack combinations—Cherry/Green Tea, Pear/Jasmine, Apricot/Orange Flower, and Peach/Ginger; in the United Kingdom, Nestlé offers a drinkable fruit yogurt named Squizzos, which sports Disney characters.[20]

9-2 Private-Label (Retailer) Brands

Private-label (retailer) brands pose an increasing challenge to manufacturers' global or local brands. European food retailers, such as Sainsbury in the United Kingdom and Albert Heijn in the Netherlands, as well as North American retailers, offer quality products with the "Sainsbury" and "ah" brands, respectively, packaged impeccably and positioned on the shelves side-by-side with popular multinational/national brands. A European case study[21] found that, in general, retailers compete primarily on price with their private-label brands, unless they are actually able to develop differentiated, high-quality store brands, thus creating consumer loyalty, which in turn translates to store loyalty.

private labels Brands sold under the brand name of a retailer or some other distributor.

In the United Kingdom, **private labels** are common. Sainsbury and Marks & Spencer have a century-long history of offering store brands perceived to be of high quality, whereas Tesco and Argyll have only recently started offering store brands. In contrast, in France, private-label brands were introduced only in the 1970s and positioned as cheap alternatives to national brands.[22] Later, French retailers such as Casino and Monoprix attempted to develop quality store brands but faced significant price competition from the national brands, leaving French consumers with the impression that store brands were inferior—a perception that was reinforced by the fact that French supermarkets, unlike their U.K. counterparts, were legally barred from using television advertising.[23]

In addition to offering quality premium store brands, retailers in developed countries also have attempted to be innovative and expand into new product categories.[24] Finally, private-label brands tend to be especially appealing to consumers during downturns in the economy, when they are more likely to make their brand selection based on price.[25] Generally, consumers worldwide have become more price conscious, demanding higher quality at lower prices. The private-label brand offering serves well this mindset, as does the proliferation of discounters such as Wal-Mart, Costco, and Toys "R" Us, which are increasing price competition by offering their own dealer brands.

9-3 Global Branding and Country-of-Origin Information

Country of origin is defined as the country with which a particular product or service is associated. The country could be the **country of manufacture,** in the case of products, or the country where the company headquarters are located, for both products and services. The key to determining a product's perceived country of origin depends on which of the two (country of manufacture or home country of the company) elicits the stronger association (see Figure 9-4). For example, many of the appliances Philips sells are manufactured in Asia; however, the Philips' headquarters are in the Netherlands. The country of origin for Philips appliances, then, is not the particular country in Asia where they are manufactured, but the Netherlands. A new, unknown brand, however, will be associated more strongly with the country of manufacture.

In the absence of other product information, the country of origin of a product or service affects consumers' evaluations of that product or service. Country-of-origin information constitutes a product trait that is external to the product itself, acting as a surrogate for product quality, performance, reliability, prestige, and other product characteristics that cannot be directly evaluated.[26] In general, products manufactured in highly industrialized countries are perceived as being of higher quality and having greater prestige than those manufactured in developing countries. Consumers from highly developed countries tend, in general, to evaluate own-country products more favorably than products from other countries. The opposite is true for consumers in developing countries and newly marketizing economies[27] who evaluate own-country products as inferior to products from developed countries.

When consumers have additional product information, however, such as brand name, or if they purchase the product at a store known for its quality—and especially premium-quality—products, country-of-origin information is no longer a primary source consumers use for product quality evaluation. And, increasingly, with products manufactured using components made in various countries and assembled in yet other countries, determining the "true" country of origin of a product is difficult. For example, BMWs for the U.S. market are manufactured in South Carolina, rather than in Bavaria; Michelin tires are also manufactured in South Carolina; and many software products used by U.S. businesses are developed in India.

country of origin The country with which a particular product or service is associated.

country of manufacture The country in which a particular product is manufactured.

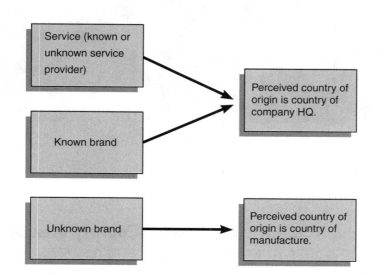

F i g u r e   9 - 4
Country-of-Origin Effects

Figure 9-5

Destination Nonmarketing: Auschwitz (a), the largest concentration and death camp complex, is rarely associated with the country where it is located—Poland. Located close to the town of Oswiencim, on the Vistula River, the camp is, nevertheless, toured daily by international visitors. Arbeit Macht Frei (b)—Work Makes You Free—is the message reigning upon the entrance to the camp.

(a)

(b)

Finally, in some cases there may be a preference not to advertise the country of origin. Obviously, Poland would prefer not to be associated with the most infamous Nazi death camp (see Figure 9-5).

9-3a Product-Country and Service-Country Stereotypes

product-country stereotypes
Product-specific stereotypes that associate the country of origin as a certification of quality.

Kenyan or Colombian coffee, Chinese tea, German beer and electronics, French perfume, Italian fashion, Swiss chocolate, and Russian caviar are examples of strong **product-country stereotypes** of quality held by consumers in the United States. Among such stereotypes shared elsewhere in the world are Iranian pistachios and rugs, Polish vegetables, Israeli oranges, and Czech and Italian crystal, to name a few. Such stereotypes are product specific and do not apply usually to other products from that particular country.

Advertisements often emphasize these stereotypes. In the United States, Colombian coffee is touted as a certification of quality. Petrossian in New York stresses its reputation as the authentic retailer of Russian Beluga and Sevruga caviar. Toblerone chocolate stresses its European origins, despite the fact that it is an Altria (Kraft Jacobs Suchard) brand. Häagen-Dazs chocolate-dipped ice cream is really a product produced locally, in the United States; its name suggests an association with Europe, again affirming the quality association with European chocolate. But sometimes a product's Italian reputation may be the only thing Italian about it (see International Marketing Illustration 9-1).

Services also are stereotyped. Eastern European cosmeticians, for example, are very popular in the West. Names such as Ilona of Hungary, Frederick Fekkai, and Erno Laszlo cosmetics are prominent on Madison and Fifth Avenues in New York. Tourists going to Eastern Europe often use the services of local beauticians (see Figure 9-6) or even go for extended stays to spas specializing in mud baths and life-renewal therapies.

Unfortunate negative stereotypes also exist. French waiters have received unfair evaluations in the United States (see Figure 9-7). Their demeanor is merely a reflection of their competence and their elegance.

9-3b Country of Origin and Ethnocentrism

We have learned about **ethnocentrism** as a company philosophy—as an approach to international marketing as an extension of domestic marketing with minimal adaptation to the needs of the international consumers and the peculiarities of the local market. This

> **ethnocentrism** The belief that one's culture is superior to another and that strategies used in one's home country (presumably a developed country) will work just as well internationally.

International Marketing Illustration 9-1

Italian Olive Oil from Spain and Greece: A New Perspective on Country of Origin

Superb Italian olive oils have achieved a remarkable reputation worldwide: Italian olive oil is a strong product-country stereotype of quality that helps it command a high price and sell well. Berio olive oil is exported from the fabled Italian countryside—a countryside with tanker trucks that bring the oil from Spain, Tunisia, and Greece for processing and export. No, the Berio olive oil does not come from Lucca in the celebrated olive-growing Tuscany where the Berio olive oil factory is located. In fact, Italy does not grow enough olives to even satisfy the Italian market, let alone export the product to the rest of the world. Less than 20 percent of the Berio brand olive oil is made with Italian olives. Berio's rival, Bertolli, also has its roots in Lucca . . . and uses foreign oil.

Berio's management justifies that it is not important where the olives are picked and pressed, but, rather, where the oil is refined and blended; the oil acquires its Italian cachet through processing by skilled Italian experts. This is a rather novel country-of-origin argument and one that the marketplace has not yet altogether dismissed because Belgian chocolate made with cocoa from the Ivory Coast is, in fact, Belgian, and not African chocolate.

This deceptive marketing strategy may be challenged in the future, however. Italian olive oil producers are up in arms because Italian exporters are more likely to purchase cheaper oil from abroad than from the promoted Tuscany olive groves. And consumers in the United States are being deceived by advertising that claims the oil is "born in the Tuscany Mountains."

Source: Clifford J. Levy, "The Olive Oil Seems Fine. Whether It's Italian Is the Issue," *The New York Times,* May 7, 2004, p. A4.

Figure 9-6
Polish beauticians are world famous. Using dated equipment, fresh natural products, and impeccable dexterity, this beautician works wonders on tourists, as well as locals.

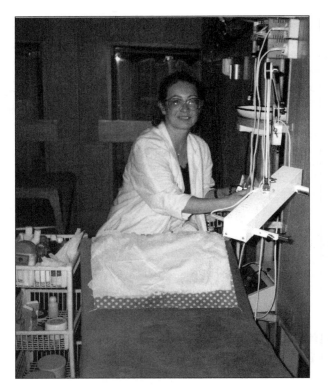

Figure 9-7
A waiter on the Champs Elysées, graciously and competently serving beer on a busy July 14 (a French national holiday).

second definition of ethnocentrism, used in relation to country of origin, is related to consumers' beliefs that purchasing foreign products is morally wrong.[28] Ethnocentric consumers believe that purchasing imported products hurts the economy, causes loss of jobs, and is unpatriotic, and consumers purchasing foreign products are worthy of contempt.[29] This concept then translates into a preference for products from one's own country—i.e., "buy American"—and a rejection of products with a foreign country of origin. This attitude may exist at the individual consumer level or at the aggregate societal level.

Governments also frequently engage in practices in which they favor locally produced products, service providers, etc., in the performance of their tasks. In section 9-4, similar restrictions and related philosophies are explored in the area of services.

9-4 The Service Side: Tariff and Nontariff Barriers to Entry

This section examines challenges that service providers face in their international involvement. These challenges, or **service barriers,** in one form or another, represent a manifestation of ethnocentrism at the firm level, at the government level, or at the consumer level. Among such challenges are[30]

service barriers Barriers encountered by services in different markets, such as requirements for local certification, local providers, and other requirements that favor local over international service providers.

- The requirement to use national services. This requirement is a form of protectionism: Company or government policies provide implicit or explicit preference for a domestic supplier, which makes it difficult for international service providers to survive.
- The prohibition against the employment of foreign nationals, or other barriers—for example, demanding a local certification such as Certified Public Accountant, which requires a degree in accounting from a U.S. institution as well as passing the CPA exam.
- Direct competition from government providers, such as a local government monopoly over natural gas and electricity.
- Restrictions on movement—for example, limiting access for tourists in a particular region or the number of flights allowed into the country.
- Tariffs imposed on international service providers.

Frequently, the challenges posed to international service providers can be attributed to the close cultural link between a society and services.[31] Section 9-5 addresses the relationship between products, services, and culture.

9-5 Products, Services, and Culture

Service encounters are primarily social encounters, and rules and expectations related to services vary from culture to culture.[32] Studies in marketing revealed that it is important for international service providers to understand the factors that affect customer considerations in service evaluations and to emphasize the various dimensions of service quality accordingly.[33] To illustrate, Japanese consumers do not expect special treatment in a medical environment. Medicine is perceived as a public good, and it would be selfish of anyone to expect special attention. Similarly, the Japanese also hold doctors in very high esteem, and customers expect and accept rudeness from doctors.[34] They also expect to be treated with a greater degree of formality by all service providers compared to consumers in the United States, whereas consumers in the United States prefer a greater degree of service personalization.[35]

Culture also influences the perception and evaluation of a brand in a particular country. Kent cigarettes continue to hold a high market share and are prominent in Romania due to the status they held as commodity money and a prestige product before the fall of communism.[36] Pepsi-Cola and Coca-Cola continue to market their diet brands as Pepsi Light and Coca-Cola Light in much of the rest of the world, where the word "diet" refers to a medically restricted diet. In Rwanda, Fanta Citron is a preferred mixer for most hard liquor. Housewives in the United Kingdom are "hoovering" when they are vacuuming (regardless of the brand of vacuum cleaner they are using), and they buy Jello in a semi-gelled, rather than powder, format.

Culture also determines the degree of brand loyalty. Consumers from more collectivist cultures, such as Latin American and Asian consumers, tend to prefer established brands and purchase them in the maturity stage. European consumers tend to be very brand name conscious and are especially loyal to top brands. In urban areas, high-priced designers such as Prada, Escada, Dolce & Gabana, and Diesel jeans are common among middle- and upper-middle-class consumers who might otherwise live in small rental apartments.

Chapter 10, "International Product and Service Strategies," addresses strategies of manufacturers and service providers aimed at meeting the challenges imposed by culture.

9-6 Protecting Brand Names

Brand names are valuable assets to a company. Companies pay millions to protect their brand names from dilution, by registering them anywhere they are present and defending them in court, primarily because counterfeit merchandise harms the brand's reputation as well as company profits. The Uruguay round of the General Agreement on Tariffs and Trade (GATT) addressed standardizing global trademark legislation that is now incorporated under the World Trade Organization (WTO) umbrella. The question that remains is whether individual governments can and will enact this legislation. To illustrate, Yiwu, a city five hours from Shanghai, is one of the largest wholesale centers of China, where 200,000 distributors purchase up to 2,000 tons of goods daily; it also is China's counterfeit capital, where counterfeit products bearing established brand names—such as Procter & Gamble's Safeguard soap and Rejoice shampoo, Gillette razor blades, and other brands belonging to companies such as Philip Morris, Anheuser-Busch, Prada, Robert Bosch, Kimberly-Clark, and Nike—are sold at a fraction of their genuine counterparts' cost.[37] Counterfeiters in China range from manufacturers of shampoo and soap in back rooms to large state-owned enterprises and/or joint-venture partners making their profits selling knockoffs of soft drinks and beer; to factories producing car batteries, motorcycles, and even mobile CD factories with optical disk machines. These products are distributed all over the world, including the United States.[38]

9-6a Identifying Types of Counterfeiting

Examples of counterfeiting are design counterfeiting and brand name counterfeiting.

Design Counterfeiting

design counterfeiting Copying designs or scents of another company.

Copying designs or scents, known as **design counterfeiting,** is quite common and risk free. The polo-style shirt is replicated by many companies, with a design that approximates the polo rider. The design of women's Peugeot watches is close to that of the Rolex Oyster Perpetual. Unknown perfume manufacturers suggest that their brand is similar in scent to a particular brand of perfume, which they name in their product packaging and advertising.

Brand Name Counterfeiting

brand name counterfeiting Selling counterfeit products as brand name originals.

At the next level is **brand name counterfeiting.** In Cairo, for about a dollar one can purchase simple, cotton shirts with the Christian Dior name on the label. Purses with names such as Prada, Fendi, and Louis Vuitton are sold practically on the steps of the actual retailers, in many capital cities, as are fake Rolex watches. Bazaars in Istanbul and Cairo are known for their "quality" fakes. Hong Kong markets where counterfeit products are sold are very popular with tourists. Counterfeit products even make it to flea markets in the United States. In different countries, Pizza Huts and Domino's Pizza restaurants are quite different from the originals, and are not legitimate franchises.

Multinational businesses need to address several factors that contribute to the counterfeiters' success:

- Consumer factors
- Technology factors
- Distribution factors
- Local-government factors

Consumer Factors

On the consumer side, there is a high willingness to purchase counterfeit goods. Studies have shown, for example, that a large proportion of consumers are likely to select a counterfeit apparel item over a genuine good when there is a price advantage, primarily because function risks are low for apparel, whereas prestige gains are high.[39] In this sense, products that are visible and/or consumed publicly are more likely to be in demand than products that are less visible and/or consumed publicly.

Moreover, consumers in emerging markets are less likely to notice the difference between a prestige brand and a counterfeit brand.[40] In fact, retailers themselves, in these markets, might be unaware of any difference between prestige brands and counterfeits.

Technology Factors

The spread of advanced production technology (affordable, quality, color-copying machines), as well as production lines supplied by pirates or know-how stolen from joint-venture multinationals required to transfer technology to local partners, has made it possible for counterfeiters to make perfect replicas of the original products. Frequently, neither the manufacturer nor the consumers can tell fakes from the real product.[41] Especially problematic is the fact that advanced technologies allow for the marketing of fake car parts, as described in International Marketing Illustration 9-2.

International Marketing Illustration 9-2

Taking Counterfeiting to New Heights

Global counterfeiting is at an all-time high: It is estimated to account for 7 percent of world trade, or US$500 billion a year. Counterfeiters from China, Taiwan, India, and South Korea have managed to create knockoffs not just for clothing, apparel items, and videos, but also for car parts, which now account for $12 billion a year in sales. Bootleggers are selling the most frequently used parts, such as fluids, brake pads, fan belts, oil and fuel filters, spark plugs, batteries, and windshields, all packaged with fake logos. These products are selling rapidly in North America, but the largest market for these products is the Middle East; fake Ford break pads go for $30, whereas the legitimate product costs $47.

The problem facing large automobile manufacturers, however, is not just the loss of sales: If someone purchases a fake part, which causes injury to the passengers, these leading auto makers have to prove that the parts are not theirs.

If fake parts are a concern to automobile manufacturers, then soon they should worry about fake automobiles—automobile knockoffs. Pirates in Shanghai are knocking off entire motor vehicles: Only months before General Motors started selling its Chevrolet Spark in China for $7,500, a $6,000 knockoff version, the Chery QQ, looking the same but missing essential accoutrements such as an airbag, started circulating on the streets of China. And, surprisingly, the manufacturer of the Chery QQ was partially owned by GM's Chinese partner.

Counterfeiters are using acceptable technology to manufacture these goods. And they are investing primarily in computer scanners to duplicate trademark labels that they can then attach to these knockoffs.

Sources: Murray Hiebert, "Chinese Counterfeiters Turn Our Fake Car Parts," *Wall Street Journal*, March 3, 2004, p. A14; Joann Muller, "Stolen Cars," *Forbes*, Vol. 173, No. 3, February 16, 2004, p. 58.

Distribution Factors

Supply chains are not adequately controlled. Traders use Internet chat rooms and unauthorized dealership networks to sell the products and mix counterfeit products with legitimate products sold on the secondary gray market.[42]

Local-Government Factors

Governments in many developing countries are reluctant to crack down on counterfeiting, especially when state-owned enterprises are involved in the operations. In the case of China, for instance, local governments hesitate to crack down on product pirates because they create thousands of jobs and keep the local economy going; and, even when local authorities take action against counterfeiters (most of whom evade taxes), persuading them to close down the state-owned factories engaging in illegal production is impossible.[43]

Counterfeit products are openly available in many developing countries. Here, consumers, as well as customs representatives inspecting the counterfeit product shipments, are not familiar with many international brand names. Further, customs officials in many developing countries very often are not sufficiently trained in identifying illegal trade in mass-market products. And, as mentioned, counterfeit products are also widely available in developed countries; the prevailing reason is that in the industrialized countries, customs officers inspect the contents of only a small fraction of the goods that go through customs.

9-6b Combating Counterfeiting

Multinational companies have used a number of strategies to combat counterfeiting. Lobbying the U.S. government, as well as the governments involved, is a first step. This process involves filing appeals to the World Trade Organization and lobbying other governmental organizations in the United States and abroad regulating trade. The outcome is uncertain, however. For example, even though member countries of the World Trade Organization are expected to abide by the organization's antipiracy provisions, they are not entirely successful in combating the sales of counterfeit products.

Alternatives involve a concerted action on the part of companies to combat counterfeiting by changing a product's appearance to differentiate authentic products from fakes. Budweiser embedded in its beer bottles special images that appear only when the product is chilled, rendering them difficult to copy; Microsoft included holograms on its software boxes and inside user manuals, but pirates quickly learned the trick.[44]

The most successful attacks have been launched with the cooperation of local governments. In 2000 in China, a raid was launched by seven battery makers, including Gillette, Energizer, and Panasonic, with the help of 200 government agents, on 21 factories in a southwestern city. As a result of the raid, 150 pieces of manufacturing equipment and three million counterfeit batteries (with Russia as their destination) were confiscated.[45]

9-7 International Perspectives of Industrial Products and Services

Marketing industrial products and services across borders has certain similarities to the marketing of consumer goods. However, there are also important differences. For example, in the marketing of consumer products, culture plays a key role, and firms must be aware of norms, values, and traditions in the target country. However, cultural differences are not readily relevant in the production process, in the types of products that businesses purchase, such as major equipment, buildings, land, accessory equipment, fabricated and component parts, process material, maintenance and repair parts, operating supplies, raw materials, goods for resale, and business services. Culture is relevant when it comes to the selection of suppliers. Typically, the decision to purchase industrial products rests with management—and often with top management at the company's headquarters in the home country, for the most expensive products—and the purchase process often takes several months.

In many countries, the national government in the country of operation has substantial input in the supplier decision, favoring national suppliers over foreign businesses. National government input can be even more restrictive when it comes to the purchase of business services. For professional services, which include legal services, auditing and consulting services, and medical services, the national government can directly restrict the company to local service suppliers, or it can require that the respective service providers have local licenses and other credentials, which could essentially mean hiring local businesses. For operating services, which include Internet services, telephone service, shipping, and insurance, and which are typically contracted out for a fixed period of time, the national government can require the business to hire local providers. If not, the business can handle those services using the most cost-effective approach, which could still mean resorting to local services or even outsourcing them to a third country where labor costs are lower. Many companies launch a request for bids for these types of services on an annual basis, and the national government could require that, all things being equal, the national company must be selected.

Industrial consumers are manufacturers, wholesalers, retailers, government agencies, and nonprofit organizations. Unlike consumer markets, business-to-business markets are characterized by fewer buyers and a larger purchase volume. In addition, the business-to-business market has important geographic concentrations: The world banking centers and advertising centers are concentrated in New York, London, and Tokyo; and the world insurance centers are Geneva, London, and Munich. And demand for industrial products is derived from demand for consumer products and thus is much more volatile: Small changes in demand for consumer products can lead to substantial changes in demand for industrial products. Plus, fluctuations in the world marketplace readily affect industries worldwide. For example, the surplus of steel in China and the former Soviet Union has dealt a blow to the steel industry in industrialized countries, to the point that most have contemplated protectionist measures.

In designing industrial products and services for international markets, firms must consider the formal buying process, starting with the identification of needs, establishment of specifications, identification of product solutions and vendors, evaluation and selection of vendors, and negotiation of purchase terms. The decision to purchase a particular product is contingent on the entire package offering—the product, the service contract and availability of replacement parts, and the product price. For example, in the process of identifying product solutions and vendors, the firm will need to evaluate whether the product comes with installation, training, and other after-sales service. Even the local availability of aftermarket replacement parts may constitute an important factor in the purchase decision. Replacement parts are often very expensive, but, if they are readily available locally at a significantly lower cost than having to ship them to Thailand from New Jersey, the respective brand will become much more attractive.

9-7a Product Standards

The discussion in section 9-1, "Standardization Versus Adaptation," is less relevant in industrial marketing because common industrial consumer needs have led to a high degree of standardization of industrial products and services. In addition, the world industrial community is attempting to create standards for each industry. And, with quality taking an important place in the competition for global markets, businesses are adhering to the international quality standards set by the International Organization for Standardization (ISO), which was established in 1946 as a nongovernmental federation of national standards bodies.

The organization issues the **ISO 9000 certification,** which addresses quality management, whereby quality refers to all product or service features that are required by the customer. In ISO terms, quality management implies that the organization ensures that the

ISO 9000 certification
Certification that specifies that the organization must meet customer and regulatory requirements and follow its policies and procedures while advancing quality through continuous improvement.

products or services it sells satisfy customer requirements and comply with any regulations applicable to those products or services. In broad terms, ISO 9000 specifies that the organization must meet customer and regulatory requirements and follow its policies and procedures while advancing quality through continuous improvement. It addresses issues such as the phases of product development from the initial design phase to the delivery phase. It also requires performance measurement throughout the process through performing internal audits, monitoring customer satisfaction, and taking corrective action.[46]

In 1992, the United Nations Conference on Environment and Development (UNCED) requested that the ISO introduce the ISO 14001 four years later; this would be the first of the ISO 14000 family of environmental management system standards designed to help businesses reduce their impact on the environment and to facilitate sustainable development and foster international trade by providing an international system of standards. **ISO 14000 certification** guidelines discourage multinational firms from engaging in hazardous environmental practices, such as locating plants that generate hazardous emissions in poor countries with weak environmental regulations, and ensure that corporate policies promoting environmentally sound, efficiency-embracing, innovative technologies and processes will contribute to establishing twenty-first century production and distribution systems that are far less environmentally degrading and wasteful. To receive this certification, multinational companies will have to develop environmental management systems (EMS) similar to the ISO 9000 standards for total quality management and a policy that stresses a commitment to continual improvement and prevention of pollution, assurances that the company will comply with relevant laws and regulations, and a framework for setting and regularly reviewing environmental objectives and targets; the respective policy must be documented, communicated to all employees, and made available to the public.[47]

Both ISO 9000 and ISO 14000 address the production process, rather than the product; however, it is implied that the process affects the product. In the context of both, certification refers to the issuing of a certificate by an independent external body that has audited the organization's management system and verified that it conforms to the requirements of the standards. The auditing body then registers the certification in the client's register. ISO 9000 and ISO 14000 are implemented by about 610,000 organizations in 160 countries. The top 10 countries with ISO 9001–2002 certificates are listed in Table 9-1.[48]

ISO 14000 certification
Certification that a company follows guidelines that discourage firms from engaging in hazardous environmental practices, and ensures that corporate policies promoting environmentally sound, efficiency-embracing, innovative technologies and processes will contribute to establishing twenty-first century production and distribution systems that are far less environmentally degrading.

Table 9-1

Top 10 Countries with ISO 9001–2002 Certificates

China	40,997
Japan	16,813
Italy	14,733
Germany	10,811
United Kingdom	9,301
Spain	8,872
Australia	7,024
France	6,529
Switzerland	5,060
United States	4,587

Source: www.iso.ch

Region	Total	Percent Share	Number of Countries
Africa and West Asia	23,534	4.19	51
Central and South America	13,550	2.44	33
North America	53,806	9.58	3
Europe	292,970	52.16	50
Far East	148,573	26.45	20
Australia and New Zealand	29,204	5.20	2

Table 9-2 **ISO 9000 Certifications Worldwide**

Source: www.iso.ch

Table 9-2 lists the distribution of ISO 9000 certifications worldwide. Note that Europe has the largest share of ISO 9000 certifications, followed by the Far East. A reason behind Europe's lead in this regard is the fact that the European Union's directives on quality management and environmental management pressure companies into becoming ISO 9000 and ISO 14000 certified.

Summary

- **Describe drivers for international standardization and offer an overview of the international standardization–local adaptation continuum and respective company strategies.** The emergence of uniform market segments, such as global consumers (global teenagers, the global elite), increased international travel, and a general consumer preference for products of higher quality at a lower price, led to opportunities for global standardization strategies. Such strategies offer numerous benefits, primarily the capability for a firm to market its goods at lower costs and higher profits. A purely global strategy, however, will invariably result in ignoring specific segment preferences and in targeting strategies that have a higher likelihood of failure. Some adaptation can be attempted using a global localization strategy, where the main module of the strategy is maintained, while making minor modifications from market to market. Sometimes, however, adaptation may be required (mandatory), or the adaptation is necessary to better meet the needs of the local market.

- **Examine country-of-origin effects on brand evaluations in relation to product stereotypes and consumer ethnocentrism.** Country-of-origin information is used in making product evaluation inferences in situations in which very little other information (brand name, for instance) is available to evaluate the product. Country information also can be used to exclude products from the consideration set. For example, ethnocentric consumers, who believe that purchasing foreign products is morally

wrong, will refuse to purchase products unless they are made in their own home country.

- **Examine challenges faced by service providers in international markets.** Service providers face numerous barriers to entry in international markets. In addition to tariffs, international service providers may be prohibited from hiring international employees, or they may be required to have certain certifications that are difficult to obtain and can be obtained only locally. They might also face direct competition from government providers, such as a local government monopoly, or they could face restrictions on movement.

- **Address issues related to brand name protection and the reasons behind widespread international counterfeiting.** Counterfeiting, ranging from direct copying to design counterfeiting, is flourishing due to improved technology, inadequate channel control, lax enforcement locally and worldwide (despite World Trade Organization involvement), and consumer demand.

- **Address the marketing of industrial products and services and related product and service standards.** Industrial products and services are marketed differently than consumer products and services are: They are not as culture dependent and are more standardized. In an effort to create quality standards for products worldwide, the ISO 9000 certification addresses quality management standards, and the ISO 14000 certification addresses environmental management standards.

Key Terms

adaptation
brand name counterfeiting
core product strategy
country of manufacture
country of origin
design counterfeiting
ethnocentrism

global consumers
global localization
global standardization
glocalization
ISO 9000 certification
ISO 14000 certification
mandatory adaptation

modular adaptation
nonmandatory adaptation
private labels
product-country stereotypes
regional standardization
service barriers

Discussion Questions

1. Describe the global standardization–local adaptation debate. What are the drivers for globalization and for adaptation? Explain.
2. Give examples of mandatory and nonmandatory adaptations.
3. How do private-label (retailer) brands compete with international and local brands? Give examples.

4. Discuss the different barriers to entry that international service providers face worldwide.
5. What are the reasons behind counterfeiting, and what efforts are taking place to combat it? Are they successful?

Chapter Quiz (True/False)

1. Overlapping media among countries makes it easier to create awareness of a product.
2. Global branding creates different images for the product in the different regions where the product is sold.
3. A product's country of origin is always the country where the product was manufactured.

4. Multinational companies often try to combat counterfeiting by differentiating their products with signature traits.
5. Wal-Mart and Tesco products sold under the respective company's umbrella name are known as private-label brands.
6. Culture is essential in the marketing of industrial products.

Multiple Choice

1. Girls around the world participating in similar pastimes such as in-line skating or playing with Barbie dolls are an illustration of
   a. differentiated consumer preferences.
   b. global consumers.
   c. international production.
   d. none of the above
2. Ford's success in promoting "world cars" like the Ford Focus is a successful example of
   a. international positioning.
   b. international travel.
   c. satisfying consumer preferences.
   d. all of the above
3. Promoting its products globally and altering parts of their promotion based on specific areas is common of a company focused on
   a. nonmandatory adaptation.
   b. global standards.
   c. glocalization.
   d. none of the above

4. The following is an example of mandatory adaptation for the United States market:
   a. U.S. automobile emission standards
   b. 110 volts
   c. NTSC television
   d. all of the above
5. Philips is headquartered in the Netherlands, but many of its appliances are manufactured in Asia. The country of origin of Philips
   a. is the Netherlands.
   b. is the country in Asia where the product is manufactured.
   c. depends on the perception of the consumer.
   d. none of the above
6. Which of the following are examples of products that businesses purchase?
   a. major equipment, buildings, land
   b. accessory equipment and fabricated and component parts
   c. process material and maintenance and repair parts
   d. all of the above

You can find the correct answers to these questions by taking the quiz and then submitting your answers in the Online Edition. The program will automatically score your submission. Where you miss a question, the program will provide the correct answer, a rationale for the answer, and the section number in the chapter where the topic is discussed.

Endnotes

1. Gary van Deursen, "The Globalization of Design," *Appliance Manufacturer,* Vol. 43, No. 3, March 1995, pp. 10–11.

2. The three assumptions listed were initially stated by Theodore Levitt, "The Globalization of Markets," *Harvard Business Review,* May–June 1983, pp. 92–102.

3. David A. Aaker, *Managing Brand Equity: Capitalizing on the Value of a Brand Name,* New York: The Free Press, 1991.

4. Ibid.

5. van Deursen, "The Globalization of Design," pp. 10–11.

6. Ibid.

7. Shaoming Zou and Aysegul Ozsomer, "Global Product R&D and the Firm's Strategic Position," *Journal of International Marketing,* Vol. 7, No. 1, 1999, pp. 57–76.

8. Ibid.

9. Susan Segal-Horn, "The Limits of Global Strategy," *Strategy & Leadership,* Vol. 24, No. 6, November–December 1996, pp. 12–17.

10. Ibid.

11. Segal-Horn, "The Limits of Global Strategy," pp. 12–17.

12. Ibid.

13. John S. Hill and Richard R. Still, "Adapting Products to LDC Tastes," *Harvard Business Review,* March–April 1984, pp. 92–101.

14. Christopher Lovelock and George S. Yip, "Developing Global Strategies for Service Businesses," *California Management Review,* Vol. 38, No. 2, 1996, pp. 64–87.

15. Ibid.

16. Cyndee Miller, "Chasing the Global Dream," *Marketing News,* Vol. 30, No. 25, December 2, 1996, pp. 1–2.

17. Ibid.

18. This is yet another example of adaptation, this time by Coca-Cola, for consumers in Europe, to whom the term "diet" signifies medically imposed eating restrictions.

19. Segal-Horn, "The Limits of Global Strategy," pp. 12–17.

20. Donna Gorski Berry, "Global Dairy Food Trends," *Dairy Foods,* Vol. 99, No. 10, October 1998, pp. 32–37.

21. Ryan Mathews, "A European Case Study," *Progressive Grocer, Special Volume: Branding the Store,* November 1995, pp. 8–9. This article discusses a study conducted by INSEAD on trends in the food industry in the United Kingdom and France.

22. Ibid.

23. Ibid.

24. John A. Quelch and David Harding, "Brands Versus Private Labels: Fighting to Win," *Harvard Business Review,* Vol. 74, No. 1, January–February 1996, pp. 99–109.

25. Mathews, "A European Case Study," pp. 8–9.

26. For a review of the country-of-origin effect literature, see Lalita A. Manrai, Dana-Nicoleta Lascu, and Ajay K. Manrai, "Interactive Effects of Country of Origin and Product Category on Product Evaluations," *International Business Review,* Vol. 7, 1998, pp. 591–615.

27. Ibid.

28. Terrence A. Shimp and Subhash Sharma, "Consumer Ethnocentrism: Construction and Validation of the CETSCALE," *Journal of Marketing Research,* Vol. 24, No. 3, August 1987, pp. 280–289.

29. Ibid.

30. For an in-depth description of these and additional restrictions, see Lee D. Dahringer, "Marketing Services Internationally: Barriers and Management Strategies," *Journal of Services Marketing,* Vol. 5, No. 3, Summer 1991, pp. 5–17.

31. P. B. Kenen, *The International Economy,* Englewood Cliffs, NJ: Prentice Hall, 1989; and Ikechi Ekeledo and K. Sivakumar, "Foreign Market Entry Mode Choice of Service Firms: A Contingency Perspective," *Journal of the Academy of Marketing Science,* Vol. 26, No. 4, 1998, pp. 274–292.

32. John A. Czepiel, "Service Encounters and Service Relationships: Implications and Research," *Journal of Business Research,* Vol. 20,

1990, pp. 13–21; and Kathryn Frazier Winsted, "Evaluating Service Encounters: A Cross-Cultural and Cross-Industry Exploration," *Journal of Marketing Theory and Practice,* Vol. 7, No. 2, Spring 1999, pp. 106–123.

33. Naresh K. Malhotra, Francis M. Ulgado, J. Agrawal, and I. B. Baalbaki, "International Services Marketing: A Comparative Evaluation of the Dimensions of Service Quality Between Developed and Developing Countries," *International Marketing Review,* Vol. 11, No. 2, 1994, p. 515.

34. Frazier Winsted, "Evaluating Service Encounters," pp. 106–123.

35. Ibid.

36. Guliz Ger, Russell W. Belk, and Dana-Nicoleta Lascu, "The Development in Consumer Desire in Marketizing and Developing Economies: The Cases of Romania and Turkey," in L. McAllister (ed.), *Advances in Consumer Research,* Association for Consumer Research, Vol. 20, 1993, pp. 102–107.

37. Dexter Roberts, Frederik Balfour, Paul Magnuson, Pete Engardio, and Jennifer Lee, "China's Pirates: It's Not Just Little Guys—State-Owned Factories Add to the Plague of Fakes," *Business Week,* Issue:No. 3684, June 5, 2000, pp. 26, 44.

38. Ibid.

39. Peter H. Bloch, Ronald F. Bush, and Leland Campbell, "Consumer 'Accomplices' in Product Counterfeiting," *Journal of Consumer Marketing,* Vol. 10, No. 4, 1993, pp. 27–36.

40. Roberts, Balfour, Magnuson, Engardio, Jennifer and Lee, "China's Pirates," pp. 26, 44.

41. Ibid.

42. Ibid.

43. Ibid.

44. Ibid.

45. Ibid.

46. www.iso.cf

47. Dennis Rondinelli and Gyula Vastag, "International Environmental Standards and Corporate Policies: An Integrative Framework," *California Management Review,* Vol. 39, No. 1, 1996, pp. 106–122.

48. www.iso.ch

49. With contributions from Christianne Goldman, Ryan Ganley, Leslie Ramich, and Akshay Patil.

50. Material available at www.philips.com.

51. www.philips.com

52. Bill Griffeth, *Philips Electronics—CHM & CEO—Interview,* Dow Jones Business Video, January 9, 2002, p. 1.

53. Hoover's Online, www.hoover.com, February 19, 2002.

54. Ibid.

55. Ibid.

56. Ibid.

57. Jennifer B. Simes, "Philippines a Key Hub, Says Philips," *Computerworld Philippines,* Dow Jones Interactive, December 10, 2001, p. 1.

58. "Brand Building," www.philips.com, p. 1.

59. "A Serious Responsibility," www.philips.com, p. 1.

60. Beth Snyder Bulik, "Philips Simplifies for New U.S. Effort," *Advertising Age,* Vol. 75, No. 28, July 12, 2004, p. 3.

61. Ibid.

62. Michael McCarthy, "Philips Can't Lose with Puppies, Beatles," *USA Today,* www.usatoday.com, January 15, 2001, p. 2.

63. Tobi Elkin, "Building a Brand," *Vision Magazine,* www.ce.org/, July/August 1999, pp. 1–2.

64. See "Owning the Right Image," www.news.philips.com, p. 1, for a more extensive analysis of the Philips communication strategy.

65. Tobi Elkin, "Philips to Sponsor U.S. Soccer Games," www.adage.com, June 19, 2001, p. 1.

Case 9-1

Royal Philips Electronics[49]

Background

Royal Philips is the world's third-largest consumer electronics firm, following market leaders Matsushita and Sony. The Philips brands include Philips, Norelco, Marantz, Sonicare, and Magnavox. The company was established in 1891 in Eindhoven, in the Southern region of the Netherlands, primarily as a manufacturer of incandescent lamps and other electrical products. The company first produced carbon-filament lamps, and, by the turn of the century, it had become one of the largest producers in Europe. Later, the company diversified into many other areas, such as electronics, small appliances, lighting, semiconductors, medical systems, and domestic care products, among others. The company headquarters moved to Amsterdam in the 1980s, but its lighting division continues to occupy the center of Eindhoven (see Figure 9-8).

Around the early 1900s, Philips started to diversify its offerings to radio valves and X-ray equipment, and later to television. Later, Philips developed the electric shaver and invented the rotary heads. Philips also made major contributions in the development of television pictures, its research work leading to the development of the Plumbicon television camera tube, which offered a better picture quality. It introduced the compact audiocassette in 1963 and produced its first integrated circuits in 1965. In the 1970s, its research in lighting contributed to the development of the PL and SL energy-saving lamps. More recent Philips innovations are the LaserVision optical disc, the compact disc, and optical telecommunication systems.[50]

Philips expanded in the 1970s and 1980s, acquiring Magnavox (1974) and Signetics (1975), the television business of GTE Sylvania (1981), and the lamps division of Westinghouse (1983). Currently, Philips operates in more than 60 countries, with more than 186,000 employees, and is market leader in many regions for a number of product categories—for example, lighting, shavers, and LCD displays.[51]

In the 1990s, Philips carried out a major restructuring program and changed from highly localized production to globalized production; this change translated into a more efficient concentration of manufacturing—from more than 100 manufacturing sites to 36, and to multiple sites for production, 2 in Latin America, 6 in Europe, and 4 in Asia (China).

Another important change was the appointment of Gerard Kleisterlee as president of Philips and chairman of the Board of Management in 2001. Kleisterlee has been seen as a Philips man, following a traditional Philips career path that had been embraced by company employees until the 1980s. He was trained locally, at the Eindhoven Technical University, in electronic engineering, and he has worked with the company for more than three decades. According to Martien Groenewegen, former research and development engineer with Philips, Kleisterlee is perceived by present and former employees as taking the company back to its original path to success. In fact, in one interview, Kleisterlee mentioned that the company was concentrating on its initial core activities with a focus on its key areas of profitability; this is a different type of restructuring from earlier attempts, when the company pursued "wrong activities."[52] Mr. Groenewegen contends that the perception among employees and the industry is that Philips, under Kleisterlee's leadership, will have a strong product orientation and that it would support an environment in which product innovation will constitute a primary focus of the company. That has been, historically, Philips' proven path to success.

Philips offers consumer products, such as communications products (cordless phones, mobile phones, fax machines), electronics (Flat TV, Real Flat TV, digital TV, projection TV, professional TV, DVD players and recorders, Super Audio CD, VCRs, satellite receivers, CD recorders/players, home theater systems, Internet audio players, shelf systems, portable radios, clock radios, PC monitors, multimedia projectors, PC cameras, PC audio, CD rewritable drives, DVD drives, among others); home and body care products (vacuum cleaners, irons, kitchen appliances, shavers, oral healthcare products), and lighting products. Its professional products include connectivity, lighting, medical systems (such as magnetic resonance imaging, ultrasound equipment, X-rays), semiconductors,

Figure 9-8

Philips Lighting reigns in downtown Eindhoven.

and other products, such as security systems, manufacturing technologies, automotive products, broadband networks, and so on.

The Competition

Among Philips' competitors are Matsushita, Sony, Hitachi, and Thomson. Matsushita Electric Industrial is the world's number-one consumer electronics firm. In North America, Matsushita makes consumer, commercial, and industrial electronics (from jukeboxes to flat-screen TVs) under the Panasonic, Technics, and Quasar brands. Matsushita sells consumer products (which account for 40 percent of sales) such as VCRs, CD and DVD players, TVs, and home appliances. It also sells computers, telephones, industrial equipment (welding and vending machines, medical equipment, car navigation equipment), and components such as batteries, semiconductors, and electric motors. The Matsushita group includes about 320 operating units in more than 45 countries. Its products are sold worldwide, but Asia accounts for more than 70 percent of sales.[53]

Sony is another competitor whose PlayStation home video game systems account for nearly 10 percent of the company's electronics and entertainment sales. Sony, the world's second-largest consumer electronics firm after Matsushita, also makes several other products, including semiconductors, DVD players, batteries, cameras, MiniDisc and Walkman stereo systems, computer monitors, and flat-screen TVs. The company's TVs, VCRs, stereos, and other consumer electronics account for more than 65 percent of sales. Sony's entertainment assets include Columbia TriStar (movies and television shows) and record labels Columbia and Epic. The company also operates insurance and finance businesses.[54]

Hitachi, another large player in the consumer electronics industry, is a leading manufacturer of both electronics components and industrial equipment. The company manufactures mainframes, semiconductors, workstations, elevators and escalators, power plant equipment, and also metals, wire, and cable. Hitachi produces consumer goods, such as audio and video equipment, refrigerators, and washing machines. Similarly to Philips, Hitachi is focusing on developing Internet-related businesses and expanding its information technology units, which account for more than 30 percent of sales.[55]

Finally, Thomson Multimedia is another major competitor and leading manufacturer of consumer electronics (which account for nearly 80 percent of sales), including TVs, video cameras, telephones, audio products, DVD players, and professional video equipment. Thomson Multimedia also produces displays and TV components. Its products, which are sold in more than 100 countries, include brands such as RCA in the United States and Thomson in Europe. Almost 60 percent of the company's sales are in the United States.[56]

Philips' Brand Image

Philips' primary mission is to "continually enhance people's lives through technology and innovation."[57] This philosophy is also reflected in its tagline "Let's make things better," launched in 1995.[58] Philips focuses on the multisensory impact of its products and their power to create memories and spur emotions to touch people's lives on a very personal level; Philips also aspires to be the world's leading eco-efficient company in electronics and lighting.[59]

Philips is a household name in European markets, with an 86 percent brand recognition. However, even in Europe, the brand is adopted by "older females with lower technology usage."[60] Under the leadership of Kleisterlee, its CEO, Philips has been simplifying its systems, processes, and products;[61] it has also revolutionized its communication with its target market to position the company and its brands as hip, cool, and technologically advanced.

This strategy is most obvious in the United States, where the company, as recently as 1996, was virtually unknown, compared with competitors Sony and RCA; the brand was associated with milk of magnesia, petroleum, or screwdrivers.[62] After spending millions to build brand awareness, Philips has successfully achieved recognition among consumers in the United States as a brand that makes exciting products that improve people's lives. Its effort to win U.S. consumers started in 1998, when Philips spent $100 million in advertising, sponsorships, movie tie-ins, and retail promotions worldwide to boost brand awareness.[63] In the same year, Philips embarked on its Star campaign in an attempt to create a more human, imaginative, and seductive brand image. Using dynamic state-of-the-art products, the Philips campaign was able to reach consumers on a very personal level, thus gaining their trust, loyalty, and brand preference. The campaign resonated very well with its target market: well-educated, independent, and carefree consumers.[64] Today, Philips uses an aggressive global marketing campaign shot and produced by Omnicom Group's DDB Worldwide with an emphasis on the United States; its overarching theme is simplicity, and its goal is to increase sales to $50 billion by the year 2009.

Another venue for communicating with its target market was Philips' five-year sponsorship of the U.S. Soccer Federation as of June 2001. This sponsorship helped Philips reach more of its young target consumers and more female consumers. Philips thus has 30-second air spots on ABC and ESPN during soccer broadcasts, as well as a presence on stadium billboards, and logo visibility on all training kits; and the Philips' branded goal cameras are highly visible.[65]

Analysis Suggestions

1. Use the globalization versus adaptation arguments to support Philips' strategies worldwide. What are some of the advantages of its new globalization strategy?
2. Some may argue that Philips is a Pan-European brand that is trying to make inroads into the United States. Find support for and against this argument.
3. Offer suggestions to Philips regarding the strategies that it can use to create a unified, resonant global brand.

International Product and Service Strategies

Chapter Objectives

By the end of this chapter, you should be able to

1 Evaluate the stages of the international product life cycle and identify the locus of operations and target markets at each stage.

2 Identify the different dimensions of the international product mix with company illustrations.

3 Examine the new product development process and the activities involved at each stage in international markets.

4 Examine degrees of product newness and address international diffusion processes.

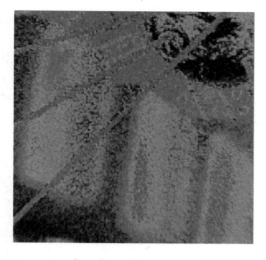

R ed Bull, an Austrian energy drink, has systematically taken over energy drink marketing around the world. The drink was adopted by consumers in the rest of Europe in the early 1990s and took the U.S. market by storm in 1997; it was, a decade later, in nearly every retail shop in the United States. In less than three years, Red Bull single-handedly created and then propelled the energy drink category to $75 million in sales.[1]

The international marketing environment creates complex challenges for products and services. For example, during the product life cycle, firms must coordinate their marketing activities with international trade and investment decisions to remain price competitive in the face of increased competition from manufacturers in developing and developed countries alike. New product development decisions involve consumers in target markets that differ from home-country consumers in their attitudes, interests, and opinions; the challenges of new product/service launches are amplified by the complexities of the marketplace and the competition from both local and multinational firms. And managing the product mix and the product portfolio in line with company strategy and the demands of different consumers offers many dilemmas to brand managers. This chapter attempts to shed light on some of these challenges.

10-1 The International Product Life Cycle (IPLC)

Products pass through distinct stages, during which profits may rise and fall, respectively; as a consequence, products require different marketing strategies in each stage. The **international product life cycle (IPLC)** involves a complex relationship between the product life cycle stage and international trade and investment. At a basic level, the premise of the IPLC is as follows: Firms from developed, industrialized countries produce products for domestic consumption in the early stage of the product life cycle primarily because product specifications and the manufacturing process are not yet stable. As the product advances to the maturity stage, product specifications and the manufacturing process stabilize. At this point, price competition becomes intense, and international markets emerge, prompting firms to move production abroad to benefit from lower manufacturing costs.[2]

Figure 10-1 describes the international trade and investment activity of an international corporation and of local competition during each stage of the international product life cycle (from the perspective of the international corporation). During the introduction and growth stages, production takes place in the home country or in another industrialized country, and the company exports the products to developing countries. At maturity, manufacturing moves abroad, and the product is imported to the home country and other industrialized countries. Local competitors then emerge; they compete with the international corporation in its home country or in other industrialized countries. During the decline stage, international sales keep the company afloat.

international product life cycle (IPLC) A product life-cycle theory, which states that firms from developed countries engage in domestic production in the early stage of the product life cycle, marketing the product to industrialized countries; as the product reaches maturity, product specifications and the manufacturing process stabilize, price competition becomes intense, and markets in developing countries become essential to the firm's success.

Figure 10-1

The International Product Life Cycle (IPLC) and the International Corporation

Introduction and Growth Stages:	Early Maturity:	Late Maturity:	Decline:
MNC manufactures product in developed countries; exports to developing countries	MNC moves production to developing country; begins importing to home country	Developing country competitor exports product to MNC home country; competes with MNC imports	Developing country markets remain viable target markets for MNC; MNC home country market is diminishing

Sales

Time

10-1a The Product Introduction Stage

introduction stage The first stage of the international product life cycle when products are developed and marketed in industrialized countries.

During the **introduction stage,** products are developed in industrialized countries and supported by firms' substantial research and development budgets and by highly skilled product research teams. To quickly recover the high costs of product development and launching, a firm markets products in industrialized countries to consumers who can afford the high prices charged to recover the high costs, while it still has control of the market (it is the only manufacturer or one of the few manufacturers of the product). According to the initial IPLC theory (see section 10-1, "The International Product Life Cycle [IPLC]"), these products were first marketed in the products' country of origin. Assuming a reasonable adoption rate in highly industrialized countries, the product also becomes available in developing countries, where it is exported by the firm. Smart phones are currently in this early growth stage.

10-1b The Growth Stage

growth stage The stage of the international product life cycle characterized by increasing competition and rapid product adoption by the target market.

The **growth stage** is characterized by increasing competition, with new product variants offered to the market, as well as rapid product adoption by the target market. Toward the end of this stage, the focus is on developing economies of scale in the manufacturing process; price competition increases at this point and a standard is reached. Examples of products in the growth stage of the IPLC are PDAs (Personal Digital Assistants). At the end of the growth stage, the product is standardized; that is, a particular standard is reached, and products are manufactured to conform to this standard. In the case of VCRs, the VHS format became the standard. DVD/CD players, now in the maturity stage, were initially introduced as DVDs; at this point, the DVD/CD combination is standard. For PDAs, it is possible that the standard will be a PocketPC-type product such as the Hewlett-Packard PDA, but the jury is still out.

During the growth state, production continues to take place in industrialized countries and manufacturers in industrialized countries continue to export their products in developing countries.

10-1c The Maturity Stage

Usually the longest stage in the product life cycle, the **maturity stage** is characterized by a slowdown in sales growth as the product is adopted by most target consumers and by a leveling or decline in profits primarily due to intense price competition. At this point, manufacturing moves to developing countries to save on labor costs. For example, the U.S. electronics company Motorola selected Krakow, Poland, as its first European software center and the location of a chip plant,[3] while Siemens AG, Macronix, and Intel Corp. are engaging in semiconductor manufacturing in Thailand, in a consortium with a local company.[4] Products manufactured abroad are then imported in the home country and other industrialized countries; these products successfully compete on price in the respective developed countries. Examples of products in this category are television sets, hi-fi equipment, and video cameras, among others.

As companies establish strategic alliances with firms from developing countries or engage in local manufacturing under other forms, such as contract manufacturing, or through a wholly owned subsidiary, they train local talent and are likely to create local competition. Competitors from developing countries will then sell products in industrialized countries, competing directly with the multinational firm in its home market and in other developed countries. Examples of successful companies from developing countries exporting their products in developed countries abound. Shenzhen Electronics Group, a Chinese company, sells its television sets, hi-fi equipment, and quartz watches in the United States.[5] In other examples, "Made in India" is a sign of high-quality software; in this market, top software companies include subsidiaries of U.S. companies, such as Motorola India Electronics Ltd. and IBM Global Services India, as well as local companies such as Satyam Computer Services Ltd., Tata Consultancy Services, and Wipro Infotech.[6]

> **maturity stage** A stage of the international product life cycle characterized by a slowdown in sales growth as the product is adopted by most target consumers and by a leveling or decline in profits primarily due to intense price competition.

10-1d The Decline Stage

Products in the **decline stage** are rapidly losing ground to new technologies or product alternatives. Sales and, consequently, profits are declining at this stage, and a firm might consider whether its presence in the market is warranted. However, having an international presence during the decline stage, particularly in developing countries, could be an advantage. One of the main benefits of going international and engaging in international marketing is the ability of a firm to extend the product life cycle. A product may be in the decline stage in the lead country, where it was developed, as well as in other industrial economies, and, at the same time, in a stable maturity stage in most developing countries.

Conceptually, the international product life cycle makes sense: Products are produced in developed countries where they are first adopted; then they are later made available in developing countries. However, consumers in today's industrializing nations do not wait for unrolling of small electronics gadgets on the basis of the life cycle addressed here; these consumers want their portable cell phones and other devices right now. For example, wireless telephones have made tremendous advances in transition economies because the traditional wired systems often have reception problems—more so than wireless phones. Nations in Europe, Latin America, and Asia are often ahead of the United States on several fronts—e.g., public transport, satellite clocks, etc.

> **decline stage** The stage of the international product life cycle in which products are rapidly losing ground to new technologies or product alternatives, causing a decrease in sales and profits.

10-2 Managing the International Product and Service Mix

The product portfolio of a firm is usually diversified into products that are in different stages of the product life cycle, such that profits from successful mature products can be used to invest in new products and products that have a lower market share. Most multinational corporations tend to have both local and global brands that they nurture through their life cycle. The international **product mix** is the complete assortment of the

> **product mix** The complete assortment of products that a company offers to its target international consumers.

product line All the brands the company offers in the same product category.

product consistency The extent to which a company's different product lines are related, use the same distribution channels, and have the same final consumers.

product length The total number of brands in the product mix.

product width The total number of product lines that a company offers to its target international consumers.

product depth The number of different offerings for a particular brand.

products that a company offers to its target international consumers, and it has a number of important dimensions. One important dimension of the product mix is the **product line,** a number of related brands in the same product category. Companies use different line strategies to achieve market share and profitability goals; for example, companies engage in line extensions to target consumers who otherwise cannot afford a particular product. In the fashion realm, for example, numerous top-line designers target the masses with bridge offerings (secondary, more affordable lines): Escada with Laurel, Ann Klein with Ann Klein II, Donna Karan with DKNY, Armani with Emporio Armani, etc.

To illustrate the remaining product dimensions, we will use the example of Unilever (www.unilever.com), one of the largest consumer product companies in the world. Unilever is actually composed of two companies, Unilever NV and Unilever PLC, operating as one company linked by a series of agreements and common shareholders, and headquartered in London and Rotterdam, respectively.[7] Although Unilever is organized primarily into two divisions, the foods division and the personal care division, the company has a number of product lines that are addressed as separate strategic business units.

Another important dimension of the product mix is **product consistency;** this term refers to the extent to which the different product lines are related, use the same distribution channels, and have the same final consumers. The Unilever brands are consistent within each of the company divisions. DiverseyLever, the company's professional cleaning product (see Table 10-1), is probably the only product that might break this pattern of consistency.

The other dimensions of the product mix, as illustrated by the Unilever example in Table 10-1, are product length, width, and depth.

10-2a Length

The **product length** is the total number of brands in the product mix—all the brands sold by the company. Counting the Unilever brands in Table 10-1, the total product length is 38.

10-2b Width

The **product width** is the total number of product lines the company offers. Counting the different product lines in Table 10-1 (culinary products, frozen foods, ice cream, tea, margarine, household care products, detergents, deodorants, shampoos, personal care, oral care, fragrances, diagnostics, and professional cleaning products), the total product width is 14.

10-2c Depth

The **product depth** refers to the number of different offerings for a product category. For example, Lipton tea comes in at least three variants: Lipton Yellow Label, Lipton Ice Tea, and Lipton Brisk. The depth of the tea category (the Lipton brand), therefore, is 3. Product depth for the tea line is thus calculated by adding all the variants under the Lipton brand.

Companies alter their product mix by purchasing existing international or local brands. For example, Unilever purchased the Ben & Jerry's Ice Cream brand. Companies also develop new brands and products that they can add to their portfolio. Section 10-3 discusses new product development.

10-3 New Product Development

To maintain their competitive advantage and to ensure survival and growth locally, regionally, or globally, companies must develop and introduce new products and services that meet the needs of their markets. International new product development is a costly process that involves the firm at all levels. If successful, product/service development is the key to a company's success and future.

Product Area	Brand Names	
Culinary products	Ragu Spaghetti Sauces Calvé Whisky Cocktail Hellmann's Mayonnaise Knorr Soups	**Table 10-1** **Unilever Products**
Frozen foods	Findus 4 Salti in Padella Gordon's Tenders	
Ice cream	Magnum Solero Bryers Ben & Jerry's	
Margarine	I Can't Believe It's Not Butter Rama margarine Becel spreads	
Tea	Lipton	
Household care	Domestos Cif	
Detergents	Omo Ala Snuggle Comfort	
Deodorants	Rexona/Sure Axe Dove	
Shampoos	SunSilk ThermaSilk Organics	
Personal care	Lux Dove Vaseline Intensive Care Pond's	
Oral care	Mentadent Signal Close-Up	
Fragrances	Valentino Cerruti Calvin Klein	
Diagnostics	Unipath fertility products	
Professional cleaning	DiverseyLever	

In general, new product development involves substantial risks and costs; the complex environment of the international marketplace adds considerably to both the risks and costs. Consider, for example, the case of Freeplay Energy, a company that started in Cape Town, South Africa, now headquartered in London, United Kingdom, which developed wind-up, self-powered radios for the African market under the name Freeplay Energy. The product initially failed in Africa, where consumers preferred to purchase batteries, rather than incur a one-time expenditure of about $50 for such a radio; the company, however, remained in business primarily due to its success in the United States and

Europe.[8] After refocusing on developed markets, Freeplay developed its products with a sophisticated, Western consumer in mind. With the initial product, the radio had to be wound 20 seconds to produce 30 minutes of radio time; a lighter, smaller version produced one hour of playing time. Subsequent to its success in Europe, the product started selling in developing countries as well. The product is marketed using different strategies worldwide: In Japan and the United States, the product is marketed as part of earthquake and tornado survival kits; in Germany, interest in the product is fueled by environmental concern; whereas in the United Kingdom, consumers take pride in owning such an invention.

Interestingly, the same company made a second attempt to fulfill the needs of the African market: Freeplay developed a self-powered generator intended to enable consumers in developing countries to charge their satellite telephones. The entrepreneurs developing this product believe that most of the growth in cell phones is in the developing world; however, most African countries cannot afford the infrastructure needed, leaving satellite communication fueled by either expensive disposable batteries or self-powered technology as the only options. This and many other Freeplay products are today used to increase self-sufficiency for consumers in developed countries.

The two examples involving Freeplay's innovations illustrate some of the complexities involved in developing new products internationally. The following are examples of risks and difficulties companies face when developing new products:

- International and local competitors could appropriate the product/service idea and deliver the final product or service to the market more swiftly, economically, and with stronger company backing (brand reputation, financial support) than the initial product/service developer.

- International target consumers might not respond as anticipated to the offering (as in the case of Freeplay's wind-up radio) because it does not meet their needs, because they cannot afford it, or because they prefer to adopt a product later in the product life-cycle stage.

- Local governments or the home-country government might impose restrictions on product testing procedures (in the case of pharmaceuticals, for example).

- The technological infrastructure of the market is substandard and cannot support the new product.

The steps that companies typically follow in the product development process are essentially the same as those involved in domestic product development. Figure 10-2 illustrates the international product development process. At each step, the process can be either terminated or restarted for each individual product idea; consequently, a product must go through each stage to reach the international product launching stage. Throughout the product development process, maintaining a strong market orientation is important: A thorough understanding of consumers' needs and wants and of the competitive situation and the nature of the market is critical to product success.[9]

10-3a Generating New Product Ideas

generating new product ideas
Seeking ideas using different strategies as the first step in the new product development process.

The first step in the new product development process is **generating new product ideas.** Depending on the products provided and/or company philosophy, ideas will be sought using different strategies. Most product and service firms are driven by the marketing concept, and their product development decisions are based on identifying the needs, wants, and desires of consumers. For technology-driven firms, the focus is more likely to be on the product itself, and thus the research and development division is likely to be responsible for developing product ideas. Even in this second instance, however, products are developed with the needs of the consumer in mind. Freeplay Energy, with its wind-up radio, is an example of a product-focused company. An inventor created the radio independent of the market, and a marketer identified a market for the product—consumers

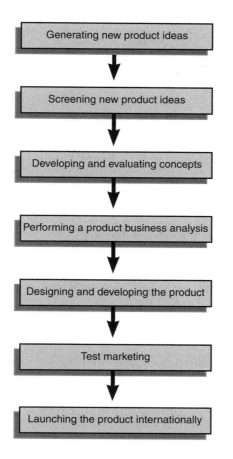

Figure 10-2
Steps in the New Product
Development Process

in Africa who do not have electricity, use batteries for their radios, and could benefit from using wind-up radios.

Companies use multiple sources for ideas. Among the most common are consumers; competitive analyses; and some additional sources such as channel members, company employees, and so on.

Consumers

The most obvious sources for ideas are consumers in the home-country market of the firm. Other sources of product ideas are consumers in the company's international markets. Although, traditionally, products of U.S. multinational firms were driven entirely by consumers in the United States, these companies are now increasingly drawing upon consumers around the world for new product or service ideas. A growing number of companies are developing products for one market and successfully marketing them in markets that are substantially different. Häagen-Dazs developed a caramel-flavored ice cream called Dulce de Leche for Argentina; the company brought this flavor to the United States, where, in stores that carry it, it is second only to vanilla, and to Europe, where it is moving from seasonal-flavor to year-round-flavor status.[10] In other examples, Nike found that a soccer boot designed and worn by Ronaldo, a player on the Brazilian soccer team, was very popular with consumers in the United States. Similarly, Levi Strauss, the quintessential all-American jeans manufacturer, offered a dark version of denim jeans that was very popular for a few years with consumers in Japan to U.S. consumers, who responded very favorably to it.[11]

Competitive Analyses

Competition represents an obvious source for product and service ideas. Products that are in the test market phase or that are just being launched are always vulnerable to having their ideas copied. For example, Kao, a Japanese detergent manufacturer, developed a super-absorbent diaper, causing Procter & Gamble's Pampers to lose its lead in the Japanese market; however, Procter & Gamble promptly developed its own super-absorbent version of Pampers, selling it aggressively worldwide.[12]

Additional Sources

Other sources of ideas are channel members, who are closer to consumers than the manufacturer; company employees, such as sales personnel, engineers, or even top management; inventors; consultants; nonprofit research laboratories; universities; and research firms, among others. Research conducted by the firm in the form of brainstorming sessions and qualitative research also may be used in the process of generating product ideas.[13]

10-3b Screening New Product Ideas

screening new product ideas Eliminating product ideas that do not fit with the target consumers and/or the overall mission of the organization.

In the process of **screening new product ideas,** it is best to consider both the extent to which the product fits with the target consumers, as well as with the overall mission of the organization.[14] At this stage, a checklist is usually developed to screen out product ideas that do not meet these criteria.

In the screening process, the following factors should be taken into consideration:[15]

- The product to be developed should be superior, delivering unique benefits to users, rather than a "me-too" undifferentiated product. Such superiority is derived from design, features, attributes, specifications, and product positioning.
- The target market should be a large, attractive, growth market, where the product is perceived as important, where demand for it has been stable over time, and where customers are profitable and price-insensitive.
- There should be a fit between the new product requirements and the resources, skills, and experiences of the firm with regard to management capabilities, technical support, research and development, and manufacturing skills, as well as sales and distribution skills and resources in the company or the firm's channel of distribution.

Factors that lead to a lower success rate normally are evaluated unfavorably in the screening process; these factors, however, are commonplace for firms targeting international markets. International involvement often takes the firm into unfamiliar territory: The company targets new customers, serves unfamiliar customer needs, uses new channels, and meets new servicing requirements. Success rates for such products are lower.[16]

10-3c Developing and Evaluating Concepts

developing and evaluating concepts Determining how consumers will perceive and use a new product; a step in the new product development process.

The next stage, **developing and evaluating concepts,** is an important step for firms developing products for international markets. Key activities at this stage are to determine how the product will be viewed by consumers and how it will be used; this information can be determined by having the target consumers test the idea to gauge its usefulness.[17] Typically, the process involves developing a detailed description of the product and asking prospective consumers to evaluate it and to indicate their willingness to purchase the hypothetical product. Most often, this is done using a focus group of representative target consumers.

Even in cases in which firms are exporting products initially developed for the home-country market, it is essential that they engage in market research. The shortening of the product life cycle and the intensity of international competition increase pressure on exporters to evaluate and reevaluate their market in light of rapid technological change and to conduct concept-testing research that ranges from formal methods, such as focus groups, to ad hoc information gathering.[18]

One method that is frequently used at this stage is conjoint analysis. In this method, respondents receive descriptions of different hypothetical products with varying levels of the same attributes, which they are then asked to rank. Analysts can determine the ideal combination of attributes, ascertain the importance of each attribute, and, assuming the data were collected from a sufficiently large sample of the target population, estimate market share.

10-3d Performing a Product Business Analysis

Performing a product business analysis should include calculating projected project costs, return on investment, and cash flow and determining the fixed and variable costs for the long term.[19] However enthusiastic the target consumers queried, if these figures do not fit the company budget, the project will be high risk. For many product categories, product price is a critical characteristic; at this stage, it is important to identify the price level at which revenue or profit best fit the manufacturer's goals.[20]

performing a product business analysis Calculating projected costs such as return on investment and cash flow, and determining the fixed and variable costs for the long term.

10-3e Designing and Developing the Product

At the next stage, **designing and developing the product,** product prototypes are developed. It is important that product prototypes precisely match the concept description developed in the concept development and evaluation stage; if the company strays from the initial description, testing the revised product description is crucial.[21]

The product now acquires a name—a brand identity—and the marketing mix is developed. The cross-functional team developing the product—research and development, engineering, operations, marketing, finance—must come together for this process.[22] This team must be focused on the project in such a way that a large percentage of team members' time is devoted to the project, rather than to other projects; it also is important that the team acts as a unit, focusing on project, rather than departmental, interests.[23]

For multinational companies, coordination takes place across subsidiaries, or in conjunction with international partners. Companies such as Boeing and Motorola coordinate research and development activities globally by establishing worldwide information systems to coordinate product and design development; for example, in developing the Boeing 777, the company used real-time computer-aided technology to design components jointly with Japanese partners.[24] Companies also tend to encourage communication among research and development facilities in different countries; Procter & Gamble and Unilever, for example, require extensive communication and information sharing among units.[25] Products must fit client needs and specifications, so coordinating with clients is essential. In one example, the Airbus A380 was designed to hold more people and handle more cargo, creating efficiencies for the airlines. The issue that still must be resolved is where to park this enormous aircraft (see International Marketing Illustration 10-1).

designing and developing the product Developing product prototypes and giving the product a name, a brand identity, and a marketing mix; a step in the new product development process.

10-3f Test Marketing

Test marketing a product can provide a good indication of how the product will be received when it is in the market, but this stage can also be expensive, time consuming, and open to competitive sabotage.[26] The following are test marketing options firms can choose to evaluate the reaction of the market to their product. At the lower involvement level is simulated test marketing, which is not as costly and does not give competition much information about the product. Controlled test marketing is limited to a few stores, is thus also less costly, and gives only limited exposure of the product to competition. Actual test marketing necessitates important strategic decisions and commitments that involve channel members, intensive promotion, and high promotional expenses; test marketing could create conditions for the product to be vulnerable to competitive reactions.

test marketing Testing new-product performance in a limited area of a national or regional target market to estimate product performance in the respective country or region.

Simulated Test Marketing

Because 8 out of 10 products fail, simulated test markets are often used to reduce the risks a company would incur in terms of marketing, sales, and capital expenses; in terms of cannibalization of the parent brand through line extension; and in terms of competitive reaction

International Marketing Illustration 10-1

Parking an Aircraft on Steroids

The Airbus 380 is touted as the world's largest airplane, the world's only twin-deck airliner, with a dedicated three-deck 150-ton long-range freighter. This giant is more fuel efficient than the average person's car: Its modern technology and economies of scale provide 15 percent lower seat-mile costs than today's most efficient aircraft. Thus, it is capable of offering passengers luxury travel at much more affordable prices—a cruise ship for the skies, the company claims.

The plane, which seats 555 passengers comfortably in a three-class interior layout, will enter into service in 2006. This superjumbo double-decker aircraft advertises itself as 50 percent larger than the Boeing 747, with plenty of extra space that would allow passengers to lounge about in cozy conference rooms and attend chic in-flight gatherings.

In reality, however, the airlines could choose to pack 880 passengers in the A380, which, in all likelihood, they will if they are going to opt for running a highly profitable operation. Already, the airlines have placed orders for more than 100 aircraft, clearly eying these profits.

Yet when such an aircraft is in use, it requires an entirely new infrastructure to support it. For example, airports must increase their baggage handling capacity and increase the number of customs and immigration personnel to handle customs at one time. Taxiways and gates need to be modified to accommodate an airplane that has 12 doors and four aisles. To date, however, only 13 airports worldwide can accommodate the A380, and the company estimates that, by 2009, there may be only 22 airports in the world with the capacity to handle the aircraft, assuming that the airports receive the necessary and substantial investments.

Sources: Joe Sharkey, "Where Do You Park a 747 on Steroids?" The New York Times, May 4, 2004, p. C7; www.airbus.com; Ham Granlund, "Are Airports Ready for A380?" Aviation Week & Space Technology, Vol. 160, No. 16, April 19, 2004, p. 6.

---

simulated test marketing Test marketing simulating purchase environments where samples of target consumers are observed in their product-related decision-making process.

to the new product.[27] Among the **simulated test marketing** research systems employed today are LITMUS, which is used especially for new packaged goods, consumer durables, and services; ASSESSOR, which is used for packaged goods; BASES, which is used primarily for food and health and beauty products; and ESP, which is used primarily for packaged goods.[28]

To illustrate, the LITMUS simulated test marketing study recruits about 600 representative consumers who participate in a research study in a central facility in a number of markets.[29] After responding to questions about their product-related attitudes and purchase behavior, they view advertising of the new brand and of competitive brands that are embedded in a television program. The respondents then comment on the television program and advertising and then proceed to a simulated store stocking test brands and competitive brands where they can buy the products at a substantial discount. The proportion of individuals purchasing the test brand is then used to estimate product trialability.

Controlled Test Marketing

controlled test marketing Test marketing that involves offering a new product to a group of stores and evaluating the market's reaction to it.

Usually conducted by a research firm in industrialized countries, **controlled test marketing** involves offering a new product to a group of stores and evaluating the market reaction to it (consumer reaction as well as competitive reaction). In the process, different aspects of the marketing mix are varied—price, in-store promotion, placement in the store, etc. A more informal controlled test marketing involves simply asking a number of stores to carry the product for a fee; depending on the outcome, the manufacturing firm may decide to produce the product on a larger scale, or not.

Actual Test Marketing

A number of important decisions are involved in full-blown test marketing. Companies at this stage must decide on the cities that are most appropriate for testing the product, based on the availability of retailers and other necessary distribution and logistics service providers, and on availability of the infrastructure needed to conduct the test market, such as the necessary media, research firms, direct mail providers, etc. Multinational companies do not limit test marketing nor product launching to their home countries. For example, Pepsi-Cola International test marketed its no-sugar Pepsi Max in Northern Italy and the United Kingdom.[30] The duration of the test market also may vary, from a few months to a year or more, depending on company goals and budget. In the case of Pepsi Max, the product was tested in the United Kingdom for one year.[31]

For companies selling financial products in industrialized countries and for companies that cannot afford large-scale testing in the marketplace, test marketing may be limited to direct mail. For example, MasterCard continually tests new products in the Netherlands and Germany by using direct mail. This strategy also appeals to service providers from developing countries. For example, Mexican exporters often use direct mail to test a market in the United States or Canada; however, this approach is problematic because the national mail service can be unreliable, ZIP codes are missing from database lists, etc.[32] Test marketing exclusively using direct mail works well when it is aimed at a narrow, well-defined target market. Although this approach is possible in Europe, Canada, and the United States, where segmentation is a precise science, based on refined methods of demographic and psychographic assessment, in developing countries, such well-defined databases are not always available.[33]

Although test marketing can provide valuable information for the manufacturer, anticipating product performance in the short run, its usefulness is often questioned given the high expense it necessitates. In a rapidly changing competitive environment, being first in the market constitutes an important competitive advantage: the first-mover advantage: As such, the company is the first to attract consumers and to commit channel members for its new product. A company is also vulnerable to competitive reaction during the test marketing stage. On one hand, competition could appropriate the product idea and be the first to offer the product to the market; on the other, competition could sabotage the new brand, cutting prices for all competitive offerings.

Test marketing, nevertheless, can be a reliable predictor of national market share, costs, and profitability, and it can be a tool to assess and compare alternative product strategies. Yet, surprisingly, this tool is frequently overlooked in international marketing.[34] Among errors to avoid in international test marketing are incorrect forecasts, unrealistic market conditions, incorrect media translations, and choice of the wrong test market.[35]

10-3g Launching the Product Internationally

Strategies for **launching the product internationally** have an impact on later product performance; products launched using a successful strategy have a higher rate of success and score high ratings on profitability, technical success, and positive impact on the company.[36] Goodness of launch is characterized by the following, in order of impact: high service quality, on-time shipment and adequate product availability, quality sales force and enough sales effort and support, quality of promotion, and sufficient promotional effort.[37]

launching the product internationally Introducing a new product to the international market as the last step in the new product development process.

Product Launch Decisions: Consumers and Countries

In international marketing, an important decision at the launching stage is which countries to launch the product in. Whereas, in the recent past, most launching was aimed at consumers in the manufacturers' home countries, increasingly, multinationals launch products in countries that have the best consumer-product fit. In the case of Pepsi Max, Pepsi-Cola International launched the product in Australia, Ireland, and Holland, rapidly gaining market shares in these three countries between 3 percent and 4.8 percent.[38] The company aimed the brand at health-conscious consumers still looking for a caffeine kick.

Timing of Launch

Another important decision is the timing of the new product launch. Companies often attempt to gain the first-mover advantage by being the first to launch the new product. Alternatively, they could engage in later entry. The advantage of this approach is that the competitors would have to incur the costs of informing the market about the new product and its features; also, the company could market the product as a "me-too" product, reducing advertising costs significantly.

Marketing Mix Decisions

Other important decisions at the product-launching stage involve setting the price that the target consumer is willing to pay for the product. Prices might be higher if the product is launched in industrialized countries with a wealthy consumer base—typically on par with competing products. For consumers in emerging markets, the product is usually launched at a lower price, to initiate trial. When Pepsi Max was first introduced in Romania, the product was available at a relatively low price.

Firms typically choose to vary their product mix from one market to another. For example, in the United States, Mentos are available primarily in one flavor—mint. In the rest of the world, they are available in numerous flavors. On the other hand, Kraft's famous Jacobs Coffee is available only in Europe, in multiple flavors (see Figure 10-3).

Promotion—in the form of sales promotion, personal selling, and advertising—is crucial during the launching process. When Pepsi Max was launched in Romania, company representatives set up tables in front of the Academy of Economics, a premier business school located in the capital city, offering samples to consumers and offering cases of the product at a discounted price. Worldwide, Pepsi-Cola International backed the launch of Pepsi Max by more than $10 million in advertising, channeled through BBDO, a New York advertising agency.[39]

Finally, channel members constitute an important element of the marketing mix during the launching stage. Decisions such as shelf positioning, often contingent on the pay-

Figure 10-3

In the United States, Mentos are available primarily in one flavor—mint. Jacobs Coffee, on the other hand, is not available here, even though it is a Kraft (U.S. company) product. In Europe, these two brands are very popular and are available in multiple varieties.

ment of slotting fees to retailers, as well as questions on inventory, trade allowances, and financing, among others, are addressed at this stage. As will be seen in Chapter 11, "Managing International Distribution Operations and Logistics," there are significant variations in the channels of distributions worldwide for individual product categories, with fragmented channels in markets such as Japan, concentrated channels in command economies, etc. This factor adds to the complexity and expense of the product-launching effort.

10-4 Degree of Product/Service Newness

Innovation is thought of as the creation of a better product or process and may range from the substitution of a cheaper material in an existing product to a better way of marketing, distributing, or supporting a product or service.[40] **Degree of product/service newness** refers to the extent to which a product or service is new to the market. Organizations that have a good record of innovation pursue innovation systematically, actively searching for change and supporting creative individuals who are internally driven.[41]

Innovation takes on many forms, and marketing literature uses various classifications for different categories of innovation. At a basic level, new products and services can be classified in one of five categories:[42]

- **New product to existing market, new product to existing company**—These categories account for 33.7 percent of products.
- **New line**—This category represents a new product or product line to a company, but for a company already operating in that market. It accounts for 16.8 percent of products.
- **New item in an existing product line** for the company—This category accounts for 11.9 percent of products; these products are likely to have the highest success rate (83 percent) and the greatest impact on company sales and profit.
- **Modification** of an existing company product—This category accounts for 18.8 percent of products.
- **Innovation**, new product to the world—This category accounts for about 18.8 percent of products.

Another popular classification organizes innovation into the radical, dynamically continuous, and continuous categories. **Radical innovations** (also known as *discontinuous innovations*) create new industries or new standards of management, manufacturing, and servicing, and they represent fundamental changes for consumers, entailing departures from established consumption.[43] Examples of radical innovations are the Internet and endoscopy/endoscopic surgery. **Dynamically continuous innovations** do not alter consumer behavior significantly, but they represent a change in the consumption pattern; cell phones are an example of such innovation. **Continuous innovations** have no disruption on consumption patterns and involve only product alterations, such as new flavors, or a new product that is an improvement over the old offering. They usually are congruous, in the sense that they can be used alongside the existing systems; for example, a new Microsoft Windows version will work with computers that are only a few years old or older computers with enhanced capacity. Geox shoes, described in International Marketing Illustration 10-2, are an example of a continuous innovation.

Most of the innovation taking place today is continuous. However, a relatively recent radical innovation, the Internet, has revolutionized all aspects of the marketing mix, with important implications for international marketing. As a distribution tool, it renders products accessible instantly worldwide, regardless of the firm's experience and size. It is an equal-opportunity distribution tool for companies from industrialized and developing countries alike, allowing for creative and innovative market penetration.

In one example demonstrating how the Internet can be used successfully in promoting developing country exports, the International Trade Center organized the world's first

degree of product/service newness The extent to which a product is new to the market in general or to a group of consumers.

new product to existing market A product never before offered to the market.

new product to existing company A new product that the company offers to the market; the product competes with similar competitor offerings.

new line A new product category offered by the company.

new item in an existing product line A new brand that the company offers to the market in an existing product line.

modification The alteration of an existing company product.

innovation A product new to the world.

radical innovation The creation of new industries or new standards of management, manufacturing, and servicing that represent fundamental changes for consumers, entailing departures from established consumption.

dynamically continuous innovation Innovation that does not alter significantly consumer behavior but still entails a change in the consumption pattern.

continuous innovation Product innovation where there is no disruption in consumption patterns; such innovations involve product alterations such as new flavors or new products that are improvements over the old offerings.

International Marketing Illustration   10-2

An Innovation That Could Relaunch the Italian Economy

Mario Moretti Polegato, a former winemaker in Northern Italy, was attending a wine convention in Nevada and went hiking to explore the area. He was hot and uncomfortable, so he poked some holes in his sneakers to cool off. This led him to go into the shoe business with a new product idea. He decided to bring to the world an innovation: a patented membrane on the soles of his Geox brand shoes. The Geox membrane has dozens of tiny openings that allow sweat to evaporate while blocking water entry, thus making them more breathable than other shoes—a difficult-to-prove claim. This membrane is referred to as the "Geox breathes" ("Geox respira") patented system. Moretti Polegato claims that this material is superior to leather, which aspirates water and keeps feet wet. The membrane he patented blocks water entry.

The company has been growing by leaps and bounds, faster than any other Italian shoe company, projecting sales of 15 million pairs a year in the short term. At the basis of its growth is the company's international expansion; in fact, the Geox brand is already present in 68 countries. Moretti Polegato's goal is to open several stores in the United States (the company's flagship store opened in New York City in May 2004), one of the largest world markets for shoes. It is also planning to open more than 100 stores in China, and in many other countries.

Moretti Polegato claims that his is an innovation that could relaunch the Italian economy, which is quite a claim, considering that most of the Geox shoes are manufactured in Romania and Slovakia. Yet, using an image-based marketing strategy in a market where image is essential, he may just be successful. The Geox stores are located in Via Montenapoleone in Milan and on Madison Avenue in New York, next to Prada, Gucci, and Armani shops. Geox shoes are available at higher end shops; for example, in the United States, they are sold at Nordstrom's and Dillard's.

Sources: Eric Sylvers, "Not Footloose but Fancy-Free, An Italian Comes Calling," *The New York Times,* March 18, 2004, pp. W1, W7; www.geox.biz; www.geox.com.

online coffee auction, selling Brazilian specialty coffee to bidders around the world via the Internet; the auction drew buyers around the world and generated high prices for Brazilian growers.[44] In another example, a small entrepreneur in rural Transylvania, Romania, used the Internet to identify retailers of custom-made hardwood borders (used in more elaborate wood flooring) in the United Sates. After requesting samples and prices via email, the entrepreneur placed orders for similar hardwood borders with a local Transylvanian furniture manufacturer and, subsequently, approached the same U.S. retailers, offering them their products at considerably lower prices.

10-5 Product Diffusion

Product diffusion refers to the manner in which a product is adopted by consumers worldwide—the speed of adoption by various groups. The consumer adoption process is addressed in section 10-5c, "Consumer Adopters." A number of factors influence the speed of product adoption in different countries; they are discussed in sections 10-5a through 10-5c.

10-5a Product Factors

In general, a number of attributes of an innovation are likely to accelerate the rate of adoption of a product or service.[45] First, the new product or service must offer a *relative*

Country (Market) Factors

Product Factors

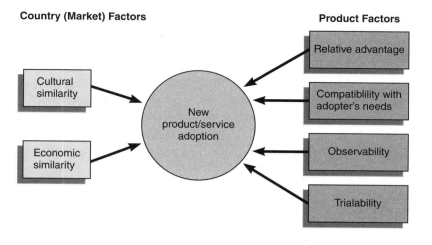

Figure 10-4
Determinants of New
Product/Service Adoption

advantage compared to the other offerings available on the market and must be *compatible with the needs of consumers.* In addition, the product/service use must be *observable* (or communicable to others) and have a high **trialability** (for example, consumers can try the product on a limited basis, by renting it, for instance). Both product and country determinants of adoption rates are illustrated on Figure 10-4.

10-5b Country (Market) Factors

New products tend to be adopted at different rates in different international markets. Countries where the product or service is first introduced and adopted are referred to as **lead countries,** and countries where the product or service is adopted at a later stage are known as **lag countries.** This process is similar to the traditional two-step **diffusion process,** whereby products are first offered to wealthy consumers and, subsequently, to the mass market. By analogy, consumers in wealthy, industrialized countries (lead countries) adopt the product first, whereas consumers in developing countries (lag countries) adopt the product later.

Generally, the diffusion rate tends to be faster in lag countries. Consumers in lag countries learn from the experiences of adopters in lead countries; for example, the dissemination of information on the benefits of retail scanners in the United States led to a very rapid diffusion of scanners in Europe, Japan, Australia, and Latin America.[46] The later the product or service is introduced in a lag country, the faster the adoption rate.[47] In addition, products and services are adopted at faster rates in lag countries that are culturally similar or that have similar economies.[48] And, although in the past geographic proximity was an important determinant of product diffusion in lag countries, international travel and media spillover across national borders are diminishing more and more the effect of geography on the product and service diffusion process.[49]

10-5c Consumer Adopters

Target consumers—national, regional, or worldwide—can be segmented based on the manner in which they adopt new products throughout the respective products' life cycle. The segments are

- **Innovators**—These few (2.5 percent of the total market) risk takers can afford to pay the higher purchase price charged by companies during the introduction stage of the product (to recoup investment costs). In developing countries, these consumers are the well-to-do business owners or leading government ministers and their families.
- **Early adopters**—The next consumers to purchase the product tend to be opinion leaders in their communities who take risks, but with greater discernment than innovators. They constitute about 13.5 percent of the total population.

trialability The ability of the consumer to experience a product with minimal effort.

lead countries Countries where a product or service is first introduced and adopted.

lag countries Countries where a product or service is adopted after already being introduced in lead countries.

diffusion process The process by which a product is adopted by consumers worldwide.

innovators Risk takers who can afford to pay the higher purchase price charged by companies during the introduction stage of a product; they account for 2.5 percent of the total market.

early adopters Consumers who purchase a product early in its product life cycle and who tend to be opinion leaders in their communities who take risks, but with greater discernment than innovators; they account for 13.5 percent of the total market.

- **Early majority**—These consumers, who account for 34 percent of the total market, are more risk averse than individuals in the first categories but enjoy the status of being among the first in their peer group to buy what will be a popular product.

- **Late majority**—These consumers, who account for 34 percent of the total market, are individuals of limited means who are likely to adopt products only if the products are widely popular and the risk associated with buying them is minimal. The products themselves are much more affordable at this stage.

- **Laggards**—These consumers, who account for 16 percent of the total market, are the last to adopt new products and do so only in late maturity. In general, laggards are risk averse and very conservative in their spending.

The categories of adopters vary greatly in markets of different development levels. For example, all categories of consumers have significantly higher means in highly industrialized countries, compared to consumers in developing countries. Nevertheless, the segments are similar in terms of their risk proneness, their status in society, and their wealth relative to the rest of the consumers in the country where they live.

Chapter Summary

- **Evaluate the stages of the international product life cycle and identify the locus of operations and target markets at each stage.** Most products are introduced in developed countries, where consumers can afford the high costs charged by manufacturers to recoup product development costs. During growth, the international company faces increasing competition worldwide from products also produced in the developed country. At maturity, standardized products compete primarily on price; manufacturing moves overseas to take advantage of cheaper labor. The company has a sales focus on emerging markets. In a product's middle and late maturity stages, competitors from developing countries enter the company's world markets and compete for consumers. In the product's decline stage, the company seeks new markets in countries of lower development levels.

- **Identify the different dimensions of the international product mix with company illustrations.** Companies use different product mix strategies for different markets. The product mix refers to the totality of brands the company offers to its target markets. A company such as Unilever offers products in many categories—for example, coffee, ice cream, detergent, and others—but does not offer many varieties of each. Unilever, thus, has low depth but high product width, and its product offering is not very consistent because it includes products for very different uses. Other companies may offer high depth in certain markets and have a very limited offering in yet other markets.

- **Examine the new product development process and the activities involved at each stage in international markets.** The new product development process starts with idea generation, in and outside the company; the next step involves idea screening using predetermined criteria, followed by concept development and evaluation. Product business analysis determines the extent to which the product is likely to be viable. In the next stage, product design and development, product prototypes are developed and evaluated by target consumers. Test marketing involves great expense on the part of the company; it also leaves the company vulnerable to competitive idea theft. Often, companies use international markets as testing grounds for new products. The final stage, launching, requires significant commitment to the product and to the target market.

- **Examine degrees of product newness and address international diffusion processes.** There are different types of new products: products that are new to an existing market or new to an existing company; new lines, i.e., new products or product lines to a company but for a company already operating in that market; new items in an existing product line for the company; modifications to an existing company product; and innovations, i.e., products that are new to the world. New products are first diffused in lead countries, typically industrialized countries where consumers can afford the products; here, the diffusion rate is slow. The countries where the product is adopted last are known as lag countries; in these countries, the diffusion rate is faster because consumers learn from the adoption experiences of consumers in lead countries.

Key Terms

continuous innovation
controlled test marketing
decline stage
degree of product/service newness
designing and developing the product
developing and evaluating concepts
diffusion process
dynamically continuous innovation
early adopters
early majority
generating new product ideas
growth stage
innovation

innovators
international product life cycle (IPLC)
introduction stage
lag countries
laggards
late majority
launching the product internationally
lead countries
maturity stage
modification
new item in an existing product line
new line
new product to existing company

new product to existing market
performing a product business analysis
product consistency
product depth
product length
product line
product mix
product width
radical innovation
screening new product ideas
simulated test marketing
test marketing
trialability

Discussion Questions

1. Describe the international product life cycle and the activities involved in developed and developing countries.

2. What are the activities involved at each stage of the new product development process? Where are most new products developed?

3. Many products are advertised in the United States as "new and improved." What does this description mean in terms of new product classifications?

4. Describe the differences between lead and lag countries in terms of adoption status and adoption rate.

Chapter Quiz (True/False)

1. A product line is defined as the complete assortment of products that a company offers to its target international consumers.

2. Product length is defined as the total number of product lines that a company offers.

3. Test marketing has a number of disadvantages: It is expensive, time consuming, and subjects the company to competitive sabotage.

4. Product trialability interferes with the diffusion process.

Multiple Choice

1. Smart phones are relatively expensive; companies are presently selling them to consumers in industrialized countries. In which stage of the international product life cycle are smart phones?
  a. product introduction
  b. growth stage
  c. maturity stage
  d. decline stage

2. DVD players are most likely in which stage of the international product life cycle?
  a. growth stage
  b. maturity stage
  c. decline stage
  d. product introduction

3. Ann Klein II is an example of a
  a. line extension.
  b. product mix.
  c. product length.
  d. none of the above

4. The many different flavors of Unilever's Ben & Jerry's ice cream illustrate Ben & Jerry's
  a. product length.
  b. product width.
  c. product depth.
  d. all of the above

5. New product ideas can be found through
  a. competitive analyses.
  b. international employees.
  c. international customers.
  d. all of the above

6. When a company screens new product ideas, what are the most important factors to consider?
  a. unique benefits to users
  b. product requirements versus resources
  c. narrowly specified target markets
  d. a and b

You can find the correct answers to these questions by taking the quiz and then submitting your answers in the Online Study Guide Edition. The program will automatically score your submission. Where you miss a question, the program will provide the correct answer, a rationale for the answer, and the section number in the chapter where the topic is discussed.

Endnotes

1. Kenneth Hein, "Bull's Market," *Brandweek*, Vol. 42, No. 22, May 28, 2001, pp. 21, 23.

2. See Raymond Vernon, "International Investment and International Trade in the Product Cycle," *Quarterly Journal of Economics*, Vol. 80, No. 2, 1966, pp. 190–207, and another article by the same author, "The Product Cycle Hypothesis in a New International Environment," *Oxford Bulletin of Economics and Statistics*, Vol. 41, 1979, pp. 255–267.

3. Milton Keynes, "Motorola Chooses Poland for New Site," *Corporate Location*, European Edition, May/June 1998, p. 7.

4. Faith Hung, "Consortium Looks to Build Thailand Fab—Siemens, Intel and Macronix Want to Jumpstart Country's Semi Industry," *Electronic Buyers' News*, Issue 1214, June 5, 2000, p. 4.

5. "Let 100 Firms Boom: China's Enterprise Groups Await Economic Reform," *Far Eastern Economic Review*, 1991, Vol. 153, No. 36, 1991, pp. 56–58.

6. Michael Cusumano, "'Made in India' a New Sign of Software Quality," *Computerworld*, Vol. 34, No. 9, February 28, 2000, p. 36.

7. Unilever is described in detail at www.Unilever.com, a source for some of the material in this section.

8. These examples are detailed in Harriet Marsh, "Adapting to Africa," *Marketing*, March 30, 2000, p. 39.

9. Robert G. Cooper, "New Products: What Distinguishes the Winners?" *Research Technology Management*, Vol. 33, November/December 1990, pp. 27–31.

10. David Leonhardt, "It Was a Hit in Buenos Aires—So Why Not Boise?" *Business Week*, Vol. 3594, September 7, 1998, pp. 56–57.

11. Ibid.

12. C. Samuel Craig and Susan P. Douglas, "Configural Advantage in Global Markets," *Journal of International Marketing*, Vol. 8, No. 1, 2000, pp. 6–26.

13. Gordon A. Wyner, "Product Testing: Benefits and Risks," *Marketing Research*, Vol. 9, No. 1, Spring 1997, pp. 46–48.

14. Lisa Susanne Willsey, "Taking These 7 Steps Will Help You Launch a New Product," *Marketing News*, Vol. 33, No. 7, March 29, 1999, p. 17.

15. See Cooper, "New Products" pp. 27–31.

16. Ibid.

17. Willsey, "Taking These 7 Steps," p. 17.

18. F. H. Rolf Seringhaus, "Comparative Marketing Behaviour of Canadian and Austrian High Tech Firms," *Management International Review*, Vol. 33, No. 3, 1993, pp. 247–270.

19. Willsey, "Taking These 7 Steps," p. 17.

20. Wyner, "Product Testing," pp. 46–48.

21. Robert S. Doscher, "How to Create New Products," *Target Marketing*, Vol. 17, No. 1, 1994, pp. 40–41.

22. Willsey, "Taking These 7 Steps," p. 17.

23. Robert G. Cooper, "How to Launch a New Product Successfully," *CMA*, Vol. 69, No. 8, 1995, pp. 20–23.

24. Shaoming Zou and Aysegul Ozsomer, "Global Product R&D and the Firm's Strategic Position," *Journal of International Marketing*, Vol. 7, No. 1, 1999, pp. 57–76.

25. Ibid.

26. Willsey, "Taking These 7 Steps," p. 17.

27. Kevin J. Clancy and Robert S. Shulman, "It's Better to Fly a New Product Simulator than Crash the Real Thing," *Planning Review*, Vol. 20, No. 4, July/August 1992, pp. 10–16.

28. Ibid.

29. The LITMUS test is the creation of Kevin J. Clancy, who describes the procedure used in Clancy and Shulman, "It's Better to Fly a New Product Simulator," pp. 10–16.

30. Harriot Lane Fox, "Global Roll-Out for Pepsi Max," *Marketing*, April 7, 1994, p. 2.

31. Ibid.

32. Stacey Ramirez, "Hand Outs," *Business Mexico*, Vol. 6, No. 5, May 1996, pp. 12–16.

33. Ibid.

34. Tamer S. Cavusgil and Ugur Yavas, "Test Marketing: An Exposition," *Marketing Intelligence and Planning*, Vol. 5, No. 3, 1987, pp. 16–20.

35. Ibid.

36. Robert G. Cooper, "Debunking the Myths of New Product Development," *Research Technology Management*, Vol. 37, No. 4, July/August 1994, pp. 40–50.

37. Ibid.

38. Fox, "Global Roll-Out for Pepsi Max," p. 2.

39. Ibid.

40. Nicholas Valery, "Survey: Innovation in Industry: Industry Gets Religion," *The Economist*, Vol. 350, No. 8107, February 20, 1999, pp. S5–S6.

41. Ibid.

42. See Cooper, "Debunking the Myths," pp. 40–50.

43. See Michael-Jorg Oesterle, "Time-Span Until Internationalization: Foreign Market Entry as a Built-in-Mechanism of Innovations," *Management International Review*, Vol. 37, No. 2, 1997, pp. 125–149.

44. "World's First Internet Coffee Auction a Success," *International Trade Forum*, Issue 1, 2000, pp. 37–38.

45. See Everett M. Rogers, *Diffusion of Innovations*, 3rd Edition, New York: Free Press, 1983.

46. Jaishankar Ganesh and V. Kumar, "Capturing the Cross-National Learning Effect: An Analysis of an Industrial Technology Diffusion," *Journal of the Academy of Marketing Science*, Vol. 24, No. 4, 1996, pp. 328–337.

47. Hikorazu Takada and Dipak Jain, "Cross-National Analysis of Diffusion of Consumer Durable Goods in Pacific Rim Countries," *Journal of Marketing*, Vol. 55, No. 1, 1991, pp. 48–54.

48. Jaishankar Ganesh, V. Kumar, and Velavan Subramanian, "Learning Effect in Multinational Diffusion of Consumer Durables: An Exploratory Investigation," *Journal of the Academy of Marketing Science*, Vol. 25, No. 3, 1997, pp. 214–228.

49. Ibid.

50. Case designed with input from Anne Carson, Todd Fowler, Kim Hribar, Liz Manera, and Brian Thoms.

51. Sarah McRitchie, "Europe Shrinks to Expand," *Dairy Foods*, Vol. 100, No. 1, January 1999, pp. 75–79.

52. Ibid.

53. Ibid.

54. McRitchie, "Europe Shrinks to Expand," pp. 75–79.

55. Ibid.

56. Ibid.

57. Ibid.

58. Ibid.

59. Donna Gorski Berry, "Global Dairy Food Trends," *Dairy Foods*, Vol. 99, No. 10, October 1998, pp. 32–37.

60. Ibid.

61. Ibid.

62. www.campina-melkunie.nl

Case 10-1

Campina, Naturally[50]

Campina is one of the leading dairy companies in the world and one of the few that produces only dairy products. A European company that remains close to its Dutch roots, Campina's image evokes picturesque Dutch cow pastures and healthy lifestyles. The company's history can be traced to Southern Holland, in the Eindhoven area; a dairy cooperative with the name "De Kempen" was created in 1947 and used the brand name "Campina." In 1964 the cooperative merged with another cooperative in the Weert region in Holland and formed Campina (named after a regional moor—its meaning is "from the land"). After several consecutive mergers—more recently, with Melkunie Holland—Campina Melkunie (or Campina, as it is informally known) became the largest dairy cooperative in the Netherlands.

In the Netherlands alone, Campina boasts 7,500 member dairy farmers. The farmers own the cooperative: Campina must buy all the milk the farmers produce, while the farmers must finance the cooperative, and, in return, they obtain a yield of the products sold. Campina itself is a nonprofit organization. Member farmers receive all the company profits. They have voting rights in the company that are proportional to the amount of milk they deliver, and they are represented by the Members' Council, the highest managerial body of the cooperative.

The separation between Campina, the operating company, and its cooperatives is evident: Campina is headquartered in Zaltbommel, in an industrial park in Southern Holland, while the dairies are located close to the consumers they serve, in different areas of the country (see Figure 10-5).

Industry Trends

Consolidation is a dominant trend of the dairy industry. The number of dairy companies is falling, and the production capacity of those that remain is increasing and becoming more efficient.[51]

Figure 10-5
Campina Truck in Eindhoven

The European Union remains the world's top dairy producer, manufacturer, and trader of dairy products; because the EU is a mature dairy market, the emphasis is on value growth and processing milk into products with high added value.[52] As such, Campina's strategy and general mission, "adding value to milk," fit well with this trend. Of the world's top 25 dairy organizations, 14 have their headquarters in Europe.[53]

The degree of concentration varies significantly, however, from region to region. In Scandinavia and the Netherlands, a handful of major cooperatives dominate. In Greece, there are more than 1,000 dairy businesses, of which more than 700 make cheese. In Germany, the industry has changed from numerous small, localized firms to most milk processors either collapsing or merging. In France, the top five control 55 percent of milk production. And in Scandinavia, the major players wield even more control: In Denmark, MD Foods and Klover Maelk control 95 percent of milk production, and in Sweden, Arla handles 80 percent.[54]

Another important trend is the focus on convenience (a packaging issue) and on value-added nutrition for functional foods (a product ingredient issue). Changes include creating new packaging and unique containers for innovative products. For example, German-based Schwalbchen Molkerei offers Go! Banana, the first milk-energy drink made from fresh milk and real, pureed bananas, packaged in 330 ml Tetra Prisma cartons with fluted sides. Spain's Pascual Dairy offers milk-based energy drink Bio Frutas in two flavors: Tropical and Mediterranean. German milk processor Immergut produces Drinkfit Choco Plus, a vitamin-fortified, chocolate-flavored milk, in the same carton. The United Kingdom company Miller offers dual-compartment, side-by-side containers of refrigerated yogurt, while a drinkable fruit yogurt from Nestle SA is offered in the United Kingdom under the name Squizzos, sporting Disney characters in a triangular-shaped package that is easy to tear, squeeze, and drink.[55]

Cheese is also presented in innovative packaging. Baars, a subsidiary of the BolsWessanen Group, a United Kingdom–Dutch company, launched a smooth, flavorful medium/mature cheddar cheese, named Maidwell, that does not crumble; it is sold in an attractive, innovative, clear-plastic, resealable pack. Rumblers, a convenient all-in-one breakfast product manufactured by U.K. company Ennis Foods Ltd., is also available in an innovative package that holds cereal and fresh, semiskimmed milk separately, all in one pack.[56]

Functional ingredients (health foods or ingredients that enhance the nutritional value of products) represent yet another important trend in the dairy industry: Dairy products represent the most important sector, accounting for 65 percent of sales in a sector that is very buoyant given the consumer interest in health and diet.[57] The leading companies in Europe in this domain are Campina Melkunie (Netherlands), Nestle (Switzerland), and Danone (France).[58] Worldwide, Japan leads in the functional foods

continued

trend and is the only country with a regulatory policy on such foods: FOSHU (Foods for Specified Health Use).[59] There is a tradition of lactic acid bacteria culture drinks and yogurts in Japan, and many of these fermented drinks and yogurts contain other functional ingredients, such as oligofructose, calcium, and DHA, which is a polyunsaturated fatty acid derived from fish oil that is said to improve learning, lower blood pressure, help prevent cancer, and lower serum cholesterol.[60] And from Dairy Gold, Australia, comes Vaalia Passionfruit Smoothie, a low-fat milk-based drink containing 25 percent fruit juice, acidophilus and bifidus cultures, and insulin.[61]

Meeting Competitive Challenges at Campina: Adopting a Market Orientation

Historically, milk production was supply driven, and excess milk was used to produce cheese and powder; this strategy led to excess cheese/commodities on the market and the need for subsidies. Campina initiated a change in this practice. Since the late 1980s, the company has been demand driven: Farmers are assigned production quotas that they are not allowed to exceed.

In other attempts to adopt a market orientation, Campina decided to eliminate all milk powder production because milk powder is a low-margin commodity. Instead, the company is focusing on building the brand to ensure recognition by consumers as a value offering and as a quality brand name.

According to R. J. Steetskamp, Director of Strategic Business Development at Campina, the company examines consumer behavior to determine where to fit Campina products in consumers' lives. As such, Campina offers four categories of products:

1. **Indulgence products.** This category constitutes an important growth area for the company. Campina produces numerous milk-based desserts, with the exception of ice cream—primarily due to the product's seasonality and the logistics strategies involved in the transportation and storage of ice cream, which differ from those for the rest of the company's offerings (see Figure 10-6).

Figure 10-6
Indulgence Products

2. **Daily essentials.** This category includes Campina products that shoppers purchase routinely, such as milk, buttermilk, yogurt, coffee cream, butter, cheese, and others (see Figure 10-7). Campina, using a strategy employed by all its competitors, also sells daily essentials under dealer (store) brands, rather than under its own brand name. For example, in Holland, it sells milk, plain yogurt, butter, Gouda cheese, and vla (chocolate or vanilla custard) under the Albert Heijn brand name. Albert Heijn is a dominant, quality supermarket chain in Holland that is owned by Royal Ahold—a large conglomerate that also owns supermarket chains in the United States (BI-LO, Giant, and Stop & Shop). The company also sells daily essentials under dealer brands in Germany.

Figure 10-7
Campina daily essentials. In the Netherlands, a vla dessert is a daily essential.

3. **Functional products.** According to Mr. Steetskamp, this product category needs to be further explored and defined by the company. In this category are health foods and other milk-based nutritional supplements sold to consumers. DMV International, a Campina division present all over the world, produces pharmaceutical products, food ingredients, and ingredients used to enhance the nutrition of consumers and their pets, such as proteins and powders with different functions. All these products are milk-based, and many of them are well known. For example, Lactoval is a popular calcium supplement.

4. **Ingredients (food and pharmaceutical ingredients).** This product category is targeted at other food product manufacturers, rather than at the individual consumers. The primary purpose of the food and pharmaceutical ingredients is to enhance the quality, taste, texture, and/or nutritive content of the products manufactured by Campina's clients. The company's Creamy Creation unit specializes in blending dairy and alcohol to make various cream liqueurs, leading to both healthy and indulgent drinks. In this category fall meal replacement drinks and high protein drinks as well. With this category, Campina becomes a supplier to other manufacturers, rather than a product manufacturer distributing to supermarkets.

International Expansion at Campina

One of the most important undertakings at Campina in the past decade was to expand beyond the Netherlands. In its first expansion effort, the company bought Belgium's Comelco, another dairy cooperative. In Belgium, the company boasts the Joyvalle dairy products and milk brand and the Passendale, Père Joseph, and Wynendale cheese brands, all marketed under the Campina umbrella brand.

Campina expanded into Germany, purchasing a number of cooperatives: Sudmilch (Southern Germany), Tuffi (Western Germany), and Emzett (Berlin). In Germany, its primary brand is Landliebe; here, the company sells Landliebe milk, cream, yogurts (seasonal, fruit, plain, and in different types of containers); different types of puddings including rice pudding, ice cream, cheese, and qwark (a funny-tasting creamy cheese) plain or with fruit; yogurt drinks (with fruit flavors such as banana, cherry, lemon, peach, and orange); and different milk drinks with flavors such as vanilla and chocolate. The company also offers products such as coffee machines, cups, spoons, and others for purchase online at its site, www.landliebe-online.de. According to R. J. Steetskamp, the Campina name will be used as the umbrella brand for all the company products; as mentioned previously, the name comes from the Latin "from the land," and it is easily pronounced in all the different languages in Europe, the brand's target market. The only brands that will not be brought under the Campina umbrella brands, according to Mr. Steetskamp, are the Mona brand in the

Figure 10-8
Offerings under the Mona Umbrella Brand

Netherlands (see Figure 10-8) and the Landliebe brand in Germany because both have high brand franchise with consumers in their respective countries. Interestingly, the Landliebe brand name is close in meaning to Campina, both making reference to the land.

As a result of these acquisitions and mergers, according to Mr. Steetskamp, Campina is the market leader in Holland, Germany, and Belgium—as the company website states, "Campina is a household name in the Netherlands, Belgium and Germany."[62]

Campina has further expanded, with its own subsidiaries in the United Kingdom, Spain, Poland, and Russia, where it ultimately plans to use the Campina brand name (the Campina Fruttis brand is one of the most popular fruit yogurt brands in Russia).

Analysis Suggestions

1. Perform a product mix analysis for Campina. Calculate product length, width, and line depth and evaluate product consistency across the different lines. Refer to www.campina-melkunie.nl for additional brand information.

2. Attempt a comparison with U.S. dairy strategies: Go to your local grocery store chain and note the different brands of milk. Are indulgence products offered by the same company? (Most likely they are not.) Can you find one dairy cooperative that offers milk, butter, cream cheese, and sour cream? Explain the differences between Campina strategies and U.S. dairy cooperatives' strategies.

11

Managing International Distribution Operations and Logistics

Chapter Objectives

By the end of this chapter, you should be able to

1 Describe the functions of home-country and host-country middlemen involved in international distribution.

2 Identify the different facilitators of international distribution and logistics and describe their involvement in the international distribution process.

3 Address the challenges encountered by distribution in countries of different development levels.

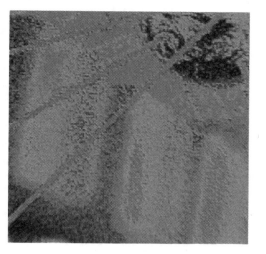

International distribution channels link manufacturers and final international consumers. Internationally, distribution channels vary greatly from one region to another and from one market to another. For most markets, consumer product channels of distribution tend to be longer than industrial product channels. Beyond this general trait, however, channel characteristics differ worldwide. The following are examples of such differences:

- In Japan, there are many more levels of distributors for consumer products than in most other countries, whereas, for most industrial goods, large export trading or export management companies deal directly with retailers.

- In socialist countries, distributors are huge state-run enterprises that often carry unrelated products.

- In Central and Eastern Europe and other emerging markets, network marketing is rapidly becoming a very popular channel of distribution. Every network marketing company is active there, with Amway leading the way.

This chapter addresses all the aspects of managing international distribution, offering an overview of the different middlemen involved in the international distribution process, the facilitators involved in international distribution and logistics, and the challenges facing the distribution process.

11-1 Issues Related to International Distribution

Some international markets have an underdeveloped distribution system for many industrial sectors and, to a lesser extent, for consumer goods. Distribution to these markets may be opportunistic and not adequately organized, or distribution channels may not exist at all. Alternatively, the complex structure of certain international channels may serve as a barrier to multinational company entry in an international market new to the company. The company first must determine whether it can use established channels or build its own.

11-1a Using Established Channels

Entering a new market can be problematic for companies. In most cases, competitors already have a hold on existing channels and are thus likely to *block* them for new entrants. In addition to competitors, there are other obstacles to using **established channels**. For example, the amount charged by distributors could be so high that the company may be unwilling to use them. This was the case for Kraft Foods International (a Philip Morris company at that time) in its attempt to enter the Hong Kong market with its Kraft brand products. Distributors (keiretsu cross-investment structures that will be examined in "The Japanese Model" in section 11-2a, "Home-Country Middlemen") charged an exorbitant amount to distribute the brand. Philip Morris refused to pay the price but also faced barriers to entry on its own; a decade later, Philip Morris yielded, deciding to use the same overpriced distributors to sell its Kraft brand in Hong Kong and then China.

established channels Distribution channels that already exist in a particular market.

The initial channel selection decision is very important: Once in a channel relationship, a company may be bound to that relationship and may not legally be allowed to change distributors.

11-1b Building Own Channels

building channels Creating new distribution channels, especially necessary in situations where there are no channels at all, or there are no channels that conform to the needs of the company.

Although **building channels** is very expensive, this strategy is especially necessary in situations in which no channels exist at all, or no channels conform to the needs of the company. The example of Coca-Cola in Eastern Europe after the fall of communism is a case in point. Although Pepsi had been present in the region since the late 1960s, Coke did not enter many of the countries until the 1990s. When Coca-Cola decided to enter this market, it found old state-enterprise channels that were selling Pepsi products, operating with low efficiency. Consequently, it decided to create its own channels of distribution that fit well with the market structure by, primarily, working with independent truck drivers who had some experience working with soft-drink retailers.

11-2 Middlemen Involved in International Distribution

home-country middlemen Intermediaries in the home country.

Depending on company involvement in a particular market, a company can use home-country middlemen or host-country middlemen. A company that uses intermediaries in its own home country is likely not to be as involved in managing the marketing mix in the country where the target market is located. **Home-country middlemen** typically provide all marketing services for firms that do not wish to enter the foreign market and/or do not have the capability to do so. Companies relying on home-country middlemen relinquish their control of the marketing mix to their distributors in the target-market foreign country.

A company using intermediaries in the host country is likely to have a presence there, in the form of a sales office, at the lowest level of direct international involvement, or in the form of a wholly owned subsidiary, at the highest level of direct international involvement. The company, by using host-country middlemen, also seeks to have a greater degree of control of the marketing mix in the target-market foreign country.

11-2a Home-Country Middlemen

Export Management Companies

export management companies Companies specializing in the export function for client companies in a particular industry.

Export management companies are highly specialized in certain industries, such as endoscopic surgery instruments or networking products, and typically represent smaller companies in a region of the country. Some of their activities include researching the international market, representing a company at trade shows and exhibitions, screening and selecting international distributors, shipping the company's product, and handling all the necessary export documentation, such as customs forms and export licensing. An example of such a firm is Amex, Inc., a company in Minneapolis, Minnesota, that offers export trading services for Midwest technology companies selling medical, networking, telecommunication, and data communication products. This type of firm works typically as a company's export department. The Office of Trading Company Affairs in the U.S. Department of Commerce can help companies identify the appropriate export management company for the companies' target country.

Trading Companies

The Japanese Model

trading companies Large companies that specialize in providing intermediary services, risk reduction through extensive information channels, and significant financial assistance to manufacturing firms.

Japanese **trading companies** have operations all around the world, ranging from finance to distribution, technology, mining, oil and gas exploration, and information. They act as intermediaries for half of Japan's exports and two thirds of its imports. Over time, they have changed from pure traders to more financially sophisticated investment holding companies.[1]

The biggest and the best of the traders are members of **keiretsus,** which are families of firms with interlocking stakes in one another; here, the trading companies' role is to act as the eyes and ears of the whole group, spotting business trends, market gaps, and investment opportunities.[2] The top sogo shoshas, or general trading companies, are Itochu Corp., Sumitomo, Marubeni, Mitsui, and Mitsubishi.[3]

Sogo shoshas (Japanese trading companies) offer their suppliers three primary services: specialization in providing intermediary services, risk reduction through extensive information channels, and significant financial assistance. Sogo shosha activities have become increasingly focused on third-country trade, increased participation in product areas requiring sophisticated distribution, and greater participation in high-risk overseas mega projects.[4]

Japanese export trading companies are presently facing competition from Honda, Sony, and Toyota, which have set up their own direct export-sales networks; consequently, the trading companies are handling a decreasing proportion of Japan's exports.[5]

The U.S. Model

In the United States, export trading companies are, in fact, consortia of smaller suppliers, service-oriented firms, multinational corporations, and quasi-public organizations or public entities.[6] In 1982, the U.S. Congress passed the **Export Trading Company Act** to encourage the formation of export trading companies to promote U.S. exports. The Office of Trading Company Affairs in the U.S. Department of Commerce can help companies identify the appropriate export trading or export management company for the company's target country; see International Marketing Illustration 11-1.

keiretsu A Japanese trading firm that consists of families of firms with interlocking stakes in one another.

sogo shosha A large Japanese trading company that specializes in providing intermediary services, risk reduction through extensive information channels, and significant financial assistance to manufacturing firms.

Export Trading Company Act Legislation, passed in 1982, that encourages the formation of export trading companies by competing firms in order to promote U.S. exports without violating antitrust regulation.

International Marketing Illustration 11-1

Aiding Export Joint Ventures: The Office of Trading Company Affairs

For companies interested in partnering with competitors to export internationally, the Office of Trading Company Affairs can provide help. Under Title III of the Export Trading Company Act, any U.S. resident, business association, group of firms, or state or local government entity may apply to this office for a Certificate of Review. The Certificate provides antitrust preclearance for the export activities of the certificate holder, essentially minimizing the application of U.S. antitrust laws to export activities and the related risk of expensive antitrust litigation. The Certificate of Review provides exporters with immunity from both government antitrust suits and with procedural advantages in private antitrust suits. The Export Trade Certificate of Review application is a free and quick process: The Department of Commerce determines whether the Certificate meets the certification standards contained in the Export Trading Company Act, obtains the concurrence of the Department of Justice, and then issues the final Certificate within 90 days.

Some of the activities that could receive the Export Trade Certificates of Review are joint establishment of export prices; exclusive agreements with domestic suppliers and/or foreign representatives; joint export marketing/selling arrangements among domestic competitors; allocation of export markets, territories, or customers; refusals to deal; exchanges of business information; and the joint licensing of technology.

Among the competitive advantages offered by export joint ventures are economies of scale, spreading of risk among the participating firms, which

continued

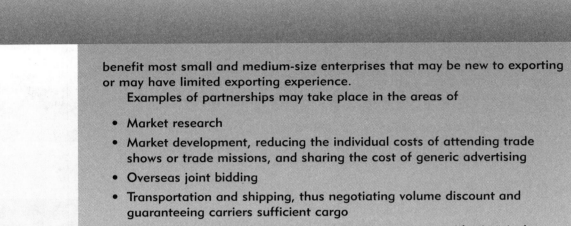

benefit most small and medium-size enterprises that may be new to exporting or may have limited exporting experience.

Examples of partnerships may take place in the areas of

- Market research
- Market development, reducing the individual costs of attending trade shows or trade missions, and sharing the cost of generic advertising
- Overseas joint bidding
- Transportation and shipping, thus negotiating volume discount and guaranteeing carriers sufficient cargo
- Establishment of uniform minimum export prices to avoid price rivalry with each other
- Service and promotional activities

In one example, an Export Trade Certificate of Review was awarded to Florida Citrus Exports of Vero Beach, Florida. Florida Citrus Exports operates as an export service umbrella for its nine members, including grower-owned cooperatives and packing houses, sharing transportation and market development costs, engaging in joint promotion, preparing joint bids, assisting each other in maintaining quality standards, and spreading the risk of international involvement. In another example, the Export Trade Certificate of Review allows the American Film Export Association of Los Angeles, California, to engage in international licensing agreements and create financing documents that are the standard for the independent film and TV industry. It permits the organization to produce a membership sales survey to measure the licensing of motion picture and television products in 33 territories; it also facilitates the sharing of credit data on more than 500 film and television buyers from 56 countries.

In an example of facilitation, the American Film Export Association ran a Regional Market in Bangkok, which opened opportunities for U.S. film companies to enter Vietnam, where cinema representatives were eager for the companies' business and were especially interested in learning how best to fight piracy. In another example, the American Film Export Association performed a study that found that countries such as Australia, France, Germany, Italy, Japan, Taiwan, Spain, and the United Kingdom can each provide revenues of $50,000 to $200,000 in theater, video, television, cable, and satellite markets.

Sources: http://www.ita.doc.gov; http://www.filmfestivals.com/afm/afnewb4.htm; http://www.mothermuse.com/markets.htm

---

brokers and agents Middlemen who bring international buyers and sellers together; they do not carry title to the product.

manufacturer's export agents Agents in the firm's home country handling the exporting function of a certain manufacturer on a commission, per deal, basis.

Home-Country Brokers and Agents

Home-country **brokers and agents** bring international buyers and sellers together in the company's home country and do not carry title to the product. They can handle different export functions and specialize in certain product categories.

Alternatively, they may represent a certain manufacturer on a commission basis for a particular deal; they are known as **manufacturer's export agents.** Or they may be buyers located in the firm's home country, representing different firms located abroad; in this case, they are known as **buying offices.**

Cooperative Export Arrangements

Cooperative export arrangements, also referred to as piggybacking or mother henning, involve exporters agreeing to handle export functions for unrelated companies on a contractual basis. Generally, cooperative exporters are large multinationals with substantial in-house know-how and resources, as well as extensive knowledge of international markets. The piggybacked products are noncompetitive with the cooperative exporter's own products but may be, nevertheless, similar; an example is an auto manufacturer in the United States who agrees to market tires or seat covers for a much smaller company that is new to international marketing.[7]

Two types of firms are generally involved in cooperative export arrangements: **complementary export agents** and **complementary export merchants.** Complementary export agents export complementary products. This category includes individual firms exporting other firms' products that are complementary to their offerings (along with their own products). If these firms carry the other firms' products for a fee/commission, they act as complementary export agents. If, instead of operating on a fee/commission, the firms actually take title to the complementary products distributed and are compensated in the form of a discount in a buy-sell arrangement,[8] they act as complementary export merchants.

Webb-Pomerene Associations of Exporters

Webb-Pomerene Associations, established under the Webb-Pomerene Act, also are involved in cooperative exporting. Webb-Pomerene Associations are composed of competing companies that join resources and efforts to export internationally. The companies are granted immunity from antitrust prosecution, under the Webb-Pomerene Act, so that they can export products manufactured in the United States to compete effectively internationally, especially in world markets in which cartels are active.

Tax Incentive-Based Structures for Internationalism

For decades, the **Foreign Sales Corporation (FSC)** has been an important instrument for internationalization, but that is likely to come to an end. The FSC was initially set up as a sales corporation overseas; establishing an FSC allowed for a portion of a U.S. tax-paying firm's foreign-source income to be exempt from U.S. income tax. To qualify for tax exemption, the FSC had to have a foreign presence, meeting certain management requirements and certain economic process requirements with regard to both the extent and nature of the sales activities undertaken abroad; and incurring abroad a minimum level of direct costs in sales activities, in areas such as marketing, advertising, and order processing.[9] After the World Trade Organization (WTO) found the FSC to essentially constitute an illegal export subsidy, which saved U.S. companies about US$5 billion per year, President Clinton signed the Extra Territorial Income (ETI) Act to replace the FSC. The ETI Act, however, did not modify the export subsidy scheme, and, consequently, the European Union (EU) challenged it before the WTO. Four years later, in March 2004, the EU imposed countermeasures consisting of customs duties of 5 percent on a list of U.S. products, followed by automatic, monthly increases by 1 percent up to a ceiling of 17 percent to be reached on March 1, 2005, if compliance had not happened in between. But, in May 2004, the U.S. Senate adopted the JOBS Act, a bill that repeals the FSC/ETI.

Export Merchants

Export merchants are intermediaries who take title to and possession of the products they carry. They are responsible for shipping and marketing the products to the target market; in this sense, they have full control over the products' international marketing mix. Generally, they can carry competing brands. One type of export merchant is the *export jobber,* who carries primarily commodity goods but does not take physical possession of the products. Another type of export merchant is the **Norazi agent,** who deals in illegal and/or gray market products. See also section 11-4b, "Parallel Imports," later in this chapter.

buying offices Buyers representing different firms located abroad.

cooperative export arrangements Agreements that involve the use of a distribution system of exporters with established systems of selling abroad, who agree to handle the export function of a noncompeting (but not necessarily unrelated) company on a contractual basis; also called mother henning or piggybacking.

complementary export agents Firms that export other firms' products that are complementary to their offerings, along with their own products, for a fee/commission.

complementary export merchants Distributors who take title to the complementary products distributed and are compensated in the form of a discount.

Webb-Pomerene Associations Associations of competing companies that are granted immunity from antitrust prosecution and that join resources and efforts to export internationally.

Foreign Sales Corporation (FSC) A sales corporation that is set up overseas; it allows for a portion of a U.S. tax-paying firm's foreign-source income to be exempt from U.S. income tax.

export merchants Intermediaries who take title to and possession of the products they carry; they are responsible for shipping and marketing the products to the target market.

Norazi agent An export agent dealing in illegal and/or gray market products.

11-2b Foreign-Country Middlemen

Foreign-country middlemen can be placed in two broad categories: merchant middlemen, who are intermediaries that take title to and possession of the products they carry, and agents and brokers, who bring buyers and sellers together but do not carry title to and take possession of the products they deal with.

Merchant Middlemen

Merchant middlemen are intermediaries who carry the manufacturer's product line in a particular country. They usually both carry title to and have physical possession of the products they distribute in the foreign target market. Companies often have close relationships with their international intermediaries; such relationships allow them to have control over their products' international marketing mix. Selecting one's middlemen carefully is important because, in many markets, the relationship with a distributor might be difficult or impossible to dissolve. A particular type of merchant middleman in a foreign country is an **import jobber,** who purchases usually commodity goods from the manufacturer to sell to the trade (wholesaler, retailer, business-to-business client) in the target market. In addition, wholesalers, retailers, and industrial consumers may import products directly for resale; as such, they act as merchant middlemen.

Agents and Brokers

A company can select from many different types of agents and brokers in its foreign target market. An agent can represent the manufacturer exclusively in this market, acting thus as a **manufacturer's representative.** This individual usually works practically as the company's sales representative and is paid on a commission basis. The **managing agent,** often called the **comprador,** has an exclusive arrangement with the company, representing its operations in a particular country; this individual does not take title to the goods and is usually paid as a percentage of sales of the company he or she manages.

11-2c Alternative International Distribution Structures

One type of alternative distribution structure is **network marketing,** a mode of distributing goods using acquaintance networks. Network marketing companies are gaining access to emerging markets all over the world, and many continue to find potential in developed countries. Because network marketing serves primarily a retailing function—all distributorships engage in selling to the final consumer—this topic will be addressed in Chapter 12, "International Retailing."

11-3 International Logistics

The international distribution function is supported by a number of service providers. Among them are distribution centers, transportation firms, home country freight forwarders and customs brokers, government agencies, nongovernmental organizations, logistics alliances, and other firms. They are described in sections 11-3a through 11-3c.

Logistics costs account for a large percentage of a company's gross revenues (between 10 and 30 percent), and for a large percentage of GDP (more than 10 percent in the United States), making logistics the single highest operating cost.[10] The U.S. Department of Commerce reports that 60 percent of all Fortune 500 companies' logistics costs are spent on transportation; thus, money saved in this area is likely to lead to lower prices for consumers.[11] The primary functions of international logistics are transportation, warehousing, inventory control, and order processing.

11-3a International Transportation

Transportation is important in international marketing. The choice of transportation determines whether products arrive at the international destination on time and in good condition. The cost of transportation is also essential because transportation costs can increase the product price in the target country. Important for transportation is the transportation infrastructure of the country where the company is doing business. Transportation networks are excellent in industrialized countries, with the countries easily accessible by rail, air, and water. Highly industrialized countries with water access have numerous sea and inland waterway ports that can handle cargo shipments efficiently. Consider, for example, the Southeastern coast of France, which has several ports: Nice/Villefranche Sur Mer, Toulon, Cannes, Marseille, Port La Nouvelle, Port Vendre, and Sète (see International Marketing Illustration 11-2).

International Marketing Illustration

11-2

Sète: One of France's Numerous Ports

The Port of Sète in Southern France is one of many ports in France that offer international access to the French market and that allow French businesses to engage in international commerce. The port handles container vessels, conventional vessels, ferries, heavy lift ships, ocean-going barges and tugs, floating pontoons, livestock carriers, navy vessels, and military cargoes, among others (see Figure 11-1).

In 2003, for example, 1,035 vessels entered the port, with a sea traffic total of 3,756,044 tons of goods, and 203,916 passengers; the total of inland waterway traffic handled at Sète was 226,063 tons. This port offers easy access to the rest of France via rail and truck. It also serves various developed local industries, among them seafood processing, wine and spirits, chemicals, building, clothing manufacturing, and aquaculture. The port is served by numerous ship-

continued

Figure 11-1
The Port of Sète in Southern France
Photo courtesy of Francis Tetard, with permission.

Figure 11-2
Sète, a less-traveled destination for cruise vessels, is gaining visibility from tour organizers due to its easy port access to the Languedoc-Roussillon region.
Photo courtesy of Francis Tetard, with permission.

ping agents, freight forwarders, terminal operators, shipyard operators, naval services, and other logistics facilitators.

The Port of Sète also handles cruise vessels along the Mediterranean coast; and from Bayonne to Dunkirk on the Atlantic, Channel, and North Sea range; to and from Morocco; and from Monaco to Sète, the latter a less-traveled destination that has much to offer (see Figure 11-2).

Sources: http://www.sete.port.fr/; http://www.agenatramp.fr/index.htm

Transportation firms are key players in international distribution, especially firms that can handle intermodal transportation, using two or more different transportation modes—truck, rail, ship (inland and sea/ocean shipping). Intermodal transportation has been greatly facilitated by containerization. For example, goods can be placed into containers at the factory, taken by truck to a train-loading facility, transported to a port, and loaded aboard a ship; after crossing the ocean, the containers are loaded on a truck and transported to their final destination. All these maneuvers can be accomplished using the initial containers—thus providing a greater protection for the products, which do not have to be shifted individually from one vessel to another—at lower cost because loading the individual products from/into vehicles is more expensive than using containers. Table 11-1 offers information on the value of U.S. international merchandise trade by mode of transportation. Note that almost half of imports into the United States, in terms of dollar amounts, enter the country by water. However, about a third of U.S. exports, in terms of dollar amounts, are transported by air.

The different transportation modes offer advantages and disadvantages in terms of flexibility, cost, and speed. Table 11-2 summarizes the flexibility, cost, and speed characteristics of each mode of transportation.

Imports	Total (in Millions of U.S. Dollars)
Water	519,607
Air	267,107
Truck	203,507
Rail	69,255
Pipeline	25,910
Other and unknown	56,573
Total Imports	**1,141,959**
Exports	
Water	198,841
Air	251,494
Truck	191,918
Rail	23,362
Pipeline	517
Other and unknown	64,894
Total Exports	**731,026**

Table 11-1

Value of U.S. International Merchandise Trade by Mode of Transportation

Sources: U.S. Department of Transportation, Bureau of Transportation Statistics, May 2002; based on total, water, and air data—U.S. Department of Commerce, U.S. Census Bureau, Foreign Trade Division.

Mode	Flexibility (in Terms of Area coverage)	Cost	Speed	Product Examples
Truck	High	Higher	Higher	Consumer goods, perishables, automobiles
Rail	Medium	Medium	Lower	Coal, gasoline, forestry products, grains, automobiles
Air	High	High	Highest	Jewelry, electronics, expensive low-volume products
Water	Low	Low	Low	Grains, gasoline, forestry products, cement and fertilizers
Pipeline	Low	Lower	Low	Oil and gasoline, chemicals, semi-liquid coal, refined products

Table 11-2

Flexibility, Cost, and Speed Characteristics of Each Mode of Transportation

Tankers, barges, and other freighters in the sea and inland waterways account for a substantial proportion of international traffic. Waterways are used for transporting over long distances high-weight, high-volume products that have a low per pound value, such as grains, gasoline, forestry products, cement, and fertilizers. Refer to International Marketing Illustration 11-2 earlier in this section, which offers a discussion of the Port of Sète.

Railways remain the primary mode for intracontinental freight transportation. Cargo that has a high-weight, high-volume, and low per pound value are transported by rail, with some exceptions. Examples of rail cargo are coal, gasoline, forestry products, and grains. Higher value products, such as equipment and automobiles, may also be transported by train (see Figure 11-3). Railways are a low-cost, lower-speed mode of transportation, and mobility is restricted to designated areas for freight handling.

Truck transportation handles smaller shipments over shorter distances (see Figure 11-4). Much of the local transportation—within cities, for example—is handled by trucks, which offer high flexibility at competitive rates. Often, trucks transport products carried by ship and rail to the final product destination. Trucks may have refrigeration and processing capabilities, which allow them to carry a variety of products, such as consumer goods, perishables, and automobiles.

Air freight is used for products that are low-volume and low-weight but high-value, such as jewelry and electronics. They are also used in situations in which handling documents or materials expeditiously is essential.

Pipelines provide a low-cost mode of transporting liquid or semi-liquid products from the source to the target market in a continuous manner, where there are no interruptions (unless interruptions are voluntary), and where intermediate storage is not necessary. Examples of pipelines are Basin, Bonito, and Capline for offshore and onshore crude oil; Harbor System and Wolverine Line for refined products; and the large, remote, and technically difficult pipeline, the Trans Alaska Pipeline,[12] a feat of engineering running from northern to southern Alaska across rough terrains and performing well in extreme weather conditions, transporting more than 1.4 million barrels of crude oil daily. Pipelines are typically owned by the producer or by joint ventures, and they are expensive to maintain.[13]

11-3b Logistics Facilitators

Moving goods from the place or origin, normally a manufacturer, to the place of sale, normally the retailer, requires some type of facilitation. The two most common logistics facilitators are distribution centers and freight forwarders, but governmental and nongovernmental organizations handle similar functions as well.

Figure 11-3

Trains carrying automobiles are often seen in Europe and the Far East.

Figure 11-4
Trucks offer high flexibility and competitive rates in Europe; however, a company should not expect delivery over the weekend even to key clients: In many countries, trucks are not allowed to drive on highways on Sundays.

Distribution centers are designed to speed up warehousing and delivery, by channeling operations to one center (hub) that is particularly well equipped to handle the distribution of products to their destination. This function is becoming a popular choice of multinational firms that have to efficiently warehouse and distribute their goods in target markets situated thousands of miles from their home country. Certain locations have become important players as hubs to a number of multinational firms. For example, Singapore is a leading regional and international logistics hub and host to virtually every major logistics player; logistics account for about 7 percent of Singapore's gross domestic product.[14]

Freight forwarders and customs brokers arrange for transportation, customs clearance, and document filing for products exported abroad. Often, they specialize in geographic locations or other areas of expertise, such as commodities—for example, flowers, seafood, and other types of perishable products. Many freight forwarders are adapting to fit the needs of their corporate consumers, pursuing different value-added techniques, such as developing distinctive competencies in terms of geography, type of business, or specific commodities. For example, Kuehne & Nagle (www.kuehne-nagel.com) is well respected for its ability to expertly handle museum art and valuable exhibition material. The company has also developed expertise with respect to arranging trade fairs and art exhibits, as well as aid and relief for developing countries. Another freight forwarder, DHL (www.dhl.com), indicates particular expertise in several industry sectors, including health care, fashion, electronics, and live animals. Recently, the company shipped 15 five-foot jellyfish to Australia.[15]

The Internet poses the greatest threat to freight forwarders and customs brokers because it provides a venue for importers to use dot-com companies to arrange for transportation, customs clearance, document filing, and other activities. Moreover, the Department of Commerce, the U.S. Customs Service, and the World Trade Organization have rulings, forms, and other useful documentation posted on the Web.[16]

In many countries, governments are directly involved in the international distribution process. Often, private distributors are not permitted by law to engage in any type of direct international transaction. This is the case for many developing countries and/or countries where national currencies are under strict control. Government involvement in distribution and logistics processes is not limited to developing countries; in many developed countries, the governments are involved in the following processes:

- As promoters of national security interests and national regulations
- As promoters of international involvement of firms, particularly of small and medium-size businesses
- As financing and insurance providers for higher-risk international ventures

In the United States, international distribution and logistics involvement are shared by a number of different government agencies—most of which are affiliated with the U.S. Department of Commerce (http://home.doc.gov):

- The International Trade Administration in the U.S. Department of Commerce offers export assistance to international firms and, in particular, to small to medium-size businesses. It offers trade education, mentoring programs for exporters (assistance from an experienced exporter), access to a market research database, country analysis information, economic data, as well as business counseling in the form of expert assistance from trade specialists. It also helps firms with export documentation (applications, licenses, declarations, etc.).
- The Bureau of Export Administration in the U.S. Department of Commerce advances U.S. national security, foreign policy, and economic interests by regulating exports of products and technologies that could affect those interests. This agency regulates exports of products such as high-platform computers and weapons, and imposes sanctions against certain countries (such as Burma, Cuba, North Korea, and Iran in the recent past); it enforces compliance with those regulations and cooperates with other nations in monitoring the trade of sensitive goods.
- The U.S. Commercial Service promotes and protects small and medium-size U.S. business interests in key export markets. It operates Export Assistance Centers, which offer companies a range of export facilitation services.
- The Export-Import Bank of the United States (Ex-Im Bank) is an independent government agency that aids the financing of international sales of U.S. products and services. It guarantees loans and makes loans to international buyers of U.S. goods; it also insures many business ventures that international or local banks will not insure due to their high risk. The Ex-Im Bank does not compete with commercial lenders and insurance firms.
- The United States Trade and Development Agency creates jobs for Americans by helping U.S. companies pursue overseas business opportunities. Although not directly involved in distribution and logistics, this agency funds feasibility studies, training, business workshops, and technical assistance aimed at infrastructure and industrial projects in developing countries, covering the cost of logistics and distribution.

Equivalent structures exist in most other countries, typically housed under the Ministry of Foreign Trade (the equivalent of the Department of Commerce).

In addition to country-specific agencies, international bodies could facilitate distribution and logistics. One example is the International Chamber of Commerce, a business organization that represents enterprises from all sectors in every part of the world engaging in international business. The ICC makes voluntary rules that govern the conduct of business across borders, and it provides important services, such as the ICC International Court of Arbitration, the world's leading arbitral institution.

Among other service providers are banks and insurance agencies financing and insuring international distribution transactions, marketing research firms providing information on the target markets and trade, and various types of consultants that specialize in facilitating international distribution and logistics activities.

In the process of setting up a firm's distribution activity in the target market, the firm needs to set up successful logistics relationships. Many **logistics alliances** in Europe have

logistics alliances Distribution alliances between two firms involving product transportation and warehousing.

been very successful and are characterized by an atmosphere of openness between the customer and the provider, mutual trust, and a clear line of communication. Successful logistics alliances typically are formed using the following steps:[17]

1. Establish objectives and selection criteria. Because choosing a logistics provider is a long-term decision, it is important to choose a partner that is likely to be a good match.
2. Identify qualified providers, with the help of consultants.
3. Express needs and wants. Here, issues such as integrating computer systems with that of the partner and other information-sharing needs should be expressed.
4. Evaluate bidders and select the partner, preferably after a site visit and interview.
5. Develop an integration plan. Because logistics involves many players, it is important to engage in systemwide integration.
6. Create a win-win relationship, based on continuous communication.
7. Measure and analyze performance.
8. Redefine goals and objectives.

11-3c Warehousing and Inventory Control

In international marketing, warehousing is of great importance. One of the critical decisions involves determining the number of warehouses and distribution centers needed to optimally implement the logistics function. In some countries, private warehouses, owned or leased by the company and operated by firms storing their own products, may be easy to come by and could provide more control and safety for the shipping firm than public warehouses. In other countries, public warehouses, used by firms that cannot afford to have their own facilities or that do not have a need for storage on a regular basis, represent a viable option: They are safe, they have the necessary capacity, and they are dependable in terms of other capabilities, such as refrigeration.

In most industrialized countries, distribution centers are an option for the international firm; they receive goods from different producers, take orders from buyers, and distribute them promptly.

Warehouses located in free trade zones or those warehouses that are themselves customs privileged facilities are typically also facilities where product assembly and packaging may be conducted.

Worldwide, companies are attempting to address customer demand while reducing inventory costs. Multinational firms adopt a just-in-time inventory system where this is possible, reducing inventory by ordering products often and in lower quantity, creating product flow rather than stock. Also, where possible and all intermediaries use the Universal Product Code (UPC), suppliers' and customers' inventory systems are linked through electronic data interchange, facilitating the flow of products. Both of these approaches aimed at reducing storage costs are widely adopted in developed countries; in developing countries, multinationals tend to adopt them, spending large sums to link suppliers to their own systems.

11-4 Challenges to International Distribution and Logistics

Firms selling across borders encounter numerous challenges. The two most cited challenges are distribution in developing countries and parallel imports.

11-4a Challenges to Distribution in Developing Countries

One challenge faced by multinationals distributing their products in developing countries is the transportation infrastructure: Dirt roads are often impassable when wet, and, in tropical climates, cool temperatures must be maintained to ensure the quality of perishable goods such as pharmaceuticals. Containerization also poses problems: Most of the ports in West Africa have shallow drafts and cannot handle larger vessels. Furthermore, unloading the products from the container may take weeks, or the container may be held indefinitely for customs inspection.[18]

11-4b Parallel Imports

parallel imports A distribution system not authorized by the manufacturer whereby the products purchased in a low-price market are diverted to other markets; also called gray market.

Parallel imports are products purchased in a low-price market and diverted to other markets by means of a distribution system not authorized by the manufacturer; this is also known as a *gray market*. A low-price market is one where the products can be purchased for a lower price either because the company is in a competitive situation in which it must lower the price or because local taxes do not significantly increase the price of the products. Most often, however, gray market goods come from authorized dealers who get rid of excess inventory, selling the products to discounters.[19]

The Netherlands, for example, is a low-price market for Similac, an infant formula manufactured by Abbott Laboratories; here, a 900-gram can of Similac sells for 6 Euros, or about $7. A can of Similac weighing 850 grams (50 grams less than the can sold in the Netherlands) sells for about $22 in the United States. The reasons Abbott Laboratories engages in the differential pricing of Similac may be numerous. First, it might be attempting to penetrate the market: Although the product is well known in the United States, it is not popular at all in Europe. Second, it is priced just less than the other, local, competing products: The company might be using a penetration-pricing strategy. Third, the Dutch government might have required the company to sell at a low price (unlikely, but possible). Consequently, the Netherlands constitutes a low-price market for Similac. If an entrepreneur decided to bring Similac from the Netherlands to sell it in the United States, he or she would be engaging in parallel imports and would have to sell the product on a gray market, not authorized by the manufacturer.

The illegal aspect of the transactions illustrated in this example clearly does not involve the product itself. Rather, what is in fact illegal is the distribution channel and the processes used to sell this product to consumers unintended by the company—U.S. consumers. When such products are available for sale in the unintended market, parallel imports then compete with the manufacturer's products intended specifically for this market, cutting into profits.

Examples of gray markets abound. In the 1970s, a thriving gray market for Mercedes-Benz automobiles existed in the United States. Automobiles manufactured for the European market were much cheaper than the ones sold through exclusive dealerships in the U.S. market. Entrepreneurs on both sides of the Atlantic took advantage of this discrepancy, transporting and converting the automobiles to U.S. specifications, obtaining the approval of the U.S. Department of Transportation, and selling the products openly to consumers in the United States.

In other examples, pharmaceutical manufacturers selling their products in the European Union have found that products sold in low markets, such as Greece, Italy, France, Portugal, and Spain, are often distributed in countries where above-average prices are charged, such as Germany, Denmark, and the Netherlands.[20]

Gray markets also can harm a company's image. Cigarettes sold for the Chinese market are likely to have a higher nicotine content and to be more addictive. Diverting these cigarettes back to the United States can harm the company's brand image. The company needs to carefully control the distribution of such products.

Multinational corporations can choose from a number of alternative actions in the process of combating parallel imports (see Figure 11-5):

- *Charge similar prices worldwide*—If price differences are not substantial enough, there will not be a gray market. Although this strategy does not quite conform to the

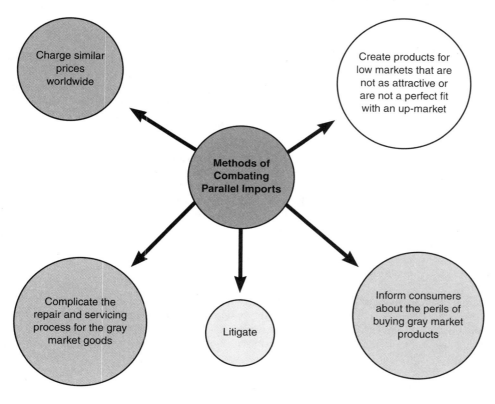

F i g u r e 1 1 - 5
Methods of Combating Parallel Imports

marketing concept—selling consumers products at prices they can afford and/or are willing to pay—it is, nevertheless, successful in preventing the success of a gray market for that particular brand.

- *Create products for low markets that are not as attractive or are not a perfect fit with an up-market*—Mercedes-Benz, after creating Mercedes USA, its subsidiary in the United States, attempted to create very different automobiles for the European and the U.S. market. To the European consumers, Mercedes offers the A-Class, which is not available in the United States, and lower-level models that are too small to meet U.S. consumers' demands for comfort. The same-level C-Class and E-Class are sold for comparable prices in the European and the U.S. markets.

- *Complicate the repair and servicing process for the gray market goods*—Individuals purchasing gray market Mercedes-Benz automobiles in the United States will find that, often, replacement parts for their automobiles must be ordered from Stuttgart, Germany, making the cost of maintenance prohibitive.

- *Inform consumers about the perils of buying gray market products*—Possible perils of gray market products might be that the product is new but technically outdated or that the product will not benefit from manufacturer warranties.

- *Litigate*—Unlike in the case of counterfeit products, litigating is often not possible in many of the integrated markets, such as the European Union, where the free movement of goods is guaranteed by law. Nevertheless, it is recommended that manufacturers keep up with the changing regulations to be able to take on unauthorized distribution when that is possible.[21] Frequently, loopholes in the national laws may allow parallel distribution, but states and localities may pass stringent gray market legislation; examples are Colorado, Michigan, and Georgia in the United States, which do not allow the importation of gray market cigarettes.[22]

Summary

- **Describe the functions of home-country and host-country middlemen involved in international distribution.** Examples of home-country middlemen involved in international distribution are export management companies, which specialize in a particular industry; Japanese trading companies, whose operations range from distribution to manufacturing, mining, and, among others, technology, and U.S. trading companies, which are export consortia of small businesses; brokers and agents who do not carry titles and export merchants who carry titles to products; cooperative export arrangements, whereby exporters handle other firms' unrelated products on a contractual basis; Webb-Pomerene Associations, which allow competitors to join forces in exporting; and Foreign Sales Corporations, which allow for a portion of a firm's foreign income to be tax exempt. Foreign-country middlemen involved in logistics are merchant middlemen, who carry title to and have possession of products, and agents and brokers, who do not.
- **Identify the different facilitators of international distribution and logistics and describe their involvement in the international distribution process.** Among facilitators are distribution centers, which use a hub for efficient channeling of operations;

transportation companies; freight forwarders and customs brokers, both in the home and the host country, who arrange for transportation, customs clearance, and export documentation; governmental and nongovernmental organizations, such as the International Trade Administration, the Bureau of Export Administration, the Export-Import Bank, and the International Chamber of Commerce, which promote and facilitate international involvement of companies.
- **Address the challenges encountered by distribution in countries of different development levels.** Multinationals operating in developing countries often must face challenges related to the transportation infrastructure, containerization (ports with shallow drafts that cannot handle large vessels), and customs inspections. In both developed and developing countries, multinationals must deal with parallel imports (gray markets), from a low-price market to another market using distribution channels not authorized by the manufacturer. Increasingly, companies are combating such distribution by charging similar prices worldwide, creating products for low markets that are not attractive to the high market, complicating repair and service processes, informing consumers about buying such products, and litigating.

Key Terms

brokers and agents
building channels
buying offices
complementary export agents
complementary export merchants
comprador
cooperative export arrangements
established channels
export management companies

export merchants
Export Trading Company Act
foreign-country middlemen
Foreign Sales Corporation (FSC)
home-country middlemen
import jobber
keiretsu
logistics alliances
managing agent

manufacturer's export agents
manufacturer's representative
merchant middlemen
network marketing
Norazi agent
parallel imports
sogo shosha
trading companies
Webb-Pomerene Associations

Discussion Questions

1. Companies either can build new channels or use existing channels in new markets they plan to serve. What are the determinants of this choice? Explain.
2. Who are the different distributors available in your home country? Who can distribute your products abroad?
3. Who are the different distributors in your target market (host country)? Who can manage a company's distribution in the host country?
4. How does the U.S. government help companies in the process of distributing their goods internationally?
5. What types of distribution and logistics challenges do firms face in the process of going international?

Chapter Quiz (True/False)

1. Using established channels can be costly for multinational firms, but paying the high price may also erect barriers to entry for competitors.
2. Home-country middlemen are instrumental in providing all international marketing services for firms that otherwise would not be able to enter a foreign market.
3. Buying offices are located in the target market country and carry title to the product.
4. The Foreign Sales Corporation (FSC) allowed for a portion of a U.S. tax-paying firm's foreign-source income to be exempt from income tax.
5. Neither merchant middlemen nor agents and brokers carry title to products.

Multiple Choice

1. What services do Japanese trading companies offer their suppliers?
   a. risk reduction
   b. specialization in intermediary services
   c. financial assistance
   d. all of the above

2. The difference between Webb-Pomerene Associations of Exporters and Cooperative Export Arrangements is that Webb-Pomerene Associations
   a. have immunity from antitrust prosecution.
   b. are formed by competing companies.
   c. both a and b
   d. neither a nor b

3. What aspect of international distribution and logistics is facilitated by containerization?
   a. distribution research
   b. freight forwarding
   c. intermodal transportation
   d. government agencies

4. DHL uses hubs that hold products it delivers regularly so it always has them on hand. This is an example of what international distribution and logistics facilitator?
   a. freight forwarders
   b. distribution centers
   c. transportation firms
   d. government agencies

5. Which government agency offers export assistance to international firms and, in particular, to small to medium-size businesses?
   a. U.S. Department of State
   b. Bureau of Export Administration
   c. U.S. Trade and Development Agency
   d. International Trade Administration

6. Which of the following constitutes a possible strategy to combat parallel imports?
   a. charging similar prices worldwide
   b. complicating the repair process for parallel imports
   c. informing customers of problems when buying gray market products
   d. all of the above

Endnotes

1. "Japanese Trading Companies: The Giants That Refused to Die," *The Economist*, June 1, 1991, Vol. 319, No. 7709, June 1, 1991, pp. 72–73.
2. Ibid.
3. Ibid.
4. Lyn S. Amine, Tamer S. Cavusgil, and Robert I. Weinstein, "Japanese Sogo Shosha and the U.S. Export Trading Companies," *Journal of the Academy of Marketing Science*, Vol. 14, No. 3, Fall 1986, pp. 21–32.
5. "Japanese Trading Companies," *The Economist*, pp. 72–73.
6. Amine, Cavusgil, and Weinstein, "Japanese Sogo Shosha," pp. 21–32.
7. Ernest R. Larkins and Fenwisk Huss, "Establishing Trade Relations in Russia," *The CPA Journal*, Vol. 65, No. 8, August 1995, pp. 26–31.
8. Ibid.
9. Rob Lee, "Boeing in the Middle," *Airfinance Journal*, Vol. 236, February 2001, pp. 34–36.
10. Sue Abdinnour-Helm, "Network Design in Supply Chain Management," *International Journal of Agile Management Systems*, Vol. 1, No. 2, 1999, pp. 99–106.
11. Ibid.
12. Randy R. Irvin, "Pipeline Owners Must Reassess Utility of Undivided-Interest Ownership," *Oil & Gas Journal*, Vol. 99, No. 30, July 23, 2001, pp. 60–65.
13. Ibid.
14. David Biederman, "Intelligent Island Links the Globe," *Traffic World*, Vol. 264, No. 10, December 4, 2000, pp. 28–31.
15. www.danzas.com
16. Lara L. Sowinksi, "It's Sink or Swim for Freight Forwarders and Customs Brokers," *World Trade*, Vol. 14, No. 2, February 2001, pp. 54–56.
17. Adapted from Prabir K. Bagchi and Helge Virum, "Logistical Alliances: Trends and Prospects in Integrated Europe," *Journal of Business Logistics*, Vol. 19, No. 1, 1998, pp. 191–213.
18. See Anthony Coia, "The Global Supply Chain Pill," *Traffic World*, Vol. 259, No. 13, September 27, 1999, p. 17.
19. Alexandra Alger, "'Gray' Watches," *Forbes*, Vol. 160, No. 3, August 11, 1997, p. 151.
20. Peggy E. Chaudry and Michael G. Walsh, "Gray Marketing of Pharmaceuticals," *Journal of Health Care Marketing*, Vol. 15, No. 3, Fall 1995, pp. 18–21.
21. Matthew B. Myers and David A. Griffith, "Strategies for Combating Gray Market Activity," *Business Horizons*, Vol. 42, No. 6, November/December 1999, pp. 2–8.
22. Marc Katz, "Gray Market Cigarettes," *NPN*, National Petroleum News, Vol. 92, No. 1, January 2000, p. 46.

You can find the correct answers to these questions by taking the quiz and then submitting your answers in the Online Edition. The program will automatically score your submission. Where you miss a question, the program will provide the correct answer, a rationale for the answer, and the section number in the chapter where the topic is discussed.

Case 11-1

Shipping Doo Kingue

Doo Kingue is a baby mountain gorilla, a member of one of the two most endangered apes in the world. There are only approximately 655 mountain gorillas alive today, all in the wild in the mountainous forests of northwest Rwanda, southwest Uganda, and eastern Democratic Republic of Congo. Mountain gorillas in this region are constantly threatened by poaching, continuous encroachment on the national parks for agricultural use, extensive harvesting of wood for fuel, and a landmine landscape as a result of fighting between the different tribes in the region. Doo Kingue, whose tribe perished as a result of water contamination, was able to survive—barely—and is currently experiencing a difficult-to-treat pulmonary infection.

The Director of Karisoke Research Center in Volcano National Park—founded by the late American anthropologist Dian Fossey in 1968 and run by the Dian Fossey Gorilla Funds, a United States Non-Governmental Organization—recently approached the National Zoo in Washington, D.C., and asked for help. The Center obtained permission from the regional government of Ruhengeri and the national government of Rwanda to send the gorilla to the National Zoo, provided the zoo takes responsibility for shipping and hospitalization. John James, one of the directors of conservation and science at the zoo, is excited about having a mountain gorilla for its primate exhibit, and Doo Kingue seems like the ideal candidate.

John's plan is to work with one of the transportation companies doing business in Sub-Saharan Africa, to bring him quickly and painlessly to Washington, D.C., and to start aggressive treatment on the pulmonary infection. Clearly, in this decision, time is of the essence. His staff is familiar with some of the companies that provide quick, reliable service for transporting animals. One of the companies he is considering is Animal Port Houston (www.pet-transport.com), a company with expertise in the relocation of pets and animals, offering services that include housing, transporting, and preparing relevant health certificates and permits. Animal-Port-Houston is a member of the American Zoo Association (AZA), the International Animal Transportation Association (AATA), the International Pet and Animal Transport Association (IPATA), the American Animal Sciences Association (AALAS), the United States Animal Health Association (USAHA), and the U.S. Air Forwarders Association.

Another company that seems a viable candidate for the transportation job is Federal Express (www.fedex.com). FedEx has recently donated the use of its express transportation network and relocated six endangered polar bears from San Juan, Puerto Rico, to their permanent zoo homes. The company flew the bears from San Juan to the FedEx Express Hub in Memphis onboard a DC-10 aircraft. Later in the day, the bears were transloaded to three other aircraft in Memphis to fly to their final destinations near Seattle, Washington; Detroit, Michigan; and Charlotte, North Carolina; respectively. FedEx Express used its customs clearance expertise to expedite the animals through U.S. Customs. John found out that FedEx Express has considerable experience in transporting animals, including elephants, rhinos, lions and gorillas. The company even transported animals to the National Zoo. In December 2000, FedEx provided air transportation, ground support, and logistical expertise to deliver two giant pandas from Chengdu, China, to the National Zoo in Washington, D.C. More recently, in 2002, FedEx transported six rare white tigers from Memphis, Tennessee, to Bangkok, Thailand, to ensure that work could continue on an endangered species breeding program.

Sources: www.scienceinafrica.co.za; Paul R. Murphy and James M. Daley, "Profiling International Freight Forwarders: An Update," *International Journal of Physical Distribution Logistics Management*, Vol. 31, No. 3, 2001, pp. 152–168; www.fedex.com.

Analysis Suggestions

1. Weigh the advantages and disadvantages of using Animal Port Houston and FedEx Express to transport Doo Kingue to Washington, D.C.
2. Arrange for intermodal transportation for Doo Kingue from Ruhengeri, Rwanda, to Kigali, the capital city of Rwanda, and to the United States. Note that none of these companies, nor any U.S. airlines, fly to Rwanda. Attempt a few routes by looking at airlines' websites, at the Animal Port Houston site, and the FedEx site to find out what markets they serve. Find out how animals can be transported from Dulles Airport to downtown Washington, D.C.

International Retailing

By the end of this chapter, you should be able to

1 Provide an overview and description of the general merchandise retailing category and offer examples and illustrations.

2 Provide an overview and description of the food retailing category and offer examples and illustrations.

3 Provide an overview and description of the nonstore retailing category and offer examples and illustrations.

4 Address issues related to legislation, taxation, and retailing practices around the world.

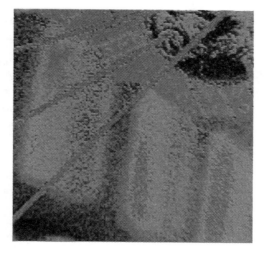

etailing is going through a process of rapid internationalization; the retailing environment worldwide is undergoing dynamic changes, with local retailers defensively countering competitive moves of enormous international chains or successfully duplicating their strategies.

Major international retailers are no longer competing only for mature markets—and for consumers in highly industrialized countries. Retailers' competitive arena has expanded to all emerging markets, where they are responding to an increasing affluence of consumers and to their increasingly sophisticated consumption-related demands. Numerous successful global retailers and consumer-product-companies-cum-retailers such as Wal-Mart (United States), Carrefour (France), Louis Vuitton Moët Henessy (France), and Royal Ahold (the Netherlands) are already present on four continents and have outlets in as many as 25 countries.[1]

This chapter offers insights into the internationalization efforts of retailers, describing different categories of retailers and their international involvement and expansion, and issues related to legislation and taxation that affect retailing operations. The chapter also illustrates retailing practices around the world.

12-1 International Expansion of Retailers

Retailers are rapidly expanding internationally to gain competitive advantage and to increase sales, profits, and overall firm performance. As they expand beyond their home-country borders, retailers also can take advantage of cost savings and learn from experiences in a way that could further enhance home-country operations. Tesco, the British retailer, for example, is using its stores in Central and Eastern Europe as a testing ground for ideas that are intended for application in the home market; the Tesco Extra in Newcastle, United Kingdom, is based on a Tesco hypermarket in Hungary.[2]

Retailers from the United States are expanding in Latin America, Asia, and Europe. Wal-Mart, for example, has adopted an aggressive strategy for international penetration: Its purchase of the Asda Group (United Kingdom) has boosted its international sales to $47 billion, which is only a fraction of its total net sales figure (fiscal year ending in January 2004) of $256 billion[3]. Although some of this growth can be attributed to its Latin American operations, Wal-Mart's primary focus remains on Europe.[4]

European retailers are rapidly gaining ground internationally as well. The 5 leading European retailers—Carrefour, Metro, Intermarché, Rewe, and Auchan—presently control a 25.4 percent share of the European grocery market.[5] European retailers are prominent in the top 100 list of global retailers as well. Among the top 15 global retail companies, there are 6 European retailers. The top 15 global retailers are ranked in Table 12-1.

The top 200 retailers worldwide are dominated by U.S. retailers, who hold 50.6 percent of the retail sales market share. Figure 12-1 shows the worldwide distribution of retail sales market share by country/region.

In the process of internationalization, many retailers are subscribing to the current trend of consolidation in the food and general merchandise sectors. Examples of such

Table 12-1   The Top 15 Global Retailers

Rank	Country of Origin	Retailers	Format	Sales (US$ millions)
1	U.S.	Wal-Mart	Discount, Hypermarket Supermarket, Superstore, Warehouse	256,329
2	France	Carrefour	Cash & Carry, Convenience, Discount, Hypermarket, Specialty, Supermarket	65,011
3	U.S.	Home Depot	DIY, Specialty	58,247
4	U.S.	Kroger	Convenience, Discount, Specialty, Supermarket, Warehouse	51,760
5	Germany	Metro	Cash & Carry, Department, DIY, Hypermarket, Specialty, Superstore	48,349
6	U.S.	Target	Department, Discount, Superstore	42,722
7	Netherlands	Ahold	Cash & Carry, Convenience, Discount, Drug, Hypermarket, Specialty, Supermarket	40,755
8	U.K.	Tesco	Convenience, Department Hypermarket, Supermarket, Superstore	40,071
9	U.S.	Costco	Warehouse	37,993
10	U.S.	Sears	Department, Specialty Mail, E-commerce	35,698
11	U.S.	Albertsons	Drug, Supermarket, Warehouse	35,626
12	Germany	Aldi Einkauf	Discount, Supermarket	33,837
13	U.S.	Safeway, Inc.	Supermarket	32,399
14	U.S.	JCPenney	Department, Drug, Mail Order	32,347
15	France	Intermarché	Cash & Carry, Convenience, Discount DIY, Food Service, Specialty, Supermarket, Superstore	31,688

Source: "2004 Global Powers of Retailing," January 2004, http://www.stores.org/m200global.asp.

consolidation are offered by Wal-Mart's acquisition of one of the largest U.K. grocery chains, the Asda Group; Royal Ahold's purchase of the Pathmark, Giant, and Stop & Shop chains in the United States; and the merger between two medium-sized French Wal-Mart look-alikes, Promodes and Carrefour,[6] to form the second largest retailer worldwide, the French retailer Carrefour, present in Argentina, Brazil, Chile, Colombia, Mexico, and the Dominican Republic in Latin America; in China, Japan, Indonesia, Malaysia, Singapore, South Korea, Taiwan, and Thailand in the Far East; Egypt, Oman,

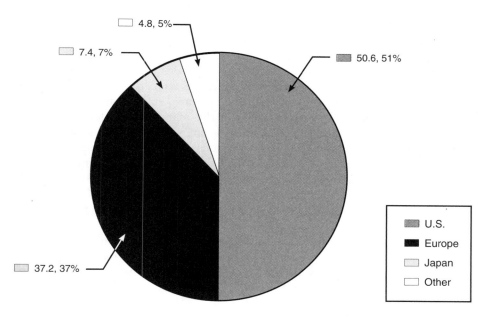

Figure 12-1
Top 200 World Retailers by Sales
Source: Adapted from "2004 Global Powers of Retailing," January 2004, http://www.stores.org/m200global.asp.

Qatar, Tunisia, Turkey, and the United Arab Emirates in North Africa and the Middle East; and France, Belgium, Italy, Switzerland, Spain, Portugal, the Czech Republic, Slovakia, Poland, Romania, and Greece in Europe.

To understand the changes in the vibrant world of international retailing, one needs to gain some insight into the many categories of retailers (local and multinational) and their modus operandi in different parts of the world. It also is important to understand how international retailing differs from retailing as defined in marketing management texts. Both of these topics are addressed in sections 12-2 and 12-3.

12-2 International Retailing Defined

International retailing is defined as *all the activities involved in selling products and services to final international consumers for their personal consumption*.

International retailing differs from local retailing as defined in marketing management in that it addresses operations of international retailers beyond home-country borders, as well as operations of local retailers in different countries worldwide—in general and/or in response to the presence or entry of international retailers aiming for their target market. As such, an examination of international retail operations must include an evaluation of all global and local retailing formats, retail practices, and an overview of local retailing environments.

12-3 Retail Formats: Variations in Different Markets

There are three main retail formats: general merchandise retailing, food retailing, and nonstore retailing. Sections 12-3a through 12-3c describe the retailers in each category and address the different international variations for each retail format, with a focus on local markets.

12-3a General Merchandise Retailing

Specialty Stores

Specialty stores offer a narrow product line and wide assortment. In this category are clothing stores (usually further specialized into women's, men's, or children's clothing stores), bookstores, toy stores, office supply stores, and consumer electronics stores, among others.

specialty stores Retailers that offer a narrow product line and wide assortment.

In many markets, specialty stores—chains in particular—are expanding at the expense of all forms of nonfood retailing. For example, specialty store chains are taking market share away from traditional department stores in the United Kingdom and France.[7] U.K. specialty retailers have made great strides in international expansion: Marks & Spencer is rapidly expanding in France, and retailers such as Virgin Records have already made substantial inroads into the U.S. market. In France, specialty stores appear to be particularly well suited to addressing the unique French lifestyle. Local players, as well as international firms such as The Gap, are very successful in this market.

For apparel retailing, many European companies are rapidly entering new markets: Mango, the Spanish retailer specializing in youth fashion, has 400 shops in 44 countries, including Israel, Eastern Europe, and South America.[8] Rival Spanish chain Zara, with its distinctive brushed-steel staircases, and Swedish chain Hennes & Mauritz are competing for these same consumers and are proving to be very successful in mature markets worldwide.

In most developing countries, specialty stores represent the main retail format. Although Western and local specialty chain stores are quite popular and have done well for decades, developing country markets are dominated by independent (usually family-owned) specialty stores, such as apparel stores, cosmetics stores, and local arts and crafts stores aimed at the tourist market, as well as other traditional retail systems as exemplified by specialized markets.

Specialized Markets

specialized markets Markets that contain specialty stores specializing in a particular product category.

Specialized markets contain specialty stores specializing in a particular product category. Examples of such markets exist worldwide, in both developed and developing countries. Examples of specialized markets are the Cairo Gold Market in the Khan El Khalili bazaar, the Jade Market in Hong Kong, and the Spice Market and Gold Market in the Covered Bazaar in Istanbul, Turkey (see Figure 12-2). Specialized markets may even cover entire cities. For example, the town of Otavalo, Ecuador, houses large and small retailers of leather goods.

In addition to these markets, local specialty stores affiliated with a project sponsored by governmental or nongovernmental organizations also are prevalent in many developing countries (see Figure 12-3). Examples may be a poultry shop partially owned by local investors selling poultry raised in a project funded by the World Bank and the United Nations Development Program aimed at helping a developing country become self-sufficient with regard to meat production, or a folk art outlet selling hand-made embroidery produced by young girls in a convent.

Department Stores

department stores General retailers that offer a broad variety of goods and wide assortments.

Department stores offer a broad variety of goods and wide assortments. Among the products they carry are clothing for men, women, and children; household appliances and electronics; kitchenware; china; home furnishings; and toys and games. Outside the United States, department stores typically also have large supermarket sections, and some may even carry fresh produce.

In the United States and Canada, department stores have suffered substantial losses since the 1990s, mostly attributed to the rise in discount stores, off-price retailers, and category killers. In an attempt to conquer new markets, however, a number of chains have been looking overseas for expansion: Sears Roebuck and JCPenney, in particular, have been looking at the Latin American market, with JCPenney opening a number of stores in Mexico and Chile.[9]

In Europe, department stores typically tend to address the needs of home markets, with efforts to expand mainly in the European Union. The United Kingdom has one of the oldest and best-established department stores in the world, accounting for 5 percent of total retail sales, and the four leading department store groups in this country control more than 65 percent of all department store trade.[10] The self-touted most famous shop in the world, Harrods department store in London (Knightsbridge), was established in

(a)

(b)

Figure 12-2

The Covered Bazaar in Istanbul, Turkey, is a prime example of a specialized market. It is divided into two main areas: (a) the general retail area and (b) the gold bazaar.

1849 and, by the end of the nineteenth century, was flourishing, selling airplanes and elephants, jewelry and pineapples, golf clubs and snuff boxes; today, it attracts an exclusive clientele to its 300 departments covering a million square feet of selling space and to its 21 restaurants.[11]

In the Netherlands, three department stores dominate: Vendex (Vroom & Dreesman), HEMA, and Bijenkorf. (The latter two belong to the KBB Group.) A similar concentration is encountered in Germany, where Karstadt (which also owns the Hertie department store chain) and Kaufhof dominate the market. French department stores are surviving despite the dominance of specialty shops and the increasing popularity of category killers and discount shops. Among the leading department stores in France are Printemps, Bon

Figure 12-3

In this specialized market, this Gypsy (Roma) retailer is selling mainly Asian clothing products at an outdoors clothing retail complex, in central Bucharest, Romania. Most owners and salespeople where this retailer is located belong to the Roma ethnicity.

Figure 12-4

Galeries Lafayette are present and successful in every large city in France; the company's international expansion attempts, however, have been problematic.

Marché, and Galeries Lafayette (see Figure 12-4). One, Galeries Lafayette, made an unsuccessful attempt to enter the U.S. market by locating in the heart of Manhattan and opened a new store in Old East Berlin—an architectural landmark in Germany's new capital. In Spain, the leading department store is El Corte Inglés, which dominates the Madrid retail scene.[12]

In Central and Eastern Europe, department stores abound; the former communist regimes found that large department stores offered economies of scale in terms of distribution and sales management. Consequently, department stores dominate the retailing environment of most large cities. With names such as Centrum or the Central Store in

Central and Eastern Europe (see Figure 12-5a) and GUM in Russia, or bearing the name of the capital city or of socialist and nationalist symbols ("Victory," "Liberty," "Unity," etc.), these stores continue to thrive in a slightly different format: In addition to their merchandise, they also have a substantial presence of leased departments. The leased departments are noteworthy in that they carry merchandise that directly competes with the store's offerings and with that of other leased departments. For example, the Bucur Obor department store in Bucharest has at least three leased departments selling chandeliers (see Figure 12-5b). Alternatively, store space may be rented to retailers that are not traditionally associated with department stores, such as automobile retailers.

In Asia, department stores have very different histories: Japanese department stores started out as kimono shops that originally sold textiles. At present, Japan's department store groups (Mitsukoshi, Daimaru, ADO, the Seibu stores and affiliates, and Takashimaya) are designed to be cradle-to-grave providers of goods and services. Japanese department stores have also expanded in China and Hong Kong, where they control 50 percent of the market. Finally, Taiwan's department stores have lagged behind; Da-Hsin and Ti-I department stores were the first to enter the market, followed by a number of newcomers, among them Far Eastern, Sesame, and Evergreen, most of which have sought affiliation with foreign (particularly Japanese) department store chains.[13]

Although department stores remain a dominant retail outlet in Asia, they are currently displaying symptoms of decline, such as oversupply, over-duplication of merchandise,

(a)

(b)

Figure 12-5

(a) This Centrum Store in Wroclaw, Poland, displays Legos and Barbie dolls. (b) At Bucur Obor in Bucharest, Romania, chandelier retailers compete in the store's leased department.

fierce competition, and declining profits. Shanghai alone witnessed the demise of five department stores in 1997. Existing department stores in this city have done well when changing their format—for example, specializing in European-style clothing and furnishings, or emulating the hypermarket environment by offering lower prices and maintaining a customer-friendly environment.[14]

General Merchandise Discount Stores

general merchandise discount stores sell high volumes of merchandise, offer limited service, and charge lower prices. Discount stores are divided into two categories: **all-purpose discount stores,** which offer a wide variety of merchandise and limited depth, and **category specialists (category killers**), which carry a narrow variety of merchandise and offer a wide assortment.

The all-purpose category is dominated by stores such as Wal-Mart, Kmart, and Target in the United States. Internationally, this retailer category tends to draw a substantial portion of profits from its supermarket section; consequently, it will be addressed in section 12-3b, "Food Retailers." In the all-purpose category, Wal-Mart has more than 1,355[15] stores internationally (many of the international stores are hypermarkets); the company is present in Canada, Mexico, Puerto Rico, Argentina, Brazil, Germany, and the United Kingdom. Wal-Mart also has a presence in China, through joint ventures, and two franchise locations in Indonesia. Its goals are to derive one third of its earnings from international operations.[16]

One of the better known international general merchandise discount stores competing with these U.S. companies is Mexico's Grupo Gigante, which, in 2003 opened 18 new stores in Mexico and 7 overseas. Its plans are to further penetrate the U.S. market and go head to head with Wal-Mart, battling for the U.S. discount store consumer.

Category specialists, also known as category killers or stores with category dominance, are large specialty stores that carry a narrow variety of merchandise and a wide assortment. Among examples of category specialists successful internationally are office supply stores, such as Staples, Office Max, and Office Depot; home improvement centers, such as Home Depot; bookstores, such as Borders, which are especially well received in East Asia; children's stores, such as Toys "R" Us, which leads sales in this product category from Scandinavia to South Africa; and furniture stores, such as Ikea, which dominates the modern, basic furniture market. Of the first category, office supply stores, Staples is present internationally in Europe, where it has 265 stores—in Germany, the Netherlands, Belgium, Portugal, and the United Kingdom.[17] Office Max has stores in Mexico, Japan, and Brazil, while Office Depot operates 32 wholly owned retail stores under the Office Depot brand name in France and 12 stores in Japan, as well as joint venture and licensing agreements for 115 Office Depot stores in Mexico, Israel, Poland, Hungary, Thailand, and Guatemala.[18]

Many of the established international specialty retailers and numerous newcomers are attracting consumers with innovative approaches to merchandising. In the furniture business, Ikea has redefined furniture retailing for more than three decades with its impressive merchandising core competencies, its sourcing economies of scale, and the savings it passes on to consumers.

Off-Price Retailers

Off-price retailers sell brand name and designer merchandise below regular retail; the products they sell may include overruns, irregular products, as well as products from previous seasons. Among examples of off-price retailers are factory outlet stores; close-out retailers, with broad, inconsistent assortments; and single-price retailers. Although this type of retailing is popular in the United States and Canada, in the rest of the world, there are only limited possibilities, other than store sales, for purchasing brand names at a discount. For example, Hugo Boss has an outlet store in Southern Germany, close to its factory, near Stuttgart, and Zurich has a famous designer outlet mall; Italy also has a few outlet stores for its famous designers. None of these examples come close in depth and

---

general merchandise discount stores Retailers that sell high volumes of merchandise, offer limited service, and charge lower prices.

all-purpose discount stores General merchandise discount stores that offer a wide variety of merchandise and limited depth.

category specialists/category killers Large general merchandise discount stores that carry a narrow variety of merchandise and a wide assortment.

off-price retailers Retailers who sell brand name products and designer merchandise below regular retail prices.

variety to the North American off-price retailer presence, but that is about to change, as more and more international consumers demand similar deals as the ones offered in the United States.

Often, American companies must build their own outlet stores in environments where this type of retail format is unknown. In the Tokyo suburb of Sagami-One, for instance, American Malls International opened an outlet mall for companies such as Guess! and Laura Ashley to sell discontinued merchandise at a discount.[19]

Catalog Showrooms

Catalog showrooms usually offer high-turnover, brand name goods at discount prices. A typical format for a catalog showroom is one in which customers order from a catalog in the showroom where the product is only displayed and then pick up the merchandise at a designated location. Internationally, the goods sold in this retail format are not typically brand name goods, but, rather, they are goods that have not sold in season through a company's catalog. For example, Neckermann and Quelle, the well-known German catalog retailers, have catalog showrooms in many of Germany's largest cities where they sell their catalog store brands. In addition, Ikea uses this strategy to sell to consumers worldwide: Customers receive a catalog, which is also available in the showroom; based on the offerings displayed in the catalog and in the showroom, customers order in the store the product they would like to purchase and pick it up from a designated location in its unassembled state.

catalog showrooms Showrooms displaying the products of catalog retailers, offering high-turnover, brand name goods at discount prices.

12-3b Food Retailers

Conventional Supermarkets

Food retailers include **conventional supermarkets,** which are self-service retailers with annual sales higher than $2 million and less than 20,000 square feet of store space. Such supermarkets abound worldwide, with local retailers and regional international retailers most prominent in this retail category.

food retailers Retailers selling primarily food products.

Superstores

The **superstores** category includes **combination stores** (food and drug) and **hypermarkets** (which combine supermarket, discount, and warehouse retailing principles). In the United States, combination stores have been quite successful; all-purpose general discount stores, such as Wal-Mart and Kmart, are often transformed into superstores to facilitate one-stop shopping for consumers. In their new, enhanced formats, these stores are known as the Wal-Mart Superstore and Big K, respectively, and they carry an extensive food selection but have a more limited refrigeration space and fresh produce offering, similar to that offered by a supermarket.

conventional supermarkets Self-service food retailers with annual sales of more than $2 million and with an area less than 20,000 square feet.

superstores Large retailers such as combination stores or hypermarkets that sell food, drugs, and other products.

These same stores have attempted, without success, to adopt a hypermarket format in the United States, by offering consumers an extensive supermarket section, with fresh produce and ample refrigeration space. However, such a format did not appeal to U.S. consumers; in the United States, the retailing equivalent of the Wal-Mart hypermarket is somewhat diluted, in the form of a superstore. As previously mentioned, Wal-Mart's presence in retail in the rest of the world is mainly in the form of hypermarkets. With its advanced distribution logistics, Wal-Mart has changed the retail market worldwide, forcing local suppliers to grow with it at a fast pace and forcing competitors to match it in its everyday-low-pricing strategy.

combination stores Medium-size retail stores that combine food and drug retailing.

Germany is a key target for Wal-Mart's international expansion. The company acquired the Wertkauf chain in 1997 and the Interspar hypermarket chain in 1998, adding almost 100 new hypermarkets.[20] In the United Kingdom, Wal-Mart purchased the Asda Group PLC, Britain's third-largest grocery chain. As of September 2004, Wal-Mart has a total of 1,520 international units; it also operates 11 stores in Argentina, 14 in Brazil, 236 in Canada, 657 in Mexico, 54 in Puerto Rico, 39 in China, 271 in the United Kingdom, 92 in Germany, and 15 in Korea.[21]

hypermarkets Very large retail stores that combine supermarket, discount, and warehouse retailing principles.

The shockwaves sent by Wal-Mart's extensive presence in Europe have led to substantial competitive and consolidation activity in the hypermarket category. The French hypermarket chain Carrefour merged with its former rival Promodes, competing for the position of the world's dominant retailer. Similarly, German retailer Metro AG strengthened its position by buying the Allkauf chain of 86 hypermarkets and the Kriegbaum Unternemensgruppe chain of 27 hypermarkets and 16 supermarkets.[22] Tesco, the British supermarket chain, is rapidly expanding with its Tesco Extra hypermarkets in Central and Eastern Europe—Poland, the Czech Republic, Hungary, Slovakia, and Latvia[23]—attempting to gain a first mover advantage in these markets.

Royal Ahold, the Dutch supermarket chain, owns, among others, a number of supermarket chains in the United States—*Stop & Shop, Giant-Landover, Giant-Carlisle, Tops, BI-LO* and Bruno's—as well as the Albert Heijn supermarkets, the Etos drugstores, and the Schuitema and Gall & Gall retail operations in the Netherlands. The company also has a presence in the Czech Republic, Slovakia, Poland, Spain, and Portugal, and has acquired a 50 percent partnership interest in the *ICA Group*, an integrated food retail and wholesale group, servicing retailer-owned and company-owned neighborhood stores, supermarkets, superstores, hypermarkets, and discount stores in Sweden, Norway, and the Baltic states.[24] Royal Ahold is rapidly selling off its operations in South America.

Also in Asia, hypermarkets Carrefour and Makro already have significant positions in Taiwan, Malaysia, Indonesia, and Thailand; and Tesco acquired a majority stake in the Lotus Supercenters in Thailand. In fact, Carrefour has more than 9,000 outlets around the world; employs 240,000 workers; and is the largest retailer in countries such as France, Belgium, Portugal, Spain, Brazil, Argentina, Taiwan, South Korea, and Indonesia. In France alone, the new Carrefour (including the recently acquired Promodes chain) represents an important employer—employing more than 600,000 people and generating a revenue equal to 15 percent of France's gross domestic product.[25]

Warehouse Clubs or Wholesale Clubs

warehouse clubs/wholesale clubs Stores that require members to pay an annual fee operating in low-overhead, warehouse-type facilities, offering limited lines of brand name and dealer-brand groceries, apparel, appliances, and other goods at a substantial discount.

Warehouse clubs, also called **wholesale clubs,** require members to pay an annual fee and operate in low-overhead, warehouse-type facilities. They offer limited lines of brand name and dealer-brand groceries, apparel, appliances, and other goods at a substantial discount. They sell to final consumers who are affiliated with different institutions, as well as to businesses (in this capacity, they are wholesalers, rather than retailers). This retailing concept is presently pioneered worldwide by Sam's Club (part of Wal-Mart) and Costco.

Sam's Club operates in 46 international locations; its most important operations are in Mexico, where it has acquired its joint-venture partner, Cifra. Sam's Club entered Mexico in 1991 with an agreement to operate warehouse clubs patterned after Sam's Club, under the Club Aurerra name in Mexico City. It is also present in the Philippines, China, Panama, and Indonesia.[26] Costco has units in Korea, Taiwan, Japan, Canada, the United Kingdom,[27] and Mexico, where it has a joint venture with the retail conglomerate Controladora Comercial Mexicana.[28] San Diego-based PriceSmart Inc. is presently forming joint ventures and licensing agreements with foreign partners to set up wholesale clubs in Latin America and Asia-Pacific countries,[29] most recently in Nicaragua and Ecuador.[30]

Convenience Stores

convenience stores Small retailers located in residential areas, open long hours, and carrying limited lines of high-turnover necessities.

Convenience stores are small retailers located in residential areas, convenient to consumers; they are open long hours, carry limited lines of higher-turnover necessities, and offer the possibility of a one-stop shopping experience. Formats of convenience stores vary worldwide (see Figure 12-6)—from small independent retailers to chains such as 7-11; from large stores offering a one-stop shopping opportunity for convenience goods and fast food to kiosks selling food items and alcoholic beverages obtained through both legal and illegal channels; from convenience stores-cum-pharmacies in a city's town square to seventh-floor apartments with a large opening in the front door selling milk, cheese, bread, and different types of chocolate. Convenience stores abound in both developing and developed countries, with many chains developing in conjunction with gas stations.

Convenience stores are fiercely competing for the Chinese consumer, as described in International Marketing Illustration 12-1.

12-3c Nonstore Retailing

Internet Retailing

Also known as **interactive home shopping** or **electronic retailing**, selling through the Internet has quickly become an important retail format. In the **Internet retailing** category, dot-com companies and traditional retailers are attempting additional market penetration by making it convenient for loyal customers to purchase their products, as well

interactive home shopping/ electronic retailing/Internet retailing Selling through the Internet using websites to increase market penetration and market diversification.

(a)

(b)

F i g u r e 1 2 - 6

The merchandise mix of convenience stores can vary greatly from one location to another. (a) At this convenience store in Poland, Ariel laundry detergent (Proctor & Gamble) dominates, and cleaning and hygiene products occupy more than half the store. (b) At another convenience store in Romania, vice products and sweets dominate, although the owners also display a dairy case and some milk products.

International Marketing Illustration 12-1

Targeting the Convenience Store Consumer in China

In most developed countries, new convenience stores have difficulty penetrating in their mature market. Even established players in this tight market must have sophisticated merchandise tracking and inventory systems, a keen attention to detail, and optimal use of limited space. In China, establishing a convenience store means simply offering the merchandise at lower prices than competition. China's $US500 billion retail sector is booming, with convenience stores revamping and reinventing themselves to appeal to the local market. Neighborhoods often have even two or three convenience stores on one street. Shanghai has 3,500 convenience stores, about half the national total, and about 2,000 of them were opened in 2002, or thereafter.

In China, convenience store retailing is nearing maturity, and cutthroat competition is the norm, with most stores competing with each other on price. There are not too many requirements for new convenience stores: They must have a product to sell and offer it at lower prices than competitors. As a result, convenience retailers survive only due to lower margins, driving down the margins of the competition in the process: Margins in China are roughly 15 percent, compared with an average 30 percent internationally.

In one example, the state-owned Liangyou chain has established a joint venture with private investors, the Buddies convenience store chain, and is battling for the Shanghai market. The Shanghai Liangyou Group was initially part of a network of rationing stations set up in the 1950s under the State Grain Administration to ration and distribute rice and cooking oil to the masses. In 1998, the Group split to form convenience stores.

In a complete turnaround, the stores have shelves up to the ceiling, giving a feeling of abundance; aisles that are five feet wide, compared to competitors' aisles, which are only three feet; and ready-to-eat displays at the counter. Store managers are given substantial freedom to decide how to organize the store to best appeal to the target market.

Source: Leslie Chang, "China's Rush to Convenience: U.S.-Trained Executive Revamps Chain to Better Take on Rivals," *Wall Street Journal*, November 3, 2003, p. A13.

as attempting market diversification by expanding their market to consumers who otherwise would not normally shop in their particular retail establishment.

With the Internet and the increase in the number of Internet users worldwide,[31] providing retailing services through a website that is accessible globally becomes much easier. Local retailers can easily become international retailers without making investments in store leases, aesthetics, atmospherics, etc.

Internet retailing provides opportunities for retail firms to define their market beyond their target regions. At the same time, it presents dilemmas with regard to customer service and control of the retail transactions (due to international and regional differences in mail reliability, and in customer orientation and skill of local service representatives, among others). Almost half (46 percent) of the current companies with e-commerce capabilities turn away international orders, primarily because they do not have a way to ship the merchandise overseas or lack the processes necessary for international shipments.[32]

In developed countries, Internet purchasing is consumption market driven and not experience driven: Consumers shop for needs and wants but do not view Internet surfing as a pleasure trip, as would consumers going to a mall or a store.[33] Consequently, shopping via the Internet for consumers in countries where attractive shopping alternatives are available, such as malls and stores with great merchandise assortment and variety, is quite different from shopping in many developing countries, where alternatives are very limited, and where both retailers and the products they sell are inferior. If it were not for the Internet and for catalog retailing, consumers in this second category would be able to purchase higher quality goods only if they went abroad.

Consumers in developed countries might also have to contend with unethical retailers. Whereas brick-and-mortar retailers can be sued in a local court of law for nonperformance, Internet retailers are more elusive; the issue of the appropriate jurisdiction further complicates the situation. Using the more established Internet retailers—the well-known brick-and-mortar retailers or the established catalog stores, such as Quelle and Neckermann from Germany and Ikea from Sweden, which are now also selling through their own web pages—may be a safer alternative.

The Internet provides a venue for émigrés shopping for their relatives in their home countries; see International Marketing Illustration 12-2.

Vending Machines

With the advent of the Smart Card, vending machine retailing has become more popular than ever (and, increasingly, more **vending machines** worldwide accept credit cards). Technology is now facilitating a more interactive consumer relationship, where videos illustrate product use and provide more information. The extent to which vending machines are used as a retail venue varies from country to country. Vending machines are used most in Japan, where they sell just about anything one can think of, including beer, sausage, rice, life insurance, eggs, cameras, pantyhose,[34] and condoms. Coke alone has one million vending machines in Japan.[35] In fact, in central locations in Japan's major cities, there are so many vending machines that they interfere with pedestrian traffic.

Vending machines are encountered in different configurations around the world. In the Netherlands, for instance, one can enter an outfit known as an Automatiek and select sausages, meatballs, salads, and beverages from the different machines, all replenished frequently by a full-time employee. In Munich, Germany, a vending machine for fresh flowers is located in the center of town. In much of the rest of the world, with the exception of the United States and Canada, cigarettes are readily available in the streets at all times of the day. In Europe, condoms are sold in vending machines outside pharmacies.

vending machines Interactive modes of retailing convenience goods.

Television Home Shopping

The **television home shopping** category includes cable channels selling to consumers in their homes, infomercials, and direct response advertising shown on broadcast and cable television. Television shopping networks, much like QVC and the Home Shopping Network in the United States, operate in many developed countries. Some offerings do not fit well in either category. For example, in a mid-1990s Romanian program, for one hour contestants had to perform different tasks, all of which involved Pepsi bottles or bottle caps. In another example, Britain's famous Harrods department store entered the home shopping business by selling its products on the TV-news channel CNBC Europe; a two-hour program called *Gold Card Television* offers shows about travel and fashion in addition to the opportunity to purchase products selected by Harrods.[36]

Western television shopping programs are also entering Asia; among the new entrants are Home Shopping Network Direct from Florida, International Shopping Network from San Diego, Interwood Marketing Group from Canada, London-based Regal Shop International and Quantum International, and Australia's International Media Management. They create or invest in television programs or 10- to 30-minute infomercials that market products ranging from cosmetics to kitchen accessories. These programs are frequently prerecorded in their country of origin and later dubbed into Asian languages.[37]

television home shopping Retailing through cable channels selling to consumers in their homes, through infomercials, and through direct response advertising shown on broadcast and cable television.

Catalog Retailing and Direct Mail Retailing

Retailers of all categories are expanding internationally through catalog sales and **direct mail retailing.** Tiffany's is expanding its direct mail operations internationally;

direct mail retailing Retailing using catalogs and other direct mail, instead of brick-and-mortar stores.

International Marketing Illustration   12-2

Retail Opportunities for Émigrés: Repatriating Food and Clothing to Home-Country Relatives

In the past, helping out relatives with money or with food packages was expensive. Traditionally, émigrés living in developed countries sent money periodically to their relatives in their home country—a developing country. Typically sent through money wire transfers or by check, the sums were often decimated by fees by the time they reached a recipient in a developing country or in an emerging market. For example, sending a check from the United States would require the recipient in Ecuador, India, or Slovakia to go to a local bank to cash it. The money would be released as long as a month later, after the check was cashed, and the recipient, who did not normally have an account at the international bank, would be charged hefty fees. It would not be unusual for the recipient of $100 check to cash out $70 or less, even if the remittance services promised free money transfer and excellent exchange rates.

In the pre-Internet past, émigrés also helped their families with food packages: Most diaspora newspapers advertised the shipping of consumer products to the home country at competitive prices (they still do today, but the Internet has taken a large bite of their business). Merz Pharma, a German pharmaceuticals firm, has been catering to East European émigrés for decades. All one had to do was pick up the phone and order the goods for delivery, paying for them with a credit card. Because shipping was involved, costs were a bit steep and prices were not quite a bargain.

Today, a greater accessibility of goods in the home country, coupled with Internet-facilitated transactions, allows émigrés to order goods for the family at competitive prices and with free shipping for orders higher than a particular amount. This variant is so attractive that it is not unusual for émigrés from Latin America and Eastern Europe to purchase food and other necessities for family members in the home country, in some cases as often as three times a month.

To illustrate, shoppers in Oregon can place grocery orders for their relatives in Argentina through Discovirtual.com, an online site of Argentine retailer Disco SA, owned by Dutch chain Royal Ahold. Peruvian supermarket chain E. Wong launched an online store that taps Peruvians abroad shopping for their families, doubling its online transactions in one year. Similarly, Brazil's Pao de Acucar found that it can sell an average of 5,000 grocery items a day through its website. And Mexico's Grupo Gigante is also actively pursuing this market.

Even though many Latinos living in developed countries do not have Internet access, it is likely that this will become big business in the future. Latino immigrants and their descendants living in the United States repatriate close to $20 billion yearly, mostly through Western Union or banks. Immigrants from Haiti and Nicaragua remit more than 20 percent of the respective home-countries' GDP yearly, that is, $810 and $610 million, respectively. Immigrants from El Salvador and the Dominican Republic remit close to $2 billion yearly. And, in Somalia, remittance companies, known as hawala, transfer $750 million to $1 billion a year from Somalis abroad to families and businesses in their home country.

E-tailers have good prospects for tapping into the remittance market.

Sources: Nicole Raymond, Di Pinheiro, and Alejandro Bianchi, "Emigres Send Food Online to Old Country—Retailers Seek to Tap into Billions Repatriated by Latino Immigrants to the U.S.," *Wall Street Journal,* November 6, 2002, p. B3; and this textbook author's experience.

its international sales account for 38 percent of the company's total revenues.[38] Marketers are using consistent marketing communications worldwide, coordinating their advertising with direct mail brochures and catalogs.[39] Traditional **catalog retailers** are expanding internationally as well. Germany's Quelle, Neckermann, and Otto Versand are actively expanding their international operations; Otto Versand, for example, offers specialty goods to consumers in Europe, the United States, and Japan.

catalog retailers Retailers selling products through mail catalogs.

The potential for catalog sales remains high internationally and is greatly enhanced by the facilitations provided by the Internet. Germany has 22 million active Internet users[40] and is among the leading countries in terms of expenditures on direct mail goods and mail order sales. Consequently, prominent U.S. catalog retailers are active in this market; among them are Eddie Bauer and Lands' End, and others, such as industrial supplies cataloger New Pig and Carol Wright Gifts, which targets older females in middle-to-lower-income households.[41]

Catalog sales provide challenges to businesses not familiar with local practices. For example, catalog and Internet retailers found that consumers in Japan expect to first receive the product and only then pay for it. The key to success of catalog retailing is adaptation to local market needs and practices. U.S. personal planner cataloger Day-Timers mails its catalogs in North America, the United Kingdom, Australia, New Zealand, Central Asia, and Germany; for its German calendars, which are translated into German, the company made Monday, rather than Sunday, the first day of the week and increased the size of the planners to accommodate Germany's larger paper sizes. Although Germans are accustomed to buying from catalogs, they are not used to the privileges considered standard in the U.S. catalog industry, such as 24-hour service, liberal return policies, or even life-time guarantees from apparel catalogers. Such guarantees were unheard of in Germany, and a group of German retailers took Lands' End to court, accusing it of "unfair" competition (and lost).[42]

In developing countries, however, many obstacles affect catalog retailing. First and foremost, the infrastructure must be sufficiently developed to warrant investment; for catalog companies, it means that telephone service and mail service must be reliable. In many countries—even in emerging markets—consumers must often purchase cell phone service because standard telephone service is inadequate or is not available. In addition, the mailing system is lax and mail is often intercepted and opened, such that only a portion of a package's content may arrive at its destination. Finally, in many developing countries, average income is a fraction of the average income in developed countries; thus, products sold via catalog, such as clothing, appliances, housewares, etc., are prohibitively expensive.

Direct Selling

In the **direct selling** retail format, a salesperson, typically an independent distributor, contacts a consumer at a convenient location such as his or her home or workplace, demonstrates product use and benefits, takes orders, and delivers the merchandise. Direct selling is in the growth stage in most of the developing world; here, a number of impediments restrict firms' capability to successfully carry out their selling activity. Among these impediments are low per capita income, unreliable postal services, high levels of bureaucracy, lack of credit cards, few telephones, and a lack of mailing lists or access to mailing lists.

direct selling Selling that involves a salesperson, typically an independent distributor, contacting a consumer at a convenient location—at his or her home or workplace, demonstrating product use and benefits, taking orders, and delivering the merchandise.

Direct selling firms are most active in growth markets, such as the emerging economies of China and Southeast Asia, Central and Eastern Europe, and Latin America. American direct selling firms, such as Avon Products, Nu Skin, and Mary Kay Cosmetics, are very active in these markets, as well as worldwide. Avon, for example, earns more than half of its revenues from markets abroad, especially from developing countries.

In recent years, however, the negative publicity surrounding pyramid schemes has led to the development of legislation that does not favor this selling approach. China, for example, has a ban on direct selling. The ban does not apply to traditional forms of direct marketing such as direct mail, catalog marketing, telemarketing, or direct-response advertising. Rather, it reflects the Chinese government's concerns about the system of independent distributor networks, door-to-door sales, and motivational meetings, and the belief that criminals use these organizations to start secret societies, swindle consumers, seek exorbitant profits, sell smuggled or fake goods, and trick customers into buying unnecessary and expensive goods.[43]

It is unfortunate that this system of selling is closely associated with pyramid money schemes; this is especially the case with network marketing. Whereas pyramid schemes do nothing in terms of production and distribution, in network-based marketing, everyone is involved, bringing in the most profit to those who have created the distribution system.

Network Marketing

network marketing/multilevel marketing Using acquaintance networks through an alternative distribution structure for the purpose of distribution.

Network marketing, or **multilevel marketing,** is a variation on direct selling and an approach to selling at the same time. It involves signing up sales representatives to go into business for themselves with minimal start-up capital. Their task is to sell more "distributorships"—that is, to identify more sales representatives from their own personal network, to buy the product, and to persuade others to buy the product. Network marketing is experiencing rapid growth, especially in emerging markets. In South Africa, for example, the poor transportation infrastructure that presents a challenge to many multinationals does not present a problem to network marketing; this and the fit with elements of traditional African culture make network marketing one of the most significant avenues for growth within the post-apartheid economy.[44] Among the most successful network marketing firms that have international operations are Amway, Herbalife International, and Equinox International.

12-4 Issues in International Retailing

12-4a Legislation and Regulation

Country regulations differ from one market to another, and legislation can have a profound impact on a firm's operations. In the case of China's ban on direct selling, leading international firms are forced to rethink their marketing strategies and offer their goods using alternative methods to direct selling. Further, in many markets (including China), retail legislation and rules differ from province to province, as well as at the national level.[45] For example, regulations allow foreign retail joint ventures to operate in more cities throughout China and to engage in wholesaling for the first time; however, most rural areas are off-limits to international retailers.[46]

Other types of regulations restrict expansion of superstores and hypermarkets (United Kingdom, France, and Belgium); limit the hours of operation to protect smaller stores (the Netherlands, Spain); require that stores locate in downtown areas (Germany); control disposal of packaging used for transportation (Germany); limit the use of promotional pricing (France, Germany);[47] and limit the period for sales. French companies, for example, rarely offer an extra product free because the amount companies are allowed to give away is limited to 7 percent of the total value. In Germany, offering three products for the price of two or other bundling offers is illegal, and cash discounts to the consumer are limited to 3 percent.

Legislation has also created stores that limit access of local consumers. In addition to shops created for the use of different categories of consumers, such as diplomatic shops or shops for the military, different countries have shops that are open to all consumers except nationals. This is the case in countries where locals are not allowed access to hard currency, which must be channeled through the Central Bank, and where all hard currency retail transactions are conducted only with expatriates. The only advantage these stores offer is that they might carry select merchandise that is not readily available in the market; however, overall, the quality of the merchandise is not necessarily higher than that of goods in the open market.

12-4b Taxation and Cross-Border Shopping

In countries where consumers are not charged duties for products they purchase from a neighboring country (if the neighboring country belongs to the same free trade area, for example), **cross-border shopping** affects most retailers in the higher-tax countries. The United Kingdom, the Irish Republic, and Denmark charge much higher taxes than the rest of the European Union members. To avoid the large value-added tax on most products for personal consumption, consumers in these countries cross borders into countries where this tax is substantially lower. In this sense, consumers' purchase decisions are driven by tax differences rather than by underlying differences in producer prices, and cross-border shopping causes an inefficient allocation of resources, leading to significant reductions in sales by domestic retailers and manufacturers, reduced profits, and job losses.[48]

In other situations, retailers in neighboring countries suffer from the low taxes imposed by a tax haven nearby. Examples of consumer tax havens are Port Said in Egypt, and Bermuda or the Bahamas in North America, among others. In setting up retail operations overseas, a company must assess and seek the most favorable environment from the taxation perspective.

Alternatively, consumers may cross borders in search of quality, variety, and novelty, as in the case of Mexican consumers purchasing products at the Imperial Valley Mall in El Centro, California, located 10 miles north of the Mexican border. The mall targets about one million potential consumers living in Mexicali, Mexico.[49]

> **cross-border shopping** Purchasing products from a neighboring country where the consumers may be charged lower duties.

12-4c Variation in Retail Practices: A Consumer Perspective

Retail practices vary from one market to another. Consumers in the United States prefer to shop less frequently and purchase products in bulk, whereas consumers in Japan prefer to purchase products in smaller quantities, packaged individually. In Asia, store demonstrations are very popular, and, in Japan and Korea, Saturday is a major shopping day, when shopping and attending the respective demonstration are a family affair. Consumers in Asia and the United Kingdom prefer products of the highest quality and are willing to pay the price. In Argentina and Saudi Arabia, consumers prefer to purchase food products at mom-and-pop stores, rather than at the supermarket, whereas in Mexico consumers continue to go to farmers' markets for fresh produce. Even bugs on fruit are important to consumers in the Philippines; they indicate that the fruit is ripe. Finally, in the United Kingdom, store name is a better indicator of quality for food products than brand name; hence, private labels are thriving for very popular stores.[50]

12-4d Variation in Retail Practice: Salespeople and Management

Sales service differs greatly from one market to another. Whereas in the United States it is customary to have friendly salespeople waiting on customers, treating them with respect; in many other countries this is not always the case. In Eastern and Southeastern Europe, for example, salespeople tend to be curt, bordering on unfriendly. A Pizza Hut employee trained in customer service according to U.S. specifications sounds terribly out of place in Poland; in fact, the language used with customers appears to be unnatural. And in a typical situation, the telephone line of a Delta Airlines office in Bucharest sounds constantly busy; upon arriving at the respective office, one would note that two telephones are off the hook permanently, while the agents are drinking coffee with friends and neglecting consumers, who are casually waited on by one agent.

In other examples, in China, the sales staff tend to be overly conscientious: If a customer forgets to pick up the change after a sale is complete, the salesperson will most likely follow him or her into the street to return the change. In other countries, the situation is quite the contrary: Salespeople keep the change and sell only those products that are priced under an even amount so that they can claim they do not have the change if a customer dares challenge them. In countries where there may be shortages of certain products, salespeople are bribed with money and other goods such as coffee, cigarettes, and perfume.

Finally, certain stores charge an admission price to ensure that individuals permitted to enter can actually afford the products sold there (an example is an antique store selling what locally would be considered masterpieces or national treasures). In these stores, it is also appropriate for customers to dress well so that they do not look "suspect." Similarly, not dressing well in environments considered upscale locally (despite the fact that, in most of the world, the respective retail environment would be perceived as average at best) could easily result in denial of service.

Summary

- **Provide an overview and description of the general merchandise retailing category and offer examples and illustrations.** In the general merchandise retailing category are a number of retailers. Specialty stores, offering narrow assortments and deep product lines, are rapidly increasing their presence internationally. From The Gap to Mango to Marks & Spencer, retailers find success well beyond their national borders. Specialized markets, specializing in one product category, are omnipresent worldwide. Department stores are experiencing a decline, with some exceptions. Innovative stores that position themselves creatively have more success; in Asia, the more successful department stores are those that position themselves as European retailers. General merchandise discount stores are rapidly expanding, with great success. Wal-Mart, in particular, has made great strides in conquering international markets. Category specialists, specializing in one product category, are also very successful in their international pursuits. Off-price stores, a staple of U.S. retailing offering brand name products at lower prices, are in great demand in other countries. Recently, such retailers have made substantial inroads into markets in Asia and Europe. Catalog showrooms, selling high-turnover, brand name goods at discount prices, are also successful internationally, with many competing players. The Ikea "model" has been the most successful to date.

- **Provide an overview and description of the food retailing category and offer examples and illustrations.** Food retailers include conventional supermarkets, which are dominated by national and regional chains. Superstores can be combination stores (food and drug) or hypermarkets, which are very successful abroad but are slow to become mainstream retailers in the United States. Warehouse clubs are becoming very popular worldwide, and many U.S. retailers in this category are doing very well. Convenience stores abound in both developing and developed countries, with many chains developing in conjunction with gas stations.

- **Provide an overview and description of the nonstore retailing category and offer examples and illustrations.** Nonstore retailing is one of the areas with the highest growth and unlimited opportunities. Internet retailing has vastly expanded opportunities for small and medium-size retailers all over the world. Vending machines are increasing in sophistication and have different formats and capabilities in each market where they are available; the products they can carry also differ. Television home shopping is attracting more audiences, and today also offers opportunities to brick-and-mortar retailers to expand. Catalog retailers are still strong, expanding rapidly beyond their home-country borders. Direct selling and network marketing are gaining ground rapidly, especially in developing countries.

- **Address issues related to legislation, taxation, and retailing practices around the world.** Retailers have many restrictions imposed on them, and those restrictions vary from one market to another. The restrictions cover hours of operation, sales activity, and pricing techniques; or the restrictions may limit access to local consumers. Retailing practices vary from one market to another: Salespeople may be more courteous and solicitous in some countries, and consumers may be more demanding in certain markets, shop more or less frequently, and may or may not rely on a product's brand name as an indication of quality.

Key Terms

all-purpose discount stores
catalog retailers
catalog showrooms
category killers
category specialists
combination stores
convenience stores
conventional supermarkets
cross-border shopping
department stores

direct mail retailing
direct selling
electronic retailing
food retailers
general merchandise discount stores
hypermarkets
interactive home shopping
Internet retailing
multilevel marketing
network marketing

off-price retailers
specialized markets
specialty stores
superstores
television home shopping
vending machines
warehouse clubs
wholesale clubs

Discussion Questions

1. What is the difference between a specialty store and a category specialist?
2. Describe the state of the department store around the globe. What strategies appear to be more successful for department stores?
3. Hypermarkets are a dominant retailing format in Europe but not in the United States. What are hypermarkets? Give examples of successful hypermarkets worldwide.
4. Direct selling and network marketing have found great success in emerging markets. What is the difference between the two categories of retailers, and how do they gain access to consumers?
5. What are some of the challenges that retailers face in international markets?

Chapter Quiz (True/False)

1. General merchandise discount store retailers sell high volumes of merchandise and offer limited services; they also charge lower prices.
2. Factory outlet shops are an example of off-price retailers.
3. Internet purchasing is experience driven in developed countries.

Multiple Choice

1. The three main retail formats are
   a. general merchandise, food, and nonstore.
   b. automotive, food, and nonstore.
   c. general merchandise, automotive, and luxury.
   d. none of the above
2. Retailers that offer a narrow product line and a wide assortment—for example, office supply stores—are examples of
   a. specialized markets.
   b. specialty stores.
   c. department stores.
   d. all-purpose discount stores.
3. Harrods of London exemplifies which of the following retail formats?
   a. specialized markets
   b. all-purpose discount stores
   c. specialty stores
   d. department stores
4. Wal-Mart, Kmart, and Target are all examples of
   a. category specialists.
   b. specialized markets.
   c. all-purpose discount stores.
   d. specialty stores.
5. Food retailers include which of the following?
   a. superstores
   b. convenience stores
   c. warehouse clubs
   d. all of the above
6. Vending machines constitute a primary mode of retailing in
   a. the United States.
   b. the Netherlands.
   c. Japan.
   d. Canada.
7. What country has a ban on network marketing?
   a. New Zealand
   b. Germany
   c. Canada
   d. China

Endnotes

1. "Global Retailing in the Connected Economy," *Chain Store Age*, Vol. 5, No. 12, December 1999, pp. 69–82.
2. Alexandra Jardine, "Retailers Go on International Shopping Trip," *Marketing*, January 20, 2000, p. 15.
3. 2004 Wal-Mart Annual Report, http://www.walmartstores.com/Files/annualreport_2004.pdf.
4. Kerry Capell and Heidi Dawley, "Wal-Mart's Not-So-Secret British Weapon; It's Using Its Asda Unit for an All-Out Assault on Europe," *Business Week*, Industrial/Technology Edition, No. 3665, January 24, 2000, p. 132.
5. "European Consolidation," *Progressive Grocer*, Vol. 79, No. 1, January 2000, p. 22.

You can find the correct answers to these questions by taking the quiz and then submitting your answers in the Online Edition. The program will automatically score your submission. Where you miss a question, the program will provide the correct answer, a rationale for the answer, and the section number in the chapter where the topic is discussed.

6. For a discussion of these mergers, see Allyson L. Stewart Allen, "Ensure Success by Studying Europe's Lessons," *Marketing News*, Vol. 34, No. 4, February 14, 2000, p. 11; and "Global Retailing," *Chain Store Age*, pp. 69–82.

7. Brenda Sternquist, *International Retailing*, New York: Fairchild Publications, 1998.

8. "Mango Hires BBJ to Boost Brand in UK Stores Launch," *Marketing*, February 17, 2000, p.4.

9. See John S. Hill and Giles D'Souza, "Tapping the Emerging Americas Market," *The Journal of Business Strategy*, Vol. 19, No. 4, July/August 1998, pp. 8–11.

10. Sternquist, *International Retailing*, 1998.

11. www.alfayed.com/harrods/

12. Dana-Nicoleta Lascu, Jose Fernandez-Olano, and Thomas D. Giese, "Holiday Shopping: A Cross-Cultural Examination of Spanish and American Consumers," in R. King (ed.), *Proceedings of the Fourth Triennial AMS/ACRA National Retailing Conference*, 1994, pp. 147–149.

13. Insights into developments in Asian department store retailing from Sternquist, *International Retailing*, 1998.

14. Andrew Ness, "Retail Space to Let," *The China Business Review*, Vol. 26, No. 3, May/June 1999, pp. 44–49; and "China: Shanghai Retail Sector in Transition," *International Market Insight Reports*, July 26, 1999, pp. 1–4.

15. 2004 Wal-Mart Annual Report, http://www.walmartstores.com/Files/annualreport_2004.pdf.

16. Mike Troy, "Wal-Mart International Sets Goals at Vendor Conference," *Discount Store News*, Vol. 37, No. 6, March 23, 1998, pp. 3, 65.

17. http://www.staples.com/about/media/overview.asp

18. www.officedepot.com

19. Peter Landers, "Stores and Stripes," *Far Eastern Economic Review*, Vol. 161, No. 52, December 24, 1998, pp. 48–50.

20. "A Foothold in Europe's Heartland," *Discount Store News*, Supplement: "Wal-Mart: Retailer of the Century," October 1999, pp. 77, 175.

21. www.walmartstores.com

22. "A Foothold in Europe's Heartland," *Discount Store News*, pp. 77, 175.

23. David Benady, "Continental Shift," *Marketing Week*, Vol. 20, No. 28, October 9, 1997, pp. 52–55.

24. http://www.ahold.com/operatingcompanies/

25. "Business: French Fusion," *The Economist*, Vol. 352, No. 8135, September 4, 1999, pp. 61–62.

26. "A Partnership for the Long Haul," *Discount Store News*, Supplement: "Wal-Mart: Retailer of the Century," October 1999, pp. 85, 179.

27. "Loyalty Helps Drive Club Sales Gains," *Discount Store News*, Vol. 38, No. 15, August 9, 1999, p. 65; and "Costco Expands into Korea," *Discount Store News*, Vol. 37, No. 14, July 27, 1998, p. 54.

28. "A Partnership," *Discount Store News*, pp. 85, 179.

29. "Rio-to-Manila-to-Jakarta," *Communications News*, Vol. 35, No. 4, April 1998, p. 64.

30. www.pricesmart.com

31. Michael J. Mandel, "The Internet Economy: The World's Next Growth Engine," *Business Week*, Industrial/Technology Edition, No. 3649, October 4, 1999, pp. 72–77.

32. Lynda Radosevich, "Going Global Overnight," *InfoWorld*, Vol. 21, No. 16, April 19, 1999, pp. 1–3.

33. "Sticking to the Web," *Chain Store Age*, Vol. 74, No. 7, July 1998, pp. 153–155.

34. Haidee Allerton, "Vending Your Way," *Training & Development*, Vol. 50, No. 9, September 1996, p.72.

35. Dean Foust, "Doug Daft Isn't Sugarcoating Things; He's Already Shaking Up Coke. But Can He Bring Back the Fizz?" *Business Week*, Industrial/Technology Edition, No. 3667, February 7, 2000, p. 36.

36. "Harrods to Start Home Shopping Business," *Direct Marketing*, Vol. 61, No. 7, November 1998, p. 16.

37. William J. McDonald, "The Ban in China: How Direct Marketing Is Affected," *Direct Marketing*, Vol. 61, No. 2, June 1998, pp. 16–19.

38. 2003 Tiffany & Co. Annual Report, http://www.shareholder.com/tiffany/annual.cfm.

39. Sarah Lorge, "A Priceless Brand," *Sales and Marketing Management*, Vol. 150, No. 11, October 1998, pp. 102–111.

40. Nielsen Netratings, http://www.nielsen-netratings.com, March 8, 2003.

41. Shannon Oberdorf, "U.S. Mailers Blitz Germany," *Catalog Age*, Vol. 15, No. 2, February 1998, p. 2.

42. Ibid.

43. McDonald, "The Ban in China," pp. 16–19.

44. Adrian Sargeant and P. Msweli, "Network Marketing in South Africa: An Exploratory Study of Consumer Perception," *Journal of International Consumer Marketing*, Vol. 11, No. 3, 1999, pp. 51–66.

45. "China: The Grandest Opening Ever," *Chain Store Age*, Supplement: "Global Retailing," December 1997, pp. 32–35.

46. "China: Shanghai Retail Sector in Transition," *International Market Insight Reports*, July 26, 1999, pp. 1–4.

47. See Sternquist, *International Retailing*, 1998; and David Reed, "Country Practice," *Marketing Week*, Vol. 20, No. 4, July 3, 1997, pp. 45–49.

48. Ian Crawford and Sarah Tanner, "Bringing It All Back Home: Alcohol Taxation and Cross-Border Shopping, *Fiscal Studies*, Vol. 16, No. 2, May 1995, pp. 94–115.

49. Connie Robbins Gentry, "Border Malls," *Chain Store Age*, Vol. 80, No. 4, April 2004, p. 81.

50. Terry Hennessy, "International Flavors," *Progressive Grocer*, Vol. 78, No. 8, August 1999, pp. 67–73.

Case 12-1

Stefanel Canada

Jean Luc Rocher, formerly with a leading department store in Montreal, is contemplating opening a clothing specialty store with European flair that would appeal to the city's large middle class. In his many years with various specialty retailers and department stores, he noted the strong appeal of European stores to the local market.

Stylish department stores abound. Holt Renfrew, for instance, founded as a hat shop in Quebec City, is known for its many exclusive designers, branded lines, and its Holt Renfrew Private Brand collections. L'Aubainerie offers excellent product selections at competitive prices. Other popular department stores are La Baie and Hoda. In addition, numerous specialty clothing stores draw Canadian consumers and Montreal visitors alike: Gap, Benetton, Abercrombie & Fitch, and Canadian clothing shops are among many retailers present in the city.

Jean Luc knows that Montreal is a mature market for clothing stores but believes that there is sufficient demand for a clothing store that carries with it personality, as well as a history of success in Europe. Ever since his last visit to Europe, where he shopped at Stefanel, a clothing specialty store on Rue de Rennes, in Paris, and on Theatinerstrasse in Munich, Jean Luc has contemplated the idea of bringing the popular chain to Canada.

Stefanel started more than 40 years ago in Ponte di Piave, close to Venice, Italy, where Carlo Stefanel produced knitwear in his factory, the "Maglificio Piave." At first, the company sold its products through Italian wholesalers. In the 1970s, the company diversified to offer sportswear, jeanswear, and prêt-a-porter collections, selling the merchandise in modern, stylish retail outlets. The company continues to produce knitwear, which is its core business, in a plant in Salgareda, Italy. In 2000, Stefanel further expanded into Germany in a take-over of Hallhuber GMBH, a clothing retail chain in Munich, and it has a 50 percent stake in Nuance, the leader in airport retailing.

The company's brand is well known in much of Europe: Its stores in many Western European countries are located centrally, in the main downtown shopping centers. They are stylish and have daring ads. Joakim Jonason, the talent behind the provocative Diesel jeans advertisements, is now in charge of the Stefanel advertising account at MADE, a Leo Burnett company. An ad aimed at movie audiences in Europe opens at dawn at the Boom Boom Circus, where the daughter of the dwarf ringmaster has just spent the night with the bearded lady's husband, resulting in chaos, until the husband wakes up from his dream. The tagline used is "Stefanel. Now you wake up." Stefanel uses "Now" in all its ads, on shopping bags and on its website.

Stefanel also has several stores in the Far East—Hong Kong, South Korea, Taiwan, and Thailand—and in the Middle East—Kuwait and the United Arab Emirates. It is currently solidifying an expansion in the former Eastern Bloc, into Croatia, the Czech Republic, Slovakia, Slovenia, Romania, and Russia. In the Americas, Stefanel is present only in Los Angeles and Chicago in the United States; in Hamilton, Bermuda; and in Santiago de Chile. A retail franchise in Canada may be attractive to the company and appeal to Canadian consumers as smart, casual clothing with European flair.

Jean Luc Rocher is presently consulting with investors to evaluate the likelihood of success of a Stefanel retail outlet in Montreal. He learned that Stefanel has important and costly requirements for new franchises. For example, the stores must be located on the main commercial streets of cities with a population of at least 50,000; they should have a surface area between 120 and 250 square meters, and numerous wide store windows. The franchise is permitted to use only Stefanel's furnishings that distinguish the store from those of other companies. Stefanel would provide the franchisee with architects free of charge; with training seminars for the store's personnel; and with shop-window designs, posters, and images. Stefanel will lease software for sales and inventory analysis and the appropriate hardware to ensure appropriate coordination and profitability. Although the company protects franchises in the sense that it limits same-store competition, Stefanel has just partnered with Pino Venture to pursue Internet shoppers.

Jean Luc's questions include: What would be the appropriate expansion strategy into the Canadian market? Would his Montreal store be the first leg in the company's international expansion into Canada? Would Stefanel sell other franchises to competitors? To what extent will Internet sales cannibalize Jean Luc's brick-and-mortar operation? How should he most effectively sell the Stefanel franchise to his investor friends?

Sources: http://www.holtrenfrew.com; http://www.hbc.com/bay; http://www.stefanel.it/; Laure Wentz, "The World," *Advertising Age*, Vol. 73, No. 37, September 16, 2002, p. 14.

Analysis Suggestions

1. Identify the retail category of Stefanel.
2. What are some of its competitors worldwide? How is Stefanel different from its competitors?
3. What is the company's international expansion strategy? How does Jean Luc Rocher's proposal fit into the company's expansion plans?

13

The International Promotional Mix and Advertising Strategies

Chapter Objectives

By the end of this chapter, you should be able to

1 Describe the international promotional mix and the international communication process.

2 Explore the international advertising formats and practices around the world.

3 Describe the international advertising and media infrastructure and infrastructure-related challenges in different markets.

4 Describe advertising strategies and budgeting decisions and offer examples of international applications.

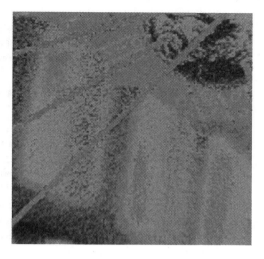

P romotion and, as an element of promotion, advertising are omnipresent in all countries of the world. From billboards on national monuments in China to little lit boats advertising shoes on the Bosphorus, to Ronald McDonald hanging his two-floor-long legs in a town square or leading a local wedding ceremony in Poland, promotion today permeates life everywhere. Promotion has become part of the world landscape, framing highways, lighting crowded downtowns, projecting glamour on walls of slums, and shading street cafés. It reaches consumers on their doorsteps, in mail or email, and via blasting stereos or drumbeats.

This chapter discusses the international promotional mix and the international communication process. Of the mix items, the chapter focuses on advertising and illustrates advertising formats, practices, and infrastructure-related issues around the world.

13-1 The International Promotional Mix

The components of the **international promotional mix** are international advertising, international salesforce management, international sales promotion, and public relations and publicity (see Figure 13-1). Companies use the promotional mix to communicate with international consumers about their products and services. In the process of expanding internationally, companies are faced with numerous challenges to their plans for communicating with the world's consumers. Many of the challenges are attributed to differences in culture. As described in Chapter 5, "Cultural Influences on International Marketing," understanding the norms, motivations, attitudes, interests, and opinions of the target market is crucial to company success in marketing to and communicating with different cultures around the globe. Companies also must be prepared to handle the challenges presented by the local media, by the local advertising infrastructure, and by the different layers of government regulating all aspects of communication with the target market.

international promotional mix The different modes of communication with international consumers about products and services, using international advertising, international salesforce management, international sales promotion, public relations, and publicity.

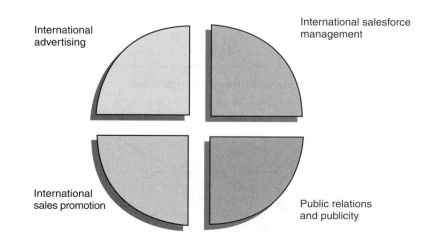

International advertising

International salesforce management

International sales promotion

Public relations and publicity

F i g u r e 1 3 - 1
The International Promotional Mix

international communication process The communication process that takes place between the product sponsor and the international target market.

sender The sponsor of an advertisement, usually represented by an advertising agency, who encodes the message into words and images and communicates it to the target market.

channel of communication The medium used to communicate a message about a product to the consumer.

medium/media The channel(s) of communication that a company uses to send to the target consumer a message about its product or services.

receiver The target market that receives the advertising message from a sender.

nonpersonal medium A channel of communication such as a print medium, a broadcast medium, or an interactive medium that does not involve contact between the seller and the consumer.

Section 13-2 describes the international communication process, and Section 13-3 presents the topic of international advertising. Chapters 14, "International Publicity, Public Relations, and Sales Promotion Strategies," and 15, "International Personal Selling and Personnel Management," will address the remaining elements of the international promotional mix: salesforce management and the expatriate salesforce, international sales promotion, international public relations, and international publicity, completing the topic of the international promotional mix.

13-2 The International Communication Process

The **international communication process** involves using the entire promotional mix to communicate with the final consumer (see Figure 13-2). Regardless of the elements of the promotional mix involved, the communication essentially has the same format. The international sponsor (**sender**), usually represented by an advertising agency, encodes a message into words and images. The message is then translated into the language of the target market and transmitted through a **channel of communication,** or **medium,** to the international consumer in the target market (**receiver**). The medium may be a **nonpersonal medium:**

● A **print medium,** such as a newspaper, magazine, billboard, pamphlet, a point-of-purchase display
● A **broadcast medium,** such as television and radio
● An **interactive medium,** such as a web page or a computer terminal on the retailer's premises

Alternatively, the channel may be a **personal medium:**

● A salesperson calling on a supplier or a door-to-door salesperson calling on consumers
● A telemarketer calling on consumers (**telemarketing**)
● A trade show, where one can address questions to an individual who is knowledgeable about the product

The international consumer (receiver) receives the message and decodes it into meaning. Ideally, the meaning of the decoded message should be identical to the meaning of the encoded message. However, **noise**—all the potential interference in the com-

Figure 13-2
The International Communication Process

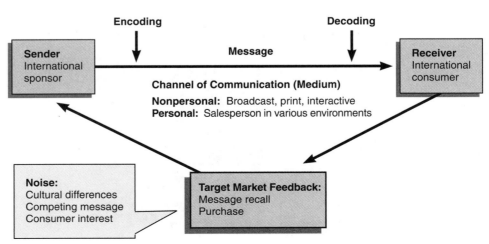

The International Communication Process

Encoding   Decoding

Sender International sponsor   **Message**   **Receiver** International consumer

Channel of Communication (Medium)
Nonpersonal: Broadcast, print, interactive
Personal: Salesperson in various environments

Noise:
Cultural differences
Competing message
Consumer interest

Target Market Feedback:
Message recall
Purchase

munication process, particularly noise attributed to cultural differences—may impede communication. During the message transmission and delivery processes, noise may interfere with proper message reception. The sponsor (sender) collects and relies on information regarding the effectiveness of the message (**feedback**) to evaluate the success of the promotional campaign; such information may be provided by sales data or by advertising research evaluating message recall rates.

Each step of the international communication process presents challenges to the message sponsor beyond those encountered when marketing to home-country consumers. First, when **encoding** the message, the source determines whether the attitudes, interests, and motivations of consumers in the international target market are different from those in the home-country target market. Manufacturers of Peugeot bicycles in France selling their product in Germany and the United States need to be aware that consumer motivations behind the purchase differ. In Germany, the main purpose of using the Peugeot bicycle is transportation. Major cities have bicycle paths on the sidewalks, and pedestrians and automobiles are not allowed to block them; bicycle paths also have their own signals at intersections. In the countryside, paths, in parallel with the main roads or highways, are reserved for bicycles. A German consumer who purchases a Peugeot bicycle will want a product that is reliable and can perform optimally, regardless of weather. Communication about the product, then, should stress durability, reliability, and quality. In the United States, a Peugeot bicycle is used primarily for recreation. Communication about the product is more likely to be successful if it focuses on a weekend recreational activity and/or on performance.

Similarly, Pizza Hut in the United States and the United Kingdom is a staple family restaurant for busy families who do not have time to cook. Pizza Hut advertising focuses on deals for the entire family. In Poland, Pizza Hut is the in-place for a techno-music dinner before consumers descend to the downstairs disco in Wroclaw, and the place for a business lunch in Warsaw's prestigious Marriott building, located strategically between stores selling haute couture. Consequently, communication about Pizza Hut in Poland should not limit itself to a family focus.

When encoding the message, one must ensure that the message is appropriately translated. In the process of translating the message, one should note that language is closely related to advertising strategy. For example, English requires less space in print and less air time for broadcast advertising (this is one of the reasons it is widely used in advertising). Translated into German, the headline, body copy, and tag line require more space for a print advertisement and more air time for a broadcast ad.

From product name to the entire marketing communication, all must be monitored to ensure that the meanings intended are the meanings conveyed. There is an explosion of naming consultancies, set up as offshoots of advertising agencies, which develop product names that are intended to work worldwide; because consumers travel everywhere, it is important that brand names are consistent in any country where they are sold.[1] From names such as Vauxhall's Nova automobile, meaning "no go" in Spanish, to airlines claiming that one will fly "naked" (as opposed to "on leather") in first class, companies have made many mistakes when communicating with international consumers.

Sending the message through the appropriate channel is frequently a challenge; the media infrastructure might be such that the most appropriate medium cannot be successfully used. In countries where mail is less reliable, such as India and Romania, it is advisable not to send direct mail containing samples. In other countries where the mailing system is reliable, such as Saudi Arabia, mail might not constitute a traditional medium for sending samples, and a direct mail package might be perceived as suspicious. In Rwanda and Burundi, the only broadcast medium available is the radio; however, international brands are rarely advertised on this medium. To reach the mass market in these two countries, the only appropriate communication medium is the billboard. Furthermore, it is preferable that the advertisement has few words and relies on pictorials to convey the message because many target consumers are illiterate.

All this competition, including other noise, such as audience inattention, from other channels of communication and from programming could negatively affect the **decoding**

print medium A nonpersonal channel of communication such as a newspaper, magazine, billboard, pamphlet, or point-of-purchase display.

broadcast medium A nonpersonal channel of communication such as television or radio.

interactive medium A nonpersonal channel of communication such as a web page or a computer terminal on the retailer's premises.

personal medium A communication channel that involves contact between the seller and the consumer.

telemarketing A personal channel of communication that involves a salesperson calling on consumers.

noise All the potential interference in the communication process.

feedback Information regarding the effectiveness of a company's message.

encoding The process whereby the advertiser puts the company's message about the product into words and images that are aimed at the target consumer.

decoding The process whereby the target consumer receives the message from the advertiser and translates it into meaningful information.

process, such that the target consumer does not fully comprehend the communication. To lessen the impact of these communication impediments, companies do the following:

- Hire research firms to evaluate the message in multiple international environments.
- Evaluate the effectiveness of the communication in attracting target market attention, using recall tests and other memory-based procedures.
- Evaluate the effectiveness of the communication in getting consumers to purchase the product.

The company then uses this feedback in modifying or designing future communication strategies.

13-3 Advertising

International advertising is becoming increasingly complex; more and more local and international companies are competing for consumers who are increasingly sophisticated and demanding. International advertising is defined as *a nonpersonal communication by an identified sponsor across international borders, using broadcast, print, and/or interactive media.*

13-3a The Media Infrastructure

media infrastructure The media vehicles and their structure in an international target market.

The **media infrastructure** provides different challenges in countries of different levels of economic development. And, even though the media structure is essentially the same in most industrialized countries, challenges still arise in terms of business practices: A medium might not be considered appropriate for advertising. For example, newspapers might not constitute the right medium for advertising a particular product in one country, whereas, in other countries, advertising a particular type of product or service might be restricted or prohibited in other media—for instance, television. Alternatively, advertising may not be very well regarded in the country where the company is launching an advertising campaign; see International Marketing Illustration 13-1.

Media Challenges

Some of the challenges firms encounter on the media front are availability, reliability, restrictions, and costs.

Media Availability

media availability The extent to which media are available to communicate with target consumers.

An important issue facing the international marketing manager is **media availability,** the extent to which the media needed for a particular communication exist locally, or if they do exist, how they can be used as intended for the company communication. Certain types of media simply might not be available in a company's target markets. In many countries in Sub-Saharan Africa, for example, there are no television stations. Alternatively, there may be one or two government-owned and/or government-controlled stations that do not permit advertising or that limit advertising to certain times. Although some television owners might have access to international satellite and cable television, especially in the emerging markets in Asia and Latin America, many more cannot afford a satellite dish or a subscription to cable television. Access to these consumers, then, is limited. And, even though more and more consumers have access to Internet advertising worldwide, such access primarily favors consumers from more developed countries, or wealthy consumers and government employees from developing countries.

Media Reliability

media reliability The probability of the media to air advertising messages on time, at an acceptable quality, and with the agreed-upon frequency.

Media reliability, the extent to which the existing media reliably reach the target consumer in the intended format and within the intended time frame, is also an important consideration. In some cases, media may be unreliable. Magazine or newspaper issues might not be printed on time, or publishers might accept more advertisements than they

International Marketing Illustration 13-1

The Status of Advertising in Germany

Germany's advertising market is the third largest in the world, behind the United States and Japan. Yet, a slow economy and modest consumer spending are negatively affecting the ad market. Moreover, German companies hold advertising in low regard: There, business strengths are linked to technical talent rather than to marketing talent. And German ad executives are not very keen on using approaches popular in the rest of the world—for example, they rarely use humor in advertising.

When the economy does not perform very well, the first to go are advertising expenditures. Companies could go without advertising for several months. Referring to Table 13-2 on page 313, note that, for the years 2002 and 2003, Germany's advertising expenditures decreased, with a modest recovery (2.5 percent growth) in 2004.

As a result, ad agencies had to change their management styles. For example, executives at Leo Burnett in Frankfurt started becoming more involved in the agency's daily business, participating in all client meetings and even attending focus groups, to express their commitment to their clients. Also, the advertising companies have become more selective about the accounts they take on instead of going after every potential business.

Sources: Erin White, "For Germany's Ad Agencies, Recovery Is Distant Prospect, *Wall Street Journal*, August 14, 2002, p. B5; Erin White and Shirley Leung, "How Tiny German Shop Landed McDonald's," *Wall Street Journal*, August 6, 2003, p. B1; Robert J. Coen, *Universal McCann's Insider Report*, December 8, 2003, www.universalmccann.com.

can print. The quality of the medium itself may be questionable. Local newspapers might not be of a high enough quality to print advertising for a global brand. Television stations might go off the air indefinitely at inopportune times, when a company's advertisement is scheduled to air. This often happens to small television stations that compete with government stations for viewers' attention.

Media Restrictions

Media restrictions refer to the different limitations that existing media pose on the sponsor. For example, the media could limit the types and number of advertisements aired or published. As mentioned in Chapter 5, "Cultural Influences on International Marketing," advertising in a number of Islamic countries might not permit the portrayal of women, whereas in other countries (China, for instance) the media do not readily encourage the advertising of feminine hygiene products. Air time might be limited; for example, the European Union allows only 12 minutes per hour for advertising on each television station.

> **media restrictions** Legal or self-imposed restrictions on the types and the number of advertisements aired or published.

Advertising also might be clustered and separated from editorial content, for newspapers or magazines, or from television programming. Many television stations in Europe, as well as in South America (Brazil, for instance), broadcast television advertising only between programs, in clusters. Consumers typically choose to engage in other activities in the home during that time. In these countries, a better venue for firms that need to send their message using visuals in broadcast media is movie advertising; cinema advertisements are typically shown before films to a captive audience. In many developing countries where the literacy rate is low, advertising is primarily limited to billboards that do not display words other than the company logo and brand name.

Media scheduling also constitutes a restriction. Lag times between the submission of the advertisement and printing could reach as much as one year for some publications, primarily due to space restrictions allotted to advertising. Also, a contract that requires a publication or a television station to print or air an advertisement on a particular date is not backed by guarantees in many countries.

Media Costs

Media costs differ greatly between countries, and even within a particular country. Factors that account for this difference range from income per capita of target market and competition for media by advertisers, to firm status (a local firm is charged less than an international firm in Eastern European countries, China, Cuba, and Vietnam).

Costs are high in countries where the advertising campaign must be translated into multiple languages. India is an interesting case in point. A campaign aimed at a more educated consumer can be communicated effectively in either Hindi or English. To reach the masses in Southern India and penetrate this target market, however, translating the advertisements into Malealam, Tamil, and Telegu would be important.

Media Formats, Features, and Trends around the World

Advertising Posters on Kiosks and Fences

Advertising posters appear on kiosks and fences in the United States to a more limited extent than in much of the rest of the world. In the United States, some kiosks display neighborhood announcements, and construction fences in larger cities display advertisements for plays, concerts, and art exhibits. In much of the rest of the world, especially in developing countries, kiosks display advertisements for the international products they sell. Kiosks are valuable and relatively inexpensive communication venues for multinationals: They are typically required to have posters displayed in exchange for having the rights to carry particular brands. Fences and other display structures are omnipresent in international capitals and small towns alike (see Figure 13-3). In France, the *affichiste* movement of modern art, whose works are displayed in major museums worldwide, used layers of posters that had been displayed for decades and then torn off walls and placed on canvas.

Advertising on the Sides of Private Homes

Typically located in high traffic areas, homes from Bangladesh to Bulgaria display advertising for international brands. This advertising constitutes a substantial source of revenue for the homeowners.

Figure 13-3

Kiosks are omnipresent in downtown capital cities and in remote village locations alike.

Advertising on Plastic Shopping Bags

Although retailers and manufacturers often display their brand names on shopping bags, another phenomenon is quickly spreading in developing countries: the use of bags (that consumers actually have to pay for!) to advertise popular television programs. The individual portrayed in Figure 13-4 sells shopping bags with characters from the U.S. soap operas *Dynasty* and *Dallas*, among others, in a Bucharest market.

Advertising on Outdoor Umbrellas

In the United States, outdoor umbrellas, if they contain any information at all, typically display the name of the restaurant where they are located. In other locations worldwide, umbrellas display international brand names, such as Marlboro, Coca-Cola, Pepsi, and others (see Figure 13-5).

F i g u r e   1 3 - 4
Sue Ellen and J. R. Ewing of the *Dallas* television series are popular in Eastern Europe, and shopping bags sporting their pictures are still considered fashionable.

F i g u r e   1 3 - 5
Outdoor umbrellas are practical and prominent modes of communication with consumers worldwide.

The Omnipresent Billboards

Although **billboards** are quite common in the United States, in other parts of the world they dominate the landscape. Elegant advertisements for Coca-Cola in Russia and for the same brand under the railway in Portugal, ads for Camel cigarettes on top of a building in Greece and in a pedestrian mall in Spain, and a Pepsi ad at a bus station urging "don't go without it"—all are examples of such advertising (see Figure 13-6). An especially interesting development is the fact that, increasingly, local ads are of comparable quality and compete effectively with ads of multinational firms. This new development is attributed to the proliferation of computer technology and lower technology costs.

Public services use billboards extensively as well. Figure 13-7 illustrates a public service advertisement for train service replacing a retailer advertisement in a train station in Southern Germany.

The Dominance of Global Media

Late-night talk show host Jay Leno's jokes are a staple around the world, as are Conan O'Brian's. CNN and Bloomberg broadcast all over the world, including in Sub-Saharan Africa. CNN is a popular television station in Ethiopia for those who can afford a television set; in fact, Addis Ababa, its capital city, often has a more accurate forecast of the next day's weather in Hong Kong from the CNN satellite than for drought-prone regions in Ethiopia itself.[2] European television stations have competitors such as CNN Europe, Sky, and NBC. Asian stations compete with global companies such as CNN, MTV, NBC,

Figure 13-6
Billboards appeal to consumers across economic strata, regardless of level of literacy.

(a)

(b)

Figure 13-7
Public service and sponsored billboards are common in train stations.

Turner Broadcasting, Walt Disney/Capital Cities ABC, and the Cartoon Channel. ESPN Asia broadcasts American basketball in the Philippines and baseball in Taiwan, and millions of Chinese viewers watch badminton and U.S. National Basketball Association games.[3] Rupert Murdoch alone owns Star Plus, Star Plus Japan, Star Chinese Channel, and Star Movies in Asia, and has, among other media interests, resonant media companies such as Fox Broadcasting, 20th Century Fox, 20th Century Television, as well as investments in BskyB, Vox Channel, El Canal Fox, Australia's Channel 7, and 130 newspapers worldwide. All these stations can sell international brands to consumers all over the world.

Magazines such as *Glamour, Cosmopolitan,* and *Mademoiselle* are published in languages ranging from Mandarin to Italian to Polish to Japanese. These magazines are vehicles for global, regional, and local advertising campaigns of multinational companies.

Infomercials and Television Shopping Networks

Infomercials and **television shopping networks** once were a North American phenomenon. Currently, infomercials and television shopping channels exist in much of the industrialized world and in many emerging markets. Not only have QVC and the Home Shopping Network expanded in Europe, Latin America, and Asia, but also local competition is growing rapidly. Home Order Television in Germany has created a strategic alliance with Quelle, the catalog store discussed in Chapter 12, "International Retailing," selling its products to television shoppers.

English in Local Advertising

Section 13-2, "The International Communication Process," stressed some of the benefits of using English for advertising. Other reasons for using English, particularly in advertising by local firms to local consumers, are to stress a cosmopolitan attitude and to endow a product or service with status. Words such as "very quick" are used in advertising for a tire inflation service (*vulcanizacion*) in Ecuador and "super wonderful" to describe the travel bags sold by a company in Poland. This is true also for product and service brand names—for example, the Romanian-American University, American Gold for a brand of gold-plated jewelry—when the products or services really have nothing to do with the

infomercials Long television advertisements (one-half to one full hour in length) that are positioned as programming.

television shopping networks Cable channels that sell products to a television audience.

Figure 13-8

Use of English in Germany, appealing to German consumers: "Highspeed zu Lowcost" Internet service.

United States, Canada, or Mexico. Figures 13-8 through 13-11 show some examples of advertisements using English in non-English–speaking countries, aimed at local consumers. Also, they show some examples of English names for retail establishments in non-English–speaking countries.

Product Placement

product placement The strategy of placing brands in movies with the purpose of promoting the products to viewers.

Product placement involves placing brands in movies with the purpose of promoting the products to viewers. Studies have found that product placement can produce a greater level of advertising recall than television advertising.[4] Year after year, films exported by the United States have swept the globe. In 1999, in spite of economic difficulties in Asia and Latin America, U.S. movies' box-office receipts were up by 17 percent, and, according to *Variety Magazine,* of 1998's most successful movies, U.S. films took the top 39 places.[5] As a result of the world dominance of Hollywood films, product placement is likely to be a venue providing high exposure for international brands.

Advertising Regulations

Advertisers encounter numerous restrictions in their efforts to deliver communication to consumers worldwide. Most regulations are imposed by national (host-country) governments. Alternatively, local firms have established traditions and self-imposed regulations that must be observed by newcomers to the local advertising scene. Among advertising restrictions are the following:

- *Comparative advertising*—The United Kingdom and Ireland have rules that appear similar to those of the United States, allowing for truthful comparative advertising that is not confusing or falsely disparaging. By contrast, continental Europe con-

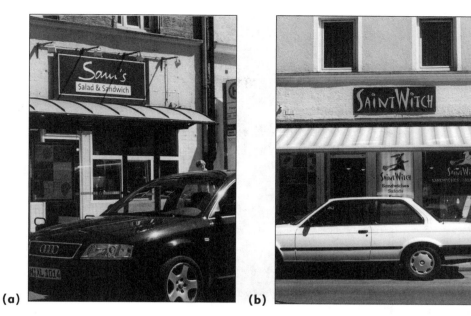

(a)   **(b)**

Figures 13-9
Sam's Salad & Sandwich (a) and
Saint Witch (b) in Munich—all
their point-of-purchase
advertising and other
communication are in English.

Figure 13-10
German Retailer, English
Communications

demns comparative advertising as denigration (comments, whether true or false, that are unduly negative), unfair competition, or unauthorized use of trademarks; therefore, for most of Europe, comparative advertising is unfair advertising.[6] In addition, the Benelux (Belgium, the Netherlands, and Luxembourg) Uniform Trademark Act forbids using another's trademark in advertising. Germany also prohibits denigrating advertising, such as Avis's "We try harder," but it allows truthful comparisons that are not negative ("as good as").[7]

- *Advertising to children*—The European Union Directive Concerning Television Broadcasting does not permit advertising that directly exhorts minors to buy a product or a service, that directly encourages minors to persuade their parents to purchase the goods advertised, that exploits the trust minors place in adults, or that shows minors in dangerous situations. Local law restricts advertising to children further: French law limits the use of children as endorsers in advertising and prohibits the use of children's heroes as endorsers.[8]

Figure 13-11

Yes Natural Mineral Water for Consumers in Bangladesh
Courtesy of Farheen Khurrum; used with permission.

- *Advertising vice products*—The European Union Directive Concerning Television Broadcasting prohibits television advertising for tobacco products and prescription drugs.[9]
- *Other regulations*—The French have regulations requiring advertisers (and all broadcasters) to keep the language pure, and not to use English terms or anglicized French terms (Franglais). Singapore does not permit advertising that is sexual in nature; the use of sex in advertising is also banned in most Islamic countries. Other challenges are posed by the need to copyright the advertising message in different languages in countries where multiple languages are spoken.

13-3b The Advertising Infrastructure

Advertising Agencies

The approach to advertising varies from one company to another, and the strategies used by different companies are numerous. Advertising decisions may be determined based on the product strategy. In one example, Henkel, a leading German manufacturer of household and cleaning products, uses a pan-European approach to advertising. The company attempts to achieve efficiency in advertising production and advertising impact by identifying how a particular product addresses target market needs (for consumers in Europe or a larger area); by assigning that specific need or benefit to one product with one brand name; by assigning that brand to one brand manager and to one advertising agency to develop and market; and by not permitting the use of that individual brand's benefit, name, or creative campaign for any other brand in the company.[10] This strategy results in the use of multiple advertising agencies, depending on the brand involved. Alternatively, the choice of the advertising agency in international markets may be based on a long-standing relationship with a particular agency in the home market; an advertising agency could follow a leading global brand anywhere in the world. This is the case of McCann Erickson, the advertising agency that has been handling the Coca-Cola account in 60 countries since 1942.[11]

A company can approach its international advertising strategy using one or more of the following options: developing local ads for the international markets in-house; developing ads using local advertising agencies, home-country agencies, or international advertising agencies with local offices; or using a combination strategy. The home-country agency and the in-house options by themselves are not likely to allow for local participation if they are located away from the target market.

The most common types of relationships between international corporations and the agencies providing advertising support are as follows:

- Hiring local advertising agencies
- Hiring international advertising agencies
- Hiring local advertising agencies to implement international agency messages

Hiring Local Advertising Agencies

A company that uses a localized strategy, targeting each individual market, is more likely to hire a local advertising agency. Hiring a local advertising agency is appropriate, especially when knowledge of the market is important. The Swedish furniture company Ikea, for example, engaged in a branding campaign aimed at the San Diego market. The company left it up to the San Diego Ikea franchise to hire a firm to build the Ikea brand in the San Diego market; it hired AM Advertising, a Los Angeles firm boasting top local talent.[12]

In a relatively uniform market, such as the Latin American market, advertisers often use Spanish and Portuguese to communicate with consumers. When a company advertises to the 25 countries of Latin America and the Caribbean, however, it is preferable to translate into each country's regional dialect to avoid presenting the company as an outsider.[13] A local agency could better design the campaign for each individual market. In addition to its knowledge of the local market, a local agency also offers the advantage of being capable of facilitating interaction with local media and government.

On the negative side, the quality of advertising is not at the level offered by a large international advertising agency. With the proliferation of technology, local companies, even in developing countries, are increasingly able to provide higher quality graphics, comparable to those produced by larger international advertisers. Nevertheless, if a company decides to hire local advertising agencies, it will not be able to coordinate a global, standardized advertising campaign.

Hiring International Advertising Agencies

In general, if a company uses a standardized (global) strategy for its products or services, it is more likely to use an international agency with local offices that can manage advertising in the respective markets. Most of the leading advertising agencies have branches in important international markets. In Eastern Europe, companies such as Saatchi & Saatchi, Leo Burnett, Young and Rubicam, and Ogilvy & Mather are represented in practically every capital city. Other companies select primarily markets of interest to their clients. For example, J. Walter Thompson is present as J. Walter Thompson/ARK Communications in Prague, the Czech Republic; as Partners J. Walter Thompson Budapest in Hungary; and as Scala JWT Advertising in Bucharest, Romania.

The five leading international advertising agencies or agency groups in terms of worldwide gross income are the Omnicom Group (U.S.), the Interpublic Group (U.S.), the WPP Group (U.K.), Dentsu, Inc. (Japan), and Young & Rubicam (U.S.). In fact, more than half of the top 50 advertising agencies are from the United States.[14]

International advertising agencies benefit from access to the parent company's experience and talent, as well as technology and research capabilities. They also can take advantage of local representatives' expertise and relationships with the media and government. Increasingly, international advertising agencies are present with more than one type of agency in important markets. For example, Rapp Collins Worldwide, the third largest marketing services agency by non-U.S. revenue, opened an office of its interactive arm, Rapp Digital, in Brazil; because Latin America is advanced from the point of view of technology, the market has high potential for interactive services.[15] Grey Global Group is present in Europe with, among others, Grey Direct, its direct marketing arm; Grey Desire, a London-based customer relationship management consultancy for Europe;[16] Grey Interactive, GCI (one of the largest public relations firms in the world); and Grey Worldwide, the company's advertising arm.

Hiring Local Advertising Agencies to Implement International Agency Messages

Hiring an international advertising agency with local offices does not preclude the use of local advertising agencies. For example, although Coca-Cola uses the Interpublic Group (primarily McCann Erickson) to design its message for advertising worldwide, it also encourages each country office to appoint local agencies to implement the brand message devised by Interpublic; in fact, Interpublic generates ideas at a global level, which are then translated by local marketers as part of Coke's "think global, act local" strategy.[17] International Marketing Illustration 13-2 offers insights into the agency choice of one of the corporate sponsors of advertisements, McDonald's.

13-3c The Advertising Strategy

Standardization Versus Adaptation in Creating Message Strategies

One of the most important decisions of firms designing their international promotional mix is whether to standardize (globalize) their promotional strategy (**standardization of the advertising strategy**), to adapt their promotional mix to each country or market (**adaptation of the advertising strategy**), or to create local campaigns. Practitioners are divided on this issue. Sponsors, as well as advertising agencies, agree that using a standardized strategy worldwide presents substantial advantages. This is most obvious from a cost perspective: Costs will be reduced considerably if companies do not need to duplicate the creative effort and the resultant communication campaign in each market. In addition, as product life cycles shrink, companies are pressured to accelerate worldwide rollout of new products; developing communication strategies for each market would delay launch.[18] Moreover, world consumers are developing common product preferences and increasingly share similar frames of references with regard to products and consumption, as they are more and more exposed to the same sources of influence (broadcast and print media, in particular, as well as blockbuster films and tourists, among others).

Advertising executives often use a standardized communication approach due to pressure from clients, especially in cases in which the companies do not have a high degree of control over international operations, or where the quality and availability of local resources are in question.[19] Nevertheless, there are some country-specific preferences: Canadian firms have a predilection for standardization or, rather, transferring the campaign; whereas German and Japanese firms are more likely to adapt campaigns locally, and firms from the United States and the United Kingdom are more likely to develop campaigns locally.[20]

Differences between countries, however, might render standardization a challenge, or even impossible. The following are barriers to advertising standardization:

- The communication infrastructure is one barrier: A particular medium might be inappropriate or not available for advertising.
- International advertising agencies might not serve a particular market.
- Consumer literacy level constitutes another major barrier: Consumers might not be able to read the body copy of the advertisement, so the information conveyed to the consumer should be visual.
- Legal restrictions and industry self-regulation might also impede standardization: Comparative advertising is not permitted in many countries, whereas, in others—Korea, for example—Confucianism forbids the public criticism of others.[21]
- Values and purchase motivations differ across countries and cultures, as illustrated in Chapter 5, "Cultural Influences on International Marketing." Targeting consumers with a campaign that stresses the good life, exemplified by driving a luxury car and having a blonde on one's side, might be inappropriate in countries where consumers are living a subsistence existence and just as improper in highly developed, cultured environments. Consumers from collectivist cultures will also question the values suggested by such ads. The decision of whether to standardize is most often contin-

standardization of the advertising strategy The process of globalizing a company's promotional strategy so that it is uniform in all its target markets.

adaptation of the advertising strategy The act of changing a company's promotional mix to each country or market, or creating local campaigns.

International Marketing Illustration 13-2

The Giant Sponsor and the Small Advertising Boutique: An Unlikely Pairing for a Global Advertising Campaign

McDonald's surprised the agency world by selecting a small advertising agency to lead its worldwide campaign. It hired the 15th largest agency in Germany, Omnicom's Heye & Partner, a company with a reputation for lacking creativity. But Heye, led by Chief Executive Jurgen Knauss, was able to gain the trust of McDonald's. McDonald's was also ready to take greater risks in its international advertising because its brand outside the United States is relatively young. Today, Heye & Partner is so closely associated with the chain that it is often referred to as the McDonald's agency. Heye also has as clients other top multinationals, such as Johnson & Johnson and Esso (Exxon), but McDonald's, one of the largest ad spenders in the world, is its top client. To best serve this client, Heye employees eat at McDonald's on a regular basis and even work behind the counter.

Going against the German tradition, which shuns humor in advertising, the Heye ads show a man stuck in traffic and a kid in another automobile making faces at him. The man, in revenge, holds up McDonald's fries and eats them demonstratively. This ad is used for most world markets, with the exception of the United States. Heye also won the McDonald's competition between several agencies for a tagline—"I'm lovin' it"—and it is used for all the company's ads in English. In another ad, aliens are shown ready to eat humans standing in line at McDonald's, with one urging the other to wait until the humans have eaten the burgers because they taste better afterward. The ads are very funny and emotional—and it is difficult to imagine that a German company came up with them. The new ad campaign communicates a youthful spirit and the idea that something is changing at McDonald's—something that its franchisees are not especially keen on.

To date, McDonald's sales have increased, posting the biggest sales gain in five years. Burger King, its competitor, on the other hand, continues to be in a slump. Although McDonald's successful Monopoly promotion and its new salad and breakfast sandwich may be partially credited for the sales increases, McDonald's and its ad executives believe that the new ad campaign has as much to do with its success.

Sources: Erin White and Shirley Leung, "How Tiny German Shop Landed McDonald's," *Wall Street Journal,* August 6, 2003, p. B1; Kate MacArthur, "McD's Sees Growth, But Are Ads a Factor?" *Advertising Age,* Vol. 74, No. 47, November 24, 2003, p. 3.

gent on the degree of cultural similarity between the sponsor and the target market:[22] Standardization of communication is recommended when similarity exists between senders and receivers in the communication process.

- Attitudes toward the product or service country of origin create another barrier; e.g., in environments where there is some level of hostility toward the United States and its economic and cultural dominance, it might be best to change an advertising campaign that stresses the product's country of origin.
- The elements of the promotional mix—particularly advertising[23]—are especially difficult to standardize because communication is language and culture specific.

Budgeting Decisions for International Advertising Campaigns

Companies use the following approaches to advertise spending decisions:

Objective-and-Task Method

objective-and-task method An advertising budgeting method in which the company first identifies advertising goals, conducts research to determine the cost of achieving the respective goals, and allocates the necessary sum for the purpose.

Companies using the **objective-and-task method** first identify advertising goals in terms of communication goals such as target audience reach, awareness, comprehension, or even purchase. As a next step, research is conducted to determine the cost of achieving the respective goals. Finally, the necessary sum is allocated for the purpose.

This method is the most popular one used by multinational corporations in the process of deciding on their advertising budgets because it takes into consideration the firms' strategies. A comprehensive international study suggests that this method is more frequently used by firms from Canada and Singapore and less frequently by Swedish and Argentinean firms.[24]

Percent-of-Sales Method

percent-of-sales method An advertising budgeting method that determines the total budget allocated to advertising based on past or projected sales.

The **percent-of-sales method** determines the total budget allocated to advertising based on past or projected sales. This method is difficult to adopt for firms entering new markets, which are more likely to benefit from budgeting methods such as competitive parity or objective-and-task. The problem with this method is that it causes advertising expenditures to decline as sales decline; at this point, the company should increase advertising spending.

For firms that have been in a particular international market for some time, this method is used by almost half of the respondents in the study on transnational advertising practices. This study found that the percent-of-sales method is most popular in Brazil and Hong Kong, and less popular in Germany.[25]

Historical Method

historical method An approach to budgeting that is based on past expenditures, usually giving more weight to more recent expenditures.

Firms using the **historical method** base their advertising budget on past expenditures, usually giving more weight to more recent expenditures. The percent-of-sales method utilizes the historical method as a first step, if the percentages allocated to advertising are based on past, rather than projected, sales. This method is not recommended for firms that operate in unstable economic, political, or competitive environments.

Competitive-Parity Method

competitive-parity method The strategy of using competitors' level of advertising spending as a benchmark for the company's own advertising expenditures.

The **competitive-parity method** uses competitors' level of advertising spending as benchmarks for a firm's own advertising expenditure. This approach is not recommended for a firm entering a new market and/or whose brands are not known locally. Moreover, this method suggests that a firm's goals and strategies are identical with those of competitors, which, most likely, is not the case.

Executive-Judgment Method

executive-judgment method A budgeting process that allocates the company's advertising budget based on the opinions of executives.

In the **executive-judgment method,** executive opinion is used in determining the advertising budget. A third of the responding firms queried in the study on transnational advertising practices reported relying on executive judgment.

Table 13-1 | U.S. Advertising Expenditures Compared to World Advertising Expenditures

Year	U.S. Ad Spending (Billion US$)	Change	World Ad Spending (Billion US$)	Change
2000	247.5	+11.3	474.3	+8.8
2001	231.3	−6.5	440.9	−7.9
2002	236.9	+2.4	450.5	+2.2
2003	249.2	+5.2	471.1	+4.6
2004	266.4	+6.9	498.3	+5.8

Source: Robert J. Coen, Universal McCann's Insider Report, December 8, 2003, www.universalmccann.com.

All-You-Can-Afford Method

Most small and medium-size enterprises entering a new market do not have the large budgets of multinational corporations. The **all-you-can-afford method** best suits the financial limitations of these firms. Unfortunately, this approach completely ignores strategic issues.

With the exception of the year 2001, advertising expenditures worldwide have increased since 2000; see Table 13-1. Note that U.S. advertising spending accounts for more than half of world totals. Table 13-2 notes changes in advertising expenditures for selected countries worldwide. Note the leaps in advertising spending for the countries of the former Eastern Bloc—Russia and Hungary, in particular—and for China and Indonesia, two large world markets with great marketing potential.

all-you-can-afford method The process of allocating the maximum amount possible to advertising; this method is used by small and medium-size corporations.

(Percent change over prior year in nominal local currencies)		
	Year	
Country	2002	2003	2004

Table 13-2

Changes in Advertising Expenditures in Selected Countries

Country	2002	2003	2004
Japan	−6.0%	+0.7%	+2.0%
Germany	−5.0	−2.0	+2.5
U.K.	+1.5	+3.0	+5.5
France	+1.0	+3.0	+2.5
Italy	−2.5	−1.0	+2.5
Spain	+2.0	+1.5	+3.5
Canada	+2.2	+2.6	+3.5
Mexico	+7.4	+12.3	+10.0
Brazil	+3.4	+5.0	+9.0
Netherlands	−2.5	+1.0	+2.0
Belgium	+6.8	+2.5	+4.0
Ireland	+7.8	0.0	+5.0
Finland	−0.5	+2.5	+2.0
Portugal	+13.2	−5.5	+5.0
Austria	−2.8	+2.5	+4.0
South Korea	+10.0	+8.0	+8.0
Taiwan	+2.0	+4.0	+6.0
India	+8.0	+14.0	+10.0
Philippines	0.0	+15.0	+15.0
Greece	+8.4%	+6.4%	+10.0%
Hungary	+18.5	+17.5	+17.5
Czech Rep.	+6.5	+5.0	+6.3
Poland	+4.8	+8.6	+10.8
Slovakia	+12.5	+11.8	+14.0
Colombia	+1.0	+2.0	+6.0
Russia	+52.7	+5.9	+12.0
China	+42.1	+42.2	+40.0
Indonesia	+35.8	+23.9	+25.0

Source: Robert J. Coen, *Universal McCann's Insider Report*, December 8, 2003, www.universal mccann.com.

Summary

- **Describe the international promotional mix and the international communication process.** The components of the international promotional mix are international advertising, international salesforce management, international sales promotion, and public relations and publicity. The international communication process involves the sender encoding a message and sending it via a medium to the receiver, who then decodes the message; the goal is to have the message sent identical to the message received. In an international communications context, the process is complicated by interferences (noise) injected by cultural and language differences between the advertiser, sponsor, and the target audiences.

- **Explore the international advertising formats and practices around the world.** International advertising—defined as a nonpersonal communication by an identified sponsor across international borders, using broadcast, print, and/or interactive media—faces many international challenges. The primary challenge is attributed to the lack of uniformity in media infrastructure, formats, and practices accepted in different markets. Among such challenges are media availability and reliability issues, such as media's inability to work with company deadlines and television going off the air frequently. The media could limit the types and the number of advertisements aired or published, or they might not permit the portrayal of women or advertising of certain products. They also might isolate advertising from programming or from editorial content. Media costs, formats, features, and trends may differ around the world.

- **Describe the international advertising and media infrastructure and infrastructure-related challenges in different markets.**

Advertising worldwide is dominated by U.S. advertising agencies; however, that fact is quickly changing. Firms from the United Kingdom and Japan are competing with large full-service agencies from the United States, and boutique advertising agencies worldwide are winning important accounts and awards for quality advertising. Multinationals today have more and more advertising agency choices. Depending on the availability of local talent and capability, companies advertising in international markets have a choice between advertising using a local agency, using an international agency, or using a local agency to advertise international agency messages.

- **Describe advertising strategies and budgeting decisions and offer examples of international applications.** An important decision facing international firms is whether to use a standardized message worldwide or to adapt the message to local markets. Standardization would lead to great economies of scale and cost savings; in reality, standardization may not be possible because of variations in the advertising and media infrastructures due to differences in consumer literacy, motivations, or consumer interests, and due to differences in advertising legislation. Advertising budgeting may involve one of the following methods: objective-and-task, whereby marketing managers set objectives and then calculate the cost for reaching the objectives; percent-of-sales, whereby the advertising budget is set as a percent of sales; historical, whereby spending is based on past expenditures; competitive-parity, whereby spending is based on competitors' spending; executive-judgment, whereby the firm's executives make the decisions; and the all-you-can-afford method.

Key Terms

adaptation of the advertising strategy
all-you-can-afford method
billboards
broadcast medium
channel of communication
competitive-parity method
decoding
encoding
executive-judgment method
feedback
historical method

infomercials
interactive medium
international communication process
international promotional mix
media availability
media infrastructure
media reliability
media restrictions
medium/media
noise
nonpersonal medium

objective-and-task method
percent-of-sales method
personal medium
print medium
product placement
receiver
sender
standardization of the advertising strategy
telemarketing
television shopping networks

Discussion Questions

1. Describe the challenges involved in the international communication process and suggest how each challenge could be addressed by a firm's international marketing manager in conjunction with an advertising agency.
2. What are some important traits of the international media infrastructure that are likely to affect local advertising strategies?
3. Describe how media formats, features, and trends differ around the world.

4. What are the advertising agency choices that international companies have for communicating with local markets? Describe each choice, its advantages, and disadvantages.
5. Ideally, multinationals should standardize their message worldwide to benefit from economies of scale and other cost savings. What prevents companies from using a standardized message worldwide?
6. How do multinational firms determine their budget for advertising?

Chapter Quiz (True/False)

1. In the international communication process, the sender can evaluate the effectiveness of the message with appropriate feedback from the target market.

2. Homeowners in Bangladesh often agree to display advertising on the walls of their homes.

3. *Glamour, Cosmopolitan,* and *Mademoiselle* are all examples of global media.

4. The European Union Directive Concerning Television Broadcasting limits all advertising of tobacco and prescription drug products in broadcast media.

5. Adaptation of the promotional strategy refers to changing a company's promotional mix so that it is uniform in most of its target markets.

Multiple Choice

1. Which of the following is a nonpersonal medium of the International Communication Process?
- **a.** personal selling
- **b.** trade shows
- **c.** television
- **d.** telemarketing

2. Which of the following refers to interference in the communication process attributed to cultural differences, competing messages, and degree of consumer interest?
- **a.** encoding
- **b.** decoding
- **c.** noise
- **d.** none of the above

3. Local newspapers that are unable to produce high enough quality in a print ad for a global brand are an example of what media challenge?
- **a.** media availability
- **b.** media costs
- **c.** media reliability
- **d.** media restrictions

4. Which of the following is not an example of media restriction?
- **a.** prohibiting advertising to children
- **b.** prohibiting the advertising of vice products
- **c.** keeping the local language pure
- **d.** All of the above are examples of media restrictions.

5. The budgeting decision that is mostly used by small and medium-sized corporations' campaigns is the
- **a.** percent-of-sales method.
- **b.** executive-judgment method.
- **c.** competitive-parity method
- **d.** all-you-can-afford method.

Endnotes

1. Sam Solley, "Developing a Name to Work Worldwide," *Marketing,* December 21, 2000, p. 27.
2. Anita Franklin, "Whose News? Control of the Media in Africa," *Review of African Political Economy,* Vol. 25, No. 78, December 1998, pp. 545–550.
3. Helen Johnstone, "Asian TV Companies Take Lead in Local Content," *Asian Business,* Vol. 32, No. 10, October 1996, pp. 26–33.
4. See Pola B. Gupta and Kenneth R. Lord, "Product Placement in Movies: The Effect of Prominence and Mode on Audience Recall," *Journal of Current Issues and Research in Advertising,* Vol. 14, No. 1, Spring 1998, pp. 47–59; and Steven J. Gould, Pola B. Gupta, and Sonja Grabner-Kräuter, "Product Placements in Movies: A Cross-Cultural Analysis of Austrian, French, and American Consumers' Attitudes Toward This Emerging International Promotional Medium," *Journal of Advertising,* Vol. 29, No. 4, Winter 2000, pp. 41–68.
5. "Business: Worrying Statistix," *The Economist,* Vol. 350, No. 8015, February 6, 1999, p. 68.
6. See Ross D. Petty, "Advertising Law in the United States and European Union," *Journal of Public Policy & Marketing,* Vol. 16, No. 1, Spring 1997, pp. 2–13.
7. Ibid.
8. Ibid.
9. Ibid.
10. William Wells, John Burnett, and Sandra Moriarty, *Advertising Principles and Practice, Fifth Edition,* Upper Saddle River, NY: Prentice Hall, 2000; and *Advertising Age,* "10 Biggest Stories of 2003," *Advertising Age,* Vol. 74, No. 51, December 22, 2003, p. 4.
11. Hillary Chura, "Coke Brands IPG as Global Ad Strategist," *Advertising Age,* Vol. 71, No. 50, December 4, 2000, p. 50.
12. David Lipin, "San Diego Ikea Hires a Local Ad Agency," *Adweek,* Vol. 50, No. 51, December 18, 2000, p. 4.
13. Peter Rosenwald, "Surveying the Latin American Landscape," *Catalog Age,* Vol. 18, No. 2, February 2001, p. 67.
14. R. Craig Endicott, "Top 25 Global Advertising Organizations: Conglomerates Beef Up Through Mergers and Acquisitions," *Advertising Age,* Vol. 70, No. 17, April 19, 1999, pp. S18–S19.
15. Cara Beardi, "Grey's Global Desire," *Advertising Age,* Vol. 71, No. 48, November 20, 2000, pp. 22, 24.
16. Ibid.
17. Cordella Brabbs, "Can Coke and IPG Truly 'Think Local'?" *Marketing,* December 7, 2000, p. 7.

You can find the correct answers to these questions by taking the quiz and then submitting your answers in the Online Edition. The program will automatically score your submission. Where you miss a question, the program will provide the correct answer, a rationale for the answer, and the section number in the chapter where the topic is discussed.

18. Anthony J. Rutgliano "The Debate Goes On: Global vs. Local Advertising," *Management Review*, Vol. 75, No. 6, June 1986, pp. 27–31.

19. Michel Laroche, V. H. Kirpalani, and Rene Darmon, "Determinants of the Control of International Advertising by Headquarters of Multinational Corporations," *Revue Canadienne de l'Administration*, Vol. 16, No. 4, December 1999, pp. 273–290.

20. Ibid.

21. Ibid.

22. Ibid.

23. Zahna Caillat and Barbara Mueller, "Observations: The Influence of Culture on American and British Advertising: An Exploratory Comparison of Beer Advertising," *Journal of Advertising Research*, Vol. 36, No. 3, May/June 1996, pp. 79–88.

24. Nicolaos E. Synodinos, Charles F. Keown, and Lawrence W. Jacobs, "Transnational Advertising Practices: A Survey of Leading Brand Advertisers in Fifteen Countries," *Journal of Advertising Research*, Vol. 29, No. 2, April/May 1989, pp. 43–50.

25. Ibid.

Case 13-1

Selling the Donnelly Brand in Romania

Donnelly's Cigarettes of Martinsville, Virginia, is planning its international expansion into a rapidly growing market, Central and Eastern Europe. The company sells the popular low-priced Donnelly brand in select Southern states, but it is currently looking for other venues for selling its brand. Encumbered with lawsuits and regulations in the United States, Donnelly is actively seeking markets that offer a higher profit potential than the home market.

Donnelly started out seven decades ago as a tobacco farm that initially sold its products to cigarette manufacturers, such as Philip Morris. It started developing its own brand of tobacco in the 1980s, providing substantial competition to the lower-priced Philip Morris brands. To the Southern U.S. market, Donnelly offers filter cigarettes, light cigarettes, menthol and menthol lights, as well as ultra lights and menthol ultra lights. The company romances the Donnelly brand's indigenous origins and it pursues profits aggressively by stressing its home-grown quality. In its advertisements, it stresses the Virginia origins of the tobacco, and its point-of-purchase advertising displays the brand's home-grown characteristics—even though Donnelly imports most of the tobacco from Asia. In its advertising for the U.S. market, Donnelly claims that it uses a large percentage of U.S.-grown tobacco, higher than that of all the Philip Morris' brands.

The family patriarch, John Donnelly, a third generation tobacco farmer with an impressive business acumen, is presently investigating modes of expansion that are likely to increase company profits. Cigarettes are under scrutiny in the United States, and Donnelly is presently dealing with lawsuits by individuals claiming that smoking the brand led to health problems. Moreover, in the United States, state governments and localities have started to ban smoking from public buildings, leading many consumers to quit and many others to decide against smoking.

In its plans to expand in Central and Eastern Europe—as with its business in the United States—Donnelly will maintain a hands-on approach to marketing the brand. Research of the business literature revealed that cigarettes are especially popular in Romania, where they are in a profitable growth stage. John Donnelly found this market especially attractive after examining this research.

Romanians have had a long-running love affair with Western cigarettes. Kent cigarettes constituted important commodity money in this market for many decades during the communist rule. Western cigarettes in general were coveted status products for Romanian smokers. Today, half of the men and one third of the women smoke in this second largest country in the region, with a population of 22 million. Romanian consumers are estimated to smoke between 25 billion and 40 billion cigarettes a year.

Research also revealed that leading Western cigarette manufacturers have set up factories to take advantage of this market. The British tobacco giant B.A.T. Industries PLC built a $70 million factory in Romania in the mid 1990s, designed to produce more than four billion cigarettes a year; the company has a market share of just under 10 percent. R.J. Reynolds Tobacco International, a U.S. firm, opened a large plant there as well. R.J.R. has a 15 percent share of the market. Philip Morris holds an 18 percent share of the Romanian market. The company dominates the Central and Eastern European market for American blend cigarettes, with 70 percent of the market share. It has cigarette plants in the Czech Republic, Kazakhstan, Poland, Hungary, the Ukraine, and Russia, but not in Romania. Another company manufacturing cigarettes in Romania is Papastratos Cigarette Manufacturing Company of Greece.

A main competitor for Donnelly is the Romanian tobacco company, Regia Autonoma a Tutunului in Romania (RATR). RATR is currently reinventing itself to appeal to Romanian consumers' nostalgia for traditional Romanian brands. The company holds 50 percent of the market share in Romania. Donnelly believes that this important market segment prefers foreign cigarettes but cannot afford them; once Donnelly sells its affordable U.S. brand to the Romanian market, many consumers smoking Romanian brands are likely to switch to the Donnelly brand.

Donnelly planned to ship the products to Romania from the port of Norfolk, Virginia, and pick them up at the Romanian port of Constanta, on the Black Sea. Even with transportation costs and with the excise duties placed on both local producers and importers and an added tax of 20 percent, the Donnelly brand would still be much cheaper than its other Western competitors. The company is planning to sell its products directly to convenience stores—mom-and-pop types that would agree to lower gross margins, which would keep prices low for Romanian consumers. The major decision that remains for the company is how to advertise in this market. Donnelly presently does all its advertising in-house in the Martinsville office complex. However, John Donnelly believes that it would be risky to use materials produced in-house in a market that is so very different from its Southern U.S. market. John Donnelly and his family are now contemplating the choice of an advertising company.

Many of the large multinational ad firms are present in Romania. Among them are Graffiti/BBDO, a division of BBDO Worldwide, among the first international firms to come to Romania; Grey Business Room, a division of Grey Worldwide; Olympic DDB; and Ogilvy Romania. John Donnelly believes that these companies have substantial expertise and capability, but their high costs are likely to infringe on company profits. Their ads would be exceptional in quality and impact, nevertheless.

The alternative would be to hire a local firm. Among prominent local firms are Ager Press S.A., a large formerly state-owned company; Andrei Advertising; Artmedia Group, a full-service advertising agency; advertigo, a full-service independent agency; and B&C Consulting, a full-service public relations and advertising

continued

agency. After examining the capabilities of the different local firms, Donnelly has found that two of them might be a better fit in terms of capability and expertise.

The first company, advertigo, is a full-service independent agency founded in 1998, serving a number of Romanian firms and a few prominent international firms and brands. Among them are 121 Marketing, Atlanta (a clothing company with brands such as Wampum Jeans, ATL, and Atlanta), Atlas Trading, Avanti Furs, Corporate Office Solutions, Corona Cosmetics, Creative Paving, and Johnson & Johnson—specifically, the company's Johnson baby, Carefree, Ob, and Neutrogena brands. The company has experts in media strategies, media planning, copywriting, design, research, as well as various business specialists. Its services span all media available in Romania.

B&C Consulting is a public relations and advertising strategy offering full service in communications and image consulting. Among its clients are the Romanian government, promoting Romania's image abroad with the B&C Consulting slogan "the strength beside you"; SNP PETROM, the large gas company, promoting its image with the slogan "the essence of movement"; and the popular Supermarket pop-rock group with its slogan "Pop-Rock Made in Supermarket." This young group creates edgy advertisements and memorable slogans in both Romanian and English.

John Donnelly must decide whether to use a multinational firm or a local firm. His family in Martinsville, the only other individuals with ownership in the company, has difficulty in offering advice. John must decide on the advertising agency before his trip to Romania in two months.

Sources: Anastasia Warpinski, "Tobacco Firms Look to Pocket Romania as Push in Central Europe Intensifies," *Wall Street Journal*, September 19, 1997, p. C1; http://www.advertigo.ro/; http://www.bcconsulting.ro/Portofoliu.html.

Analysis Suggestions

1. Should Donnelly use in-house produced advertising in the Romanian market? Why or why not?
2. What advantages would Donnelly have if it decided to use a U.S. advertising agency present in Romania? What would be the disadvantages of using a U.S. agency?
3. Which advertising agency should Donnelly choose for advertising the Donnelly brand in Romania? Explain.

14

International Publicity, Public Relations, and Sales Promotion Strategies

Chapter Objectives

By the end of this chapter, you should be able to

1 Provide an overview of international publicity and the different international public relations activities that can be used to influence it.

2 Describe the different approaches to international consumer sales promotion and the activities involved.

3 Describe the different approaches to international trade promotion and the different activities involved.

In the past, multinational firms hired advertising agencies to be in charge of the advertising function of the promotional mix, and they handled publicity and much of sales promotion in-house. Multinational companies today are attempting to coordinate all communication activities and typically hire international advertising agencies capable of coordinating their integrated marketing communications. Consequently, they are more likely to leave all public relations activities, local and international, to firms with public relations expertise. This fact is readily evident, especially in developed countries; the public relations machine

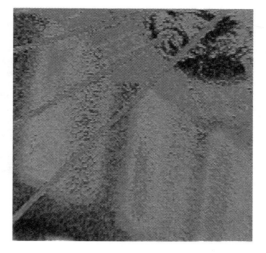

stands ready to avert any negative doubts cast on multinationals. Whereas, in the past, it took Andrew Grove, CEO of Intel, several months before addressing a glitch in the company's microprocessors, today's firms stand ready to defend their reputations and assign blame elsewhere—as in the case of the Ford Explorer and Bridgestone/Firestone tires. Covering up defects and not addressing them promptly and openly, on the other hand, can potentially lead to the demise of the company. Mitsubishi Motors Corp. was aware that some Mitsubishi trucks had clutch problems that could cause serious accidents, but instead of recalling the trucks, the company tried to cover the defects. As a result, Mitsubishi sales plunged by more than 50 percent, and its stock price collapsed; the company posted a loss of $2 billion in 2003. DaimlerChrysler, a majority owner in Mitsubishi Motors Corp., is planning to sue the company for the decline in value of its stock.[1]

Sales promotion is quickly catching on worldwide. Companies such as McDonald's and Burger King believe they are as much in the fast-food business as in the toy business,[2] coming up with new promotions and generating excitement about the newest promotional event. The Butt-Ugly Martians' appearance on the U.S. Nickelodeon television network was preceded by an intense merchandising blitz that is certain to expand beyond U.S. borders into children's stores and fast-food restaurant promotions.

This chapter addresses the topics of international publicity, public relations, and sales promotion. It addresses the effect of competent international public relations activity on generating positive publicity for a firm; in the process, it discusses the different public relations tools that international marketing managers have at their disposal. The chapter also addresses the various international consumer sales promotion tools, the degree of sales promotion standardization worldwide, and the challenges presented by engaging in sales promotional activities in different countries. It also addresses international business-to-business sales promotion and offers examples of different international promotional activities of multinational companies.

14-1 Publicity and Public Relations

This chapter addresses three of a total of five components of the promotional mix: publicity and public relations, which are closely related, and sales promotion. The other components of the promotional mix are advertising and personal selling, covered in Chapter 13, "The International Promotional Mix and Advertising Strategies," and

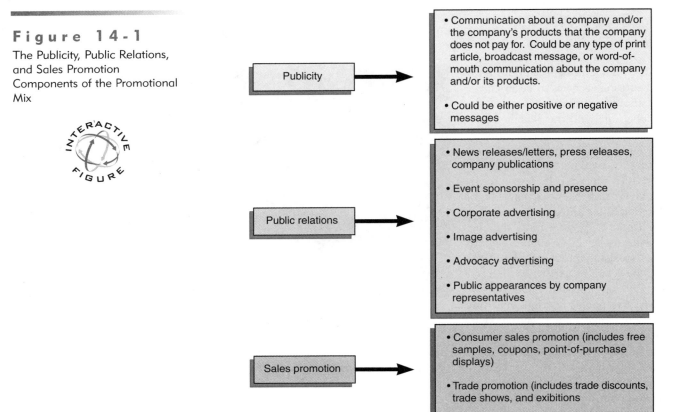

Chapter 15, "International Personal Selling and Personnel Management." Figure 14-1 illustrates the communication vehicles used by each component of the promotional mix addressed in this chapter.

14-1a Publicity

publicity Any communication about a company and/or the company's products that the company does not pay for; may be positive or negative.

Publicity is *a communication about a company and/or the company's products that the company does not pay for.* In this category falls any type of print article, broadcast message, or word-of-mouth communication about the company and/or its products; the message may be positive, negative, or a mix of both.

Multinational corporations, in particular, frequently experience negative publicity. In general, there is a negative perception of multinational firm dominance and globalization, as illustrated in the Seattle, Washington, revolts on the occasion of the 1999 World Trade Organization meetings. McDonald's experienced a classic example of negative publicity in France. In response to Europe's decision to ban hormone-treated beef, the U.S. government imposed high import tariffs on French Roquefort cheese, Dijon mustard, and foie gras. The French retaliated by, among others, vandalizing McDonald's restaurants; in their eyes, the company was a symbol of U.S. hegemony, globalization, multinationals, the power of the marketplace, and industrially produced food, at the expense of individuals' health and French peasants' livelihood.[3] In other examples, the war in Iraq further nourished anti-American sentiment in Europe, with restaurants removing Coca-Cola and Budweiser from their menus, and with the French calling American cheese "idiot cheese." Vandals in Bordeaux even torched a replica of the Statue of Liberty.[4]

Positive publicity, although difficult to come by, is very valuable. Due to its independent nature, it is more credible than advertising. A few years ago, DaimlerChrysler received free positive publicity for its luxury Mercedes automobiles when a photograph of former U.S. Secretary of State, General Colin Powell, appeared at the wheel of a Mercedes on the front page of *The New York Times*, with the caption "Do you mind if I drive?"

Table 14-1   **Strategies for Maximizing Benefits of Publicity in a Foreign Market**

General Strategies	Actions and Outcomes
Supplement ad campaigns with publicity campaigns.	The international company should establish third-party editorial credibility for products. The company should convey more information in greater detail about products.
Translate and be careful about translations.	Publishers are more likely to pick up a story if they have a good translation of the information.
Inform the managers in the home country about publicity efforts.	This strategy can be helpful in securing funds for new campaigns.
Use publicity to secure a distributor or a distribution network.	The right distributor may approach if the company indicates it is looking for distributors.
Use publicity as a sales lead.	The company may obtain sales leads if it includes detailed information, including contact information, in the press release.

Source: Adapted from Hank T. Walshak, "Publicity Is a 'Must' for International Marketers," *Marketing News,* Vol. 24, No. 14, July 9, 1990, p. 14.

The paper published a follow-up story on Powell driving the Mercedes belonging to Jordan's King Abdulla.[5] Although the impact of such publicity is difficult to measure in terms of dollars and cents, marketing executives in Stuttgart, the home of Mercedes-Benz, could rest assured that their brand received significant exposure and a credible endorsement in the U.S. market.

Marketing practitioners believe that publicity is a must in international marketing. Table 14-1 illustrates strategies that international companies should use to maximize the benefits of publicity in a foreign market.

14-1b Public Relations

International public relations is defined as *a concerted effort on the part of a company to generate good will among international publics (community, government, consumers, employees, among others) that are essential to the company.* Its main purpose is to generate positive publicity about the company.

International public relations is big business. The leading public relations firms are primarily U.S.- and U.K.-based multinationals, as shown in Table 14-2.

Much of the growth in public relations expenditures takes place in emerging markets—in particular, in the transition economies of Central and Eastern Europe. See International Marketing Illustration 14-1.

Public relations efforts fall into the following categories:

- News releases/letters, press releases, company publications
- Event sponsorship and presence
- Corporate advertising
- Image advertising
- Advocacy advertising
- Public appearances by company representatives

international public relations A concerted effort on the part of a company to generate goodwill among international publics that are essential to the company; its main purpose is to generate positive publicity about the company.

News Releases/Letters, Press Releases, Company Publications

Multinational firms must, on a regular basis, communicate with their different publics (home-country, local, and international customers; trade; stockholders; government; and community). When new products are introduced in local markets, company representatives

Table 14-2   **The Top 20 Public Relations Firms (Ranked Based on Worldwide Revenue)**

	Firm Name	2001 Worldwide Revenue	2000 Worldwide Revenue
1	Weber Shandwick Worldwide	$426,572,018	$507,438,046
2	Fleishman-Hillard Inc.	$345,098,241	$338,415,880
3	Hill and Knowlton, Inc.	$325,119,000	$302,769,000
4	INCEPTA (CITIGATE)	$266,018,371	$243,938,376
5	Burson Marsteller	$259,112,000	$303,860,000
6	Edelman Public Relations Worldwide	$223,708,535	$233,415,105
7	Ketchum, Inc.	$185,221,000	$168,247,000
8	Porter Novelli	$179,294,000	$208,157,000
9	GCI GROUP/APCO Worldwide	$151,081,645	$150,661,643
10	Ogilvy Public Relations Worldwide	$145,949,285	$169,453,900
11	Euro RSCG Corporate Communications	$124,158,504	$107,959,000
12	Manning, Selvage & Lee	$116,019,465	$118,843,522
13	Golin/Harris International	$113,247,644	$134,650,000
14	Cordiant Communications Group	$90,655,000	$79,810,000
15	Ruder Finn Group	$80,348,000	$84,125,000
16	Brodeur Worldwide	$70,001,900	$84,200,000
17	Waggener Edstrom, Inc.	$59,890,800	$57,904,000
18	Cohn & Wolfe	$57,779,000	$63,580,000
19	Rowland Communications Worldwide	$42,666,000	$45,391,000
20	Text 100 Public Relations	$33,676,739	$33,681,553

Source: Council of Public Relations Firms 2002 Industry Documentation & Rankings, http://www.prfirms.org/docs/2001rankings.

news releases Statements issued to the public to introduce a new product, touting its advantages; any other information shared with the media.

press releases Statements issued to the press to communicate news about a company and its products.

company publications Public relations publications that describe the products of a company to potential customers and summarize financial achievements.

event sponsorship The financial support of cultural or sports-related events; companies use these events to get positive publicity.

are likely to offer **news releases, press releases,** or **company publications** touting the advantages of the new products or services.

Event Sponsorship and Presence

Event sponsorship is a growing venue for international marketing communication. Nearly every important international cultural or sports-related event has the backing of multinational corporations. Brands such as Adidas, MasterCard, Visa, Rolex, Coca-Cola, Pepsi, and Heineken sponsor events ranging from World Cup Soccer to World Cup Cricket to the Davis Cup for tennis. Across continents, cultural manifestations are supported by major international brands: Vodacom, a cellular network provider in Africa, sponsored Placido Domingo, Luciano Pavarotti, and Jose Carreras during their Bravo Africa concert;[6] Vodafone, NatWest, Air Emirates, and Pepsi sponsored World Cup Cricket;[7] and Gatorade was the official sports drink of the 2000 Olympic Games and has acquired affiliations with the National Hockey League, World Cup Soccer, and Tour de France, among others.[8] GE was the primary sponsor of the 2004 Olympics. And the list continues. See Figure 14-2 for an illustration of event sponsorship.

International sponsorship is so prevalent that it has drawn the attention of artists. Near a bus stop in Kassel, Germany, a kiosk that would normally carry advertisements is actually a work by New York–based artist Hans Haacke displaying quotes from executives telling why they sponsor art shows. Hilmar Kopper, head of Deutsche Bank, says: "Who-

International Marketing Illustration

14-1

Central and Eastern Europe: A Growing Market for Public Relations

Public relations firms are relatively new in Central and Eastern Europe. Consumers, unaccustomed with promotional efforts beyond propaganda, first regarded all promotion with suspicion. Yet, with the proliferation of commercials, banners, flyers, direct mail, and other communication methods and venues, East European consumers are becoming increasingly more educated on the subject, as more and more domestic firms emerge as competitors to multinational promotion giants. Technical terms such as "PiAr" (or PR, public relations), "advertising," "marketing," and others, all borrowed from English, are now part of the everyday vernacular not just among business people, but everyday consumers as well.

Public relations firms are growing rapidly in numbers and in revenue, overcoming some of the growing pains and environmental obstacles. Among some of the obstacles the companies continue to face are the overly close relationships between magazines and PR companies. Often, companies pay journalists to write stories about them. PR agencies control the media, especially the popular lifestyle magazines where ads for the holidays and food are portrayed as editorial articles. Sponsoring companies pay for much of the travel for journalists. And publishers do not permit the journalists in their employ to write negative stories about the firms that advertise in their magazines and newspapers—i.e., to author negative publicity about their advertising clients.

The reverse situation also presents problems: Media, and newspapers in general, tend to be suspicious of PR agencies. In fact, media owners are wary of corporations and often view any type of positive publicity as something they should be paid for. Hungarian and Czech newspapers even go as far as to place barriers against PR companies and prevent journalists from having contact with them. When a company executive shares an important tip, he or she is quoted as the representative of an unnamed firm, rather than the representative of an identified firm.

Adding to the difficulties of the PR firms in Eastern Europe is the fact that their senior executives are younger than 30. They are perceived as inexperienced, and clients barely agree to pay them a fee of 15 percent on top of expenses; it is difficult to justify to clients that PR involves important work that helps companies remain competitive.

Yet, in spite of all the challenges, the public relations industry is growing by leaps and bounds, with PR firms increasing in number and successfully competing with leading international PR firms.

Sources: Maria Vornovitsky, "Advertising Changes in Post-Soviet Russia: Content Analysis," working paper; Katka Krosnar, "Hope for PR in Eastern Europe," *Marketing Magazine*, Vol. 106, No. 2, January 15, 2001, p. 6; and by the same author, "PR Struggles in Eastern Europe," *Marketing Magazine*, Vol. 106, No. 1, January 1/8 2001, p. 6.

ever pays, controls." Alain Dominique Perrin, Cartier's head, says: "It is a tool for shaping public opinion."[9]

Corporate Advertising

Corporate advertising is used to promote the company behind the different brands. One particularly memorable advertisement of this kind was designed by Philip Morris for the Chinese market on the occasion of the Chinese New Year. This ad portrayed traditional

corporate advertising A type of advertising that is used to promote the company behind the different brands.

Figure 14-2
Event sponsorship brings important revenues for national and international events—and even local events, as in this photograph: Rucanor, a European manufacturer of sportswear, is a sponsor of a youth tennis championship.

Figure 14-2
Event sponsorship brings important revenues for national and international events—and even local events, as in this photograph: Rucanor, a European manufacturer of sportswear, is a sponsor of a youth tennis championship.

Chinese dancers dancing on the Great Wall to the Marlboro theme song, which was still familiar to consumers despite the fact that Marlboro cigarettes are no longer advertised on television. At the end of the ad, the advertisement wished Chinese consumers a happy new year from the Philip Morris companies.

Image Advertising

image advertising An advertising campaign that enhances perceptions of a company in a given market by creating a positive impression on the target consumers.

Image advertising is used to enhance perceptions of a company in a given market. McDonald's used image advertising to combat the negative attitudes of consumers and farmers in France after the events described in section 14-1a, "Publicity." To address discontent with the restaurant and to dissipate the perceived link between McDonald's and the United States, the company created an advertising campaign that both made fun of Americans and stressed the fact that McDonald's avoided using genetically modified ingredients. It also stressed the French origins of McDonald's products; its slogan was "McDonald's. Born in the USA. Made in France."[10]

Advocacy Advertising

advocacy advertising Advertising a particular position or point of view.

Advocacy advertising is used by a company to stress a particular point of view. For example, one can assume that the Benetton (www.benetton.com) campaign portraying death-row inmates' perspectives on their lives, along with personal statistics that include the type and date of murder and related sentence, is in fact a statement against the death penalty. The ads portraying young people of all ages and races in colorful Benetton clothing could be perceived as welcoming the cultural diversity in our world. The ad for the French market showing a reporter interviewing an ethnic protester while he is being brutally arrested could be perceived as a protest against police brutality, and so on.

Public Appearances by Company Representatives

public appearances Company representatives' public involvement, speaking on behalf of the international firm and its products.

In addition to **public appearances** to speak on behalf of the international firm and its products, which are typical of this category, company representatives frequently attend important international events. One such event is *documenta*, an international contemporary art exhibit that takes place once every five years. At one exhibit, prominent business representatives Ronald Lauder of Estee Lauder Cos. (also an art collector); Eli Broad of SunAmerica Corp.; Ronald Rosenzweig, CEO of Anadigics Inc., an electronics company; Charles Lazarus of Toys "R" Us Inc.; and Neuberger & Berman's Arthur Goldberg reflected on exhibits such as a dead mealworm in yellowish sand and a photo of an eviscerated rabbit.[11]

14-2 Consumer Sales Promotion

Aside from advertising, personal selling, public relations, and publicity, all other sponsored communications offered to the end consumer or to the trade that stimulate purchases or improve relationships to middlemen and retailers in the short term fall into the category of **sales promotion.** Among examples of consumer sales promotion are point-of-purchase displays, free samples to initiate product trial or brand switching (see Figure 14-3), other incentives (coupons, cents-off, gifts, product tie-ins) to initiate trial or brand switching, and sweepstakes and contests. Among examples of trade (business-to-business) promotion are trade discounts, sweepstakes and contests, and trade shows.

Sales promotion activities are often conducted in conjunction with advertising campaigns, as well as with personal selling and public relations efforts. Consequently, the sales promotion effort is frequently managed by the promotional arms of leading international advertising agencies; among them are WPP's OgilvyOne and Perspectives, and Young and Rubicam's Wunderman Cato Johnson. In addition, new players are emerging, such as The Marketing Store Worldwide, which is quickly expanding in Europe, the United States, and in select markets in Latin America and Asia (Argentina, China, Taiwan).[12] However, even companies that have strong relationships with an advertising agency, such as Coca-Cola, which uses McCann Erickson for its advertising, frequently allow international subsidiaries to make their own sales promotion decisions. Coke Brazil has traditionally created all sales promotion in-house, for example.[13]

> **sales promotion** Sponsored communications to the target consumer or trade segment that stimulate purchases or improve relationships with middlemen.

14-2a Adaptation of Sales Promotion

International sales promotion campaigns fall into one of three strategies, paralleling international advertising and international product marketing strategies: global campaigns, modular campaigns, and local campaigns.

Global Campaigns

Global campaigns are rarely attempted in sales promotion. Even a company such as IBM, which wants consistent strategies worldwide, requires a priori feedback from local markets to ensure that the central strategy can be implemented.[14]

> **global campaign** A worldwide standardized advertising campaign that is not adjusted to different target markets.

F i g u r e 1 4 - 3

In this store, free samples are offered to customers to induce them to try and to purchase the pastries.

Certain types of sales promotion, such as point-of-purchase displays, lend themselves to a more standardized campaign. They do not rely on words, so different language versions are not necessary; they speak an international language by reinforcing logos and emphasizing brand image visually.[15] Yet even point-of-purchase displays need some adaptation. Smirnoff Vodka, a company that spends one sixth of its advertising budget on such displays, finds that, in the townships of South Africa, posters bleach in the sun and rain, and metal advertising plates often disappear from the walls to be used as roofs.[16]

Occasionally, the target market itself may encourage the use of a global, standardized approach. For example, in markets where multiple languages are spoken, and where English is one of the unifying languages, as in the case of India, using English for sales promotion may be appropriate. Even in countries where English is not a language used nationally, such as in Switzerland, using English as the language of the promotion may be a benefit. For example, promotions aimed at Swiss consumers often use English, rather than French, German, or Italian, because two groups of consumers would be offended if a campaign used only one of the three languages spoken in Switzerland.[17]

Modular Campaigns

modular campaign An advertising campaign that provides a template that is varied and customized from market to market.

Modular campaigns provide a template that can be varied from market to market. Even in the European market, different strategies are likely to be used in the United Kingdom than in continental Europe. For example, in continental Europe, PepsiCo included *Star Wars* characters in its Walker and Lays chips, whereas, in the United Kingdom, the same promotion offered consumers a chance to win a Jar Jar Binks toy through an in-pack scratch card.[18]

Multinational companies often launch a worldwide promotional campaign centered around one theme and then use advertising to customize the message for each individual market. For example, BBDO Mexico introduced a worldwide campaign on behalf of Pizza Hut launching its promotion of the week, such as Pizza Pooch toys, coloring books, placemats, as well as product giveaways like skateboards; local agencies then provided voice-overs to produce local language spots.[19]

Local Campaigns

local campaign An advertising campaign that is tailored to local needs; especially used in markets that media cannot easily reach.

Local campaigns are tailored to local needs, and retailer cooperation is of particular importance in ensuring that such sales promotion campaigns are successful. In the Netherlands, Albert Heijn appears to be favored as a grocery store where multinationals offer their new products and attempt to initiate consumer trials. The store, part of the Royal Ahold retail conglomerate, offers quality products aimed at the middle and upper-middle class. It was there that Procter & Gamble first introduced Bounty paper towels to Dutch consumers. Albert Heijn displayed the product prominently using point-of-purchase displays located near the cash registers and also offered the product in the paper products section of the stores. Simultaneously, the company mailed samples of Bounty in individual sheets, with different designs, in plastic bags, to selected homes. In another example, Coca-Cola representatives offered free samples of Coke and Coke Light to consumers shopping at Albert Heijn. After sampling Coke in miniature cans, consumers were able to purchase the product with a two-for-the-price-of-one promotion.

Finally, local sales promotion campaigns gain significant importance in markets that are not reached by other media and where sales promotion constitutes a primary form of communicating with the final consumers.

14-2b The Online Venue for Sales Promotion

Online sales promotion is quickly becoming a pervasive mode of communication with prospective consumers. Whether the promotion involves sweepstakes, printed coupons, promotional pricing, or other strategies, companies find that consumers around the world respond well to aggressive online promotions. Most of the communications firms (the former traditional advertising firms) now serve their clients by providing to target consumers extensive interactive sales promotion that is in line with the company's other types of communications.

14-2c Legal and Ethical Issues in Consumer Sales Promotion

To a certain degree, adaptation to local markets is necessitated by legal requirements. Even in economically and politically integrated markets, such as the European Union, sales promotion–related legislation differs from one country to another. In Germany, for example, "buy one, get one free" offers are illegal; in France, premiums are restricted to 7 percent of the product's value; and, in Belgium, retail sales can run for only a month and prices cannot be cut below one third.[20]

The European Commission has yet to decide on the process of harmonization of rules applying to sales promotion throughout the member countries: The European Commission of the European Union issued a Green Paper on European Union Consumer Protection in 2001 and a much criticized draft regulation on sales promotion. In 2002, the International Chamber of Commerce (ICC) revised the International Code for Sales Promotion; the Code was initially introduced in 1973. See International Marketing Illustration 14-2 for more information about the ICC's and European Commission's efforts to promote high standards of ethics in marketing.

Sweepstakes based on pure chance are deemed illegal in Holland,[21] Canada, Sweden, and Belgium,[22] whereas, elsewhere in the world, additional legal requirements for sales promotion strategies diverge. Puerto Rican law, for instance, requires rules for all promotions to be printed in both English and Spanish, and both versions should be printed in a general circulation newspaper at least once a week for the duration of the campaign. Quebec requires sponsors to provide French translations, to pay a duty based on the total value of the prize pool, and to post a bond to run a promotion.[23] All paperwork regarding point-of-purchase displays must be legalized by going through embassies in the Middle East, while displays going to Eastern Europe must be marked as not being for resale to avoid additional customs duties.[24]

Often the companies themselves are responsible for creating a bad reputation for sales promotion. Sales promotions aimed at emerging markets over time have been questionable. For example, common in developing countries in Sub-Saharan Africa and Eastern Europe are local consumers wearing fur jackets and hats promoting luxury automobiles, investment funds, and airlines, whose products and services they could not possibly afford, and expensive cigarettes they should not spend their limited income on. In another example, in Eastern Europe in the early 1990s, a Pepsi Game was aired on prime-time television, occupying at least one hour of viewing time on Pepsi trivia, when consumers had little alternative programming to watch. And umbrellas advertising cigarettes are often displayed in restaurants adjacent to elementary schools.

Historically, there are also examples of flagrant violations of businesses' ethical responsibilities in their management of sales promotion. A case in point is that of Nestlé, a multinational food-product company, which successfully lured new mothers in Sub-Saharan Africa to adopt the company's baby formula. Women dressed as nurses offered free samples to new mothers in maternities, urging them to feed formula to their infants as a replacement for breast milk. Lack of sanitary conditions for formula preparation, as well as the high cost of the product, ultimately led to the death of many infants. What is especially interesting in this case is the fact that the negative publicity for the company was generated abroad, where consumer groups brought this issue to international media attention, rather than on the African continent.

14-2d The Future of Consumer Sales Promotion

With time, it is becoming increasingly clear that sales promotion is emerging as an important component not only of a company's promotional strategy, but also of its brand strategy. Brand managers are noting that sales promotion tools can actually contribute to strength-

International Marketing Illustration   14-2

Promoting High Ethical Standards in Marketing: The ICC International Code of Sales Promotion and the European Union Green Paper on Consumer Protection

The International Chamber of Commerce (ICC) attempted to establish self-regulatory codes to complement the existing framework of national and international law. The code is intended as a basis for self-regulation, but it can also be used as a reference document for legal and administrative bodies. Sales promotions are required to abide by the following rules, among others:

- Be legal, decent, honest, and truthful and aimed at avoiding disappointment and complaints.
- Be framed in such a manner that they would not abuse public trust or exploit the public's lack of experience or knowledge; this is especially true when it comes to children.
- Make it easy to identify the terms of the offer and its true value to consumers and to intermediaries.
- Be administered with adequate resources and with the appropriate supervision.
- Respect the privacy of consumers.
- Be safe for consumers.
- Not be imposed on intermediaries; if the intermediaries do accept the promotion, they should have all the necessary means to effectively run the respective promotion.

Similarly, the European Commission published the Green Paper on European Union Consumer Protection. The green paper acknowledges that regulations on sales promotions (i.e., discounts, simple reductions, rebates, joint-offers, free gifts, coupons, vouchers, and commercial contests and games) are subject to different national rules. The primary difference is in terms of information requirements, although certain practices are wholly or partially prohibited in some member countries but permitted in others. The EU created a Draft Regulation on Sales Promotion that came under fire from businesses and consumers. For example, the Draft Regulation requires that consumers receive information on promotional efforts only if they ask for it; otherwise, they would not receive it. This is seen as unfair both to businesses and to consumers. The Draft Regulation also allows promoters to collect personal data without parents' consent, allowing them to take advantage of children.

Sources: http://www.iccwbo.org/home/statements_rules/; http://europa.eu.int/.

ening brand perceptions and attitudes; consequently, companies such as Ford, Kraft Jacobs Suchard, and L'Oreal are involving sales promotion firms when deciding on brand strategies.[25] Important growth is anticipated especially in the area of point-of-purchase displays. As research suggests that European and U.S. consumers make more than 50 percent of their purchase decisions at the point of sale, point-of-purchase expenditures constitute an increasingly higher percentage of overall promotional expenditures worldwide.[26]

14-3 International Trade Promotion (Trade Shows and Exhibitions)

Most sales promotion addressed in section 14-2, "Consumer Sales Promotion," is primarily aimed at the final consumer—although sweepstakes and contests, as well as incentives such as price-off reductions, also may be aimed at the trade. **Trade shows and exhibitions** belong to the category of business-to-business promotion. They are also referred to as *international trade promotion*—sales promotion aimed at the trade. Trade shows and exhibitions are usually held annually in formats in which companies purchase exhibit space to display and demonstrate their offerings to the target market. For U.S. industrial firms, trade shows and exhibitions account for one fifth of the overall communication budget, and one fourth for European industrial firms.[27] Trade shows and exhibits constitute a proven promotional tool capable of having a direct positive impact on sales.[28] There are numerous trade shows for most industries. To illustrate the extent to which companies have opportunities for exhibiting their work, Table 14-3 offers a partial listing of trade shows for a typical month of June.

Trade shows and exhibitions offer potential buyers and sellers a chance to meet face-to-face, as they bring many decision makers to a single location for a limited time, enabling firms to get their message to a large number of people at one time.[29] In a typical promotional environment, the seller must pitch the product to the buyer; for trade shows and exhibits, however, the visitors are the ones who approach the seller, searching for new products and suppliers.[30] Finally, trade shows and exhibits provide a neutral location for doing business and bring together managers from different departments in buyers' organizations, thus increasing the probability of meeting every decision maker who will influence the buying decision.[31]

Country and state governments are often involved in ensuring that national/local companies are represented at important fairs. In the United States, the Department of Commerce is actively involved in promoting U.S. companies abroad using trade shows as

> **trade shows and exhibitions**
> Business-to-business promotions that usually are held annually in formats where companies purchase exhibit space to display and demonstrate their offerings to the target market.

| Table 14-3 | A Partial Listing of Industry Trade Shows in June 2004 |

Trade Show	Industry	Location
Entech Pollutec Asia	Multiple industry sectors	Bangkok, Thailand
BIO Annual Convention	Biotechnology	San Francisco, U.S.
Expo Comm Wireless Spain	Multiple industry sectors	Vancouver, Canada
26th Annual ISA Expo Control	Multiple industry sectors	Mexico City, Mexico
Boat Show	Pleasure boats/accessories	St. Petersburg, Russia
Fieldays	Agricultural machinery and equipment	Wellington, New Zealand
Eurosatory	Defense industry equipment	Paris, France
Asian Elenex	Multiple industry sectors	Hong Kong, China
Metav	Machine tools/metalworking equipment	Dusseldorf, Germany
SMT/Hybrid/Packaging	Electronics industry products/test equipment	Nuremberg, Germany
Expo Medica Hospital	Medical products	Mexico City, Mexico
China International Consumer Electronics Show	Consumer electronics	Qingdao, China
Optatec	Laboratory scientific instruments	Frankfurt, Germany
FILMART	International film and TV market-catalog show: films/videos	Hong Kong, China
Intersolar	Renewable energy equipment	Freiburg im Breisgau, Germany
ISPO: International Trade Fair for Sports Equipment and Fashion	Multiple industry sectors	Munich, Germany
Networld Interop	Multiple industry sectors	Tokyo, Japan

Source: http://www.ita.doc.gov/doctm/

venues. Usually, the U.S. government shares the cost of the exhibits by sponsoring a national pavilion at the different fairs.

As mentioned, trade shows and exhibitions are organized annually or at set intervals, and tend to be specialized in one domain. The Frankfurt Book Fair, for example, draws publishers and authors on all topics from around the world every fall to the city of Frankfurt, Germany. The *documenta*, mentioned in section 14-1a, "Publicity," takes place every five years, and the Venice Biennale takes place biannually; both exhibits show art works of contemporary artists. In other examples, DRUPA is an annual trade exhibition for the graphic arts industry, and Interkama is an international trade fair for industrial communication, automation, measurement, and analytics. Messe Dusseldorf, in Dusseldorf, Germany, for example, specializes in international trade shows for machinery, as well as for the medical, fashion, and services industries.

The World Exposition (the World Fair) cuts across domains and is one of the most important venues for exhibiting new ideas, technology, and art in an environment where numerous countries are represented. The city of Hanover, Germany, hosted the most recent World Fair, Expo 2000, an exhibition of art, science, and culture (see Figure 14-4). The theme of the fair was "Humankind—Nature—Technology: A New World Arising" and its aim was to focus on creating guiding principles for living in the twenty-first century. Projects stemming from the Expo are taking place around the world, emphasizing the use of environmentally friendly technology.

More than 170 countries were represented at Expo 2000, and more than 50 countries built their own pavilions. Businesses were prominently represented at the fair. Among those present with impressive pavilions were appliance manufacturer Bosch, the German telephone company Deutsche Telekom, the automobile manufacturer DaimlerChrysler, and German publisher Bertelsmann. Countries worldwide also were represented: Uzbekistan and Turkmenistan displayed artisanal work and music, the Romanian pavilion displayed wine and clothing from a Transylvanian village, and the Colombian pavilion offered quality coffee to visitors. The Netherlands pavilion was one of the most important attractions at the fair; it consisted of a stacked landscape, with flowing water and trees on the highest floor.[32] Among the millions of visitors at the Expo were heads of state (Chancellor Gerhard Schröder of Germany visited the Expo numerous times) and royalty (Queen Beatrix of the Netherlands, Queen Margrethe of Denmark, Prince Rainier of Monaco, and Prince Phillippe of Belgium, among others).

Expo 2005 is organized in Seto, Japan, in the Aichi Prefecture, and Expo 2010 will take place in Shanghai, China.

Summary

- **Provide an overview of international publicity and the different international public relations activities that can be used to influence it.** Publicity is a promotional tool that companies do not pay for; rather, publicity is a result of companies' performance and/or perception in world markets. For companies conducting business internationally, publicity in one country may have important repercussions on company perception in all the markets where the companies are present. Publicity can be positively influenced by using appropriate public relations tools, such as releasing relevant company publications, press releases, news releases; engaging in appropriate public appearances; and hiring agencies to design image advertising and corporate advertising that reflects company philosophies and strategies.
- **Describe the different approaches to international consumer sales promotion and the activities involved.** International consumer promotions are becoming very popular worldwide. Such activities include point-of-purchase displays, free samples to initiate product trial or brand switching, and other incentives (coupons, cents-off, gifts, product tie-ins) designed with the purpose to initiate trial or brand switching. Promotional activities can be global in nature; modular, with some adaptation in select markets; and local, designed with local consumers in mind.
- **Describe the different approaches to international trade promotion and the different activities involved.** International trade promotion, aimed at the business-to-business market, can involve trade shows and exhibitions, as well as trade discounts, sweepstakes, and contests. Trade shows provide a neutral environment where buyer and seller can meet face-to-face, in a low-pressure situation in which the buyer is most likely to approach the seller, rather than vice versa.

Key Terms

advocacy advertising
company publications
corporate advertising
event sponsorship
global campaign

image advertising
international public relations
local campaign
modular campaign
news releases

press releases
public appearances
publicity
sales promotion
trade shows and exhibitions

Discussion Questions

1. Describe the relationship between international public relations activities and international publicity.
2. What are the different public relations tools that an international firm can use to fend off negative publicity?
3. Describe some of the international consumer promotion activities that international firms currently engage in, while addressing ethical issues and international standards involved.
4. How does international business-to-business sales promotion (trade promotion) benefit international companies and target consumers?

Chapter Quiz (True/False)

1. Communication about a company that the company does not pay for is defined as publicity.
2. The main purpose of public relations is to generate *positive* publicity about a company.
3. Companies must consider legal and ethical issues with consumer sales promotions. In Germany, "buy one, get one free" offers are illegal.
4. Trade shows are an example of consumer sales promotion.

Multiple Choice

1. Royal Dutch Shell was one of the official sponsors of Ferrari's Formula One team, endorsing Michael Schumacher in the year 2002. This is an example of
   a. press release.
   b. company publications.
   c. event sponsorship.
   d. advocacy advertising.

2. According to the text, what international organization often uses advocacy advertising?
   a. McDonald's
   b. Benetton
   c. Visa
   d. Adidas

You can find the correct answers to these questions by taking the quiz and then submitting your answers in the Online Edition. The program will automatically score your submission. Where you miss a question, the program will provide the correct answer, a rationale for the answer, and the section number in the chapter where the topic is discussed.

3. Which of the following is an example of sales promotion?
   a. product tie-ins
   b. free samples
   c. cents-off
   d. all of the above

4. Which of the following types of sales promotion can be varied from one market to another?
   a. local campaigns
   b. modular campaigns
   c. global campaigns
   d. none of the above

5. What percent of Europeans and U.S. consumers make their purchase decision at the point of sale?
   a. 50
   b. 60
   c. 30
   d. none of the above

6. What city will host the World Fair Expo 2010?
   a. San Francisco
   b. London
   c. Shanghai
   d. Munich

Endnotes

1. Arun Sudhaman, Ross Rowbury, and James R. Weeks, "Mitsubishi Drives into Gridlock of Problems," *Media*, June 18, 2004, p. 19.

2. cf. Doug Porter, Executive Vice President, Leo Burnett, in charge of the McDonald's account.

3. See Jon Henley, "Flip Flop, " *The New Republic*, Vol. 222, No. 1, January 3, 2000, p. 24.

4. Erin White, "Europeans Take a Satiric Jab at the U.S.," *The Wall Street Journal*, April 28, 2003, p. B1.

5. "How the General Put a Pedal to the Metal," *The New York Times*, February 26, 2001, p. A8.

6. "Bravo Pretoria," *Finance Week—South Africa*, January 22, 1999, p. 11.

7. Ian Darby, "Cricket World Cup L8m Short in Sponsorships," *Marketing*, March 25, 1999, p. 7.

8. Debbie Howell, "Gatorade vs. the Beverage Giants—Going Head-to-Head in Sports Drinks," *Discount Store News*, Vol. 39, No. 3, February 7, 2000, p. 58.

9. Thane Peterson and Sandra Dallas, "Tycoons on the Trail of the Next de Kooning," *Business Week*, Vol. 3541, August 25, 1997, p. 16E2.

10. Ibid.

11. Ibid.

12. "Pushing Back the Business Frontiers," *Marketing*, October 1997, pp. 49–50.

13. James Curtis, "Coke's Brazilian Sales Pitch," *Marketing*, May 7, 1998, pp. 39–41.

14. "Pushing Back," *Marketing*, pp. 49–50.

15. Daney Parker, "Popular Choice," *Marketing Week*, Vol. 19, No. 10, May 31, 1996, pp. 39–40.

16. Ibid.

17. Rob Furber, "Centre Shop," *Marketing Week*, Vol. 22, No. 38, October 21, 1999, pp. 51–54.

18. "Pushing Back," *Marketing*, pp. 49–50.

19. Margaret McKegney, "Pizza Hut Casts Puppies in Global Kids Campaign," *Advertising Age*, Vol. 71, No. 33, August 7, 2000, p. 16.

20. Ken Gofton, "How Euro Rules Will Change SP," *Marketing*, October 5, 2000, pp. 60–61.

21. Furber, "Centre Shop," pp. 51–54.

22. Warner Bernhard, "Crossing the Border," *Brandweek*, Vol. 37, No. 48, December 16, 1996, pp. 37–38.

23. Maxine Lans Retsky, "Global Promotions Are Subject to Local Laws," *Marketing News*, Vol. 31, No. 10, May 12, 1997, p. 8.

24. Parker, "Popular Choice," pp. 39–40.

25. Paul Gander, "Internal Examination," *Marketing Week*, Vol. 22, No. 21, June 24, 1999, pp. 57–60.

26. Robin Cobb, "POPAI Gets Right to the Point," *Marketing*, September 18, 1995, pp. 37–40.

27. D. Jacobson, "Marketers Say They'll Boost Spending," *Business Marketing*, Vol. 75, March 1990, pp. 31–32.

28. See C. M. Sashi and Jim Perretty, "Do Trade Shows Provide Value?" *Industrial Marketing Management*, Vol. 21, 1992, pp. 249–255; and Srinath Gopalakrishna and Gary L. Lilien, "A Three-Stage Model of Industrial Trade Show Performance," *Marketing Science*, Vol. 14, No. 4, Winter 1995, pp. 22–42.

29. Aviv Shoham, "Performance in Trade Shows and Exhibitions: A Synthesis and Directions for Future Research," *Journal of Global Marketing*, Vol. 12, No. 3, 1999, pp. 41–57.

30. Ibid.

31. Ibid.

32. The United States was not represented at the Expo 2000 World Fair, primarily because U.S. companies did not want to create their own pavilion and did not want to be in a U.S. pavilion; they claimed that they were international companies.

Case 14-1

Promoting Coke in South Africa

Johan Timmermans, sales director for Coca-Cola South Africa, was hired to revive Coke sales in South Africa in March 2001. Sales were stagnating, and numerous new brands were emerging in the marketplace, poised to compete successfully with Coke products on price.

South Africa was Coca-Cola's first stop on the African continent in 1928. The company set up the first bottling and distribution plant in Johannesburg and has expanded its business in the country ever since, employing more than 10,000 people. The company's presence in South Africa created many more jobs in the country: For every job created by the production and marketing of Coke products, 10 additional jobs, on average, were created in South Africa in related industries.

The Coca-Cola Company sells numerous nonalcoholic brands to South African consumers. Among them are Coca-Cola (with its Light and Vanilla Coke versions), Fanta (with its Orange, Grape, and Pineapple versions), Sprite, Tab, Sparletta, Lemon Twist, Schweppes, Mixers, Fresca, Minute Maid, Powerade, Bibo, Milo, Krest, Splash, Bonaqua, and Vitango, among others. Its product mix in South Africa is more extensive than in the United States because, in South Africa, the company also bought out a number of popular regional competitors.

A year after joining Coca-Cola South Africa, in 2002, Johan Timmermans was approached by Coca-Cola bottlers who were concerned that their sales were stagnating. The company has four bottlers: Amalgamated Beverage Industries (ABI), Coca-Cola Fortune, Forbes, and the Cook Group. Thirty-one plants and two canning operators support the Coke infrastructure, and co-packers are used for selected alternative packages. The bottlers are active participants in Coke promotions and even created the Bottler HIV/AIDS Program as a response to the AIDS crisis that has devastated Africa. The program offers an aggressive awareness and prevention campaign and access to medical treatment and the necessary drugs.

The bottlers asked Johan Timmermans to identify promotions that would clearly set their brand apart from those of the competition. Johan contacted Riverside Technologies in Wilton, Connecticut, for ideas on technological modifications that would set the brand apart. Riverside came up with modules that could be inserted into the packaging; these modules would sing and announce the winner of a Coke promotion. Consumers who purchased the winning cans were instant winners of Panasonic Hi-Fis. The winning cans were filled with carbon dioxide and water, to replicate the weight and feel of a real can, and were assembled into the Coke can by Schmalbach-Lubeca Continental Can in Bonn, Germany. Fifty talking cans were produced for the promotion and were distributed nationally.

In just the first month of the promotion, sales of Coke cans rose by 3.2 percent, Diet Coke cans, by 18.6 percent, and Fanta, by 3.8 percent compared to the previous year. This was in line with the theme of the promotion, "This summer only Coca-Cola talks," literally—and figuratively, in terms of sales.

In the spring of 2004, Johan Timmermans coordinated with its advertising agencies another promotion that was not as popular with South African consumers. The promotion asked them to nominate the most inspiring person they knew to carry the Olympic Flame in Cape Town on June 12. Moreover, distributors were not involved in the promotion, and they felt that a more aggressive and creative approach was needed to resuscitate Coke sales again. Johan set up a meeting with representatives of the four bottlers to discuss innovative sales promotions. In preparation for the meeting, Johan Timmermans reviewed the arsenal of consumer promotion strategies that Coca-Cola South Africa could use.

Sources: Adapted from Andrew Kaplan, "Case Study: Drumming Up Sales," *Beverage World*, Vol. 122, No. 1724, March 15, 2003, p. 99; http://rsa.coca-cola.com; http://www.cocacola.co.za/.

Analysis Suggestions

1. What are the different types of consumer promotions that can be used to increase sales for Coca-Cola South Africa?
2. Are there any types of sales promotions that may not be effective or should not be used in a country characterized by a wealth gap, with a substantial proportion of the population under the poverty line? Explain.
3. As a consultant to Johan Timmermans, create a promotional campaign that has a reasonable likelihood of success in this market.

International Personal Selling and Personnel Management

Chapter Objectives

By the end of this chapter, you should be able to

1 Examine companies' expatriate management strategies.

2 Describe the different types of employees suited for a company's international operations.

3 Address issues related to expatriate management, such as motivating international employees and ensuring successful assignment performance and repatriation.

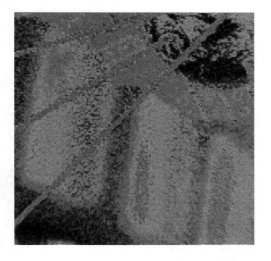

International sales representatives are often the frontline personnel in a firm's relationship with an international target market. Their expertise, ability, demeanor, and appearance all convey information that is integral to the firm's product or service offering and help shape the firm's relationship with the target market, distributors, suppliers, and local government agencies overseeing the firm's operations. Frequently, sales representatives are expatriates, crossing cultural divides and bridging cultures on behalf of the firm, often in unfamiliar settings, where the culture and marketing practices differ from those in the sales representatives' home country. Expatriate sales representatives must survive the challenges posed by the new environment, continuously adapt to its changing demands, and play by the host-country rules while representing the company and selling its products and services in a foreign market.

Local sales representatives also have challenges as the company's frontline personnel. Although, as nationals of the host country, they understand the market and its intricacies, as representatives of the company, they also need to understand the company's home country and organizational culture, as well as its marketing practices.

This chapter addresses issues related to managing expatriate employees, motivating them for optimal performance, and ensuring their successful repatriation to the home country.

15-1 International Presence and Personnel Issues

From a company perspective, hiring expatriates or locals is a function of the company's involvement in the market. The company's presence in the market—entry mode—and its commitment to the market are important considerations in determining (a) the size of the sales team and (b) the types of sales representatives the company employs. Companies primarily involved in exporting are likely to engage in only minimal international sales activity. An example of such an activity might be sending representatives to an international trade show, to exhibit the firm's products.

Companies using a home-country middleman, such as an export trading company or an export management company, rely on the salesforce of the intermediary for international sales and limit sales activity to the domestic market. The situation is similar if host-country middlemen such as foreign-country brokers or agents are used. However, when using all the other types of host-country middlemen, such as manufacturers' representatives and distributors, the company directly engages in some level of personal selling. When using host-country distributors, the respective company hires sales representatives who call on the distributors.

Personal selling is an important component of international marketing communications, especially for business-to-business transactions. Salespeople are the Chanel saleswoman selling the French brand in a leased department in a U.S. department store, the representative of the Coke bottler selling Fanta to a Burundi bottled drinks retailer, the

Figure 15-1

An order taker in this Dutch butcher's shop can suggest that buyers purchase different meat cuts.

order taker Individual who processes routine sales orders from the customer.

order getter Individual who actively generates potential leads and persuades customers to purchase the firm's products.

electronic data interchange (EDI) Relationship whereby buying and selling firms are able to share important data on production, inventory, shipping, and purchasing.

Air India ticketing agent at JFK airport in New York, and the Polish manufacturer selling upholstery to the Fiat plant in Italy. Personal selling involves a face-to-face interaction between the seller and the buyer and, in industrial sales, their respective teams. As such, the interaction between the two parties will be affected by their national cultures.

In the international selling context, the **order taker,** the individual who processes routine orders from the customer, is likely to be a local employee who is familiar with the local customs and culture. The order taker in Figure 15-1 is in charge of selling the meat cut requested by the customer. That does not mean that he has no initiative: He can suggest different cuts and can persuade the buyer to buy a larger quantity of the product.

Order getters, individuals who actively generate potential leads and persuade customers to purchase the firm's products, can be local or international staff who are highly skilled technically, as well as trained in conducting negotiations. In international marketing, most order getters work in the business-to-business area as field salespeople, going to customers to solicit business. Order getters selling to other businesses would go to their clients' places of business. Order getters selling to consumers directly would go to consumers' homes; for example, direct marketers such as Avon and multilevel marketers such as Amway hire salespeople to sell products to their network of friends.

In developed countries, telemarketing is also popular in selling products. For telemarketing campaigns to be successful, companies need to have access to a reliable telephone system.

After a sale is closed, companies sign contracts that address the terms of the transaction, costs involved, and the term of the relationship. In many countries, a written contract does not mean much: Sellers and buyers can readily choose to ignore the agreement without any penalty. The legal systems may endorse contracts but not defend them. In many cultures, a contract may have little value, while someone's word is fully reliable. In many countries outside the United States, trust relationships are expected, and company executives are insulted at the suggestion the agreement should be noted in a written contract (see Figure 15-2).

Companies can also set up an **electronic data interchange (EDI)** relationship, whereby buying and selling firms are able to share important data on production, inventory, shipping, and purchasing. EDI relationships are possible primarily if the firms have the appropriate resources and trust their local partner with the information. Most firms in developed countries have established some type of EDI relationship for optimal performance. In many countries, switching vendors is difficult; consequently, one of the

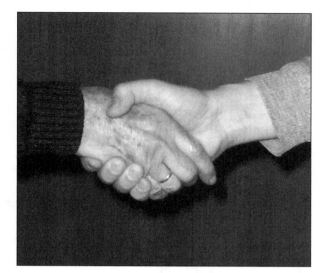

Figure 15-2
In many countries, a handshake is more valuable than a written contract.

restrictions EDI imposes—i.e., the obstacle involved in switching vendors because of the high cost of linking with a new vendor—is a moot point.

Depending on the tasks involved and the type of buyer-seller relationships the company establishes in the process of conducting its business in different international markets, the company needs to determine the types of salespeople it should hire for optimal performance. The foreign salesforce of the multinational corporation could include *expatriates* (home-country nationals and third-country nationals) and *host-country nationals*.

15-1a Expatriates

Expatriates working in a particular foreign country belong to two categories: One category is the *home-country national*, successful as a sales representative in the home country, assigned overseas. An example would be a U.S. Philip Morris employee engaging in sales in the company's Hong Kong operations. Representing the second category is the *third-country national*, a truly international salesperson, the expatriate who works in numerous countries. An example would be a Latin American salesperson who previously worked in sales in Italy and Spain calling on Colgate-Palmolive's trade accounts in Bulgaria.

> **expatriate** An employee working in a foreign country.

Home-Country Nationals

Home-country nationals—known also as *parent-company nationals*—are preferred by companies whose products are at the forefront of technology, and when the selling function relies on extensive training and highly specialized information. In general, in situations in which a greater interdependence exists between an overseas unit and corporate headquarters, firms are more likely to dispatch home-country nationals; this is also true for situations in which complex operations are involved, there is a greater political risk, and there is a greater level of competition.[1]

> **home-country national** A local employee who works in his or her home country for the international corporation.

A disadvantage of hiring home-country nationals for international operations is the high cost involved. In addition to the regular salary and commission the employee would have received in the home country, numerous incentives are considered standard for international assignment. A cost-of-living allowance, a housing allowance that often permits hiring household help, and a substantial education allowance for children, which pays for education at expensive international private schools, are standard. Other standard perks are an annual or biannual home-leave for the entire family, or an annual visit from immediate family members living in the home country. In addition, the firm also is expected to pay for the costs of selling the employee's home in the home country, for storing furniture, and/or for moving household goods overseas, making it very expensive for the firm to send the employee overseas.

Even sending an employee overseas for five months can be costly to the company. In one example, a Motorola employee working for a Siemens-Motorola joint venture in Dresden, Germany, was housed in a hotel for his entire stay, rented an automobile, and had a living allowance that even included a phone card to keep in touch with family in the United States. In addition, the company paid for two business-class round-trip leave tickets back to the United States, team-building exercises, and trips to London and Prague, among others. These costs were covered in addition to salary, bringing the overall company costs to more than $100,000 for the five months.

Among other disadvantages of hiring home-country nationals are

- The numerous cultural barriers faced by the home-country nationals in the country of assignment
- The expenses involved in training the home-country nationals in the culture (and, often, language) of the country of assignment
- The lack of local personal connections to the important decision makers in the government and the local trade
- The difficulty of finding quality employees willing to take on international assignments because they are reluctant to uproot their families, or because they fear that they will lose visibility and status at the head office (international companies offer many incentives to overcome this impediment)

Third-Country Nationals

third-country national An employee working in the country of assignment who is not a national of that country nor of the country in which the corporate headquarters of the company he or she works for are located.

Third-country nationals are employees working temporarily in an assignment country, who are not nationals of that country, nor of the country in which the corporate headquarters of the company they work for are located.[2]

Third-country nationals are "professional expatriates." They are accustomed to constantly adapting to new environments. They speak numerous languages, are familiar with customs and business practices in different environments, and have learned, through their vast international experience, to adopt optimally for international assignments. In certain countries, third-country nationals are more likely than home-country nationals and locals to be on international corporations' payrolls. Examples of such countries are the United Arab Emirates and Saudi Arabia, where international companies hire highly skilled employees from India, Pakistan, Egypt, and the Philippines. One study found that expatriates working in Saudi Arabia typically save for future consumption and gear most of their purchases toward home-country consumption.[3]

Often, third-country nationals are competent company employees transferred from a subsidiary of the company operating in another country. Usually, third-country nationals cost less than home-country nationals (but more than locals) because they are not as likely to forgo the high salaries of the company's home country and expatriate allowances typical for home-country employees. And they are less likely to be a costly early return for the company, due to difficulty in adaptation to the local environment.

In the case of both home-country nationals and third-country nationals, it should be noted that many governments, primarily in developing countries, dictate the number (usually, percentage) of foreign nationals that a foreign firm operating in the respective country is permitted to hire. In the case of third-country nationals, it is not uncommon for local governments to delay visas or otherwise complicate the hiring process. In all these situations, firms are forced to rely heavily on host-country nationals (locals) and may tap into international sales talent and expertise only to a limited extent.

15-1b Host-Country Nationals (Locals)

host-country national A local employee who works in his or her home country for the international corporation.

The local salesperson who works in his/her home country for an international corporation is a **host-country national.** An example would be the Hungarian brand manager schooled in a university in the United States, working for Procter & Gamble (www.pg.com) in Hungary. This individual understands the U.S. business environment, has been well trained technically at an accredited U.S. institution, and is willing to return to his/her home country to work for a U.S. multinational firm.

Increasingly, international firms appear to prefer local employees to expatriates. Cost is only one consideration. Frequently, locals with similar levels of education and training are available for employment at a fraction of the cost of expatriates. Host-country nationals also speak the local language and often have a well-developed network within the local industry and government. And, as mentioned in section 15-1a, "Expatriates," some host governments restrict the number of foreign nationals working in the country; thus, host-country nationals also fit with the country's employment policies.

Many international firms compete for the types of individuals described here. Although the multinational company will deem it appropriate to remunerate host-country nationals below the level of expatriates, not offering them the appropriate motivation to remain with the company will increase their risk of flight to a competitor.

15-1c Another Alternative: Long-Distance International Selling

Selling via the Internet or mail is an important venue for approaching new customers overseas. Costs of distance selling are lower—companies do not have to dispatch salespeople abroad and spend on cross-cultural training—allowing for greater market coverage. However, distance selling is difficult to coordinate internationally, often largely due to cultural differences. For example, a financial salesperson seeking new customers in the Netherlands would have a difficult time penetrating the market, primarily due to the fact that sales have traditionally been exclusively handled by local agents and brokers at local branch offices.[4] This difficulty was already addressed in the area of financial sales in the European Union. The European Commission advanced regulation that promotes pan-European consistency and fosters trade in the region; among other things, the regulation covers consumers' right to reflection on the offer and contract for 14 days, as well as consumers' right for withdrawal without any penalty if they were subjected to unfair pressure or were not aware of all the conditions of the sale.[5]

15-2 Managing International Employees

15-2a Managing Relationships

Managing internationals—expatriates and host-country nationals—is no easy task for multinational corporations. Companies that attempt to transplant personnel policies proven successful in the home country will run against obstacles in different international environments. Establishing quotas, assigning management responsibilities to employees within the firm, or even simply addressing employees by first names could prove to be challenges for the firm. Issues related to culture, such as national character, could come into play: Rolling up one's sleeves and working on the assembly line will result in an instant loss of status for the manager in Southeast Asia, Eastern Europe, and South America. Problems related to social class or caste will bring additional challenges: Placing a pariah (untouchable) in charge of a Brahman in India may be problematic, as would be placing someone of peasant origins in charge of someone from the intellectual class in Eastern Europe (even if training and education justify such an assignment).

15-2b Understanding the International Buyer-Seller Relationship

In a personal selling environment, challenges also arise in the **international buyer-seller relationship.** Certain approaches to selling work better than others. For example, a hard sell is not likely to be successful in most Asian countries, where modesty, a humble attitude, and

international buyer-seller relationship The distribution between the buyer and the individual involved in personal selling.

respect are seen as valuable traits. Looking one's counterpart directly in the eye—a sign of honesty in the United States—is likely to be perceived as an aggressive stance in Asia. In one's first encounter with a Chinese counterpart, it is advised that business cards be exchanged; when one takes the Chinese manager's business card, one should do so with both hands and read it, as a sign of respect. The U.S. manager is advised to have business cards written in English and Chinese when dealing with the Chinese.

In other examples, Italians typically enjoy engaging in the negotiation process and want to feel that they are special customers. They want to have a special deal; offering them a bottom-line price at first is a strategy that will most likely meet with failure.[6] The strategy of focusing on closing the deal and aiming toward the next sale is unlikely to work in Latin America, where individuals prefer to take time to build a relationship with suppliers.[7] In this environment, it is best to first socialize, to build a relationship of friendship and trust, preferably involving the family. In the Middle East, this approach also works well, although it most often does not involve the family.

15-2c Understanding Cultural Values and the Relationship between Buyer and Seller

National Character, Organizational Culture, and Personality

national and regional character A set of behavior and personality characteristics shared by individuals of a certain country or region.

The level of psychological overlap in communication between buyer and seller will vary across three dimensions: **national character, organizational culture,** and **individual personality.**[8] A personal selling situation involves *content* and *style*. Content includes substantive aspects of the interaction, such as suggesting, offering, or negotiating product-specific utilities and expectations, whereas style refers to rituals, format, mannerisms, and ground rules of the buyer and seller during the course of their interaction.[9] An interaction between buyer and seller is satisfactory if the two parties are compatible on these two dimensions.[10] In cross-cultural sales interactions, content and style are shaped by national character, organizational culture, and the personality of the individuals involved in the interaction.[11]

organizational culture The shared norms and values that guide collective behavior in organizations, and enduring traits that characterize individuals, motivating them to act or react to stimuli in the organization and in the environment in a particular manner.

Chapter 5, "Cultural Influences on International Marketing," described national character in terms of personality traits shared at the national level. The dimensions identified as constituting national character are individualism, power distance, uncertainty avoidance, and masculinity/femininity.[12] Organizational culture refers to shared norms and values that guide collective behavior in organizations.

individual personality Enduring traits that characterize individuals, motivating them to act or react to external stimuli in a particular manner.

Personality refers to enduring traits that characterize individuals, motivating them to act or react to external stimuli in a particular manner. Congruency within the three dimensions between the buyer and seller is likely to result in the most successful transaction, whereas discrepancy is likely to result in a low chance for success.[13] To have a higher chance for success in international markets, a company could select a target market with a national character similar to that of its own home country, target companies with similar organizational culture, and hire international salespeople with the appropriate personality traits, as will be described in section 15-3a, "Recruiting Expatriates."[14]

Low- and High-Context Cultures

As mentioned in Chapter 5, "Cultural Influences on International Marketing," individuals from cultures with a low context of communication use formal, direct communication that is verbally expressed, whereas individuals from cultures with a high context of communication use less verbal information to convey the message, relying instead on cues such as gestures and facial expressions. In the latter case, status of the speaker, individual background, values, associations, and so on are very important in completing the message conveyed, thus linking the message to the context in which it was delivered.[15] Negotiators from high-context cultures, such as those of Latin America and Asia, are less programmatic and less rigid, especially in time management, contract signing, and closing deals, whereas negotiators from low-context cultures follow

Western logic, with the negotiation terminating when an agreement is formally reached and in writing.[16] Furthermore, individuals from high-context cultures are less confrontational and place greater emphasis on interpersonal interaction than individuals from low-context cultures.[17]

15-3 Successfully Managing Expatriates

International management experts estimate that the cost of a failed expatriate assignment is in the millions of dollars and that more than 50 percent of expatriate assignments fail.[18] The direct costs associated with each expatriate turnover are estimated to be between $55,000 and $150,000; and indirect costs—such as reduced productivity and efficiency, lost sales, reduced market share, diminished competitive position, unstable corporate image, and tarnished corporate reputation—are even greater.[19]

Firms could attempt to minimize their early return rate by engaging in the appropriate training and development strategies for expatriates. Such strategies should involve the use of effective selection and screening criteria for recruiting expatriates, training them and preparing them for the international assignment, motivating them for peak performance, and ensuring their successful **repatriation** (see Figure 15-3).

repatriation The return of the expatriate employee to the home country.

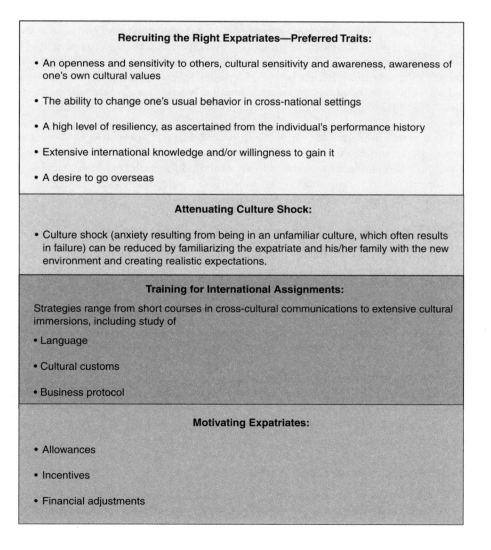

Recruiting the Right Expatriates—Preferred Traits:

- An openness and sensitivity to others, cultural sensitivity and awareness, awareness of one's own cultural values

- The ability to change one's usual behavior in cross-national settings

- A high level of resiliency, as ascertained from the individual's performance history

- Extensive international knowledge and/or willingness to gain it

- A desire to go overseas

Attenuating Culture Shock:

- Culture shock (anxiety resulting from being in an unfamiliar culture, which often results in failure) can be reduced by familiarizing the expatriate and his/her family with the new environment and creating realistic expectations.

Training for International Assignments:

Strategies range from short courses in cross-cultural communications to extensive cultural immersions, including study of

- Language

- Cultural customs

- Business protocol

Motivating Expatriates:

- Allowances

- Incentives

- Financial adjustments

Figure 15-3

Successful Expatriate Management

15-3a Recruiting Expatriates

In the process of recruiting expatriates, companies should select those individuals who have traits such as

- An openness and sensitivity to others, cultural sensitivity and awareness, awareness to relate across cultures, awareness of their own cultural values[20]
- The ability to change their usual behavior in cross-national settings[21]
- A high level of resiliency,[22] as ascertained from the individuals' performance histories
- Extensive international knowledge and/or willingness to gain it[23]
- A desire to go overseas[24] and willingness to work in areas where there is political instability and/or a strong anti-American sentiment

Typically, potential recruits for international assignments—from within or outside the company—are given batteries of personality tests and are subjected to interviews to determine their motivation for an international assignment. Those prospects who are primarily interested in completing the assignments to earn promotions are not likely to be as successful as those who are eager to experience different environments.

15-3b Attenuating Culture Shock

culture shock A pervasive feeling of anxiety resulting from one's presence in a new, unfamiliar culture.

Culture shock, which frequently accounts for early repatriation, is defined as *a pervasive feeling of anxiety resulting from one's presence in a new, unfamiliar culture.* Culture shock could result in feelings of inadequacy, reluctance to experience the environment, and fear of failure, among others. Cross-cultural communication experts advise companies that culture shock can be diminished when employees know what to expect in their new environment. Companies need to provide some familiarity with the physical and social environment (local customs, in particular) to the prospective expatriates to attenuate culture shock.

The family, in particular, must be prepared for the international assignment. Whereas the expatriate employee interacts within the company and has a company culture around him/her, the spouse and children often find themselves isolated, lacking support. International Marketing Illustration 15-1 addresses issues related to the accompanying spouse and expatriate compensation.

15-3c Training for International Assignments

Companies use different strategies in training their employees for international assignments. The strategies range from short courses in cross-cultural communications to extensive cultural immersions. For example, Procter & Gamble, Motorola, Microsoft, and Hewlett-Packard require extensive cross-cultural training courses for their international salespeople, whereas other companies require employees to read books and other materials on the cultures before departure for the sales mission.[25] When the Abril Group, a diversified media company, sends its salespeople to Brazil, a country where it does much of its business, it requires them to participate in a 10-day Portuguese immersion program, studying the country's language, culture, and customs.[26]

In training expatriates for international assignments, a company must assess the fit between the individual salesperson and the client the person will call on. See International Marketing Illustration 15-2 for a number of important cultural elements that must influence the recruitment and selection of salesforce personnel.

15-3d Motivating Expatriates

The success of an international assignment is predicated on a high degree of motivation. The intrinsic (internal) aspects of motivation for an international assignment are addressed in the recruiting process, which ensures that only those candidates who have the appropriate traits (see section 15-3a, "Recruiting Expatriates") are deployed. The

International Marketing Illustration

15-1

The Financial and Legal Cost of the Expatriate Spouse

Expatriate employees often ask their employer to find their spouse a job in the country of assignment. The employer may agree to find the spouse a job either with the same subsidiary or with an affiliate company located within a reasonable geographic proximity.

From a legal perspective, finding employment for a spouse may be problematic for the employer. The marriage may end in divorce, and the company will be in a bind, continuing to accommodate the spouse. Or the spouse can claim that he/she is owed additional salary and compensation because, in fact, he/she is also an expatriate employee. Companies are covered if a written agreement makes clear that the request is, in fact, an accommodation for the accompanying spouse and that the spouse is not entitled to special benefits.

The company will also find that the costs of bringing the expatriate with an accompanying spouse are much higher than bringing the expatriate alone. Consider the cost of living allowance (COLA) of an expatriate from New Zealand living in France. The cost of living allowance for this individual increases by 13 percent from a single to a married individual and by more than 27 percent for a married individual with two children (see Table 15-1). Note that this amount does not include other costs such as the cost of education in private school for the children or hardship allowances.

Table 15-1 — Cost of Living Allowance for an Expatriate from New Zealand Working in France in 2004

New Zealand Annual Salary Range (New Zealand Dollars, $US1= NZD1.5)	Cost of Living Allowance in France			
	Single	Married	Married +1	Married +2
49,500–50,500	18,636	21,105	22,423	23,740
50,500–51,500	18,877	21,379	22,713	24,048
51,500–52,500	19,119	21,653	23,004	24,355
52,500–53,500	19,361	21,926	23,295	24,663
53,500–54,500	19,602	22,200	23,586	24,971
. . .				
68,500–69,500	22,718	25,730	27,336	28,942
69,500–70,500	22,926	25,965	27,586	29,207
70,500–71,500	23,133	26,200	27,836	29,471
71,500–72,500	23,341	26,436	28,086	29,736

Source: http://www.air-inc.com/compensation/col.html; William A. Carmell, "Expatriate Compensation/The Accompanying Spouse," http://articles.corporate.findlaw.com/articles/file/00014/009536.

International Marketing Illustration 15-2

Hiring the Right Person for a Company's International Salesforce

A number of cultural elements are important to consider in the process of recruiting and selecting international salesforce personnel. Among them are the ethnic composition of the salesforce, the religious orientation and social class of the employees, as well as their gender:

- *Ethnic composition*—Managers should be aware of the ethnic composition in the country and match the salespeople with the customers appropriately; this is especially important in countries where there is cultural and ethnic diversity, such as India and Indonesia, and where the ethnic groups do not get along well.
- *Religious orientation*—Managers should match individuals with similar religious backgrounds to have the greatest impact.
- *Social class*—Countries with long social histories base social class on different criteria, such as seniority (Japan and other Asian countries), caste (India), or other criteria that the marketer should be aware of.
- *Education*—In many countries—Japan, most countries in Europe, for example—educational systems are more elitist, and an appropriate match based on education is essential for optimal appeal to the target market.
- *Gender status*—Many countries keep women in the background and do not involve them in business. Consequently, it would be a mistake to have women in a salesforce that sells products to male decision makers in countries such as Japan and most of the countries of North Africa and the Middle East.

Source: Jeffrey E. Lewin and Wesley J. Johnson, "International Salesforce Management: A Relationship Perspective," Journal of Business and Industrial Marketing, Vol. 12, No. 3/4, 1997, p. 236.

---

company controls the extrinsic aspects of motivation, such as compensation, leave and family policies, career incentives, etc.

In terms of compensation, certain companies attempt to use uniform policies worldwide. For instance, IBM uses a sales compensation plan that links 140,000 salespeople from North America, Latin America, Europe, and the Asia Pacific region, allowing sales managers to act locally and think globally. Their compensation is derived from team performance in a regional or industry group (20 percent), personal contribution to customer solutions and use of business partners (60 percent), and challenges and contests (20 percent).[27]

Other companies offer numerous compensation incentives above those used for assignments in the home country, thus making the international assignment very attractive. Among such incentives are those described next and illustrated in Figure 15-4.

Cost-of-Living Adjustment/Post Adjustment

cost-of-living adjustment/post adjustment A compensation incentive whereby the company adjusts expatriate salaries to reflect the cost of living in the new environment at standards in the expatriate's home country.

For many companies, the **cost-of-living adjustment** is above and beyond that justified by the local conditions. This type of compensation, also referred to as **post adjustment,** includes payment for household help, such as maids, cooks, gardeners, night watchmen, etc.

Housing Allowance

housing allowance A compensation incentive whereby the company covers part, or the entire cost, of housing for the expatriate employee while abroad.

Often, companies cover part or the entire cost of housing for the expatriate employees while abroad. Even if the **housing allowance** does not cover permanent housing, it most likely covers the cost of staying at a quality hotel until housing becomes available.

Education Allowance

The **education allowance** covers the cost of children's education at an international private school. U.S. companies pay the education allowance for their employees primarily so that they will be on par with employees working for European multinationals. Many European firms pay for high-quality education for their employees' children, regardless of whether they are in their home country or overseas, and for as long as they are attending school.

Home-Leave Allowance

The **home-leave allowance** pays for the family abroad to vacation in the home country. The company also may pay for the children remaining in the home country to attend school to visit the family member or members posted abroad.

Moving Allowance

Household moving expenses to the country of assignment are usually covered. The **moving allowance** also may cover storage in the home country. Some companies also arrange for the sale of the expatriate's home, often incurring losses if the housing market is in a slump.

Repatriation Allowance

The **repatriation allowance** covers expenses for moving to the home country. In addition, the repatriation allowance may consist of a considerable sum paid to the expatriate simply for returning from the international assignment.

Other Types of Allowances

Expatriates also can benefit from other types of allowances. Such allowances may, for example, cover family membership in a social and/or health club designed primarily for expatriates and for well-to-do locals.

Noncompensation incentives are very important. Multinational corporations frequently offer as incentive to the expatriate a guaranteed promotion in the company ranks

education allowance A compensation incentive whereby the company agrees to cover the cost of children's education at an international private school in the country of assignment or at a boarding school in the expatriate's home country.

home-leave allowance A compensation incentive that pays for the expatriate and his or her family to vacation in the home country.

moving allowance A compensation incentive whereby the company pays for the household moving expenses to the country of assignment and, at the end of the assignment, back to the home country.

repatriation allowance A compensation incentive whereby the company covers expenses involved in moving back to the home country, as well as, frequently, a large sum paid for successfully completing the international assignment.

upon his or her successful return from the country of assignment. Companies also must address career-related concerns of the accompanying spouse. In an effort to recruit the best candidates for international posting, companies often offer spouses positions in the companies congruent with their talents and objectives to ensure the continuity of their careers.

15-3e Obstacles to the International Sales Mission

Once in the country of assignment, expatriates must learn the culture quickly and not gravitate toward home-country expatriates.[28] When they are living in the expatriate community, however, such situations may be unavoidable. First, if the expatriates are assigned to a country where restrictions are imposed on interactions with foreigners, such as Saudi Arabia, China, and Cuba, the expatriate community is likely to be the only forum for social interaction.

Expatriates may be drawn toward their home-country expatriate community in other countries as well. For example, for U.S. expatriates, many home-country offices and representatives play an important part. Among them are the United States Embassy, the various other offices present in a particular country in conjunction with the embassy (the Unites States Information Agency, the United States Agency for International Development, the Fulbright Office, and other agencies), as well as others associated with the embassy—the cultural, the military, and the commercial attaché. One responsibility of U.S. officers within these respective positions and structures is to organize activities that involve the participation of U.S. expatriates. Expatriates are invited to various functions, activities, and celebrations to participate and to represent the United States. Often, there are even American schools for expatriates' children and American clubs. The Marine House, which houses the marines stationed at the embassy, periodically shows American movies, accompanied by receptions. Most often, a recreation center is open to American expatriates so that they can play pool, watch American football games, and reminisce about life in America.

At the very least, one can find a website that unites expatriates in a particular region. Expat Forums is such an example, helping individuals cope with their foreign assignments and compare benefits, other company practices, and costs. Although the forum is open to any participants, most are U.S. expatriates. Other sites aimed at expatriates help them to "live abroad as they would in their home country."

All these factors have the potential to impede expatriates' immersion in the local culture. An extreme outcome would be the expatriate who is isolated and lives primarily for his or her return to the home country; the only motivation for this individual's international presence is strictly monetary, or is linked to the international assignment as a precondition for promotion. Individuals in this predicament are more likely to fail than those who actively participate in the life and culture of the host country.

Yet another extreme is the expatriate who has "gone native." In extreme cases, this individual may refuse to return to the home country, insisting on remaining abroad in the company's service, and in some situations even serving locals to the detriment of the company.

15-3f Repatriation Issues

Upon repatriation, expatriates often find themselves working in a company that has changed drastically during their absence. They find that their corner offices are occupied by their former underlings or by professionals new to the company, and that they do not quite fit into their new work environment. They also suffer a loss of status in their home environment. Whereas, during their international assignment, expatriates and their families were involved in a close, elite social environment that was reserved for the local international community, upon return, they often find themselves to be no more than average dwellers in nondescript suburbia. At this point, they may experience **reverse culture shock,** a feeling of anxiety associated with a longing for the international environment left behind, or fear of not adapting in the new environment and/or losing one's job due to lack of fit.

reverse culture shock Anxiety experienced after returning to the home country, associated with a longing for the international environment left behind and with the difficulty of readjusting to the home country and to corporate life at one's firm.

Companies often try to soften the reverse culture shock experienced by expatriates—especially professional expatriates, who are often reluctant to return to their home country. Strategies used by companies to better prepare the expatriates for repatriation involve, among others, offering a substantial incentive package, such as a raise upon return; guaranteeing a promotion; and/or providing a repatriation grant.

One of the most important actions of the company may be to keep the expatriates "in the loop" for the duration of their assignments.[29] This can be accomplished by flying them back to headquarters on a regular basis, preferably for extended stays, and keeping them on a regular mailing list for intra-office and intra-company communication. Expat Forums recommends ongoing communication to avoid the renegade syndrome and the "out-of-sight, out-of-mind" mindset, and arranging for a mentor in upper management.

Summary

- **Examine companies' expatriate management strategies.** Managing international employees requires using appropriate personnel management policies—a process complicated by obstacles presented by the international environment. Decisions such as assigning management responsibilities to employees, establishing quotas, or even simply addressing employees by their first names could prove to be a challenge. To further complicate matters, local culture and national character will affect relationships between management at each tier of the organization, as will social class or caste.
- **Describe the different types of employees suited for a company's international operations.** A company will hire three types of employees for its international operations. Expatriates are home-country nationals groomed from within the firm's national operations; these employees are familiar with firm policy, operations, goals, and objectives and are likely to best represent company interests. Third-country nationals are professional expatriates who adapt easily regardless of the environment to which they were assigned. On the downside, they need to learn both about the local environment and the company's culture, procedures, and goals. Locals (host-country nationals) are familiar with the host-country operating environment and have relationships already established with the national government and other important agency representatives; they also are the employees most likely to sell out the company by creating a local competitor.
- **Address issues related to expatriate management, such as motivating international employees and ensuring successful assignment performance and repatriation.** To ensure top performance, companies need to appropriately train and motivate expatriates. Training in the local language, however superficial, may benefit the expatriates, as will cultural training; all will minimize culture shock. Appropriate motivation will also improve performance. Some typical perks for expatriates are a housing allowance, moving allowance, education allowance, post-adjustment pay, and home-leave pay. In addition, the employees should be prepared for re-entry in the firm and home country at the end of the assignment, to minimize reverse culture shock.

Key Terms

cost-of-living adjustment
culture shock
education allowance
electronic data interchange (EDI)
expatriate
home-country national
home-leave allowance

host-country national
housing allowance
individual personality
international buyer-seller relationship
moving allowance
national and regional character
order getter

order taker
organizational culture
post adjustment
repatriation
repatriation allowance
reverse culture shock
third-country national

Discussion Questions

1. Describe the three types of employees a company is likely to send to a foreign post. What are their strengths and weaknesses?
2. Discuss some of the management and culture-related challenges involved in international salesforce management? How do companies address those challenges?
3. How do international companies select and train employees for international assignments?
4. What are some of the methods that international firms use to motivate employees for international assignments, and how do these companies ensure that employees face minimal culture shock upon repatriation?

Chapter Quiz (True/False)

1. A third-country national is also known as a local.
2. An advantage of hiring home-country nationals for international operations is that they are less expensive for the company.
3. Expatriates working in a particular foreign country are either home-country nationals or host-country nationals.
4. Organizational culture refers to personality traits shared at the national level.
5. Reverse culture shock is a feeling of anxiety experienced after returning to the home country.
6. In low-context cultures, what is said is precisely what is meant.

Multiple Choice

1. In Asian countries, what approach to selling would work best?
   a. confident, persuasive
   b. modest, exhibiting a humble attitude
   c. serious, formal hard sell
   d. none of the above
2. What are some preferred traits of expatriates?
   a. sensitivity to others
   b. willingness to gain international knowledge
   c. high level of resiliency
   d. all of the above
3. How do companies motivate expatriates?
   a. guaranteed promotion
   b. travel and other allowances
   c. finding spouses employment in the country of assignment
   d. all of the above
4. To relieve reverse culture shock, companies can
   a. keep an employee updated with office emails.
   b. offer promotion on return to the home country.
   c. fly an expatriate back regularly for meetings.
   d. all of the above

Endnotes

1. Nakiye Boyacigiller, "The Role of Expatriates in the Management of Interdependence, Complexity and Risk in Multinational Corporations," *Journal of International Business Studies*, Vol. 22, No. 3, Third Quarter 1991, pp. 357–381.
2. Calvin Reynolds, "Strategic Employment of Third-Country Nationals," *HR: Human Resource Planning*, Vol. 20, No. 1, 1997, pp. 33–93.
3. Dana-Nicoleta Lascu, Lalita A. Manrai, and Sugandha Kamalapuri, "Purchase Behavior of Expatriate Consumers in Saudi Arabia: An Exploratory Study," in W. D. Herrington and R. Taylor (eds.), *Marketing Advances in Theory, Practice, and Education*, Mount Pleasant, MI: Society for Marketing Advances,1998, pp. 128–134.
4. "EC Proposed Legislation No Guarantee for Distance Selling," *International Insurance Monitor*, Vol. 52, No. 1, 1991, p. 2.
5. Ibid.
6. Cynthia Kemper, "Global Sales Success Depends on Cultural Insight," *World Trade*, Vol. 11, No. 5, May 1998, pp. S2–S4.
7. Erika Rasmusson, "Can Your Reps Sell Overseas?" *Sales and Marketing Management*, Vol. 150, No. 2, February 1998, p. 110.
8. Sudhir H. Kale and John Barnes, "Understanding the Domain of Cross-National Buyer-Seller Interactions," *Journal of International Business Studies*, Vol. 23, No. 1, First Quarter 1992, pp. 101–131.
9. Jagdish N. Sheth, "Cross-Cultural Influences on the Buyer-Seller Interaction/Negotiation Process," *Asia Pacific Journal of Management*, Vol. 1, No. 1, 1983, pp. 46–55.
10. See Rosann L. Spiro and Barton A. Weitz, "Adaptive Selling: Conceptualization, Measurement, and Nomological Validity," *Journal of Marketing Research*, Vol. 16, No. 3, August 1990, pp. 355–369; and Kale and Barnes, "Understanding the Domain," pp. 101–131.
11. Kale and Barnes, "Understanding the Domain," pp. 101–131.
12. Geert Hofstede, *Culture's Consequences: International Differences in Work-Related Values*, London: Sage Publications, 1980.
13. Kale and Barnes, "Understanding the Domain," pp. 101–131.
14. Ibid.
15. Alma Mintu-Wimsatt and Julie B. Gassenheimer, "The Moderating Effect of Cultural Context in Buyer-Seller Negotiation," *Journal of Personal Selling Sales Management*, Vol. 20, No. 1, Winter 1999, pp. 1–9.
16. Ibid.
17. See Edward Hall, *Beyond Culture*, Garden City: NY: Anchor Press/Double Day, 1976; and Mintu-Wimsatt and Gassenheimer, "The Moderating Effect," pp. 1–9.
18. Rasmusson, "Can Your Reps," p. 110.
19. Earl Naumann, "A Conceptual Model of Expatriate Turnover," *Journal of International Business Studies*, Vol. 23, No. 3, Third Quarter 1992, pp. 499–531.
20. David M. Noer, *Multinational People Management*, Washington, D.C.: Bureau of National Affairs, 1975.
21. Nancy J. Adler and John L. Graham, "Cross-Cultural Interaction: The International Comparison Fallacy?" *Journal of International Business Studies*, Vol. 20, No. 3, Third Quarter 1989, pp. 515–537.
22. Noer, *Multinational People Management*, 1975.
23. Stephen J. Simurda, "Finding an International Sales Manager," *Northeast International Business*, Vol. 1, No. 3, 1988, pp. 15–16.
24. Rasmusson, "Can Your Reps," p. 110.
25. Kemper, "Global Sales Success," pp. S2–S4.
26. Rasmusson, "Can Your Reps," p. 110.
27. Michele Marchetti, "Global Gamble," *Sales and Marketing Management*, Vol. 148, No. 7, July 1996, pp. 64–65.
28. Rasmusson, "Can Your Reps," p. 110.
29. Lambeth Hochwald, "Luring Execs Overseas," *Sales and Marketing Management*, Vol. 152, No. 2, February 2000, p. 101.

You can find the correct answers to these questions by taking the quiz and then submitting your answers in the Online Edition. The program will automatically score your submission. Where you miss a question, the program will provide the correct answer, a rationale for the answer, and the section number in the chapter where the topic is discussed.

Case 15-1

The Expatriate Spouse: Managing Change

Geena Sorenson, a former Madison Avenue executive and spouse of a Kraft Foods expatriate from the company's New York headquarters assigned to Shanghai, found herself counting the hours until her first home leave scheduled in exactly nine months. She missed visiting her circle of friends and former classmates at New York University, spending her Saturday mornings visiting the Chelsea art galleries, buying her bagels hot at Tal Bagels, and experiencing the quiet trepidations of the city on a Sunday morning. Instead, she was counting the hours until her return, unable to fit into the local environment of an equally vivacious Shanghai. She felt much like the lonely characters of the movie *Lost in Translation,* unable to understand her environment, spending long hours in a high-rise apartment and waiting on her busy husband, who was rarely home.

Reading the different journals and magazines for expatriates and looking at the readily available online literature, she found that the cost of sending a family to an international location is as high as $1 million. And yet companies are not as skillful in the selection and preparation procedure as one might think. A foreign assignment presents problems for the entire family—Geena could relate. The employee should be capable to cope, to learn how to lead, motivate, and work with staff from other cultures. The spouse, if female, may have to deal with living in a male-dominated culture; and it is often likely that her world will be limited to the local expatriate community. China, which is by far the most popular new destination for foreign assignments, is quite a problematic posting because expats face not only language and cultural barriers, but also challenges when it comes to housing, transportation, education, and medical care.

Geena also found that, in spite of China's status as an important destination for expatriates, the number of its expatriates are decreasing, primarily for two reasons. One, expatriates are increasingly hired on local terms, without the traditional expat package. Expatriates tend to have less pay and a shorter-term package and thus are less likely to accept the assignment. And, two, jobs are increasingly going to well-trained nationals.

In her search, Geena discovered a website, Expats in China, which offered an overview of the expatriate life in China, similar to the materials provided by her husband's company in the training materials for the assignment. She also found useful referrals for various services she could potentially use in the future, a digest of the local and national news from various sources, but not much else. Other expatriate sites were also only marginally useful.

Using her entrepreneurial skills, Geena decided to create an agency that would address the needs of spouses like her, attempting to understand the local environment in spite of the culture shock, but also longing for her home country. The purpose of the agency would be to facilitate integration and dialogue about integration in a society that is culturally dissimilar.

Sources: Rensia Melles, "Lost in Translation," *Canadian HR Reporter,* Vol. 17, No. 5, March 8, 2004, p. 14; "Hong Kong, A Classic Case of Expatriate Change," *International Money Marketing,* March 2004, p. 16; "Where Next for the Expat?" *International Money Marketing,* March 2004, p. 14; http://www.expatsinchina.com/.

Analysis Suggestions

1. Is Geena experiencing culture shock? Explain. If the answer is yes, what can she do to lessen its impact?
2. What are the costs of bringing a spouse along for an assignment? Would the company be better off if the spouse remained in the home country? Explain.
3. How should Geena's agency help in addressing the needs of expatriate spouses. Offer ideas and activities that would benefit the large group of spouses accompanying expatriates in China.

International Pricing Strategy

Chapter Objectives

By the end of this chapter, you should be able to

1 Identify pricing-related internal challenges facing international firms.

2 Identify pricing-related challenges imposed by competition on international firms.

3 Identify pricing-related challenges imposed by the political and legal environment on international firms.

4 Identify pricing-related challenges imposed by the economic and financial environment on international firms.

5 Address international pricing decisions of international firms.

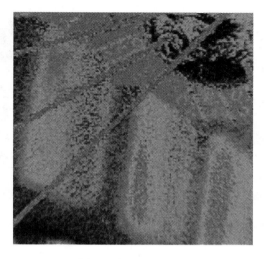

Pricing is especially important in international marketing strategy decisions, due to its effect on product positioning, market segmentation, demand management, and market share dynamics.[1] The international pricing decision is complex: Numerous internal and external variables, such as the nature of the product, the location of production plants, the type of distribution system used, and the economic climate, must all be evaluated before determining the final price of products and services.[2] Pricing decisions are further affected by currency fluctuations and by exchange rate controls in individual markets.

This chapter addresses challenges that international firms face internally when setting prices. It also addresses the impact of the international competitive, political and legal, and economic and financial environment on firm pricing decisions. Finally, it evaluates pricing policies of firms for different international markets.

16-1 Pricing Decisions and Procedures

Pricing decisions are determined by the location of production facilities and the companies' abilities to track costs.

16-1a Production Facilities

The location of production facilities determines the extent to which companies can control costs and price their products competitively. Multinationals usually can afford to shift production to take advantage of lower costs and exchange rates, whereas small to medium-size firms are often limited to exporting as the only venue for product distribution.[3] Companies can and often do price themselves out of the market in certain countries, especially if they do not shift production to a low-labor-cost, low-tax country. As an example, Marc Controls, to lower the price of its products, purchases raw materials in Korea, China, and India and ships them to the United States for manufacturing; its products are competitively priced when sold on the German market, but they are considered overpriced in most of Asia.[4]

16-1b Ability to Keep Track of Costs

Product components often are manufactured in different countries. Often, the final products are assembled in a particular country—which is frequently not the company's home country—and then sold all over the world. It is consequently difficult for financial officers to keep track of product costs.[5]

16-2 Environment-Related Challenges and Pricing Decisions

Pricing decisions are affected by all the external elements in a company's international environment. An international company must react effectively to changes in the competitive environment, in the political and legal environment, and in the economic and

The Competitive Environment	• **Gray market/parallel imports** as a competitive threat • **Dumping** as a competitive threat
The Political and Legal Environment	• **Transfer pricing** • The price of protectionism
The Economic and Financial Environment	• Inflationary pressures on price • Fluctuating exchange rates • Shortage of hard currency and **countertrade**

financial environment. Figure 16-1 addresses examples of different challenges in the international firm's environment that affect the firm's pricing decisions.

16-2a The Competitive Environment

Competition

International and local competition often pose serious concerns to multinational firms. If competition can keep product prices low by manufacturing in a low-labor-cost country, firms must meet this challenge and maintain a low price, potentially at a loss. At a retail level, and especially in service environments, companies often are challenged by local competitors offering legal copycat products at a much lower price. For example, Pizza Hut is challenged in every market in Poland by a local pizza chain that offers almost identical products, such as Neapolitan pizza, at a fraction of Pizza Hut's offering.

Frequently, challenges at the retail level may be difficult to identify. Here's an example of such a challenge: Firms operating in markets where retailers are likely to keep the change price their products under the even number of the banknote that would normally be used in purchasing those products. For example, in Egypt, Romania, and Turkey, among others, retailers are unlikely to give back small change, or even any change at all, to customers. In such an environment, a company using an even-pricing strategy will be at a disadvantage because retailers will choose to sell competitors' products. This is the case even if the company's prices are below competitors' prices.

Gray Market/Parallel Imports as a Competitive Threat

A firm engaging in a differential pricing strategy could be vulnerable to competition from unauthorized channels. In fact, differential pricing (price discrimination) by the manufacturer has been identified as a main cause of parallel importing—diverting products purchased in a low-price market to other markets (**parallel imports**) by means of a distribution system not authorized by the manufacturer, otherwise known as a **gray market**.[6] See Figure 16-2.

A manufacturer may charge different prices in different markets for the same product

parallel imports/gray market
A distribution system not authorized by the manufacturer whereby the products purchased in a low-price market are diverted to other markets.

- To meet the needs of target consumers who have a limited purchasing power.
- To keep the product price competitive in markets that are actively targeted by competition.
- Due to changes in the exchange rate in countries where the products are sold; the product is likely to be cheaper in the countries with the weakest currency.
- Due to the fact that it offers discounts to wholesalers buying higher quantities.

- Due to differences in wholesale prices in different markets; for example, wholesale prices for luxury goods are relatively high in the United States, compared to wholesale prices in the rest of the world.

Gray markets or parallel imports are common in the United Kingdom, and elsewhere in the world; see International Marketing Illustration 16-1.

Dumping as a Competitive Threat

Firms also can face challenges from companies **dumping** products in their target market. Dumping is an important factor affecting pricing decisions. A typical example of dumping involves a foreign company that enjoys high prices and high profits at home as a result of trade barriers against imports; the company uses those profits to sell at much lower prices in foreign markets to build market share and suppress the profitability of competitors with open home markets.[7] According to the World Trade Organization, dumping should be condemned if it threatens to cause injury to an established industry in a particular market and/or if it delays the establishment of a viable domestic industry.[8]

Antidumping policies differ somewhat from country to country. China, according to its Antidumping and Anti-Subsidy Regulations set forth by the State Council, defines dumping as the subsidization of exports resulting in substantial injury, or the threat of substantial injury, to an established domestic industry, or substantially impeding the establishment of a comparable domestic industry.[9] According to the Chinese, dumping is involved if a product is sold at a price below its normal value, where normal value may be based on production costs plus reasonable expenses and profit, or on the comparable price in the exporting country for an identical or like product; if there is no comparable price for the product in the exporting country, reference is made to the price at which the exporter sells a similar product in a third country.[10]

Similarly, the United States Department of Commerce, the government branch responsible for determining whether products are dumped on the U.S. market, considers that dumping takes place if products are priced only minimally above cost, or at prices below those charged in the producing country. The European Commission, in charge of antidumping regulation in the European Union, requires a vote of the Council of Ministers for action against dumping activity and other unfair trade practices.

dumping Selling products below cost to get rid of excess inventory and/or to undermine competition.

International Marketing Illustration 16-1

Parallel Imports: A Perspective

In the United Kingdom, one can buy Coke produced for the Middle East, Russian Head & Shoulders shampoo, South African Colgate toothpaste, and Brazilian Dove soap.

Tesco even purchased Levi Strauss jeans in the United States to sell them at a discount in its U.K. stores; the stores sold about 15,000 pairs of Levi's jeans a week for half the price charged in specialty stores approved by Levi Strauss. Levi Strauss filed a lawsuit at the European Court of Justice, joined by Zino Davidoff, the perfume maker. The Court ruled that selling Levi's jeans meant for U.S. consumers was wrong.

As a result of the Court's decision, Tesco and the public were outraged. Tesco was seen as attempting to level an uneven ground where jeans were sold as premium goods in Europe and mass-merchandised in the United States, thus cheating U.K. consumers. Even attempts by Levi Strauss to explain that it is costly to sell jeans in the United Kingdom, due to the limited availability of retail space, were met with significant consumer skepticism.

All in all, the international brand often speaks the wrong language in much of the world. Consumers may recognize that the brand looks somewhat different, but they are always glad to get a bargain: The brand name alone provides the guarantee. This debate will linger and, possibly, the only way to circumvent parallel imports is to closely control distribution. Gucci, the upscale Italian clothing manufacturer, was practically destroyed by loose licensing and overexposure in discount retailers. However, it was able to take charge of its situation, ending contracts with third-party suppliers, controlling its distribution well, and opening its own stores. This strategy worked so well that it is difficult to find discounted Gucci products today.

Sources: "Market Report: Parallel Lines," *In-Store*, September 2003, p. 21; "Business: Trouser Suit; Parallel Imports," *The Economist*, Vol. 361, No. 8249, November 24, 2001, p. 76.

Dumping challenges and charges abound. China, Japan, and South Korea have often been challenged for dumping products in the United States and Europe. China is currently fighting back, enforcing its antidumping legislation to protect local industry from international competition; one target of Chinese scrutiny is U.S. newsprint.[11] Another point of contention centers on calculating product prices in nonmarket and transition economies, such as those of China and Russia. There is a strong disagreement on exactly how to determine product costs in a state-owned or directed economy; the U.S. Department of Commerce is attempting to address this unknown by making reference to tangible measures, such as product price in the product's home country, or in other markets.[12]

As established by the World Trade Organization, after determining that price discrimination did indeed occur and that a particular local industry was injured by the dumping activity, governments are entitled to impose **antidumping duties** on the merchandise. Similar to these are **countervailing duties,** which are imposed on subsidized products imported into the country. Such subsidizing could, for example, take the form of government aid in the processes of production and/or distribution.

Enforcement of antidumping regulation is particularly intense when the economy is not faring well and when price competition is intense. In the recent past, the United States Department of Commerce and the International Trade Commission scrutinized

antidumping duties Duties that must be paid by firms as a punishment for engaging in unfair price competition.

countervailing duties Duties imposed on subsidized products imported into a country.

numerous importers' pricing practices, using strict criteria to determine whether the importer had committed price discrimination and, if so, if it resulted in injury to a particular local industry. Electronics, textiles, and steel, among others, originating in countries from Japan to Russia to China to Mexico, have been at the center of antidumping action in the past few decades. In the case of Mexico, the current administration has imposed prohibitive and unreasonable antidumping duties on imports of cement, in spite of the shortage of cement in the United States; instead, builders in the United States must rely on suppliers from Asia, who take on average 44 days to deliver the product at a U.S. port.[13]

In spite of a more strict enforcement, companies continue to be affected by pricing actions of importers taking advantage of loopholes in the antidumping legislation. To avoid price discrimination charges, the importers modify their products slightly so as not to permit them to be directly compared with products sold in other countries at higher prices.

16-2b The Political and Legal Environment

Governments regulate prices charged by multinational firms. Regulations and restrictions exist with regard to many pricing decisions, ranging from dumping to setting limits on wholesalers' gross margins and on the product's retail price. As mentioned in Chapter 12, "International Retailing," Wal-Mart has been challenged in the European Union for charging prices that are too low (just above cost) and that drive competition out of business. Price promotions are severely restricted, limiting the manufacturers' ability to boost sales in the short term and to help retailers renew their inventories.

Multinational companies also are affected by local government subsidies to local manufacturers, in particular, to producers of agricultural products and to exporting firms. Subsidies lower the price charged in international markets for products and challenge the competitive position of firms operating in the same industry. Finally, governments can also impose tariffs and other duties on products in certain industries, especially if those industries are in infancy in the respective countries. Governments defend such action under the **infant industry argument,** which permits setting high tariffs on imports that challenge emerging local producers.

In general, governments use numerous strategies in their attempts to restrict the repatriation of profits by multinationals and to tax and/or to encourage the reinvestment of profits. One way that companies can bypass such restrictions is through the use of transfer pricing.

Transfer Pricing

Transfer pricing is a pricing strategy used in intra-firm sales: The pricing of products in the process of conducting transactions between units of the same corporation, within or beyond the national borders of the parent company, is known as transfer pricing and regarded as a legitimate business opportunity by transnational corporations.[14] Developing countries often bring the issue of transfer pricing to the attention of international trade bodies as a strategy that could help a multinational company under-report profits and decrease its tax burden in countries where it has foreign direct investment, thus evading taxation. Instead of pricing products at cost, products can be priced *at market level,* known as **market-based transfer pricing,** where the price reflects the price products sell for in a particular market; *at cost,* known as **cost-based transfer pricing,** where the cost reflects not the cost incurred by the company, but the estimated opportunity cost of the product; or products can be priced using a combination of the two strategies.

The Price of Protectionism

Protectionism adds to the final price paid by consumers. In spite of the Uruguay round of trade liberalization and the strides made by the World Trade Organization, protectionist actions continue to increase the costs of goods, and hence the price for the final consumer. Europe's economy, for example, is almost as protected as it was 10 years ago, and

infant industry argument A protectionist strategy aimed at protecting a national industry in its infancy from powerful international competitors.

transfer pricing A pricing strategy used in intra-firm sales for commercial transactions between units of the same corporation, within or beyond the national borders of the parent company.

market-based transfer pricing A pricing strategy used in intra-firm sales for commercial transactions between units of the same corporation, within or beyond the national borders of the parent company, whereby products are priced at market cost, rather than at the cost incurred by the company.

cost-based transfer pricing A pricing strategy used in intra-firm sales for commercial transactions between units of the same corporation, within or beyond the national borders of the parent company, where the costs reflect not the costs incurred by the company, but the estimated opportunity costs of the product.

its costs are as high as 7 percent of the gross domestic product of the European Union—some $600 billion.[15] To illustrate, the EU's banana-import restrictions cost European consumers up to $2 billion a year, or about 55 cents per kilogram of bananas.[16] In other examples, European beef farmers receive large subsidies, while tariffs of up to 125 percent are imposed on beef imports; in addition, the EU has a ban on hormone-treated beef from the United States. The costs incurred by European beef consumers for subsidies, tariffs, and other restrictions amount to $14.6 billion a year in the form of higher prices and taxes, or around $1.60 per kilogram of beef.[17]

These figures are high in the United States as well, especially in service industries such as shipping and banking.[18]

16-2c The Economic and Financial Environment

Inflationary Pressures on Price

An inflationary environment places strong pressures on companies to lower prices; often, pricing competitively may mean that companies are not producing a profit. During inflationary periods, firms often find that they must decide between maintaining a competitive presence in a market and weathering the downside of the economic cycle or abandoning the market, which is a high-cost, high-risk proposition. Companies operating in Latin America in the 1980s and early 1990s often faced challenges posed by inflation.

Fluctuating Exchange Rates

Fluctuating exchange rates provide both challenges and opportunities to firms trading in the global arena. Companies that do not pay attention to fluctuations in exchange rates could find that their profits are greatly eroded during the time lapsed between contract negotiations and the actual product delivery. Including a percentage that covers exchange rate fluctuations when specifying the product price is one strategy companies use to address the unpredictability of such fluctuations.

Traditionally, firms specified all transactions in a strong, stable, hard currency—usually the dollar. Since the dollar's ups and downs in the 1970s and 1980s, however, other currencies have emerged as standards for exchanges. Increasingly, pricing decisions are facilitated by the advent of successful venues for regional integration, such as the European Union and MERCOSUR (the Southern Cone Common Market). Member countries have adopted a single currency, in the case of the European Union, or, in the case of MERCOSUR, they are attempting to peg the currency of member countries relative to each other. The advent of the Euro in the European Union has greatly facilitated transactions in the region.

Shortage of Hard Currency and Countertrade

Developing countries face a significant shortage of hard currency reserves. **Hard currency** is currency that is accepted for payment by any international seller; **soft currency** is currency that is kept at a high artificial exchange rate, overvalued, and controlled by the national government. This situation, compounded by the inability to borrow from international banks or other sources such as the International Monetary Fund, has led developing countries to resort to **countertrade** to remain active in international trade and to address the needs of local consumers. Moreover, as global markets are growing competitive, increasingly, the balance of power is shifting from sellers to buyers; in the process, buyers require sellers to engage in reciprocal purchases, known as countertrade.[19]

Countertrade involves selling a product to a buyer and agreeing to accept, in return for payment, products from the buyer's firm or from the trade agency/institution of the buyer. Countertrade has been traditionally associated with companies from countries in the former Soviet Bloc and from other countries with a tightly controlled soft currency. The classic countertrade example is the one initiated by PepsiCo with the former Soviet Union. In the late 1960s, Nikita Khruschev, then president of the Soviet Union, was

hard currency Currency that is accepted for payment by any international seller.

soft currency Currency that is kept at a high artificial exchange rate, overvalued, and controlled by the national central bank.

countertrade A form of trade whereby a company sells a product to a buyer and agrees to accept, in return for payment, products from the buyer's firm or from the trade agency/institution of the buyer.

impressed by the taste of Pepsi and agreed to an exchange of Pepsi syrup and bottling equipment in return for Stolichnaya vodka. This exchange was an example of successful countertrade conducted over decades.

Countertrade is on the increase worldwide; it is estimated that the percentage of the total world trade financed through countertrade transactions is just more than 20 percent.[20] Many developing countries rely heavily on countertrade in their international trade activity; for example, as much as 70 percent of Russian industrial activity involves barter.[21]

A typical countertrade exchange today would involve a seller from a developed, industrialized country and a buyer from a developing country where hard currency is scarce and tightly controlled by national institutions, such as the Central Bank and the Ministry of Foreign Trade. Usually, firms in the developing country are unable to secure bank loans that would finance imports of products deemed to be unessential, such as consumer products. In many developing countries (even in countries with a greater access to hard currency—primarily due to the export of natural reserves, such as oil and diamonds), governments actually mandate countertrade as a form of payment for firms purchasing imported goods.

It should be noted that countertrade is an important venue for firms in developed countries as well. For example, firms in the United States and Western Europe use countertrade exchanges routinely.[22]

The Position of the U.S. Government on Countertrade

The United States, in line with the mandates of the General Agreement on Tariffs and Trade (GATT) and the World Trade Organization (WTO), has a policy that opposes government-mandated countertrade. The U.S. government interferes only in the case of firms that operate with U.S.-government financing or firms that have contracts with the U.S. government. In this case, the U.S. government could compromise the competitive position of U.S. firms, which are at a disadvantage in developing countries compared to their Japanese and European competitors.[23] However, the U.S. government does not deter firms from engaging in countertrade with private parties. Furthermore, the U.S. government supports countertrade for the sale of weapons and aircraft (countertrade constitutes the key form of trade internationally for defense equipment) and for agricultural surplus.[24]

Countertrade Brokers

Often, countertrade is conducted with the help of countertrade brokers because it is rare that a perfect match can exist for product exchanges and because the exchanges themselves are complex. Exchanges could range from paying sausages to rock stars for their performances, and bringing French high fashion to Russian consumers by selling quality Russian crystal to Saudi merchants. In the second example, the barter of French high fashion for Russian crystal is mediated by Saudi parties, who pay cash for the product to the French couturiers.

Numerous companies specialize in brokering barter deals. Located in many financial centers, such as London and New York, as well as in countries that have traditions of brokering barter agreements, such as Sweden, these brokers can put together intricate exchanges. Among the major U.S. corporate barter firms doing large-volume business are the firms of Argent Trading; Active International; Media Resources International; and Tradewell, Inc.[25] These barter agents or brokers, known in the trade as commercial trade exchanges, typically utilize extensive computerized databases to locate and match demand and supply.[26]

Advantages of Countertrade

Countertrade offers substantial advantages to the involved parties. Countertrade allows firms from industrialized countries to sell their products in markets in the developing world that otherwise would not be accessible. Many countries that have a shortage of hard currency and that otherwise cannot secure bank loans to finance imports restrict the import of products considered nonessential by using foreign exchange controls and/or other barriers. Countertrade can help an exporting company bypass such restrictions.

In addition to offering an opportunity to many developing countries to participate in trade, countertrade also offers individuals from developing countries access to consumer products. Ministries of Foreign Trade in many developing countries tend to favor *heavy* industry imports and to restrict *light* industry imports, especially imports of soft consumer goods. For example, countertrade makes it possible for consumers in developing countries to have access to brand name clothing and small appliances and to attend concerts of popular rock stars.

Disadvantages of Countertrade

Among the disadvantages of countertrade are the following:[27]

- Companies countertrading with an indebted nation may find that foreign lenders have prior claim on goods offered as part of the countertrading agreement.
- Countertrade arrangements frequently restrict profit margins and, often, during negotiations, price setting is difficult because not all cost factors are known in advance.
- Countertrade practices encourage economic inefficiency and are a cumbersome and time-consuming way of doing business.
- Prices are distorted as deliveries, which could take place over time, are made without reference to changes in technology, taste, quality, market structure, or competing products.
- Companies may receive inferior quality products as payment because rigorous quality control may not be a practice in the trading partner's enterprise.
- Exchange partners can, in the long term, become competitors.
- Countertrade agreements often require long and expensive negotiations.

Often, the goods firms receive as payment are unrelated to the products they sell, and the firms have no expertise in marketing these products; for example, Caterpillar Tractor received Algerian wine in exchange for its products but was unable to sell it in the U.S. market.

Types of Countertrade

The different types of countertrade usually involve monetary exchange to a certain degree. Barter is the only type of exchange that does not involve monetary exchange. At the next level are clearing agreements and switch trading, which involve the transfer of currency, usually a mutually-agreed-upon hard currency. All other types of countertrade are based on direct monetary exchange.

Barter

Barter can be traced back for centuries as a form of exchange. It involves a simple, non-monetized exchange of goods and/or services between two parties. Although no money is involved in the exchange, the parties calculate the value of the goods in a particular currency and attempt to achieve value parity for the exchanged goods.

Clearing Agreement

A clearing agreement, also known as a **clearing account,** is a somewhat complex form of countertrade. Under this form of countertrade, a third party, usually a barter agent or some other type of broker, creates clearing accounts that represent trade credits for the respective parties, and companies trade in and out as necessary.[28] Under a clearing agreement, countries are likely to trade products up to a certain amount stated in a particular,

barter A simple, nonmonetized exchange of goods and/or services between two parties.

clearing account A complex form of countertrade whereby countries trade products up to a certain amount stated in a particular, mutually-agreed-upon hard currency and within a given time frame, and, when an imbalance occurs and one country owes money to the other, swing credits are paid in an agreed-upon hard currency, known as the clearing currency; also called a clearing agreement.

mutually-agreed-upon hard currency, and within a given time frame. When an imbalance occurs and one country owes money to the other, **swing credits** are paid in an agreed-upon hard currency, known as the **clearing currency.**

Switch Trading

Switch trading involves buying a party's position in a countertrade in exchange for hard currency and selling it to another customer.[29] Professional switch trading firms purchase products that are not accepted by the seller as payment for products and, for a commission, sell them on the market at a discount.

Compensation

Compensation involves payment in products and in cash, usually in a mutually-agreed-upon convertible currency. The firm compensated using this system is at lesser risk—especially if the proportion of cash is high—than the firm that is entirely dependent on the sale of the products it receives from the trading partner.

Counterpurchase

Counterpurchase involves two exchanges that are paid for in cash; as such, counterpurchase involves two parallel contracts—hence, its name of **parallel barter.** The seller agrees to purchase products that usually are unrelated to its business from the buyer and sell them on international markets. The purchase could be for the total sum of the products sold or for a fraction thereof. The exporter agrees to buy goods from a shopping list provided by the importer; the list typically consists of light manufactures and consumer goods. In one example, Volkswagen sold 10,000 cars to the former East Germany and agreed to purchase, over a period of two years, goods for the value of the automobiles, from a list of goods provided by the East German government.[30] Another illustration of counterpurchase is the classic countertrade example whereby PepsiCo sold its syrup to Russia in the late 1960s; the export agreement stated that PepsiCo would subsequently import Stolichnaya vodka to be sold in the United States.[31]

The advantage of counterpurchase is that, typically, the seller is paid up front, in cash; the seller also has a specified, limited period (usually no more than a year) to sell the goods obtained through the exchange. Many governments of developing countries mandate counterpurchase as a requirement for firms exporting products to them. For example, in the past Indonesia required 100 percent counterpurchase on state contracts higher than $500,000, except where aid funds were involved; however, due to pressure from GATT and governments of industrialized countries, this policy has changed.[32]

Offset Purchase

Offset purchases involve large hard currency purchases, such as the purchase of defense equipment, airplanes, telecommunications networks, railway or road building, and other expensive civil engineering projects, by a developing country. The seller agrees, in return for the sale of its offering, to purchase products that are valued at a certain percentage of the sale, ranging from 20 percent, which is quite typical, to as much as 100 percent for highly competitive deals. China, for example, often imposes offsets for its purchases. Other examples of offset purchases may involve sourcing some of the production locally, transferring technology to the importing country, or marketing different products sourced in the purchasing country.[33]

An example of an offset agreement is the sale of DC-9s by McDonnell Douglas to the former Yugoslavia in the 1960s; to secure the order, McDonnell Douglas agreed to help sell products sourced in Yugoslavia to buyers in the United States to generate capital to help finance the purchase of the passenger planes.[34]

Buyback Agreements

In a **buyback agreement,** the seller builds and provides a turn-key plant, as well as the manufacturing know-how, the necessary equipment, patents, and licenses necessary for

---

swing credits Amounts paid within the framework of a clearing agreement by the country that owes money to the other when an imbalance occurs.

clearing currency The agreed-upon currency used to pay swing credits in a clearing account or agreement.

switch trading The process of buying a party's position in a countertrade in exchange for hard currency and selling it to another customer.

compensation The payment in products and in cash, usually in a mutually-agreed-upon convertible currency.

counterpurchase/parallel barter A form of trade that involves two exchanges paid for in cash; it involves two parallel contracts whereby the seller agrees to purchase products that are usually unrelated to its business from the buyer and sell them on international markets.

offset purchase A large, hard-currency purchase, such as the purchase of defense equipment, airplanes, telecommunications networks, railway or road building and other expensive civil engineering projects whereby the seller agrees, in return to purchase products that are valued at a certain percentage of the sale.

buyback agreements Agreements whereby the seller builds and provides a turnkey plant and is paid up front part of the cost of the plant in an agreed-upon convertible currency; in return, the seller agrees to purchase specific quantities of the plant's output over an extended period of time.

production and distribution of the product. The seller is paid up front part of the cost of the plant in an agreed-upon convertible currency, which is typically obtained by borrowing from international banks or the International Monetary Fund. The seller agrees to purchase specific quantities of the plant's output over an extended period of time. An advantage of this type of countertrade to the seller is that it has the know-how in terms of marketing and distributing the products because the company operates in a similar business.

An example of a buyback is that of two British firms, ICI and Davy Powergas, which in 1977 sold a methanol plant to the Soviet Union for $250 million and agreed to purchase 20 percent of the plant's output in the years 1981 to 1991, for a total of $350 million.[35]

16-3 International Pricing Decisions

16-3a Price Setting

Setting prices internationally tends to be intuition- and experience-driven and highly decentralized. The skill in pricing lies in exploiting differences in consumers' willingness to pay; consequently, it is important for marketing managers to be familiar with the price elasticities of their products in a particular international market.[36]

Important determinants of the final price are currency fluctuations. Managers must decide what their reactions should be to currency fluctuations: Should they adjust their prices based on these fluctuations, or should they fix the prices on their home country currency or the currency in the country of production? Should they pass on price increases to customers or choose a lower profit? Due to the instability of currencies, many sales contracts have exchange rate clauses that address exchange rate fluctuations and exchange risk. Periodic examinations of exchange rate trends determine the adjustments necessary to align prices accordingly.

Additional important determinants of the final price are the prices paid down the chain of distribution, in business-to-business transactions. In these transactions, buyers and sellers need to agree to the terms of sale and on the terms of payment. The terms of sale determine what is and what is not included in the price quotation and when the seller takes possession of the goods. In a business-to-business environment, a buyer can correctly evaluate price deals on their face value only when fully taking into account the terms of sale and the terms of payment offered by the seller. Consequently, these considerations constitute important competitive tools when quoting prices: It is very helpful to be aware not only of the prices that competitors set, but also the terms of sale and terms of payment quoted. Moreover, it is important to note that businesses in certain markets may have a preference for one type or category of quote over another, and that certain markets may not be well equipped to handle a higher level of risk, for instance.

Incoterms (International Commercial Terms) Terms of sale used in transactions.

The terms of sale are stated using **Incoterms**—the International Commercial Terms, described in International Marketing Illustration 16-2. As a general trend, marketers tend to be more inclined to quote more inclusive terms—the D-terms in the Illustration.

Other important determinants of the final price are the terms of payment offered by the seller. Handling the payment is often one of the last items to be considered in the international transaction and, as a result, it is sometimes given less weight. The methods of payment are typically determined by the company's reasons for going international, the company's strategy in the respective market, and its expected return. The company needs to find out what forms of payment are preferred in a particular market and are acceptable for the buyer; this information will also shed light on the partner's financial strength.[37] International Marketing Illustration 16-3 examines the different terms of payment in international transactions.

In setting prices, companies need to examine existing competition, the labor market and materials costs, the buying power of consumers, and the goal of the company with regard to the respective target market. The company may price products higher or lower in the home market; it could engage in aggressive export pricing, skimming, or penetration pricing; or it could use standardized pricing worldwide or local pricing. These strategies are described next.

International Marketing Illustration

16-2

Terms of Sale

Incoterms apply both to domestic and to international transactions. They were first devised by the International Chamber of Commerce (ICC, based in Paris, France) in 1936 and, since then, have been updated a number of times, most recently in the year 2000. These terms of sale are also referred to as "Incoterms 2000."

The terms are further organized into E-terms, implying that the seller makes the goods available at the seller's plant, factory, place of business. The E-term *EXW—Ex Works* (factory, warehouse, etc.)—states that the title and risk pass to the buyer from the seller's factory, plant, or warehouse. The seller's merchandise is not cleared for export, and the seller does not load merchandise on a vehicle. Ex Works is used for any mode of transportation, and it requires the minimum responsibility of the seller.

Prices are also quoted using F-terms, meaning that the seller delivers goods to the carrier that the buyer appoints. Among the F-terms are *FCA—Free Carrier* (a place after the origin point)—whereby the title and risk pass to the buyer at the point when the seller delivers goods that have been cleared for export to the carrier designated by buyer. The seller loads the goods on the buyer's vehicle, and the buyer receives the seller's arriving vehicle unloaded. A product that is delivered *FAS—Free Alongside Ship* (at port, after all port charges)—requires the title and risk to pass to the buyer after the merchandise is delivered alongside the ship by the seller. This term is used for sea or inland waterway transportation. The seller is in charge of export clearance. *FOB—Free on Board* (port, after all port charges)—means that the title and risk pass to the buyer once delivered on board the ship by the seller—after the goods pass the ship's rail. This term is used for sea or inland waterway transportation. The seller is in charge of export clearance.

C-terms denote that the seller must arrange for transportation without assuming the risk of loss. *CFR—Cost and Freight* (destination port)—means that the title, risk, and insurance cost pass to the buyer when delivered on board the ship by the seller. The seller pays transportation costs to the destination port. *CIF—Cost, Insurance and Freight* (destination port)—means that the title, risk, and insurance costs pass to the buyer when delivered on board the ship by the seller. The seller pays transportation and insurance costs to the destination port. CFR and CIF are used for sea or inland waterway transportation. *CPT—Carriage Paid To* (place at destination; includes all port charges)—means that the title, risk, and insurance costs pass to the buyer when delivered to the carrier or seller. The seller pays transportation and insurance costs to the destination port. A product delivered *CIP—Carriage and Insurance Paid To* (place at destination; includes all port charges)—means that title and risk pass to the buyer when delivered to the carrier or seller. The seller pays transportation and insurance costs to the destination port. Both CIP and CPT are used for any mode of transportation, and the seller is obligated to clear the goods for export.

D-terms imply that the seller bears all the costs and risks to bring the goods to a location agreed upon by the buyers. *DAF—Delivered to Frontier* (border of

continued

country)—means that the title and risk pass to the buyer who is responsible for import clearance. This term is used for any mode of transportation. *DES— Delivered Ex Ship* (on board ship to destination port)—means that the title, risk, and responsibility for vessel unloading and import clearance pass to the buyer when the seller delivers goods on board the ship to the destination port. *DEQ— Delivered Ex Quay* (Wharf), Duty Paid (destination port, includes duties and taxes but not destination charges and delivery)—means that the title and risk pass to the buyer when delivered on board ship at the destination by the seller. The buyer clears the merchandise for import and pays for all formalities, duties, taxes, and other charges. The seller delivers goods on dock at the destination and clears merchandise for import. The terms *DES* and *DEQ* are used for sea or inland waterway transportation.

DDU—Delivered Duty Unpaid (destination; excludes all duties and taxes)— means that the title, risk, and responsibility for the vessel's discharge and import clearance pass to the buyer when delivered on board the ship at the destination point by the seller. Finally, *DDP—Delivered Duty Paid* (buyer's door; includes all charges)—means that the title and risk pass to the buyer when the seller delivers goods to the destination. The seller is responsible for import clearance. The terms *DDU* and *DDP* are used for any mode of transportation.

Now consider three identical shipments with identical prices for each shipment, quoted for EXW (Dieburg, Germany), CIF (Norfolk, Virginia), and DDP (Norfolk, Virginia) for Stihl merchandise shipped from Dieburg, Germany, to Norfolk, Virginia. The best deal for the buyer is the DDP (Norfolk).

Sources: http://www.iccwbo.org/incoterms; International Chamber of Commerce, *Incoterms 2000*, Paris: ICC Publishing, 2000; John Murray, Jr. "Risk, Title, and Incoterms," *Purchasing*, Vol. 132, No. 10, June 19, 2003, p. 26; John Shuman, "Incoterms 2000," *Business Credit*, Vol. 102, No. 7, July/August 2000, p. 50.

Prices Higher in the Home Market

Setting prices higher in the home market than in the international market is justified by, among others, one or a combination of the following:

* A lower labor or raw material cost in the international market
* Strong local competition in the international market
* A lower buying power of host-country consumers relative to consumers in the company's home market
* A firm goal to increase market share by using a penetration pricing strategy in the international market, as is most likely in the example offered in Figure 16-3

Prices Lower in the Home Country

Setting prices lower in the home country, compared to company prices in the international market, is justified, among others, by one or a combination of the following:

* There may be no cost advantages to producing overseas, such as economies of scale and labor to justify a lower price.

International Marketing Illustration 16-3

Terms of Payment

Buyers and sellers can agree to a number of methods of payment in international transactions:

- *Cash in Advance*—This is the most advantageous payment option for the seller, but not for the buyer. It is used for sellers' markets primarily or for high-risk buyer environments.
- *Open Account*—This method entails delivering goods or services without a guarantee of payment; the buyer and seller had conducted transactions in the past, and there is an expectation of continued business for both. The Basic Open Account entails payment reasonably soon after the shipment arrives or within an agreed-upon period. This method is very risky for the seller, who must choose buyers well.
- *Consignment with Open Account*—Sellers can reduce risk with this type of Open Account because they still own the merchandise. However, the costs of recovering the goods are typically high in international transactions.
- *Documentary Collection*—With this method, title and possession pass to the buyer when the documents attesting to the title and the shipping documents pass as well. These documents can be a bill of lading, a commercial invoice, an insurance certificate, or a certificate of origin. The payment document, known as a bill of exchange or draft, requiring the buyer to pay immediately (sight draft) or at a specified time (time draft), is sent through the seller's bank to the buyer's bank after the goods have been shipped. The buyer then pays the sight draft or accepts the time draft, the documents are released to the buyer, and the buyer can take possession of the goods.
- *Letter of Credit (L/C)*—With this method, the letter is drawn by the buyer's bank, which guarantees to pay the seller for the merchandise upon the presentation of documents stipulated in the letter that provide evidence of shipment, adherence to the purchase order, and even inspection, if so stipulated. The bank releases the funds when all the conditions of the sale are met. Most L/Cs are irrevocable, in the sense that neither party can change it without the consent of the other parties.

It should be mentioned that the risk of selling to international buyers, especially using cash in advance or on open account, can be alleviated by purchasing insurance using the many different sources discussed in Chapter 2, "An Overview of the International Marketing Environment."

Source: Adapted from "Getting Paid or What's a Transaction For?" *World Trade*, Vol. 12, No. 9, 1999, pp. 42–48.

- There may be few or no challenges from competition in the international market.
- The market potential might be limited.
- Buyers in the international market can afford the higher price.

One strategy used by multinational firms to penetrate an attractive international market is aggressive export pricing.

F i g u r e 1 6 - 3

In the Netherlands, Similac is made by Abbott Laboratories, where it is sold for about $7, while U.S. buyers of Similac pay more than $22. Why? Only Abbott knows, and the company is not telling. It's no wonder that savvy parents who travel to Holland bring back Dutch Similac for their children rather than pay the U.S. prices.

aggressive export pricing A pricing strategy that prices products below market price in order to penetrate new markets.

dynamic incremental pricing A pricing strategy whereby a company assumes that it will have certain fixed costs whether or not it exports its products overseas and does not factor in its international price marketing and promotion costs for domestic distribution, nor its full overhead.

local pricing A pricing strategy in which different prices are charged in different markets, reflecting differences in consumer purchase power, distribution costs, tax systems, or other market traits.

standardized pricing A pricing strategy in which the same price is charged for a product regardless of local market conditions.

16-3b Aggressive Export Pricing

To gain market share and/or to remain competitive in international markets, companies often engage in **aggressive export pricing.** One example of aggressive export pricing is **dynamic incremental pricing,** whereby a company assumes that it will have certain fixed costs whether or not it exports its products overseas; as such, the company does not factor in its international price marketing and promotion costs for domestic distribution, nor its full overhead.[38] The company allows for the product cost to reflect only the *variable cost* of taking the product abroad (thus using variable-cost pricing), rather than the *full cost* of the product (that is, full-cost pricing). Companies from Japan, Taiwan, and South Korea exporting semiconductor chips to the United States gained high market share rankings using aggressive export pricing.[39]

Exports priced well below fair market value, however, might place the company at risk for dumping challenges. The U.S. Department of Commerce challenged a Japanese company selling active matrix computer screens at 63 percent less than fair value.[40]

16-3c Standardized Pricing Versus Local Pricing

Enormous price differentials exist between countries. Companies charge different prices for their products to meet the needs of consumers and to fit their purchase power and to account for differences in distribution systems, market position, and tax systems; this type of pricing is known as **local pricing.**[41] In different markets, certain pricing traditions are followed. For example, in luxury markets in the United States, products are priced using even numbers—for example, $500 for a pair of Prada shoes. When those shoes go on sale, they are priced using odd pricing, such as $199. Alternatively, products in most discount outlets and in grocery stores are priced using odd pricing. In Europe, the odd/even pricing strategies are not used; even pricing is preferred because it facilitates calculation. See Figure 16-4.

Even in unified markets such as the European Union, price differentials exist: If a person living in France purchases a car elsewhere, he or she can save 24.3 percent on a Citroën (a French automobile), 18.2 percent on a Peugeot (another French automobile), or 33 percent on a Volkswagen Jetta (a German automobile).[42]

In spite of the obvious advantages of tailoring the price to the budget of the consumer, many companies selling high-end technology products opt for using a **standardized pricing** strategy. IBM, Toshiba, Hewlett-Packard, and Compaq all use a regionally standardized pricing plan.[43] In addition to the cost benefits of standardized pricing, this strategy is also a deterrent to gray market activity; by charging a uniform price worldwide, manufacturers no longer have to deal with parallel imports from a market where the company charges a lower price.

Figure 16-4
Odd/even pricing strategies are not used in many markets to differentiate between products. In Europe, even pricing is preferred because it facilitates calculations. In Asia, odd pricing reflects the mark-ups at the different distribution levels.

penetration pricing A pricing strategy in which a product is first priced below the price of competitors' products in order to quickly penetrate the market at the competitors' expense and then raised to target levels.

skimming strategy A pricing strategy in which a product is priced above that of competitors' products, when competition is minimal, to quickly recoup investments; consumers responding to skimming strategies are more concerned with quality, uniqueness, and status, rather than price.

16-3d Penetration Pricing and Skimming Strategies

Multinationals that have sales-based objectives, attempting to gain a high sales volume, are likely to use **penetration pricing.** Firms using this strategy price the product at first below the price of competitors to quickly penetrate the market at their competitors' expense. Compaq was able to quickly capture the European market by using this strategy. In the Netherlands, for example, Compaq offered deals unmatched by any brand name competitor and coupled this pricing strategy with excellent warranties and support.

Alternatively, firms may have pricing objectives that are centered on generating a high profit and recovering the costs of product development quickly. Companies thus use a **skimming strategy,** pricing the product above that of competitors, when competition is minimal. In general, consumers responding to skimming strategies are more concerned with quality, uniqueness, and status, rather than price.

Summary

- **Identify pricing-related internal challenges facing international firms.** Product pricing is partially determined by the location of the production facilities; companies that do not move production to take advantage of low-cost labor are likely to price themselves out of the market. Because products are manufactured in one country, assembled in another, and then modified in yet another country, keeping track of product costs is difficult. Companies need to keep track of costs and ensure that the maximum profitability is achieved.

- **Identify pricing-related challenges imposed by competition on international firms.** Products can face challenges from legitimate competitors; from gray markets, whereby a company's products from a low-priced market are sold through unauthorized channels in a high-priced market, competing with authorized distributors; and from dumping activities of competitors who price their products below cost to gain competitive advantage.

- **Identify pricing-related challenges imposed by the political and legal environment on international firms.** Governments often regulate prices charged by multinationals, thus setting limits on wholesalers' gross margins and on the products' retail price and restricting price promotions. Governments can impose tariffs and other duties, thereby increasing the prices charged by the international firm.

- **Identify pricing-related challenges imposed by the economic and financial environment on international firms.** Multinational companies are facing many challenges; among them are inflationary pressures on price, fluctuating exchange rates, and even the inability of governments to guarantee payment in hard currency. For the latter, a viable solution is countertrade, whereby a company accepts payment in kind, in product output of a company, or in some other format, in return for the products it sells or for setting up operational factories in the respective country.

- **Address international pricing decisions of international firms.** International firms use different pricing strategies in different markets. They may set prices higher in the home country if they want to penetrate new international markets or if the international markets cannot afford high prices. Or prices may be higher in international markets if those markets can afford it and pricing is in line with competitors' pricing, or if the international markets are not perceived as offering viable long-term opportunities. Companies need to make decisions such as determining whether aggressive export pricing is an appropriate strategy or whether they should use standardized prices throughout or local prices in their target markets.

Key Terms

aggressive export pricing	countervailing duties	parallel barter
antidumping duties	dumping	parallel imports
barter	dynamic incremental pricing	penetration pricing
buyback agreements	gray market	skimming strategy
clearing account	hard currency	soft currency
clearing currency	Incoterms	standardized pricing
compensation	infant industry argument	swing credits
cost-based transfer pricing	local pricing	switch trading
counterpurchase	market-based transfer pricing	transfer pricing
countertrade	offset purchase	

Discussion Questions

1. What are gray markets? How do distributors using parallel imports affect a multinational firm's operations in the target market?
2. What is dumping? Why do international companies use dumping strategies in select target markets?
3. Countertrade helps a company do business in markets that otherwise would be inaccessible. What are the different approaches to countertrade that a manufacturer of telecommunications equipment could use to penetrate such markets?
4. What are the different motivations behind a company setting prices higher or lower in the home country?

Chapter Quiz (True/False)

1. Dumping is defined as selling products at cost to get rid of excess inventory and/or to undermine competition.
2. Dumping represents a problem if it threatens to cause injury to an established industry in a particular market and/or if it delays the establishment of a viable domestic industry.
3. Hard currency is currency that is accepted for payment by any international seller.
4. Countries with a shortage of soft currency reserves are more likely to engage in countertrade.
5. Aggressive export pricing involves pricing products below market price to penetrate new markets.

Multiple Choice

1. Which of the following is NOT an external economic or financial factor affecting pricing decisions?
   a. inflation pressure on price
   b. shortage of hard currency
   c. transfer pricing
   d. fluctuating exchange rates

2. A manufacturer may charge different prices in different markets for the same product
   a. to meet target market needs.
   b. due to changes in the exchange rate.
   c. due to differences in wholesale prices.
   d. all of the above

You can find the correct answers to these questions by taking the quiz and then submitting your answers in the Online Edition. The program will automatically score your submission. Where you miss a question, the program will provide the correct answer, a rationale for the answer, and the section number in the chapter where the topic is discussed.

3. What company was responsible for initiating a countertrade relationship with the Soviet Union in the late 1960s?
   a. McDonald's
   b. PepsiCo
   c. Philip Morris
   d. none of the above

4. What type of countertrade involves buying a party's position in a countertrade in exchange for hard currency and selling it to another customer?
   a. compensation
   b. switch trading
   c. counter purchase
   d. offset purchase

5. If a firm's objectives are centered on generating high profit and recovering product development costs quickly, it is likely to use which one of the following international pricing strategies?
   a. skimming
   b. penetration pricing
   c. standardized pricing
   d. competitive pricing

Endnotes

1. Terry Clark, Masaaki Kotabe, and Dan Rajaratnam, "Exchange Rate Pass-Through and International Pricing Strategy: A Conceptual Framework and Research Propositions," *Journal of International Business Studies*, Vol. 30, No. 2, Second Quarter 1999, pp. 249–268.
2. Virginia Citrano, "The Right Price," *CFO*, Vol. 8, No. 5, May 1992, pp. 71–72.
3. Ibid.
4. Ibid.
5. Ibid.
6. For an extended discussion on parallel imports, see Chapter 11, "Managing International Distribution Options and Logistics."
7. Greg Mastel, "The U.S. Steel Industry and Antidumping Law," *Challenge*, Vol. 42, No. 3, May/June 1999, pp. 84–94.
8. Ibid.
9. Lester Ross and Susan Ning, "Modern Protectionism: China's Own Antidumping Regulations," *The China Business Review*, Vol. 27, No. 3, May/June 2000, pp. 30–33.
10. Ibid.
11. Ibid.
12. Ibid.
13. *Wall Street Journal*, "Housing Surge Threatened by a Shortage of Cement," *Wall Street Journal*, September 9, 2004, p. A 17.
14. Messaoud Mehafdi, "The Ethics of International Transfer Pricing," *Journal of Business Ethics*, Vol. 28, No. 4, December 2000, pp. 365–381.
15. *The Economist*, "Finance and Economics: Europe's Burden," Vol. 351, No. 8120, May 22, 1999, p. 84.
16. Ibid.
17. Ibid.
18. Ibid.
19. Dorothy A. Paun, Larry D. Compeau, and Dhruv Grewal, "A Model of the Influence of Marketing Objectives on Pricing Strategies in International Countertrade," *Journal of Public Policy & Marketing*, Vol. 16, No. 1, Spring 1997, pp. 69–82.
20. Sam C. Okoroafo, "Determinants of LDC-Mandated Countertrade," *International Marketing Review*, Vol. 5, Winter 1988, pp. 16–24.
21. David Woodruff, *Money Unmade: Barter and the Fate of Russian Capitalism*, Ithaca: NY: Cornell University Press, 1999.
22. John P. Angelidis, John P. and Nabil A. Ibrahim, "Countertrading between United States and Western European Firms: An Empirical Analysis of the Benefits and Pitfalls," *International Journal of Management*, Vol. 18, No. 2, 2001, p. 252.
23. Paun, Compeau, and Grewal, "A Model of the Influence of Marketing Objectives," pp. 69–82.
24. Ibid.
25. Janet Aschkenasy, "Give and Take," *International Business*, Vol. 9, No. 8, September 1996, pp. 10–12.
26. Richard E. Plank, David A. Reid, and Frank Bates, "Barter: An Alternative to Traditional Methods of Purchasing," *International Journal of Purchasing and Materials Management*, Vol. 30, No. 2, Spring 1994, p. 52.
27. Nabil A. Ibrahim and John P. Angelidis, "Countertrading with Eastern Europe: A Comparative Analysis of the Benefits and Pitfalls," *International Journal of Commerce & Management*, Vol. 6, No. 3/4, 1996, pp. 22–40.
28. Plank, Reid, and Bates, "Barter: An Alternative," p. 52.
29. Jean F. Hennart, "Some Empirical Dimensions of Countertrade," *Journal of International Business Studies*," Vol. 21, No. 2, Second Quarter 1990, pp. 243–270.
30. Ibid.
31. Aschkenasy, "Give and Take," *International Business*, pp. 10–12.
32. "Indonesia to Reform Countertrade Policy," *Project Trade and Finance*, No. 153, January 1996, p. 15.
33. Hennart, "Some Empirical Dimensions," pp. 243–270.
34. Aschkenasy, "Give and Take," pp. 10–12.
35. Hennart, "Some Empirical Dimensions," pp. 243–270.
36. Simon Herman, "Pricing in a Global Setting," *Marketing News*, Vol. 29, No. 21, October 9, 1995, pp. 21–22.
37. "Getting Paid or What's a Transaction For?" *World Trade*, Vol. 12, No. 9, 1999, pp. 42–48.
38. Citrano, "The Right Price," pp. 71–72.
39. Ibid.
40. Ibid.
41. Herman, "Pricing in a Global Setting," pp. 21–22.
42. Ibid.
43. Jack Sweeney, "PC Vendors Bend Pricing for Overseas Customers," *Computer Reseller News*, No. 614, January 23, 1995, p. 3.

Case 16-1

Travel Turkey: Pricing Decisions in a Changing Environment

Erdogan Eser, a former hotel sales manager with Hilton, decided to return to his home country, Turkey, to establish a travel agency called Travel Turkey. With an office in Taksim Square in the center of Istanbul, the travel agency is actually a broker between foreign tour operators and lodging operators in Turkey. Lodging operators—managers of hotels, bed and breakfasts, inns, and resorts—have voiced concerns about foreign tour operators, especially about the lack of guarantees when it came to occupancy. Similarly, foreign tour operators felt that their needs were not appropriately addressed by lodging operators. As a broker, Erdogan would be able to address concerns on each side and benefit each party by creating optimal matches. Travel Turkey will benefit from Erdogan's many years in the travel industry and from his extensive network of colleagues and friends in the travel business. Even though Turkey has experienced its own economic and political problems, the country remains quite attractive to tourists and is a preferred destination for many tourist groups.

Turkey's tourism has experienced an impressive boom since the early 1980s. The total number of tourists to the country approaches 10 million yearly. Turkey is an attractive destination, located at the crossroads of Asia and Europe, offering centuries of cultural and historical sites. It is a dynamic destination of sun, sea (Aegean and Mediterranean), and archeological sites. The government has offered significant incentives to businesses to increase bed capacity, and it enacted Law 2634 to encourage the development of tourism in 1982; this support is still readily available.

The major players in Turkey's expanding tourism are Western European package tour operators, one of Erdogan's main target markets. These operators coordinate their activities with airlines and travel agencies in France, Germany, and the United Kingdom, in particular. The relationship between Turkish lodging operators and the European tour operators is not always smooth: A study of 200 Turkish lodging operators revealed the difficulties that are often encountered in their relationship with Western tour operators:

Types of Problems	Number of Times Cited
Cancellations	113
Delayed payments	126
Pressure to accept low prices	129
Artificial price competition	129
Reduced number of rooms blocked	118
Requests for complimentary rooms	65
Requests for last-minute reservations	116

Erdogan Eser will also target U.S. travel agencies, especially church groups visiting European capitals—a market that, in spite of safety concerns, remains relatively solid. There are still concerns and numerous reports that Americans are verbally attacked on the street in much of Europe by locals who oppose U.S. military policies around the world. Newspapers advise U.S. travelers: If you're heading overseas, be prepared to have discussions with people who think America is the devil. If the past 100 years were widely considered the American Century, this new century is rapidly shaping up as the Anti-American Century. However, Erdogan feels that the right price would bring these tourists to the shores of the Bosphorus. After all, Greece and Turkey are among the hottest destinations for Christians: the ruins of Ephesus in Turkey, where Mary is said to have spent her last days, are especially popular. Travel Turkey could partner with Travel Dynamics International, which specializes in these types of tours.

Another important target market is the Eastern European travel operators who coordinate shopping trips to Istanbul. Eastern European consumers often take short trips to Istanbul to purchase quality leather products of Turkish provenance and knockoffs of top international brands. They may purchase products for their own and their family's use, or they may purchase for resale. Regardless, the buses always return to Russia, the Ukraine, and Romania full of merchandise.

Erdogan's plans are to assure lodging operators of large occupancy levels and obtain large discounts. He will then assure tour operators of rooms at reasonable rates that would meet their needs. For example, for a week in Istanbul, he would arrange with the Conrad hotel, the Ciragan Palace (a Kempinski Hotels property), and Swissôtel to book 100 rooms, each at 70 Euros. For spending a week at one of these hotels, he would charge the tour operators as follows:

- Western European tour operators would pay 100 Euros per room per night.
- Eastern European tour operators would pay 90 Euros per room per night.
- U.S. tour operators would pay $130 per room per night.

One of the first to meet Erdogan in his capacity as travel agent, a U.S. tour operator, Jack Maloney, who heads a church travel agency in Cincinnati, was concerned that the dollar price for the three hotels was rather high. His feeling was that because his Ukrainian colleague, another tour operator, was charged only 90 Euros, his business should be charged the same amount. Moreover, even a tourist off the street would be able to book a room at the Conrad, for instance, for only $150 for a Conrad Saver rate—not much less than the deal he was getting. True, those are all premium properties and five-star hotels, but charging different prices for the East European operators seemed unfair, and Jack's travel agency would not be able to make a sufficient profit.

As a result of this meeting, Erdogan Koc decided to rethink his pricing strategy. Were there any international laws that did not allow him to charge different prices to different clients? This was never a concern in Turkey. And, at his previous job with the Hilton, charging different rates was customary. Was it ethical to give a break to the Eastern European tour operators? Was it unethical to charge the U.S. operators higher amounts given that the dollar continues to lose in value relative to the Euro?

Sources: Marco R. della Cava, "Ugly Sentiments Sting American Tourists as Europeans Cite Frustrations with U.S. Policy," *USA Today*, March 4, 2003, pp. 1–2; Gene Sloan, "Cruise Lines Are Forced to Bail Again," *USA Today*, March 4, 2003, p. 10b; Dan Reed, "American Wants to Get the Low-Fare Word Out," *USA Today*, March 4, 2003, p. 8A; Elizabeth Bernstein, "The Other Holy Lands—Spiritual Tourists Skip Israel for Sites in Cuba, Turkey; Keeping Kosher in China," *The Wall Street Journal*, December 6, 2002, p. W4; Kurtulus Karamustafa, "Marketing Channel Relationships: Turkey's Resort Purveyors' Interactions with International Tour Operators," *Cornell Hotel and Restaurant Administration Quarterly*, Vol. 41, No. 4, 2000, pp. 21–32.

Analysis Suggestions

1. Are there any legal or ethical concerns that might preclude Travel Turkey to charge different prices to different travel agents for the same room? Is it ethical or legal to charge different prices based on the home country of the tour operators and their respective tourists?
2. What can Erdogan do if the dollar continues to fall relative to the Euro?
3. How can Travel Turkey ensure against foreign exchange risk and maintain its Eastern European and U.S. clients?

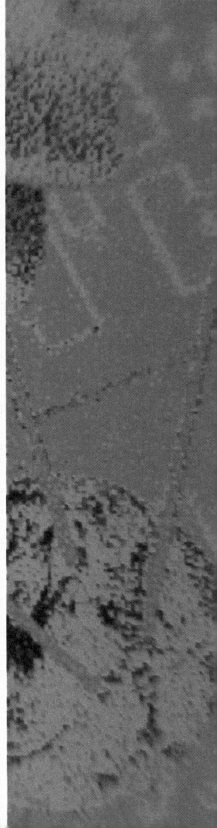

part 5

International Marketing Strategy: Implementation

17 Organizing and Controlling
International Marketing Operations
and Perspectives for the Future

17

Organizing and Controlling International Marketing Operations and Perspectives for the Future

Chapter Objectives

By the end of this chapter, you should be able to

1 Identify the factors in a firm's external and internal environment that determine the organizational design best suited for international operations.

2 Describe different organizational designs and offer examples of designs that different international firms have adopted.

3 Identify formal and informal controls necessary to ensure that company operations are in line with company goals and objectives as stated in the strategic plan.

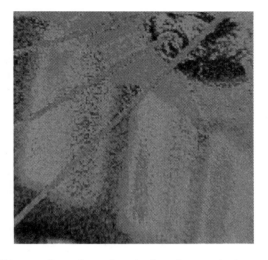

Multinational companies today are confronted with aggressive competition for markets worldwide. To meet the challenges of intensifying competition, multinationals have been forced to alter their organizational structures and to adapt their standards to the new environment, aligning executive compensation with the companies' new goals.

Ford, responding to rapid changes in the global economy, implemented a major reorganization, ending competing regional fiefdoms by consolidating engineering, design, and development within new global divisions. Motorola, faced with aggressive Asian competitors and falling profits, adopted a similar plan, replacing decentralized and competing businesses with three distinct global groups focusing on retail customers such as cell phone users, telecommunications companies, and government and industrial clients. Procter & Gamble initiated the broadest overhaul in its industry, transforming four business units based on geographic regions into seven global entities based on product lines such as Baby Care or Food & Beverage.[1]

This chapter addresses the process of organizing for international marketing and controlling international operations, offering examples of organizational structures of firms worldwide.

17-1 Organizing for International Marketing Operations

Firms need to consider organizational designs that fit with their external environment and with company characteristics and goals. Organizational design is determined by numerous factors in the firms' operating environments. Among such factors are those in the firm's environment, such as competition, environmental stability, similarity with the home country, common regional traits and/or regional integration, and availability of qualified labor. Factors within the firm also affect organizational design—in particular, the priority given to internationalization. These factors are described in sections 17-1a, "Factors in the Firm's Environment," and 17-1b, "Factors within the Firm."

17-1a Factors in the Firm's Environment

Competitive Environment

In environments characterized by intense competition, where decisions must be made quickly to counter competitive moves, a decentralized organization would allow for the most immediate reaction. In a decentralized organization, each subsidiary operates as a profit center and has full charge of its market. Such an organization permits direct offense on competition, or immediate defensive action in reaction to competitive moves. High flexibility is essential to react to changes quickly. However, even in a highly competitive international environment, centralization helps firms avoid duplication and lower costs. Activities such as finance and research and development benefit from centralization. Even firms that have at one point adopted a decentralized model to compete effectively in the international market have rethought their strategies and opted for a centralized model. Section 17-2d, "The Matrix Structure," addresses changes at Philips, a multinational company that decided to move from a decentralized organization to a centralized organization to effectively compete internationally.

Environmental Stability

Countries characterized by unstable political environments or countries where government policies are unstable, countries that are characterized by high inflation and high unemployment, and countries with unstable currency require companies to adapt quickly to the changing environment. Such companies need to be able to take immediate action to adapt to the new environments and need an **organizational structure** that allows them to react quickly.

Environmental Similarity with the Home Country

Companies operating in countries that are similar to their home country are likely to use similar strategies; these companies would opt for an organization that integrates operations between the home and host countries.

Common Regional Traits and/or Regional Integration

Companies can organize their operations with a regional focus in countries that share language, religion, or other cultural similarities; countries that share a border; or countries that are members of a regional alliance.

Availability of Local Qualified Labor

Companies operating in countries that have ample educated and qualified labor will delegate more control to local operations and have organizational structures that allow for more local control.

17-1b Factors within the Firm

Organizational design also is determined by company traits. A firm that considers internationalization a priority is likely to have an organizational structure with regional divisions in charge of particular countries. Other organizations involved in international business might have only an international division that oversees international operations. Companies that are only minimally involved in international business might have only a small international department.

Companies are likely to maintain their organizational structure when they go international. An organization that is hierarchical and centralized is likely to have a centralized international organization. An organization structured based on product lines is also likely to maintain this structure for its international operations.

17-2 Examining International Organizational Designs

Multinational companies use four types of formal structures in their international **organizational designs:** international divisions, worldwide regional divisions, product divisions, and the matrix structure.

17-2a The International Division Structure

Firms with an **international division structure** have two main divisions: the domestic division and the international division. When firms become involved in international business by exporting products overseas, they typically assign responsibility for all international operations to an export department (this is known as an export department structure). As their international involvement increases, they will most likely have an international division in charge of all their international operations. These firms are still

organizational structure The outcome of the organization of reporting and coordination within a company.

organizational design The organization of reporting and coordination within a company.

international division structure An organizational structure whereby firms have separate domestic and international divisions.

primarily focused on domestic operations, but their international operations have an important standing, at the same level with all other divisions. In an international division structure, all foreign subsidiaries report directly to a single division responsible for international operations, which is separate from domestic operations.

17-2b The Worldwide Regional Division Structure

A **worldwide regional division structure** configures operations either by geographical region or by country. Under this model, subsidiaries report directly to the single division responsible for operations in the country or geographic region. Although this structure allows for some duplication of activities and thus might increase costs, managers consider this organization to be very effective in creating competitive advantage for the firms.[2] A particular advantage of the worldwide regional division structure is that it is better equipped to immediately process and respond to country-specific information and conditions than other formal structures—at some cost to product-related information—because of its strong regional focus.[3]

Frito-Lay, one of the PepsiCo family of companies, has a worldwide regional division structure. The Frito-Lay Company, headquartered in the United States, oversees all the functional areas, i.e., marketing, manufacturing, research and development, finance, etc. The regional divisions—Frito-Lay North America, headquartered in the United States; Frito-Lay Europe/Africa/Middle East, headquartered in Geneva, Switzerland; and Frito-Lay Latin America/Asia Pacific/Australia—oversee all regional operations, country subsidiaries, and offices (see Figure 17-1).

This type of structure is helpful for firms that have similar congruent product lines, such as Frito-Lay, or for services. The Guggenheim museum also has this type of structure, with the Guggenheim New York (the main museum and Guggenheim Soho), Guggenheim Venice (Italy), Guggenheim Bilbao (Spain), Guggenheim Berlin (Germany), and the Guggenheim Virtual Museum, an online museum for virtual exhibitions and artists' projects.

> **worldwide regional division structure** An organizational structure whereby operations are organized by region or by country, and where subsidiaries report directly to the single division responsible for operations in the country or geographic region.

17-2c The Product Division Structure

In a regional or worldwide **product division structure,** subsidiaries report to the product division (strategic business unit) with responsibility for the particular products. In the past, this structure was common for high-tech companies or multinational companies with diversified portfolios. However, increasingly, this format is replaced by the matrix structure. Even companies that once were identified as typical examples of the product division structure, such as Sun Microsystems and Whirlpool, have adopted a matrix structure.

> **product division structure** An organizational structure whereby subsidiaries report to the product division (strategic business unit) with responsibility for the particular products.

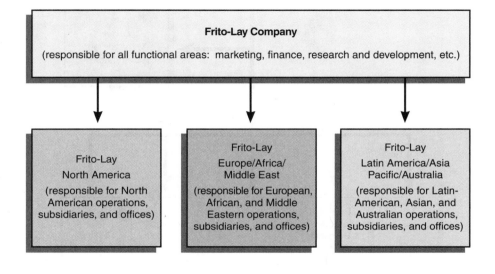

Frito-Lay Company

(responsible for all functional areas: marketing, finance, research and development, etc.)

| Frito-Lay North America (responsible for North American operations, subsidiaries, and offices) | Frito-Lay Europe/Africa/ Middle East (responsible for European, African, and Middle Eastern operations, subsidiaries, and offices) | Frito-Lay Latin America/Asia Pacific/Australia (responsible for Latin-American, Asian, and Australian operations, subsidiaries, and offices) |

Figure 17-1
Worldwide Regional Division Structure: Frito-Lay

17-2d The Matrix Structure

matrix structure An organizational structure whereby each operational unit reports to both region/country managers and product managers.

The **matrix structure** takes into account the multiple dimensions involved in doing business internationally—functional areas, product, and region/country. In a matrix structure, two dimensions are integrated such that each operational unit reports to both region/country managers and product managers.

Many large multinationals have had a matrix structure for decades—among them Philips Electronics, Unilever, Electrolux, IBM, Texas Instruments, and Procter & Gamble. And, in recent years, many more multinationals have adopted this organizational structure—among them, BASF, Disney, and Rockwell International. This type of format works especially well for firms that have global brands as well as local brands; such companies need to coordinate marketing activities worldwide involving the global brands and need to focus on the local market for the local brands.

Unilever's matrix structure is organized based on products (Home and Personal Care Products and Bestfoods products) and on regions around the world. Its divisions are Home & Personal Care, Africa, Middle East & Turkey; Home & Personal Care, Asia; Home & Personal Care, Europe; Home & Personal Care, North America/Latin America; Unilever Bestfoods Africa, Middle East & Turkey; Foodservice; Ice Cream and Frozen Foods; Latin America & Slim·Fast worldwide; Unilever Bestfoods, Asia; Unilever Bestfoods, Europe; and Unilever Bestfoods, North America.[4]

In another example of a matrix structure, Philips is organized into five divisions (see Figure 17-2), each run separately. The divisions are Philips Lighting, Philips DAP (Domestic Appliances & Personal Care), Philips Semiconductors, Philips Consumer Electronics, and Philips Medical Systems. The company initially ran its operations in different regions, with production, sales, and marketing coordinated separately for North America, Latin America, Asia, Africa, and Europe for each of the five divisions. In addition, the company had a separate division for research and development.

Philips has been streamlining operations through a concerted effort to centralize its global operations. The company has reduced the number of business units and creation

Figure 17-2

The Philips Organization: The organization runs its divisions— Philips Lighting, Philips DAP (Domestic Appliances & Personal Care), Philips Semiconductors, Philips Consumer Electronics, and Philips Medical Systems— separately.

Source: Adapted from www.philips.com.

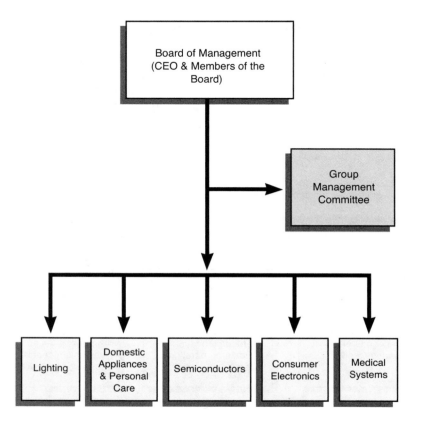

Table 17-1	A Comparison between the Organization for Consumer Electronics in 2003 and 2004

2003 Organization for Consumer Electronics	2004 Organization for Consumer Electronics
Decentralized business planning, logistics, and accounting	Centralized business planning, logistics, and accounting
7 business units	3 business units
21 creation teams	12 creation teams
Individual R&D approach for each team	Aligned R&D roadmaps
Distinct regional marketing programs	Coherent global marketing approaches
Undifferentiated business modes	Business model adapted to life cycle
In-house infrastructure	Outsourced, shared service centers
Large, company-owned consumer service organization	Outsourced consumer service

Source: www.philips.com

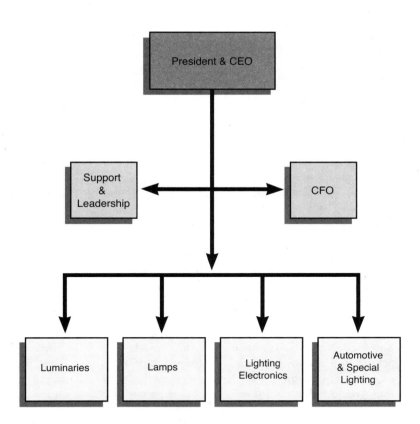

Figure 17-3

The Philips Lighting Organizational Chart

Source: Adapted from www.philips.com.

teams in each division and outsourced its customer service department. Table 17-1 illustrates the divisions of Philips. To illustrate, Philips Consumer Electronics, one of the company's five divisions, reduced the number of business units from 7 to 3, the number of creation teams from 21 to 12, and made other important changes, such as aligning research and development roadmaps and outsourcing and sharing service centers and consumer services.

Philips Lighting, another Philips division and its principal business historically, reorganized around the different subdivisions: luminaries, lamps, lighting electronics, and automotive & special lighting (see Figure 17-3).

Likewise, Nokia recently adopted a matrix structure to keep up with competition from China and to maintain its market share. Although Nokia and Motorola have sold more cell phones to customers worldwide, Chinese brands are rapidly increasing in popularity and taking market share from both. See International Marketing Illustration 17-1.

17-3 Controlling International Marketing Operations

Controls are necessary to ensure that international company operations are in line with company goals and objectives, as stated in the company's strategic plan. Yet, controlling international operations and ensuring that performance standards are met throughout the company are complex tasks. Adding to the complexity are the following:

- Local units and a regional focus often add intermediate levels of management and staffing that further complicate the management, communication, and evaluation processes.
- Multinational companies are likely to have subsidiaries and branch offices in countries where the external environment is changing at different rates, having a differ-

International Marketing Illustration   17-1

Using the Matrix Structure as a Competitive Tool

Nokia recently engaged in global restructuring, creating a new matrix structure in which four business lines—mobile phones, multimedia, networks, and enterprise solutions—are overlaid over three supporting groups—customer and market operations, technology platforms and research, and venturing and business infrastructure. The company found itself in a position in which its global market share, estimated to be between 15 and 20 percent, was going down from a leading position and getting close to that of Motorola; hence the company decided to restructure. At the same time, China's Ningbo Bird and TLC are just below 10 percent and catching up fast in the highly competitive market.

The battle between cell phone makers is raging in every major international market. In China, for example, domestic cell phone manufacturers have more than 40 percent of the market. And Ningo Bird, based in the central coastal city of Ningbo, China, ships more than 11 million cell phones per year. At the same time, China Mobile Communications Corp., the largest wireless operator in the country, just ordered phones from national manufacturers that it will sell bundled with service plans. This effort is likely to further boost sales of Chinese brands and increase their market share worldwide, at the expense of Nokia and Motorola. This picture is quite different from that of the 1990s, when Nokia commanded as much as 80 percent of the market share in China.

Nokia believes that a matrix structure will enable it to take into account the multiple dimensions involved in doing business internationally: functional areas, product, and region/country. In a matrix structure, these dimensions are integrated such that each operational unit reports to both region/country managers and product managers.

Sources: Adapted from Alfred Hille, "Nokia Faces Up to China's Challenges," *Media*, January 16, 2004, p. 1; and Evan Ramstad, "Two Tech Concerns in China Lose Luster," *Wall Street Journal*, March 2, 2004, p. A16.

ent impact on company operations; thus, standards and measures instituted for evaluation purposes are often not comparable across countries.

- Given the distance of subsidiaries from headquarters, there is a tendency to resist influence in both directions, such that subsidiaries often fight to retain autonomy in decision making and performance evaluation, while the headquarters may resist input from the subsidiaries in the planning and evaluation process.

Difficulties imposed by the complexity of the international management context can, to a certain extent, be offset by instituting the appropriate formal and informal controls.

17-3a Formal Controls

Instituting **formal controls** involves the following process:

- Establishing performance standards
- Measuring performance
- Addressing discrepancies

Establishing Performance Standards

The first step in establishing formal controls involves establishing **performance standards** in light of the company's projected market potential. Parameters must be developed in the strategic plan for evaluating dimensions of the external environment for the purpose of setting standards based on that potential. The evaluation must include a continuous assessment of competitive intensity (local and international competitors in the market), political stability, developments in the economy, regional and local trade, and other developments that directly affect company performance. In many emerging economies, currencies have fluctuated widely over the past few years, and many of these economies have seen major political overhauls; hence, it is difficult to accurately measure outcomes and evaluate managerial performance. Moreover, postprivatization restructuring may take a long time to complete and may produce soft outcomes, so outcome measurability becomes problematic, thereby complicating management evaluation.[5]

Measuring Performance

Actual performance is measured based on established standards. At this point, measures such as sales, profit, and market share are assessed for the target market in a particular country or region and measured against previous performance and/or against competitors. These assessments are compared with company goals and objectives for the target market as expressed in the company plan.

Addressing Discrepancies

At the final stage of this process, discrepancies between standards and performance are corrected. If the standards were unreasonable or were not reached due to unanticipated changes in the external environment, they will be adjusted accordingly for the next assessment period. Lessons from the company's experience in other parts of the world and lessons learned from other companies' experiences are useful at this stage. For example, studies have found that the performance of European and Japanese multinationals is positively correlated with corporate policies emphasizing innovation and globally standard product designs with local adaptation.[6] A company that may be very keen on a standardized international product strategy may benefit from adapting its offer to suit local preferences. The company may also need to offer more innovative products to the target market. Both the local adaptation strategy and the focus on innovation need to be coordinated with company headquarters; in fact, for many firms, innovation takes place at the company's national headquarters.[7] For example, Procter & Gamble has 22 innovation centers in 12 countries worldwide.[8]

formal controls Systematic controls, such as performance standards and measurement, used in international marketing to ensure that international company operations are in line with company goals and objectives.

performance standards A priori measures against which firm performance is evaluated.

17-3b Informal Controls

informal controls Systematic controls, such as dialogue between the headquarters and the international field operations, used in international marketing to ensure that international company operations are in line with company goals and objectives.

In addition to the controls described in section 17-3a, "Formal Controls," companies also can use **informal controls** to ensure that there is a fit between the standards and actual performance. The following are examples of informal controls a company can use:

- Establishing frequent contact between the home-country headquarters and the regional and/or local office. Such contact serves as a means to better coordinate activities and ensure clear communication of expectations in both directions.

- Rotating managers to different assignments to obtain the maximum benefit from international experience. One often-used strategy is to hire third-country managers (from a country other than the home or the host country) to oversee new or problematic operations; these individuals have the flexibility and experience but not the biases that association with the home or host country of the company would create. In general, moving expatriates from one subsidiary to another will offer valuable exchange in information to be used as input into the control function.

- Training the employees and inculcating a management culture that is consistent with company goals and objectives. Management development training can be used to share the mission and objectives of the company expressed in the relevant performance terms. For example, a company can focus on company growth or profitability objectives, on innovation, on the relationship with the target customer, or on any other dimension that the company deems important.

17-4 International Marketing: Future Perspectives

The world economy has experienced revolutionary changes in the past few decades, with the growth of the technology sector. The Internet and related technologies have expanded the realm of international marketing and dramatically increased access to new markets. World markets are expected to continue to benefit from the expansion in opportunities facilitated by e-commerce.

Research conducted by Nielsen found that more than 385 million people around the globe are using the Internet, with almost one third of those in the United States.[9] See Table 17-2.

It is expected that e-commerce will increase dramatically worldwide. The adoption of the Internet will continue to be the most rapid in highly industrialized countries, where it will achieve 100 percent penetration. It will be rapid in emerging markets and especially in those markets where English is widely spoken; countries such as China, Brazil, India, and many countries in Latin America anticipate significant increases in usage.

Yet, in spite of extensive Internet access worldwide, companies are not equipped to handle sales. About 46 percent of companies with e-commerce capabilities turn away international orders because they do not have the processes in place to fill them. About $10 million are turned away annually by companies faced with language and cultural barriers that hinder basic communications, or they have difficulty handling the destination country's import and tax regulations or export controls in the home country. In addition, payment mechanisms are cumbersome, and there is a high rate of credit card theft, adding to the company's risk.[10]

Many changes will take place in the product arena, where product life cycles will continue to manifest their current accelerating trend. International firms must be prepared for rapid new product introductions simultaneously in world markets, regardless

Table 17-2	Internet Use in Selected International Markets			
Country	**Active Users (in Millions)**	**Average Time per Month**	**Average Number of Sessions Per Month**	**Percentage of Internet Penetration**
United States	110.9	13 hr 17 min	24	70.4
Japan	26.6	11 hr 44 min	21	50.4
Germany	22.0	10 hr 57 min	21	54.9
United Kingdom	17.5	8 hr 52 min	17	60.6
Canada	10.5	10 hr 8 min	22	63.9
France	9.5	10 hr 37 min	21	38.0
Italy	9.2	9 hr 36 min	18	50.9
Brazil	7.5	11 hr 9 min	16	10.8

Source: Nielsen Netratings, http://www.nielsen-netratings.com, March 8, 2003.

of the markets' levels of development. As seen in International Marketing Illustration 17-1, the battle for market share for market leaders often takes place in developing countries. The Illustration portrayed Nokia as losing market share in China, negatively affecting its competitive stance worldwide. When new products such as cell phones or smartphones are introduced, developing countries and emerging markets will be important battlegrounds.

As the world population grows, there will be significant changes in the consumption process. Environmental concerns will become critical, and pollution as well as the shortage of raw materials will place constraints on marketers. In the future, it is likely that substantial attention will be paid to environmental protection, and marketers will have to adapt their strategies to respond to consumers' and governments' environmental demands.

In terms of promotion, firms will compete on their ability to resonate themes that appeal to world consumers, and most efforts will be in the area of integrating their messages. Integrated marketing communications are becoming standard for both international consumer product companies and for business-to-business communications. Furthermore, consumers will expect extensive information on the websites of companies with which they do business.

With regard to distribution, companies will continue to pursue measures to reduce distribution costs by adopting just-in-time inventory systems and creating product flows rather than stocks. They will also coordinate their inventory systems with suppliers and clients through electronic data interchange. Moreover, companies will have to abide by post September 11, 2001, security measures, which will further reduce merchandise theft.

Entertainment will be especially important when communicating with consumers in all retailing environments; see International Marketing Illustration 17-2.

Finally, the future will be characterized by greater price competition and broader price alignment, as local businesses and multinationals compete over markets. This competitive surge is likely to be accompanied by increased governmental scrutiny.

International Marketing Illustration 17-2

Shoppertainment: The Future of Retailing

Brand experiences are thought to be the future of international marketing. Shoppertainment is the logical blend of retailing and leisure that increases the guests' length of stay and, very importantly, the total spending on the retailer's premises. World retail brands and consumer product companies in the new millennium are aiming to create entertaining in-store environments that delight customers and increase the likelihood of repeat visits and spending.

Shoppertainment takes different forms. A factory outlet center in Livingston, Scotland, has one of the largest indoor ferris wheels in the world. A large shopping center in Kent has a nondenominational prayer "Quiet Room" with hair- and feet-washing facilities for Muslim guests. Girl Heaven, owned by Australian LendLease, has hot pink, glitter-flecked floors and training counters that teach teens the latest nightclub dance moves and make-up and hairstyle trends. Common are themed food courts, onsite jugglers and face painters, shuttle trains to parking lots, and onsite day-care centers. Large bookstores are partnering with Starbucks and other similar chains to attract shoppers who will drink coffee, leaf through a few magazines, and, ultimately, purchase a few books.

Retailers worldwide are competing with online shopping and e-commerce, especially in developed countries. They are also competing for shoppers with limited time who expect a memorable and pleasant shopping experience. In the future, the competition will extend to emerging markets and developing countries, and marketers will need to devise global strategies for entertaining consumers as they engage in consumption: Experiential consumption will be the norm worldwide.

Source: Allyson L. Stewart-Allen, "Europe Says 'That's Shoppertainment,'" *Marketing News*, Vol. 33, No. 17, August 16, 1999, p. 7.

Summary

- **Identify the factors in a firm's external and internal environment that determine the organizational design best suited for international operations.** Organizational design is determined externally by the competitive environment: Intense competition requires a company to react quickly, and it can do so effectively if it has a decentralized structure. Companies operating in environments plagued by high inflation, unemployment, and political instability must be organized to be able to react quickly to changes. Multinational companies are likely to have similar operating structures to those in their home country if the countries where they operate are culturally similar to their own country. Companies that have competent, educated, local employees are likely to delegate more control to local opera-

tions. Companies that operate in a region with common traits, or within a regional bloc, will most likely organize the company with a regional focus. Firm traits such as degree of focus on international operations or its organization in the home country also have an impact on organizational structure.

- **Describe different organizational designs and offer examples of designs that different international firms have adopted.** The four organizational designs for international operations are the international division structure, for firms with limited international involvement that are likely to have an export department; firms with a worldwide regional division structure, which operate either by region or by country; firms with a product division structure, where subsidiaries report to the product division with responsibility for the respective product; and firms with a matrix structure, which combine functional areas, product, and region in their organization.

- **Identify formal and informal controls necessary to ensure that company operations are in line with company goals and objectives as stated in the strategic plan.** Formal controls involve establishing performance standards, measuring performance,

and addressing discrepancies by either changing the standards to correct for differences in market traits, or changing executive compensation to reflect firm priorities. Informal controls involve maintaining contact between headquarters and international operations, rotating managers to share experience with new operations, and appropriately indoctrinating new employees in the company's culture.

Key Terms

formal controls
informal controls
international division structure

matrix structure
organizational design
organizational structure

performance standards
product division structure
worldwide regional division structure

Discussion Questions

1. List the factors that influence organizational design. Describe how each factor influences the design.
2. Compare the international division structure and the regional division structure. What would make a company move from an international division structure to a regional division structure?
3. How does the matrix structure differ from the other three organizational structures? Explain.
4. Discuss the formal and informal controls used to ensure that international marketing operations are in line with company goals and objectives.

Chapter Quiz (True/False)

1. Companies operating in countries characterized by unstable political environments or countries where government policies are unstable need an organizational structure that allows them to react quickly.
2. Companies operating in countries that have ample educated and qualified labor are more likely to be centralized.
3. A worldwide regional division structure has two main divisions: the domestic division and the international division.
4. An advantage of the worldwide regional division structure is that it is better equipped to immediately process and respond

to country-specific information and conditions than other formal structures.
5. In a regional or worldwide matrix division structure, subsidiaries report to the product division (strategic business unit) with responsibility for the particular products.
6. Informal controls are used in international marketing to ensure that international company operations are in line with company goals and objectives.

Multiple Choice

1. Which of the following companies has a worldwide regional division structure?
   a. Frito-Lay
   b. Coke
   c. Eli Lilly
   d. none of the above
2. Which of the following companies has a matrix structure?
   a. IBM
   b. Unilever
   c. Disney
   d. all of the above

You can find the correct answers to these questions by taking the quiz and then submitting your answers in the Online Edition. The program will automatically score your submission. Where you miss a question, the program will provide the correct answer, a rationale for the answer, and the section number in the chapter where the topic is discussed.

3. What is the process for instituting formal controls?
   a. measuring performance, establishing standards, addressing discrepancies
   b. establishing standards, measuring performance, addressing discrepancies
   c. addressing discrepancies, establishing standards, measuring performance
   d. none of the above

4. In spite of extensive Internet access worldwide, companies are not equipped to handle sales due to
   a. language and cultural barriers.
   b. difficulty handling the destination country's import and tax regulations.
   c. difficulty in handling export controls in the home country.
   d. all of the above

Endnotes

1. Jeffrey E. Garten, "Cutting Fat Won't Be Enough to Survive This Crisis," *Business Week*, No. 3603, November 9, 1998, p. 26.
2. Allen J. Morrison, David A. Ricks, and Kendall Roth, "Globalization Versus Regionalization: Which Way for the Multinational?" *Organizational Dynamics*, Vol. 19, No. 3, Winter 1991, pp. 17–29.
3. Bruce T. Lamont, V. Sambamurthy, Kimberly M. Ellis, and Paul G. Simmonds, "The Influence of Organizational Structure on the Information Received by Corporate Strategists of Multinational Enterprises," *Management International Review*, Vol. 40, No. 3, Third Quarter 2000, pp. 231–252.
4. www.Unilever.com
5. Ravi Dharwadkar, Gerard George, and Pamela Brandes, "Privatization in Emerging Economies: An Agency Theory Perspective," *Academy of Management: The Academy of Management Review*, Vol. 25, No. 3, July 2000, pp. 650–669.
6. Masaaki Kotabe, *Global Sourcing Strategy: R&D, Manufacturing, and Marketing*, New York: Quoruom Books, 1992.
7. *Annual Report, Procter & Gamble*, 2000.
8. "R&D's Formula for Success," www.pg.com/science, September 24, 2004.
9. Nielsen Netratings, http://www.nielsen-netratings.com, March 8, 2003.
10. Lynda Radosevich, "Going Global Overnight," *InfoWorld*, Vol. 21, No. 16, April 19, 1999, pp. 1–3.
11. With contributions from Tiffany Allen, Jessica DiTommaso, Kate Hopkins, Dana Lascu, Paula Munafo, and Amber Summers.
12. www.siemens.com
13. Hoover's, Siemens AG-industry conglomerates, www.hoovers.com.
14. Hoover's, Medical Equipment Snapshot, www.hoovers.com.
15. Hoover's, Siemens Medical Solutions., www.hoovers.com, September 29, 2004.
16. www.siemens.com
17. Welcome to Siemens, www.usa.siemens.com.
18. "All-Digital Hospital Will Include Wide Range of Equipment, Software from Siemens," *Hospital Material Management*, Vol. 27, No. 10, 2002, pp. 1–5.
19. Hoover's, OSRAM GmbH, Company Capsule, www.hoovers.com.
20. Management's Discussion and Analysis, www.siemens.com.
21. Automation and Control, www.siemens.com.
22. Ibid.
23. "Siemens Automation," Hoover's Database, www.hoovers.com, February 12, 2002.
24. "Power," Siemens Business Segments, www.siemens.com, January 23, 2002.
25. Ibid.
26. "Siemens Power," Hoover's Database, www.hoovers.com, February 12, 2002.
27. Hoover's Online, "Siemens AG—Information and Communications," www.hoovers.com.
28. Ibid.
29. Siemens web site, "Siemens Business Services," www.siemens.com.
30. Hoover's Online, "Siemens Buys DSL Company to Spur Internet-Related Growth," www.hoovers.com, February 18, 2002.
31. Hoover's Online, "Siemens Debuts Program to Build Revenue-Generating Applications for Next Generation Converged Network Solution," www.hoovers.com, February 18, 2002.
32. Baines Stewart, "Roland Koch: Company Man," Responsive Database, *Communications International*, www.rdsweb1.rdsinc.com, July 2000, pp. 42–44.

Case 17-1

Siemens: Organizational Issues for the International Market[11]

Siemens, a German company whose business portfolio comprises industries such as information and communications, automation and control, power, transportation, medical, lighting, and financing and real estate, has spearheaded innovation in many domains. It linked the first long-distance telegraph system in Europe in 1848; it completed a 6,600-mile telegraph line from London, United Kingdom, to Calcutta, India, in 1870; and it created the first electrified railway and one of the first elevators.[12] The company , had its beginnings in the mid 1800s, when Werner von Siemens developed the pointer telegraph, which enabled him to lay the cornerstone of the company; the Siemens & Halske Telegraph Construction Company was founded in Berlin in 1856. Today, Siemens, headquartered in Munich, Germany, is a multinational corporation with a presence in more than 190 countries, employing more than 480,000 people; it has a balanced business portfolio whose operating groups include Automation and Drives, Power Generation, Transportation Systems, Medical Solutions, Financing and Real Estate, Information and Communication Networks, Information and Communication Mobile, and Siemens Business Services.[13]

Siemens and the Medical Equipment Industry

The medical equipment industry consists of different products, services, and solutions for integrated health care; in this category are makers and distributors of medical supplies, instruments, and equipment. Siemens Medical Solutions ranks fifth in sales among manufacturers of medical equipment, behind GE Medical Solutions, Baxter, Tyco Healthcare, and Medtronic.[14] Siemens Medical Solutions makes and markets a wide range of medical equipment, including MRI (magnetic resonance imaging) systems, radiation therapy equipment, and patient monitoring systems; its Ultrasound unit produces imaging equipment for cardiology, radiology, gynecology, and urology, and the company offers information technology to doctors, hospitals, and clinics through Siemens Health Services.[15]

Siemens entered into a partnership with HealthSouth Corporation in the United States to create the world's first all-digital hospital: Siemens serves as the primary technology provider and supports the hospital in health-care information technology applications and infrastructure, medical equipment, telecommunications, and "smart" building techniques.[16] The hospital offers such services as an Internet connection to every bed for videoconferencing and a wireless wellness monitor to evaluate the health status and indicate the exact location of each patient.[17]

In another example, Alegent Health in Omaha, Nebraska, is standardizing its eight hospitals using Siemens equipment and software. Alegent will spend $150 million on diagnostic, surgical, lighting, building, and climate control equipment, as well as on information technology.[18]

Siemens and the Lighting Industry

In the lighting area, Siemens specializes in lighting sources and the associated electronic control gear, offering products such as general lighting solutions, automotive lighting (an industry in which the company is ranked first), photo-optic lamps, and display lighting. In this sector, it competes with GE Lighting, Matsushita Electric Works, and Philips Electronics.[19] Siemens' focus in this industry is on innovative products, such as e-business, and expansion into Asia and Eastern Europe. Its latest joint venture in opto-semiconductors with Osram Sylvania helped the company during difficult economic conditions.[20]

Siemens and the Automation and Control Industry

Siemens is the world's largest supplier of products, systems, solutions, and services in the industrial and building technology sector: Its four major automation markets consist of manufacturing, process, building, and logistics automation. Siemens Automation and Control is divided into four sub-groups: Automation and Drives, Industrial Solutions and Services, Siemens Dematic, and Siemens Building Technologies.[21] Its major products include industrial networks, human/machine interfaces, power controls and supplies, industrial components, AC/DC drives, motion-control products, analyzers, scales, motors and pumps, circuit breakers, transformers, and residential electric products such as surge protectors and meters. The company's products range from airport logistics to consumer daily life: Its Smart Homes have electronic butlers who greet homeowners at the door, lock up when commanded, and answer the telephone, while their fire detectors can differentiate between the smoke from a cigar or a fire.[22] Top competitors in this segment of the business include Emerson, GE Industrial Products and Systems, and Schneider.[23]

Siemens and the Power Industry

Siemens Power Generation (PG) is an important player in the global power plant development business, focusing on the design and construction of fossil-fueled plants, which account for about 75 percent of sales.[24] Siemens PG manufactures gas and steam turbines, compressors, catalysts, and other electrical products and builds nuclear, hydroelectric, biomass, and combined heat and

continued

power plants.[25] Siemens' competitors in the power industry include companies such as ALSTOM, GE Power Systems, HOCHTIEF, Schneider, ABB, and Fluor.[26]

Siemens and the Financial Services Industry

In the financial services sector, Siemens specializes in innovative corporate financing and related risk management. Siemens offers financial services such as leasing, factoring, asset securitization, pension advisory, insurance, investment management, treasury and financing services, equity investment, project and export financing, and e-financing. Siemens Financial Services focuses on sales and corporate financing. Siemens specializes in balance sheet and liquidity management for large international companies and develops products and services for each client, involving the client, business partners, and, when necessary, public agencies and other service providers such as banks. The Siemens Financial Services ventures in India and the United States have been especially profitable.

Siemens Transportation

The transportation sector of Siemens is divided into two groups: Transportation Systems and Siemens VDO Automotive AG. Through these two different groups, Siemens offers transportation solutions and systems, such as modular vehicles for light rail and mainline systems, technology for driverless subways and computer-controlled electronic interlockings, and optical sensor systems and GPS-based service and diagnostic concepts, among others.

The products offered by the transportation sector of Siemens are mass transit, regional passenger rail, main line and high-speed traffic, turn-key systems, and a service sector that includes service on infrastructure and telecommunications equipment. Siemens partners with the automotive industry to create innovative solutions and systems integration.

Siemens and the Information Technology Industry

Siemens' information technology division, which accounts for approximately 37 percent of Siemens' total sales,[27] is organized into three groups: Information and Communication Networks, Information and Communication Mobile, and Siemens Business Services. Information and Communication Networks provides products such as broadband access gear, e-business systems, network management systems, professional consulting services, security systems, switches, and telephone systems.[28] The Information and Communication Mobile group specializes in core network equipment, intelligence network equipment, mobile networking systems, and wireless modules. Siemens Business Services specializes in business and enterprises services, consumer services, public sector services, and service provider and network operator services; and the group's e-business Solutions and Services addresses five core areas: supply chain management, enterprise resource management, business information management, customer relationship management, and electronic commerce.[29]

A few years ago, Siemens bought Efficient Networks, a United States firm specializing in digital subscriber line (DSL) technology—which allows Internet transmission and voice calls to take place at the same time. In January 2001, Siemens also introduced its first cell phone into the United States; Siemens is the third biggest producer of handsets in Europe.[30]

A recent Siemens initiative is the SURPASS program, which will enable it to increase the services that it provides to its customers in the packet-based network area. The company will use SURPASS technology and combine it with applications delivered by outside vendors (Broadsoft, Comverse, Iperia, LongBoard, Pactolus, Tornado Development, and Ubiquity).[31] According to Roland Koch, CEO of Siemens' Information and Communication Networks, there are great opportunities in the mobile arena, and the business is just in its beginning stages.[32]

In this sector, Siemens competes with Alcatel, Ericsson, and Nokia in offering communications products for public networks, homes, and businesses; in the broader IT sector and business services, Siemens competes with Accenture, Affiliated Computer Services, Atos Origin, BearingPoint, Capgemini, Deloitte Consulting, and EDS.

Analysis Suggestions

1. Perform an analysis of the Siemens product portfolio and comment on the Siemens branding strategy. Refer to www.siemens.com for additional information.
2. Siemens competes internationally with an international design that is best suited for its long-term international goals. Provide an analysis of Siemens' organizational design.

Appendix A

The International Marketing Plan

Overview

The international marketing plan is an essential element of a company's strategic plan, an effort to maintain a fit between company objectives and capabilities and the continuously changing international environment. Students are advised to first focus on corporate planning and, subsequently, on the specific international marketing strategy.

The steps outlined in this blueprint are general and should be adapted based on the information available and based on the industry and on the country conditions at the time of the analysis.

Step 1: Analyzing the Company and Country Background

As a first step, the marketing plan should include a brief company background, with a focus on the product that will be marketed internationally and the country where the product will be introduced.

The company should rely on its mission statement to articulate its vision and principles for its international endeavors, underscoring the distinctive differentiating aspects of the business and the company's approach to its different stakeholders: consumers, employees, society. It should rely on its overall goals and objectives to create the specific goals and objectives for the international market. The company objectives may be to enter new international markets or to increase market share in its existing markets. Or they may involve focusing on research and development in order to bring leading-edge technology to the marketplace worldwide. Objectives can also be expressed in terms of societal outcomes, such as increasing literacy or reducing world hunger, depending on the focus of the business.

The ultimate organizational goal is creating profit for the company and wealth for its shareholders. Company goals could include increasing productivity and production volume, lowering labor costs by moving production to countries with low-cost labor, maximizing consumption of consumers worldwide, and, as a result, increasing sales.

In the process of achieving these organizational goals, companies compete to offer a wide variety of goods and services and a maximum number of choices for consumers. As they compete, they lower prices that consumers pay for their products to gain market share.

This step of the analysis could include the following information:

- Brief profile of the company
- Brief product profile
- Brief country background
- Rationale for introducing the product to the respective country

Step 2: Analyzing the Environment

In the second step, the local and regional environment must be assessed to evaluate the country and target market attractiveness. At this stage, the local economy and the trade, political, and legal infrastructures are evaluated to determine the extent to which investing in the country constitutes a sound decision. The social-cultural environment also is assessed to identify the most viable marketing strategy to use in the respective country. Finally, the competitive environment is examined; here, the competitive intensity (local and international) and the existing and potential barriers to entry imposed by the competition are evaluated to determine the resources needed for market penetration.

This step of the analysis could include the following information:

Economic and Trade Analysis

Population statistics and relevance of demographics to company plans

Economic development statistics (GNP, GDP, economic growth) and relevance to company plans

Overview of industrial and agricultural sectors, national resources, and labor

Analysis of transportation and telecommunication infrastructure

General analysis of the marketing support structure:

    Distribution and logistics

    Promotion infrastructure

    Marketing research suppliers

Trade trends:

    Membership in regional and international trade organizations

    Trade patterns (imports, exports, foreign direct investment) and rate of growth

    Barriers to trade

Political and Legal Analysis

Political stability:

    Legitimacy of political elite

    Diversity of ethnic groups with divergent interests

    Degree of political repression

    Nationalism

    Stability of government policies

Type of legal system

Transparency of the legal system

Degree of ambiguity of commercial laws

Degree to which laws are followed and enforced

Socio-Cultural Analysis

Languages and dialects and implications for marketing

Social institutions and implications for the company:

> Family
>
> Social class
>
> Social status
>
> Social groups and group dynamics

Religion, norms, and value systems and marketing implications

Target Market and Competitive Analysis

Target consumer analysis (product use, shopping behavior)

Existing distribution patterns for product category and availability of local distributors (wholesalers, retailers, logistics companies)

Existing promotion patterns for product category and availability of local promotion talent and media

Degree of competitive intensity

Competitor marketing strategies

Competitive barriers

Step 3: Evaluating the International Business Portfolio

The third step involves evaluating the different strategic business units of the international company. At this stage, the company must identify the products that have great promise in the marketplace and need additional resources, the products that are performing well in a mature market, and those that are not and must be divested. Establishing a strategic fit with the market is essential: Companies may have the resources to support a particular strategic business unit, but if the unit does not fit with the company's long-term goals, or if selling the unit would generate resources that could be invested to further the company's goals, the company may consider selling this particular business. Companies periodically review their different businesses and make decisions on whether to acquire new ones or divest those that might be unprofitable or that do not represent a good fit with the company.

Each business unit must develop its own mission statement, focusing on the strategic fit between resources and the company goals with regard to its international target markets. The mission statement of the business unit should be more specific than the corporate mission statement, focusing on the brand or product itself.

An important step in the analysis process involves identifying the company's strengths, weaknesses, opportunities, and threats (SWOT). Students should first examine the microenvironment of marketing, addressing its strengths and weaknesses; more specifically, students should examine strengths and weaknesses related to the company, consumers, suppliers, middlemen, and other facilitators of marketing functions and to the competition. Next, students should examine threats and opportunities in the international socio-demographic and cultural environment, the economic and natural environment, the technological environment, and the political and legal environment.

To facilitate the analysis, students can use Tables A-1 and A-2 for each region or country.

Step 4: Developing the International Marketing Plan

The marketing plan focuses on the strategic business unit the company has selected: a product or service that the company has proposed to analyze. It involves the following:

Setting marketing objectives (express objectives in terms of sales, profit, and market share) based on corporate goals and objectives and market potential

Product decisions

> Decisions on standardization versus adaptation
>
> Product mix decisions (short and long term) for the market

Promotion decisions

> Advertising objectives
>
> Media decisions
>
> Message decisions

Distribution decisions

> Decisions on whether to use existing channels or to build distribution
>
> Decisions on wholesalers, retailers, warehousing, and logistics firms
>
> Logistics decisions (intermodal transportation, freight forwarders, customs brokers, insurance agents, other facilitators)

Pricing decisions

> Identifying local market traits and needs and product cost
>
> Developing an international marketing budget based on cost
>
> Identifying human and capital resources needed for local operations

Identifying International Marketing Objectives

Marketing objectives could be defined in terms of dollar sales or units sold, profit, or in terms of market share.

Defining the Marketing Strategy

The marketing strategy involves identifying international segments that are similar with regard to key traits and those who would respond well to a product and related marketing mix (market segmentation); selecting the segments that the company can serve most efficiently and developing products tailored to each (market targeting); and offering the products to the market, communicating, through the marketing mix, product traits and benefits that differentiate it in the consumer's mind (market positioning).

At this stage, students should identify the different international market segments, select the segments that represent the best fit with the company goals and objectives for the respective international market, and design the strategies aimed to serve these segments more effectively than competitors.

Table A-1	Microenvironment, Country A	
	List of Strengths	**List of Weaknesses**
Company		
Consumers		
Suppliers		
Middlemen		
Other facilitators		
Competition		

Table A-2	Macroenvironment, Country A	
	List of Threats	**List of Opportunities**
Socio-demographic and cultural environment		
Economic environment		
Natural environment		
Technological environment		
Political environment		
Legal environment		

Developing the Marketing Mix for the International Market

At this stage, international marketing mix decisions address product, price, promotion, and distribution strategies that will be used for entering the international target market and the controls needed to evaluate marketing performance.

Product: Decide on design, features, brand name, packaging, and service components for a particular market.

Refer to Chapters 9, "Products and Services: Branding Decisions in International Markets," and 10, "International Product and Service Strategies."

Place: Decide on the types of channels used, market coverage, assortment, transportation and logistics, and inventory management.

Refer to Chapters 11, "Managing International Distribution Operations and Logistics," and 12, "International Retailing."

Price: Decide on the price, discounts, and credit terms.

Refer to Chapter 16, "International Pricing Strategy."

Promotion: Decide on advertising, personal selling, sales promotion, public relations, and publicity that the company should pursue.

Refer to Chapters 13, "The International Promotional Mix and Advertising Strategies," 14, "International Publicity, Public Relations, and Sales Promotion Strategies," and 15, "International Personal Selling and Personnel Management."

Step 5: Establishing Methods for Implementation and Control of the International Operation

Students should suggest how marketing plans can be turned into marketing action programs to accomplish the international marketing objectives.

The company will set performance standards and related controls to ensure that performance is in line with market potential given the country-specific operating environment.

This step of the analysis could include the following information:

• Standards for operation in light of market potential
• Proposed performance measures in light of goals and objectives
• Methods for addressing discrepancies

Glossary

A

accessibility The ability to communicate with the international target market.

acculturation The act of learning a new culture; encompasses intercultural interaction and adaptation.

actionability The extent to which the target market segment is responsive to the marketing strategies used.

adaptation The strategy of altering a product to better meet the needs of a local market.

adaptation of the advertising strategy The act of changing a company's promotional mix to each country or market, or creating local campaigns.

adiaphoras The norms that refer to customs that a foreign national may engage in but is not necessarily expected to do so.

advertising effectiveness research Studies conducted to examine the effectiveness and appropriateness of advertisements aimed at individual markets.

advocacy advertising Advertising a particular position or point of view.

African Development Bank A bank, headquartered in Abidjan, Ivory Coast, that has as a primary goal poverty reduction in Africa, providing support and expertise in agriculture, human resources, and health services, with an emphasis on small business. (See www.afdb.org.)

aggressive export pricing A pricing strategy that prices products below market price in order to penetrate new markets.

all-purpose discount stores General merchandise discount stores that offer a wide variety of merchandise and limited depth.

all-you-can-afford method The process of allocating the maximum amount possible to advertising; this method is used by small and medium-size corporations.

analogy method A method for estimation that relies on developments and findings in similar markets or where the product is in the same life-cycle stage.

Andean Common Market (AnCom) A trade group of the Andean countries that aspires to become a common market; it is currently in the process of agreeing upon common external tariffs. (See www.comunidadandina.org.)

antidumping Legislation designed to counter unfair price competition; lengthy antidumping investigations can also serve as an impediment to trade.

antidumping duties Duties that must be paid by firms as a punishment for engaging in unfair price competition.

antitrust laws Laws designed to prevent anticompetitive activities, such as the creation of monopolies and cartels.

appearances An individual's physical attire and overall grooming.

applications positioning The marketing of a very precise product application that is differentiated in the consumers' minds from other products that have a more general use.

Arab Maghreb Union (AMU) An attempt, in the early 1980s, at creating a free trade area in the Southern Mediterranean area; it was not successful due to conflict.

arbitration Binding procedure for conflict resolution involving an independent third party; a faster and less costly procedure than a lawsuit.

ASEAN Free Trade Area (AFTA) A free trade agreement signed by members of the Association of Southeast Asian Nations (ASEAN). (See www.aseansec.org.)

Asian Development Bank A bank, headquartered in Manila, the Philippines, that focuses on the private sector in Asia, sponsoring projects aimed at increasing access to technology and improving the functioning of government in the region. (See www.adb.org.)

Asia-Pacific Economic Cooperation (APEC) A trade group including all major economies of the Asia-Pacific region, it is a forum for economic cooperation and has as its goal the gradual reduction of barriers to trade and investment between member countries. (See www.apec.org.)

assimilation The act of abandoning all home-country traditions while learning a new culture.

Association of Southeast Asian Nations (ASEAN) A successful example of integration in Asia, creating an environment that promotes mutual involvement in industrial development in the region and a free trade area composed of Brunei, Cambodia, Indonesia, Laos, Malaysia, Myanmar, the Philippines, Singapore, Thailand, and Vietnam. (See www.aseansec.org.)

attribute/benefit positioning Positioning that communicates product attributes and benefits, differentiating each brand from the other company brands and from those of competitors.

automatic import license A license granted freely to importing companies but may be used by government for the purpose of import surveillance, thus discouraging import surges, imposing administrative and financial burdens on importers, and delaying shipment.

B

back translation The translation of translated text back into its original language, by a different individual, to ensure that the instrument has been translated as intended.

barter A simple, nonmonetized exchange of goods and/or services between two parties.

benefit segmentation The process of identifying international market segments based on important differences between the benefits sought by the target market from purchasing a particular product.

big emerging markets (BEMs) Large markets characterized by rapid economic development and high potential; big emerging markets set the pace for the economy in their geographic region.

bilateral agreement Regional trade cooperation between two countries aimed at reducing or eliminating trade barriers for all or for selected products.

billboards Advertisements in public areas appearing on large posters or electronic panels.

blocked currency A strategy that does not allow importers to exchange local currency for the seller's currency or a currency that the seller is willing to accept as payment (hard currency).

bourgeoisie A dominant social class, which, according to Marxist-Leninist theory, establishes lucrative means of production and achieves high productivity at the expense of exploited workers.

boycott An action calling for a ban on consumption of all goods associated with a particular company and/or country.

brand awareness research Research investigating how consumers' knowledge and recognition of a brand name affect their purchasing behavior.

brand name counterfeiting Selling counterfeit products as brand name originals.

brand name generation and testing The testing of brand names and logos, necessary when companies market their products internationally.

broadcast medium A nonpersonal channel of communication such as television or radio.

brokers and agents Middlemen who bring international buyers and sellers together; they do not carry title to the product.

building channels Creating new distribution channels, especially necessary in situations where there are no channels at all, or there are no channels that conform to the needs of the company.

buyback agreements Agreements whereby the seller builds and provides a turnkey plant and is paid up front part of the cost of the plant in an agreed-upon convertible currency; in return, the seller agrees to purchase specific quantities of the plant's output over an extended period of time.

buyer behavior research Research examining brand preferences and brand attitudes.

buying offices Buyers representing different firms located abroad.

C

capitalism A stage of economic and political development, which, according to Marxist-Leninist theory, is characterized, in its early stages, by an emerging bourgeoisie, the shift of production from the agrarian sector to the industrial sector, and, in its later stages, by imperialism, where capital loses its national identity by crossing borders and establishing monopolies.

catalog retailers Retailers selling products through mail catalogs.

catalog showrooms Showrooms displaying the products of catalog retailers, offering high-turnover, brand name goods at discount prices.

category killers Large general merchandise discount stores that carry a narrow variety of merchandise and a wide assortment; also called category specialists or stores with category dominance.

category specialists Large general merchandise discount stores that carry a narrow variety of merchandise and a wide assortment; also called category killers.

causal research Research that examines cause-and-effect relationships.

Central American Common Market (CACM) An economic agreement between Central American countries; this agreement includes plans for forming a regional economic union similar to the European Union, and to advance regional and international trade.

channel of communication The medium used to communicate a message about a product to the consumer.

channel performance and coverage studies Studies investigating whether existing channels are appropriate for communication, if channels exist at all, or whether they are appropriate for international marketing communications.

chronemics The timing of verbal exchanges.

clearing account A complex form of countertrade whereby countries trade products up to a certain amount stated in a particular, mutually-agreed-upon hard currency and within a given time frame, and, when

an imbalance occurs and one country owes money to the other, swing credits are paid in an agreed-upon hard currency, known as the clearing currency; also called a clearing agreement.

clearing currency The agreed-upon currency used to pay swing credits in a clearing account or agreement.

code law Comprehensive written laws that specify what constitutes legal behavior.

collectivism The degree to which individuals prefer to act in the interest of the group, rather than in their own self-interest.

combination stores Medium-size retail stores that combine food and drug retailing.

common law Laws that are based on prior court rulings (legal precedents).

common market A market composed of member countries, characterized by the unrestricted movement of goods, labor, and capital.

Common Market for Eastern and Southern Africa (COMESA) An agreement between 20 member countries aimed at achieving economic integration; COMESA is currently eliminating all tariff and nontariff barriers to trade and is in the process of adopting common external tariffs.

Commonwealth of Independent States (CIS) A political agreement between the twelve non-Baltic countries of the former Soviet Union. (See www.cis.minsk.by.)

communism A stage in economic and political development, which, according to Marxist-Leninist theory, is characterized by state and cooperative ownership of all means of production and property.

company publications Public relations publications that describe the products of a company to potential customers and summarize financial achievements.

comparative advantage The premise that countries benefit from specialization in an industry where they have comparative advantage and from trading with one another.

compensation The payment in products and in cash, usually in a mutually-agreed-upon convertible currency.

competitive pricing analyses Pricing studies that determine the price the market will bear for the respective product category.

competitive-parity method The strategy of using competitors' level of advertising spending as a benchmark for the company's own advertising expenditures.

competitor positioning The process of comparing the firm's brand with those of competitors, directly or indirectly.

complementary export agents Firms that export other firms' products that are complementary to their offerings, along with their own products, for a fee/commission.

complementary export merchants Distributors who take title to the complementary products distributed and are compensated in the form of a discount.

comprador A foreign agent with an exclusive arrangement with a company, representing its operations in a particular country; also referred to as a managing agent.

concentrated targeting The process of selecting only one market segment and targeting it with one single brand.

concept development and testing studies Concept tests usually performed in developed countries evaluating the product/service offering and the related marketing mix in light of the different international target markets.

conceptual equivalence The extent to which meanings remain the same in different cultural environments.

confiscation The foreign government seizure of company assets and/or investors' assets without any compensation.

consortia A company created with the participation of three or more companies; allowed in underserved markets or in domains where the government and/or the marketplace can control its monopolistic activity.

consumer segmentation studies Research conducted to identify market segment profiles.

content analysis Method that assesses the content of advertisements in a medium with verbal and/or visual content.

continuous innovation Product innovation where there is no disruption in consumption patterns; such innovations involve product alterations such as new flavors or new products that are improvements over the old offerings.

contract manufacturing A relationship between two companies wherein one company contracts with another to manufacture products according to the contracting company's specifications and for a specified period of time.

controlled test marketing Test marketing that involves offering a new product to a group of stores and evaluating the market's reaction to it.

convenience stores Small retailers located in residential areas, open long hours, and carrying limited lines of high-turnover necessities.

conventional supermarkets Self-service food retailers with annual sales of more than $2 million and with an area less than 20,000 square feet.

cooperative export arrangements Agreements that involve the use of a distribution system of exporters with established systems of selling abroad, who agree to handle the export function of a noncompeting (but not necessarily unrelated) company on a contractual basis; also called mother henning or piggybacking.

cooperative exporting Using the distribution system of exporters with established systems of selling abroad who agree to handle the export function of a noncompeting (but not necessarily unrelated) company on a contractual basis; also called mother henning and piggybacking.

copyright The rights to an original work of art (literature, music, film, design, and other works), enabling the owner to reproduce, sell, perform, or film the work.

core product strategy The strategy of using the same standard core product/service worldwide, but varying certain aspects of the offering (product ingredients, advertising) from market to market.

corporate advertising A type of advertising that is used to promote the company behind the different brands.

corruption laws Laws designed to prevent multinational corporations from using unethical means to obtain competitive advantage in a particular market.

cost analyses Methods used for projecting the cost of research.

cost-based transfer pricing A pricing strategy used in intra-firm sales for commercial transactions between units of the same corporation, within or beyond the national borders of the parent company, where the costs reflect not the costs incurred by the company, but the estimated opportunity costs of the product.

cost-of-living adjustment A compensation incentive whereby the company adjusts expatriate salaries to reflect the cost of living in the new environment at standards in the expatriate's home country; also called post adjustment.

Council of Ministers The decision-making body (the legislature) of the European Union, composed of one minister from each member country.

Council of Mutual Economic Assistance (CMEA) A trade agreement between the countries of the Soviet Bloc that disintegrated after the fall of communism. CMEA was an economic body similar in nature to a free trade area, and approached what would be considered a political union.

Council of Nations The constitutional council of the European Union consisting of representatives from parliaments of EU member states. (See www.europa.eu.int.)

counterpurchase A form of trade that involves two exchanges paid for in cash; it involves two parallel contracts whereby the seller agrees to purchase products that are usually unrelated to its business from the buyer and sell them on international markets; also called parallel barter.

countertrade A form of trade whereby a company sells a product to a buyer and agrees to accept, in return for payment, products from the buyer's firm or from the trade agency/institution of the buyer.

countervailing duties Duties imposed on subsidized products imported into a country.

countervailing duty actions Investigations initiated to determine whether imports are sold below fair prices as a result of foreign subsidies and the subsequent establishment of measures to offset subsidies.

country of manufacture The country in which a particular product is manufactured.

country of origin The country with which a particular product or service is associated.

creeping expropriation A situation characterized by bureaucratic red tape and corruption, an unreliable judicial system, and shifting regulations, where foreign government actions discourage foreign investment, especially investment in nonessential sectors.

cross-border shopping Purchasing products from a neighboring country where the consumers may be charged lower duties.

cultural variability The classification of cultures on a number of dimensions, or continuums; Hofstede classified cultures on the dimensions of collectivism, masculinity, power distance, and uncertainty avoidance.

culture The continuously evolving totality of learned and shared meanings, rituals, norms, and traditions among the members of an organization or society.

culture shock A pervasive feeling of anxiety resulting from one's presence in a new, unfamiliar culture.

currency and capital flow controls All protectionist activities involving the control of capital and hard currency flows in and out of a particular country.

customs union A market composed of member countries imposing identical import duties and sharing import regulations.

D

data collection instrument The instrument used to collect data, such as a printed questionnaire, a paper-and-pencil measure, or an electronic measurement device.

decentering The successive translation (by different translators) of an instrument between the original language and the language of administration with the purpose of obtaining an instrument that is closest in meaning to the original.

decision support system A coordinated collection of data, systems, tools, and techniques, complemented by supporting software and hardware designed for the gathering and interpretation of business and environmental data.

decline stage The stage of the international product life cycle in which products are rapidly losing ground to new technologies or product alternatives, causing a decrease in sales and profits.

decoding The process whereby the target consumer receives the message from the advertiser and translates it into meaningful information.

degree of product/service newness The extent to which a product is new to the market in general or to a group of consumers.

Delphi method A method of forecasting sales by asking a number of experts to estimate market performance, aggregating the results, and sharing this information with the said experts; the process is repeated several times, until a consensus is reached.

demographic segmentation The process of identifying market segments based on age, gender, race, income, education, occupation, social class, life-cycle stage, and household size.

department stores General retailers that offer a broad variety of goods and wide assortments.

depth interview A qualitative research method involving extensive interviews aimed at discovering consumer motivations, feelings, and attitudes toward an issue of concern to the sponsor using unstructured interrogation.

descriptive research All research methods observing or describing phenomena.

design counterfeiting Copying designs or scents of another company.

designing and developing the product Developing product prototypes and giving the product a name, a brand identity, and a marketing mix; a step in the new product development process.

developed countries Highly industrialized countries with well-developed service sectors, mature markets, and intense competition; they are characterized by the World Bank as high-income, with a GNP per capita of US$9,266 and above.

developing and evaluating concepts Determining how consumers will perceive and use a new product; a step in the new product development process.

developing countries Countries that are primarily agrarian, often neglected or under-served by large multinationals, and characterized by the World Bank as low-income countries, with a GNP per capita of less than US$755.

differential exchange rate The rate imposed by the local government to promote imports of desirable and necessary goods; it also can be the difference between the black market exchange rate and the official government rate.

differential response The extent to which international market segments respond differently to marketing strategies.

differentiated targeting A targeting strategy identifying market segments with different preferences for a particular product category and targeting each segment with different brands and different marketing strategies.

diffusion process The process by which a product is adopted by consumers worldwide.

direct exporting An export entry mode whereby a firm handles its own exports, usually with the help of an in-house exporting department.

direct mail retailing Retailing using catalogs and other direct mail, instead of brick-and-mortar stores.

direct selling Selling that involves a salesperson, typically an independent distributor, contacting a consumer at a convenient location—at his or her home or workplace, demonstrating product use and benefits, taking orders, and delivering the merchandise.

distribution alliance A nonequity relationship between two firms, in which one firm handles the other's distribution or some aspect of the distribution process.

domestic marketing Marketing that is focused solely on domestic consumers and on the home-country environment.

domestication The process initiated by a foreign government leading to the gradual transfer of ownership and management to locals.

drive-to-maturity stage A stage in economic development, described by Rostow, as characterized by the technological and entrepreneurial skill to produce anything society chooses to produce.

drivers in the business environment Elements in the business environment, such as competition, technology, and labor costs, causing the firm to become involved internationally.

dumping Selling products below cost to get rid of excess inventory and/or to undermine competition.

dynamic incremental pricing A pricing strategy whereby a company assumes that it will have certain fixed costs whether or not it exports its products overseas and does not factor in its international price marketing and promotion costs for domestic distribution, nor its full overhead.

dynamically continuous innovation Innovation that does not alter significantly consumer behavior but still entails a change in the consumption pattern.

E

early adopters Consumers who purchase a product early in its product life cycle and who tend to be opinion leaders in their communities who take risks, but with greater discernment than innovators; they account for 13.5 percent of the total market.

early majority Consumers who enjoy the status of being among the first in their peer group to purchase a popular product; they account for 34 percent of the total market.

ecology The manner in which society adapts to its habitat, i.e., the distribution of resources within an industrialized country versus a developing country; the desire for efficiency, space-saving devices, or green products.

Economic Community of West African States (ECOWAS) A free trade agreement that strives to achieve economic integration in West Africa; domination by Nigeria, civil unrest, and regional conflict have served as impediments in the group's success. (See www.ecowas.int.)

education allowance A compensation incentive whereby the company agrees to cover the cost of children's education at an international private school in the country of assignment or at a boarding school in the expatriate's home country.

electronic data interchange (EDI) Relationship whereby buying and selling firms are able to share important data on production, inventory, shipping, and purchasing.

electronic retailing Selling through the Internet using websites to increase market penetration and market diversification; also called interactive home shopping and Internet retailing.

embargo The prohibition of all business deals with the country that is the target of the embargo, endorsed or initiated by the company's home country.

emerging countries Middle-income countries with a GNP per capita of US$766 to US$9,265, and with emerging markets that have great potential.

emerging markets Countries that are developing rapidly and have great economic potential; the World Bank characterizes them as middle-income countries, with a GNP per capita of US$766 to US$9,265.

emic instrument A data collection instrument constructed for each nationality to measure a particular factor; it is the best measure for culture-specific phenomena.

employment protection Protection of local employment by not granting import licenses for products competing with similar, locally produced, goods.

encoding The process whereby the advertiser puts the company's message about the product into words and images that are aimed at the target consumer.

enculturation The process by which individuals learn the beliefs and behaviors endorsed by their own culture.

entry mode The approach to international expansion a company chooses based on desired control and on the risk it can afford.

established channels Distribution channels that already exist in a particular market.

ethnocentric orientation Company strategies consistent with the belief that domestic strategies, techniques, and personnel are superior to foreign ones and therefore provide the most effective framework for the company's overseas involvement; companies adopting this perspective view international operations and customers as secondary to domestic operations and customers.

ethnocentrism The belief that one's culture is superior to another and that strategies used in one's home country (presumably a developed country) will work just as well internationally.

etic instrument A culture-free data collection instrument that can be used to measure the same phenomenon in different cultures.

Euroland The nickname of the European Monetary Union. (See www.europa.eu.int.)

European Atomic Energy Community A precursor to the European Union, it addressed issues related to the use and control of atomic energy.

European Bank for Reconstruction and Development A bank headquartered in London, United Kingdom, which has as main goals reforming and strengthening markets in the transition economies of Central and Eastern Europe. (See www.ebrd.com.)

European Central Bank The bank of the European Union charged with enacting monetary policy for the twelve countries that share a common currency, the Euro. (See www.europa.eu.int.)

European Coal and Steel Community An agreement that represents an early attempt at tariff reduction between members of the European Union.

European Commission The body of the European Union in charge of initiating and supervising the execution of laws and policies. (See www.europa.eu.int.)

European Council The highest policy-making body of the European Union. (See www.europa.eu.int.)

European Court of Justice The Supreme Court–equivalent of the European Union. (See www.europa.eu.int.)

European Exchange Rate Mechanism (ERM) A precursor of the Euro, a float that included the Euro, the then-theoretical currency of the European Union; the float allowed for variability in each currency.

European Free Trade Association (EFTA) A free trade agreement between Iceland, Liechtenstein, Norway, and Switzerland; previously, Sweden, Austria, and Finland were also members, but they have since joined the European Union. (See www.efta.int.)

European Monetary Union (EMU) A union composed of the members of the European Union who adhere to the joint monetary policy enacted by the European Central Bank and who have adopted the Euro as the single currency. (See www.europa.eu.int.)

European Parliament The Parliament of the European Union, composed of members elected every five years by direct universal suffrage; seats in the Parliament are allocated among member states based on their population. (See www.europa.eu.int.)

European Union An economic union consisting of most of the Western European countries; it is the only agreement that has achieved full economic integration and is now pursuing political integration. (See www.europa.eu.int.)

event sponsorship The financial support of cultural or sports-related events; companies use these events to get positive publicity.

exclusives The norms that refer to activities that are appropriate only for locals and from which individuals from a foreign country are excluded.

executive-judgment method A budgeting process that allocates the company's advertising budget based on the opinions of executives.

expatriate An employee working in a foreign country.

experimental research Research that examines cause-and-effect relationships; it has the highest validity and reliability of all types of research.

exploratory research Research conducted early in the research process that helps further define a problem or identify additional problems that need to be investigated.

export management companies Companies specializing in the export function for client companies in a particular industry.

export marketing Involvement in international marketing limited to the exporting function; although the firm actively seeks international clients, it considers the international market an extension of the domestic market and does not give it special consideration.

export merchants Intermediaries who take title to and possession of the products they carry; they are responsible for shipping and marketing the products to the target market.

Export Trading Company Act Legislation, passed in 1982, that encourages the formation of export trading companies by competing firms in order to promote U.S. exports without violating antitrust regulation.

expropriation The foreign government seizure of company assets with partial reimbursement, usually not at market value.

external secondary data Data collected for purposes other than the problem at hand.

F

feedback Information regarding the effectiveness of a company's message.

femininity The degree to which a national culture is characterized by nurturing, rather than assertive, values.

feudalism A stage in economic and political development, which, according to Marxist-Leninist theory, is characterized by the dominance of feudal lords, who own the land and its dwellers.

firm-specific drivers Elements specific to the firm, such as product life cycle, causing the firm to become involved internationally.

focus group interview A qualitative research approach investigating a research question using a moderator to guide discussion within a group of subjects recruited to meet certain characteristics.

food retailers Retailers selling primarily food products.

foreign consumer culture positioning The positioning of a particular brand as symbolic of a desired foreign culture.

Foreign Corrupt Practices Act Legislation that makes it illegal for companies and their representatives to bribe government officials and other politicians or candidates to political office, either directly or through third parties.

foreign exchange permit A permit that is generally provided by a country's Central Bank in conjunction with the Department of Trade (Ministry of Foreign Trade) and that gives priority to imports of goods considered to be in the national interest.

Foreign Sales Corporation (FSC) A sales corporation that is set up overseas; it allows for a portion of a U.S. tax-paying firm's foreign-source income to be exempt from U.S. income tax.

foreign trade zones Tax-free areas in a country that are not considered part of the respective country in terms of import regulations and restrictions.

foreign-country middlemen Intermediaries who help distribute products in a target foreign market.

formal controls Systematic controls, such as performance standards and measurement, used in international marketing to ensure that international company operations are in line with company goals and objectives.

franchisee The recipient party to a franchise who pays royalties in return for the right to use the franchisor's brand name and related trademarks.

franchising The main international entry mode for the service industry, whereby the franchisor gives the franchisee the right to use its brand name and all related trademarks in return for royalties.

franchisor The owner of the franchise who gives the franchisee the right to use its brand name and all related trademarks and its business know-how, such as secret recipes and customer interfacing techniques, in return for royalties.

free trade agreement An agreement whose goal is the reduction in, or even elimination of, customs duties and other trade barriers on all goods and services traded between member countries.

Free Trade Area of the Americas (FTAA) A plan to create a free trade association by 2005 that would comprise all member countries of the 34 democratic nations of North, Central, and South America. (See www.ftaa-alca.org.)

functional equivalence The difference in the purposes for which products may be used in different country environments.

G

gender roles The roles that women and men are expected to hold in a society.

General Agreement on Tariffs and Trade (GATT) The international trade agreement promoting trade and eliminating trade barriers, opening markets to international business, and creating a forum for resolving trade disputes; GATT issues are now addressed by the World Trade Organization. (See www.wto.org.)

general merchandise discount stores Retailers that sell high volumes of merchandise, offer limited service, and charge lower prices.

generating new product ideas Seeking ideas using different strategies as the first step in the new product development process.

geocentric orientation Company strategies that are consistent with the belief that the entire world, without national and regional distinctions, constitutes a potential market with identifiable, homogeneous segments that need to be addressed differentially.

geographic segmentation Market segmentation based on geographic location, such as country or region.

gift giving The norms regarding the gifts that are appropriate to give to others.

global campaign A worldwide standardized advertising campaign that is not adjusted to different target markets.

global consumer culture positioning Marketing programs appealing to individuals who want to be part of a global consumer culture by purchasing a brand that is a symbol of that culture.

global consumers The homogeneous consumer group worldwide sharing similar interests and product/brand preferences.

global elite A psycho-demographic group worldwide characterized by high income and desire for status brands and exclusive distribution.

global localization The practice of global branding and localized marketing adaptation to differences in local culture, legislation, and even production capabilities.

global marketing International marketing activities that do not have a country or region focus and that are possibly due to the emergence of global consumer segments and efficient global allocation of company talent and resources.

global standardization The standardization of products across markets and, ultimately, to the standardization of the marketing mix worldwide; more commonly called glocalization.

global youth segment A psycho-demographic global group of teenagers considered to be astute consumers with precise desires for brand name clothing products and entertainment.

glocalization The standardization of products across markets and, ultimately, to the standardization of the marketing mix worldwide; also called global standardization.

gray market A distribution system not authorized by the manufacturer whereby the products purchased in a low-price market are diverted to other markets; also called parallel imports.

greenfielding Developing a brand new subsidiary.

Group of Seven (G7) A group of the seven most industrialized countries: Canada, France, Germany, Italy, Japan, the United Kingdom, and the United States; the group also includes Russia and it is often also referred to as a G8. The group addresses issues such as biotechnology and food safety, economic development, arms control and nonproliferation, organized crime, drug trafficking, terrorism, environmental issues, digital opportunities, microeconomic issues, and trade. (See www.g7.utoronto.ca.)

growth stage The stage of the international product life cycle characterized by increasing competition and rapid product adoption by the target market.

H

haptics The use of touch while conversing.

hard currency Currency that is accepted for payment by any international seller.

high mass consumption A stage in economic development, described by Rostow, as characterized by leading sectors shifting toward durable goods.

high-context cultures Cultures in which the context of a message—the message source, the source's standing in society or in a group, his or her expertise, tone of voice, and body language—are all meaningful parts of the message.

historical method An approach to budgeting that is based on past expenditures, usually giving more weight to more recent expenditures.

home-country laws Laws of a company's home country that follow the international company all over the world.

home-country middlemen Intermediaries in the home country.

home-country national A local employee who works in his or her home country for the international corporation.

home-leave allowance A compensation incentive that pays for the expatriate and his or her family to vacation in the home country.

host-country laws Local laws; laws of the different countries where a company operates.

host-country national A local employee who works in his or her home country for the international corporation.

housing allowance A compensation incentive whereby the company covers part, or the entire cost, of housing for the expatriate employee while abroad.

hypermarkets Very large retail stores that combine supermarket, discount, and warehouse retailing principles.

I

ideology The manner in which individuals relate to their environment and to others, including their attitudes toward time, space, possessions, and referent others.

image advertising An advertising campaign that enhances perceptions of a company in a given market by creating a positive impression on the target consumers.

imperatives The norms referring to what individuals must or must not do in a certain culture.

imperialism A stage of economic and political development, in which, according to Marxist-Leninist theory, capital loses its national identity by crossing borders.

import jobber A merchant middleman who purchases commodity goods from the manufacturer to sell to the trade (wholesaler, retailer, business-to-business client) in the target market.

import quota The maximum quantity (unit limit) or value of a product that may be imported during a specified period.

import/export analysis Research that aids companies in identifying the necessary logistics that serve their needs in a timely and cost-effective manner.

Incoterms (International Commercial Terms) Terms of sale used in transactions.

indirect exporting An export entry mode whereby a company sells its products in the company's home country to intermediaries who, in turn, sell the product overseas.

individualism The degree to which people in a country prefer to act as individuals, in their self-interest.

individual personality Enduring traits that characterize individuals, motivating them to act or react to external stimuli in a particular manner.

infant industry argument A protectionist strategy aimed at protecting a national industry in its infancy from powerful international competitors.

infomercials Long television advertisements (one-half to one full hour in length) that are positioned as programming.

informal controls Systematic controls, such as dialogue between the headquarters and the international field operations, used in international marketing to ensure that international company operations are in line with company goals and objectives.

innovation A product new to the world.

innovators Risk takers who can afford to pay the higher purchase price charged by companies during the introduction stage of a product; they account for 2.5 percent of the total market.

intellectual property rights Laws protecting the rights of the inventor or of the firm employing the inventor to use and sell an invention for a specified period of time.

interactive home shopping A venue for selling through the Internet using websites to increase market penetration and market diversification; also called electronic retailing and Internet retailing.

interactive medium A nonpersonal channel of communication such as a web page or a computer terminal on the retailer's premises.

Inter-American Development Bank A bank headquartered in Washington, D.C., aiding companies in the Americas that do not ordinarily deal with the large development banks; this bank is involved in funding private sector projects, modernizing governments, strengthening institutions, and eliminating technology barriers. (See www.iadb.org.)

internal secondary data Data collected by a company to address a problem not related to the current research question.

international buyer-seller relationship The distribution between the buyer and the individual involved in personal selling.

international communication process The communication process that takes place between the product sponsor and the international target market.

international division structure An organizational structure whereby firms have separate domestic and international divisions.

international laws Rules and regulations that countries agree to abide by, addressing agreements among countries with regard to trade, protection of property, and other issues in the political and economic sphere.

international market potential studies Studies conducted to evaluate the potential that a particular country offers for a company.

international marketing The processes involved in the creation, production, distribution, promotion, and pricing of products, services, ideas, and experiences for international markets; these processes require a substantial focus on international consumers in a particular country or countries.

international marketing research The systematic design, collection, recording, analysis, interpretation, and reporting of information pertinent to a particular marketing decision facing a company operating internationally.

International Monetary Fund (IMF) Traditionally the lender of last resort; the IMF also has assumed the position of mediator between debtors and creditors, imposing stabilization programs; debt-reduction guidelines; ceilings for bank credit, budget deficit, borrowing, and international reserves; and development programs for borrowing countries. (See www.imf.org.)

international product life cycle (IPLC) A product life-cycle theory, which states that firms from developed countries engage in domestic production in the early stage of the product life cycle, marketing the product to industrialized countries; as the product reaches maturity, product specifications and the manufacturing process stabilize, price competition becomes intense, and markets in developing countries become essential to the firm's success.

international promotional mix The different modes of communication with international consumers about products and services, using international advertising, international salesforce management, international sales promotion, public relations, and publicity.

international public relations A concerted effort on the part of a company to generate goodwill among international publics that are essential to the company; its main purpose is to generate positive publicity about the company.

Internet retailing Selling through the Internet using websites to increase market penetration and market diversification; also called interactive home shopping and electronic retailing.

introduction stage The first stage of the international product life cycle when products are developed and marketed in industrialized countries.

Islamic law A system of law based on the interpretation of the Koran, Islam's holy book, and on interpretations of the practices and sayings of the prophet Muhammad.

ISO 9000 certification Certification that specifies that the organization must meet customer and regulatory requirements and follow its policies and procedures while advancing quality through continuous improvement.

ISO 14000 certification Certification that a company follows guidelines that discourage firms from engaging in hazardous environmental practices, and ensures that corporate policies promoting environmentally sound, efficiency-embracing, innovative technologies and processes will contribute to establishing twenty-first century production and distribution systems that are far less environmentally degrading.

J

joint venture A corporate entity created with the participation of two companies that share equity, capital, and labor, among others.

jurisdiction The country and/or legal body where a particular dispute should be adjudicated, according to the country's law, or according to the legal body's principles, respectively.

jury of expert opinion An approach to sales forecasting based on the opinion of different experts.

K

keiretsu A Japanese trading firm that consists of families of firms with interlocking stakes in one another.

kinesics The movement of part of the body in order to communicate.

L

lag countries Countries where a product or service is adopted after already being introduced in lead countries.

laggards Consumers who are the last to adopt new products and do so only in late maturity because they are risk averse and very

conservative in their spending; they account for 16 percent of the total market.

language The vehicle used for communication in a particular culture; includes spoken and written language and nonverbal communication.

late majority Individuals of limited means who are likely to adopt products only if the products are widely popular and the risk associated with buying them is minimal; they account for 34 percent of the total market.

Latin American Free Trade Association (LAFTA) An attempt by Latin American countries to establish a free trade association; its demise is attributed to the economic disparity between member countries and to protectionist policies.

Latin American Integration Association (LAIA) Latin America's largest trade agreement striving to establish bilateral and multilateral agreements aimed at reducing tariff and nontariff barriers.

launching the product internationally Introducing a new product to the international market as the last step in the new product development process.

lead countries Countries where a product or service is first introduced and adopted.

licensee The purchaser of the license who pays royalties to the licensor for the rights to use the licensor's technology, know-how, and brand name.

licensing An international entry mode that involves a licensor, who shares the brand name, technology, and know-how with a licensee in return for royalties.

licensor The owner of a product license who agrees to share know-how, technology, and brand name with the licensee in return for royalties.

local campaign An advertising campaign that is tailored to local needs; especially used in markets that media cannot easily reach.

local consumer culture positioning Positioning that associates the brand with local cultural meanings, reflecting the local culture, and portrayed as consumed by locals and/or depicted as locally produced for local people.

local content requirement A protectionist measure requiring that a certain percentage of the products imported are locally produced.

local pricing A pricing strategy in which different prices are charged in different markets, reflecting differences in consumer purchase power, distribution costs, tax systems, or other market traits.

logistics alliances Distribution alliances between two firms involving product transportation and warehousing.

low-context cultures Cultures in which what is said is precisely what is meant so that the verbal message carries the full meaning of the sentence.

M

Maastricht Treaty The treaty credited with establishing the European Union, eliminating all tariffs; establishing common external tariffs; allowing for the free movement of capital and labor within its territory; and setting regulations involving common trade policies, common agricultural and industrial policies, and common monetary and fiscal policies between member countries. (See www.europa.eu.int.)

managing agent A foreign agent who has an exclusive arrangement with a company, representing its operations in a particular country.

mandatory adaptation The adaptation of products to local requirements so that the products can legally and physically function in the specific country environment.

manufacturer's export agents Agents in the firm's home country handling the exporting function of a certain manufacturer on a commission, per deal, basis.

manufacturer's representative An agent who represents the manufacturer exclusively in the foreign target market.

manufacturing alliance A nonequity relationship between two firms, in which one firm handles the other's manufacturing or some aspect of the manufacturing process.

maquiladora Customs-privileged contract manufacturing facilities in Mexico that take advantage of low-cost labor.

market-based transfer pricing A pricing strategy used in intra-firm sales for commercial transactions between units of the same corporation, within or beyond the national borders of the parent company, whereby products are priced at market cost, rather than at the cost incurred by the company.

marketing alliance A nonequity relationship between two firms, in which one firm handles the other's marketing or some aspect of the marketing process.

Marxist-Leninist development model A development model attributed to Karl Marx and Vladimir Lenin which maps the development of society from an agrarian, traditional society to a society characterized by shared ownership of the means and outcomes of production and an equitable resource allocation; advancement from one stage to another is based on class struggle and transfer of ownership from one class to another and, ultimately, to the state.

masculinity The degree to which a national culture is characterized by assertiveness, rather than nurturing.

materialism Individuals' degree of concern with material possessions.

matrix structure An organizational structure whereby each operational unit reports to both region/country managers and product managers.

maturity stage A stage of the international product life cycle characterized by a slowdown in sales growth as the product is adopted by most target consumers and by a leveling or decline in profits primarily due to intense price competition.

measurability The ability to estimate the size of a market segment.

media availability The extent to which media are available to communicate with target consumers.

media infrastructure The media vehicles and their structure in an international target market.

media reliability The probability of the media to air advertising messages on time, at an acceptable quality, and with the agreed-upon frequency.

media research Studies that evaluate media availability and appropriateness of the medium for a company's message.

media restrictions Legal or self-imposed restrictions on the types and the number of advertisements aired or published.

mediation Nonbinding procedure for conflict resolution involving an independent third party.

medium/media The channel(s) of communication that a company uses to send to the target consumer a message about its product or services.

merchant middlemen Different intermediaries who carry the manufacturer's product line in a particular country; they both carry title to and have physical possession of the products they distribute.

Ministry of Foreign Affairs The international institutional equivalent of the State Department; it coordinates a country's involvement in international relations.

Ministry of Trade The international institutional equivalent of the Department of Commerce; it coordinates a country's international trade relations.

modification The alteration of an existing company product.

modular adaptation The localization across markets of the product by offering parts (modules) that can be assembled worldwide in different configurations, depending on the needs of the market.

modular campaign An advertising campaign that provides a template that is varied and customized from market to market.

monetary union A form of economic integration characterized by the establishment of a common central bank enacting monetary policy for the group.

monochronic time The interpretation of time as linear, such that individuals do one thing at a time, and in sequence.

monopolistic capitalism A stage of economic and political development, in which, according to Marxist-Leninist theory, multinational companies establish monopolies and expand internationally with the goal of subjugating developing countries.

Most-Favored-Nation Status Favored trade status previously granted by Congress for imported products from selected countries, which are not party to a preferential trade agreement with the United States.

mother henning Using the distribution system of exporters with established systems of selling abroad who agree to handle the export function of a noncompeting (but not necessarily unrelated) company on a contractual basis; also called piggybacking and cooperative exporting.

moving allowance A compensation incentive whereby the company pays for the household moving expenses to the country of assignment and, at the end of the assignment, back to the home country.

multilateral forums and agreements Agreements that involve multiple countries, have an informal structure, and/or do not necessarily have regional integration as their goal.

multilevel marketing Using acquaintance networks through an alternative distribution structure for the purpose of distribution; also called network marketing.

multinational marketing Marketing in different countries without coordinating across operations.

N

national and regional character A set of behavior and personality characteristics shared by individuals of a certain country or region.

nationalism An expression of fierce nationalist sentiment in a country where a company is operating, which poses an implicit threat to the company and its operations.

nationalization The takeover of company assets by a foreign government with the aim of creating a government-run industry.

network marketing Using acquaintance networks through an alternative distribution structure for the purpose of distribution; also called multilevel marketing.

new item in an existing product line A new brand that the company offers to the market in an existing product line.

new line A new product category offered by the company.

new product to existing company A new product that the company offers to the market; the product competes with similar competitor offerings.

new product to existing market A product never before offered to the market.

news releases Statements issued to the public to introduce a new product, touting its advantages; any other information shared with the media.

noise All the potential interference in the communication process.

nonautomatic import license A license issued on a discretionary basis to restrict imports of a given product and/or from a particular country.

nonmandatory adaptation The strategy of adapting a product to better meet the needs of the local market, without being required to do so.

nonpersonal medium A channel of communication such as a print medium, a broadcast medium, or an interactive medium that does not involve contact between the seller and the consumer.

nontariff barriers All measures, other than traditional tariffs, used to distort trade flows, used to increase prices of imports, and thus favor domestic over foreign products.

nonverbal communication All communication that is not written or spoken; includes body language, gestures, facial expressions, eye contact, and silence.

Norazi agent An export agent dealing in illegal and/or gray market products.

norms Rules that dictate what is right or wrong, acceptable or unacceptable in a society.

North American Free Trade Agreement (NAFTA) An agreement between the United States, Canada, and Mexico, aiming to eliminate tariff and nontariff barriers between the countries. (See www.nafta-sec-alena.org.)

North Atlantic Treaty Organization (NATO) A military agreement between countries that were, initially, not part of the Soviet Bloc. (See www.nato.int.)

O

objective-and-task method An advertising budgeting method in which the company first identifies advertising goals, conducts research to determine the cost of achieving the respective goals, and allocates the necessary sum for the purpose.

observational research A research approach used frequently in international markets, whereby subjects are observed interacting with a product and the related components of the marketing mix.

obstacles to internationalization Impediments that the firm may encounter in the process of internationalizing.

oculesics The use or avoidance of eye contact during communication.

off-price retailers Retailers who sell brand name products and designer merchandise below regular retail prices.

offset purchase A large, hard-currency purchase, such as the purchase of defense equipment, airplanes, telecommunications networks, railway or road building and other expensive civil engineering projects whereby the seller agrees, in return to purchase products that are valued at a certain percentage of the sale.

offshore assembly plants Plants located in customs-privileged bonded areas in countries with low labor costs, where products are manipulated and re-exported.

olfactions The use of odors to convey messages.

open-ended questions Questions with free-format responses that the respondent can address as he or she sees appropriate.

order getter Individual who actively generates potential leads and persuades customers to purchase the firm's products.

order taker Individual who processes routine sales orders from the customer.

orderly market arrangements Protectionist measures involving intricate processes for establishing quotas in the textile and apparel industries.

Organization for Economic Co-operation and Development (OECD) An economic multilateral agreement. (See www.oecdobserver.org.)

Organization of the Petroleum Exporting Countries (OPEC) Industry-specific (oil) multilateral agreement aimed at managing the output and price of oil. (See www.opec.com.)

organizational culture The shared norms and values that guide collective behavior in organizations, and enduring traits that characterize individuals, motivating them to act or react to stimuli in the organization and in the environment in a particular manner.

organizational design The organization of reporting and coordination within a company.

organizational structure The outcome of the organization of reporting and coordination within a company.

orientations Individuals' positioning relative to their counterparts during conversation.

outsourcing The strategic use of outside resources to perform activities that are usually handled by internal staff and resources.

Overseas Private Investment Corporation (OPIC) U.S. government corporation that provides loans, guarantees and insurance to U.S. corporations investing in countries that present high political risk.

P

paralinguistics The nonverbal aspects of speech that include intonation, accents, and the quality of voice.

parallel barter A form of trade that involves two exchanges that are paid for in cash; it involves two parallel contracts whereby the seller agrees to purchase products that are usually unrelated to its business from the buyer and sell them on international markets; also called counterpurchase.

parallel imports A distribution system not authorized by the manufacturer whereby the products purchased in a low-price market are diverted to other markets; also called gray market.

parallel translation The process of translating the original instrument by different translators and comparing the translations.

paratariff measures Additional, nontariff fees that increase the costs of imports in a manner similar to tariffs.

patent Protection of the rights of the inventor or of the firm employing the inventor to use and sell an invention for a specified period of time.

penetration pricing A pricing strategy in which a product is first priced below the price of competitors' products in order to quickly penetrate the market at the competitors' expense and then raised to target levels.

percent-of-sales method An advertising budgeting method that determines the total budget allocated to advertising based on past or projected sales.

performance standards A priori measures against which firm performance is evaluated.

performing a product business analysis Calculating projected costs such as return on investment and cash flow, and determining the fixed and variable costs for the long term.

personal medium A communication channel that involves contact between the seller and the consumer.

piggybacking Using the distribution system of exporters with established systems of selling abroad who agree to handle the export function of a noncompeting (but not necessarily unrelated) company on a contractual basis; also called mother henning and cooperative exporting.

plant/warehouse location studies Studies that evaluate the appropriateness of plant or warehouse location to ensure that it is in accordance with the limitations of the national environment and with the needs of a company.

point-of-sale–based projections Market share and other relevant market dimensions assessed by the use of store scanners in weekly and biweekly store audits.

political risk The risk associated with actions of local, regional, and/or parastatal governing bodies affecting the international company, and with the overall economic and political stability within a particular country.

political union The highest level of regional integration; it assumes a viable economic integration and involves the establishment of viable common governing bodies, legislative bodies, and enforcement powers.

polycentric orientation Company strategies predicated on the assumption that each country's market is unique and should be addressed individually, with a country-specific marketing mix.

polychronic time The interpretation of time as fluid, such that individuals can accomplish multiple tasks at once.

post adjustment A compensation incentive whereby the company adjusts expatriate salaries to reflect the cost of living in the new environment at standards in the expatriate's home country; also called cost-of-living adjustment.

postures Individuals' physical postures during conversation.

power distance The manner in which interpersonal relationships are formed when differences in power are perceived.

press releases Statements issued to the press to communicate news about a company and its products.

price controls Strategies requiring a product to sell for a particular price in the local market; price control strategies are typically used to increase the prices of imports to match the minimum prices of local competition.

price elasticity studies Studies examining the extent to which a particular market is price sensitive.

price/quality positioning A strategy whereby products and services are positioned as offering the best value for the money.

primary data Data collected for the purpose of addressing the problem at hand.

primitive society The first stage of economic and political development, characterized, according to Marxist-Leninist theory, by the joint tribal ownership of primitive means of production centered on agricultural tasks.

print medium A nonpersonal channel of communication such as a newspaper, magazine, billboard, pamphlet, or point-of-purchase display.

private labels Brands sold under the brand name of a retailer or some other distributor.

product class positioning A strategy used to differentiate a company as a leader in a product category, as defined by the respective company.

product consistency The extent to which a company's different product lines are related, use the same distribution channels, and have the same final consumers.

product depth The number of different offerings for a particular brand.

product division structure An organizational structure whereby subsidiaries report to the product division (strategic business unit) with responsibility for the particular products.

product length The total number of brands in the product mix.

product line All the brands the company offers in the same product category.

product mix The complete assortment of products that a company offers to its target international consumers.

product packaging design studies Studies that evaluate consumers' reaction to a package, the extent to which the package adequately communicates information to the consumer, and the distribution implications of the package.

product placement The strategy of placing brands in movies with the purpose of promoting the products to viewers.

product testing Studies that estimate product preference and performance in a given market.

product user positioning A positioning strategy that focuses on the product user, rather than on the product.

product width The total number of product lines that a company offers to its target international consumers.

product-country stereotypes Product-specific stereotypes that associate the country of origin as a certification of quality.

profit analyses studies Studies that estimate product profit in specific international markets.

protection of markets with excess labor The erection of barriers to imports of products competing with local offerings in an effort to protect local jobs.

protection of markets with excess productive capacity A protectionist measure used to prevent foreign buyouts, invoking the protection of local labor.

protectionism All actions by national and local governments aimed at protecting local markets from foreign competitors.

proxemics The amount of physical space individuals require to feel comfortable in the process of communication.

psychographic segmentation The use of values, attitudes, interests, and other cultural variables to segment consumers.

public appearances Company representatives' public involvement, speaking on behalf of the international firm and its products.

publicity Any communication about a company and/or the company's products that the company does not pay for; may be positive or negative.

purchase behavior studies Research aimed at evaluating consumers' reaction to and interaction with a company's products.

Q

qualitative research Research that uses nonsystematic processes, such as nonrandom sampling and open-ended data, as well as involves the researcher as participant.

quantitative research A structured type of research that involves either descriptive research approaches, such as survey research, or causal research approaches, such as experiments.

R

radical innovation The creation of new industries or new standards of management, manufacturing, and servicing that represent fundamental changes for consumers, entailing departures from established consumption.

receiver The target market that receives the advertising message from a sender.

regiocentric orientation Company strategies that view world regions as distinct markets that share economic, political, and/or cultural traits that will respond to a regionwide marketing approach.

regional standardization The use of a uniform marketing strategy within a particular region.

reliability The extent to which data is likely to be free from random error and yield consistent results.

religion A society's relationship to the supernatural.

repatriation The return of the expatriate employee to the home country.

repatriation allowance A compensation incentive whereby the company covers expenses involved in moving back to the home country, as well as, frequently, a large sum paid for successfully completing the international assignment.

research approach The method used to collect data.

reverse culture shock Anxiety experienced after returning to the home country, associated with a longing for the international environment left behind and with the difficulty of readjusting to the home country and to corporate life at one's firm.

Rostow modernization model An economic development model attributed to Rostow, according to which each stage of economic advance is a function of productivity, economic exchange, technological improvements, and income.

S

sales forecast Projected sales for a particular territory.

sales potential studies Studies forecasting optimal sales performance.

sales promotion Sponsored communications to the target consumer or trade segment that stimulate purchases or improve relationships with middlemen.

salesforce compensation, quota, and territory studies Different studies pertaining to personal selling activities; they are crucial in helping to determine the appropriate strategies for certain international markets.

salesforce composite estimates Research studies wherein sales forecasts are based on the personal observations and forecasts of the local salesforce.

sample size The number of study participants necessary to obtain a high study reliability.

sampling frame The list from which sample units are selected.

sampling procedure A decision involving the selection of sampling units.

sampling unit The entity included in the study; it may be individuals or representatives belonging to particular groups.

sanctions Punitive trade restrictions applied by a country or a group of countries against another country for noncompliance.

screening new product ideas Eliminating product ideas that do not fit with the target consumers and/or the overall mission of the organization.

secondary data Data collected to address a problem other than the problem at hand.

segmentation The process of identifying consumers and/or international markets that are similar with regard to key traits, such as product-related needs and wants, and that would respond well to a product and related marketing mix.

self-reference criterion Individuals' conscious and unconscious reference to their own national culture, to home-country norms and values, and to their knowledge and experience in the process of making decisions in the host country.

sender The sponsor of an advertisement, usually represented by an advertising agency, who encodes the message into words and images and communicates it to the target market.

service barriers Barriers encountered by services in different markets, such as requirements for local certification, local providers, and other requirements that favor local over international service providers.

simulated test marketing Test marketing simulating purchase environments where samples of target consumers are observed in their product-related decision-making process.

skimming strategy A pricing strategy in which a product is priced above that of competitors' products, when competition is minimal, to quickly recoup investments; consumers responding to skimming strategies are more concerned with quality, uniqueness, and status, rather than price.

slavery-based society A stage of economic and political development, which, according to Marxist-Leninist theory, emerges as a result of tribes' dominance over other tribes: Dominant tribes claim ownership of conquered tribes and their property.

social structure The organization of relationships in a society.

socialism A transition stage of economic and political development, characterized, according to Marxist-Leninist theory, by the disappearance of private property and its replacement with collective, state property.

soft currency Currency that is kept at a high artificial exchange rate, overvalued, and controlled by the national central bank.

sogo shosha A large Japanese trading company that specializes in providing intermediary services, risk reduction through extensive information channels, and significant financial assistance to manufacturing firms.

South African Customs Union (SACU) A customs union that includes Botswana, Swaziland, Lesotho, and Namibia. The group's main trading partner is South Africa, and member countries have partially or entirely tied their currencies to the South African rand.

Southern African Development Community (SADC) A free trade organization that promotes economic cooperation among a coalition of 14 of Africa's more affluent and developed nations, designed to foster increased economic and governmental stability through the use of collective peace-keeping forces.

Southern Cone Common Market (MERCOSUR) A free trade agreement in South America that has met with considerable success; MERCOSUR is presently in the process of becoming a viable customs union. (See www.mercosur.org.uy.)

special economic zones Customs-privileged manufacturing facilities in China where multinational companies can take advantage of low-cost labor.

specialized markets Markets that contain specialty stores specializing in a particular product category.

specialty stores Retailers that offer a narrow product line and wide assortment.

spoken/written language The language used in conversation/the language used in written communications.

stability over time The extent to which preferences are stable, rather than changing, in a market segment.

standardization of the advertising strategy The process of globalizing a company's promotional strategy so that it is uniform in all its target markets.

standardized pricing A pricing strategy in which the same price is charged for a product regardless of local market conditions.

standards as barriers to trade Trade barriers imposing performance, environmental, or other requirements that are primarily aimed at imports.

status concern The value placed on symbols of status and on the attainment of high status in a society.

strategic alliance Any type of relationship between one or more companies attempting to reach joint corporate and market-related goals; term used to refer to most nonequity alliances.

studies of premiums, coupons, and deals Studies that help identify the practices in each target country where a promotion is planned by investigating the practice and legality of premiums, coupons, and special deals.

substantiality The extent to which the market is large enough to warrant investment.

superstores Large retailers such as combination stores or hypermarkets that sell food, drugs, and other products.

survey research Descriptive research that involves the administration of personal, telephone, or mail questionnaires.

swing credits Amounts paid within the framework of a clearing agreement by the country that owes money to the other when an imbalance occurs.

switch trading The process of buying a party's position in a countertrade in exchange for hard currency and selling it to another customer.

T

take-off A stage in economic development described by Rostow as one in which economic growth becomes the norm and improvements in production lead to the emergence of leading sectors.

target market Consumers and/or international markets that are similar in aspects relevant to the company.

target marketing The process of focusing on those segments that the company can serve most effectively and designing products, services, and marketing programs with these segments in mind.

tariffs Taxes imposed on goods entering a country.

telemarketing A personal channel of communication that involves a salesperson calling on consumers.

television home shopping Retailing through cable channels selling to consumers in their homes, through infomercials, and through direct response advertising shown on broadcast and cable television.

television shopping networks Cable channels that sell products to a television audience.

test marketing Testing new-product performance in a limited area of a national or regional target market to estimate product performance in the respective country or region.

third-country national An employee working in the country of assignment who is not a national of that country nor of the country in which the corporate headquarters of the company he or she works for are located.

time orientation The manner in which individuals view time in relation to accomplishing tasks.

time series and econometric models Models that use the data of past performance to predict future market demand.

trade secrets Intellectual property such as know-how, formulas, special blends, and other elements that are not registered, and are thus not protected by law.

trade shows and exhibitions Business-to-business promotions that usually are held annually in formats where companies purchase exhibit space to display and demonstrate their offerings to the target market.

trademark A brand name, mark, symbol, motto, or slogan that identifies a particular manufacturer's brand and distinguishes it from the competitors' brands in the same product category.

Trade-Related Aspects of Intellectual Property Rights (TRIPS) An international agreement, under the World Trade Organization, that sets out minimum standards for the legal protection of intellectual property. (See www.wto.org.)

trading companies Large companies that specialize in providing intermediary services, risk reduction through extensive information channels, and significant financial assistance to manufacturing firms.

traditional society A stage in economic development defined by Rostow as one in which the economy is dominated by agriculture and relatively few exchange transactions occur.

transfer pricing A pricing strategy used in intra-firm sales for commercial transactions between units of the same corporation, within or beyond the national borders of the parent company.

transitional society A stage in the economic development process described by Rostow as characterized by increased productivity in agriculture and by the emergence of modern manufacturing.

trialability The ability of the consumer to experience a product with minimal effort.

U

uncertainty avoidance The extent to which individuals are threatened by uncertainty, risk, and ambiguous situations and thus adopt beliefs, behaviors, and institutions that help them to avoid the uncertainty.

undifferentiated targeting A targeting strategy aiming the product at the market using a single strategy, regardless of the number of segments.

United Nations organizations The totality of United Nations bodies created to maintain international peace and security; to develop relations among nations; to achieve international cooperation in solving international economic, social, cultural, or humanitarian problems; and to encourage respect for human rights and fundamental freedoms using the venues offered by the different UN organizations. (See www.un.org.)

United States Agency for International Development (USAID) An independent agency of the federal government that supports the economic development of and trade with developing countries aligned politically with the United States. (See www.usaid.gov.)

United States Department of Commerce The U.S. governmental agency that oversees and promotes trade, offering export assistance and counseling to U.S. businesses involved in international trade, providing country information and country specialists, and bringing buyers and sellers together.

United States State Department The foreign affairs arm of the United States government, in charge of promoting relations with other governments. (See www.state.gov.)

usage segmentation The process of segmenting markets based on the extent to which consumers are nonusers, occasional users, medium users, and heavy users of a product.

use positioning The process of marketing a very precise product application that differentiates it in the consumers' minds from other products that have a more general use.

user status segmentation The process of determining the status as users of competitors' products, ex-users, potential users, first-time users, and regular users.

V

validity The extent to which data collected is free from bias.

values Enduring beliefs about a specific mode of conduct or desirable end-state that guide the selection or evaluation of behavior.

vending machines Interactive modes of retailing convenience goods.

voluntary export restraints A government's self-imposed export quotas to a particular country that are established to avoid more severe protectionist action by the respective importing country.

voluntary import expansion A government's response to protectionist threats from another country whereby it agrees to open markets to imports and/or to increase foreign access to a domestic market to avoid more severe protectionist action.

W

warehouse clubs Stores that require members to pay an annual fee operating in low-overhead, warehouse-type facilities, offering limited lines of brand name and dealer-brand groceries, apparel, appliances, and other goods at a substantial discount; also known as wholesale clubs.

Webb-Pomerene Associations Associations of competing companies that are granted immunity from antitrust prosecution and that join resources and efforts to export internationally.

West African Economic and Monetary Union (WAEMU) One of the first attempts at economic integration in Africa. Although it is successful as a monetary union that has adopted a single currency, trade is quite modest within the WAEMU. (See www.dakarcom.com/EconReports/econ_waemu.htm.)

wholesale clubs Stores that require members to pay an annual fee operating in low-overhead, warehouse-type facilities, offering limited lines of brand name and dealer-brand groceries, apparel, appliances, and other goods at a substantial discount; also known as warehouse clubs.

wholly owned subsidiary The entry mode that affords the highest level of control and presents the highest level of risk to a company; it involves establishing a new company that is a citizen of the country where the subsidiary is established.

World Bank The World Bank Group, headquartered in Washington, D.C., that is one of the largest sources of funds for development assistance aimed at the poorest countries worldwide. (See www.worldbank.org.)

World Trade Organization (WTO) The largest and most influential international trade organization whose primary goal is ensure the free flow of trade; WTO's agreements (negotiated and signed by member countries, ratified in their parliaments) represent trade rules and regulations and act as contracts guaranteeing countries trade rights and binding governments to trade policies. (See www.wto.org.)

worldwide regional division structure An organizational structure whereby operations are organized by region or by country, and where subsidiaries report directly to the single division responsible for operations in the country or geographic region.

Index

Page numbers in italics identify illustrations. An italic *t* next to a page number (e.g., 241*t*) indicates information that appears in a table.